# Higher Education, Emerging Technologies, and Community Partnerships:

## Concepts, Models and Practices

Melody A. Bowdon
*University of Central Florida, USA*

Russell G. Carpenter
*Eastern Kentucky University, USA*

D1625636

Information Science
**REFERENCE**

| | |
|---|---|
| Senior Editorial Director: | Kristin Klinger |
| Director of Book Publications: | Julia Mosemann |
| Editorial Director: | Lindsay Johnston |
| Acquisitions Editor: | Erika Carter |
| Development Editor: | Myla Harty |
| Production Editor: | Sean Woznicki |
| Typesetters: | Mike Brehm, Keith Glazewski, Natalie Pronio, Jennifer Romanchak, Deanna Zombro |
| Print Coordinator: | Jamie Snavely |
| Cover Design: | Nick Newcomer |

Published in the United States of America by
    Information Science Reference (an imprint of IGI Global)
    701 E. Chocolate Avenue
    Hershey PA 17033
    Tel: 717-533-8845
    Fax: 717-533-8661
    E-mail: cust@igi-global.com
    Web site: http://www.igi-global.com/reference

Library of Congress Cataloging-in-Publication Data

Higher Education, Emerging Technologies, and Community Partnerships: Concepts, Models and Practices / Melody A. Bowdon and Russell G. Carpenter, editors.
    p. cm.
  Includes bibliographical references and index.
  Summary: "This book is a comprehensive collection of research with an emphasis on emerging technologies, community value, and corporate partnerships, providing strategies to implement partnerships"--Provided by publisher.
  ISBN 978-1-60960-623-7 (hardcover) -- ISBN 978-1-60960-624-4 (ebook) 1. Education, Higher--Effect of technological innovations on. 2. Distance education--Computer-assisted instruction. 3. Educational technology. 4. Community educa-tion--United States I. Bowdon, Melody A., 1967- II. Carpenter, Russell G., 1979-
  LB2395.7.H54 2011
  378.1'03--dc22
               2011000121

British Cataloguing in Publication Data
A Cataloguing in Publication record for this book is available from the British Library.

# Table of Contents

### Section 1
### Innovative Models for Technology-Based University Collaboration with K-12 Schools

**Chapter 1**

*Rachael Wendler, University of Arizona and Desert View High School, USA*
*Aria Altuna, University of Arizona and Desert View High School, USA*
*Timothy Crain, University of Arizona and Desert View High School, USA*
*Oksana Perez, University of Arizona and Desert View High School, USA*
*Savannah Sanchez, University of Arizona and Desert View High School, USA*
*Jalina Vidotto, University of Arizona and Desert View High School, USA*

**Chapter 2**

*Curtis L. DeBerg, California State University, Chico, USA*

**Chapter 3**

*Jill Russell, College of Mount St. Joseph, USA*
*Karen Glum, Seven Hills Middle School, USA*
*Jennifer Licata, Seven Hills Middle School, USA*
*David Russell, Avian Research & Education Institute, USA*
*Jenny Wohlfarth, University of Cincinnati, USA*

**Section 4**
**Transcending Boundaries of Technologies and Using Technologies to Transcend Boundaries in Partnerships**

**Section 5**
**Using Digital Technologies to Cross Generational and Cultural Divides**

### Section 6
### Universities, Digital Technologies, and the Public Good

# Detailed Table of Contents

### Section 1
### Innovative Models for Technology-Based University Collaboration with K-12 Schools

**Chapter 1**

> *Rachael Wendler, University of Arizona and Desert View High School, USA*
> *Aria Altuna, University of Arizona and Desert View High School, USA*
> *Timothy Crain, University of Arizona and Desert View High School, USA*
> *Oksana Perez, University of Arizona and Desert View High School, USA*
> *Savannah Sanchez, University of Arizona and Desert View High School, USA*
> *Jalina Vidotto, University of Arizona and Desert View High School, USA*

This case study demonstrates how Web 2.0 tools, such as Google Wave and other programs that allow participants to collaboratively create documents, provide an architecture of participation that supports a PAR approach to assessing and improving community partnerships.

**Chapter 2**

> *Curtis L. DeBerg, California State University, Chico, USA*

This case study describes an international partnership among four main stakeholders: (1) a nonprofit organization called Students for the Advancement of Global Entrepreneurship (SAGE), (2) high school students and their teachers, (3) university students and (4) the private sector, including corporations, foundations, and individual philanthropists.

This case study describes a partnership between the Avian Research and Education Institute (AREI), College of Mount St. Joseph (MSJ), University of Cincinnati (UC), and science teachers at The Seven Hills Middle School. This partnership enabled the teachers to implement a Bird Studies program and empowered the students to become citizen scientists.

# Chapter 4

One-to-one computing has emerged as a controversial framework for integrating technology in education. The Cambridge Friends School XO laptop pilot program is a collaboration between the Digital Literacy Project (DigiLit), a non-profit and Harvard College student organization, and the Cambridge Friends School (CFS), an independent K-8 school. This chapter examines both positive and negative features of the program, as well as a model for implementation of similar programs.

To stimulate student interest in science, technology, engineering, and math (STEM) disciplines, the University of Central Florida (UCF) partnered with the Crooms Academy of Information Technology (CAIT), a public magnet high school that emphasizes technology education for a diverse student population. Using digital tools and a service-learning model, UCF chemistry and biology students partnered with CAIT students to debunk science myths, perform laboratory experiments, and engage in an experiential oyster reef restoration project.

**Section 2**
**Service-Learning with Emerging Technologies**

This case study reviews a hybrid face-to-face (F2F) and virtual collaboration between the state of Hawai'i's Division of Forestry and Wildlife and a team of university technical writing students to identify specific features of the hybridity that shaped the collaboration. In a course focused on organizational authorship, students were tasked with learning about the organization's workplace culture to successfully represent its ethos in a report on the history of forestry in Hawai'i.

    *Matthew W. Turner, The University of Alabama in Huntsville, USA*
    *Michael P.J. Benfield, The University of Alabama in Huntsville, USA*
    *Dawn R. Utley, The University of Alabama in Huntsville, USA*
    *Cynthia A. McPherson, The University of Alabama in Huntsville, USA*

The capstone senior design class in the Department of Mechanical and Aerospace Engineering at The University of Alabama in Huntsville (UAH) is taught as a distributed Integrated Product Team (IPT) experience. Engineering students are teamed with students of different disciplines within UAH and with students at universities in other states and Europe. Because of the distributed nature of these teams, the IPT students must use a variety of technologies to communicate.

    *Pat Byrne, National University of Ireland Galway, Ireland*
    *Lorraine McIlrath, National University of Ireland Galway, Ireland*

This chapter presents findings from an established service-learning module at the National University of Ireland, Galway, in a postgraduate IT degree programme. It describes the context at a local and national level for embedding service-learning within IT while likening it to the process of tightrope walking, involving the complexity of balance and control in a sometimes uncertain terrain.

    *Emily Wexler Love, University of Colorado at Boulder, USA*
    *Debra Flanders Cushing, University of Colorado Denver, USA*
    *Maggie Sullivan, Partnering High School, Colorado, USA*
    *Jode Brexa, Partnering High School, Colorado, USA*

This chapter describes a university/high school partnership focused on digital storytelling. It also explains the multi-stage process used to establish this successful partnership and project. The authors discuss the central role that technology played in developing this university/high school partnership, a collaboration that extended the impact of a digital storytelling project to reach high school students, university students, educators, high school administrators, and the local community.

This case study analyzes critical success factors for digital technology projects in service-learning courses at Pace University, a leading school of computer science and information systems in New York City. The study argues that the factors of collaboration, pedagogy, project management, strategy, and technology are foundational not only to implementing and generating meaningful benefits from projects, but also to ensuring durable and fruitful partnerships with nonprofit organizations.

The University of Richmond, a mid-size liberal arts institution, had a longstanding institutional commitment to civic engagement. Campus location and curricular issues once made the popular model of service-learning, direct service to fellow citizens in need, too restrictive, and not a good fit for many of the university's courses. Campus leaders wanted to create community partnerships that would accommodate the wide range of pedagogical needs on campus, connect to every discipline, and still maintain healthy and sustainable partnerships in the community. This case study describes their collaboration with community leaders to launch ConnectRichmond, a network hub with many Web 2.0 features.

# Chapter 12

This chapter develops a model of service-learning that focuses on serving the information and communication technology (ICT) needs of community organizations, and contrasts it with the traditional service-learning model used in universities, questioning if it is a more effective way of meeting nonprofits' ICT needs. The authors evaluate their model's utility from the perspective of a technology empowerment "stepstool" where nonprofit organizations can move from simply using existing technology better, to shaping the technology, to creating their own technology. The chapter then goes on to discuss attempts to implement versions of this model at the University of Wisconsin, discussing their strengths and weaknesses, and paying particular attention to the limitations of doing this work within an institutional framework.

## Section 3
## Online Learning And Professional Development

**Chapter 13**

*Kristine Blair, Bowling Green State University, USA*

This chapter provides a constructive critique of the gap between the institutional rhetoric of technology and the academic reality of delivering curriculum digitally. As part of the analysis of the material conditions within the academy that inhibit the development of engaged online pedagogies, including ones with the potential for service-learning and community literacy components, this chapter establishes benchmarks for both institutions and units, not only to assess and sustain the success of such initiatives, but also to foster the professional development training of current and future faculty to foster online learning as an important example of the scholarship of teaching, learning, and engagement.

**Chapter 14**

*William P. Banks, East Carolina University, USA*
*Terri Van Sickle, Tar River Writing Project, USA*

The following case study explores the impact of a university-school-community partnership developed in an online environment in order to address the immediate need of high school teachers in North Carolina to become more knowledgeable about responding to student writing in online and digital environments. Using a grassroots, teachers-teaching-teachers model fostered by the National Writing Project, members of the Tar River Writing Project, in partnership with a university faculty member and an administrator from a local public school district, developed and implemented an online professional development workshop to improve teacher response practices.

**Chapter 15**

*Kathleen Schisa, Syracuse University, USA*
*Anne McKinney, University of Illinois at Urbana-Champaign, USA*
*Debbie Faires, San Jose State University, USA*
*Bruce Kingma, Syracuse University, USA*
*Rae Anne Montague, University of Illinois at Urbana-Champaign, USA*
*Linda C. Smith, University of Illinois at Urbana-Champaign, USA*
*Marianne Sterna, San Jose State University, USA*

Web-based Information Science Education (WISE) is a collaborative distance education model that increases the quality, access and diversity of online education opportunities. The WISE Consortium is a group of graduate Library and Information Science (LIS) programs founded on three pillars: quality, pedagogy, and collaborations (Montague & Pluzhenskaia, 2007). This chapter outlines the approach to achieving these three pillars and the assessment mechanisms used to measure the consortium's success.

# Chapter 16

Teachers are increasingly expected to work with children with varying disabilities in the least restrictive environment – most commonly, the general education classroom. Yet, teachers who did not major in special education remain unprepared to meet the needs of children with disabilities in the classroom because they received no relevant formal field experiences during their pre-service years. As a result, unknowledgeable teachers may retain damaging stereotypes of persons with disabilities, hold a reduced sense of teacher efficacy to include all learners, and in the end, be less willing to work with exceptional students in their classes. This chapter provides an overview of a Florida-based project that aims to connect communities, nonprofit organizations, university pre-service teachers, and persons with disabilities using high-tech, high-touch service-learning.

This chapter provides the Technology-Enhanced Community (TEC) Partnership Model to enrich higher education. The TEC Partnership Model addresses the incorporation of community resource professionals into coursework to provide authentic learning experiences for students. The model is situated in a case study of an online Human Rights Education course, designed to serve the needs and academic interests of K-12 practitioners, community practitioners, and students in a variety of disciplines. This chapter describes the experiences and impact from both perspectives of the partnership and provides examples from the Human Rights Education course to show the model in practice.

# Chapter 18

This chapter describes the central role technology played in the Tennessee Public Health Workforce Development Consortium project in terms of fostering inter-organizational cooperation and collaboration and providing measurable educational impact. The chapter also illustrates the project's role in forming community partnerships, as well as explaining the best practices/strategies learned from this project.

This case study describes an innovative and effective e-mentoring program for beginning teachers that has enhanced Western Carolina University's (WCU) school-university teacher education partnership. With national data indicating that nearly one-half of beginning teachers leave the classroom within five years, schools and universities are faced with the challenges of providing the support needed to keep new teachers in the classroom and developing them into effective professionals.

While many K-12 teachers, especially those in elementary education, have extensive academic training and work experience in effective pedagogy, there is a concern that their discipline-specific knowledge may not be as robust as is necessary to address the needs of today's students in a competitive, global environment. This is especially true in the STEM fields (science, technology, engineering, and math). To address this need, Florida's Manatee County School District partnered with Embry-Riddle Aeronautical University (ERAU) and Nova Southeastern University (NSU) to develop the ScienceMaster program. The ScienceMaster program leveraged existing university expertise in science-related online education to provide in-service professional development for teachers, especially teachers in low-performing elementary schools.

**Section 4**
**Transcending Boundaries of Technologies and Using Technologies to Transcend Boundaries in Partnerships**

This chapter argues that to align social media with community partnership building, all participants must develop a critical sensibility about these media. This sensibility must rearticulate social media to leverage their use toward the goals of the community action. A more thoughtful understanding of social media and their potentials and constraints can help to foment stronger, sustainable partnerships between higher education and community partners.

When people in the United States seek to collaborate with partners in the Democratic Republic of Congo (DRC), even good intentions cannot overcome differing expectations for how people use technologies to facilitate communication – both interpersonal and among social groups. This case study looks at an ongoing collaboration between a faculty member at the University of Minnesota and two NGOs working in the DRC: First Step Initiative, providing microloans to women entrepreneurs, and Pact, an international development organization.

This case study outlines the partnership between the Minnesota Department of Corrections and St. Cloud State University. As higher education underwent significant changes in technology and distance education delivery during the 1990s, the print-based correspondence course was rapidly being converted to online delivery, leaving offender students without higher education access or options. The university-corrections partnership created an innovative and unique program through reverse-engineering online general education courses into print-based materials.

Sierra Leone currently has one of the highest child mortality rates in the world. Among those children who have the greatest chance of survival are those who have access to life's basic needs. Because the government of Sierra Leone does not provide child welfare programming, non-governmental organizations (NGOs) are lifelines for millions of children. Few studies have explored the barriers facing these NGOs or have used participatory action research methods to do so. This case study serves agencies working to address barriers to individual and community health in war-torn and developing countries.

In traditional software, hardware, and program development processes, the project evaluator has been relegated to a peripheral role at the end of the process. Today's complex interactive media projects require a different evaluation model, one that situates the project evaluator firmly at the center. From this vantage point, the evaluator subtly guides a technologically sophisticated integration of people, institutions, technologies, and cultural assumptions. Instead of the summative role—verifying that milestones and objectives have been met—the 21st-century evaluator is cast in a formative role as a problem finder.

# Chapter 26

Phenomenal changes have occurred in higher education (HE) since the emergence of e-learning, thus necessitating change in teaching and learning approaches. The rate of change, demands, and pressures of the workplace brought by these ICTs, and the need for continual self improvement, job market competition, and job relevance have created an unprecedented demand for HE. There seem to be mythical ideas about the potential effects of e-learning and the proximal and contingent contextual factors that might affect its use, especially in Africa.

**Section 5**
**Using Digital Technologies to Cross Generational and Cultural Divides**

This chapter presents an anthropological case study of the response to rapidly changing technologies by members of a distributed network of 35 technology-based afterschool programs throughout California. University-Community Links (UC Links) is a collaborative effort among university campuses and local communities to develop a network, both physical and virtual, of afterschool program sites for underserved youth in California. While each UC Links program is a physical setting with its own set of learning activities developed in response to the cultural, linguistic, and educational concerns of the local community, the UC Links network as a whole serves as a larger virtual context for defining and pursuing shared goals and objectives and communicating information about effective uses of new digital technologies for afterschool learning.

In 2006, the University of Maryland, Baltimore County (UMBC) entered into a unique partnership with Retirement Living Television (RLTV). Initially driven by the practicalities of bringing a new broadcast network to air, the relationship came to influence the role of new media technology in teaching and learning on the UMBC campus. The Charlestown Project brought university students and senior citizens together to create short digital movies. The project also became a catalyst for creating human connections beyond the campus and across generations. Along the way, students formed new attitudes towards aging and community, and the campus attained an increased awareness of the power of digital storytelling.

# Chapter 29

This case study chronicles the activities of a community-university partnership that supports the University of California, San Diego's threefold mission of teaching, research, and service while directing educational resources to underrepresented communities. This partnership, instantiated in a research project widely known as La Clase Mágica, involves a broad spectrum of institutional units seeking to bridge the digital, cognitive, and employment gaps that exist between middle-class mainstream communities and those at the margins. The case study examines the project's history and philosophy, theoretical framework, commitment to collaboration, assessment, and impact over the past two decades.

# Chapter 30

This chapter investigates the Schools Intergenerational Nurturing and Learning (SIGNAL) project at Liverpool Hope University and its impact on communities of learning within some of the most deprived areas of the United Kingdom. Embracing the wide aims of Citizenship Education in England, SIGNAL encompasses intergenerational and partnership activities, volunteerism, values education, and entrepreneurial learning shaped to assist with the unique issues faced by diverse school communities. Central to the project is the engagement of service-learning (SL) focussed student teachers, and their use of Information and Communication Technology (ICT).

## Section 6
## Universities, Digital Technologies, and the Public Good

**Chapter 31**

*Trey Conner, University of South Florida St. Petersburg, USA*
*Morgan Gresham, University of South Florida St. Petersburg, USA*
*Jill McCracken, University of South Florida St. Petersburg, USA*

Drawing on experiences of creating a partnership between the University of South Florida St. Petersburg and a social service organization, Mt. Zion Human Services, Inc., the authors of this chapter moved from a plan for installing and directing a program of networking technologies—refurbished computers scavenged by professors, servers built from components by students, operating systems and software coded by the open-source programming community, and communications technologies that enable an open-source "bazaar" or ecology of writing in the client-based classrooms—to a plan for participating in and responding to the dynamics of the social and cultural networks that emerge vis-à-vis technology.

**Chapter 32**

*Cheryl Cates, University of Cincinnati, USA*
*Kettil Cedercreutz, University of Cincinnati, USA*
*Anton C. Harfmann, University of Cincinnati, USA*
*Marianne W. Lewis, University of Cincinnati, USA*
*Richard Miller, University of Cincinnati, USA*

Cooperative Education (the systematic alternation of school and work) creates ongoing partnerships between institutions of higher education and their corporate partners. The beauty of co-op is that it allows feedback on student work performance while the student is enrolled in an academic program. The objective of this project was to use emerging digital technologies to capture partnership information and channel it back to faculty in charge of curriculum development for summative and formative purposes. The project was funded by the U.S. Department of Education's Fund for the Improvement of Postsecondary Education (FIPSE) through the grant Developing a Corporate Feedback System for Use in Curricular Reform.

**Chapter 33**

*Alfredo Alejandro Careaga, Ibero-American Network for Sustainable Development, Mexico*
*Alberto Ramirez-Martinell, Ibero-American Network for Sustainable Development, Mexico*

In this chapter, the authors present the Network of Digital Production Centers, a modular, scalable scheme for the development of educational and cultural content in schools and nongovernmental organizations (NGOs) in the state of Veracruz, Mexico. The chapter describes its goals, philosophy, its operations, and its growth plans, as well as the results achieved during the first phase of its implementation. The authors frame the project within the overall objectives of its funding institution, the Ibero-American Network for Sustainable Development, an NGO that began this project with the goal of transforming traditional content consumers into developers and producers of educational and cultural digital materials..

# Chapter 34

Universities can enhance the return on the public investment that they represent by collaborating with their natural allies in addressing pressing social issues. That work can be further enhanced by harnessing appropriate digital technologies. In this chapter, the authors profile a current example of a community-led, multi-layered partnership that was formed to strengthen the infrastructure of the charitable sector in Canada. In particular, the chapter demonstrates that the "habit of partnerships" combined with the "habit of technology" is a potent strategy for addressing community needs.

# Chapter 35

New methods of involving large numbers of citizens in public decision-making using information and communications technologies have spurred academic and professional interest. This chapter will describe the case of the Citizen Panel, a public-involvement project in which a municipal government and university combined their capacities to create a significant new opportunity for public involvement in public policymaking. Technology was used to broaden access to participation in, and awareness of, the Citizen Panel. Technology application included development of a video version of the information resources used by the Citizen Panel, posting key information on the website, hosting a Facebook group discussion, and live broadcast of panel sessions by Web streaming.

In 2005, Clemson University's SC LIFE Project and South Carolina's Florence School District Three began a collaborative project to catalyze research among teachers and students in the rural community. This project piloted the concept of using Web-based videoconferencing to allow university faculty to facilitate research in a precollege setting. This technology removed the more than 200 mile distance between the partners as an impediment to the participation of district teachers and students in Clemson University programs. To prepare teachers for the research, an online course was developed and disseminated from Clemson University via Macromedia Breeze.

**Conclusion**

The concept of remediation, as outlined by Jay David Bolter and Richard Grusin, offers a lens through which we might analyze and reinvent 21st-century partnerships. Accordingly, I argue that as we look to the future, community-university partnerships will gain momentum as centralizing educational venues, while emerging technologies will offer mediated spaces where academic, professional, and nonprofit institutions merge to provide learning opportunities that engage both sides. In this chapter, I situate the multiliteracy space—in this case the Noel Studio for Academic Creativity at Eastern Kentucky University—as a model for community-university partnerships that employ emerging technologies to develop communication skills

# Foreword

As I write this, it is the autumn of 2010 and we are all, apparently, waiting for Superman! *Waiting for Superman* is the title of a documentary that is being released this fall that has been getting much attention. In fact, this film seemed to crowd out all the other films playing at my local multiplex recently. I had gone there to view another one of the popular films this autumn-*The Social Network*. This film also has some ties to education that I'll discuss later.

When I walked into the box office to buy my ticket for the film that chronicles (some say, fictionalizes) the start-up of Facebook, I was amazed to see what appeared to be children's drawings tacked up all over the walls and windows. When I walked into the concession area, I saw what looked like a huge cardboard yellow school bus with cartoon-like figures of children popping up in the windows. I soon realized that these were not real pieces of artwork created by children, but faux kiddie art, all part of a marketing campaign to sell the coming attraction—*Waiting for Superman*. The entire lobby had been transformed into what seemed like an elementary classroom, complete with gold stars affixed to every visible surface. There was even some kind of appeal to give support to the children who were apparently at risk by our current public school system with a website that allowed for donations. So the film distributors were able to make us feel good about helping at the same time they were selling their film.

I was able to see the documentary a few days later, and I was underwhelmed by it. It reminded me that I had seen another intersection of the Superman film and Facebook. I had happened upon the episode of *Oprah* in which Mark Zuckerberg, founder of Facebook, announced that he plans to give $100 million to the Newark public school system. During that hour-long broadcast, all the guests, including the mayor of Newark and the governor of New Jersey, provided a litany of the failures of the public schools. The main criticism focused on teacher incompetence. This was a major theme of *Waiting for Superman*, as well, with blasts against tenure and teachers' unions. In the documentary, there were the now well-known "undercover" shots of the teachers waiting for disciplinary hearings in the New York City schools who are forced to show up each day in a holding pen somewhere, sleeping the day away.

What bothered me most about the film (as well as the *Oprah* episode) was that there were no "solutions" suggested. It was like sitting through a 90-minute documentary on how awful heart disease is with very little specifics on how one might fight heart disease. (It's all the nurses' union's fault!) And *Waiting for Superman* doesn't have a happy ending. The pay-off montage at the end of the film cuts among several different lotteries going on to determine which students will get to be admitted to the various charter schools portrayed in the film. The odds are against the kids as, in each of these situations, there are far more families interested in attending the schools than there are seats. We are left to be outraged as most of the kids walk away as education lottery losers.

xxvi

There is a kind of implied "hero" in the film, however. It is a memory of Geoffrey Canada, in fact, that gives the film its title. He tells a story about being a child and finding out from his mother that Superman is a fictional character. It was a profound realization to him as a child, and presumably a motivating realization to him as an adult; if there is no Superman to help humanity, he thought, it would be up to him and the Harlem Children's Zone to help the kids of Harlem, one block at a time. It is certainly not my desire to criticize such a noble notion. And it is significant to me that Canada has been trained and has experience as a classroom teacher.

But the implied hero of the film is never really fully unmasked. We are led to believe that there are some amazing things going on in these charter schools, and we see clips of uniformed kids sitting in rows listening to their teachers. But what exactly are they doing that is so great? What are Superman's secrets? We only get three real specific answers during the film. One aspect of these schools' successes, predictably, is that charter schools can fire incompetent teachers more quickly than can schools in which there are teachers' unions. The film doesn't explain at all how these schools determine how to evaluate teachers, but the bottom line is that they can apparently get rid of "dead weight" more quickly. The second idea that is briefly described is that (some) of these schools don't believe in tracking students. There are many educators I know who would agree with this principle. There is no explanation of how they meet the needs of all students, however, in an untracked environment. There is just a proud statement on the part of a principal that all kids are held to the same standard. Period. Problem solved! Finally, in a brief profile of the KIPP schools, they show the same video clip I've seen every time the KIPP schools are described--the "teacher across the hall" from the KIPP founders when they were teaching in the public schools (interestingly) who created rap songs to teach multiplication facts. There is the same clip played of the teacher frozen in time standing at the blackboard while the kids chant the rhymes she's created with little explanation made, from a human learning perspective, as to why this might be an effective teaching strategy.

In 102 minutes, these were the only specific examples that I could see about what these supposedly exemplary schools are doing that others should emulate. (There is one more, but I don't think it really counts—the filmmakers completely advocate the idea that we should have a longer school day and more school days in the school year. I don't see this as really counting, because it doesn't really speak to the content of the school day.)

But if we're all waiting for Superman, shouldn't we have some notion of what he's going to be doing? All we are to determine, from the selected clips we're shown is that a very old fashioned teacher-directed, textbook dependent curriculum and instruction system is the "superman" we've all been waiting for.

I'm guessing that the teachers described in this book probably wouldn't be interested in help from such a retro "superman." I'm under the assumption that if such a superman showed up at their doors, they'd think twice before letting him in. Many of us interested in uses of new media in schools would actually view the desks in rows portrayed in this film without a computer in sight as actually putting those students "at risk" just as much as our supposedly sinister public schools do. Many educators are increasingly coming to terms with the fact that kids are reading more minutes a day from a screen than they are from a page. These new-literacies teachers are taking schools in directions that are quite different from the recitation model that seems never to be out of style with many charter school proponents, even as it continues to bear almost no resemblance to the ways we humans read, write, and interact on a daily basis. Sure, it may lead to increased test scores (although, even the filmmakers point out, this isn't universal), but what resemblance do these tests bear, anyway, to the "real world" in which such concrete "answers" are just a keystroke away?

The teachers, professors, and community leaders who have contributed to this book are moving away from a call-and-response model of de-contextualized "fact checking" to a way of teaching that is becoming more and more integrated with life outside of schools. Whether it's working on community-based projects, participating in e-mentoring, or building bridges between the educational silos that have been so separate, these educators are changing the conversation. These kinds of visionary educators are realizing that school doesn't have to be divorced from our lives afterschool, that, while social media can in some cases be isolating, these new forms of representation can also break down walls that cordon us off and keep schools artificial and contrived. The writers contributing to this book are working across international, political, and institutional boundaries to identify creative and resourceful strategies for promoting collaboration between higher education and the communities it serves beyond the classroom.

Interestingly, the other film that I saw at the multiplex, *The Social Network*, even while it was set in an institution of learning—Harvard University—contained only one scene set in a classroom. And in this one scene, the lead character, Mark Zuckerberg, stalks out of the class after showing up the professor who dares to call on him when he thinks Zuckerberg isn't paying attention. Indeed, such a teacher-driven environment is portrayed as hopelessly irrelevant to the life of such a genius, who must retreat to a dorm room to create the platform that will grow to 500 million users. An interesting mission like creating Facebook certainly couldn't be done within the "old school" lecture hall. So Zuckerberg had to leave and, ultimately, he never graduated. To his credit, he is now pumping millions of dollars into a public school system. One can only hope that some of the Newark teachers will read this book. Make no mistake, it would be a great thing if more of the Newark kids get to graduate and go on to college. But it would be sad if they emerge in their uniforms into a world that is unrecognizable to them. They would end up winning the lottery, but losing their relevancy. They would end up, like Canada, realizing that Superman is fictional but without the abilities and experiences to move forward. Unless, of course, they've learned what they need to learn beyond the schoolroom door.

*William Kist*
*Kent State University, USA*

**William Kist** *is an associate professor at Kent State University, where he teaches literacy methods courses for pre-service teachers in the area of English Education in the Adolescence to Young Adult Education Program. He also teaches graduate students in the Master of Arts in Teaching (M.A.T.) program and in curriculum and instruction. He has been a middle school and high school language arts teacher, a language arts and social studies curriculum coordinator, and a consultant and trainer for school districts across the United States, both independently and as a consultant for the National Council of Teachers of English. Dr. Kist has been active on the state and national levels as a literacy educator, founding and facilitating the Ohio Language Arts Supervisors' Network and currently serving as director for the Commission on Media for the National Council of Teachers of English. Focusing on new literacies—broadening our conceptions of "literacy" to include alternative media such as video, blogging, and text messaging—Dr. Kist's new book,* The Socially Networked Classroom, *explores classroom uses of social networking in classrooms. He has presented nationally and internationally, with over 40 articles and book chapters to his credit; his profiles of teachers were the essence of his book* New Literacies in Action (2005), *which was chosen as a National Council of Teachers of English Select Book.*

# Preface

During the early boom of Web-based education in the late 1990s, both in the United States and in other nations such as the United Kingdom and Australia, there was a flurry of publications on the subject of university and industry partnerships, with a focus on ways in which online learning might break down barriers and lead to new models of collaboration and engagement across heretofore clearly delineated borders. Despite the interest in such endeavors this moment generated, few such partnerships materialized and fewer still have been effectively documented. Some might argue that this outcome is attributable to the proprietary nature of most course management systems, which steadfastly maintain a wall between campuses and the outside world. Others might say that partnerships across sectors are inherently unsustainable because the differences are simply too significant. Whatever the reasons, there has been little documentation of effective technology-based partnership practice within the literature of higher education. This collection is meant to bring attention to exceptional projects around the world that demonstrate ways in which colleges and universities can leverage resources of time, energy, and intelligence to create mutually beneficial collaborations with industry, nonprofit, and other groups in their local and global communities.

My co-editor and I join with the 88 teachers, professors, community leaders, and others who have written the chapters in this collection to argue that technologies are being used in compelling ways to forge partnerships between college students, staff and faculty members, and the communities around them. As we enter the second decade of the 21st century, we see a moment of growing opportunity for connection. Though progressively more formal course management options are owned and operated by large corporations, each year, many faculty members move their classes out of these structures and into the blogosphere. Social networking programs like Facebook and Twitter are increasingly central to the lives of faculty, and mobile technologies are ubiquitous, blurring lines among work, school, and pleasure. Second Life, a virtual world built by technologically savvy entrepreneurs, and similar interfaces are appropriated frequently by educators interested in exploring their potential for teaching and learning. As entities of all types struggle to survive in increasingly difficult economic times, there is a chance for innovative and intellectually, economically, and socially beneficial collaborations among academic institutions on all levels and nonprofit and profit-driven organizations in their communities. These opportunities are the focus of this volume.

## WHAT WE'VE LEARNED FROM THE EDITING AND COLLABORATION PROCESS

The first feature that might strike readers about this volume is its considerable length. When we started this project in mid-2009, we reached out to listservs, blogs, and other digital community venues in search of exemplary partnership projects from around the world. We were thrilled to receive the many proposals that came in over the course of the fall of 2009 and the process for selecting those we would highlight was challenging. What we found through our efforts is that committed people everywhere are working to improve education and other opportunities for their fellow citizens through innovative uses of digital technologies. The examples that emerged from our rigorous review process to become part of this volume underscore a number of important lessons about community partnerships. Below I will summarize a few of these lessons that are effectively demonstrated in the chapters that follow.

*College and high school students today are taking a lead in the process of creating valuable partnerships that make a difference in local and global communities.* We hear a great deal of speculation about the attitudes and abilities of the Millennials, a moniker used to describe people born between 1980 and 2000, which includes most current traditional-aged college and high school students. Many chapters in this book will demonstrate that young people today are contributing significantly to the world through their creativity, hard work, and commitment. Chapter One is written by Rachael Wendler and a team of high school student researchers from Tucson, Arizona—Aria Altuna, Timothy Crain, Oksana Perez, Savannah Sanchez, and Jalina Vidotto. The chapter describes the group's efforts to study a service-learning partnership between high school and university students and to identify ways to improve the learning impacts for both groups of students. The chapter underscores the energy, intelligence, and technical expertise these emerging leaders bring to the table, and makes crucial points about the ways in which digital tools, including Google Wave, can be used to harness and direct those resources. In Chapter Two, Curtis DeBerg describes the profound global impact of Students for the Advancement of Global Entrepreneurship (SAGE), an organization that brings high school and university students and their teachers together with representatives from the private and nonprofit sectors to encourage collaboration, all with a goal of improving the world. DeBerg describes SAGE as "a transnational social movement organization (TSMO) that includes youth and adults who believe that humanitarian capitalism and social entrepreneurship provide one promising avenue to alleviate poverty and to contribute to world peace." The chapter identifies compelling ways in which participants use digital technologies to work together toward these ends. Recent Harvard graduate Katelyn Foley describes another student-run project in Chapter Four. Foley and a group of her fellow students recognized a lack of access to computers in a small local school, formed a campus organization to raise money to address that need, and provided the equipment resources and their own labor and knowledge to help students in the school to improve their technological and social skills. Foley takes up the one-to-one computing debate in this piece, which describes a sustained and, indeed, expanding partnership for education that addresses the need for technical training not only for primary school students but for their teachers as well.

*Creating a successful partnership is challenging.* Anyone in higher education who has attempted to create a genuine partnership with an organization outside of the academy can attest to the complexity of the balance required to secure mutual benefit. Just managing the logistics and working through the politics to get the appropriate parties to a shared table is challenge enough, but those steps are only the beginning. Throughout this book, authors offer insights about the importance of recognizing the values and expectations of community partners and of figuring those elements into every stage of project development. In Chapter Twelve, Katherine Loving, Randy Stoecker, and Molly Reed offer a model of technology-based service-learning that prioritizes the immediate technology needs of nonprofit partners and suggests strategies for helping those organizations to not only receive technical assistance through the process, but also to play a role in shaping the emerging tools for their own needs and expectations. Students working together on these projects learn about technology and partnerships through genuinely addressing the needs of their community partners. In Chapter Twenty-Seven, Charles Underwood and Leann Parker apply an anthropological methodology to study the responses to changing technology across 35 sites hosting technology-based afterschool programs for underserved youth in California. Their analysis suggests, among other points, that the unique attributes of each site shape the technological and programmatic approach needed to create a successful university and community partnership. Similarly, Pat Byrne and Lorraine McIlrath describe in Chapter Eight a successful service-learning project at the University of Ireland, Galway, that pairs Master's students in Information Technology with local community organizations to address specific technology needs that impact the organizations' ability to provide services needed in the community. The authors place this project within the context of the history of service-learning in Ireland and provide data from interviews with both students and community partners to offer insights into strategies for making technology-focused partnerships successful for everyone involved, including student awareness of the realities of the technical conditions in the organizations' sites.

While collaboration is a valued process for all of our authors, *not all partnerships are equally effective*. Many university leaders face mounting pressure to form partnerships with local businesses and nonprofit organizations as available resources contract in the current economic situation, but partnership for partnership's sake is not inherently valuable. Authors in many of the chapters that follow offer solid criteria for evaluating the potential of a given current or potential partnership and support the notion that in some cases it is better to discontinue or redirect a partnership rather than to maintain one that is problematic for any of the parties involved. James Lawler argues in Chapter Ten that a set of critical factors shapes the effectiveness and value of a technology-focused, service-learning partnership; he suggests that faculty members can apply these criteria as they form new partnerships and assess existing ones. While Lawler's ideas are geared toward computer and technology courses in particular, the lessons presented will resonate with service-learning teachers across campuses. Trey Conner, Morgan Gresham, and Jill McCracken reflect in Chapter Thirty-One that even when an initial partnership turns out to be a less than perfect fit, value can still emerge from the process for the local community. They describe an experience of initially helping to establish a computer network with a local social services organization and then stepping back to watch a human network emerge. Ultimately, the university's role in the project changed from a major player to a peripheral role in a collaboration that took on a life of its own. The authors offer a model for redefining partnership through a community capacity-building lens, and underscore the importance of maintaining focus on project goals from the community partner's perspective.

Partnerships are not always easy to initiate or to sustain, but *partnerships with primary and secondary schools can be some of the most valuable and effective*. Education at all levels today face budget challenges, and institutions of higher education are often in a unique position to leverage the expertise of their faculty and students to enhance curricula at the lower stages. This kind of work can provide learning and research opportunities for students and teachers on all levels. Chapter Three authors Jill Russell, Karen Glum, Jennifer Licata, David Russell, and Jenny Wohlfarth describe an exciting science education effort among two universities, a research and education institute, and a middle school. These team members engage middle school students in a bird-banding project that captures their attention and sparks their interest in the natural world. The chapter explains how digital technologies allow these young researchers to work as citizen scientists, collecting and tracking data that contributes to conservation efforts in and beyond their region. Web-conferencing technology allows the students to participate virtually in a conservation expedition in Alaska, and the faculty and researchers involved have a fascinating vantage point for watching learning and science in action. In Chapter Five, my co-authors

Meghan Griffin, Erin Saitta, Linda Walters, and I provide an overview of our project, Engaging STEM, which uses digital technologies, including handheld video cameras and Web conferencing, to connect undergraduate chemistry students with virtual lab partners in a local technology magnet high school and invites college biology students to produce educational videos about marine life for students at the same school. We describe ways in which technology makes our partnership sustainable and engaging for all of the students involved.

*Successful partnerships between universities and other groups can be invaluable in the promotion of intercultural communication and support for underserved populations.* In Chapter Nine, Emily Wexler Love, Debra Flanders Cushing, Jode Brexa, and Maggie Sullivan describe ways in which their partnership has challenged university service-learning students to engage multicultural high school students, many of whom struggle with written and spoken English skills, in sharing their experiences with their communities through digital storytelling. They explain the evolution of their partnership from a hesitant beginning to a sustained collaboration that has proved valuable for college and high school students and their communities. Caroline Collins, Olga Vásquez, and James Bliesner make related points in Chapter Twenty-Nine, where they describe *La Clase Mágica,* an afterschool educational activity that brings University of California-San Diego students together with residents of five underserved neighborhoods in the city. The programs take place at a Catholic Mission, a community center on the U.S./Mexico border, two affordable housing complexes, and an American Indian Reservation. These authors argue that the process of making technology and other kinds of educational support available to the children and families in these communities enhances the lives of several generations of residents and secures benefits for the university as well.

The authors of many chapters make the point that *technological tools have different practical and theoretical meanings for different populations,* and underscore the importance of taking that reality into consideration when we plan our partnership efforts. Amy Kimme Hea demonstrates this point effectively in Chapter Twenty-One when she argues that all parties in a technology-based partnership need to develop a critical sensibility about the media used in a project to collaborate effectively. After offering a robust theoretical framework for this recommendation, she demonstrates her point through the example of students in a client-based professional writing course who are developing a social media campaign for a local business. The students and partners discover that while they may share a basic understanding of how the technology functions, their ideas about how this tool can and should be used in the community sometimes conflict. Kimme Hea suggests that helping students and partners become more aware of their interpretation of these tools through formal reflection can help to alleviate this problem. Bernadette Longo offers a related insight in Chapter Twenty-Two as she describes her graduate students' experiences of working with women attempting to start small businesses in their home country, the Democratic Republic of Congo. Longo explains that her students had to reevaluate their use of cellular phones as a tool for communication as they worked with these entrepreneurs for whom cellular minutes were precious and to whom common American mobile phone features such as games, texting, and e-mail were of little or no value. She explores the educational and partnership value of careful analysis of the function of technologies across cultures and advocates for continued purposeful efforts of collaboration and research.

While some chapters in the volume, such as those noted above, argue for the importance of thinking carefully about the kinds of tools we use for specific purposes, others argue that *the collaboration process itself can be much more important than the selection of particular tools.* In Chapter Seventeen, Amy Garrett Dikkers and Aimee Whiteside offer the example of their online human rights education course that uses a range of technologies to bring public school teachers, nonprofit leaders, and human rights experts from around the world together to create an exemplary educational experience. The authors reflect on the complexity of working with such a varied group of participants and emphasize best practices for remaining flexible in pedagogical practice and use of technology. Chapter Thirty by John Patterson offers a model for engaging teachers-in-training as technology educators in their local communities in the United Kingdom. Drawing on more than a decade of programming, Patterson argues that the selection of relevant specific tools varies according to the local setting and is less important to the process than the initiative's critical role in building community engagement in public education and training of future educators.

While the specific kinds of tools used in a given context may vary significantly, *access to digital tools of any kind remains an issue in many communities and contexts.* Patricia Aceves, Robert Aceves, and Shannon Watson offer a fascinating analysis of challenges related to technology and education access in correctional facilities. Describing the relevant curricular and financial history of higher education access in the Minnesota corrections system, the authors explain in Chapter Twenty-Three that over time the old model of correspondence courses, once a viable option for incarcerated students, has been replaced on most campuses with online learning, leaving these students who are forbidden access to the Internet with few or no options for pursuing an education. The chapter explains the process educators used to convert online courses back to a print-based model permissible within prisons, and describe the benefits and costs of this conversion process. Ashley Walker and Jody Oomen-Early present a different perspective on the importance of access to technology in Chapter Twenty-Four, which focuses on their use of PhotoVoice with nongovernmental organization (NGO) workers in Sierra Leone in a community-based research project. Facing one of the highest child mortality rates in the world, these NGO caregivers have developed critical expertise in medical and social management. By providing digital cameras and training in how to use them, the researchers on this project offered communities an opportunity to document their knowledge, reflect upon their experience together, and share their perspectives with policy makers. The authors highlight the challenges of finding sufficient electricity to keep the cameras charged and on the cultural complexities of capturing images in pictures, but more significantly they demonstrate the potential to initiate social change through technological empowerment and through engaging local leaders in educational work.

Indeed, several of our authors make the point that *capacity building for technology use remains a critical objective in many parts of the world.* James Kariuki Njenga and Louis Cyril Henry Fourie offer a vision of online learning in Africa, particularly in South Africa, in Chapter Twenty-Six. They describe the increasing demand for workforce development through higher education and a number of challenges ranging from lack of reliable sources of electricity to strict governmental policies related to communication technologies, limited bandwidth, and pedagogical barriers. The authors ask if e-learning is truly a viable current option in their country and others in the region and speculate on what might be required to make it a widely available option. In Chapter Thirty-Three, Alfredo Alejandro Careaga and Alberto Ramirez-Martinell describe the model their organization has developed for bringing digital tools to remote areas of Mexico to build human and technological capacity. Their network of mobile digital production centers offers "a modular, scalable scheme for the development of educational and cultural content in schools and nongovernmental organizations (NGOs) in the state of Veracruz, Mexico." The projects described in this chapter explain how taking technology into undeveloped areas can have the three-fold impact of helping to provide education to local residents, allowing outsiders to become aware of the residents' stories and situations, and offering both groups opportunities to collaborate on mutually beneficial environmental and cultural sustainability projects.

As noted above, though access to technology is a critical global issue, simply securing access is only a beginning place for creating solid technology-based partnerships. *Educators and partners need to be involved with shaping and developing the tools that impact our communities.* In Chapter Twenty-Five, Karla Kitalong describes her work as an evaluator for a National Science Foundation-funded research project that examines ways in which middle school students engage with educational technologies in an informal (non-school) setting. She argues that the 21st century evaluator "not only confirms that project goals and objectives have been met, but also evaluates collaborative processes and facilitates collaborations among the myriad stakeholders." Kitalong's analysis suggests that educators across the disciplines need to engage with industry and nonprofit agency partners to design communication tools of the future for a range of settings and offer strategies for handling situations in which the perspectives of stakeholders collide. In the book's conclusion, Chapter Thirty-Seven, my co-editor Russell Carpenter describes the cutting-edge learning and collaboration space he administers at Eastern Kentucky University to argue that higher education administrators on all levels need to be involved in imagining and creating spaces where students, faculty members, college staff, community members, and industry partners can come together to discover models for solving problems that affect them all.

Not all educational spaces are physically tangible, of course. When we began to conduct our own relevant research and to receive proposals for the book it became clear that *online education is increasingly a staple of academic training for professionals, and it is extremely challenging.* In Chapter Thirteen, Kristine Blair articulates the institutional pressures to increase online instruction on many campuses and the corresponding challenges that make it difficult for administrators and faculty alike to maintain appropriate workloads while delivering high-quality educational experiences for students. Drawing on her experience as a department chair, Blair argues that "21st-century colleges and universities need to develop ways to align technology with both pedagogy and policy to bridge the divide between the academy and the community to maintain our relevance in both realms in the digital age." Will Banks and Terri Van Sickle describe in Chapter Fourteen their process of moving a decades-old model for training K-12 writing teachers into an online environment that makes resources more easily accessible for teachers throughout North Carolina. The authors argue, furthermore, that in addition to making available training that would not otherwise have been offered, the online format creates a good forum for training teachers to respond to writing in an online environment. The authors offer a number of best practices, though they do not advocate that all training of this sort be placed online. In Chapter Sixteen, Trae Stewart, Rebecca Hines, and Marcey Kinney describe their success with a teacher training program that incorporates a range of digital communication tools, including Web conferencing and online discussion boards to create what they call "high-tech, high-touch service-learning with special populations." Pre-service teachers around the state of Florida engage in face-to-face encounters and online learning experiences that prepare them to work with exceptional students. The university team works closely with the local affiliates of a national nonprofit organization to leverage community resources to provide training and services to a wide range of people. Technology is a critical element of the training model.

Despite the exciting activities many chapters describe, others underscore a reality that underlies all of our efforts: *funding problems today are making partnerships simultaneously critical and difficult to sustain.* In Chapter Fifteen, Kathleen Schisa and Anne McKinney describe a multi-state collaboration among graduate programs in library and information science that takes advantage of the expertise and resources on numerous campuses to offer students unprecedented access to training with experts around the nation. These authors describe how their team of collaborators from California, New York, and Illinois developed a system that allows students on campuses in all three states to take online classes together, maximizing the potential offerings available to each student and the sustainability of each university's program. The authors explain in detail the complex and impressive system that allowed each participating institution to collect tuition, award credits, and otherwise take advantage of this system. They also explain some of the challenges associated with sustaining this kind of cross-institutional endeavor. Chapter Eighteen highlights another multi-campus educational undertaking; this time in the area of public health. The authors, Aleshia Hall-Campbell, Pamela Connor, Nathan Tipton, and David Mirvis, describe the successes between 2003 and 2009 of the Tennessee Public Health Workforce Development Consortium, a collaborative effort among three universities and a government entity. The chapter describes the critical role technology played in making this collaboration possible, and explains how the multi-strand model of programming offered learning opportunities for a wide range of constituencies. Public health education became a shared focus among the parties involved. In Chapter Twenty, Thomas Cavanagh describes a program in which two universities partnered with a public school district to provide professional in-service training in the science, technology, engineering, and mathematics (STEM) fields for teachers, particularly those in low-performing elementary schools. This program brought these teachers into contact with experts from around the state. Cavanagh explains the grant-funded system that allowed teachers to opt to either take individual courses and modules or to pursue a Master's degree. He describes assessment outcomes for the program, which exceeded its initial goals in many ways. Unfortunately, all of these programs, which have innovatively attempted to leverage resources from multiple campuses to address significant community education needs, have ultimately ended or been significantly curtailed or modified due to funding problems. These stories underscore the need for new program development approaches and funding models among as well as within colleges and universities.

Though the adoption of new technologies often signals the decline of old models of interaction, one important lesson that emerged from our work was that online engagement is not a substitute for face-to-face connections. Many of our authors understand technologies as a way to facilitate and supplement this in-person engagement, and several argue that *a hybrid approach combining in-person and online engagement is the best model for creating successful partnerships.* Jim Henry presents a model of collaboration using cloud-based document development tools in a service-learning technical writing class in Chapter Six. The author describes the ways in which his students successfully created a document in collaboration with a representative from the Hawai'i Division of Forestry and Wildlife primarily online, but he underscores the importance of the hybrid model for the success of the project, explaining that initial and periodic in-person meetings started the project in the right direction and kept all parties focused on shared goals. Henry asserts that these in-person elements were and are critical to collaborative client-based document development success. In Chapter Seven, Matthew Turner, Michael Benfield, Dawn Utley, and Cynthia McPherson present a model for international collaboration between students in engineering and other disciplines at the University of Alabama at Huntsville, their industry-based clients, and students in Europe as they work on an engineering capstone design course. The authors offer significant teaching-focused recommendations for project planning. They compare the effectiveness of a number of digital collaboration tools used by the students and, ultimately, conclude that students prefer what they call "informal" collaboration tools, but even more importantly, that collaborations across the board are more successful when they include at least one face-to-face meeting. When in-person meetings aren't possible, synchronous sessions using videoconferencing afford some increased success in the collaborations. The program described in Chapter Nineteen relies heavily on "online face-to-face" initial orientation (synchronous Web conferencing) for a distance-based mentoring program supporting beginning teachers in North Carolina. Janice Holt, Lori Unruh, and Michael Dougherty offer detailed analysis of the challenges of recruiting and retaining new teachers in rural areas and of the impacts of the program their university team has developed for providing highly relevant assistance to teachers around their state through this system. Though budgetary constraints make it difficult to create actual in-person encounters for their teams, this program offers an alternative to previous models that provided only matches based on convenience and proximity and, instead, enables leaders to match participants based on their roles and interests. Strategic use of technology makes the program possible.

As we reviewed the materials for this project we consistently noted *the importance of the role of the university as a responsible citizen within a community*. Theresa Dolson describes in Chapter Eleven the challenge her suburban university faced as they worked to connect with real needs in their community. Like so many campuses, the University of Richmond is geographically isolated from the most critical needs in the town where it is located, which made it challenging to identify problems to work on and to arrange logistics for service-learning activities and other kinds of engagement. Dolson describes ConnectRichmond, an interactive website that resulted from collaboration between the university and the city and that facilitates meaningful connections between local nonprofit organizations facing real challenges and faculty and staff members on campus. This creative use of technology helped to establish the university as more of an active citizen and created stronger ties between the campus and the city. In Chapter Thirty-Two, Cheryl Cates, Kettil Cedercreutz, Anton Harfmann, Marianne W. Lewis, and Richard Miller describe a robust system used at the University of Cincinnati for channeling performance feedback from cooperative education processes back into the curriculum to create a closed assessment loop that builds strong partnerships between the university and the businesses where students are placed, as well as providing excellent learning experiences for students. This project demonstrates the role of the university as a partner to local industry and underscores the importance of using university research capabilities to assess and improve the contributions our students make to their work with partners. In Chapter Thirty-Four, Lois Gander and Diane Rhyason argue that, "the widespread adoption of technologies among universities' allies, competitors, students and faculty that characterizes the electronically defined era will compel universities to adopt both the habit of partnerships and the habit of technology." Their analysis of the history and impacts of the Legal Resource Centre in Alberta, Canada, demonstrates ways in which universities can partner with citizen groups to improve the process and outcomes of democracy. Marco Adria and Yuping Mao offer different perspectives on related programming in Alberta in Chapter Thirty-Five. The authors offer an intriguing definition of community that focuses on cross-sectional representation of citizens in a university partnership. They focus on the "citizen panels" whose collaboration with the university and a municipal government incorporated social networking, Web conferencing, digital video production, and other digital technologies to create an environment to support and foster citizen involvement in local government. Each of these examples demonstrates that colleges and universities can be integral parts of their local communities and that the outcomes from those collaborations can be powerful.

Anyone exploring this book will find that it not only features compelling concepts, models, and practices of the use of emerging technologies to forge partnerships between higher education institutions and community organizations, but that it also includes a number of inspiring and informative narratives of the hard work of all contributors to these projects. This reality underscores a final observation that is central to this book: *telling stories is a valuable process*. In Chapter Twenty-Eight, William Shewbridge describes a project that brought college students and senior citizens in his community together to create short digital movies. The seniors had an opportunity to share stories of their lives with the students, who worked to engineer and distribute the final products. Through this technology-based project, all participants gained a sense of the value of sharing our experiences with others. Cora Allard, Deborah Whittington, and Barbara Speziale share an example in Chapter Thirty-Six of a university, public school and community collaboration that included the use of Web-conferencing and asynchronous bulletin board tools to connect people across the state of South Carolina in the SC Life project. Students of all ages around the state worked together to tell the often vexed story of the role of tobacco in the state's economy and culture. Their collaboration created an artifact that is a testament to their work together and will provide important information for current and future generations. The project was made possible through innovative uses of digital technology.

## CONCLUSION

Not since the launch of Sputnik in 1957 has American education faced such a demand to develop a productive and well-trained workforce for managing international competition and nationwide challenges as we do today, and other nations around the world face similar situations. In this moment of economic recession, universities and colleges of every size and sort around the country are struggling to maintain enrollments, retain talented faculty members, and continue to pursue excellence in research and education. Meanwhile, industries of all kinds are being forced to rethink corporate missions and shuffle priorities to remain profitable and whole. Public school districts are expected to continue to educate an American populace with growing economic and social needs while their resources are steadily being cut. Non-profit organizations are asked to provide services for more and more needy people while their base of donations is steadily declining. All of these groups and institutions face different difficulties, but in this volume we argue that one important strategy for helping these groups to survive and thrive beyond these challenges is to promote innovative cross-category partnerships among them. We see thoughtful use of emerging and established digital technologies as an important piece of this collaboration in the future, and we look forward to seeing what resourceful and dedicated leaders will do to address these concerns.

*Melody A. Bowdon*
*University of Central Florida, USA*

# Acknowledgment

First, we want to acknowledge the support and assistance of the IGI Global staff members who made the process of putting together this book enjoyable and efficient. Editorial Assistant Myla Harty, in particular, helped us to stay on track as we moved into production. Her assistance and patience were invaluable.

Sincere thanks to editing assistants from the University of Central Florida David Dadurka, Arwen Main, and Nicole Tallman, each of whom worked hard to get this manuscript ready for production. Their attention to detail, commitment to professionalism, and supportive attitudes kept us on our toes and ensured the project's success.

We value the support provided by our editorial board, including Dianna Baldwin, Shelley Billig, Kristine Blair, Sarena Seifer, and Trae Stewart. This team helped us to identify excellent potential authors and to review proposal and manuscript submissions. Other manuscript reviewers whose assistance we deeply appreciate include Marco Adria, Brian Blackburne, Maggie Boreman, Aminata Cairo, Thomas Cavanagh, Lisa Day-Lindsey, Amy Garrett Dikkers, Michael Dougherty, Sheri Dressler, Mary Ann Eastep, Doreen Fisher, Jim Gleason, Charlotte Gray, Morgan Gresham, Meghan Griffin, Glenda Gunter, Amy Kimme Hea, James Henry, Naim Kapucu, Kathy Keltner, MaryAnn Kolloff, James Lawler, Bernadette Longo, Katherine Loving, Yuping Mao, Eric Main, Alex McClimens, Rudy McDaniel, Lorraine McIlrath, Don Merritt, Rick Mott, James Kariuki Njenga, Clancy Ratliff, Erin Saitta, J. Blake Scott, Randy Stoecker, Terry Thaxton, Kelvin Thompson, John Venecek, John Weishampel, Rachel Wendler, Adrian Wurr, and Lisa Zideck. Special thanks to J. Blake Scott for his support and contributions throughout the process.

Our deepest appreciation goes to the 86 authors who contributed to this volume. We thank them for the hard work they put into creating and revising their chapters and cases, but even more for the amazing efforts represented in these words. We are humbled to think of the number of communities, schools, organizations, and individuals around the world who are touched by the projects described here. We have gained great insight and inspiration through the process of working closely with this inspiring group of people who are making a difference in the world. It has been a privilege.

Finally, we would not have been able to complete this project without the help and support of Barbie Carpenter, David Fenenbock, the University of Central Florida and Eastern Kentucky University.

*Melody A. Bowdon*
*University of Central Florida, USA*

# Section 1
## Innovative Models for Technology-Based University Collaboration with K-12 Schools

# Chapter 1

# An Architecture of Participation:
## Working with Web 2.0 and High School Student Researchers to Improve a Service–Learning Partnership

**Rachael Wendler**
*University of Arizona and Desert View High School, USA*

**Oksana Perez**
*University of Arizona and Desert View High School, USA*

**Aria Altuna**
*University of Arizona and Desert View High School, USA*

**Savannah Sanchez**
*University of Arizona and Desert View High School, USA*

**Timothy Crain**
*University of Arizona and Desert View High School, USA*

**Jalina Vidotto**
*University of Arizona and Desert View High School, USA*

## ABSTRACT

*This case study, collaboratively authored by a university researcher and five high school students, presents a model for assessing community partnerships that employs Web 2.0 technologies to facilitate participatory evaluations. A research team of high school students undertook an evaluation of a service-learning partnership titled Wildcat Writers that sponsors online writing exchanges between high school and college English courses. The evaluation project used a participatory action research (PAR) approach, which involves (1) including community members as equal co-researchers, (2) respecting experiential knowledge, and (3) working toward mutually-conceived positive change. This case study demonstrates how Web 2.0 tools that allow participants to collaboratively create documents provide an architecture of participation that supports a PAR approach to assessing and improving community partnerships.*

DOI: 10.4018/978-1-60960-623-7.ch001

## INTRODUCTION

"Who you are changes what you see." This observation by high school student researcher Aria Altuna holds important implications for the assessment of service-learning (SL) programs. All forms of inquiry are shaped by the perspective and background of the inquirer, as science theorist Haraway (1998) has reminded us. In service-learning assessments, the evaluator's worldview influences the choice of the outcomes to examine, the collection methods, and the approach to interpreting data. We cannot pretend that factors such as college or community affiliation have no impact on our assessments. Yet as service-learning scholars Cruz and Giles (2000) have noted, community-university partnership evaluations are traditionally carried out solely by university representatives. Cruz and Giles have explained that when university members conduct evaluations, academic issues such as student learning, faculty performance reviews, and institutional goals take center stage, while the perspective of the community remains relatively untapped. The focus becomes "Where's the learning in service-learning?" rather than also "Where's the service in service-learning?" (Cruz & Giles, p. 28). Because assessments often form the basis for program planning, the university's needs and ways of understanding the world therefore steer the partnership—an imbalance we find deeply problematic.[1]

To resist this hierarchy in university and community relationships, and to develop partnerships responsive to community needs and perspectives, we suggest actively involving community members in the design and implementation of program evaluations. This participatory process can be supported by Web 2.0 technologies—tools that go beyond technical facilitation to foster the participatory approach to knowledge needed for collaborative meaning-making. As software designer and IT entrepreneur Kapor (2006) has famously observed, "Architecture is politics." Changing the power dynamics of the university-community relationship requires finding tools that are structured to promote democratic ways of thinking and interacting. We argue that Web 2.0 technologies have the potential to encourage more balanced program assessments.

This chapter traces the efforts of a research team of five high school students (Aria, Timothy, Oksana, Savannah, and Jalina) and one graduate student researcher (Rachael) to collaboratively evaluate a service-learning partnership between the University of Arizona and five local high schools. The service-learning partnership, Wildcat Writers, pairs high school and college English classes for online writing exchanges. As representatives of the community being "served" by the partnership, the high school student researchers provided invaluable leadership and insight in the project, and the graduate student (who is also the coordinator of Wildcat Writers) offered guidance in research methods and access to teachers and administrators. Together, we crafted research questions, designed evaluation tools, collected and analyzed data, and presented our findings to key stakeholders in our program. Together, we also composed this book chapter to detail our project for others who may be interested in our approach. Our composition process follows our participatory philosophy, as this chapter was authored collaboratively on a Web 2.0 tool called Google Wave. We all brainstormed for each section of the piece, and then certain groups took on primary authorship for each part of the chapter. The student researchers crafted the section on Wildcat Writers and the student research team, along with portions of the conclusion, and Rachael wrote the other sections, incorporating quotations from the student researchers. Our case study intentionally uses a "we voice," because although this approach may gloss over the differences that naturally arise on a diverse team (Cahill, Rios-Moore, & Threatts, 2008, p. 93), we are committed to the participatory feel and enriched perspective that a "we voice" gives our description of the project.[2] We first provide background on Wildcat Writers and outline the process we undertook as a research team. We then describe the need for a participatory action research (PAR) approach to evaluation, and we demonstrate how Web 2.0 tools can be integrated with PAR approaches to knowledge through examples from our own work. Finally, we address the limitations of 2.0 technologies and participatory evaluations, and conclude by highlighting key outcomes of our project, along with future possibilities for the field of service-learning.

## WILDCAT WRITERS AND THE STUDENT RESEARCH TEAM

Wildcat Writers is a program that connects high school and college students online to exchange pieces of writing. One goal of the program is to help teachers better understand and bridge the gap between high school and college writing, so that high school students will be better prepared for college composition. The program also strives to motivate students to be interested in writing, and to connect the university with the community; Wildcat Writers wants to help high school students feel more comfortable about the idea of college and encourage university students to become more involved with the larger community. The partnership began in 2004 with a single collaboration between a graduate student and a high school teacher, and eventually expanded to be an official part of the University of Arizona's Writing Program.[3] Currently upwards of a thousand students and twenty-eight teachers are involved each year. The program incorporates service-learning scholar Deans' (2000) model of community writing, which includes three forms of writing exchange: writing *for*, where students write for their partners; writing *about*, where students write about their experiences of interacting with their partners; and writing *with*, where students work collaboratively with their partners to produce a single piece of writing. Sample projects include photo essays, letters about college life, public arguments, reflection journals, and zines. To connect students we use technologies such as e-mail, blogs, Nings, VoiceThread, Glogster, Edmodo and GeoGraffiti.[4] Whereas college students may often be perceived only as role models to high school students, Wildcat Writers allows both parties to benefit one another, creating a more equal partnership. The program has expanded greatly, but before this year there was not yet any official research to determine the effects of the program.

The Wildcat Writers student research team was established with the purpose of evaluating and improving the Wildcat Writers program. We, the five high school sophomores on the team, were recruited by Rachael for our exceptional writing skills and desire to be involved in the community. We met with Rachael before and after school in the computer lab, using our ingenuity, creativity and the help of pizza-flavored goldfish to develop, evaluate, and implement different research methods to improve Wildcat Writers. Our group also used this time to train ourselves and acquire certification with the University of Arizona IRB (Institutional Review Board). We had various collaborations with the university where we interviewed professors such as the director of the writing program, participated in graduate classes where we presented our use of PAR and 2.0 technology, and used university resources such as the library.

The process of constructing our research project began with a logic model, a tool applied in professional evaluations to better understand the inputs, activities, and outputs of a given program.[5] This allowed us to identify the possible strengths and weaknesses of Wildcat Writers. Using the logic model, we produced potential research questions and voted to choose the best: (1) Are the high school students enjoying the partnership? Why or why not? (2) Has the partnership made the high school students more interested in attending college? (3) Are the high school students becoming more interested in writing? and (4) Has the partnership helped the high school students better understand and appreciate college writing? These questions served as a base for crafting further questions for the surveys and later for directing our focus groups.

As a research team, we placed high importance on having students themselves conduct the research and delve into the subject at hand. As high school students, we are better able to gain insight and understanding of the situation as pertains to the Wildcat Writers participants, as opposed to a possibly intimidating professor. Our initial contact with the students began with the surveys, through which we sought to discern the effects the participants experienced as a result of Wildcat Writers. When presenting the surveys in classrooms, we were the ones to enter the room and explain the purpose and necessity of the survey and consent forms. We used the guidelines expressed throughout the IRB certification to explain the specifics of the survey. Between the pre- and post-surveys, we conducted focus groups. Each group consisted of about five students and was led by one member of the research team. Through half-hour sessions we were able to gain honest opinions and feedback.

Upon receiving the results of both pre- and post-surveys and student responses shared through focus groups, we analyzed and coded the data. Using this data we formed our recommendations for Wildcat Writers. Our suggestions included changing the way the program is introduced to both high school and college participants, moving the campus visit for high school students to the beginning rather than end of the semester, and tying Wildcat Writers assignments to the course grade for accountability, among other changes. After we finalized our recommendations, we presented this data to participating teachers, community partners, administrators, and eventually at a conference at the university.

## TOWARD A NEW APPROACH: PARTICIPATORY ACTION RESEARCH

We believe our model, though not universally applicable, has the potential to move beyond many of the problems of traditional service-learning assessments. Evaluations of community-university partnerships have historically focused on college student impact. A wide variety of survey scales and strategies have been developed to address the question of student learning (Bringle, Phillips, & Hudson, 2003; Toncar, Reid, Burns, Anderson, & Nguyen, 2006). Cruz and Giles (2000) have suggested that this focus on students rather than community is largely due to political reasons, because the fledgling field of service-learning has struggled to prove its validity as a pedagogical approach in order to justify institutional support (p. 28). Therefore, when community impact is included in assessments, it is usually only one variable among many others (Cruz & Giles, p. 29). Common approaches to gauging community attitudes toward service-learning include questionnaires mailed out to site staff, interviews of organization leaders, and evaluations of student work by nonprofit supervisors (Cohen & Kinsey, 1994; Ferman & Hill, 2004; Oates & Leavitt, 2003). In other words, when community members are involved in evaluations, they remain mostly on the sidelines as a secondary data source.

Some innovative work has moved beyond this university-centered model. For example, a group of scholars originating from Portland State University (Driscoll, Holland, Gelmon, & Kerrigan, 1996; Gelmon, 2000; Gelmon, Holland, Driscoll, Spring, & Kerrigan, 2001; Holland, 2001) has crafted a detailed chart of assessment questions and objectives for *each* major stakeholder group in service-learning: students, faculty, institutions, and community partners. Another step forward is the publication of *The Unheard Voices: Community Organizations and Service Learning* (Stoecker & Tryon, 2009), a book devoted solely to community perspectives in partnerships. The book explores key themes that arose from a series of interviews with nonprofit staff who have participated in service-learning projects.

However, even though progress in honoring community perspectives has been made, studies that incorporate community voices often suffer from a problem *defining* "community." The people receiving the services of nonprofits are often melded with the staff—service-learning scholarship seems to assume that the staff perspective is a sufficient representation of the community. Yet the vast majority of nonprofit staff is white and middle class, and most clients do not share this background (Toupin & Plews, 2007, p. 7). Given our interest in how position changes perception, we are concerned that the views of community members themselves are not being heard in service-learning assessments. As Martin, SeBlonka and Tryon (2009) noted in *Unheard Voices,* "As far as we know, there are no studies of client experiences with short term service-learning" (p. 62). These community perspectives are certainly not incorporated regularly into assessment design, and thus we are left with an impoverished view of our programs. Stoecker and Tryon (2009) have explained that not knowing the effects of service-learning means that we risk doing more harm than good, burning bridges, and "ultimately undermin[ing] the entire effort of service-learning" (7).

Scholars in service-learning are beginning to call attention to the lack of community input on assessment and the need for change (Bowdon, 2008; Cruz & Giles, 2000; Driscoll et al., 1996; Ferman & Hill, 2004; Gelmon, 2000). Bowdon has argued that in order to create sustainable and meaningful partnerships, we must work with community members to research our impact. We feel one particular method of community-based inquiry provides an especially generative framework for service-learning assessment: participatory action research (PAR). Brabeck (2004) defined PAR as "an enterprise that engages researchers and com-

munity members as equal participants; combines popular, experiential knowledge with that of an academic, 'rational' perspective; and seeks to join community members in collective action aimed at radically transforming society" (p. 43). PAR has evolved both from theorists in the Majority World who view PAR as a libratory approach to inquiry (Fals-Borda, 2001; Freire, 2000) and from Western scholars from the fields of social psychology, management, and organization theory who have pursued PAR as a more effective model of improving organizations (Lewin, 1948; Senge & Scharmer, 2001). Today PAR is a thriving approach to research employed across disciplines and communities. A sister field to PAR, Participatory Evaluation (PE), may also prove helpful to service-learning assessment, as it offers a model of evaluating programs with the help of those impacted by the programs.[6]

Many scholars have written on assigning participatory projects to service-learning students (Kinnevy & Boddie, 2001; Reardon, 1998), but we join the growing scholarship that addresses the possibilities of using PAR and PE to research the service-learning program itself (Giles & Cruz, 2000; Marullo et al., 2003; Payne, 2000). We see PAR as a generative framework for assessing community-university partnerships, because as student researcher Oksana notes, "PAR involves the people being affected." This collaboration fosters more accurate evaluations: Student researcher Savannah argues that involving high school students in our project provided "a true insider's view" in creating assessment methods, and incorporating both community and university representatives on the team created a "full, spherical perspective" on the program. The students were able to contribute substantially to the process because PAR emphasizes experiential rather than "objective" knowledge, creating space for personal stories and feelings to be treated as data. As student researcher Jalina writes, "PAR is a way of doing research without feeling disconnected." Furthermore, and perhaps most importantly, PAR's focus on producing transformative action kept us keenly aware of our goal to improve a program that directly affects students at five Tucson high schools, which serve a very high proportion of low-income, Latino/a, and Native American students—all groups severely underrepresented in higher education.

As our research team attempted to implement a PAR approach, we ran into the challenge of developing concrete methods for putting participatory theory into practice. In particular, we needed a way of working with documents collaboratively, because we would be crafting research tools, entering and analyzing data, and writing presentations together. As the IText group of digital writing scholars has argued, the process by which texts are created shapes organizations almost as much as the texts themselves (Geisler et al., 2001, p. 280). We knew we needed more than one set of hands on the keyboard. This led us to explore the possibilities of Web 2.0.

## SIX CURSERS, ONE SCREEN: WEB 2.0 AS SYNERGIST FOR PARTICIPATORY INQUIRY

Student researcher Oksana aptly explains why we used Web 2.0 technologies during our research: "PAR and Web 2.0 are soul-mates!" Web 2.0 provides a structure especially fit for PAR assessments of community partnerships. The term "Web 2.0," coined by Tim O'Reilly and Dale Dougherty, does not have a cut and dry definition, but is rather a "gravitational core" of concepts; it is "more an attitude than a technology" (O'Reilly, 2005, The Web as platform, para. 1). As Cormode and Krishnamurthy (2008) have explained, "The essential difference between Web 1.0 and Web 2.0 is that content creators were few in Web 1.0, with the vast majority of users simply acting as consumers of content, while *any* participant can be a content creator in Web 2.0" (Introduction, para. 4). This means that in contrast to Web 1.0 tools, which are intended for one-way information dissemination, Web 2.0 technologies are characterized by an architecture of participation. Web 1.0 technologies include Encyclopedia Britannica, Mapquest, and websites without comment features, while tools such as Wikipedia, Google Maps, and Facebook move closer to the ideal of Web 2.0.

For our research project, we chose a 2.0 technology called Google Wave that allows users to build texts in community through collaborative, real-time editing. We utilized this tool to draft a variety of documents, such as our team contract, interview and focus group questions, surveys, presentations, and this chapter. Wave also provided a virtual space for discussing ideas, dividing and tracking tasks, communicating over school breaks, and planning meetings. While Google announced that it was discontinuing development on Wave a few months after we completed our project, Wave is only one among a range of Web 2.0 collaborative composition tools that can be used to foster participatory evaluations. Similar tools available at the time of this writing include wikis, Google Docs, NotePub, Writeboard, and Zoho. Our discussion in this chapter will address both Google Wave in particular, as an example of how a specific technology can be analyzed for affinity with PAR ideals, and Web 2.0 generally.

To deeply understand the implications of working with 2.0 technologies, we need to follow technology critic Feenberg's (1991) call and move beyond a simple concept of programs as neutral tools controlled by the user. Instead, we use Selber's (2004) "cultural artifact" metaphor of technology, considering the "political, social, and even psychological assumptions embodied in computers" as well as the contexts in which technologies are used (p. 86). Technology designs and contexts implicitly shape the behaviors and worldviews of users. This active role of digital tools is especially important considering, as Selfe and Selfe (1994) have argued, the way interfaces function as Pratt's (1991) "linguistic contact zones": "social spaces where cultures meet, clash, and grapple with each other, often in contexts of highly asymmetrical relations of power, such as colonialism, slavery, or their aftermaths as they are lived out in many parts of the world today" (p. 34). Given the highly political nature of technology, we want to be attentive to the ways that 2.0 tools both promote equality and subtly encourage hierarchy. In many ways, we see 2.0 technologies as a positive force.

To begin, Web 2.0 forwards new ways of conceptualizing knowledge. Dede (2009) has referred to the shift in epistemology between Web 1.0 and Web 2.0 as "seismic," tracing the move from "Classical" notions of knowledge wherein "there is only one correct, unambiguous interpretation of factual interrelationships" discovered by scholars, to a Web 2.0 epistemology, where knowledge is defined as "collective agreement" among ordinary users (p. 80-81). People work together to create content rather than simply reading what has been produced by experts. As education scholar Eijkman (2009) has written, "Web 2.0's privileging of non-foundational knowledge construction challenges conventional thinking about the nature of knowledge, learning, and academia's role as the supreme arbiter of 'true' and 'valid' knowledge" (p. 94). This aligns neatly with PAR's commitment to valuing community members as experts. Student researcher Tim explains that instead of relying solely on Rachael, the university representative, "We use Google Wave…so we can all build off each others' knowledge." For example, we practiced collaborative knowledge generation as we crafted interview questions for the UA writing program director. We began by creating a list of potential questions in a Google Wave document, and then we each read through the list and put emoticons next to the questions we liked. The group copied and pasted questions with more than two emoticons to the top of the document and worked together to delete duplicates, color code the questions based on theme, and arrange them so they progressed smoothly. Google Wave includes a playback feature that

shows the development of drafts over time, and if you were to push the playback button on this document, you would watch six brightly colored cursers jump around the page as the interview questionnaire slowly takes shape. This playback visually represents the philosophies of Web 2.0 and PAR in action.

Web 2.0 tools also have the potential to present new ways of understanding knowledge by extending what counts as data. One method is the 2.0 tendency to "combine facts with other dimensions of human experience, such as opinions, values, and spiritual beliefs" (Dede, 2009, p. 80). In the online world of comments, links, and blogs, these types of knowledge are considered legitimate. Student researcher Tim emphasizes the overlap with PAR: "Just like in PAR, 2.0 accepts experiences and opinions as knowledge and shares the idea that everyone has information to give." During our process, members of the research team shared stories and personal reflections on our subject, often through informal additions to Google Wave documents. Student researcher Oksana writes, "We've used Google Wave to read one another's ideas and opinions and even stated our opinions about their opinions. That's a lot of opinions, but that's what PAR and Web 2.0 are all about." Many online editing programs, including Google Wave, also make possible the expansion of data by accepting texts authored in multiple languages. This welcoming of non-English texts runs in contrast to the ways that many tools "devalue linguistic diversity and inscribe nonstandard language users as Other within the interface... and the culture" (Selfe & Selfe, 1994, p. 489). For example, though Wave's interface is only available in English, the spell checker supports multiple languages, and even recognizes and legitimates the practice of switching languages in mid-sentence, a pattern common in many community settings. Forms of knowledge (such as stories and emotions) and languages (such as mixed Spanish and English) that are traditionally excluded from meaning-making can therefore be included.

The interfaces of 2.0 tools are another aspect to consider when trying to support non-dominant modes of thinking, as interfaces shape the way users process and organize information. As Selfe and Selfe (1994) have argued, interfaces often use hierarchical presentations of knowledge, "a perspective characteristically—while not exclusively—associated with patriarchal cultures and rationalistic traditions of meaning making" (p. 492). In contrast, Selfe and Selfe identify associative patterns of knowledge construction as more inclusive. Some 2.0 tools feature highly associative structures. For example, in Google Wave, instead of replying systematically to messages, users can interject at any point in the text to make connections and add remarks. Portions of the document can be easily highlighted and transformed into a new conversation, or linked to another draft through hypertext. Furthermore, rather than storing documents in separate folders, Wave employs a collective tagging process that allows any user to label a draft and any draft to hold many tags, encouraging multiple associations with each document.

As Web 2.0 works to equalize knowledge production, it has the potential to create space for more egalitarian connections between people. As in several other 2.0 tools, Google Wave's edit function allows multiple users to work on the same text without explicitly attributing changes to particular users.[7] This means that while in edit mode, the group treated Rachael's contributions on Wave with the same scrutiny as text produced by the students, because the authors were unidentified. We were therefore able to remove some of the extra weight attached to ideas offered by the university "authority."

We also attempted more egalitarian interaction in the process of having the student researchers sign consent forms that presented the expectations, risks, and benefits of participating in the evaluation.[8] Consent documents and contracts usually work against participatory approaches (Blake, 2007; Martin, 2007), because people must sign a document that outlines the project before having a chance to give input on its design. Instead, Rachael placed the skeleton of the consent form on Google Wave and worked with the students to edit and add material. The document thus became a mutually-designed agreement rather than a contract owned by the researcher. While we used this strategy to compose an IRB consent form, the same method could work for any opening document or contract that details the evaluation process and goals for participants.

From the authoring of the initial consent form to the composition of this case study, our team has consistently worked on 2.0 tools to guide our research process. No one technology offers a perfect solution, however. For example, we were forced to switch from Wave to Google Documents in order to input and organize our survey data, as Wave does not allow collaborative editing of spreadsheets. The lack of spreadsheet functionality was a major drawback of Google Wave, but it was by no means the only one. We turn now to a discussion of the limitations of 2.0 tools and PAR for service-learning assessments.

## LIMITATIONS OF PAR AND WEB 2.0

If we simply present the potential benefits of participatory technologies, we risk contributing to what Hawisher and Selfe (1991) have described as an irresponsibly positive "rhetoric of technology" (p. 55) that represents digital spaces as sites of idealized democratic exchange. We also perpetuate the incorrect assumption that newer technology always fosters more efficient and effective work (Turnley, 2007, p. 117). If we want to engage participatory methods and technologies responsibly, we must honestly address the ways they can potentially undermine assessment projects. The truth is that during the period we used Wave, it was still a very "buggy" program, and there were days we could have accomplished our work more easily with a pen and paper (Wave "ate" student researcher Jalina's initial contribution to this chapter, for example). Using a collaborative editing tool was also not a cure-all for the unequal power dynamics in our group; as Kelly (1993) has noted in her work on student researcher initiatives, "Researchers and teachers can never stop being authorities or having authority" given the societal context that surrounds the research project (p. 21). PAR and 2.0 technologies may help to mitigate the hierarchy, but it can never be completely eliminated. We must also remember that the *use* of the tool determines the power dynamics of the group more than the tool itself. A university evaluator could work with community members on a 2.0 program in a very anti-participatory manner, without allowing them to contribute meaningfully to the project. The Web 2.0 tool cannot do all the work of power sharing.

Given that use plays such a large role in the potential of 2.0 technologies, practitioners must assess the context where the tool will be used when considering limitations. We recognize that while we felt our attempt to use a collaborative editing program for participatory evaluation was generally effective, the success of our project depended fully on our particular context. Our method will not transfer without complication to other situations. Selber (2004) has explained, "As with any form of literacy, computer practices do not travel seamlessly or unproblematically across contexts, cultures, and communities" (p. 22), and the same concept holds true for research methods (Sullivan & Porter, 1997, p. 69). For example, PE requires a significant time commitment from community members, something not everyone is able or willing to contribute (Gelmon et al, 2001, p. 89; Kinnevy & Boddie, 2001, p. 45). Or, evaluators working with data that might be considered personal because of cultural norms or the nature of the nonprofit agency (e.g., a shelter for homeless youth) might have to reconsider moving data online given privacy issues. Furthermore, attempting a participatory assessment on 2.0 technologies necessitates a certain amount of digital literacy and access on the part of community participants. The student researchers for our project were well prepared because of a grant program at their school that offers high-achieving students free laptops, which are then integrated into classroom instruction. Just down the street, however, another high school in the same district struggles with a severe lack of working computers and digital instruction. Attention to issues of digital access and literacy is especially important for service-learning PE, because the communities where we are negotiating power dynamics are often the same communities negatively impacted by the digital divide. Working on a 2.0 program, however much that program may foster participatory modes of thinking, may actually reinforce unequal power dynamics if the university representative has substantially more experience working online and does not actively find ways to share authority. Community members may end up dependent on the university representative for help navigating the digital landscape, or they may have limited access to computers to do the work. In some contexts, markers and flipchart paper might be a better approach, as everyone has the same level of familiarity with these tools.

No discussion of the limitations of participatory methodologies can be complete without addressing concerns related to the validity of results. Traditional evaluators who craft scales by testing for unidimensionality of scale items, convergent and discriminant validities, and reliability may feel that many participatory evaluations produce "less scientific" results. Of course, it would be possible to go through this kind of highly rigorous process with community members, but many PE practitioners choose to take a more organic approach. We argue that the results are still useful, however. Brunner and Guzman (1989) have also argued for the distinctive value of PE results:

*Participatory evaluation does not produce traditional objective knowledge.... Reality is not described from the point of view of a neutral observer. Instead, it is interpreted by passionately involved people who have a stake in the success of the project. The resulting knowledge is not valid because the method with which it was obtained is replicable or because the theoretical constructs, operational definitions, variables, and indicators match. Instead, this knowledge is validated in action, and it has to prove its usefulness by the changes it accomplishes. (p. 16)*

We agree, and we ask service-learning scholars to consider judging evaluation methods by the results they produce. In the final section, we discuss some of the outcomes of our project.

## THE LIFEWORLD SPEAKS BACK: OUTCOMES AND FUTURE DIRECTIONS

We see three main outcomes of the work our research team has completed. First, our project demonstrates to the high school administration that the university is truly invested in the Wildcat Writers program, and especially in making sure that the program serves the goals of the high school. As our proposal and approval documentation for this project has passed the desks of various school district officials, and as we present on our project, we have raised the profile of the Wildcat Writers program while showing that the program is committed to the community.

Second, the research project has provided significant educational benefits. Rachael, the graduate student, has learned to practice participatory action research, while the high school students have received support in research methods and writing skills. Student researcher Tim notes, "The greatest improvement I have noticed while participating in this research group is my ability to think critically." Beyond academic skills, participatory projects have the potential to promote empowerment among those who contribute, as outlined by the "Wingspread Declaration of Principles

for Youth Participation in Community Research and Evaluation" (Sabo Flores, 2008, p. 8). Our project has also been educational for university students and faculty in that it presents the high school students as holders of valuable knowledge and skills, challenging stereotypes of high school students, especially stereotypes of youth from the south side of Tucson. As student researcher Aria reflects, "Our project brings equality to the high school and college students."

And finally, we believe we have significantly improved the Wildcat Writers service-learning program. Our evaluation allowed us to suggest changes in the way Wildcat Writers is introduced to participants, as we found they needed a more comprehensive orientation to the program. Additionally, we recommended changes to the partner selection process, such as incorporating student-authored bios, so participants have a greater chance of being paired with someone compatible. We also learned that students should be paired with a partner very early in the semester, because when teachers made the pairings later, the relationships between students were not as strong. A key insight was the need to change the timing of the campus visit to the beginning of the program rather than the end, in order to more thoroughly familiarize the high school students with their partners and build a stronger foundation for the semester. Finally, our team suggested that teachers enhance their practice by providing structures to ensure students respond to their partners in a timely matter.

We find these changes especially meaningful because they stem from the community members themselves. Bland and Atweh (2003), drawing on Habermas' theory of communicative action, have written of the potential of student researchers to have input into systems of power. Habermas described a "systems world," comprised of institutions that do not necessarily reflect the values of our "lifeworlds," the daily experiences of people. The systems world has colonized our lifeworld, injecting its principles and metaphors (e.g. productivity, accountability) into the way we live. Our project, along with other participatory evaluations, holds the potential for the lifeworlds of community members to push back and impact the systems world. The students' thoughts, experiences, and opinions are incorporated into the new administrative system of the service-learning program. We see hope in this model.

Much more research has yet to be done in this area. We second the call in *Unheard Voices* for deeper studies into the community experience of service-learning, especially that of community members themselves. There is also a need for more work on service-learning assessment, the ways technologies can shape assessments, and the potentials of participatory strategies to offer greater community input in university collaborations. The field of service-learning is ripe to move in such directions. We return to Aria's insight in the beginning of this chapter, "Who you are changes what you see," to suggest that as the field changes, our perspectives will also change. Service-learning continues to gain legitimacy and the pressure to prove student outcomes is lessening, which means our research and assessment agendas are primed to open up. The field is ready to see communities and community impact as more central aspects of service-learning, and to look *with* and not simply *at* community members as these questions are asked—perhaps through participatory technologies. We hope that this case study has demonstrated, through both the means of its composition and its content, the potential for community members to contribute considerable insight to this conversation.

## ACKNOWLEDGMENT

The authors would like to thank Maria Elena Wakamatsu, NJ Utter, Dawn Maddock-Pea, Peggy DeChecko, Adela Licona, Anne-Marie Hall, Michael and Jennifer Sanchez, Kimberly and Michael Crain, Denise Vidotto, Virginia Gaitan, and the Wildcat Writers students and teachers who participated in our study. This project would have been impossible without your support.

## REFERENCES

Blake, M. (2007). Formality and friendship: Research ethics review and participatory action research. *ACME: An International E-Journal for Critical Geographies, 6*(3), 411–421.

Bland, D. C., & Atweh, W. (2004). A critical approach to collaborating with students as researchers. In E. McWilliam, S. Danby, & J. Knight (Eds.), *Performing education research: Theories, methods, and practices* (pp. 331-344). Flaxton, Qld: Post Pressed.

Bowdon, M. (2008). Introduction. In M. Bowdon, S. H. Billig, & B. A. Holland (Eds.), *Scholarship for sustaining service-learning and community engagement* (pp. xiii–xix). Charlotte, NC: Information Age Publishing.

Brabeck, K. (2004). Testimonio: Bridging feminist and participatory action research principles to create new spaces for collectivity. In M. Brydon-Miller, P. Maguire, & A. McIntyre (Eds.), *Traveling companions: Feminism, teaching, and action research* (pp. 41–52). Westport, CT: Praeger Publishers.

Bringle, R., Phillips, M., & Hudson, M. (Eds.). (2003). *The measure of service learning: Research scales to assess student experiences.* Washington, DC: American Psychological Association.

Brisolara, S. (1998). The history of participatory evaluation and current debates in the field. *New Directions for Evaluation, 80,* 25–41. doi:10.1002/ev.1115

Brunner, I., & Guzman, A. (1989). Participatory evaluation: A tool to assess projects and empower people. *New Directions for Program Evaluation, 42,* 9–18. doi:10.1002/ev.1509

Cahill, C., Rios-Moore, I., & Threats, T. (2008). Different eyes/Open eyes: Community-based participatory action research. In J. Cammarota & M. Fine (Eds.), *Revolutionizing education: Youth participatory action research in motion* (pp. 89–124). New York, NY: Routledge.

Cammarota, J., & Fine, M. (Eds.). (2008). *Revolutionizing education: Youth participatory action research in motion*. New York: Routledge.

Cohen, J., & Kinsey, D. (1994). Doing good and scholarship: A service-learning study. *Journalism Educator, 48*(4), 4–14.

Cormode, G., & Krishnamurthy, B. (2008). Key differences between Web 1.0 and Web 2.0. *First Monday, 13*(6). Retrieved July 19, 2010, from http://www.uic.edu/htbin/cgiwrap/bin/ojs/index.php/fm/article/view/2125/1972

Cruz, N. I., & Giles, D. E. (2000). Where's the community in service-learning research? *Michigan Journal of Community Service Learning,* Special Issue, 28-34.

Deans, T. (2000). *Writing partnerships: Service-learning in composition*. Urbana, IL: NCTE.

Dede, C. (2008). A seismic shift in epistemology. *EDUCAUSE Review, 43*(3), 80–81.

Driscoll, A., Holland, B., Gelmon, S., & Kerrigan, S. (1996). An assessment model for service-learning: Comprehensive case studies of impact on faculty, students, community, and institution. *Michigan Journal of Community Service Learning, 3*, 66–71.

Eijkman, H. (2008). Web 2.0 as a non-foundational network-centric learning space. *Campus-Wide Information Systems, 25*(2), 93–104. doi:10.1108/10650740810866567

Eijkman, H. (2009). Using Web 2.0 to decolonise transcultural learning zones in higher education. *Campus-Wide Information Systems, 26*(3), 240–255. doi:10.1108/10650740910967401

Fals-Borda, O. (2001). Participatory (action) research in social theory: Origins and challenges. In P. Reason & H. Bradbury (Eds.), *Handbook of action research: Participative inquiry and practice* (pp. 27–37). Los Angeles, CA: SAGE Publications.

Feenberg, A. (1991). *Critical theory of technology*. New York, NY: Oxford University Press.

Ferman, B., & Hill, T. L. (2004). The challenges of agenda conflict in higher-education-community research partnerships: Views from the community side. *Journal of Urban Affairs, 26*(2), 241–257. doi:10.1111/j.0735-2166.2004.00199.x

Freire, P. (2000). *Pedagogy of the oppressed* (Ramos, M., Trans.). New York, NY: Continuum International Publishing Group. (Original work published 1970)

Geisler, C. (2001). IText: Future directions for research on the relationship between information technology and writing. *Journal of Business and Technical Communication, 15*(3), 269–308. doi:10.1177/105065190101500302

Gelmon, S. (2000). Challenges in assessing service-learning. *Michigan Journal of Community Service Learning,* Special Issue, 84-90.

Gelmon, S., Holland, B., Driscoll, A., Spring, A., & Kerrigan, S. (2001). *Assessing service-learning and civic engagement: Principles and techniques*. Providence, RI: Campus Compact.

Haraway, D. (1988). Situated knowledges: The science question in feminism and the privilege of partial perspective. *Feminist Studies, 14*(3), 575–599. doi:10.2307/3178066

Hawisher, G., & Selfe, C. (1991). The rhetoric of technology and the electronic writing class. *College Composition and Communication, 42*(1), 55–65. doi:10.2307/357539

Holland, B. (2001). A comprehensive model for assessing service-learning and community-university partnerships. *New Directions for Higher Education, 114*, 51–60. doi:10.1002/he.13.abs

Kapor, M. (2006, April 23). Architecture is politics (and politics is architecture). *Mitch Kapor's blog.* Retrieved July 19, 2010, from http://blog.kapor.com/index9cd7.html?p=29

Kelly, D. M. (1993). Secondary power source: High school students as participatory researchers. *The American Sociologist, 24*(1), 8–26. doi:10.1007/BF02691942

Kinnevy, S. C., & Boddie, S. C. (2001). Developing community partnerships through service-learning: Universities, coalitions, and congregations. *Michigan Journal of Community Service Learning, 8*(1), 44–51.

Lewin, K. (1948). *Resolving social conflicts.* New York, NY: Harper and Row.

Martin, A. SeBlonka, K., & Tryon, E. (2009). The challenge of short-term service learning. In R. Stoecker, E. A. Tryon, & A. Hilgendorf (Eds.), *The unheard voices: Community organizations and service learning* (pp. 57-72). Philadelphia, PA: Temple University Press.

Martin, D. (2007). Bureacratizing ethics: Institutional review boards and participatory research. *ACME: An International E-Journal for Critical Geographies, 6*(3), 319–328.

Marullo, S., Cooke, D., Willis, J., Rollins, A., Burke, J., Bonilla, P., & Waldref, V. (2003). Community-based research assessments: Some principles and practices. *Michigan Journal of Community Service Learning, 9*(3), 57–68.

O'Reilly, T. (2005, September 30). What is Web 2.0: Design patterns and business models for the next generation of software. *O'Reilly.* Retrieved July 19, 2010, from http://oreilly.com/web2/archive/what-is-web-20.html

Oates, K. K., & Leavitt, L. H. (2003). *Service-learning and learning communities: Tools for integration and assessment.* Washington, DC: Association of American Colleges and Universities.

Payne, D. A. (2000). *Evaluating service-learning activities and programs.* Lanham, MD: The Scarecrow Press.

Pratt, M. L. (1991). Arts of the contact zone. *Profession, 91*, 33–40.

Reardon, K. M. (1998). Participatory action research as service-learning. *New Directions for Teaching and Learning, 73*, 57–64. doi:10.1002/tl.7307

Sabo Flores, K. (2008). *Youth participatory evaluation: Strategies for engaging young people.* San Francisco: Jossey-Bass.

Sandy, M., & Holland, B. A. (2006). Different worlds and common ground: Community partner perspectives on campus-community relationships. *Michigan Journal of Community Service Learning, 13*(1), 30–43.

Selber, S. A. (2004). *Multiliteracies for a digital age.* Carbondale, IL: Southern Illinois University Press.

Selfe, C. L., & Selfe, R. J. (1994). The politics of the interface: Power and its exercise in electronic contact zones. *College Composition and Communication, 45*(4), 480–504. doi:10.2307/358761

Senge, P. M., & Scharmer, C. O. (2001). Community action research: Learning as a community of practitioners, consultants, and researchers. In P. Reason & H. Bradbury (Eds.), *Handbook of action research* (pp. 195–206). Los Angeles, CA: SAGE Publications.

Stoecker, R., & Tryon, E. A. (2009). Unheard voices: Community organizations and service learning. In R. Stoecker, E. A. Tryon, & A. Hilgendorf (Eds.), *The unheard voices: Community organizations and service learning* (pp. 1–18). Philadelphia, PA: Temple University Press.

Stoecker, R., Tryon, E. A., & Hilgendorf, A. (Eds.). (2009). *The unheard voices: Community organizations and service learning.* Philadelphia, PA: Temple University Press.

Sullivan, P., & Porter, J. (1997). *Opening spaces: Writing technologies and critical research practices.* Greenwich, CT: Ablex Publishing Corporation.

Toncar, M. F., Reid, J. S., Burns, D. J., Anderson, C. E., & Nguyen, H. P. (2006). Uniform assessment of the benefits of service learning: The development, evaluation, and implementation of the Seleb Scale. *Journal of Marketing Theory and Practice, 14*(3), 223–238. doi:10.2753/MTP1069-6679140304

Toupin, L., & Plews, B. (2007). Exploring the looming leadership deficit in the voluntary and nonprofit sector. *The Philanthropist, 21*(2), 128–137.

Turnley, M. (2007). Integrating critical approaches to technology and service-learning projects. *Technical Communication Quarterly, 16*(1), 103–123. doi:10.1207/s15427625tcq1601_6

## ENDNOTES

[1] See Stoecker & Tryon (2009) and Sandy & Holland (2006) for two studies attempting to equalize this imbalance through large-scale investigations of non-profit staff perspective on service-learning.

[2] A "we voice" also provides a more honest representation of the shared labor of our project.

[3] Wildcat Writers is also part of GEAR-UP (Gaining Early Awareness and Readiness for Undergraduate Programs), a federal grant project.

[4] Each of these technologies allows for different kinds of interaction. E-mail and blogs facilitate the exchange of and response to basic texts. Nings are networking tools that combine profiles, comment walls, photo-sharing, and discussion boards. VoiceThread allows students to post, annotate, and respond to visual images, while Glogster provides a space for students to create visual arguments. Edmodo uses a Facebook-style interface to allow students to post and reply to material. With GeoGraffiti, students can comment on specific geographic locations, a helpful tool in place-based pedagogies.

[5] See Sabo Flores (2008) for a description of how to utilize logic models in participatory evaluations.

[6] Other fields with rich literatures that inspired our work include transformative participatory evaluation (TPE), youth participatory action research (YPAR), youth participatory evaluation (YPE), and the students as researchers movement (Bland & Atweh, 2004; Brisolara, 1998; Cammarota & Fine, 2008; Kelly, 1993; Sabo Flores, 2008).

[7] However, the "reply" function does label text by its author.

[8] The student researchers had to sign IRB consent forms because they would be potentially working on this publication. Usually service-learning practitioners interested in PE need not worry about engaging with the IRB if the project will not be published or presented in an academic forum.

# Chapter 2
# SAGE:
## An International Partnership Linking High School Students, Universities and the Private Sector through Social Enterprise

**Curtis L. DeBerg**
*California State University, Chico, USA*

## ABSTRACT

*This case study describes an international partnership among four main stakeholders: (1) a nonprofit organization called Students for the Advancement of Global Entrepreneurship (SAGE), (2) high school students and their teachers, (3) university students and (4) the private sector, including corporations, foundations, and individual philanthropists. SAGE, incorporated as a nonprofit charitable corporation, is a global network with the following mission: to help create the next generation of entrepreneurial leaders whose innovations and social enterprises address the world's major unmet needs. SAGE started as a California-only initiative in 2003, but has now grown to operate in eight U.S. states and 19 countries. This would not be possible without available technology. The model provided here can be implemented by others who are interested in utilizing technology to build Transnational Social Movement Organizations (TSMOs), resulting in the creation of social capital to solve local problems.*

## INTRODUCTION

The next generation of entrepreneurial leaders, guided by creative educational design including service-based learning, can drive global innovation and positive social change through partnerships among educators, the social sector and the private sector. To develop the next generation of entrepreneurial leaders, we can use available technology to engage today's high school and university students in social entrepreneurship as a catalyst for

DOI: 10.4018/978-1-60960-623-7.ch002

partnership and collaboration for societal change. By leveraging existing technology, as well as the underutilized capacity in universities to provide the human capital necessary, we can rapidly scale up and amplify the effects of this innovation to produce a future replete with social entrepreneurs.

This case study describes a global partnership that is successful, in large measure, because of two primary technological tools: a centralized Web site (http://sageglobal.org) and an electronic listserv (sagemail@lists.csuchico.edu). The Web site serves as a hub for information such as guidebooks, PowerPoint presentations, brochures, schedules, sample grant proposal templates and examples of successful social enterprises. While the Web site serves as the primary hub, many of the participating countries have created their own Web sites to address local needs. Furthermore, the listserv allows over 500 subscribers in 19 countries to directly communicate and engage in transnational dialogue. Subscribers include high school teachers and students, university professors and students, NGOs, government officials, business leaders and individual philanthropists. Together, they share ideas and projects that can be replicated in other parts of the world.

The partnership involves four primary stakeholders: (1) a nonprofit organization called Students for the Advancement of Global Entrepreneurship (SAGE), (2) high school students between the ages of 13 and 19, (3) universities (especially professional programs like business) and (4) the private sector, including corporations, foundations and individual philanthropists. SAGE, incorporated as a 501(c)(3) charitable corporation in California, has the following mission: to help create the next generation of entrepreneurial leaders whose innovations and social enterprises address our world's major unmet needs. SAGE is now operating in eight U.S. states and 19 countries.

The model described here can be implemented by others who are interested in utilizing available technology to build Transnational Social Movement Organizations (TSMOs). According to Smith (2001), TSMOs:

*provide a mechanism for articulating, recognizing and confronting transnational differences in viewpoints and priorities that are caused by class, race, gender, and national political contexts. The ability to engage in such transnational dialogue—either face-to-face or via newsletter or via e-mail—is a necessary component for the formation of social capital and for the strengthening of a global civil society. (p. 206)*

SAGE is an example of a TSMO, in that it offers a new way of thinking about how to educate the next generation of leaders, with social enterprise as the focal point.

In this case study, I describe how social capital is being generated by teenagers from around the world as they create social enterprises that address local problems. By providing a platform for youth to describe their innovations on a regional, national and world stage, with business leaders acting as jurists and evaluators, SAGE has become a networked nonprofit as opposed to a traditional nonprofit. According to Wei-Skillern and Marciano (2008):

*Networked nonprofits are different from traditional nonprofits in that they cast their gazes externally rather than internally. They put their mission first and their organization second. They govern through trust rather than control. And they cooperate as equal nodes in a constellation of actors rather than on relying on a central hub to command with top-down tactics. (p. 43)*

## HISTORY OF THE PROJECT

Preparing young people for a successful future—this is the job of public education throughout the civilized world. However, ever-increasing pressures have dictated priorities in public spending, and resources that normally ensure a well-rounded education for all students have been stretched thin. Key subject areas such as math, science and languages continue to be prioritized, but in this chapter I contend that educators in all disciplines can help their students adopt a global worldview while preparing them to become social entrepreneurs, productive workers and active citizens in a global economy.

A challenge for educators is to identify relevant in- and out-of-classroom learning opportunities where students can link theory to practice. As global markets expand and global tensions rise, there might be no more important time than now to help today's youth develop an international perspective, while encouraging them to pursue their individual passions and talents. Based on this belief, I founded the SAGE organization in 2003, with a belief that social enterprise should be a valued topic to be taught in secondary schools, either as course content or as an afterschool activity.

From 1997 to 2002, SAGE operated as a small program (under a different name) only in California. Starting in 2003, however, it expanded beyond California and has now grown to include a total of eight states and 19 countries. Countries include Canada, China, DR – Congo, Ghana, Israel, Malaysia, Nigeria, Northern Ireland, Philippines, Russia, Singapore, South Africa, South Korea, Tanzania, Uganda, Ukraine, United States, Zambia and Zimbabwe. Without the ability to share information on the web and to communicate via e-mail, this program would not have been possible. Furthermore, this program could not be possible without support from the private sector, including corporations, foundations and individuals, and universities who provide mentors to the younger students.

## THE FOCUS ON HIGH SCHOOL STUDENTS

One reason SAGE focuses on high school-aged youth is because "teenagers are the single most influential group in a low-income community" (Bornstein, 2004, pp. 176-177). Moreover, the International Labor Organization (2009) estimates that about 85.3 million young men and women were unemployed throughout the world in 2006. Also, the ILO estimates that 59 million young people between 15 and 17 years of age are engaged in hazardous forms of work.

High school youth are the primary focal point because they are the *future* entrepreneurs, employees, investors, customers and citizens. SAGE's conceptual foundation relies heavily on social entrepreneurship, as a discipline, and experiential education, as a teaching strategy. My goal in starting SAGE was driven by three primary outcomes: (1) greater awareness among global youth of the power of socially responsible business and entrepreneurship to improve their lives; (2) greater social capital contributed by the participants and greater social assets enjoyed by the community; and (3) stronger links among local education and business activists to effect meaningful changes in their communities by being linked to the global SAGE network.

## SOCIAL ENTERPRISE AS THE MAIN TOPIC

Social enterprise has been defined many different ways, but in this case study I adopt the view offered by Dees (2003):

*Any form of social entrepreneurship that is worth promoting broadly must be about establishing new and better ways to improve the world. Social entrepreneurs implement innovative programs, organizational structures, or resource strategies that increase their chances of achieving deep, broad, lasting, and cost-effective social impact.*

This view focuses on innovation and impact, whether or not the enterprise relies on earned income strategies. In other words, both profit-seeking businesses and nonprofit seeking businesses (NGOs) can be considered entrepreneurial if they are innovative and seek social impact.

By focusing on youth and social impact, SAGE's goal is to increase the number of social entrepreneurs, as well as productive workers who have the mindset of a social entrepreneur. Productive employment of youth will not be solely in the private and public sectors. Instead, they will also be working in Drucker's (1994)*social sector.* Table 1 provides a taxonomy of five types of organizations ranging from private sector, for-profit businesses to public sector (nonprofit) government organizations. In between, we have three hybrid organizations: for-profit businesses, but with a strong sense of social responsibility; nonprofit businesses, but with significant earned income capacity; and nonprofit organizations, with little or no revenue-generating capacity.

The three hybrid organizations identified in Table 1 are part of the social sector. Drucker predicted a more entrepreneurial 21st century, in which we would see a shift in the balance of power. The power would shift from the company to the "knowledge worker." In the knowledge society, these knowledge workers will not depend so much on their employers from the private sector or the public sector to meet their health care, education and social needs. Rather, they will depend on a new, social sector, whose institutions aim to create human health and well-being.

I posit that 21st century growth in the social sector will in large part be credited to two actors: (1) humanitarian capitalists and (2) social capitalists. I define humanitarian capitalists as leaders of for-profit businesses who view themselves as socially responsible and who proactively implement sustainable business practices. Companies like these understand their social responsibility

to improve communities while making profits. Rather than focusing solely on "single bottom line" profits, these companies adopt a broader view of success that focuses on the "triple bottom line"—profits, people and planet (Savitz & Weber, 2006). Contrast this with social capitalists, who are leaders of organizations whose primarily motivation is not to maximize financial wealth for shareholders; rather, their main goal is to maximize social impact. But one way to maximize social impact, of course, is through earned income strategies that can sustain the organization.

Taken together, humanitarian and social capitalists can be classified under what Bill Gates refers to as creative capitalism. According to Gates:

*Governments and nonprofit groups have an irreplaceable role in helping [the world's poor], but it will take far too long if they try to do it alone. It is mainly corporations that have the skills to make technological innovations work for the poor. To make the most of those skills, we need a more creative capitalism: an attempt to stretch the reach of market forces so that more companies can benefit from doing work that makes more people better off. We need new ways to bring far more people into the system—capitalism—that has done so much good in the world. (Gates, 2008, p. 40)*

SAGE's goal is to increase the number of social and humanitarian capitalists, starting with teenagers. One proven way to engage students is by giving them a role and voice in their own education. Today's world is rich in career opportunities in both the private and social sectors, and actively engaging students in community projects is consistent with the views of school reformers who have learned that students want more personal involvement (Noguera, 2004) and who are most vibrant when creating or thinking about something new (Intrator, 2004). By doing so, faculty members who are themselves social entrepreneurs are encouraging their students to become social entrepreneurs.

*Table 1. Drucker's organizations linked to entrepreneurship and capital*

| Business and Nonbusiness Organizations in a Democratic Society (according to Drucker, not all organizations are entrepreneurial) | Drucker's Sectors | Entrepreneurial Organizations (founders are opportunity finders/innovators) | Main Source of Capital (Financial, Social) | Measured By | Primary Value Perspective |
|---|---|---|---|---|---|
| 1. For-profit; primary stakeholder => shareholder/investor; goal is to maximize wealth for investors | Private Sector | Business entrepreneurs | Financial | Net income (i.e., profit; earnings); stock price | Short-term profits to maximize shareholder wealth |
| 2. For-profit; humanitarian capitalism => primary stakeholder => shareholder/investor, but concern for other stakeholders; goal is to first maximize wealth for investors, but ancillary goal is to add value for customers, employees, suppliers, community | Private/Social Sector | Business entrepreneurs with humanitarian perspective | Financial, then Social | Net income and stock price first, and then nonfinancial performance measures such as triple bottom line income and balance sheet goodwill | Short-term and long-term profits; good community standing |
| 3. Nonprofit, with a revenue-generating capacity; social capitalism; primary stakeholder => targeted clients in the community; primary goal is to maximize value for target clients, but to also finance their operations (in part) from retained profits | Social Sector/Private Sector | Social entrepreneurs with a profit making component | Social, then Financial | Nonfinancial performance measures first, then net income | Benefits to clients; profits and contributions to sustain operating capacity |
| 4. Nonprofit; no revenue-generating capacity (funding comes entirely from donations, government funding (e.g., development aid); primary goal is to maximize value for targeted clients in the community | Social Sector | Social entrepreneurs | Social | Nonfinancial performance measures | Benefits to clients; contributions to sustain operating capacity |
| 5. Government (local, state, federal, global); collects funds through taxes; primary goal is to balance stakeholder "health" (safety, health, environment, culture) through compliance (making rules and enforcing them) | Public Sector | Innovative organizations constrained by government mandate | Social | Public "good" (safety, education, transportation, social security) | Benefits to citizens, but constrained by budgets |

## THE ROLE OF TECHNOLOGY

Today's technology has made a program like SAGE possible. Community partnerships are now defined not only as the local community, but also the online global community. Communication among members of the SAGE network is achieved through Web page updates, on-line registration for events, listservs, e-mail, text messaging, Facebook groups and Skype (Skype calls are free when made computer to computer, and very inexpensive when calling from a computer to a telephone). To date, SAGE has been able to rely on an active national and global advisory board and a dedicated staff of volunteers to maintain quality. Effective communication with state and national SAGE coordinators, and the advisory boards, has been achieved primarily with listservs and general e-mail. The staff consists of veteran university students who have at least two years of experience with the SAGE program as part of their service-learning activities. Communication with staff has been achieved primarily with text messaging and voicemail.

Entry into the network typically occurs when a high school student or teacher discovers SAGE on the Internet and inquires about the program. The same is true for a university professor or an executive with an NGO who inquires about how to start a SAGE program in their region or country. The SAGE home office immediately replies to these queries and offers advice on how to proceed. If a high school is located in an area where SAGE does not have a state or national coordinator, then we invite that high school to launch SAGE on a trial basis and then work to find a SAGE host university and regional coordinator.

## ORGANIZATIONAL STRUCTURE

SAGE is governed by nine board members, who in turn have retained me as the CEO. Two other officers include the COO and CFO. The board meets four times a year (three times via teleconference; since not all board members currently use Skype, we have not yet used this for group meetings), and communicates regularly via e-mail. Each of the 19 countries participating in SAGE has a National Coordinator, who provides the board with advice and direction via a listserv explicitly devoted to national coordinators.

Figure 1 provides a diagram of how the entire community can become involved in SAGE. At the heart, of course, is the high school student SAGE team. The younger students are assisted upstream by university students who are assigned to high schools as mentors. The university students can be part of a service-learning class, a civic engagement class or a student organization where service is a key part of their mission.

The high school students are also assisted, laterally, by their high school teacher (or adviser), and by a group of leaders from the business and civic community who volunteer to serve on the team's business advisory board. Together, the combined group of high school teachers, university mentors, and community leaders helps the high school student team identify, launch and operate their for-profit and social enterprises during the academic year.

At the end of the year, the high school student teams are invited to a regional tournament, where they describe their most successful ventures to a new group of business and civic leaders who serve as tournament judges (i.e., panelists/evaluators) of the written annual report and 13-minute oral presentation. It is important to note that many of the evaluators are recruited from companies and foundations that support the program. For example, some of the current sponsors include Target Corporation, Enterprise Rent-a-Car, Wells Fargo, Allstate, Bank of the West, Deloitte and the Sierra Health Foundation of Sacramento.

## COMMUNITY IMPACT

SAGE brings entrepreneurial teams of teenagers into the community, under the direction of their teacher and university student mentors. Community impact has been largely dependent on the strength of each team's local partnerships and the dedication of the teacher leading the program. Each year, SAGE provides prize money to the best enterprises.

As an example, the best social enterprise in 2009 was presented to a team from the Philippines. The award-winning project was "Palm Frond Cement-Bonded Block (PFCBB) Production." In search of an alternative that would arrest the rising cost of construction materials and to answer the

*Figure 1. The SAGE partnership model: Bringing high schools, universities and the business community together [Excerpted from SAGE 2008 Annual Report Page 4 www.sageglobal.org/doc/SAGEAnnual-Report2008.pdf]*

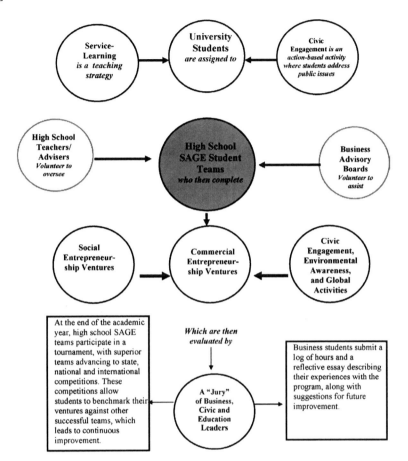

environmental and health problems caused by the burning of palm fronds, PFCBB was developed. The extraction process utilizes the inner portion of the frond as a substitute aggregate in fabricating concrete blocks while the cleaned frond is utilized as a substitute for plywood. PFCBB is best recommended for non-load bearing walls like partition walls, fences and pig pens. The product was introduced in Barangay Ceram (on the island of Mindanao) and the SAGE team trained over 100 male participants on the skills needed in the fabrication of PFCBB. The team also educated the residents on the environmental and health hazards caused by improper burning of the agricultural residue.

According to Reblando (2009), in an August 2009 article in the *Manila Bulletin*, Governor Teng Mangudadatu of Sultan Kudarat commended the team for winning the prestigious SAGE Philippines cup and hailed the invention as a breakthrough in the construction industry whose benefit would redound to the people, especially the poor. "Certainly, this invention of a new cement block which is lightweight yet fire-resistant, would eventually solve the problem on lack of shelter in the country plagued by high price of construction materials," Mangudadatu said. The governor said he would order the provincial engineering office to find out how to manufacture palm frond cement blocks and test it for a construction project in the province.

## EDUCATIONAL IMPACT ON HIGH SCHOOL STUDENTS

SAGE operates in approximately 1,000 high schools throughout the world. With an average SAGE team of about 15 students each, this program directly impacts about 15,000 students per year. Though it is difficult to assess the impact SAGE makes on the individual learning of each participant, as measured by traditional exams, there is ample evidence of impact through authentic assessment. SAGE offers a unique from of assessment. In order to be competitive, students must design projects that meet ten specific judging criteria. Table 2 provides a summary of the criteria.

Unlike most forms of academic assessment, which is made by teachers, the evaluators are business and community leaders who serve as competition judges. Furthermore, high school students are strongly encouraged to observe as other teams make their multimedia presentations. By observing other teams, students are able to benchmark their own program, which in turn leads to improvement in future years.

When teachers incorporate SAGE activities into an existing course, students are asked to reflect on their work through project papers and plans, written journals and oral presentations. As the SAGE tournament approaches, there are other means for incorporating structured reflection into the service-learning projects, such as the written annual report preparation process and regional/national presentations, and mentoring activities.

Consider the reflections of Nidya Baez, a student from Oakland, who said this about her SAGE experience: "I'm so proud of my school! It makes me feel motivated, but what makes me feel the best is that all the other students saw everything, took part, and feel empowered to make a difference. Now I [am] motivated to continue with

other projects, to help others, and to work hard and to make an impact" (Baez, 2007). And consider Veronica Garcia: "I learned things like teamwork and that we can unite for the better. I know that we are making a difference. Our hard work does matter" (Garcia, 2007). Baez and Garcia were members of the 2004 SAGE World Cup champion team from the Fremont Business Academy. Both recently graduated from University of California Berkeley and are social entrepreneurs in the San Francisco Bay Area.

Unlike other high school classroom projects, which are completed at the end of a semester, SAGE teams are strongly encouraged to *sustain* their best projects from year to year. In fact, two of the ten judging criteria require that teams continue their best social and for-profit enterprises from one year to the next. Consider the worlds of teacher, Teri Jones, from Santa Monica High School: "SAGE competitions have been a fantastic addition to our classes, and the competition is what drives the students to reach new heights" (Jones, 2009).

Benefits to high schools include more motivated and inspired student, energized faculty, a greater sense of collaboration between the schools and the community at large, and positive public relations. As an example of the value for an educational institution, consider this excerpt from one of Nigeria's leading magazines, which interviewed the principal of the national champion high school team from Nigeria:

*Saidu Garba, the principal of the school, could not hide his feelings when he spoke to the magazine last week. He said SAGE was the best thing that had happened to the school in the last three years, stressing that the group had made the school famous as a skill-acquisition centre. Garba said poverty had been the major problem of majority of Nigerians, and saw programmes like that of SAGE as a feasible way out of mass poverty. Now a child who is involved in SAGE programmes and cannot further his education would not become a*

*Table 2. Ten SAGE judging criteria [Excerpted from Page 4 of the SAGE Information Handbook for Advisers 2009-2010: http://sageglobal.org/doc/SAGEHandbook2009-2010.pdf ]*

| How effective were the students in demonstrating that they: | Written Annual Report * | Oral Presentation |
|---|---|---|
| (1) planned and operated at least one<u>new</u>, *commercial business*; in doing so, the students showed that they *learned* about entrepreneurship and business, and were able to *apply* their knowledge and skills to plan and implement their business; the primary purpose of a commercial business is profit; a secondary purpose can be to solve a social problem. | 4 | 4 |
| (2) planned and operated at least *one<u>continuing</u>, commercial business*; in doing so, the students showed that they *learned* about entrepreneurship and business, and were able to *apply* their knowledge and skills to plan and implement their business (Note: If this is a SAGE team's first year, it may "opt out" of this criterion and ask judges to weight Criterion (1) a total of 20 points). | 4 | 4 |
| (3) planned and operated at least one<u>new</u> *social venture*; in doing so, the students showed that they *learned* about social entrepreneurship and socially-responsible business, and were able to *apply* their knowledge and skills to plan, implement and sustain their venture. The primary purpose of a social venture is to solve a social problem; a secondary purpose may be to make a profit. | 4 | 4 |
| (4) planned and operated at least one<u>continuing</u> *social venture*; in doing so, the students showed that they *learned* about social entrepreneurship and socially-responsible business, and were able to *apply* their knowledge and skills to plan, implement and sustain their venture (Note: If this is a SAGE team's first year, it may "opt out" of this criterion and ask judges to weight Criterion (3) a total of 20 points). | 4 | 4 |
| (5) Included at least one type of "global" component in their activities during the year (e.g., did students work with students or businesses from another country to import/export products; did they study how free markets work in an economy other than their own; did they understand which organizations are the key policymakers in a global economy?). | 4 | 4 |
| (6) Understand the importance of civic engagement in a democratic society, and that each citizen can exercise their freedom by registering to vote and participating in public elections? | 4 | 4 |
| (7) Understand the importance of being responsible stewards of the environment in a market economy? | 4 | 4 |
| *How effective were the students in:* | | |
| (8) Utilizing their resources, including at least one or two "consultants/mentors" from a nearby college or university, and a Business Advisory Board (each team should have at least three active BAB members, at least two of whom come from the private sector) to help them identify, deliver, assess and present their projects? | 4 | 4 |
| (9) Utilizing mass media (e.g., newspapers, TV, radio, billboards, newsletters, a Web site devoted to SAGE)? Attach newspaper articles to the annual report. | 4 | 4 |
| (10) Measuring the results of their projects (e.g., pre- and post-tests; financial statements)? | 4 | 4 |
| TOTAL POSSIBLE POINTS | 40 pts | 40 pts |
| How effective were the students in their responses to judges' questions during the Q and A period? **20pts** | | |

Written Annual Report _____ (40 points maximum)

Oral Presentation _____ (40 points maximum)

Q & A Period _____ (20 points maximum)

Total _____ (100 points maximum)

*liability to society. He has something to fall back on because of the skill element of the programme." He said that the programme had caused a change in the career choice of many of the students. Some of them now prefer to continue their education in vocational schools. Garba said the successes recorded by SAGE had encouraged teachers and*

*educators to start campaigning for the inclusion of entrepreneurship skill acquisition in the secondary school curriculum for the benefit of all students. (Ibeneme, 2009, p. 33)*

In the United States, SAGE was nationally recognized as a featured program in the "Promising Practices in Afterschool System" (see http://www.afterschool.org/).

The PPAS System is an effort to find and share good things that go on in afterschool programs countrywide. Funded with support from the Charles Stewart Mott Foundation, it is one of approximately 100 practices that have been recognized as promising. The SAGE activity was highlighted as the "Featured Program" in May 2004.

## VALUE OF THE PROJECT FOR UNIVERSITIES

The Association to Advance Collegiate Schools of Business (AACSB) is the premier standard-setting body for universities seeking accreditation (AACSBb, 2006). The AACSB encourages business schools to pursue their own diverse missions, with the ultimate goal that business education prepares students to contribute to their organizations and the larger society. It also recognized that challenges for business education are similar to the challenges faced by other organizations including global economic forces, differences in organizational and cultural values, cultural diversity among employees and customers, and changing technology in products and processes.

SAGE has made a strong contribution to the mission of the College of Business at California State University, Chico. In a January 2008 letter to the dean at CSU, Chico, extending maintenance of accreditation until 2012, the AACSB explicitly cited SAGE as a program to be commended as an effective practice.

The program is also consistent with the recommendations offered by the AACSB's Peace through Commerce Task Force report (AACSBa, 2006). This report addressed how business education may be able to contribute to a "world of good." Because private sector businesses seek new opportunities and markets, they are innovative in finding effective solutions that transcend

personal and cultural differences. Creating new value "can inspire collaboration between strangers and sometimes even between those who might have regarded each other as enemies. Once people work together and learn that people are essentially the same, regardless of their backgrounds, making war is likely to become far less attractive than making money" (AACSBa, 2006: 7). The ability to find mutually beneficial opportunities often depends on one's network, and when people of different backgrounds and perspectives decide to work together, this is known by sociologists and political scientists as "bridging social capital" (Putnam, 2000b, 1).

The Peace through Commerce Task Force (AACSB, 2006a) called on business schools to teach the importance of nonfinancial measures of corporate performance. The report stated: "Management education should also offer students opportunities to explore the underlying philosophical, nonfinancial aspects of business. By integrating these concepts into the educational experiences of students, schools can produce more globally conscious leaders and heighten understanding—and even prospects for peace" (AACSBa: 6). The AACSB listed SAGE as an effective practice in contributing to its peace through commerce initiative (see http://www.aacsb.edu/resource_centers/peace/practices.asp).

## A LOOK AHEAD

The SAGE board of directors met in June 2010 to explore ways to improve and expand its reach. Among the topics on the agenda were how technologies can successfully foster collaboration among the different partners in SAGE projects and how the best projects can be shared. One of the board members is a successful Silicon Valley software entrepreneur who is now retired, and he has agreed to focus his energy on Web infrastructure. Namely, he will focus on the creation of (1) online document repositories (e.g., summaries of successful projects; business plans; annual reports) and (2) online forms linked to spreadsheets as small databases. After the basics are set up, we will then encourage all members of the SAGE network—including community members and student partners—to contribute articles and ideas, thereby allowing members to engage one another across time and space and culture.

We will also encourage more collaboration directly among SAGE teams, similar to what the SAGE team from Mercer Island High School in Washington did this year. Mercer teamed up with a high school SAGE team from Cape Coast, Ghana, through e-mail and video conferencing to start a global trading company dedicated to "connecting the world, one school at a time." They wrote a business plan, formed a hypothetical corporation, sold stock and created a venture to trade goods with a SAGE school in Ghana. They also added Malaysia as a trading partner to expand their relationships with international students.

*Another significant change is designed to increase the impact and sustainability of the business ventures. To increase impact, SAGE teams will now choose to conduct one or both of two separate competitions:*

- **Social enterprise businesses (SEBs):** Social enterprises directly address social needs through their products or services or through the numbers of disadvantaged people they employ; they can be legally structured either as nonprofits or as for-profit businesses, but in either case must be profitable.
- **Socially responsible businesses (SRBs):** Socially responsible businesses are always legally structured as for-profit businesses; they do not directly address social needs through their products or services or through the numbers of disadvantaged people they employ; instead, they create

positive social change indirectly through the practice of corporate social responsibility (e.g., creating and implementing a philanthropic foundation; paying equitable wages to their employees; using environmentally friendly raw materials; providing volunteers to help with community projects; and so on).

To increase sustainability, each team will be allowed to enter the same business for a maximum of three years. This change not only increases the probability that ventures will be sustained, but it also has the added benefit of preventing long-term dominance by a single team. In both competitions, teams will be judged on their ability to demonstrate measurable success in two principal areas:

- **Marketplace viability:** The business must either have achieved profitability already or have defined a believable path toward profitability.
- **Social impact:** The business must demonstrate significant social impact, either through their products and services or through the numbers of disadvantaged people they employ (as a SEB) or through the practice of corporate social responsibility (as a SRB).

Another substantial change made by the board initially involves only SAGE teams in the USA. State tournaments will be discontinued starting in 2011. Instead, the state tournaments will be replaced by a larger and better-publicized national tournament that will take place in Chicago each year. Mentoring by university students will continue to include on-site visits by the older students to the SAGE teams, but we will urge more mentoring through webcam videoconferencing using Yahoo and Skype. This is another example of how we will use technologies to foster and sustain the relationships among high school students and their university partners.

To date, SAGE has not yet made a concentrated effort to use technology to teach and support actual collaborations among participants. With the changes adopted by the board, however, this will be improved. Further, we plan to create a new special competition—in addition to the special competitions now that award prize money to the best social ventures and best environmental ventures—to recognize teams that have been the most effective and innovative in using technology to collaborate with other SAGE teams.

## CONCLUSION

This case study described an international partnership that encourages youth to become social and humanitarian capitalists. This partnership would not be nearly as effective without the ability to share information and communicate using today's technology in the partnership. The SAGE program offers a new way of thinking about how high school educators can engage students in hands-on, real-world activities. The program encourages teenagers to create social and business ventures under the direction of consultants from the nearby university and business community. With today's technology, SAGE participants can make connections with people from other countries and cultures, and garner new resources to facilitate their ventures.

SAGE has established a blueprint model for how education can take the lead in creating new international networks that focuses on the next generation of leaders; it is a transnational social movement organization (TSMO)that includes youth and adults who believe that humanitarian capitalism and social entrepreneurship provide one promising avenue to alleviate poverty and to contribute to world peace. The SAGE network is vital to each participating country, in that each country's association with the international program gives them access to resources that they may not otherwise have. In essence, SAGE provides a bridge for youth from different cultural, ethnic and political backgrounds to add to their social capital.

In conclusion, this chapter explained how the SAGE program can be implemented by entrepreneurial educators who want to help their students become better prepared for life, a life that will be increasingly dependent upon interaction with people from other countries.In conclusion, we offer the words of Thomas Friedman (2005):

*Give young people a context where they can translate a positive imagination into reality, give them a context in which someone with a grievance can have it adjudicated in a court of law without having to bribe the judge with a goat, give them a context in which they can pursue an entrepreneurial idea and become the richest or the most creative or most respected people in their own country, no matter what their background, give them a context in which any complaint or idea can be published in the newspaper, give them a context in which anyone can run for office—and guess what? They usually don't want to blow up the world. They usually want to be part of it. (pp.458-459)*

## REFERENCES

Association to Advance Collegiate Schools of Business. (2006a). *A world of good: Business, business schools and peace.* Report of the AACSB International Peace through Commerce Task Force. Retrieved February 15, 2010, from http://www.aacsb.edu/publications/thoughtleadership/peace-english.pdf

Association to Advance Collegiate Schools of Business. (2006b). *Eligibility procedures and accreditation standards for business accreditation.* AACSB International, January 1, 2006.

Baez, N. (2007). *E-mail sent to author.* October 20, 2007.

Bornstein, D. (2004). *How to change the world: Social entrepreneurs and the power of new ideas.* New York, NY: Oxford University Press.

Dees, J. G. (2003). *Social entrepreneurship is about innovation and impact, not income.* Center for the Advancement of Social Entrepreneurship. Retrieved February 15, 2010, from http://www.caseatduke.org/articles/1004/corner.htm

Drucker, P. F. (1994). The age of social transformation. *Atlantic Monthly, 274*(5), 53–80.

Friedman, T. L. (2005). *The world is flat: A brief history of the twenty-first century.* New York, NY: Farrar, Straus and Giroux.

Garcia, V. (2007). *E-mail sent to author.* October 26, 2007.

Gates, B. (2008, August 11). How to fix capitalism. *Time Magazine*, 40-45.

Ibeneme, E. (2009). *SAGE team of JSS Jikwoyi emerge winner of FCT SAGE exhibition* (pp. 32–34). TELL.

International Labor Organization. (2009). *Youth employment: Breaking gender barriers for young women and men.* Retrieved February 15, 2010, from http://www.ilo.org/wcmsp5/groups/public/dgreports/gender/documents/publication/wcms_097919.pdf

Intrator, S. (2004). The engaged classroom. *Educational Leadership, 62*(1), 20–25.

Jones, T. (2009). *E-mail to author.* September 9, 2009.

Noguera, P. A. (2004). Transforming high schools. *Educational Leadership, 61*(8), 26–31.

Reblando, B. M. (2009, August 15). Sultan Kudarat students invent new cement block. *Manila Bulletin*, 2009. Retrieved February 15, 2010, from http://www.mb.com.ph/node/216005/

Savitz, A. W., & Weber, K. (2006). *The triple bottom line: How today's best-run companies are achieving economic, social and environmental success-and how you can too.* San Francisco, CA: John Wiley & Sons.

Smith, J. (2001). Global civil society? Transnational social movement organizations and social capital. In B. Edwards, M. W. Foley, & M. Diani, M. (Eds.), *Beyond Tocqueville: Civil society and the social capital debate in comparative perspective* (pp. 194–206). Hanover, NH: University Press of New England.

Wei-Skillern, J., & Marciano, S. (2008). The networked nonprofit. *Stanford Social Innovation Review, 6*(2), 38–43.

## KEY TERMS AND DEFINITIONS

**Humanitarian Capitalist:** A profit-seeking person or organization who understands the importance of environmental and social value, but puts financial returns above social impact.

**Service-Learning:** A learning strategy used by educators to actively engage students in the community, with an eye toward reinforcing classroom theory with real-world experience.

**Social Capital:** Value created as a result from the strength of one's network, and the willingness of those in the network to work together to find mutually beneficial opportunities; these opportunities can result in financial, social or environmental returns. Furthermore, using today's technology, social capital can be created much more rapidly and efficiently.

**Social Capitalist:** A profit-seeking person or organization who puts social value above financial returns.

**Social Entrepreneur:** An innovative and creative individual who strives to make a positive societal impact; this person can be a humanitarian capitalist, a social capitalist, or someone who works for a nonprofit organization.

**Students for the Advancement of Global Entrepreneurship (SAGE):** A global network with the following mission: to help create the next generation of entrepreneurial leaders whose innovations and social enterprises address our world's major unmet needs.

**Transnational Social Movement Organization (TSMO):** A group of individuals and organizations that identify and confront an unjust or unfair societal need that has international implications; such an organization is a necessary component for the formation of social capital to strengthen a global civil society; using today's technology, TSMO's can be much easier to form, and more efficient to operate.

# Chapter 3
# Birds, Bands, and Beyond

**Jill Russell**
*College of Mount St. Joseph, USA*

**Karen Glum**
*Seven Hills Middle School, USA*

**Jennifer Licata**
*Seven Hills Middle School, USA*

**David Russell**
*Avian Research & Education Institute, USA*

**Jenny Wohlfarth**
*University of Cincinnati, USA*

## ABSTRACT

*This case study describes a partnership between the Avian Research and Education Institute (AREI), College of Mount St. Joseph (MSJ), University of Cincinnati (UC), and science teachers at The Seven Hills Middle School. This partnership enabled the teachers to implement a Bird Studies program and empowered the students to become citizen scientists. The partners used various technologies to establish and maintain an ongoing relationship between the field and classroom, so that students interacted with field ornithologists face-to-face and virtually via the Internet. In the classroom, students assisted researchers as they color-banded birds that visited the school's wild bird garden. The students then monitored the banded birds, communicated with the researchers, posted updates on the class wiki, conducted biweekly bird counts and submitted data to eBird, created eField Guides, completed inquiry projects, and presented their data at a school event and a community bird festival.*

## CONTEXT OF PROJECT

One challenge in science education is to engage students in learning experiences that are relevant to them and to local and global communities.

DOI: 10.4018/978-1-60960-623-7.ch003

Conducting science that produces valuable results to the community is motivating and empowering for learners and helps them understand and value the role of science in society (Stoecker, 2002). This study describes how students partner with community members, both face to face and virtually, to become citizen scientists who contribute meaningful data to the community (through local university-based research projects, national research initiatives, etc.). To accomplish this, the partnership established the following goals: 1) empower students to function as scientists, 2) (re)connect students with the natural world in a way that helps them recognize and value the interconnectedness of humanity and nature, 3) help students develop a sense of place—both locally and globally, and 4) provide students with opportunities for authentic collaboration with community partners. The students' successful completion of bird-based inquiry projects and their creation of eField Guides that identify and describe the bird species they learned about demonstrate our achievement of these goals.

The key to getting students to *understand* and not just *know* science is to frame the content in such a way that students generate questions—for example, "Why do researchers band birds?"—that lead them to investigate the answers on their own (Weick, 1984; Kaplan, 2000; Newell, 2003). These exploratory questions could easily be answered by the science teachers or the partnering ornithologists, and they were. But by color-banding the

birds at the Seven Hills bird garden, the students began to construct answers for themselves. They documented birds with color bands (for example, "Kiwi" the Tufted Titmouse has a lime-green band), made observations ("I think it was funny that the size of the peanut was bigger than Kiwi's beak," as seen in Figure 1) and formulated questions on their own (How will different textures on the perches affect the feeding behavior of the birds?).

In addition to inspiring students to launch their own inquiries, this project used technology to create an ongoing relationship between the field and the classroom and empowered learners to study birds as scientists. Not only did they share their ideas, questions and work with the field researchers, but they were also able to be in the field with them, "virtually" participating in multiple research projects. As the 40 middle school students progressed in their studies of the banded birds in the school's bird garden, they became more interested in the other projects the researchers were engaged in. For instance, the project's two partner scientists were part of a 15-person team that conducted a search for Ivory-billed

*Figure 1.*

BIRDCAM 01     08/28/07 09:34 AM

Woodpeckers in the Florida panhandle. The Seven Hills students completed a study that determined how many trees were necessary to provide food for a pair of Ivory-billed Woodpeckers and were able to share their data with the team as it conduced research transects in Florida. At the same time, the field researchers were able to share images of trees that had the horizontal markings indicative of Ivory-billed eating behaviors. Through these technological interactions, students were able to experience science in a way that allowed them to be a part of a project, instead of just being passive observers.

## Technology as a Catalyst

It is one thing to *want* to use videoconferencing with researchers in remote field stations and quite another thing to actually make it happen. Figuring out which technologies would best help us was the most complicated and time-consuming aspect of this project. Three representatives from the Instructional Technologies (IT) department at MSJ and two staff members at Seven Hills tested various hardware and software tools over a four-month period to get clear audio and visual communications running smoothly. As a result, we used numerous forms of technology to enable interaction and collaboration between the Seven Hills students and the partners at AREI, MSJ and UC. Examples include:

- laptops with either built-in or external cameras, video cameras, and external microphones
- monthly video conferencing (using Skype and cellular broadband, or Ethernet connections) to bring the students into the field with the scientists
- SnapzProX and CamStudio to record video conferences
- WingScapesBirdCams to capture visits to the middle-school bird feeders by banded and other birds

- iMovie, iTunes and iPhoto to create eField Guides identifying the birds that came to the feeders
- wikis to share eField Guides, inquiry projects and bird photos with partners, parents and the community
- the Internet to report bird count data to the Cornell Lab of Ornithology (eBird website)
- Excel software to create data tables and graphs as part of the independent bird inquiry.

Using Skype to video-conference with the field scientists was key to developing a reciprocal relationship between the Seven Hills students and the researchers. We initially introduced the two researchers (one scientist from AREI and one researcher from MSJ) to the students via a Skype session at the Seven Hills school (see Figure 2) in which they discussed the importance of studying birds and bird banding. The researchers then visited the middle school and color-banded the birds that came to the feeders in the school's bird garden. The middle-school students spent the day interacting with the bird banders and discussing various aspects of bird biology. In Figure 3, for example, AREI scientist Dr. Dave Russell discusses feather features of a Tufted Titmouse. Students then created inquiry projects to answer the questions they generated throughout the day, and posted these on the class wiki to receive feedback from the scientists. Figure 4 shows some of their posts, including their reports on the individual birds banded at the school. This use of technology to create community partnerships directly supports the outreach missions of both AREI and MSJ. The community partners, therefore, had the responsibility of prompting the students in this exploratory, uninhibited, and active form of learning.

As one can imagine, using electronic equipment in the field posed unique challenges. Complications such as weather, cold batteries and low broadband coverage hindered live video-confer-

*Figure 2.*

encing on several dates. The researchers tested a laptop with an external video camera from various field stations in the U.S. and were able to connect with the students at Seven Hills using a cell phone link to broadband. Unfortunately, tall trees and spotty broadband coverage in many sites made it difficult to establish and maintain a strong signal. Several transmissions experienced delays and a separation of audio from video because of slow uploading and downloading speeds. The project partners also had difficulty recording each live

*Figure 3.*

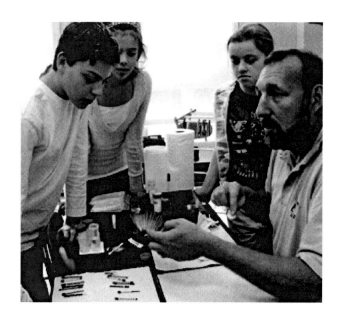

*Figure 4.*

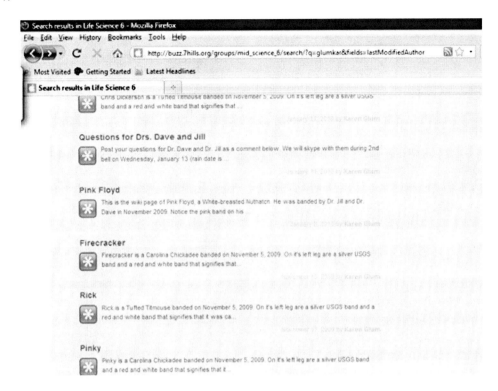

session in the field due to limitations in functional memory in the laptops.

We also discovered that satellite transmission worked better than broadband service when broadcasting from most locations. The current satellite coverage available is adequate for our needs at most field sites we plan to incorporate into the field interactions. However, when we're in ultra-remote locations—such as Barrow, Alaska, where we may communicate with the students in future field sessions—we will be beyond the arc of satellite coverage and may need to rely on broadband access.

## Community Connections and Impact

Generally, the Seven Hills middleschool science students' educational interactions with the community are one-sided, with the students functioning as recipients of information, not as partners or contributors to the learning process. For example,

the students have met with and learned from representatives from the county's soil and water conservation district, solid-waste management district, and various science and conservation nonprofits. The Bird Studies program, however, has enhanced the students' connection to the community by enabling them to develop a more interactive, two-way connection with scientists in the field.

The two scientist partners at a nonprofit organization like AREI have proven to be ideal partners for such a program. AREI's mission is to protect and conserve avian populations through research, education and advocacy. In order to accomplish this, AREI utilizes bird banding to introduce nature and the environment to citizens—of any age—through the perspective of a bird's eyes. Small, brightly colored avian gems create an immediate bond that opens minds and allows the scientists to illustrate important environmental concepts and problems.

Unfortunately, too many kids in the U.S. arenot aware of these important issues, and may not have any idea how interesting nature really is, because they have not spent time exploring it. Regardless of the cause, "nature deficit disorder" (Louv, 2005)—this lack of interaction with wild things—has been studied to the extent that it sparked the passage of the U.S. *No Child Left Inside Act* (110th United States Congress, 2008) as an amendment to the National Environmental Education Act. By interacting with Seven Hills middleschool students via Web conferencing and at the school's bird garden, the partnering scientists have helped them appreciate, learn, and develop a sense of responsibility and love for the living world. Understanding where birds go, how they get there, and what they need to survive inspires open discussions on habitat, pollution, geography, physiology, and conservation—concepts that are usually only words in a textbook—and lays the foundation for students to become informed global citizens. Likewise, learning about migration helps students understand the inherent global interconnectedness of the natural world.

Parental feedback on this partnership has indicated that the students' families are also becoming more aware and appreciative of the relationship between humanity and nature, as the students engage family members to help them monitor birds at home. Several students and their families have participated in community bird counts (such as the Cornell Lab of Ornithology's and National Audubon Society's Great Backyard Bird Count) and community-sponsored bird walks (such as those organized by the Queen City Young Birders Club in Cincinnati). The study of birds has enabled students and parents to connect in a way that typically—and unfortunately—occurs less and less frequently during early adolescence. Empowering educational projects like the Bird Studies program allow students to be experts, sharing their knowledge with parents, thereby generating real parental interest in what the students are able to share. This type of experience, valued by both

the students and the parents, creates meaningful common ground.

## Educational Impact

When you empower people to take actions that help solve real problems, they are more engaged in their own learning process, as suggested by the Environmental Citizenship Behavior Model (Hungerford, 1990). Validation of students' success by the community beyond the classroom generates pride and motivation in the students. The result is that the Seven Hills students have become more invested in their learning experiences. The proof is in their changed attitudes and behaviors. When asked their opinions about the program, students made such comments as "I enjoyed looking at pictures, doing our experiment [and] iMovies, having Dr. Jill and Dr. Dave, and just…EVERYTHING! I cannot wait for the spring when we continue our bird unit." Meanwhile, the partnership has generated new ideas, behaviors, attitudes and interests inside and beyond the classroom. Students often race to the windows of the classroom to grab binoculars and see which birds are at the feeders. Never before have the sixth-grade students been so excited about science, and their excitement is contagious. Students in other grades have asked to be present during the sixth-grade bird banding sessions. Seventh graders now regularly ask questions about the birds in the garden outside their classroom window and inquire about the work being done by the sixth grade. Teachers from other disciplines and even from The Seven Hills Upper and Lower Schools have become involved in the Bird Studies program by attending bird-banding activities, investigating the school's garden birds with their own students, and designing interdisciplinary projects and units that focus on birds.

We found that the use of various technologies has helped engage and motivate the students, enabling them to learn more deeply and communicate with others in novel ways. For example, the

Birdcams provide glimpses into the lives of the birds in the school garden that would otherwise be inaccessible. Interactions between birds captured on camera, such as a confrontation between a European Starling and Red-bellied Woodpecker, both satisfy and drive student curiosity about the relationships that unfold in the school's garden. iMovie software allows students to incorporate these images and videos into a product that is functional and fun. Reports about local bird species, produced on iMovie, become eField Guides (see Figure 5) that are convenient and appealing to students who load them onto iPods and iPhones. The Internet site eBird, which collects and shares data managed and used by the Cornell Lab of Ornithology, provides a way for students to report, view and interact with research findings, making science and scientists much more accessible. The students' work receives immediate validation and their data becomes the source of their own inquiries and those of other citizen and professional scientists. Wikis, meanwhile, enable students to share their ponderings, opinions, questions, and work. Particularly appealing to students are the wiki's free-form opportunities where student expression is both unsolicited and unencumbered by teacher expectations and requirements. Here students freely and playfully express their excitement about birds and the Bird Studies program.

## Value for the Educational Institutions

The technologies used in this project allow our educational institutions to work together in forming a bridge between higher learning and middleschool. College professors generally have no idea what technology students are mastering in middle school, and middleschool teachers have no idea what technology is incorporated in college science courses. Since we know that students learn better when they are interactively engaged, incorporating camera, audio, video, wikis and

*Figure 5.*

web conferencing into a collaborative learning experience creates multiple ways to connect them to nature and science. For instance, Seven Hills students were able to feel like they were a part of the Ivory-billed Woodpecker expedition not only because they were video-conferencing with researchers in the field, but also because they could actually see the area the researchers were in and could hear the sounds of the swamp. At the same time, the students were able to post questions on the class wiki that the partners could read and respond to at a later date. In addition, undergraduate biology students in an MSJ Basic Birding class used the eField Guides created by the sixth-graders as a tool for learning basic observation skills. Because of this partnership, we have been able to integrate technologies at both the middleschool and college level that form a continuum for interactive learning.

The value of the partnership for the middle school is that it generates interest, excitement and attention for the school's science program. Seven Hills strives to be an active participant in the global and local community, but unfortunately such interactions are often limited to monetary or material contributions to a cause, rather than educational partnerships forged between groups of learners. What excites the teachers about the work with AREI and MSJ is that the science is occurring through legitimate partnerships that connect communities previously separated by geography, age and expertise. Other Seven Hills teachers see the program's potential for interdisciplinary collaboration and recognize it as a meaningful tool in creating an immediate, positive and lasting impact on students. For instance, the scientists took blood samples from some of the school's banded birds as part of an ongoing research project at MSJ that is focused on sexing monomorphic species (species in which males and females look identical). The Seven Hills high school biology class will be running the DNA gels from these blood samples as part of that research project. In addition, sixth-grade teachers in many disciplines (language arts, math, geography, visual art, theater) worked collaboratively to incorporate birds into their curricula. The year-long bird study culminated in a "Sixth Grade is for the Birds" day on campus, which featured projects the students generated throughout the year in the various disciplines and provided parents and the school community with a chance to celebrate the students' work.

The Bird Studies partnership was a perfect fit for MSJ, whose mission includes educating students through interdisciplinary liberal arts and professional curricula while emphasizing values, integrity, and social responsibility. Several MSJ undergraduates have interacted with the Seven Hills students and have begun to develop mentoring relationships outside the classroom. The project's use of such technologies as Skype, meanwhile, are serving as a model for MSJ, and the college plans on making Web conferencing available to all faculty in the next fiscal year.

This partnership has also generated interest from local and regional media. "Cincinnati Edition," a weekly program broadcast by Cincinnati's National Public Radio (NPR) affiliate, featured the partnership in a recent story. In addition, the project's partnership with a journalism professor at the University of Cincinnati will lead to future articles in both mainstream and academic publications. The word is getting out: MSJ has recently received inquiries from high school students who are interested in biology and bird conservation projects.

## OVERVIEW OF BEST PRACTICES

The key aspect to making this partnership a success was the creation of design standards to establish the goals/outcomes of the partnership before doing anything else. This kept all of the partners focused on the same outcomes for the project. Community organizations generally have clearly defined mission statements, researchers use specific techniques to test their hypotheses and teachers have specific learning outcomes in mind for their students. In our case, AREI's mission is to protect and conserve avian populations through education, research, and advocacy; the research goals of the MSJ faculty member include helping monitor bird populations through bird banding and educating students about the environmental and conservation issues affecting avian populations; and the goals of the Seven Hills teachers are to empower their students as citizen scientists and increase their connection to the natural world.

Bringing these like-minded groups together provided the framework for designing a project like the middle-school bird garden, which enabled all three groups to achieve their goals. We chose birds, but partnerships like this could be connected to any subject. Content is important, but enthusiasm and excitement are the critical elements that draw in and capture all parties involved in such partnerships. In addition, local universities and colleges have huge reservoirs of untapped enthusiasm—students with lots of energy who might lack confidence in their depth of knowledge. Engaging these students in such projects—whether for credit or community service hours—can enhance the multi-institutional appeal of such partnerships, helping everybody learn more deeply. With sound direction and mentoring, the college students are able to funnel their excitement into the project, adding another layer of engagement to the scientific inquiries.

Our project benefited from a clear, shared sense of the learning activities and the knowledge and skills we wanted to develop in the students. We designed each activity and interaction to have meaningful relevance to students, while also focusing on producing scientific results that would be valuable to local and global communities.

Our best practices included:

1. Video-conferencing to maintain a relationship between the field scientists and the Seven Hills students. Students shared their ideas, questions and work and were able to "virtually" be in the field with the scientists as they participated in multiple research projects. Giving the students meaningful, real roles in data gathering transformed them from passive learners into active partners who contribute valuable data to the scientific community—both locally and globally. Not only did the students interact with real research scientists, but they also got to know them as people. Through this connection, the students were empowered to take pride in their role as authentic citizen scientists.

2. Color-banding the birds that came to the bird feeders in the Seven Hills bird garden helped the students recognize and value the interconnectedness of humanity and nature. Through their own observations and inquiry projects, they discovered how human behavior can impact birds. Something as simple as forgetting to fill the bird feeders before a big snowstorm, for example, taught the students the importance of food availability for bird survival. Students also learned to observe. Instead of ignoring bird calls as they walked to their classes, they began to notice the birds and recognize the calls of the different species. A new connection developed between the Seven Hills students and the birds around the school. Students recognized the colored bands, transforming individual birds into familiar friends; they even named the banded birds and genuinely cared about them. Soon, the students wanted to take care of the birds and help fill the bird feeders. This behavior spilled over at home, where some students pressed their parents to put up bird feeders so they could document the birds that came into their yard. The eField Guides that students created became treasured digital scrapbooks and journals that captured the meaningful connections the students made with the birds, which were celebrated in photographs and writing. The students connected with birds and nature in a way that the middle-school

science teachers and research scientists had never seen before.

## FUTURE RESEARCH DIRECTIONS

This project has proven to be immensely valuable as a model for middleschools to establish partnerships with other schools, colleges and universities and nonprofit organizations in their communities. The students have formed relationships with field researchers and college professors that will, we hope, inspire them to continue their education beyond high school. Some students and their families have even accompanied the researchers to bird-banding stations outside of school. In fact, one teacher and student from Seven Hills traveled with the partnering scientists to Alaska this summer to participate in field studies in Fairbanks and Barrow. The student was able to experience, firsthand, how the scientists find and identify birds in a remote location that is critical to migratory breeding. The teacher, meanwhile, connected with educators in various cities throughout the state to establish an ongoing relationship between the schools, with hopes to share data, findings, and inquiries in future collaborations. It is our hope to extend our partnerships so that students in several cities and remote areas are able to collaborate in meaningful research about bird migration and conservation science.

## REFERENCES

Hungerford, H. A., & Volk, T. L. (1990). Changing learner behavior through environmental education. *The Journal of Environmental Education*, *21*(3), 8–22.

Kaplan, S. (2000). Human nature and environmentally responsible behavior. *The Journal of Social Issues*, *56*(3), 491–508. doi:10.1111/0022-4537.00180

Louv, R. (2005). *Last child in the woods: Saving our children from nature-deficit disorder*. Chappel Hill, NC: Algonquin Books.

Newell, R. (2003). *Passion for learning: How project-based learning meets the needs of 21st century students*. Lanham, MD: The Scarecrow Press, Inc.

Stoecker, R. (2002). Practices and challenges of community-based research. *Journal of Public Affairs*, *6*(1), 219–239.

110th United States Congress. (2008). *H.R. 3036: No Child Left Inside Act of 2008*. Civic Impulse LLC. Retrieved November 27, 2009, from http://www.govtrack.us/congress/bill.xpd?bill=h110-3036&tab=summary

Weick, K. (1984). Small wins: Redefining the scale of social problems. *The American Psychologist*, *39*(1), 40–49. doi:10.1037/0003-066X.39.1.40

## ADDITIONAL READING

Conservation, R. A. R. E. Inc. (2009). *About RARE*. Retrieved November 27, 2009, from RARE: inspiring conservation: http://rareconservation.org/about/

Jacobson, S. K. (2006). *Conservation Education and Outreach Techniques*. Oxford: Oxford University Press. doi:10.1093/acprof:oso/9780198567714.001.0001

Patuxent Wildlife Research Center. (2010, February 28). *Why Band Birds?* Retrieved February 28, 2010, from Bird Banding Laboratory: http://www.pwrc.usgs.gov/BBL/homepage/whyband.cfm

Russell, J. (2004). *Outreach*. Retrieved February 28, 2010, from Avian Research and Education Institute (AREI): http://www.avianinstitute.com/?page_id=76

Russell, J. (2007). *Front of the Class*. Retrieved February 28, 2010, from College of Mount St. Joseph Mount News: http://www.msj.edu/view/faculty/behavioral--natural-sciences-faculty/biology-faculty/jill-russell-phd/jill-russell.aspx

The Seven Hills School. (2005). *The Seven Hills School*. Retrieved February 28, 2010, from The Seven Hills School: http://www.7hills.org/Default.asp?bhcp=1

Wiggins, G., & McTighe, J. (2005). *Understanding by Design*. Alexandria: Association for Supervision and Curriculum Development.

## KEY TERMS AND DEFINITIONS

**Bird Banding:** A universal technique for studying the movement, survival and behavior of birds by attaching a small, individually numbered, metal band to their legs.

**Bird Banding for Education:** Banding birds at a school provides the opportunity for students to touch nature and connect in a way not previously available to them.

**Project-Based Learning:** Students ask their own questions and design experiments to answer those questions while teachers and partnering scientists serve as facilitators of their learning.

**Scientific Collaborations:** Partnerships with real-world scientists that enable students to develop relationships that empower them to continue their education.

**Student Scientists:** Students conduct science that produces results of value to the community, which is motivating and empowering for learners and helps them understand and value the role of science in society.

# Chapter 4
# Using the XO Laptop to Build a Digital Bridge Between Primary Schools and Universities

**Katelyn Foley**
*Harvard University, USA*

## ABSTRACT

*One-to-one computing has emerged as a controversial framework for integrating technology in education. The Cambridge Friends School XO laptop pilot program is a collaboration between the Digital Literacy Project (DigiLit), a non-profit and Harvard College student organization, and the Cambridge Friends School (CFS), an independent K-8 school. This chapter will examine both positive and negative features of the program, as well as a model for implementation of similar programs. DigiLit introduced low-cost XO laptops to two grade levels and designed laptop-based lesson plans. The author also investigated the XO's effects on collaborative behavior, finding that laptops influenced mobility and sharing of information during group activities. As part of the pilot, students tested new software and completed a survey about the design of an open-source spreadsheet program. The partnership between DigiLit and CFS has provided a platform for researching child-computer interaction and for developing a laptop-based curriculum.*

## INTRODUCTION

One-to-one computing refers to a classroom setup in which there is one handheld device (i.e., computer, laptop, PDA) per student or teacher. This movement hails from the early stages of digital technology in education. In 1985, Apple implemented the first large-scale K-12 one-to-one computing program through the Apple Classrooms of Tomorrow (ACOT) initiative. More recently, in 1997, Microsoft introduced Anytime Anywhere Learning (AAL), which provided laptops for teachers and students. These and other ubiquitous computing programs have ushered in an era in which technology is readily accessible in schools.

DOI: 10.4018/978-1-60960-623-7.ch004

Since the 1980s, the meaning of one computer to one student or teacher has changed dramatically, as laptops have replaced desktops and wireless Internet has become a feature of many American classrooms. Low-cost computing is a recent phenomenon sparked by the XO, a $200 laptop designed by the nonprofit organization One Laptop per Child (OLPC). This child-friendly laptop has spurred on a new market for low-cost laptops, including Intel's Classmate and Asus' Eee, which also retail for around $200.

Despite the recent drop in costs associated with one-to-one computing, these programs have remained controversial due to conflicting reports on their classroom impact. A number of studies suggest that one laptop per student can enhance 21$^{st}$ Century skills and improve writing ability (Penuel, 2006). However, these and other studies have found that the success of these programs is highly dependent on support for teachers, who act as "gatekeepers" to educational change (Cuban, 2004, p. 106). Integration of computers into existing curricula is a gradual process that depends on teacher comfort with technology in the classroom (Sandholtz, Ringstaff, & Dwyer, 1997). The challenging nature of this process is underscored by findings showing that most teachers in one-to-one classrooms are still adapting course material to laptop computers (Penuel, 2006). While today's children are digital natives, or "'native speakers' of the digital language of computers, video games and the Internet," teachers are digital immigrants, "who speak an outdated language (that of the pre-digital age) [and] are struggling to teach a population that speaks an entirely new language" (Prensky, 2001).

We will explore a collaborative model for one-to-one computing program initiation that includes nonprofit and student organizations at universities. This case study will look at how university students can partner with primary schools to facilitate laptop integration through technical support, teacher training, and curriculum development. We will investigate the use of the low-cost XO laptop for this type of initiative, specifically exploring its effects on collaborative behavior and how its open-source software can be tailored to children through a user-centered design approach.

## BACKGROUND

### The Low-Cost XO Laptop

One Laptop per Child's XO (Figure 1) is a low-cost, environmentally friendly children's laptop. In an effort to bridge the digital divide, over 1.4 million XO laptops have been distributed to children in over thirty countries around the globe (One Laptop per Child, 2009). Specifically designed for the developing world, the XO is energy efficient and durable, allowing it to withstand high temperatures and exposure to water. It also boasts a rotating screen that allows configurations for e-book reading and gaming, as well as standard laptop use. In addition, the XO is the only laptop with wireless mesh network technology that allows offline peer-to-peer communication.

Even though the XO was designed with the developing world in mind, its low cost and effective, child-friendly software give it potential to positively impact the American educational landscape. According to data released by the U.S. Census Bureau in 2009, there was an average of 3.9 students per computer in public and private schools during the 2005-2006 school year. Although American students have access to computing resources at school, many are still not able to take ownership of computers by having their own laptops that they can use at school and at home.

### History of the Digital Literacy Project

While the XO laptop has tremendous potential in the classroom, the current lack of teacher and student support limits students' ability to use this technology as a gateway to the world. After learning about the One Laptop per Child project,

*Figure 1. XO laptop specifications (Adapted from One Laptop per Child)*

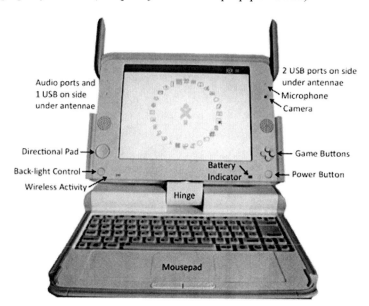

MacKenzie Sigalos and I (Harvard College Class of 2010 and 2009, respectively) co-founded the Digital Literacy Project (DigiLit) to address this unmet need. DigiLit is a 501(c)(3) nonprofit and Harvard College student organization that initiates and supports laptop pilot programs at schools around the world. By developing training materials and laptop-based curricula for teachers and students, we seek to encourage sustainable technology practices. The overall goal is to seamlessly integrate technology into the classroom, so that it becomes a tool rather than a short-lived toy.

DigiLit has grown steadily since it was founded in the fall of 2008. After becoming an officially recognized student organization in November 2008, my co-founder and I were granted advising through Harvard's Public Service Network and permission to host on-campus events. We recruited team members mainly from Harvard, but opened volunteer information sessions to the Boston community at large. As of the summer of 2010, our team consists of 27 undergraduate students and alumni from Harvard College, Massachusetts Institute of Technology, and Carnegie Mellon University. We were a team of 12 undergraduates at the time this research was completed.

As a student organization, we raised funds for over 70 XO laptops through online marketing during our first year. Using our Website (www.DigiLiteracy.org) and various blogs, we asked participants in One Laptop per Child's "Give One Get One" program to donate their "Get One" laptop to our pilots. In order to broaden our eligibility for grants and foundation funding, we applied for 501(c)(3) status and received federal designation as a nonprofit in December 2009. The Harvard Transactional Law Clinic provided pro bono legal services throughout this application process, and a foundation seed grant covered incorporation fees. Our dual status as a 501(c)(3) and student organization has given us credibility off-campus, as well as a strong university base that provides mentorship and manpower.

## Cambridge Friends School XO Laptop Pilot Program

DigiLit launched its first laptop pilot program at the Cambridge Friends School (CFS) in Cambridge,

MA, during the fall of 2008. The CFS XO laptop pilot program is the first one-to-one computing program at the school, even though several grade levels share a laptop cart that can be borrowed by a classroom. My co-founder and I chose CFS because of its open-minded approach to education and its close proximity to Harvard's campus.

After contacting the Head of School via e-mail with a program proposal, we began meeting with school administrators during the summer of 2008. We pitched the program to teachers in October 2008, and the sixth grade teachers volunteered their classes for the initial pilot. Throughout the planning period, the school was extremely supportive; the Head of School presented the program to parents at a PTA meeting, and the teachers welcomed additional technology resources.

DigiLit worked with the sixth grade during the 2008-2009 academic year and with the fourth grade during the 2009-2010 academic year (Table 1), after finding that sixth graders were too old for the laptops.

## Research Background and Limitations

Evaluation of the CFS XO laptop pilot program was made possible by a grant from the Harvard College Research Program. Over the course of two semesters, I worked with Professor Eric Mazur of the Harvard School of Engineering and Applied Sciences to develop objective survey and interview protocols that were approved by Harvard's Institutional Review Board (IRB). This research is limited by the fact that I was both a deliverer and an evaluator of the program.

## Sixth Grade Pilot

In October 2008, DigiLit volunteers began training the two sixth grade teachers. This training was intended to open a dialogue about the challenge of authentically integrating the XO into the curriculum. A key finding of the 2001 CEO Forum on Education and Technology is that "technology can have the greatest impact when integrated into the curriculum to achieve clear, measurable educational objectives" (Meyer, 2007). In accordance with this finding, we showed teacher show the XO could interface with individual lessons to accomplish learning goals.

By meeting with teachers, DigiLit volunteers created a bundle of open-source software tailored to sixth grade syllabi. Most of the fall was devoted to classroom simulations and curriculum workshops. In the spring, we began visiting CFS two days per week in order to lead classroom activities and provide technical support. During the eight-week pilot, we collected images, video, instructor surveys, and interview results as a means of measuring the XO's effects on student dynamics, particularly collaborative behavior.

## Fourth Grade Pilot

In the fall of 2009, we choose to move the one-to-one computing program to the fourth grade, where it could be a better fit for students' age group and interests. Through a partnership with the New Delhi-based Software for Education, Entertainment, and Training Activities (SEETA), we had the opportunity to test SocialCalc, an open-source spreadsheet activity, in the two fourth grade classrooms. Previous research suggests that

*Table 1. Cambridge friends school demographics*

| Grade Level | Teachers | Students |
|---|---|---|
| Sixth Grade (2008-2009 academic year) | 2 (1 female, 1 male) | 28 (13 female, 15 male) |
| Fourth Grade (2009-2010 academic year) | 2 (2 female) | 27 (12 female, 15 male) |

children's exploratory nature strengthens their ability to test and evaluate software, especially programs designed for a young audience (Hatch, 2008). We developed social studies lesson plans that integrated SocialCalc into existing course material and led classroom activities. In order to gauge how fourth graders navigated SocialCalc, we designed a survey that allowed students to rate the program in several areas, as well as propose new features. This research supported a user-centered design approach (Mazzone, Xu, & Read, 2007) in which interview results were sent to the SocialCalc developers to shape future releases of the program.

## Community Support

The Boston area is home to the One Laptop per Child headquarters, as well as an active community of educators, students, and computer scientists who are interested in the XO. The CFS XO laptop pilot is one of the first local pilots and thus has allowed many community members who are working on software or curriculum development to apply their work to the pilot. Over the course of the pilot, DigiLit has formed partnerships with local institutions and international organizations. One Laptop per Child hosted curriculum workshops for the DigiLit team, students from Olin College of Engineering provided on-site technical support, and students from Boston University School of Management aided in the design of media kit and fundraising materials. Without community support, this laptop program would not be feasible.

## ONE-TO-ONE COMPUTING AND THE XO LAPTOP

### Impact on Learning, Curriculum Integration, Ownership

One of the concerns about one-to-one computing is that it can undermine a learning environment

with distractions such as video games, Internet, and messaging capabilities. Both educational and recreational software are available for the XO laptop, including a program that allows students to chat over the mesh network. In the past, handheld devices with local or no messaging technology, such as classroom response systems and graphing calculators, have been successfully integrated into the classroom. However, some schools have banned cell phones and iPods because they cause distractions and provide a means of cheating. Aligned with these restrictions are data showing that multitasking associated with web surfing and messaging can lead to decreased retention of a class lecture (Hembrooke & Gay, 2003).

In addition to their potential as a classroom distraction, laptops and other handheld devices can limit collaborative behavior. Students in one-to-one classrooms have been observed to work alone more often than in classrooms where laptops are shared (Russell, Bebel, & Higgins, 2004). Another study showed that handheld devices limit interaction between group members but that shared displays facilitate collaboration in small groups (Liu & Kao, 2007). Together, these data reinforce notions that one-to-one computing might have a negative effect on group work and on students' abilities to build effective relationships with teachers and peers.

Another significant concern regarding one-to-one computing is authentic integration of laptops into curriculum. Recent studies suggest that teachers who are uncomfortable with a one-to-one environment use laptops mainly for word processing and teacher-centered activities (Donovan, Hartley, & Strudler, 2007). In this context, laptops are often presented to students as a reward for completing an assignment or as a special addition to an activity. When we modified existing lessons to include the XO laptop, it was difficult to incorporate the XO as a tool rather than a glamorous afterthought. In an instructor survey, a sixth grade teacher noted that "[t]he project could have gone more smoothly if we allotted more time

*Table 2. Most-used software during the pilot*

| Computer Program (open-source) | Description |
|---|---|
| Browse | Internet browser |
| Memorize | Matching game creation |
| Record | Image, video, and sound recording |
| SocialCalc | Spreadsheet activity |
| WikiBrowse | Offline encyclopedia version of Wikipedia |

for the students to experiment with the XOs and then had more time to design lessons that were a better match for the curriculum."

Finally, the success of a one-to-one computing is heavily dependent on software. In the past, development of software for children has relied on adults who work with kids, such as educators and psychologists. As a result, there is a dearth of research on how to guide children through the software design process and on how child-designed solutions for software compare with those designed by adults (Hatch, 2008). Previous research suggests that children can be active participants in software requirements gathering and in testing (Druin, 1999; Hanna, Risden, & Alexander, 1997). However, common use of closed-source software that is not tailored to a young audience prevents children from being actively involved in software customization.

## Implementation of One-to-One Computing at CFS

In both pilots, we found that CFS administrators were more enthusiastic about the program than teachers. In order to address teacher concerns about program implementation, we organized training workshops for sixth grade (2008-2009 academic year) and fourth grade (2009-2010 academic year) teachers. Instead of focusing on technical skills, DigiLit volunteers introduced open-source computer programs that are compatible with the XO's Sugar operating system. Initial workshops were structured around software capabilities so that teachers could compile a bundle of thirty programs

that were a good fit for their curricula (Table 2), selectively eliminating recreational software that might pose a distraction in the classroom.

After we loaded the software bundle, teacher workshops transitioned into simulations of the classroom experience. Based on syllabi, we designed sample lesson plans and tested them with teachers. These lesson plans integrated the XO into existing course material by utilizing its hardware and software to achieve clear goals. We found that distilling the objectives behind specific lessons facilitated inclusion of laptops. Once objectives were identified, we could choose appropriate digital avenues for fulfillment of these objectives. Subsequent workshops gave teachers the opportunity to develop and share their own lesson plans.

Once XOs were introduced to students, DigiLit volunteers taught lessons and provided in-class technical support. Although class activities were initially less structured, they became more formal as teachers and students gained confidence with the machines. It is important to note that neither sixth nor fourth graders were allowed to take XO laptops home because teachers were concerned that they would forget to bring them back to school. Although this model has prevented loss of laptops, we feel that it has also limited students' ability to explore and take ownership of their XOs.

It is also important to note that DigiLit continued teacher workshops after students received XO laptops. Neither sixth nor fourth grade teachers felt prepared to design lesson plans that incorporated the XO. In instructor surveys and strategy meetings, teachers said that they would have liked to participate in more curriculum workshops before XOs were introduced to students. This finding underscores the challenging nature of technology-driven curriculum redesign.

## Sixth Grade Pilot: Evaluation of Collaborative Learning

As part of the sixth grade pilot, we conducted four student interviews (n=2) in order to examine the XO laptop's effects on collaborative behavior. Our interviews were designed to help us understand the object (motive), subject (human activity), tools, rules (constraints), community, and division of labor within the context of collaborative activities with and without XOs (Greenhow & Belbas, 2007).In order to supplement our small sample size, we also used images, video, and classroom observations as part of our analysis.

Our interviews and qualitative studies suggest that the XO facilitated sharing of information, as well as communication between sixth grade students. In addition, students noted that XOs improved their efficiency when working on group activities. However, there were no substantial differences in the division of tasks, student willingness to help peers, or conceptions of team dynamics. In an instructor survey, a sixth grade teacher stated that XOs were most helpful for "small group activities where the team had a specific task to work on together." Notably, the XO hardware played a significant role in group work. One student mentioned that the portable nature of the XO allowed students to move around the classroom. The other student stated that the rotating screen facilitated communication:

*[XOs affected the way we communicated] because you can't really turn [a computer screen] and show your group mates, but with the XO, you can turn it and still be writing to show them.... It made it a lot more easier to communicate rather than if we were working on desktops....*

This response suggests that the rotating screen on XOs, which was initially designed for e-book reading and gaming, might also play a role in sharing information.

## Fourth Grade Pilot: User-Centered Software Design

In addition to teacher support and classroom integration, we have found that piloting software in a classroom setting can yield valuable feedback about usability. Employing a user-centered design approach, we completed one round of usability and defect testing for SocialCalc, an open-source spreadsheet program. In this case, design refers to solving problems on an existing system rather than engineering a new system. Fourth grade students (n=23) participated in three fifty-minute lessons in which they used the program to graph different sets of data that they gathered online. In this context, the one-to-one computing framework facilitated technology immersion and a co-discovery format. After three lessons over the span of two weeks, students were asked to complete a survey that included a questionnaire with a modified Likert scale (Figure 2) and a drawing intervention in which they could draw new features or changes to existing features.

*Figure 2. Likert scale with child-friendly pictures*

*Figure 3. SocialCalc questionnaire results*

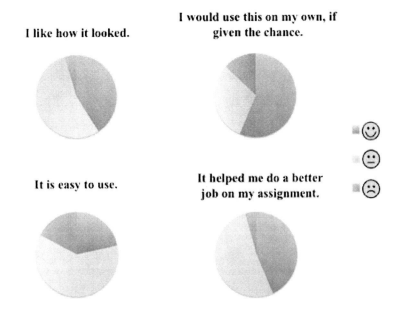

Ratings of the first four statements indicate that this age group (eight- to nine-years-old) found SocialCalc challenging (Figure 3). These ratings will be used as a basis for comparison when the next release is tested. Trends in new features include an emphasis on choice. Students wanted more control over font and chart colors. In addition, students were confused by error messages when they did not select the correct data set. They wanted the program to give them better feedback about their mistakes. Three out of 23 students stated that the program did not need improvements. This feedback will go to the SocialCalc developers at SEETA, allowing the CFS pilot to positively impact the development of open-source software for children.

### Balancing Program Expansion with Sustainability

During the 2010-2011 academic year, the CFS XO laptop pilot program will double in size to include the third and fourth grades. DigiLit will continue to support the program until it is inde-

pendent of outside volunteers. In order to further ensure sustainability, DigiLit is currently working with One Laptop per Child Australia, a nonprofit organization that does parallel work in Australia, to design the first global education portal for XO laptop users. Specifically designed for teachers, the portal offers software demo videos, lesson resources, online courses, and Facebook-style social networking. The training and curriculum resources developed for CFS will be available on the portal upon its launch in the fall of 2010.

### FUTURE RESEARCH DIRECTIONS

Our future research will be focused on further explorations of the XO's effects on collaborative behavior, as well as other dimensions of the classroom dynamic. In order to follow up on our initial studies, we would like to use video to analyze student body language during XO-based activities, particularly group assignments. In addition, we would like to investigate whether or not the XO's unique peer-to-peer mesh network can foster an environment of shared learning by allowing students to share and simultaneously edit writing assignments. Teacher surveys showed that students were already using the mesh network to chat with each other during free time.

One area that we were not able to explore in depth is teacher-student dynamic. Despite common beliefs that the presence of computers in the classroom can hinder effective relationships between teachers and students, previous work has shown that one-to-one computing programs can increase teacher-student interaction (Zucker & McGhee, 2005). This area of study is significant because a major concern with technology in education is a general dehumanization and mechanization of the classroom experience.

In addition, technology implementation has been previously linked to a shift towards constructivism (Ravitz & Becker, 2000). However, many of these studies have been survey-based without classroom observation or teacher interviews. In our study, we did observe that XO laptops were often used for self-guided activities that allowed children to build or engage in inquiry-based learning. Some examples of these activities were science experiments, mapmaking, and storytelling. Since constructivism is more a style of learning than a style of teaching, it may be beneficial to learn about the way that students view laptop versus non-laptop assignments in this context.

Our future software usability research will focus on iterative phases of software testing. A new release of SocialCalc was recently distributed,

allowing us the opportunity to complete a second round of testing.

## CONCLUSION

Over the course of two years, the Digital Literacy Project has developed a close relationship with the Cambridge Friends School. CFS administrators and teachers have provided mentorship that has helped a small nonprofit expand to other communities. The teaching and curriculum development experience gained by DigiLit volunteers has given the team the skills needed to initiate other laptop pilots. In the fall of 2009, DigiLit introduced XO laptops to an after-school program in the low-income Mission Hill neighborhood in Boston. Through a partnership with the Inter-American Development Bank, the organization set up a computer lab for deaf students at the Managua-based Nicaraguan Deaf Association in January 2010. DigiLit will continue to work closely with CFS by supporting one-to-one computing in both the third and fourth grades.

The CFS XO laptop pilot has allowed us to identify best practices that have informed other XO laptop pilots. Our framework is based on two phases of implementation: teacher training and classroom integration (Figure 4). We found that focusing on the capabilities of software to achieve clear goals, as well as classroom simulations, gave teachers more confidence when using this new technology in the classroom. Curriculum

*Figure 4. Best practices derived from the CFS XO laptop pilot*

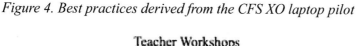

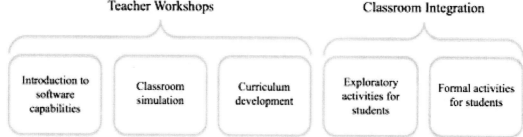

workshops should be supplemented with sample lesson plans that cover a wide range of subjects and software. We are currently working on a curriculum portal that will offer more extensive tutorials and lesson plans for teachers in one-to-one classrooms, particularly those who use the XO laptop.

Our instructor surveys suggest that exploratory assignments facilitate student introduction to XO laptops. In addition to informal activities, we have found that allowing students free time to play with XOs boosts their focus during more structured assignments. Although CFS students were not permitted to take XOs home, we believe that at-home exploration will not only give students the chance to use laptops for homework assignments but it will also promote family involvement in the school community.

Like any handheld device, the XO laptop is ultimately a tool. Its durability, size, and low cost make it a potential candidate for one-to-one computing programs in both domestic and international classrooms. By selectively investigating the XO's effects on different types of activities, one may identify a set of activities for which this laptop is most effective. In our study, we found that the XO facilitated certain aspects of collaborative work. As a result, we have tailored future curriculum design to group activities.

A user-centered approach was helpful in identifying problematic features of a new computer program that had not been identified in initial testing. Our results are aligned with other findings that children want control, social experiences, and expressive tools in technology (Druin, 1999). Although children are often left out of the software testing process, their candid feedback can provide insight into features that are not tailored to a young age group.

Although the CFS XO laptop pilot program is primarily a collaboration between DigiLit and CFS, the program has received support from students at local universities beyond Harvard. Students at Olin College of Engineering and at Boston University School of Management have shared their technical and business expertise. In addition to university support, software developers at the New Delhi-based SEETA have worked with DigiLit to pilot SocialCalc.

A highly digitally literate group, university students have many opportunities to share their technology skills with primary schools. This model demonstrates how university students, as part of a non-profit or student organization, can implement a one-to-one computing program, conduct on-site research in the classroom, and garner the community support needed to make technology a sustainable feature of K-12 classrooms.

# REFERENCES

Cuban, L. (2004). *The blackboard and the bottom line: Why schools can't be businesses.* Cambridge, MA: Harvard University Press.

Druin, A. (Ed.). (1999). *The design of children's technology.* San Francisco, CA: Morgan Kaufmann Publishers.

Greenhow, C., & Belbas, B. (2007). Using activity-oriented design methods to study collaborative knowledge-building in e-learning courses within higher education. *International Journal of Computer-Supported Collaborative Learning, 2*(4), 363–391. doi:10.1007/s11412-007-9023-3

Hanna, L., Risden, K., & Alexander, K. J. (1997). Guidelines for usability testing with children. *Interaction, 4*(5), 9–14. doi:10.1145/264044.264045

Hatch, R. J. (2008). *Discovering differences in software designed by children versus software designed by adults.* Doctoral dissertation. Available from ProQuest Dissertations and Theses database. (UMI No. 3371427)

Hembrooke, H., & Gay, G. (2003). The laptop and the lecture: The effects of multitasking in learning environments. *Journal of Computing in Higher Education, 15*(1), 46–64. doi:10.1007/BF02940852

Liu, C. C., & Kao, L. C. (2007). Do handheld devices facilitate face-to-face collaboration? Handheld devices with large shared display groupware to facilitate group interactions. *Journal of Computer Assisted Learning, 23*(4), 285–299. doi:10.1111/j.1365-2729.2007.00234.x

Mazzone, E., Xu, D., & Reed, J. (2007). Design in evaluation: Reflections on designing for children's technology. *British Computer Society: Proceedings of the 21st BCS HCI Group Conference.*

Meyer, R. C. (2007). *A case study of one-to-one computing: The effects on teaching and learning.* Doctoral dissertation. Available from ProQuest Dissertations and Theses database. (UMI No. 3289413)

One Laptop per Child. (2009, December 22). *Deployment statistics.* Retrieved February 21, 2010 from http://wiki.laptop.org/go/Deployments

Penuel, W. R. (2006). Implementation and effects of one-to-one computing initiatives: A research synthesis. *Journal of Research on Technology in Education, 38*(3), 329–348.

Prensky, M. (2001). Digital natives, digital immigrants. *Horizon, 9*(5), 1–6. doi:10.1108/10748120110424816

Ravitz, J., & Becker, H. J. (2000). *Evidence for computer use being related to more constructivist practices and to changes in practice in a more constructivist-compatible direction.* Paper presented at the annual meeting of the American Educational Research Association, New Orleans, LA.

Russell, M., Bebell, D., & Higgins, J. (2004). Laptop learning: A comparison of teaching and learning in upper elementary classrooms equipped with shared carts of laptops and permanent 1:1 laptops. *Journal of Educational Computing Research, 30*(4), 313–330. doi:10.2190/6E7K-F57M-6UY6-QAJJ

Sandholtz, J. H., Ringstaff, C., & Dwyer, D. C. (1997). *Teaching with technology: Creating student-centered classrooms.* New York, NY: Teachers College Press.

U.S. Census Bureau. (2009). *Computers for student instruction in elementary and secondary schools.* Retrieved February 21, 2010, from http://www.census.gov/compendia/statab/cats/education.html

Weiser, M. (1996). *Ubiquitous computing.* Retrieved February 21, 2010, from http://www.ubiq.com/hypertext/weiser/UbiHome.html

Zucker, A. A., & McGhee, R. (2005). *A study of one-to-one computer use in mathematics and science instruction at the secondary level in Henrico County Public Schools.* Arlington, VA: SRI International.

## KEY TERMS AND DEFINITIONS

**Collaboration:** The process by which two or more people actively work towards a common goal.

**Digital Divide:** The gap between those who have access to technology and those who do not.

**Digital Immigrants:** Non-native speakers of digital technologies who have not yet attained the fluency of a native speaker.

**Digital Literacy:** Proficiency in computer and internet use.

**Digital Natives:** Native speakers of digital technologies.

**One-to-One Computing:** One handheld device (i.e. computer, laptop, PDA) per student or teacher.

**User-Centered Design:** Design methodologies that include end users as designers.

**XO Laptop:** A low-cost laptop designed by One Laptop per Child (OLPC) that runs a Linux-based operating system called Sugar.

# Chapter 5
# Engaging STEM:
## Service–Learning, Technology, Science Education and Community Partnerships

**Meghan Griffin**
*University of Central Florida, USA*

**Erin Saitta**
*University of Central Florida, USA*

**Melody Bowdon**
*University of Central Florida, USA*

**Linda J. Walters**
*University of Central Florida, USA*

## ABSTRACT

*To stimulate student interest in science, technology, engineering, and math (STEM) disciplines, the University of Central Florida (UCF) partnered with the Crooms Academy of Information Technology (CAIT), a public magnet high school that emphasizes technology education for a diverse student population. Using digital tools and a service-learning model, UCF chemistry and biology students partnered with CAIT students to debunk science myths, perform laboratory experiments, and engage in an experiential oyster reef restoration project. This chapter provides an overview of project activities, implementation and the value of using technology. Challenges are detailed to offer a model for future community partnerships. The chapter concludes with a set of best practices for future projects.*

## HISTORY AND CONTEXT

Service-learning is a relatively well-established pedagogical approach in the humanities, social sciences and pre-professional fields, but has only recently begun to gain traction in U.S. physical and life science curricula. At the University of Central Florida (UCF), service-learning has been a commonly accepted pedagogy for several years, but, in keeping with national trends, rarely expanded into the STEM disciplines until recently. In the summer of 2009, UCF secured a small seed grant from Florida Campus Compact

DOI: 10.4018/978-1-60960-623-7.ch005

to launch Engaging STEM, an initiative designed to enlist interdisciplinary faculty teams in science, technology, engineering, and math courses to collaborate with instructors at Crooms Academy of Information Technology (CAIT), a local public high school, to support learning for students on both campuses. During the 2009-2010 academic year, UCF and CAIT students in mathematics, chemistry and biology partnered on projects ranging from debunking common science myths to a collaborative oyster reef restoration project. The use of technology in these service-learning partnerships and the challenges that arose as the projects were developed and implemented will be discussed in this case-study.

## Technology to Create a Product

During Engaging STEM's first year, some of the science projects consisted of university students using technology to produce a teaching tool that was shared with high school students. One of the projects involved UCF biology students who reached out to CAIT students through video-based lessons. These lessons related to marine biology and included topics such as coral reef diseases, invasive species, harmful algal blooms, open-ocean aquaculture and environmental awareness. UCF students researched the topics, created scripts with age-appropriate, engaging storylines and recorded their video presentations, which were then used to teach content to CAIT students with accompanying interactive discussion.

Rather than adding a new assignment to the course, the professor in this case modified an existing one. Her previous "hot topics in marine biology" class oral presentation assignment became an opportunity for students to use inexpensive digital movie cameras that plugged directly into PC computers (Flip-Cams™) provided through grant funding to create instructional and entertaining videos about the relevant topic of their choice to share with CAIT students. Together the student teams produced six short films that instructors at CAIT and other schools can use to supplement their existing curricular materials.

## Technology to Engage a Dialogue

Taking Engaging STEM in a different direction, three of the projects utilized technology to engage in live conversation through web conferencing. As part of a discussion section of their required coursework, approximately 100 Chemistry I students at UCF worked on a project called Chem-Mysteries. After collecting information from CAIT students regarding chemistry perceptions and beliefs, UCF students worked in teams to dispel misconceptions through live video conference presentations. CAIT students used their laptops to watch UCF students perform demonstrations and explain the truths behind common chemistry myths.

The following semester, in an effort to make the partnership more interactive, 22 UCF Chemistry II laboratory students worked as virtual lab partners with CAIT students in a real-time, kinetics-based interactive laboratory experiment. Students at both locations were divided into groups, conducted experiments, and shared and analyzed data through web-conferencing software.

Similarly, UCF Marine Biology students partnered with CAIT students on an oyster reef restoration project that began through web-conferencing tools. This project used the technology as a springboard to communication, which culminated in a face-to-face experiential education event at the end of the semester on the National Day of Service. CAIT students volunteered their Saturday to visit the UCF campus, meet the college students and ask them about all aspects of college life while collaboratively participating in the construction of oyster reef mats that will be used to help restore damaged oyster habitats in central Florida.

## Technology as an Integrated Approach

We learned a great deal from the initial projects described above. In all but one of the projects, technology was able to alleviate the need for student travel. The fact that with the use of web-conferencing technology each group of students can participate at their own institutions could be important if similar programs were to occur in remote or rural areas (Dalgarno, Bishop, Adlong & Bedgood, 2009). On the other hand, direct student-to-student contact was limited, which may be the reason many students requested more interaction with each other. Moving forward, technology is being incorporated in an integrated way. In spring 2011, the service-learning project in the Chemistry II laboratory course, for example, will span over two months with multiple opportunities for student interaction. University students will meet K-12 students over the Internet through web conferencing, keep in touch with them through video messages made with Flip cameras, and spend a lab period with them in person during a school field trip to UCF. This integrated approach is intended to promote a deeper connection to the community partner while enabling both populations to reach content goals.

## DETAILS ABOUT THE TECHNOLOGY IN ENGAGING STEM

Emerging technologies played a crucial role in the science partnerships between UCF and CAIT students and teachers. Adobe Connect was the primary web-conferencing medium used for real-time interaction between students across campuses. Adobe Connect allowed for live video and chat interaction between student groups. While the sessions were not glitch-free, Adobe Connect has a manageable learning curve so that students and faculty can adapt to the interface, bringing discussion and interactivity to the foreground

rather than the technology itself. UCF student teams used Flip cameras to record their video presentations. Author Griffin, a UCF graduate student with technical writing expertise, developed a brief manual that explained best practices for filming that the students could refer to and pointed them to online tutorials for troubleshooting and video editing.

## Required Technology

For live broadcasts using Adobe Connect, students needed a computer with Internet access, a webcam, a microphone, and speakers. Students without webcams or microphones participated using the text-based chat function. This cut down the chaos of too many people speaking at once while still allowing a constant flow of communication. Adobe Connect allows all participants to access the web-based platform via URL and does not require that they download software. Only the host of the session, in this case the UCF instructor, needs an account. In most cases, institutions pay a fee and then license individual instructors at a set cost per faculty member.

## Flexibility

CAIT served as an ideal pilot partner for the Engaging STEM initiative because of the school's focus on technical literacy. Even though students at CAIT were able to use their individual laptops issued to all students as freshmen, it is possible to modify activities for partnerships in more traditional settings where students do not have access to individual terminals. Adobe Connect proved to be a convenient tool for engaging both the UCF and CAIT student populations while mitigating the need for transportation between campuses or background checks for visitors to the public high school. This preserves school resources and cuts down on the project's carbon footprint. Many free or less expensive web-conferencing tools also exist and new ones are emerging regularly.

The key considerations for our approach were identifying a tool that was permissible at the high school (in light of URL restrictions, etc.) and that allowed multiple groups to connect with each other simultaneously.

## IMPACT ON STUDENTS AND FACULTY

Through the Engaging STEM initiative, UCF students experienced multiple possibilities for advanced study in the sciences, including science teaching possibilities that are not part of the regular curriculum. CAIT students had a chance to reconsider misperceptions regarding science careers and learned about what college-level science courses might entail. Using web-conferencing tools, UCF students modeled that science attracts a diverse student population with multiple areas of interest and that science education can be interesting and even enjoyable.

Using an interactive, collaborative approach facilitated through Adobe Connect, students and faculty connected for discussion and partnered experiments. Research has indicated that populations underrepresented in science, including women and ethnic minorities, may prefer collaborative learning methods with an emphasis on socially based and connected knowledge (Cabrera, Colbeck, & Terenzini, 2001). Implementing the ChemMysteries project and oyster restoration topics allowed both student populations to experience a range of topics and diversity of methodologies employed within the scientific community.

For CAIT students, engaging with UCF students enhanced their high school curriculum and modeled college-level learning. With a personal connection to college-level science education, the university learning environment was somewhat demystified and more accessible to this diverse high school population. As a result, the CAIT students involved may no longer rely solely upon popular representations and misunderstandings of

science careers and professionals, but will have a better understanding of science education in relation to the diverse population, interests, and approaches of UCF science students and faculty. Studies have shown that hands-on programs can improve students' attitudes towards science, which is important because students with positive attitudes towards science have been reported to achieve higher scores on science assessments (Neathery, 1997; Schwartz-Bloom & Halpin, 2003; Bredderman, 1982; Herron & Nurrenbern, 1999; Reid & Shah, 2007).

Engaging with CAIT students allowed UCF students to teach forward newly acquired content knowledge, aiding in long-term retention and building upon course lecture and lab exercises. The biology students who filmed video lessons, for example, used course principles to address issues that were relevant, interesting, and engaging for them. This aligns with literature reporting college student learning gains through service-learning (Bringle & Hatcher, 2009; Esson, Stevens-Truss & Thomas, 2005; Hatcher-Skeers, 2002; Kalivas 2008). Along with the science education principles that were reinforced, UCF students also engaged with new technologies including video production software and Adobe Connect. While learning about the tools was not part of the course learning objectives, the Engaging STEM project provided additional technical literacy support and exposure to UCF science students. One student was hired immediately after graduation specifically because of his Biology BS degree combined with video production experience.

For instructors at both UCF and the CAIT, the partnership and engagement with technology allowed for experimentation with new pedagogical approaches and alternative strategies for teaching familiar content. One CAIT instructor, for example, expressed frustration with a kinetics laboratory experiment that was unreliable. Using Adobe Connect, the CAIT high school students were able to engage in an alternate kinetics experiment using virtual lab partners, and the high school instructor was exposed to alternate methods for teaching kinetics. In addition, instructors at both institutions learned the Adobe Connect technology themselves, acquiring a flexible tool for connecting with students.

For UCF faculty, these partnerships allowed faculty to try something different, avoid an instructional rut, and to become co-learners with their students as they implemented new instructional techniques. Science faculty reported initial concern over teaching using technology—for example, they did not want to spend time teaching video camera operations rather than biology fundamentals. Engaging knowledgeable students to demonstrate technologies to their peers and allowing for out-of-class experimentation with the equipment, these faculty members were able to implement technical literacy into their courses without foregrounding the use of technology to an extent that course content was overshadowed.

## OVERVIEW AND BEST PRACTICES

While the Engaging STEM science partnerships were successful, several important issues emerged as overarching best practices for this type of collaboration.

Flexibility played a key role for instructors and for students. As in any project relying upon emerging technologies, adaptation to changing conditions was essential on the parts of instructors and students at both institutions. Unexpected Internet connectivity problems, equipment failure, and technical glitches are part of the electronic production process and cannot be completely mediated in an electronic learning environment. Instructors at both institutions had to be flexible, think creatively, and work through imperfect situations as they emerged. Instructors came to view these moments of technological failure as opportunities to model resourcefulness and creativity for students.

For UCF faculty, using technology without foregrounding technology created a continuous challenge. Enlisting the help of graduate assistants and technologically savvy students proved a useful strategy for implementing new technologies. Allowing for creative adaptation is precisely what affords a biology professor who has never used a Flip-Cam to assign recording assignments to students. When imperfection is allowed and even expected, students and faculty alike enjoy the freedom to experiment with new forms of technology.

In working with high school teachers, college-level instructors must remember that secondary teachers are knowledgeable and experienced in classroom management and educating students, and that any service-learning project must enrich the existing high school curriculum. When projects met the high school instructor's content needs, all parties were able to benefit. By focusing on the high school content needs, the partnerships remained symbiotic. In other words, college-level instructors could not focus exclusively on the activities that would be most beneficial for their students, but had to remain committed to the learning and teaching objectives of the high school partners.

As the partnership between the University of Central Florida and the CAIT continues through the Engaging STEM initiative, projects will be improved and new projects are expected to develop. The next phase for the collaboration will involve assessing the effectiveness of the initiative in relation to student learning outcomes in both UCF and CAIT populations. Overall, the use of technology has proved to be an essential component of the alliance in allowing for synchronous and interactive conversations about shared scientific discovery and applications.

# REFERENCES

Bredderman, T. (1982). What research says: Activity science—the evidence shows it matters. *Science and Children, 20*(1), 39–41.

Bringle, R. G., & Hatcher, J. A. (2009). Innovative practices in service-learning and curricular engagement. *New Directions for Higher Education, 147*, 37–46. doi:10.1002/he.356

Cabrera, A. F., Colbeck, C. L., & Terenzini, P. T. (2001). Developing performance indicators for assessing classroom teaching practices and student learning. *Research in Higher Education, 42*, 327. doi:10.1023/A:1018874023323

Dalgarno, B., Bishop, A. G., Adlong, W., & Bedgood, D. R. Jr. (2009). Effectiveness of a virtual laboratory as a preparatory resource for distance education chemistry students. *Computers & Education, 53*, 853–865. doi:10.1016/j.compedu.2009.05.005

Esson, J. M., Stevens-Truss, R., & Thomas, A. (2005). Service-learning in introductory chemistry: Supplementing chemistry curriculum in elementary schools. *Journal of Chemical Education, 82*(8), 1168. doi:10.1021/ed082p1168

Hatcher-Skeers, M., & Aragon, E. (2002). Combining active learning with service learning: A student-driven demonstration project. *Journal of Chemical Education, 79*(4), 462. doi:10.1021/ed079p462

Herron, J. D., & Nurrenbern, S. C. (1999). Chemical education research: Improving chemistry learning. *Journal of Chemical Education, 76*(10), 1353. doi:10.1021/ed076p1353

Kalivas, J. H. (2008). A service-learning project based on a research supportive curriculum format in the general chemistry laboratory. *Journal of Chemical Education, 85*(10), 1410–1415. doi:10.1021/ed085p1410

Neathery, M. F. (1997). Elementary and secondary students' perceptions toward science and the correlation with gender, ethnicity, ability, grade, and science achievement. *Electronic Journal of Science Education, 2*(1), 11.

Reid, N., & Shah, I. (2007). The role of laboratory work in university chemistry. *Chemistry Education and Research Practice, 8*(2), 172–185.

Schwartz-Bloom, R. D., & Halpin, M. J. (2003). Integrating pharmacology topics in high school biology and chemistry classes improves performance. *Journal of Research in Science Teaching, 40*(9), 922–938. doi:10.1002/tea.10116

# Section 2
# Service–Learning with Emerging Technologies

# Chapter 6
# Hybridizing F2F and Virtual Collaboration Between a Government Agency and Service-Learning Technical Writing Students

**Jim Henry**
*University of Hawai'i at Mānoa, USA*

## ABSTRACT

*This case study reviews a hybrid face-to-face (F2F) and virtual collaboration between the State of Hawaii's Division of Forestry and Wildlife and a team of university technical writing students to indicate specific features of the hybridity as it shaped the collaboration. In a course focused on organizational authorship, students were tasked with learning about the organization's workplace culture to successfully represent its ethos in a report on the history of forestry in Hawai'i. Moments and modes of collaboration are discussed chronologically as they enabled successful report writing, featuring key components: clearly stipulating terms of collaboration through service-learning, assessing fit between the course and the organization, emphasizing the need for onsite visits by students to ascertain the workplace culture, conducting swift follow-up on challenges in meshing the virtual with the face-to-face, and leveraging each mode of collaboration synergistically rather than discretely.*

## INTRODUCTION

Traditional gulfs between the campus and the community produce writing scenarios that fail to take advantage of the kinds of knowledge produced in each, yet as Spinuzzi has observed in his discussion of "distributed work" (2007), alliances bridging the two are certain to emerge increasingly. These alliances, often enabled through service-learning, can benefit from collaboration that merges face-to-face (F2F) interaction with the virtual possibilities

DOI: 10.4018/978-1-60960-623-7.ch006

afforded by Web 2.0 technology, as illustrated by this case study set in Hawai'i. In a state comprising seven islands, virtual collaboration is indispensable to composing state government reports. For technical writing students partnering with a government agency and seeking to adequately reflect that agency's organizational culture and *ethos*, face-to-face interaction between students and organizational workers is key. This case study traces the collaboration between my technical writing students partnered through service-learning with the Department of Land and Natural Resources/ Division of Forestry and Wildlife (DOFAW) in Hawai'i to identify key modes and moments of interaction that met the goals of both the Division and the course. After a brief depiction of the context of the project, a timeline of events reveals important interconnections between virtual and F2F collaboration, noting both breakthroughs and challenges afforded by technology. The study concludes with summary comments on the educational impact of the project, the community impact of the project, and the value of the project in forming community partnerships.

## CONTEXT OF THE PROJECT

The format for this technical writing course emphasized teaching technical *authorship* (Henry, 1995), with a goal of helping students "internalize the complexities of working in real contexts" (Clark, 2004, 320). On a Tuesday/Thursday schedule in a 16-week semester, this format devoted the first half of the semester to teaching technical writing fundamentals such as audience, purpose, and genre, with a strong emphasis on organizational authorship as it requires technical writers to represent an organization's *ethos* adequately and ethically. In the second half of the semester, I placed students in teams of two or three into organizational contexts to complete collaborative technical writing projects, so that they could enact the principles learned during the first half of the

semester in a rhetorical context that enabled them to perceive the reciprocal nature of workplace culture and document production (Kleimann, 1993). I articulated the course with the campus service-learning office, which solicited community partners at mid-semester. Once partners were identified around the seventh week, students and I collaborated with the organization's point of contact to propose an appropriate writing project. Projects embraced a wide range of genres, yet the central course premises of writing "for," "with" (Deans, 2000) or "as" (Bowdon & Scott, 2003) the community organization figured alongside that of learning the organization's culture to represent its *ethos*, or character. Academic writing most often positions students as singular authors, leaving them ill-prepared for the mostly collaborative writing of the workplace (Ede & Lunsford, 1990; Rainey, Turner, & Dayton, 2005), so learning outcomes for this course included collaborating effectively as a team and with the organization to produce technical documents that achieved clarity, cohesion, and readability, while also meeting the goals for the document as established by the organization.

## TIMELINE OF MOMENTS AND MODES OF COLLABORATION

Because the hybrid collaboration produced a synergy that emerged over time, key elements of this synergy are best located along a timeline, as follows:

### Step 1: Listserv Solicitation

At week 6, I solicited collaborators from the community via a Web 1.0 tool—the campus service-learning listserv. This solicitation briefly explained the course format, designated the availability period of weeks 8-16, and listed the specific kinds of writing that might work in a collaborative venture. (Experience had shown that this last information was an important ingredient in first contact; SL listservs often reach a very broad constituency, some of whom have worked with SL students from other courses with very different learning objectives. The solicitation emphasized that technical writing should be the key focus of the collaboration.)

## Step 2: E-mail Follow-up

This solicitation brought a response from Forester Ron Cannarella, of the Division of Forestry and Wildlife, detailing some projects that required technical writing and querying me as to appropriateness. Mr. Cannarella also offered to visit the class in person to present them, which to me suggested a strong possibility for a collaborative fit in the form of a point of contact who would be actively engaged in the project. (Previous experience had produced one or two instances in which an organization's point of contact made a valid case by e-mail yet failed to engage regularly and meaningfully with the technical writing student team, rendering the project less instructive than it might be. Research has shown, moreover, the importance of recognizing community partners as co-educators [Sandy & Holland, 2006].)

## Step 3: Face-to-Face Presentation

Mr. Cannarella soon thereafter visited class to explain a needed report detailing the history of forest management in the state. The presentation and Q's & A's that followed gave him the opportunity to informally assess the fit from his perspective, even as students and I were doing the same. *Any* historical representation of Hawai'i is remarkably complex—given the fiftieth state's former status as an independent kingdom before U.S. annexation that paved the way for statehood—and the discussion that followed his presentation revealed moments when the terms of complexity for this project were implicitly being probed, as when one student asked if the history could include pre-contact with Europeans. Mr. Cannarella's

response that the history *should* include details from this period, along with his other elaborations on the details of the report, established an initial intellectual orientation that all parties—students, Mr. Cannarella, and I—found inviting. Just as this orientation suggested a postcolonial understanding of history (and by extension of historical accounts), so did it suggest an organizational *ethos* amenable to a service-learning project encouraging student engagement on the civic and intellectual level along with the professional (see Turnley). Three students expressed interest in this project immediately, and a team was established during week 7.

## Step 4: Meetings On Site to Establish the Hybrid Working Framework

Teams were required to arrange an onsite visit and meet with their points of contact as soon as possible, following best practices for bolstering relationships in distributed work (Jackson 1996). They also had to submit a full project proposal to me and a formal letter of understanding detailing responsibilities and rights to the point of contact. Only two of the students could make this first site visit during week 8 of the semester, and their report back to me revealed that they were a bit overwhelmed by the complexity of the project as described. The mode of collaboration, moreover, was still to be determined, and Mr. Cannarella was ready to embark on a Web 2.0 venture, replacing their chains of e-mails and attachments with a less cumbersome and more efficient protocol for producing reports—a virtual document housed on the Web and accessible to all collaborators.[1] Mr. Cannarella had suggested a blogging tool with which he had novice familiarity, and one of the students had prior experience with it, so they had tentatively set up a shell. Yet attempts to use it proved daunting for all parties. Recognizing that a holdup in establishing a virtual collaborative tool could possibly delay effective collaboration by a week or two—far too much of a delay with respect to the semester timeline—I organized another onsite visit immediately with two of the three students. At that meeting, I proposed using Google Docs, primarily because I had experience using this Web 2.0 tool through campus committee report writing. Neither Mr. Cannarella nor the students had prior experience with the tool, and at that meeting I demonstrated its basic setup and possibilities for collaborative work. Because Google Docs emulates Microsoft's toolbar menus in its graphic user interface, collaborators found themselves able to apprehend the basic setup and possibilities rather quickly, and they agreed to use this tool as their primary mode for collaborative writing. Thus the Web 2.0 composing tool served as a major catalyst at a key moment in collaboration, providing an interface that was intuitively easy to learn and available 24/7/365 to any of the collaborators for asynchronous contributions. The following sections review elements of both asynchronous (virtual) and synchronous (F2F) collaboration during weeks 9-16 as each shaped teaching and learning among collaborators.

## Step 5: Fully Implementing the Web 2.0 Composing Tool

The report on forest history was projected to be quite comprehensive and detailed, with a due date to its Washington, D.C.-audience set for fifteen months later. Thus the scope of the writing exceeded the contributions that student technical writers could supply in one semester's work, yet the nature of the report—a series of sections that could be drafted initially by individual writer/researchers—enabled a collaboration within students' reach and one deemed valuable by both the forester and me. A key first step was setting up an outline to enable this "divide and conquer" approach (Lay, Wahlstrom, Rude, Selfe, & Selzer, 2006, p. 145) to collaborative writing. During this second F2F meeting at the Division headquarters in week 9, Mr. Cannarella suggested several possible topics for this history while students took notes and I entered the topics into an outline in

Google Docs. We then discussed this evolving outline, querying the forester on the nature of specific topics, what kinds of information would likely be needed for each, and how students could most expeditiously begin drafting. Mr. Cannarella was able to witness as the students and I engaged as writers and writing coach, and I demonstrated how I would likely insert comments into the draft when I saw a needed revision. In fact, this F2F session enabled all parties to view the comment function as it enabled "meta-commentary"—comments *about* the report rather than part of it—that would then become part of an asynchronous virtual discussion to support teaching and learning that targeted course learning outcomes and the division's goals for the report. These F2F contacts also helped to establish the "human relationship" key to distributed work (Nardi & Whitaker, 2002, p. 84), enabling a "social and professional context that makes distributed collaboration possible" (Paretti, McNair, & Holloway-Attaway, 2007, p. 332).

## Step 6: Exploiting the Hybrid Form for Drafting and Revising, Teaching and Learning

Once the Google Docs outline was in place, students chose specific topics and began researching and drafting sections of the report. By week 10 of the semester, I had expanded my role to online writing coach and editor by inserting comments specific to technical writing principles as students updated their drafts. The forester was able to track the students' progress, and he inserted comments specific to the content.

Two weeks into the collaboration, Mr. Cannarella was on vacation 6,000 miles and six time zones away from the students, making real-time collaboration difficult. But because the Web 2.0 document was fully accessible at any time in its most current version, he was able to continue to engage the students by providing additional resources. Some of those resources were newly created reports by DOFAW that were being posted online as this collaboration was taking place, so the students had access to the most current information available. These additional written sources also gave students multiple examples of how DOFAW represented organizational *ethos,* thus providing valuable models for them to emulate and for me to consider in my comments both virtually and when we met face to face in class. In this sense, the Web 2.0 document and its support sources positioned me as an *interpreter* of written organizational *ethos,* and with my experience as a consultant to industry, I was able to point out features contributing to the *ethos* that might have escaped students. At the same time, the support documents, though historical in many cases, were not exactly the same in nature as the actual history of forest management they were composing—and therefore only approximations of an appropriate *ethos* for that document. Explaining the complexities of why and how this was so would have been impossible in an embedded comment in the collaborative report, I realized, revealing a drawback of the technology with respect to virtual teaching and learning. Teaching issues and topics such as this one required F2F meetings in class, where our oral dialogue could enhance the learning that was transpiring via the 2.0 application. The team was required to compose its own style sheet for the writing, and these F2F meetings also allowed me to check in on those style sheets and make suggestions for adjustments.

To supplement their learning about organizational *ethos* that was transpiring virtually and via such F2F meetings in class, students made several trips to the Division headquarters over the next three weeks to familiarize themselves with the Division and its employees, and with the on-site resources in print form. These trips to the brick-and-mortar office enabled the students (and me) to gain a sense of the organizational culture by studying its "artifacts," including "everything from physical layout, the dress code, the manner in which people address each other, the smell and feel of the place, its emotional intensity, and other

phenomena" (Schein, 1990, p. 111). While student were on site, moments emerged when technology aided both their interpretation of local culture and the structuring of the document—as when I captured the forester's notes on a white board during the second F2F meeting by photographing them on my smartphone, then later reviewing them in class with the students. Students were required to take notes on their time on site, to supply one of their deliverables for the course: a "working paper" that documented their evolving understandings of the workplace culture, intended both to deepen their understanding of the division—and to situate themselves intellectually with respect to it—and to render their writing more compatible with the division's *ethos.* I used this working paper and my own insights gleaned in part by reading the forester's suggestions to teach to the student team in weekly F2F team meetings held in class. Davis and Hardy have recommended that instructors "try to keep movement between the two types of spaces [virtual and f2f] fluid and easy to negotiate" (2003), and this teaching approach that dedicated at least twenty minutes per week per writing team in class was an attempt to do so.

For example, during the second F2F meeting and in follow-up comments inserted in the evolving online draft, Mr. Cannarella had identified a number of key contributors to forestry management during the past couple of decades who could provide valuable information for the report. I then assigned readings on conducting interviews to this technical writing team and held one in-class meeting to enable students to propose some questions and try out some interviewing techniques. Students conducted their interviews by cell phone and in person while taking notes and garnering interviewees' e-mail addresses for short follow-ups; then they drafted full paragraphs that went into the report.

Back on island, Mr. Cannarella was now teaching the knowledge of his workplace both face-to-face, when the technical writing students would arrive at division headquarters to consult necessary documents or archives on a weekly basis, and virtually, when he would place a comment or recommendation into the evolving report. I could at times act on these comments directly in F2F sessions by suggesting how students should go about responding to his recommendations, shaping my teaching as part-interpreter, part recommender. At other times the students took the lead on the follow-up, gaining confidence in representing the organization through their onsite visits and affirming feedback—virtual and F2F—from both forester and me. As students composed, errors in grammar, style, usage, or punctuation occasionally made their ways into the report, and in these instances I would insert what Godwin-Jones, in discussing a best practice for teaching 2.0 writing, calls "indirect feedback" (2008, p.10): I would highlight such errors and explain them in the comments, leaving it to the student writers to interpret this virtual teaching and make the necessary changes. (Students were also required to maintain evolving personalized editing checklists for specific errors, so that they could systematically check future writing for an identified error. When students failed to execute the needed changes successfully or seemed to be straying from their style sheet, I held brief F2F sessions in class to teach the mini-lesson.)

This collaboration thus blended teaching driven by technical writing principles and organizational needs with a learner-centered approach to instruction, leveraging students' prior educational experiences to tap their "contributory expertise" (Henry, 1998; Kleimann, 1993, p. 69) as part of the collaboration. One of the student writers was an exchange student from the University of Alaska hoping to become a park ranger one day, and she brought knowledge of conservation to the report that appeared in two of its sections. Another student was a Native Hawaiian who integrated his culture's precepts on sustainability into the report as well, inserting Native Hawaiian proverbs that resonated with the forester's (and the division's) understandings of the *ethos* of the report (Henry,

2010). That students arrived at these contributions *entirely* independently of any virtual or F2F coaching by Mr. Cannarella or me marked a moment when the "personal" and "civic" dimensions of critical service-learning identified by Turnley took form in a deliverable for the organization; that Mr. Cannarella deemed the passages excellent contributions confirmed that these students could not only appropriately represent organizational *ethos* but also *inflect* it. As will be seen below, this collaboration also inflected organizational practices for collaborative writing.

## Step 7: End of Semester Assessment by Students and Instructor

At the course conclusion, the student technical writing team provided a self-assessment of the group's work to me. Their report showed how their understanding of this history of forest management authored by DOFAW grew over the seven weeks: initially they had imagined a narrative similar to those encountered in singly-authored histories, and their experience working on this report enabled them to ascertain how organizationally-authored histories differ in content and tone. They also emphasized the difficulty of matching three students' schedules for trips to the headquarters and noted that they never were able to muster a meeting on site when all members were present. From this perspective, the Web 2.0 technology provided an invaluable site where they could all meet asynchronously. And because each student was visiting headquarters on his or her own, they were independently developing an understanding of the organization's culture that they could discuss during class meetings.

In self-assessing the "most valuable part" of their learning experience as required on the syllabus, this team of twenty-somethings stated:

*In terms of meeting the learning outcomes of the Technical Writing course, the firsthand research was one of the most successful aspects of our*

*project. We learned how to conduct a personal interview and then how to synthesize that primary research into a technical document.*

The shifts between online and F2F work barely surfaced in this self-assessment, subsumed under the topic of "firsthand research." Yet the foregoing analysis shows that their "firsthand" work was in fact part flesh-and-blood/brick-and-mortar, part virtual. Craig (2007) has observed that the user-centered approach to teaching afforded by Web 2.0 technologies reflects this generation's approach to learning; assessment of such learning thus requires a review of apt uses of such technology. One way to do so is by reviewing iterations of the report available through Google Doc's archived histories, which in this case shows sustained contributions that made use of one another's work. In this sense, their "technical writing" revealed itself to be an elaborate interplay of contributions shaped by both F2F and virtual collaboration.

Another way to assess the success of this hybrid collaboration is to hold its dynamics and deliverables up to standards for successful professional writing identified through empirical research. One such set identifies "habits of mind" of successful writers, which includes the following: persevere, attempt challenges, embrace learning, exhibit keen interest in subject, engage in collaboration, understand how to write in complicated contexts, respond positively to critique, and engage in metacognition (Walters, Hunter, & Giddens, 2007). The student writers who collaborated in this hybrid F2F/virtual project demonstrated each of these habits of mind on more than one occasion, and in many cases throughout the entire project. I can confirm these habits after participating so actively in their processes along with seeing iterative products.

## EDUCATIONAL IMPACT OF THE PROJECT

The educational impact of this collaboration was significant. Students were able to pursue the parallel goals of learning the workplace culture and representing it appropriately, all the while participating quite actively in the drafting of a high-stakes report. For me, this new genre—a collaborative, virtual document now available to a desktop, laptop, or mobile phone—emerged as a new tool for instruction by enabling the roles of online writing coach backed up by in-classroom project manager in weekly meetings with the team. At times, comments in the online document—either by me, Mr. Cannarella, or students—were perceived by other parties to the collaboration as somewhat inscrutable, necessitating phone calls or F2F action to clarify. In other words, the 2.0 technology, partly because of its simultaneous access to all, opened the door for misunderstandings (much as a Wiki does). Yet the time lost in those instances was far outweighed by an accessibility that enabled people working on very different schedules to remain current as collaborators. Moreover, for students, the forester, and me, the revision history available through Google Docs enabled us to shift between local issues in any part of the text and the bigger organizational structure that evolved as they progressed. The availability of the document via any mobile phone with browser capabilities enabled all parties to consult the document even when no computers were immediately available—a feature that became valuable during telephone interviews.

## COMMUNITY IMPACT OF THE PROJECT

This collaboration had a huge impact on work practices at DOFAW. Mr. Cannarella and the other project staff now use Google Docs extensively, and it has become a mainstay of their workflow.

By his accounting, he has tested a number of other 2.0 applications, yet with respect to DOFAW's workplace culture, Google Docs has proven easiest to learn and to implement effectively. Mr. Cannarella is located in Honolulu on the island of O'ahu, and DOFAW's principal technical writer on this project is located on the island of Kaua'i. Their main Forest Service contact was at the time on sabbatical in Massachusetts. With a cell phone, free conference calling and an open Google document, they could brainstorm an issue in real time and then have a reference document to work from to produce a final product. Having witnessed the pressures they are under to produce, I sense that another part of our value to their organization was simply the time we—the students and I—had available to approach any challenges or questions raised by the technology as part of our learning about technical "writing," then to convey our thoughts to the organization. Had we had more time to experiment with other kinds of collaborative platforms (see Godwin-Jones for a list current as of 2008), our hybrid collaboration might have changed somewhat. But the ways in which teaching and learning were inflected would have most likely remained quite similar, given the overarching structure of the course and its required learning outcomes. The specific Web 2.0 technology is less significant than the opportunities it affords and its interface with other evolving technologies, and future collaborations could well take place on those technologies that prove themselves to be most adaptable and easy to use.

The experience at DOFAW, as reported by Mr. Cannarella, has been that Google Docs is useful to a point, but for formatting a final product (printed document, spreadsheet, presentation) they must pull it down into a desktop word processing application as soon as possible due to the formatting limitations of the Web 2.0 platform. The "track document history" feature has proven to be especially useful in helping them to account for time spent on a given project by providing a permanent record of who made changes and when. More and more, staff have been encouraged to bring a wireless-capable laptop to a meeting, where a common Google Doc is created; people add their thoughts, copy and paste URL's to relevant documents, and walk out with a finished document that has the "buy in" of all present. That document can then be shared with someone who wasn't in the meeting, providing access to the collective experience of all of the contributors. Thus, collaboration has been taking place in real time, face to face, and after the fact by a third party with seamless integration.

## VALUE OF THE PROJECT IN FORMING COMMUNITY PARTNERSHIPS

When the project was completed, Mr. Cannarella reported, he met with each of his colleagues who had been interviewed by the students. Without exception, the professionals within DOFAW expressed how much they had appreciated the interaction with the students, and how personally fulfilling it was for them to have an opportunity to pass on their experience to an interested person. The passing of oral history is an important aspect of local culture in Hawai'i, where elders are respected as *kupuna*, or keepers of traditional knowledge, and where oral tradition is kept in high regard. This understanding was shared by the old-timers and students alike, and particularly so by the Native Hawaiian student. Invisible to many of those at DOFAW who had served as "firsthand sources" to the students was the complex F2F/virtual collaboration emerging from their interactions and resulting ultimately in a draft report that melded personal writing effort with organizational *ethos*.

The bond between the workplace and the university also endures. The forester and I each gained a richer sense of the writing challenges, opportunities, goals, and hopes of one another. Our face-to-face meetings and our virtual interactions laid the basis for ongoing collaboration:

another team of technical writing students joined the DOFAW report team in the spring 2010 semester and supplemented the previous spring's work with several more sections of the report. Our collaboration has prompted the forester to signal other future writing projects amenable to such hybrid collaboration, forecasting possible long-term partnership that could even take new forms such as internships and directed studies.

## REFERENCES

Bowdon, M., & Scott, B. (2003). *Service-learning in technical and professional communication.* New York, NY: Addison Wesley Longman.

Clark, D. (2004). Is professional writing relevant? A model for action research. *Technical Communication Quarterly, 13*(3), 307–323. doi:10.1207/s15427625tcq1303_5

Craig, E. M. (2007). Changing paradigms: Managed learning environments and Web 2.0. *Campus-Wide Information Systems, 24*(3), 152–161. doi:10.1108/10650740710762185

Davis, E., & Hardy, S. (2003). Teaching writing in the space of Blackboard. *Computers and Composition Online.* Retrieved July 10, 2010, from http://www.bgsu.edu/cconline/DavisHardy/index.html

Deans, T. (2000). *Writing partnerships: Service-learning in composition.* Urbana, IL: NCTE.

Diehl, A. (2006, February 2). What is Web 2.0 and how will technical writers be impacted? *Content Matters, 1*(2). Retrieved July 11, 2010, from http://www.msu.edu/user/diehlamy/atw/ezine/

Ede, L., & Lunsford, A. (1990). *Singular texts/plural authors: Perspectives on collaborative writing.* Carbondale & Edwardsville, IL: Southern Illinois University Press.

Goodwin-Jones, R. (2008). Emerging technologies—Web-writing 2.0: Enabling, documenting, and assessing writing online. *Language Learning & Technology, 12*(2), 7–13. Retrieved July 11, 2010, from http://llt.msu.edu/vol12num2/emerging.pdf

Harris, K. R., Santangelo, T., & Graham, S. (2010). Metacognition and strategies instruction in writing. In H. S. Waters, & W. Schneider (Eds.), *Metacognition, strategy use, & instruction* (pp. 226–256). New York, NY: Guilford.

Henry, J. (1995). Teaching technical authorship. *Technical Communication Quarterly, 4*(3), 261–282.

Henry, J. (1998). Documenting contributory expertise: The value added by technical communicators in collaborative writing situations. *Technical Communication, 45*(2), 207–220.

Henry, J. (2010). Greening the subject of/through technical writing. *Academic Exchange Quarterly, 14*(1), 140–146.

Jackson, K. (1996). Managing distributed documentation. *Society for Technical Communication Conference Proceedings.* Retrieved July 9, 2010, from http://www.stc.org/confproceed/1996/PDFs/PG6162.PDF

Kleimann, S. (1993). The reciprocal nature of workplace culture and review. In R. Spilka (Ed.), *Writing in the workplace: New research perspectives* (pp. 56-70). Carbondale & Edwardsville, IL: Southern Illinois University Press.

Lay, M., Wahlstrom, B., Rude, C., Selfe, C., & Selzer, J. (2006). *Technical communication* (3rd ed.). New York, NY: McGraw Hill.

Nardi, B. A., & Whitaker, S. (2002). The place of face-to-face communication in distributed work. In P. Hinds, & S. Kiesler (Eds.), *Distributed work* (pp. 83–110). Cambridge, MA: MIT Press.

Paretti, M. C., McNair, L. D., & Holloway-Attaway, L. (2007). Teaching technical communication in an era of distributed work: A case study of collaboration between U.S. and Swedish students. *Technical Communication Quarterly, 16*(3), 327–352.

Rainey, K., Turner, R., & Dayton, D. (2005). Do curricula correspond to managerial expectations? Core competencies for technical communicators. *Technical Communication, 52*(3), 323–352.

Sandy, M., & Holland, B. A. (2006). Different worlds and common ground: Community-partner perspectives on campus-community partnerships. *Michigan Journal of Community Service Learning, 13*(1), 30–43.

Schein, E. (1990). Organizational culture. *The American Psychologist, 45*(2), 109–119. doi:10.1037/0003-066X.45.2.109

Spinuzzi, C. (2007). Guest editor's introduction: Technical communication in the age of distributed work. *Technical Communication Quarterly, 16*(3), 265–277.

Turnley, M. (2007). Integrating critical approaches to technology and service-learning projects. *Technical Communication Quarterly, 16*(1), 103–123. doi:10.1207/s15427625tcq1601_6

Walters, M., Hunter, S., & Giddens, E. (2007). Qualitative research on what leads to success in professional writing. *International Journal on the Scholarship of Teaching and Learning, 1*(2). Retrieved July 11, 2010, from http://academics. georgiasouthern.edu/ijsotl/v1n2/articles/walters/media/

## ENDNOTE

[1] WWW scholars generally identify the turn from 1.0 to 2.0 as constituted by uses that have gone beyond that of the Web as storage house to that of the Web as platform enabling new ways to interact with content. (For more details, see Diehl 2006, Wendler *et al.,* this volume.) Against the burgeoning of ways to interact with content offered by 2.0 designers, Google Docs might be considered "2.0 lite." Yet a central document housed on a server, password-protected and accessible to all collaborators from any device with Internet browsing capabilities is a definite step beyond documents created in MWord, saved to a local hard drive, and circulated by e-mail. Unlike proprietary-neutral 2.0 applications that merely seek out content in new ways (for example, RSS feeds that locate other third-party content that those parties freely provide and deliver it to a chosen device), Google Docs does stipulate in its terms of service that even though users retain copyright they nonetheless grant Google the right to "perpetual, irrevocable, worldwide, royalty-free, and non-exclusive license to reproduce, adapt, modify, translate, publish, publicly perform, publicly display and distribute any Content which you submit, post or display on or through, the Services" (Google Docs Terms of Service). Suspecting no doubt that such language might avert users, Google has added a "Terms of Service Highlights" that states: "Google does not assert any ownership rights in your content. What belongs to you, stays yours. We do require that you give us a licence to the content you post so that we can host it and, if you ask us to, make it available to others."

# Chapter 7
# Integrated Product Teams at The University of Alabama in Huntsville

**Matthew W. Turner**
*The University of Alabama in Huntsville, USA*

**Michael P.J. Benfield**
*The University of Alabama in Huntsville, USA*

**Dawn R. Utley**
*The University of Alabama in Huntsville, USA*

**Cynthia A. McPherson**
*The University of Alabama in Huntsville, USA*

## ABSTRACT

*The capstone senior design class in the Department of Mechanical and Aerospace Engineering at The University of Alabama in Huntsville (UAH) is taught as a distributed Integrated Product Team (IPT) experience. Engineering students are teamed with students of different disciplines within UAH and with students at universities in other states and Europe. Because of the distributed nature of these teams, the IPT students must use a variety of technologies to communicate. The authors of this chapter found that the students prefer familiar, informal, contemporary forms of communication, including Google Groups/ Sites, Skype, instant messaging, e-mail, phone calls, and text messaging for team communication and project management, and reject more formalized forms of communication, even if advanced features are offered. Most importantly, the authors found that the effectiveness of all forms of technology based communication tools is greatly enhanced when the students have the opportunity to personally meet prior to the design semester.*

DOI: 10.4018/978-1-60960-623-7.ch007

# INTRODUCTION

The capstone senior design course in the Mechanical and Aerospace Engineering (MAE) Department at The University of Alabama in Huntsville (UAH) offers students a unique design, teaming, and collaboration experience. This class, referred to as the Integrated Product Team (IPT) class, has collaborative efforts with other departments on campus and multiple external university partners, foreign and domestic. The IPT class teaches students how to implement and affect the design process; furthermore, because of its structure, the IPT class shows students the importance of communication and collaboration, and some best practices for doing both. The use of technology as a communication tool is prevalent in the IPT class – it allows the students to communicate with the instructors, external professional mentors, and students at partner universities.

Currently, the IPT class has three collaborative efforts on campus. As credit for their senior design course, students from the Electrical and Computer Engineering (ECE) Department at UAH serve as the electrical and communications design experts for the team. Students in the UAH English Department's technical editing class provide editing and writing support for the documents teams must prepare (Norman & Frederick, 2000). ECE and editing students directly integrate into the MAE teams, attend team meetings, and participate as full team members. Graduate students in Engineering Management (EM) observe the IPTs as part of their graduate research. In addition, these graduate students offer collaboration advice to the undergraduate students.

The IPT class currently has three external university partners. Ecole Supérieure des Techniques Aéronautiques et de Construction Automobile (ESTACA) University in Paris, France, has been an engineering partner to the IPT class for 11 years (Frederick, et al., 2002). ESTACA has a five-year, master-level program; therefore, their students could be equated to first-year graduate students specializing in space transportation systems. Southern University in Baton Rouge (SUBR), Louisiana, has been a mechanical engineering partner for the past six years. Beginning in Fall 2009, the newest partnership – with undergraduate science students at the College of Charleston (CoC), in Charleston, South Carolina – provides the science rationale, goals, and objectives for the project. The projects for this class are real world, where the fundamental objectives of the mission are to accomplish science-related goal(s). The science students, therefore, define the basic mission objectives and determine instruments that can measure and accomplish their scientific goals (Benfield et al., 2010; Turner et al., 2010). The engineering students design the vehicle (spacecraft, lander, rover, etc.) that houses the science instruments and transports them to the appropriate environment or celestial body.

The IPT class has experimented with several technologies to facilitate collaboration within the IPTs and between the IPTs and their distance partners, including formalized and institutional networks and tools. Students, however, prefer simpler and more familiar tools to those that are more powerful and offer more options. They also prefer less formal and more social forms of collaboration. Moreover, when collaborating with professionals external to the class, students typically prefer asynchronous communication, such as e-mail, because it allows them time to think about their questions and responses. Most students are uncomfortable with professional teleconferences, but the discomfort can be mitigated through preparedness for the meeting. (We often suggest that the students hold several asynchronous discussions and do their research before a teleconference.) This discomfort can also be exacerbated when students are involved in a meeting that has both face-to-face and remote call-in participants. The additional intimidation of face-to-face participants may disquiet some students; however, they almost always benefit from being an observer to a discussion between subject matter experts. Although the students efficiently and effectively use the communication tools, we still find that the most fruitful discussions occur during a face-to-face meeting between a subject matter expert (mentor) and well-prepared students. The student teams function best when the on-campus collaborators are directly integrated into the teams; furthermore, when the students have physically visited the external university partners prior to the design semester, the collaborations and designs are much improved.

For example, in preparation of the Spring 2010 semester of the design class, one instructor and eight students visited ESTACA University in Paris, France, in November 2009, but, due to scheduling conflicts, we were unable to visit Southern University in Baton Rouge, Louisiana (Turner et al. 2010). Normally, our working relationship with Southern University is more productive (better integration, iteration, and more thorough designs) than with ESTACA, because of the differences in time, culture, and language. However, during the Spring 2010 semester, the working relationship with ESTACA was more productive than with Southern University. We postulate that this is because of the personal relationships established during their meeting; our students communicated with the French students more often and in greater detail than with the students from Baton Rouge. In an effort to increase productivity between UAH and SUBR, a UAH IPT instructor visited Baton Rouge during the Spring 2010 semester. This visit provided a basic understanding for the project – a starting point and common vocabulary – between the UAH and SUBR students; however, there was very little increase in overall communication and collaboration, because the students, themselves, were not able to meet face to face.

This chapter describes the communication and collaboration tools used by the IPTs, discusses the advantages and disadvantages of each, and presents some lessons learned through their years of use. Any conclusions, with respect to different technologies or tools, come directly

from first-hand experience or conversations with the students. The students complete surveys that measure overall team growth, performance, and effectiveness; however, no surveys have specifically measured the effectiveness of technological tools. Most of the university partnerships described in this chapter have evolved over the years. When designing and developing partnerships, the IPT administration seeks like-minded professors/ instructors of courses that would complement the program – i.e., courses that would enhance the "real world" aspects of the program. Most communication and collaboration between instructors (whether local or remote) occurs via email or telephone; therefore, the instructors' use of communication technology is not a focus of this chapter.

## BACKGROUND

The IPT class, in its current form, began in 1993 (Frederick & Sanders, 1993), covering a total of 25 different design projects since that time. Approximately 90% of these projects have come directly from customers at the Redstone Arsenal or NASA Marshall Space Flight Center in Huntsville, Alabama (Benfield & Turner, 2009). The goal of the class is to have "real world" design projects for the students. Real world experience includes (1) having a professional customer who shapes the design specifications and interacts with the students, (2) incorporating design reviews in which eight to ten professionals evaluate the students' designs, and (3) utilizing professional mentors to help the students with discipline-specific questions and issues. Unlike service-learning, which focuses on meeting some need in a community, this class simulates the research and development process in engineering firms in which performance or mission specifications are given to the engineering teams who then design a product to meet those specifications. The "real world" aspect is part of the attraction of this class to local government and commercial engineering organizations who partner with us. Approximately 76% of our graduates live and work in the Huntsville area after obtaining their baccalaureate degrees. It is, then, in the best interest of the local engineering organizations to support the IPT so that our graduates are prepared for real world engineering when they exit the classroom.

## OVERVIEW OF THE USE OF TECHNOLOGIES

Because this class functions as a distributed integrated product team spanning multiple departments, states, and countries, technology plays a vital role. The specific technology, and its use in the class, depends on the particular partner's role in the course (Middleton & Frederick, 1999). In most cases, the propensity to use a specific technology might depend on the partnership – whether the partner is (1) local or remote, (2) college peer or professional mentor, (3) science or engineering focused, etc. However, since the student teams comprise on-campus and remote partners, a team will typically use the "least common denominator" approach to the choice in technology. That is, a team will use a technology that is acceptable to all parties, even if some or a majority of the team can use a more advanced technology. In addition to communicating about their projects, students must share files, answer weekly surveys, and submit weekly activity reports. Technologies available to the IPTs and their partners include our university's course management system (CMS) and e-mail system, Google applications such as Google Forms and Groups, Facebook, Instant Messenger, video chat software such as Skype and iChat, phones, and text messages.

## Asynchronous Communication: Course Management, File Sharing, and E-mail

UAH currently uses ANGEL as its course management system (CMS); in the past, WebCT was used. UAH students have automatic access to ANGEL and the IPT instructors have always given external students proper user privileges within ANGEL. However, students from other universities are reluctant to use ANGEL because

1.  the log-in procedure is perceived as a hassle,
2.  this particular CMS is unfamiliar to most external students,
3.  some students have never used a CMS (e.g., French students); therefore, the CMS itself and the concept of a CMS are unfamiliar to the students.

In all cases, we have found that simple usergroups (e.g., Google Groups, Google Sites) are familiar, and easy-to-learn, for all students. Furthermore, Google applications offer some online storage space (approximately 100 MB) for the students to exchange files. The ubiquity of Google and its applications allows it to serve as the default communication system for the students, irrespective of their locations.

As part of the IPT course, all students take weekly surveys and must submit weekly activity reports. We originally placed these surveys within the ANGEL system, utilizing ANGEL's online assessment and survey tools. A significant drawback to using ANGEL's survey tools, in addition to login issues, is the way data is reported. To make the data useful, we must manually format and postprocess the data once it is exported from ANGEL.

We have found that Google Forms, which do not require the student to log-in to complete the survey, were not only more user-friendly, but offered improved data export features as well. The data entered into a Google Form is sent to a Google Spreadsheet, which can be saved locally as an Excel spreadsheet, or processed on the Google servers. One disadvantage is that, while ANGEL allows a survey or assessment to be accessible for a specified period of time and reused for a specified period of time, a Google Form is accessible as long as it is open on the Internet. However, to mitigate this, Google Forms automatically inserts a time/date stamp into every entry, which allows instructors to determine whether a student completed a survey or assessment within the proper time frame. Even with the inability to limit student access to surveys, the advantages (user-friendliness, data formatting) of Google Forms far outweigh the disadvantages. While we find Google Forms efficient for surveys, we continue to use the ANGEL CMS for coordination and filesharing with UAH students.

E-mail remains the most prevalent form of asynchronous communication and file transfer among the students. All students are issued university e-mail accounts, and most have their own personal accounts as well. E-mail is relatively easy to use and readily available, and all students are familiar with webmail and/or desktop e-mail applications; however, in most of the IPT teaming situations, e-mail is not the optimal form of communication among the students. We encourage the students to form Internet forums, such as a Google Group, for their teams. In the past, the instructors created web forums inside the UAH ANGEL course management system, but these forums were seldom used because of login issues and distance students' problems with using the CMS. Internet forums are advantageous for several reasons, including

1.   All team members are able to read all team communications. This ensures that all team members, even the remote partners, are "on the same page" as far as the engineering design is concerned.
2.   Internet forums provide an automatic archive of all communications, for students and instructors.

3.   Most Internet forums offer some file storage space.
4.   Internet forums allow the instructor and the Engineering Management observer to monitor the communications within the team.

Most Internet forums, e.g., Google Groups, offer e-mail updates of conversations, and the ability to submit responses directly to the forum via standard e-mail; therefore, it would seem reasonable that students would automatically start a web forum for their team at the beginning of the semester. However, fewer than half of the IPTs start Internet forums on their own because the forum requires some initial setup. Despite this response, we feel that the time spent with the initial setup is overshadowed by the benefits offered by the forum, and therefore strongly encourage, sometimes require, the students to start a forum for their team. Many teams later realize the benefits of the Internet forum. Some teams put forth the extra effort to create a Web site, via Google Sites, for their teams. This helps to create a strong sense of camaraderie and teamwork (Benfield and Utley, 2005; Fortune et al., 2005).

Although most filesharing occurs via e-mail or online groups, recently many of the students have started using Dropbox, a file-sharing tool that synchronizes a specified folder across the Internet. With Dropbox, a student can have a folder on the team's computer on campus, and this folder can be synchronized to the student's personal computer, and to other team members' computers. So, as a file is added to the folder on one computer it is updated to all computers with the synchronized folders, with up to 5 GB of data storage space being offered free from Dropbox. Dropbox is a cross-platform, easy-to-use tool for backups, synchronization, and version control; however, it can create a false sense of communication because students can transfer files to one another with no explanation of the content or the context. Furthermore, with Dropbox, students feel that online groups are unnecessary, which further erodes communication.

Ideally, students would use a combination of Dropbox and an online group. The online groups offer the communication with limited file-sharing capabilities, and Dropbox offers file sharing with essentially no communication. Therefore, a marriage of the two would be best with students using the online groups for communicating that files have been updated and Dropbox for file sharing.

E-mail is used almost exclusively for communication between students and their professional mentors and Review Board members, typically because the professionals prefer it. E-mail allows students time to consider their questions and responses, and it gives the professionals the flexibility to respond to the students at their convenience.

## Synchronous Communication: Phone Calls, Instant Messaging, Video Chatting

Students use online conferencing and chatting tools most often for conversations.

ESTACA University in Paris, France, is the most remote IPT partner with a seven-hour time difference. UAH and ESTACA students typically prefer instantaneous forms of digital communication – video chatting (usually via free software applications like Skype or iChat), and instant messaging (IM). Phone calls and text messages have also proven to be very fruitful, yet are used much less often. The students prefer video-chats and IMs to phone conversations because, for standard voice phone calls, the students must use university facilities or pay for the international call themselves. However, in all cases of international synchronous communication, because the chats occur in English, the French students prefer to receive the questions or topics of conversation prior to the conversation so that they can prepare answers or comments (Middleton, Frederick, & Norman, 2000).

The remote partners in the U.S., CoC and SUBR, prefer familiar, usually free, forms of instantaneous communication – Skype, iChat and IM. Text messaging and cellular phone calls are more common with CoC and SUBR because these students are in the U.S. The engineering departments at UAH and SUBR also have an Internet video teleconferencing link, where students can share presentations, video, and audio. While the students know of its capability and availability, this system is often unused. Students feel that it is too "formalized" because they have to gain access to the facility through an instructor or administrator. Similarly, students would rather use the desktop sharing portion of Skype than use WebEx or GoToMeeting because the students would be required to contact the instructors to gain access to the WebEx or GoToMeeting accounts. The students prefer simpler forms of communication that do not require approval or intervention of the instructors or the institution.

Design reviews, where the students present their design solutions to the external professional Review Board, utilize professional Internet meeting software, such as WebEx or GoToMeeting. After years of trial, the instructors prefer GoToMeeting because it is much more user friendly than WebEx. While WebEx offers secure connections and is more commonly used at NASA, providing an advantage when teams work with NASA partners, the secure connections are not needed in a classroom exercise, and all external partners seem to be comfortable with GoToMeeting. The exact features of each software differ from version to version – so any enumeration here would become quickly out-of-date; however, it is our experience that university partners prefer GoToMeeting (for its ease of use), while civil-service and professional partners prefer WebEx (because of their familiarity with it in their professional environment).

## Observation Technology

The Engineering Management (EM) graduate students observe the engineering teams (Benfield, 2003; Benfield & Utley, 2005), in-person and via video/audio recordings. Each engineering team at UAH has a team room within our dedicated IPT laboratory, with 24-hour access to their rooms. Because the teams are in competition against each other, the rooms are locked and acoustically isolated. When the engineering teams have a meeting, they are recorded (audio and video) for later viewing. During class-time, EM students are in the room with the undergraduate engineering teams for observation (Utley, Farrington, & Frederick, 2002). While recording the team meetings is vital for the engineering management research, the EM students report that the most effective observations take place in person.

## CONCLUSION

Local and remote partners in the IPT collaboration prefer familiar, informal, contemporary forms of digital communication, including Google Groups, Skype, instant messaging, email, phone calls, and text messaging. Students tend to avoid more formalized, institutional forms of communication, even if the tool is more advanced. This preference for non-institutional forms of communication is consistent with the individual students taking pride in and developing groups/sites for their team. While the students make good use of the available technologies, as instructors, we have found that the effectiveness of all technology based communication tools is enhanced when the students have the opportunity to personally meet prior to the collaboration semester. Even if it lasts only a few hours, the personal meeting gives the students a connection that fosters team development, which results in better collaboration and designs.

E-mail is and will remain the dominant form of online communication in the classroom context. For some situations, e-mail is sufficient; everyone involved in the class already has an e-mail address, where most other services would require registration (and, coincidently, an e-mail address). Furthermore, as discussed, e-mail is appropriate when the students communicate with professionals. However, we believe that Internet forums and groups, such as Google Groups and Google Sites, are better communication and collaboration tools for the following reasons:

1. All messages can be read by all team members more easily.
2. Online storage is usually available with online groups.
3. All team communications are automatically archived and can be used by students, instructors, and engineering management observers. There is a "permanent record" of the teams' conversations.
4. Instructors can passively observe the communications more easily.
5. Instructors can more easily send messages to an entire team, or to all the students in a class.

Based on our years of experience with large projects requiring complex collaboration between local and remote partners, we identify several best practices to make the process work efficiently and productively:

• Avoid overly complex or proprietary Internet forums, such as those offered by a university's course management system, and online groups that are too similar to social networking sites, like Facebook or MySpace. Overly complex or proprietary forums often go unused, and forums that offer too many social networking services tend to be used for the wrong purposes. Applications like Google Groups, while technically limited, offer the right number of communication and collaboration features without extraneous elements that would cause confusion or divert focus.

- Utilize programs that complement online groups. Since most online web groups do not offer enough online storage, a program such as Dropbox can serve as an excellent backup tool for the students' data.

- Encourage teams to find their own best way to communicate. Allowing some freedom in finding the right tools and applications gives students greater ownership in their team and project and facilitates productivity (Benfield and Utley, 2007, and Fortune, et al., 2005).

- Arrange for remote partners to meet in person whenever possible. Years of experience have taught us that distributed team collaboration efforts work best when the team members have met, in person, prior to or at the beginning of the collaboration semester.

- When true face-to-face meetings are not possible, video teleconferences, such as Skype or iChat, are recommended for initial meetings. Ready availability of webcams and high-speed Internet combined with free video teleconferencing software allows any two people or groups to have a virtual face-to-face meeting. In these cases, if the instructor is managing the initial meetings between the student groups, we have found it most efficient if the instructor uses the same technology that students will later use as this helps to introduce the students to the technology. Subsequent communication can take place via Internet forums, email, or telephone; however, we feel that an initial face-to-face meeting, real or virtual, is important to establish a working relationship.

- We also encourage instructors to give students enough freedom to allow for open communication in the initial meeting of distributed partners, whether that meeting is real or virtual. That is, once the conversations have reached a self-sustaining level, instructors should leave the room and allow the students to take control of the meeting.

## REFERENCES

Benfield, M. P. J. (2003). *Determining the development of engineering teams.* Paper presented at the American Society for Engineering Management 2003 Conference, St. Louis, MO.

Benfield, M. P. J., & Turner, M. W. (2009). *Senior design concepts for a lunar exploration transportation system (LETS) for the NASA Marshall Space Flight Center.* Paper presented at the 47th AIAA Aerospace Sciences Meeting, Orlando, Florida. (AIAA-2009-568).

Benfield, M. P. J., Turner, M. W., Runyon, C. J., & Hakkila, J. (2010). *The new frontiers academic AO experiment.* Paper presented at the Lunar and Planetary Institute's 41st Lunar and Planetary Science Conference, The Woodlands, TX.

Benfield, M. P. J., & Utley, D. R. (2005). *Describing team development in science and engineering organizations.* Paper presented at the American Society for Engineering Management 2005 Conference, Norfolk, VA.

Benfield, M. P. J., & Utley, D. R. (2007). *The team phase change theory–a new team development theory.* Paper presented at the 2007 Industrial Engineering Research Conference, Nashville, TN.

Fortune, J., Utley, D. R., & Benfield, M. P. (2005). *Modeling teams: An investigation into teaming theories and their application.* Paper presented at the American Society for Engineering Management 2005 Conference, Norfolk, VA.

Frederick, R. A., Jr., Pawlak, M.-S., Utley, D. R., Corsetti, C. D., Wells, B. E., & Landrum, D. B. (2002). *International product teams for aerospace systems design.* Paper presented at the 38th AIAA/ASME/SAE/ASEE Joint Propulsion Conference and Exhibit Indianapolis, Indiana. (AIAA 2002-4337).

Frederick, R. A., Jr., & Sanders, J. (1993). *The effective use of mentors in undergraduate design.* Paper presented at the 1993 ASME Winter Annual Meeting, AES Vol. 30/HTD Vol. 226, Thermodynamics, Analysis, and Improvement of Energy Systems, (pp. 219-225). New Orleans, LA.

Middleton, R. L., & Frederick, R. A. (1999). *UAH experiences in network-based classes.* Paper presented at the Southeastern Research Universities Association, Fall Workshop.

Middleton, R. L., Frederick, R. A., & Norman, R. L. (2000) *UAH network-based engineering classes for international design teams.* Paper presented at The Huntsville Simulation Conference, Simulation in the New Millennium, The Practice and the Effect, The Holiday Inn at Research Park, Huntsville, Alabama.

Norman, R., & Frederick, R. A. (2000). Integrating technical editing students into a multidisciplinary engineering project. *Technical Communication Quarterly, 9*(2), 163–189.

Turner, M. W., Benfield, M. P. J., Runyon, C. J., & Hakkila, J. (2010). *The Mars sample return integrated product team academic experiment.* Paper presented at the Lunar and Planetary Institute's 41st Lunar and Planetary Science Conference, The Woodlands, TX.

Utley, D. M., Farrington, P. A., & Frederick, R. A. (2002). *Using an undergraduate design course as an experimental environment for team development research.* Proceedings from the 2002 American Society for Engineering Management National Conference, Oct. 2002, (pp. 88-92).

## KEY TERMS AND DEFINITIONS

**Asynchronous Communication:** Communication where users input comments that will be read and responded to at a later point in time.

**Course Management System:** An online repository for one or more classes at an institution of higher learning.

**Distributed Teams:** Non-collocated individuals working together toward a common goal or endpoint.

**Integrated Product Team (IPT):** Multidisciplinary group of people who are collectively responsible for delivering a defined product or process. The students in our class come from different disciplines, and work together as an IPT to solve an engineering problem. The senior design course in Mechanical and Aerospace Engineering at The University of Alabama in Huntsville has adopted the nickname "IPT" when referring to the class.

**Internet Forum:** An online discussion site. Sometimes referred to as a "message board" or an "online group." It originated as the modern equivalent of a traditional bulletin board. From a technological standpoint, forums or boards are web applications managing user-generated content.

**Review Board:** A voluntary group of experienced professionals from the public and private sector, independent of the university/institution, who review the written reports and oral presentations of the student design solutions.

**Synchronous Communication:** Communication where users can carry an instantaneous and real-time conversation – comments can be replied to in real-time.

**Technical Mentors:** Subject matter experts who volunteer to help the students solve the science/engineering problems, with respect to their specific area of expertise.

# Chapter 8
# Tightrope Walking:
## Balancing IT within Service-Learning in Ireland

**Pat Byrne**
*National University of Ireland Galway, Ireland*

**Lorraine McIlrath**
*National University of Ireland Galway, Ireland*

## ABSTRACT

*This chapter presents findings from an established service-learning module at the National University of Ireland, Galway, in a postgraduate IT degree programme. It describes the context at a local and national level for embedding service-learning within IT while likening it to the process of tightrope walking involving the complexity of balance and control in a sometimes uncertain terrain. The findings highlight both the challenges and successes of service-learning in IT following a series of semi-structured interviews conducted with community partners, the course director and the 2008-2009 student cohort. Service-learning provides a means of connecting students' academic study with community and society with the explicit intention of promoting active and responsible citizenship (Bringle and Hatcher, 1996; Furco and Holland, 2004; Zlotkowski, 2007). Using service-learning in computing programmes is not new (Webster & Mirielli, 2007; Tan & Phillips, 2005; Scorce, 2010; Lawler et al., 2010); however, an analysis of this work taking the perspectives of multiple stakeholders and its contexts within Ireland are all original.*

DOI: 10.4018/978-1-60960-623-7.ch008

*The cable was guy-lined by a number of well-tightened cavallettis. Sometimes he loosened them so the cable would sway. It improves his balance. He went to the middle of the wire, where it was most difficult. He would try hopping from one foot to the other. He carried a balancing pole that was too heavy, just to instruct his body in change. (McCann, 2009, p. 158)*

## SERVICE-LEARNING IN IRELAND

Service-learning is a priority issue within higher education in Ireland. This has been prompted by the 'Celtic Tiger'[1] when the 1990s brought a profound change and the country benefited from a period of economic boom. Coupled with this wealth was a growing concern over perceived declines in levels of "social capital" and to counteract this there was recognition of the potential role that service-learning, as well as other civic engagement strategies within higher education could play in redressing the balance (Boland & McIlrath, 2007).

The concept of 'social capital' has been defined as "networks, together with shared norms, values and understanding that facilitate co-operation within or among groups" (OECD, 2001) and "connections among individuals – social networks and the norms of reciprocity and trustworthiness that arise from them" (Putnam, 2000). Putnam's research, gathered from data collected over half a century, indicates that since the 1960s there has been a steady decline in civic participation in such activities as voting, volunteering, giving and socialising in the US. The research points to the adverse effects of this decline and the benefits to be reaped from an increase in participation in local community. If volunteering and voting are active expressions of strong social capital, there are also worrisome trends relating to youth within Ireland. Those under the age of 29 are the least active, (after those over the age of 65), with

this being the only group to experience a drop in volunteering activity, from 16.9% to 14.7%, between 2002 and 2006. In addition, over 55% of eligible voters under the age of 25 do not vote at all (Taskforce on Active Citizenship, 2007). Over 85% of new entrants to higher education in Ireland are between the ages of 17 to 25 (HEA, 2007), and so fall within the cohort of those least active in civic engagement.

Putman's *Bowling Alone* (2000) had a profound impact on the Irish government and prompted the former Taoiseach (Prime Minister) to create the Taskforce on Active Citizenship in Ireland in 2006. The Taskforce was charged with advising "the Government on the steps that can be taken to ensure that the wealth of civic spirit and active participation already present in Ireland continues to grow and develop" (Taskforce on Active Citizenship, 2007). The following year, the Taskforce made a series of recommendations two of which concerned higher education: first, to establish a network of higher education institutions (HEIs) to be led by the Higher Education Authority (HEA) to promote, support and link civic engagement activities, including volunteering and service-learning; and second, to develop a national awards/certificate system to recognise students volunteering for community activity.

To this end, the Irish HEA, through an innovation fund, granted 1.4 million Euros to five universities to introduce, support and embed civic engagement activities across Irish higher education. Under this funding a national network entitled 'Campus Engage'[2] was established (McIlrath and Lyons, 2009). This work is at a nascent stage. It mirrors other national networks such as Campus Compact in the U.S. but is tailored to operate in an Irish cultural, social and economic context. In 2010, a national survey of institutional commitment will be undertaken so as to benchmark contemporary perspectives on commitment to social capital through civic engagement activities.

## SERVICE-LEARNING AT NUI GALWAY

On the local level, some HEIs in Ireland are experiencing serious declines in social capital. The first formal commitment to increasing social capital through civic engagement came from the National University of Ireland (NUI), Galway, in 2001. With the support of a number of benefactors (including Atlantic Philanthropies), the Community Knowledge Initiative (CKI)[3] was established within the university. This initiated "the creation of a radical new approach to the betterment of society through emphasis on three core elements of community-based research, service-learning and knowledge-sharing" (CKI Strategic Plan 2002-2005, p. 2) and was subsequently afforded prominence within the institution's Academic and Strategic Plans (2003-2008 and 2009-2012). This funding allowed the university to employ personnel to work on mainstreaming civic engagement within the curriculum across the institution (service-learning) and also on encouraging and supporting extracurricular (student volunteering) based activities. Annually the CKI undertakes a community needs analysis whereby local community groups document their needs related to the disciplines that contain a service-learning experience. These needs are subsequently mapped to members of faculty and this process ensures that the university is responding to a direct need and not saturating the community sector with an overabundance of service-learning students. Since the inception of the CKI, over thirty academic degree programmes have incorporated service-learning experiences, with the IT Project described here being one of the first to be piloted and adopted as a mainstream activity.

## IT PROJECT

Information Technology (IT) is an obvious academic area that is open for application in community groups. Since commercial IT consultancy is expensive, it is an area in which communities in Ireland have been reluctant to invest, feeling that resources might be better applied in practical community action. This is a lacuna, which IT students are in a perfect position to fill. During their course work they may gain technical skills, but they do not often gain experience of the practical application of IT in the real world. The experience of meeting end users and grappling with technology implementation in real-life settings provides valuable lessons in becoming an IT professional, and the service-learning exercise can provide appropriate opportunities for this.

At NUI Galway the programme which first integrated IT with community engagement through service-learning was the Masters in Information Technology (MIT). This is a two year postgraduate programme that was established in 1989. The programme aims to create a hybrid graduate – one who can combine technical skills with knowledge of business and behaviour sciences in order to fully understand the context in which technology is applied. MIT graduates are well placed to progress into a career in IT management; they are taught subjects in the first year covering the three strands as previously mentioned: technical, business and behavioural sciences. In order to link these often diverse elements and to give the students an opportunity to put theory into practice, a bridging module, IT Project, is introduced during the second semester. This was initially designed as a case study where students created a small hypothetical computer system. However, in this form it did not give any opportunity for the students to engage with users or to practice the professional skills expected from MIT graduates. And as it was only a paper exercise, with the product of their work never put into action, it provided limited interest and motivation for the students.

In 2003 the course director redesigned the IT Project to provide the students with a real-life "client" in the form of a not-for-profit community group who needed support in exploiting

IT resources to further advance their work. The client was chosen from the list of those who had signalled a need for IT services through the CKI, and the course director was able to select one whose needs might match the skill set of this particular cohort of students. In recent years this has included a range of diverse not-for-profit organisations and charities such as disability support groups, youth work services for disadvantaged children, an organisation that helps the homeless, and a local community street theatre company. In the pilot year the IT Project proved very successful, and has been subsequently mainstreamed as a programme requirement. This service-learning experience places great demands upon all those involved, but has proved a very rewarding exercise that catches the imagination of the course director, the students and the community groups with whom they work.

The MIT class is not large – it typically enrolls 12 students who all have a high scoring undergraduate degree. They are interviewed as to their suitability before being offered a place on the programme. A strong technical background is not a prerequisite, but an understanding of the role and need for the skills gained and the desire and ability to apply the MIT objectives are seen as important traits in incoming students. We usually get a good mix of students from various backgrounds; for example, the current cohort comes from disciplines in humanities, science, engineering and medicine.

Prior to the commencement of the IT Project, the course director meets with groups that have expressed a need for IT development through the CKI's community needs analysis and discusses the possibilities for student engagement. However, the project details are not explored in great depth as it is the role of students to communicate, specify, plan and undertake the client requirements. The course director in this way acts as a broker or mediator between the two polar points setting up a strong tensioned wire between the community and the university. She sets up the links, encour-

ages self-directed learning and gently guides the partners throughout the process of the project. The students meet the community partner, develop a project plan, and carry out the work. Acting as IT consultants, the students are encouraged to let the community group (as end users) dictate the design and form of the final product. Throughout this time the course director creates some safety nets and acts as a manager - receiving regular updates on the work, giving advice on technical aspects and ensuring all interactions go smoothly so that the partnership is strong. At the end of the project she also becomes one of the course examiners. Throughout the project the students are expected to act in a professional manner, as if they are providing a commercial service. In doing so, they learn how to integrate the elements related to the technical, business and behavioural skills as required by the programme.

To date, students have engaged with nine different community partners whose work and IT related needs have varied considerably. Some of these already had quite sophisticated software and hardware in place, while others had only a collection of donated computers with little knowledge of how to best use them for their needs. The types of project the students have undertaken include in-house staff development IT training, Website development, costing and assisting technology purchase and set-up, and creating small software applications (mainly databases) to suit local needs. In all these encounters, they have also gained the skills of dealing with external partners and have learnt that it is not the sophistication of the technology that is important to many end users, but rather its practical functionality. The community partners have reported satisfaction with the work undertaken and enjoyed the interaction with the students and the fresh perspectives they brought to the community and its issues. This was especially evident in cases when the organisation had little knowledge of current technologies and the students opened their minds to how they might exploit current trends such as social networking, blogging, use of SMS or interactive Websites.

Data related to success and challenges arising from this service-learning module were collected in 2009 from the experiences gained following five years of embedding the IT Project. All the interviews undertaken were semi-structured and individual. Interview schedules were designed for each group with overlapping characteristics and some common questions that allowed for multiple perspectives on key points. Interviews were conducted on the experience of the IT Project in the academic year 2008-2009 in order to give a representative snapshot at a mature point in the implementation of the curriculum. The interviews were recorded, transcribed and analysed thematically for common challenges and successes. What follows are some findings from the experiences. The students from this particular cohort (2008-2009) worked with two community partners on three distinct projects; one group designed and created a youth-based Website, another trained professional staff in IT skills; the final group carried out computer familiarity classes with children from disadvantaged backgrounds which were designed specifically towards the interests and hobbies of these children.

## SUCCESSES AND CHALLENGES

While the IT Project has been very successful in meeting the needs of both students and community groups, it has also provided a number of challenges for all parties involved. While some of these have been specific to the project in question, there are also issues that arise regularly and we are keen to identify common underlying causes to minimise any negative effects and to develop additional safety nets. A number of the problems we have encountered in this instance specifically related to the fact that IT is the focus of engagement. The successes and challenges fall into a number of broad and interrelated themes that include timing; matching diverse expectations, roles and responsibilities; product sustainability; and real world problem solving. These themes will be outlined in some depth in the following section with pointers to both positive (successes) and negative (challenges) consequences.

*Timing*: As identified elsewhere in the literature, timing is often a crucial factor in the success of a project. Martin et al.'s (2009) challenges relate to the undertaking of a meaningful project in a semester period while having sufficient time to prepare students. We also recognize this, and the course director puts considerable energy into making the appropriate contacts and choosing work that the students can complete and deliver fully within the duration of an academic semester (12 weeks annually between January and March). In some cases, it is possible that the students do not have to start the project from scratch, as we now have developed a number of solutions (such as computer training packages offered to particular community cohorts) in past years which we can be revised and adopted for other communities. As other work has also identified, community and semester calendars can be mismatched (Wallace, 2000; Daynes & Longo, 2004). We have had this experience in that we have had instances where students are ready to begin, but the community partner may not have the same level of urgency and cannot give the time or attention required due to their focus on other pressing community issues. There have been instances when the students delivered a working piece of software, but there was a lack of human resources in the organisation to implement it immediately. When this happens the students move on without seeing their client through the installation and initial support phases. In other cases, the 'perfect project' has come along (through an approach to CKI) at a time of year when the students are unavailable and by the time the module is being prepared, the impetus for starting it has disappeared.

While timing issues exist and will continue to present themselves as both prohibitive and proactive in terms of the IT Project, the course director and the CKI play a key role to communicate and build understandings of the limitations of the university and its semester bound challenges.

*Matching Diverse Expectations*: While timing issues can be dealt with in a coherent and coordinated manner through effective communication and management, more difficulty centres on managing the expectations of all partners – students, course director and the community. One community partner said:

*I think the big challenge is having everybody very clear on exactly what you want to achieve. Setting the goals, making them realistic, making them achievable.*

Students may underestimate the work they are undertaking, as they are often inexperienced in assessing the time taken to complete projects. Unless the course director is aware of any excessive promises made, and intervenes to safely re-scope the work, the client group will be disappointed with an incomplete or non-functioning end product. Working together in design and development helps both sides to be realistic about what can be achieved. In one instance, when a student group was designing a Website for a youth group, they used an iterative approach in gathering clients' needs and feeding back possible solutions, and this co-operative prototyping approach was found to be a very successful way to set and manage expectations. Here is how a student describes the process:

*We had an initial meeting, just had a bit of some requirements gathering and then we went away ... and we put together ... [four] sketches of layout of what we think should be in the webpage. So after we did that we put the four of them up in the [premises] for I think was a two week period and we left a feedback chart underneath each of them and then it was up to the youth council to vote on which one they preferred the best .... And*

*as soon as we knew that then we sat down again and had another meeting and just tried to figure out more things ... we were just making sure we had the requirements sorted right from the very beginning. It was most important.*

In another instance, we had a community partner who was very clear on their IT needs, and did not understand the limitations of students who were still "learning their trade" and who were incapable of the expected professional job. In this case he was disappointed by the level of sophistication of the software produced. The role of the course director is crucial as they must remain aware of both student and community interests. This allows for mediation when possible to ensure the matching of abilities and needs.

Even when the project is outlined collaboratively at the outset, "scope creep" can occur. This arises when the community organisations realise the value of what the students can do, and their ideas for the IT Project becomes more visionary over time, not realising that further sophistication usually means more time and effort. One student recognised this:

*I'd say we had about seven or eight different meetings with the staff and with the [clients] and when we'd go back generally because [community leader] was quite enthusiastic about it she would often have a new idea she'd like…….but really we had to say you know there's a time limit here and you can't put everything into it so we need to compromise on what the most important features are.*

The students are now warned that "scope creep" can cause problems with delivering a completed project, and are encouraged to set specific limits on what they are to achieve.

Enthusiasm from the students is not to be discouraged, but it may have to be managed. In one instance, we had students produce an attractive and functioning database that their client group saw no real need for – they were happy with their current manual system of recordkeeping. In such a case, it is unlikely that the product will ever be used.

*Roles and Responsibilities*: Throughout the IT project, the course director has a number of roles to play. While she acts chiefly as mediator and manager of the student group throughout the project, this is an assessed module, and at its conclusion she becomes one of the examiners of the work. In some instances, it becomes obvious that the project will not succeed, as the students have not put the requisite attention into their work. Here she is faced with the option of intervening to 'save' the situation for the community partner by actually doing the work for them. In doing so, she is denying the students the "freedom to fail." She is faced with a very difficult balancing act in a very uncertain real environment. A safety net has been developed to acknowledge that serving the community client is primary, and the students are assessed not necessarily on the final product, but rather on how they have handled the challenges posed, and what they have learned in the process. Acknowledging where a project has not been given due attention or where incorrect choices have been made is a difficult and sobering lesson that usually ensures the same errors will not occur again.

We include the community partners in the assessment process, and find that their perspectives are often different from the IT staff examiners. If a community group gains an end product that helps a lot in their work (and which comes with little effort on their behalf), they are usually effusive in their praise, which the students will interpret as success. However, their standards may not be as exacting as those of the more tech-savvy academics who realise that a different approach might have yielded a much more creative or productive outcome. Again, balance and negotiation must ensue.

*Product Sustainability*: One of the biggest challenges we face within the IT Project experience is that of follow-up and ongoing maintenance of the software products. Assuming the software does work correctly when handed over at the end of the semester, there is the possibility that problems or faults may develop when it is fully operational. The students have by then moved on, usually into the workplace. We are very insistent that completed systems are delivered with full documentation and the clients are trained, informing the students that community groups need to be self supporting and sustaining in the future.

We have had one severe problem where a Website we developed was hacked into from abroad, and the community group could not understand what was happening to their site, which had worked so successfully in the past. To our delight, when we managed to contact the student developers they immediately responded and reloaded the site, giving the community group support and help even though their project was long over. Although we cannot guarantee this will happen in every case, we saw this as a most successful outcome for this particular service-learning partnership.

*Real World Problem Solving*: Despite these shortcomings, we have found that the IT Project module consistently achieves its objectives, and is a very positive experience for all involved. It seems from our findings that students appreciate not only the real world problem solving dimension but also the fact that this is done in a community context. As one student stated, "[It's really great] going out and getting to meet the community ... and knowing you are helping people." As a learning exercise for the students as IT professionals, service-learning has provided an excellent vehicle to put their skills into practice. They are dealing with clients who are often unsure of what they need and what the technology can do for them, and experience the need to build trust and understanding with the end user and put considerable effort into the requirements gathering phase of the software development lifecycle. Actual experience teaches this need in a way that is very hard to get across in coursework. One student describes how the greatest challenge for him was

*Trying to settle on a design that was practical and did everything they wanted ... at the start they weren't too sure what they wanted themselves and they had a few crazy ideas ... and from my own experience ... I kind of knew that some of the things they were trying to get in wouldn't work.*

He also recognised that while his client partner wanted a lot, they were also unsure of what they were taking on:

*They are not very technology savvy there so they were kind of terrified really of having a website on their hands that they wouldn't be able to manage, and that they would have to upkeep on a daily basis*

In order to overcome these problems, the students needed to build trust with their client regarding what they hope to achieve. Interestingly, the client has a slightly different perspective of this particular piece of work. She believed that the student's ideas were overly complex, and that it was her role to set boundaries. She stated that,

*They had really complex in-depth website ideas that would go down level after level after level and one thing I know is keep things simple. And they did, they did come around to that, said okay these people don't know much about it, we would be better off, don't show your knowledge to the best of our ability but show what could be achieved and obtained.*

A balance was enabled whereby both sides believed that they had made a compromise, but over different issues.

## REFLECTIONS

Although often difficult to manage and demanding of new skills from the students, the IT Project module has undoubtedly been a success for the university, the students and the community partners. There have also been a number of successful outcomes that we did not initially envisage. One of these is that the clients took on a role to educate the students in their own field. One, for example, perceived her role as an educator to inform and teach the students to keep things simple regarding the technology product under development. Another facilitated the development of new knowledge related to the community context and how to deal with the community members, which in this case were children who could be disruptive. He describes how he dealt with this:

*And their eyes were opened the very first day they came in and you could see that because they weren't used to dealing with these young people. ... I had a talk with them and we do the training like child protection and all that, once they took that in ... there really weren't any issues.*

This experience is consistent with other studies such that of Sandy and Holland who found "... community partner's profound dedication to educating college students – even when it is not an expectation, part of their job description, or if the experience provides few or no short- and long-term benefits for their organization" (Sandy & Holland, 2006, p. 34).

We have found from our experiences and interviews that if the service-learning project is related to community need and university expertise then the chances of a successful partnership and process are greater. This has also been identified in the existing literature on capacity enhancing motivations from the perspectives of communities within service-learning (Tiamiyu & Bailey, 2001; Bell & Carlson, 2009). The community from the service-learning needs analysis regarded the potential partnership as meeting an IT need that would otherwise be unresolved. One community partner sums up his motivations:

*It was an identified [IT need], I'll tell you why it was an identified need....because we run a computer club in [disadvantaged community] but what was happening was young people were just coming in and playing games on computers and as far as we were concerned...yeah....it was great they were coming in and using it but they weren't actually learning anything from it. And then I thought if we wanted to bring them to a higher level we were going to need the expertise to do it. So to get the service-learning students in to do it was excellent. And their ability to teach them stuff that we would never be, we just wouldn't have the expertise background to do it at all. It was fantastic.*

Another unanticipated success highlighted was that, when possible, students made themselves available to the community beyond the end of IT Project and if there were instances where problems arose (as previously mentioned) they returned to troubleshoot and rectify problems personally or through online support. One community partner explained her immediate contact and student action:

*I emailed them saying having problems with the website and they were in, I had an email from one of them this morning, so the follow on has been above and beyond and it hasn't left us high and dry at all.*

While students may have intervened to help out in this instance, we have little data to document and support evidence of an increase in student's commitment to service-learning. The reasons why they might support an existing project may be due to ownership of the product developed, personal relationships developed through the IT project, or alternately as one student stated "just taking pride in the quality."

## CONCLUSION

While we can relate many challenges and successes, without doubt the experience of the IT Project is one that develops our programme objective of the hybrid student. It is as though being steeped in an unfamiliar community environment and through social interaction with diverse people who hold technology in a different place is where students develop their human behaviour and interaction skills.

Without doubt the role of both the course director and the CKI are crucial to the overall success of the experience from the multiple stakeholders. The role of the course director is one that is complex and involves both elements of 'control' and 'letting go' and, as previously mentioned, can resemble the challenges facing a tightrope walker. While she ultimately seeks the creation of successful IT solutions for pressing community needs, this has to be balanced against the "freedom to fail" dimension. From her experience, the role of the CKI is crucial in terms of undertaking the community needs analysis so that there is a live list of community partners to work with on an annual basis. Sustainability of the IT product is an ongoing issue and a new measure is being piloted in 2010 whereby the current cohort of students revisit the previous nine community partners to ascertain any issues which have arisen and the next steps of IT development or enhancement. Over time there has been a thickening to our community partnerships and the university through which the CKI has engaged with these agencies in multiple service-learning disciplines. For example, a major issue within our locality has been a lack of information around free public access to IT resources and another of the 2010 student groups is undertaking research to map available computer hardware sites, which should enable resource sharing by community groups.

From the perspective of the community they see the rewards to be reaped from community university engagement though service-learning and as one partner stated:

*I think you know the days of the 'sacred cow' [the university] up on the hill not being involved because students end up coming out of college knowing very little about the practical working world, that doesn't achieve anything.*

If the "sacred cow" is to become a partner with community through service-learning, then it is essential that safety nets underpin the uncertain nature of the cable to ensure a healthy tension between balance and control.

## REFERENCES

Bell, S. M., & Carlson, R. (2009). Motivations of community organizations for service learning. In R. Stoecker, & E. A. Tryon (Eds.), *The unheard voices: Community organizations and service learning*. Philadelphia, PA: Temple University Press.

Boland, J., & McIlrath, L. (2007). The process of localising pedagogies for civic engagement in Ireland: The significance of conceptions, culture and context. In L. McIlrath, & I. MacLabhrainn (Eds.), *Higher education and civic engagement: International perspectives*. Aldershot, UK: Ashgate.

Bringle, R. G., & Hatcher, J. A. (1996). Implementing service learning in higher education. *The Journal of Higher Education*, *67*(2), 221–239. doi:10.2307/2943981

Community Knowledge Initiative. (2001). *CKI strategic plan* 2002-2005. Galway, Ireland: National University of Ireland Galway.

Daynes, G., & Longo, N. (2004). Jane Addams and the origins of service learning practice in the United States. *Michigan Journal of Community Service Learning*, *11*(1), 5–13.

Furco, A., & Holland, B. (2004). Institutionalizing service-learning in higher education: Strategy for chief academic officers. In M. Langseth, & W. M. Plater (Eds.), *Public work and the academy – an academic administrators guide to civic engagement and service-learning*. Boston, MA: Anker Publishing Company.

Lawler, J., Coppola, J., Feather-Gannon, S., Hill, J., Kline, R., Mosley, P., & Taylor, A. (2010). Community empowerment and service learning practices through computer science curricula of a major metropolitan university. *Journal of Computing Sciences in Colleges*, *25*(3), 10.

Martin, A. SeBlonka, K., & Tryon, E. (2009). The challenge of short term service. In R. Stoecker & E. A. Tryon (Eds.), *The unheard voices: Community organizations and service learning*. Philadelphia, PA: Temple University Press.

McCann, C. (2009). *Let the great world spin*. London, UK: Bloomsbury.

OECD. (2001). The well-being of nations, the role of human and social capital. Centre for Educational Research and Innovation. Paris, France: Organisation for Economic Co-operation and Development.

Putnam, R. (2000). *Bowling alone*. New York, NY: Simon & Schuster.

Sandy, M., & Holland, B. A. (2006). Different worlds and common ground: Community partner perspectives on campus-community partnerships. *Michigan Journal of Community Service Learning*, *13*(1), 30–43.

Scorce, R. A. (2010). Perspectives concerning the utilization of service learning projects for a computer science course. *Journal of Computing Sciences in Colleges*, *25*(3), 75–81.

Tan, J., & Phillips, J. (2005). Incorporating service learning into computer science courses. *Journal of Computing Sciences in Colleges*, *20*(4), 57–62.

Taskforce on Active Citizenship. (2007). *Report of the Taskforce on Active Citizenship.* Dublin, Ireland: Secretariat of the Taskforce on Active Citizenship. Retrieved July 20, 2010, from http://www.activecitizen.ie/UPLOADEDFILES/ Mar07/Taskforce%20Report%20to%20Government%20%28Mar%2007%29.pdf

Tiamiyu, M. F., & Bailey, L. (2001). Human services for the elderly and the role of university-community collaboration: Perceptions of human service agency workers. *Educational Gerontology, 27*(6), 479–492. doi:10.1080/036012701316894171

Wallace, J. (2000). The problem of time: Enabling students to make long-term commitments to community-based learning. *Michigan Journal of Community Service Learning, 7*, 133–141.

Webster, L. D., & Mirielli, E. J. (2007). *Student reflections on an academic service learning experience in a computer science classroom.* Paper presented at the 8th ACM SIGITE Conference on Information Technology Education, Destin, Florida, USA.

Zlotkowski, E. (2007). The case for service learning. In L. McIlrath, & I. MacLabhrainn (Eds.), *Higher education and civic engagement: International perspectives.* Aldershot, UK: Ashgate.

## ENDNOTES

[1] The term "Celtic tiger" was first coined by Morgan Stanley in 1994 and was popularly adopted as an indicator of the new-found wealth in the Republic of Ireland which was prior to this time considered economically backward.

[2] Additional information on Campus Engage can be access at http://www.campusengage. ie.

[3] Additional information on the Community Knowledge Initiative can be accessed at http://www.nuigalway.ie/cki.

# Chapter 9
# Digital Storytelling within a Service–Learning Partnership:
## Technology as Product and Process for University Students and Culturally and Linguistically Diverse High School Youth

**Emily Wexler Love**
*University of Colorado at Boulder, USA*

**Debra Flanders Cushing**
*University of Colorado Denver, USA*

**Margaret Sullivan**
*Partnering High School, Colorado, USA*

**Jode Brexa**
*Partnering High School, Colorado, USA*

## ABSTRACT

*This chapter describes a university/high school partnership focused on digital storytelling. It also explains the multi-stage process used to establish this successful partnership and project. The authors discuss the central role that technology played in developing this university/high school partnership, a collaboration that extended the impact of a digital storytelling project to reach high school students, university students, educators, high school administrators, and the local community. Valuing a reflective process that can lead to the creation of a powerful final product, the authors describe the impact of digital storytelling on multiple stakeholders, including the 13 university students and 33 culturally and linguistically diverse high school youth who participated during the fall of 2009. In addition, the chapter includes reflections from university and high school student participants expressed during focus groups conducted throughout the project. While most participants had a positive experience with the project, complications with the technology component often caused frustrations and additional challenges. Goals for sharing this project are to critically evaluate digital storytelling, describe lessons learned, and recommend good practices for others working within a similar context or with parallel goals.*

DOI: 10.4018/978-1-60960-623-7.ch009

## INTRODUCTION AND OVERVIEW OF CASE STUDY

*"No amount of books is really going to teach you or give you the feeling in your heart that you feel when you're with those kids and start connecting with them, feeling their problems, their frustration. Like, no book is going to give you that feeling, you know? You have to go and you have to be with them and talk to them. You have to talk or it's just not going to happen." – University student reflecting on the value of working directly with youth during this project*

With recent advances in multimedia technology, creating short videos is no longer limited to professionally trained journalists and documentary filmmakers (Burgess, 2006; Lambert, 2007; Meadows, 2003; Davis, 2004), but is instead designed to "amplify the ordinary voice" (Burgess, 2006, p. 207). Creating videos through digital storytelling (a process that combines still photos, a recorded narrative, and music) enables students to inform the public about critical issues from a personal perspective. How-to manuals, project descriptions, and anecdotal comments are available on digital storytelling, yet very little research has been conducted to determine its impact on the stakeholders involved in the process. Moreover, even with the growing number of digital storytelling projects around the world, with the exception of a handful of studies (Ware, 2008; Vinogradova, 2008; Hull and Katz, 2006), little research examines culturally and linguistically diverse youth (CLD)[1] experiences with technology and how digital storytelling can contribute to building alliances between institutions of higher education and high schools. The development of such alliances enhances the educational experiences of participants through the exchange of stories, experiences, resources and expertise and presents the opportunity for undergraduate students to engage in scholarship that is relevant and useful beyond the university walls (Strand et al. 2003, p. 5).

In this chapter we describe one digital storytelling project facilitated within the context of an undergraduate service-learning course focused on community planning, education, and immigrant integration. Although this project was three years in the making, we focus specifically on the culminating semester, during which 13 undergraduate students mentored 33 CLD high school students in the creation of personal digital stories to share their voices with the community.

We write this case study as four educators who worked together on this project, two of us from universities and two of us from partnering high schools. The four of us bring complementary expertise in areas that include multicultural education, community planning, and English as a Second Language instruction. Within this chapter we each share our individual perspectives on the benefits and challenges of using multimedia technology to help CLD youth develop language and communication skills and enable them to express their views of the community. We discuss the central role that technology played in developing this university/high school partnership, a collaboration that extended the impact of the digital storytelling project to reach high school students, university students, educators, high school administrators, and the community. In addition, we include the reflections of both the university and high school students expressed during focus groups conducted throughout the project.

One of our goals for sharing this project is to begin a dialogue within academia to critically evaluate digital storytelling as an empowering teaching tool and to consider its impact on multiple stakeholders through its process and final product. In addition, we describe our lessons learned and recommend good practices for others working within a similar context or with parallel goals.

## CONTEXT AND HISTORY OF PROJECT

Messages in mass media often portray youth as deviant, unaware and unconcerned with societal issues, or just plain lazy (Kelly, 2006). For immigrant and CLD youth, the message tends to be even more negative, including assumptions that students are undocumented, are gang members, and can't speak English or succeed in school (Katz, 1997). Leaving such stereotypes unexamined can perpetuate the lack of respect from the dominant culture members, often silencing voices of the youth. To counteract negative messages targeted at teenagers, we designed a digital storytelling project to accomplish the following goals: use multi-media technology to enable CLD youth to reflect on their experiences in the community; give a public voice to a demographic of teenagers who are often silenced; and build a mutually enriching partnership among public high school students, university students, and staff from participating institutions. As noted in civic-engagement research, minority youth are less likely to participate in certain programs and benefit from opportunities due to a lack of adult support, knowledge of programs, and encouragement (Cano & Bankston, 1992, p. 8). This pattern is disturbing and provides justification for our choice to seek out students who are marginalized in this community. We strongly believe their voices matter and need to be heard. The students oftentimes feel silenced by legal status, language, and what feels like a lack of understanding about the dominant culture. Digital storytelling can counteract those obstacles by empowering students. Digital storytelling provides opportunities for students to share their stories, in their own words. Furthermore, they can describe an issue in the community to a large audience, via the Internet or in a live forum, using a dynamic and visually engaging format (Davis, 2005, p. 1). Teenagers can use digital storytelling to talk back, to rewrite and reframe the negative messages that surround them and "assert their identity" (Meadows, 2003, p. 193).

## PROJECT BACKGROUND

Although our primary focus for this chapter is work conducted during the fall semester of 2009 at two participating high schools, preliminary work for this project began over two years earlier, during the summer of 2007 when we (Cushing and Wexler Love) were asked to consult on a youth dialogue project. The dialogue project brought us together for the first time because of our interest in immigrant issues and ultimately helped to create a professional partnership, merging two distinct disciplines, education and community planning. While at times it has been challenging to identify how the disciplines intersect, our affiliation with the Children, Youth, and Environments Center for Research & Design (CYE) has supported the process by carving out a space in academia in which interdisciplinary work is privileged and valued.

Based on previous work with high school youth and pilot studies that took place during the 2007-2008 school year, we designed a project that was activity-based, relevant to young people's lives, provided opportunities for the students to acquire skills, and enabled students to share their views with the larger community. Digital storytelling became a key component of our work with high school youth because the process of creating a short movie was engaging for the majority of young people and helped us to realize our intentions listed above. Once the students knew how to create a short movie, they were able to use this skill within other academic areas and in their personal lives. They became the experts and were able to demonstrate their acquired skill set to teachers, students, family members and their communities.

In order to foster a strong university/high school partnership, we developed an undergraduate service-learning course called Immigrant Integration through Community Planning. We designed the course to enable students to critically examine the intersection of education and community planning while using the technology of digital storytelling. During the course, the undergraduate students explored issues related to community planning and design; local, national and international immigration policy; youth development; and, most importantly, the centrality of young people's voices in expressing issues relevant to their lives and their communities. The university students in this service-learning course learned how to facilitate discussions about immigration and community planning and how to create a digital story. Then as they became comfortable with the class topics and technology, they were expected to teach the high school students how to create a digital story of their own exploring these topics.

The university students participated in a service-learning project that supplemented their classroom discussions and readings and included ten weeks of mentoring CLD youth from two high school classes: Sullivan's Advancement Via Individual Determination (AVID) course at Aguila High School[2] and Brexa's English as a Second Language course (ESL) at Colina High School, the two high schools within their district with the highest percentage of minority youth. The research reported in this chapter contributes to Wexler Love's larger dissertation project. Both the school district and the University of Colorado at Boulder Institutional Review Board approved this research project. All participants and guardians signed consent/assent forms and the participants and guardians who were willing to give us permission to screen their digital stories in public and/or post them to a website signed an additional consent form.

## PARTICIPANTS

Thirty-three high school students participated in the digital storytelling project, including 17 first generation immigrants (52%), seven 1.5-genera-tion immigrants (21%) (immigrants who arrived before the age of 13), and three second generation immigrants (9%). Twenty-nine of the students also represented minority populations (88%) whose countries of origin include Mexico, El Salvador, China, Burma, and the United States. Sixteen of the students were enrolled in Sullivan's AVID class at Aguila High School. AVID is a curriculum that targets first generation college students and marginalized students with the objective of supporting their successful transition to post-secondary education. Seventeen students were in Brexa's ESL 1 class, part of the school district's only Newcomer program for recently arrived immigrants. The students at each high school site had different needs. For example, in Sullivan's AVID class we focused more on writing and developing cohesive narratives. Students in Brexa's ESL 1 class were learning English and therefore we needed to adapt the digital storytelling project so students could share their stories in their native languages and in English.

Thirteen university students participated in the service-learning course during the fall of 2009. Four of the 13 university students were minorities. Two of the university students were native Spanish speakers, and another student spoke proficient Spanish. Eight of the 13 undergraduates worked with Sullivan's AVID class and five (including the Spanish speaking students) worked with Brexa's ESL 1 class. The undergraduate students adjusted their schedules to ensure they could be at the school sites during high school class times. With the presence of Wexler Love and Cushing as the university instructors, the university mentor to high school student ratio was 1 to 2 in Sullivan's class, and 1 to 2.5 in Brexa's class. In order to meet the needs of different students and accomplish project goals within the constraints of a semester, a low ratio between college and high school students was essential.

## TECHNOLOGY AS CATALYST: DIGITAL STORYTELLING

Digital storytelling is an engaging process for both university and high school students in part because it has the appeal of being something new and in most cases results in a final product that can communicate a message. A digital story contains three main components: a narrative script that becomes the voice-over; still photos and short video clips combined to create the visual component of the story; and music that sets the mood and accentuates the overall effect of the video (Burgess, 2006, p. 207; Lundby, 2008, p. 366; Klaebe et al., 2007, p. 4). For teenagers in particular, creating a short video provides an accessible and appealing process to practice their listening, speaking, reading, writing and technology skills.

Though the final product, a 2-3 minute video, makes digital storytelling seem simple, there are many critical steps in the process. Brainstorming activities are recommended to generate ideas, followed by scriptwriting exercises to turn the ideas into compelling stories for an identified audience (Lambert, 2007, p. 5). For our project, early scriptwriting involved engaging one-on-one with high school students, asking about their daily experiences, important events, or topics of interest to them. Prompts such as "tell us what it is like to be a teenager in this community" were used to inspire student reflection.

The cost and availability of equipment and software can ultimately impact the scope of a project. While we believe that you can be creative with limited resources, insufficient resources can also lead to frustrating situations for participants and facilitators[3]. Digital cameras, computers, and moviemaking software are all important components for this project. As the high school students worked on their narratives, we encouraged them to borrow digital cameras provided by the university to visually document their lives and inspire their stories. Once their narratives were finalized, we used free sound recording and engineering softwa-

re[4] installed on individual laptops to record student narratives and create audio files. There are several different types of sound recording software available. When making our selection we considered the following factors: low cost, ease of use, PC and Mac compatibility, and functionality (allowing us to manipulate and combine music and voice tracks). Since each high school student needed access to the video software, we chose movie-making software[5] that was already available on all school district computers and therefore did not have to be downloaded or purchased. Additionally, because the software we chose was free on most PC computers, the undergraduate students could also easily access and learn the program. Students then selected music to enhance their story. Next, students used the storyboard and timeline features in the movie-making software to sync up the visual material with the narrative. Finally, students discussed appropriate outlets for showing their videos and communicating their messages.

Although we encouraged students to use their own photos in their stories, some students relied on photos downloaded from the Internet to show maps or photos of their native countries. Although we allowed this we were very aware of copyright issues. This was also true for the music students used. We encouraged the use of royalty-free music and directed them to different Websites, but many had their hearts set on a specific popular song they wanted to use. Although it is best to avoid the use of copyright-protected material, it is generally considered acceptable if it is used for educational purposes and the end product is not being sold or used to generate payment of any kind.

Both the high school and university students participating in this digital storytelling project shared powerful personal stories that vividly captured their perspectives, feelings, needs, actions, and history. We have observed that the process of creating and sharing a digital story is a complex contradiction—a simultaneously public and private artifact. Some students told deeply personal stories knowing that they would be showing their digital stories to peers, teachers, school district administrators, university students and instructors, and members of the community. The experience of creating a simultaneously public and private artifact was more especially significant for particular students. At the beginning of a class session, about three weeks into the digital storytelling project, one student, Juan, who we had assumed was not very engaged because of his tendency to not participate in group activities or one-on-one brainstorming sessions, asked Wexler Love to read his three-page narrative that was written in Spanish[6]. Juan's narrative was beautifully constructed, passionate, and raw, revealing that he was in fact very much engaged in the project. The opening sentence of his narrative read: "All around the world people emigrate to other places in search of a better future even though sometimes the only thing we find is the same death."

In his digital story, Juan shared vivid details about his journey to the United States:

*I left my village on the 28th of September 2008 at 6:00 in the morning. That was the saddest thing because there you decide to leave everything and perhaps never come back to see it. From this day I began the journey that changed me into one of the many who look for a better future in the "United States." I spent days without eating and drinking, sleeping outside with cactus spines in my skin making me a fugitive of the laws.*

In the Spanish version of his digital story, Juan went on to explicitly talk about being one of the many undocumented individuals in the United States. The student made a bilingual final product by recording his digital story in Spanish and English; however, he chose not to read his statement about being an undocumented immigrant in English. Juan's decision to not read the part of his narrative that revealed his documentation status in English demonstrated his awareness of the public aspect of creating a digital story and the potential risk involved in sharing this information. At the

same time, Juan shared he was undocumented in Spanish, and his story illustrates one example of a student sharing very personal details about his life with the option of sharing this with his classmates, teachers, and larger community. Digital storytelling literally helps students feel more seen in a community where they feel they need to be invisible, where they feel they need to hide parts of who they are to protect themselves from possible harm[7].

## MULTIPLE PERSPECTIVES: DEVELOPING SOLID PARTNERSHIPS

In this section we present our distinct perspectives on developing a solid partnership, specifically focusing on the distinct challenges and objectives.

University Instructors (Cushing and Wexler Love):

*For our undergraduate service-learning course, we wanted to seek out and develop partnerships with marginalized high school youth who might not already have a forum to share their voice with the larger community. We also wanted to enable our undergraduate students to develop mutually beneficial relationships with CLD high school youth, learning about their needs in the community while teaching them how to create digital stories. To do this successfully, we approached the project as a long-term process that required regular reflection and adjustment. For some of the university students, we learned that this was the first time they would create friendships with someone with a cultural and linguistic background that was different from their own. Because of our awareness about the demographics of our community, our course was set up to provide university students with the opportunity to reflect on their political views around immigrants and immigration within the United States. Since high quality service-learning approaches emphasize meeting mutual needs rather than forcing a relationship, it was essential that we spent time collaboratively defining the goals of this project (Honnet & Poulsen, 1989; Eyler & Giles, 1997; Howard, 2003). As university instructors, it was often challenging to meet the needs of our undergraduate students as well as our partnering high schools, while addressing the constraints imposed by each group.*

Prior to the fall of 2008, we approached two different groups in Aguila, the most diverse city in our school district, with the desire to connect our university students to CLD and immigrant youth in the community. We approached a community youth leadership organization that advises the Aguila City Council and Margaret Sullivan (third author), an ESL and AVID teacher at Aguila High School. While the youth leadership organization agreed to partner with our service-learning class, Sullivan was hesitant about giving us access to her classes; instead, she agreed to let us work with the afterschool Diversity Club that met once a week. We were fortunate to work with both groups of students (the youth leadership organization and Diversity Club), yet the partnerships were not ideal.

The youth leadership organization already had the ear of the City Council so their voices were being heard, and they met only twice a month, limiting the time they were able to focus on our project. Furthermore, the leadership group was not diverse, with only one Latino boy in the group of 16 members. The Diversity Club was comprised of the diverse youth population that was critical to the purpose of the project, but attendance at their weekly meetings was sporadic. Consistent attendance for both university students and high school students was critical to our project.

When considering our options for community partners for the spring semester of 2009, we wanted to address attendance issues and a previous lack of diversity. In a majority White community, we felt it was imperative to seek out partnerships in which marginalized voices could be heard and to provide an opportunity for university students to

work with youth who might have different experiences from their own. We relied on our network of high school teachers and administrators, which enabled us to partner with the district's only teen parent program at Front Range High School and with two Language Arts classes at Colina High School. In addition, Sullivan asked us to work with her AVID class at Aguila High School instead of the Diversity Club. This represented four different classes and nearly 60 youth.

We learned several valuable lessons during this semester. First, working with four different classes was too much to coordinate in conjunction with our undergraduate service-learning course and we found our limited technology resources spread too thin. Although the teen parents were a diverse group whose views were not typically heard in the community, these students had irregular attendance due to competing demands on their time as mothers and students.

For the fall semester of 2009 (the focus of this chapter), we continued our collaboration with Colina and Aguila High Schools. After debriefing with Sullivan immediately following the spring 2009 semester, we decided to continue to work with her in the fall. We felt the partnership was working well. We had developed clear lines of communication and were comfortable working together. Most importantly more than 50% of her new AVID class was of Latino descent and had a diverse range of cultural backgrounds in terms of immigrant status (1st, 1.5 and 2nd generation), age of arrival, and country of origin.

Although the partnership with the language arts classes at Colina High School had worked well, the teacher was not available to work with us again in the fall and we had to develop a new relationship. Because of this, we were introduced to Jode Brexa, an ESL teacher at Colina High School, who was interested in working with us to support the needs of the Newcomer immigrant students. We anticipated some challenges working with students who were just beginning to develop English language proficiency; however, we felt this was an exceptional opportunity to better understand new immigrant youth experiences in the community.

Partnering High School AVID Teacher (Sullivan):

*Before I was approached to work with Wexler Love and Cushing, I had been involved in an unsuccessful partnership with a different university in the area. Based on that experience, I promised myself never to do any community-based service-learning again in the context of my high school classroom. When a counselor asked me to meet with Wexler Love and Cushing, I did so as a professional courtesy. Wexler Love and Cushing seemed organized, and they had a clear focus on listening to the experiences of CLD youth in our community. So, I offered them a chance to work with the Aguila afterschool Diversity Club. That way, if students were not interested they could opt out of participating since it was a club rather than a required class. As Wexler Love and Cushing, along with their university students, began to work with the diversity club, I knew this was going to be a powerful experience for my students. For the first time my club members were being listened to by members of our larger community. The university undergraduates were organized and e-mailed lesson plans weekly. My club members were proud of their final projects and were excited to share them with the greater Aguila community. Their final projects were similar to the other groups of youth working on digital storytelling projects and they saw parallels between their lives and other teens in the town.*

One of the problems of running the program after school was the time-constraints that impacted the students' ability to participate in extra-curricular programming. Many of the Latino students in my school provide economic relief to their families, so attendance was irregular for the Diversity Club members. Because students who attend classes during regular school hours

have better attendance, I wanted Wexler Love and Cushing to work with my AVID class during the following two semesters. I opened my classroom to Wexler Love and Cushing because of the relationship that we had formed, the way that their students engaged with and listened to the high school youth, and the organized way in which they approached the project.

As an educator I also had to think about the AVID standards. AVID focuses heavily on the relationships between high school students and university students through Tutorials[8]. We have a hard time hiring undergraduate Tutors for the Tutorials because our school is located farther from the university than other high schools in the school district and is 30minutes away by bus. This digital storytelling project was a great opportunity to encourage university students to work with Aguila High School in order to gain their university credit and offer the intended support for my AVID students.

Given that I had been working with Wexler Love and Cushing for over a year, I was aware of the technological needs of a digital storytelling project. The first week of the fall 2009 semester I reserved the computer lab for the whole semester. In addition, the university students did not start working with us until a month into the semester, and because AVID requires students to develop different styles of writing, my students first wrote memoirs to explore how an important event had shaped their life. The assignment was an effective way to scaffold the work that the high school students would be engaged in during the digital storytelling project.

I knew the high expectations Wexler Love and Cushing held for their students from the previous semesters, and I felt comfortable stepping back from the teaching role. When the university students started working with my high school students, I transitioned out of the role of facilitator and let the university students lead. Giving the university students leadership opportunities also encouraged relationship building between the two groups of students. Such a classroom environment allowed my students the chance to connect with the university students in a more natural way during small group time. Granted, the conversations were prompted by the weekly assignments, but I was not interjecting and asking clarifying questions. My students learned more about being a university student during the small group time then they did on university tours.

Partnering High School ESL Teacher (Brexa):

*As a high school teacher of culturally and linguistically diverse students, I welcomed the opportunity to work with university educators and students. This project provided opportunities to build community partnerships through technology and for students to engage in an authentic writing experience valuing their personal stories.*

Luckily, Cushing and Wexler Love had worked with a different class at Colina High School during the previous semester, thus many of the technological difficulties had been addressed by the time their undergraduate students began to work with my students. We'd followed the district requirements of background checks for the visiting students to our campus; our administration had been informed and had approved the partnership; and my students' parents had signed permission slips for participation[9]. In addition, my colleague Jerry Hunter and I had met with Wexler Love and Cushing in pre-planning sessions to design a curriculum map, align standards, and plan weekly lessons. Together we shaped the project to meet the ESL benchmarks for the beginning English learners. Key to connecting the undergraduate students to our school's diverse population, our assistant principal also presented demographics and the academic needs of our students to Wexler Love and Cushing's class. In preparation for the technological needs of the project, I had reserved computer labs for the semester-long project, made sure we had the Windows Movie Maker software loaded on the computers, and counted

the number of cameras that we would need to borrow for the semester. Because new language learners can sometimes feel apprehensive about engaging with native English speakers, I made sure to let my students know about the upcoming project. I also prepped them on how to welcome and interact with new visitors to our classroom before the undergraduates arrived.

## MULTIPLE PERSPECTIVES ON IMPACT

Below we examine the impact of this digital storytelling project from multiple perspectives. In addition to our own reflections as educators, we provide a brief overview of the impact on participating high school students and university students.

University Instructors (Cushing and Wexler Love):

*Our objective as university instructors was two-fold: to create a rich learning experience for the participating undergraduate and high school students and to initiate change in the community based on the views of high school students. Although we could see the relationships forming between our undergraduate students and the high school youth and we were all developing an increasing awareness of the challenges of CLD adolescents in our community, we would often walk out of class questioning the impact the project would have on the larger community. What tangible change would come out of this work, if any at all?*

Digital storytelling as a product enables students to share their stories with countless individuals. Thus, at the end of the production phase of the project, we arranged to screen the digital stories at the university. After gaining permission from their parents, high school participants shared their digital stories at the university, bringing attention to this project and their work during the semester. The chief academic officer of the school district who attended this screening helped organize a presentation for the larger school community prior to an official school board meeting. Though the tangible impact of this project may not be measurable within a short-term context, the students' work has connected them and us to other organizations, groups, and initiatives focusing on immigrant issues as well as to those who might not have otherwise been aware of CLD youth experiences in our community.

On a professional level, as university instructors, this project has given us the opportunity to develop expertise in coordinating a multi-institutional project and bringing university and high school students together through a service-learning course. We have also been able to develop relationships with teachers and administrators in our local school district that will carry over into other projects and outreach work.

Partnering High School AVID Teacher (Sullivan):

*This project met many of the goals outlined by the AVID curriculum. One goal is that students practice writing for different purposes. Through the digital storytelling process, they had to choose a topic and create a written piece that would draw their audience into their world and situation. Each week, my AVID students and the university students interacted while reflecting on issues within our greater community. My students were also asked to present their digital stories to educators and administrators at our district education center, giving them the opportunity to work on their verbal presentation skills, another goal of the AVID curriculum.*

However, the introduction of technology also led to some frustrations. Each of my students borrowed a digital camera; unfortunately, though, a few were malfunctioning and students needed to share. This led to challenges for some students when trying to finish their stories on time. Also, several students struggled with the task of taking photos of youth issues in the community and they eventually downloaded pictures from the Internet.

From my perspective, an important aspect of this project was the opportunity for my high school students to share quality time with university students, thus allowing them to see that college students were almost their peers. University students provided feedback as my AVID students were combining the various components of their digital stories. I wanted my students to bond with the university students as they learned the software and created their stories. I hoped my students could imagine themselves in the university setting and could see that they have the power to change people's opinion through their words. Each of the different tasks within the digital storytelling process allowed my students to practice real life skills they will need to succeed.

Professionally this project has opened doors for me at the University of Colorado. In my role as an AVID and ESL teacher, I am working to support all of my students in thinking about college as a future option. Following the conclusion of this project, I began collaborating with another professor and a group of Latino boys on a similar project using digital photography to share their stories. Additionally, during the digital storytelling screening at the University of Colorado, I told the university students that they are welcome to come by at any point to see the students and to support them. Since this project shaped the first semester of our AVID class, we continued to talk about and explore ways to share the videos again throughout the year.

Partnering High School ESL Teacher (Brexa):

*A technology-centered classroom with university student mentor support was a unique opportunity to engage immigrant youth in the development of language and communication skills while giving voice to their unique perspectives about their communities. Students' technological expertise in my classroom ranged from limited to extensive.*

*Yet all students spent two to three days a week in the computer labs learning the movie-making software, accessing the Internet, downloading pictures and music, not to mention using digital cameras and recording equipment. Specifically, students engaged in this project through taking personal photos, discussing the message of their stories, uploading photos, editing, downloading music, and recording voice-over narratives. Because the technology component tended to focus student attention, positive classroom management resulted.*

A significant educational impact of this project was authentic language acquisition. Students practiced speaking and listening skills to communicate about the technology, writing skills to compose and edit their narratives, and reading skills to record their first and second language voiceovers. This technology-centered classroom allowed new English language learners to spend as much time as they wanted perfecting their stories, thus allowing language acquisition to progress individually, independently, and more rapidly than in a teacher-centered classroom setting.

The most important outcome, however, was the opportunity for the immigrant youth to find their voices. Recorded in students' first and second languages, these narratives allowed students to communicate about their personal interests, home, family, school, and larger community not only in words but through pictures and music. Thus, for students who were not yet proficient in English, these multiple forms of expression gave voice to individual feelings, perceptions, and perspectives in a creative way.

One of the outcomes of this project was the fuller understanding that I gained about each of my students. As Wexler Love and Cushing noted above, my students told powerful personal stories, sharing parts of their lives that I had not been fully aware of. As a result of observing their work with the undergraduate students, supporting their writing, hearing their narratives, and celebrating their achievements, I have a deeper, more personal relationship with each of them.

On a professional level, I have explored the applications of technology to my language development curriculum concurrently with my students. My learning curve has included some of the same skills my students learned: digital camera use, importing photos into the movie-making software, recording, downloading music, and uploading the final products to a Website. Because community outreach is a fundamental component to high-performing schools, this opportunity to access the extraordinary community resources provided by the University of Colorado instructors and their students created a foundation for future joint projects. In addition, I've posted the digital stories on a global Website (with permission) to connect my students with students of English as a Foreign Language in Tajikistan where I recently traveled on a State Department education grant. The potential to use digital storytelling as a vehicle for sharing global issues in communities across the globe is work I hope to explore as a result of this project.

## STUDENT PERSPECTIVES

### High School Student Perspectives

Wexler Love conducted three focus groups at each of the two high schools during November and December of 2009. At Colina High School, where the majority of high school students had arrived within months, if not weeks, of beginning this project, a native Spanish speaker assisted with the focus groups and helped with transcribing and translating student responses. The high school youth participants also completed an anonymous survey written in both English and their first language evaluating their experiences and their perceptions of the program's impact. Having all forms in both languages allowed the students to respond more fully in the language of their choice.

In the focus groups and survey, students spoke about how the digital storytelling project provided a medium through which they felt they could express themselves. One student said about the project:

*I can show how I feel about this community, express a lot of stuff that many people don't ask me or don't, well, I would say don't care because they don't ask me but I don't know if that's what happens, if that's the truth. I just think it's a way for me to express how I feel about my community[10].*

Some students talked about not feeling heard, not being consulted. Other students explicitly connected the existence of discrimination with a need to speak out in the community and agreed that digital storytelling could play a role in helping students to speak out. When asked if digital storytelling is a good way to share the voices of teenagers in the community, one Newcomer student responded, "Yes, because sometimes we Latinos are discriminated against and this is a voice in the community. We need to be heard." The digital storytelling project enabled us to ask students about their experiences and perspectives, to consult students about their lives.

Many students were overwhelmed with the technological aspects of the digital storytelling project, experiencing a steep learning curve. The following statement was shared mid semester:

*It sucks….Well I thought I was gonna put the picture in and I thought I was gonna have everything…I was hoping to get all that started at the times and everything. And it didn't happen and because I was dragging it from my camera file to there it didn't work because it didn't appear.*

Many students conveyed their appreciation for the opportunity to learn about new technology and Newcomer students at Colina High School in particular discussed the beneficial opportunities provided by digital storytelling to practice writ-ing, reading, and speaking English. When asked about the most frustrating aspects of the project, students talked about concerns with how they could most effectively convey their messages and how people would interpret what they were saying. For example, one student noted that, "Finding a picture that represents what you're talking about or symbolizing it. Sometimes it's hard."

Students displayed a critical awareness of the project, as evidenced by their thoughtful approach to each creative decision they had to make and in their reflections on how the project made them think about their place in the community. Below are two instances of students reflecting on their community awareness:

*I kind of really don't think about my community and then when we started doing this project I went back and started thinking about my community and what I did and how I felt about it. So, I think this project makes you think about your community.*

*I realized that before we did this I didn't really think of it but then when we started talking about it I realized that there's a lot of things that we teenagers can't do and stuff. And then, I don't know it just made me think a lot about how we don't have a lot of things other cities or other communities have.*

Students spoke powerfully about the different ways they feel silenced, or unheard, in the community and how digital storytelling is one medium that can counteract this. Also, through their movies, they shared meaningful ways that they do interact with the spaces and people in the community. Digital storytelling can create authentic ways for young people to connect with adults and share their perspectives. Through this project, students revealed that they want to be heard, sometimes because they feel marginalized in their own community, and sometimes because they just want their classmates and teachers to know more about them.

## Undergraduate Student Perspectives

The university students also participated in a focus group conducted by an outside facilitator. For most, this digital storytelling project was a positive experience. It gave them an opportunity to mentor CLD youth in their community and hear their stories. One university students said:

*I think one of the biggest things that this class has taught me is to just open up and let my mind value what the youth have to say, even if they are not some great intellectual or something. It's a lot about what they need, a support system.*

Many of the university students also experienced frustrations with various aspects of the project. Most expressed a desire to have more time with the high school students to build relationships and have fun with the youth. Since the first five weeks of the semester were allotted to the university students learning the digital storytelling process, they only had the last 10 weeks of the semester to get to know the youth and help them create a digital story:

*I would have liked to have gone into the school a little sooner in the semester so we could have built that bond up a little bit and then really have time to enjoy the kids. You know, the advocacy and just the volunteer work of it. Instead of it just being, you know, you've got to get this done, you've got to push them. It would have been nice to get to know them a little better.*

Some university students found digital storytelling provided a great format to reflect on their community. Because of the limited time within one semester, the process for creating a digital storytelling became just as important as having a quality digital story as a final product at the end:

*I think that even if [the high school students] don't use the digital stories to get their voice heard, it forced them to think about the issues in their community that they may not give any consideration to or think about, and it kind of brought light to those issues for both us and for them. I think that was a good thing... [The youth] had a lot of pride in what they made, what they produced. But I think that it was good even if they just took pictures or were able to translate their story into English, something like that. Just those little bits that were components were really good for those kids.*

For university students who worked with Brexa's ESL students, the project also taught them ways to overcome language barriers and learn to work with people who are different than they are.

*... we had to communicate in different ways than we probably thought we were going to have to and there was just a lot of smiling and laughing. You know half the time we had no idea what we were saying to each other. We just knew we were getting something done and just agreed that it was pretty, or this wasn't okay or this was yes and stuff like that. We couldn't understand them, they couldn't understand us and we were forced to use universal means of speaking together to be able to communicate.*

In the end, some university students felt that they did not have time to follow through with the project and see the changes that their collaborative work could have on the community and they questioned the next steps. When the impact goes beyond the constraints of the university semester schedule, it can often leave the participating undergraduate students with unanswered questions and the feeling of being cut out of a process they valued.

*We've got these digital stories; we've worked on these, what happens now? How do you use these as an avenue for social change? I mean, do those digital stories sit here from fall semester 2009 now? Cause I feel like the class was called, you know, Immigration Integration in the Community; well how is that happening? How do we see that transposed into the community? I guess that is the question that I have.*

The undergraduates finished their commitment to the digital storytelling project and the high school students when the semester ended in December of 2009. Consequently, they not all of them were able to see how the impact of the project extended well beyond the limits of the semester. In February of 2010, we invited the undergraduate students who participated in the project to a presentation of the digital stories that took place before a school board meeting. Three came and afterwards shared that it was exciting to see how the work they did in one semester continues on. In May of 2009, we invited the undergraduates who worked at Colina to an end of year party allowing them to reconnect with the high school students and hear about their future plans. All five undergraduates who worked with the students at Colina came to this celebration. It is important to recognize that due to the constraints of the semester calendar, the undergraduates' may feel that their participation is cut short. Thus, it is important to be transparent about such constraints and celebrate their achievements and schedule a shared event to publicly recognize the work they complete. Even though we reach out to former students to inform them of presentations and related events in an effort to keep them connected to the project, in reality they have other commitments as a new semester begins.

## COMMUNITY IMPACT

Another outcome of this digital storytelling project is the impact on the larger school and district communities. Students in the larger school community observed the process (photographing, recording, movie-production) in Sullivan and Brexa's classes and expressed interest. Parents expressed their support of the project and joined their students for the end-of-the semester digital story screening on the university campus. District-level administrators who attended the project screening proposed sharing the project with the larger community through a screening at the monthly School Board meeting, while the district Communications Division has proposed showing the digital stories on a local public television network. During earlier semesters we coordinated a presentation of the digital stories to city councils in two communities. Although the response by city council members was very different between the two communities and included both positive reactions and dismissive attitudes, most agreed that it was extremely valuable for the adult councils to see that youth cared about their communities and wanted to engage in them. Thus, the voices of CLD students, often silenced by limited language ability, negative portrayals, or cultural marginalization, have been heard in our community through this medium of technology.

## RECOMMENDATIONS FOR GOOD PRACTICES AND STRATEGIES

Based on our experience with this digital storytelling project we have compiled recommendations for developing university/high school partnerships within the context of a technology-based project.

- Take the time needed to develop the project and make sure everyone's needs and goals are understood by meeting well in advance to identify the objectives of the project, the potential benefits, district curriculum standards that have to be met, and the estimated time requirements for teachers, instructors, and students (both the undergraduates and high school students).
- Recognize the immense scope of creating a technology-based service-learning project.

Even though we planned 15 contact hours at each site to complete the digital stories, undergraduates had to come in on additional days in order to assist high school students in completing their videos. Plan ahead for logistical issues that may come up, such as school closings or in-service days, and consider having flex-days allotted at the end of the semester in case additional time is needed to finish.

- Be realistic with what can be accomplished during the time that you have to work together and be respectful of everyone's schedule. Although it is often wonderful when students want to continue with the project beyond the time-frame originally planned (such as one semester), this can present a challenge to other students who have scheduling conflicts and cannot continue. Make sure there is a significant ending to the project for those students who cannot continue to participate. Involve students in the process of deciding which videos to share in the public screenings.

- Focus on the process of creating the digital stories as much as the final product. Some of the students may never finish their videos due to various constraints such as absences or joining the class mid semester. By focusing on the reflective process used to create the digital stories, students are able to benefit from the project even without a final product. However, be aware that this can be frustrating for some students who are used to getting grades only for completed assignments.

- Embrace the opportunity to get to know young people through digital storytelling. Digital storytelling provides educators and community members with a window into their students' worlds. Ask the high school students and their guardians for permission to share their stories at faculty meetings. As we learned new things about each

student, others will learn that immigration issues affect each student differently. The implications of knowing young people on a deeper level are numerous. Educators and communities can more adeptly meet the needs of young people through understanding who they are, where they come from, what challenges and successes they have faced, and how they see their schools and communities. Most importantly, young people feel heard and valued in the school and community context.

- Understand and respect the limitations of the university students as facilitators of this process. Depending on their experience level, they are often learning as much as they are serving the community group. In some cases, they will need additional support in order to ensure the success of the project. During our undergraduate class time we would reflect on what happened at the high school sites, plan for future sessions, role play hypothetical and real scenarios to develop creative responses, and address any challenges that the undergraduates faced. Each time the undergraduates were at Colina, Brexa provided them with a brief typed assessment of their facilitation that offered praise and suggestions for how to improve their practice. Students at Aguila developed an open relationship with Sullivan and often discussed facilitation issues as they came up.

- Celebrate both the small and large accomplishments. An authentic showing of the final digital stories for everyone involved is a natural ending to this type of project. If possible, plan for multiple screenings with different audiences, including one in the classroom with just participating students. This will give them a chance to celebrate while talking about the process without the stress of getting the work done or presenting to adults in positions of power. In addition, positive reinforcement during each step of the process is important to keep morale high and prevent students from getting discouraged. For example, when the undergraduate students felt pressure to assist the high schools students with the tasks assigned without having the chance to just hang out together, we brought in snacks during particular sessions[11]in order to make them less formal and more like a celebration. The presence of food also lowered the stress level and gave the students a chance to get to know one another.

## CONCLUSION

As educators, the four of us wanted to counteract the impact of society's negative messages about immigrant youth. Our digital storytelling project was designed to accomplish that through meeting the following goals: use multi-media technology to enable CLD and immigrant youth to reflect on their experiences in the community; give a public voice to a demographic of teenagers who are often silenced; and build a mutually enriching partnership among public high school students, university students, and staff from participating institutions. This digital storytelling project facilitated an authentic approach to teaching, providing both university and high school students a real-world application of new skills. Integrating technology in the classroom is no longer a choice; it is a necessity. All students must have access to opportunities to engage in learning technology; without it they risk being left behind.

## REFERENCES

Burgess, J. (2006). Hearing ordinary voices: Cultural studies, vernacular creativity and digital storytelling. *Continuum, 20*(2), 201–214. doi:10.1080/10304310600641737

Cano, J., & Bankston, J. (1992). Factors which influence participation and non-participation of ethnic minority youth in Ohio 4-H programs. *Journal of Agricultural Education, 33*(1), 23–29. doi:10.5032/jae.1992.01023

Davis, A. (2004). Co-authoring identity: Digital storytelling in an urban middle school. *Then Journal, 5*(1). Retrieved from http://thenjournal. org/feature/61/

Eyler, J., & Giles, D. (1997). The importance of program quality in service-learning. In A. Waterman (Ed.), *Service learning: Applications from the research* (pp. 57–76). Mahwah, NJ: Lawerence Erlbaum Associates, Publishers.

Honnet, E., & Poulen, S. (1989). *Principles of good practice for combining service and learning: A wingspread special report*. Racine, WI: The Johnson Foundation.

Howard, J. (1993). Community service-learning in the curriculum. In J. Howard (Ed.), *Praxis I: A faculty casebook on community service-learning* (pp. 3–12). Ann Arbor, MI: OCSL Press.

Howard, J. (2003b). Community service learning in the curriculum. In *Campus Compact's introduction to service-learning toolkit: Readings and resources for faculty* (2nd ed., pp. 101–104). Providence, RI: Brown University.

Hull, G., & Katz, M. (2006). Crafting an agentive self: Case studies of digital storytelling. *Research in the Teaching of English, 41*(1), 43–81.

Katz, S. (1997). Presumed guilty: How schools criminalize Latino youth. *Social Justice (San Francisco, Calif.), 24*(4), 77–96.

Kelly, D. (2006). Frame work: Helping youth counter their misrepresentations in media. *Canadian Journal of Education, 29*(1), 27–48. doi:10.2307/20054145

Klaebe, H., Foth, M., Burgess, J., & Bilandzic, M. (2007). Digital storytelling and history lines: Community engagement in a master-planned development. In *Proceedings 13th International Conference on Virtual Systems and Multimedia*, Brisbane. Retrieved from http://eprints.qut.edu.au.

Ladson-Billings, G. (2004). New directions in multicultural education: Complexities, boundaries, and critical race theory. In J. A. Banks & C. A. McGee Banks (Eds.), *Handbook of research on multicultural education* (2nd ed., pp. 50–65). San Francisco, CA: Jossey-Bass.

Lambert, J. (2007). *Digital storytelling cookbook*. Berkley, CA: Digital Diner Press.

Lundby, K. (2008). Editorial: Mediatized stories: Mediation perspectives on digital storytelling. *New Media & Society*, *10*(3), 363–371. doi:10.1177/1461444808089413

Meadows, D. (2003). Digital storytelling: Research-based practice in new media. *Visual Communication*, *2*(2), 189–193. doi:10.1177/1470357203002002004

Solorzano, D. G., & Yosso, T. J. (2001). Critical race and latcrit theory and method: Counter storytelling. *International Journal of Qualitative Studies in Education*, *14*(4), 471–495. doi:10.1080/09518390110063365

Strand, K., Marullo, S., Cutforth, N., Stoecker, R., & Donohue, P. (2003). Principles of best practice for community-based research. *Michigan Journal of Community Service Learning*, *9*(3), 5–15.

Vinogradova, P. (2008). Digital stories in an ESL classroom: Giving voice to cultural identity. *Language, Literacy, and Cultural Review*. Retrieved on December 16, 2009 from http://www.umbc.edu/llc/llcreview/2008/2008_digital_stories.pdf.

Ware, P. (2008). Language learners and multimedia literacy in and after school. *Pedagogies: An International Journal*, *3*(1), 37–51.

Weis, T., Benmayor, R., O'Leary, C., & Eynon, B. (2002). Digital technologies and pedagogies. *Journal of Social Justice*, *29*(4), 153–167.

## ENDNOTES

[1] In the context of this chapter, we describe the youth participants in this project as *culturally and linguistically diverse* to underscore the immense diversity they brought to the digital storytelling project, their schools, and their communities. Not only did students represent five distinct countries of origin (Mexico, El Salvador, China, United States, and Burma), but there was a range of experiences in terms of culture, language, immigration status, generation status, age, and educational background that needed to be recognized as a major contribution to this work. Thus, culturally and linguistically diverse youth is a descriptor we are using to capture the great diversity students shared with us in conversations and through their digital stories that helped us to hear their voices with a better understanding of their experiences and who they are as individuals.

[2] School names have been changed to protect the identities of the student participants.

[3] During our second semester of running this digital storytelling project in the spring of 2009, we had roughly 30 cameras and 60 students participating. Although we tried to work out a complicated exchange schedule that required us to rotate cameras on a weekly basis, ultimately it caused undue frustration for students and facilitators.

[4] Audacity™

[5] Windows Movie Maker™

[6] In order to privilege student voices, we structured the assignment so students could write their personal narratives in the language of their choice. We then helped students to

translate their stories into English in order to reach a broader audience. Some students chose to create bilingual videos, reading their stories in their native languages first and English second. We chose to include translated excerpts in this chapter.

7    In this paragraph we share how an extremely political issue, immigration, is a reality in the lives of the students we work with. We believe that knowing more about how immigration affects the lives of students is critical to being more effective educators, though we also caution educators to understand the implications of students revealing information about their documentation status and remind educators that they cannot request information about documentation status from their students. Students shared their stories; we never asked about documentation status.

8    Tutorials are based on the idea of study groups. Each student is expected to arrive at class with two higher level questions from their academic learning. The study groups then use inquiry and collaboration to answer the questions. AVID prefers that the tutors are university students. The Tutorials are part of the AVID curriculum and are used on a set day each week. For example, I would do Tutorials every Tuesday.

9    Permission slips were translated into Spanish for students.

10   To improve readability the words "like" and "um" were removed from quotes when used as a discourse particle or interjection.

11   Some schools have certain restrictions on food so make sure to ask ahead of time. For example Aguila High School required us to bring individually wrapped, store-bought food.

# Chapter 10
# Critical Success Factors for Partnering with Nonprofit Organizations on Digital Technology Service-Learning Projects:
## A Case Study

**James P. Lawler**
*Pace University, USA*

## ABSTRACT

*This case study analyzes critical success factors for digital technology projects in service-learning courses at Pace University, a leading school of computer science and information systems in New York City. The study argues that the factors of collaboration, pedagogy, project management, strategy, and technology are foundational not only to implementing and generating meaningful benefits from projects, but also to ensuring durable and fruitful partnerships with nonprofit organizations. The findings from this case study will help instructors considering expansion of high-tech service-learning courses to secure innovative partnerships by encouraging all parties involved to maintain focus on service and human interactions rather than simply on technology.*

## INTRODUCTION

Civic engagement is defined in this chapter as empowering or a difference in the civic life of [a community] and developing the combination of knowledge ... and motivation to [enable] that difference ... [and as] promoting the quality of life in a community, through both non-political and political processes" (Ehrlich, 2000), a definition articulated by Project Pericles (www.projectpericles.org), an organization that promotes civic engagement among institutions of higher

DOI: 10.4018/978-1-60960-623-7.ch010

education (Liazos & Liss, 2009). Service-learning is a form of experiential learning in which academic courses are enhanced through community service (Hunter & Brisbin, 2000). In many cases, service-learning engages students in experiencing life at nonprofit organizations that help disabled or disadvantaged citizens of a community. The learning can be focused on challenging students to initiate technology-based solutions to the needs or problems of the nonprofit organizations and to reflect on their learning throughout the project process (Petkus, 2000). Student learning is improved through introspective perceptual and cognitive reflection on service experiences (Dunlap, 2006).

The focus of this chapter is maximizing the benefits of service-learning projects for nonprofit organizations. In the current economy, nonprofit organizations are confronted by budget constraints that simultaneously increase their need for and decrease their ability to support service-learning projects. To sustain their operations, these organizations need help beyond projects that "do good." They need meaningful help for sustaining their missions. This can be a problem when it comes to service-learning projects, in part because of logistical issues. Projects at nonprofit organizations rarely fit readily into the academic calendar. Short-term projects may be difficult for nonprofit organizations to manage in a semester (Tryon, Stoecker, Martin, Seblonka, Hilgendorf & Nellis, 2008), but long-term service-learning projects, especially those involving digital technology, can be difficult for faculty and students to manage due to the realities of course duration. In addition, it may be challenging for nonprofit organizations and faculty members to maintain projects across subsequent semesters, after students move on to other courses (Daynes & Longo, 2004). Short-term, semester-long service-learning projects may not even generate meaningful benefits for institutions of higher education or nonprofit organizations if students are not instructed about and significantly engaged with the missions of the nonprofit organizations (Mitchell, 2008).

The burden of effectively enabling benefits from service-learning is a challenge for institutions of higher education and for nonprofit organizations (Creighton, 2007) that if not met can negate the concept of service (Pompa, 2002).

This chapter introduces the critical success factors of collaboration, pedagogy, project management, strategy and technology, that my experience shows can help faculty and partners to secure meaningful benefits from service-learning projects and ensure fruitful partnerships between higher education institutions and nonprofit organizations. The factors are analyzed in my courses that included technology-based service-learning projects for nonprofit organizations in partnership with the Seidenberg School of Computer Science and Information Systems at Pace University (SSCSIS), a leading member of Project Pericles. Relationships between three specific nonprofit organizations and SSCSIS are analyzed in this chapter, inasmuch as these relationships are considered to be foundational to service-learning projects (Benson & Harkavy, 2000) and the technology projects initiated by them. The partnerships are grounded in personal relationships between higher education instructors and nonprofit staff members (Mihalynuk & Seifer, 2004). These partnerships are also analyzed on a spectrum of relationships that are considered in the literature to range from transactional to transformational (Enos & Morton, 2003). This chapter introduces practices that will help instructors to successfully use service-learning as a tool for teaching technology-focused courses.

## BACKGROUND

The Seidenberg School is a leading pioneer in service-learning with technology, and our courses are making a difference in nonprofit organizations in downtown New York City (Coppola, Daniels, Gannon, Hale, Hayes, Kline, Mosley, Novak & Pennachio, 2008). Projects generated through

*Table 1. Service-learning technology courses at the Seidenberg School of Computer Science and Information Systems of Pace University*

| Semesters | Service-Learning Courses | Technology Projects |
|---|---|---|
| Fall 2007 through Spring 2010 (seven semesters) | Community Empowerment through Information Systems and Technology | Assistive Communication Devices<br>Digital Art Galleries on the Internet Intranet Portals<br>Multimedia Profiles<br>Search Systems |
| Spring 2005 | Social Networking Systems on the Web | Intranet Social Media Networking Systems |
| Fall 2003 and Spring 2004 | Web Design for Nonprofit Organizations | e-Commerce Greeting Cards on Internet<br>Internet Site<br>Virtual Tours on World Wide Web |

these courses are enabling nonprofit organizations to help their clients, often disadvantaged citizens from the New York area, through novel technology solutions to an array of challenges. The author-instructor's service-learning and technology courses described in this chapter began with basic web design in 2003 and have evolved to include courses as advanced as community empowerment through information systems and technology in 2010, as defined below in Table 1.

Though the courses listed in Table 1 are customized to address the needs of the nonprofit organizations with whom the students partner, they have consistent student objectives and learning outcomes:

- Describe comfortably the concept of community service;
- Describe functions of the nonprofit organization(s) in helping disabled or disadvantaged clients in downtown New York City;
- Explain interactions and limitations encountered by the nonprofit organization(s) in helping disadvantaged clients in a budget-constrained economy, and explain limitations and needs of disadvantaged clients in interactions with society;
- Implement in partnership with the nonprofit organization(s) a project(s) furnishing the potential or reality of web and non-web

information systems and technology that may help the nonprofit organization staff in helping the disadvantaged clients in the city; and,
- Initiate informed discussion of issues and needs of practicing service in a democratic society for less fortunate people in the society.

As an instructor, I discuss the expected outcomes with the students in the first week of each course. The students meet the directors of the nonprofit organization(s) for orientation during the second week, and engage with the nonprofit organization staff and often the clients they serve in the third week of the course. From the fourth to the fifth, sixth to seventh, eighth to eleventh, and twelfth to thirteenth weeks of each course, the students work in teams to analyze, design, develop and implement projects with the clients and the organization staff. The students present the systems to the senior management of the nonprofit organization(s) during the fourteenth week.

Since 2003, the three-credit courses have engaged 177 "consultant" students in nine technology-based projects at nonprofit organization sites over 14-week periods. Through their experiences students have fulfilled core knowledge requirements at the university and engaged hundreds of disadvantaged citizens and organization staff.

These courses are considered consultative (Kenworthy-U'Ren, 2000) and project-based (Draper, 2004) in the service-learning literature, as the benefits of the technology projects are actualized through defined objectives and outcomes in a semester. The projects benefit disadvantaged clients lacking perceptions of self-development and organization staff lacking productivity resources (Lazar & Norcio, 2000). The technology projects benefit the students in learning about the problems of the disadvantaged clients and the organization staff and in learning the potential if not the reality of productivity and self-development solutions achievable through technology. Students learn about reflective citizenship, and often about social sensitivity, by working together on project teams (Kolb, 1984). Such sensitivity may continue in the future as they proceed in society (Waxer, 2008). These technology-based projects abound in benefits as a model of service-learning (Saulnier, 2004).

Though the benefits of service-learning technology projects are numerous in the literature, designing these courses can be difficult for instructors in schools of computer science and information systems (Wei, Slow, & Burley, 2007). This challenge applies to me, though I've been designing such courses since 2003. Project design is a particular challenge. Experimentation is a critical element in developing the courses, and helps to ensure that students learn about service (Freire, 1985), rather than merely technology. Furthermore, instructors have to be cognizant of the needs of the nonprofit organizations as partners (Jacoby, 1996) as they initiate projects, and nonprofit organizations have to be cognizant concurrently of the needs of their academic partners. This balance is critical if a project is to yield meaningful benefits for both sides. Further complicating matters are inconsistent definitions of service-learning in the literature on service-learning and technology-based projects. It is critical for everyone involved in a partnership to define goals and expectations collaboratively, a process I incorporate into my collaboration with nonprofit organizations.

I contend that the benefits of technology-based service-learning projects are dependent on the customization of the course design based on the needs of the partnering nonprofit organization. Moreover, I argue that this customization is dependent on the factors of collaboration, pedagogy, project management, strategy and technology, as defined in Table 2.

*Table 2. Critical success factors of service-learning technology projects at the Seidenberg School of Computer Science and Information Systems of Pace University*

| Factors | Sub-Factors |
|---|---|
| **Collaboration** | Extent of commitments of institution of higher education, nonprofit organization and Center for Community Action and Research; engagement and mentoring of disadvantaged clients; and perception of project urgency in enabling a bona fide partnership |
| **Pedagogy** | Extent of customization of course; education of students on nonprofit organization problems; flexibility in pedagogy; maturity and orientation of students; and reflection of students, in enabling implementation of evolving technology |
| **Project Management** | Extent of communication forums; course as a project; flexibility in scheduling; meaningfulness of projects; and ownership of projects, in enabling meaningful productive and self-developmental technology |
| **Strategy** | Extent of program planning before semester; planned programs after semester; programs for students; public relations; and recognition of students, in enabling fruitful long-term partnership strategy |
| **Technology** | Extent of availability of productivity technology for nonprofit organization staff; self-development technology for disadvantaged clients; technology training of organization staff; support through nonprofit organization technology department; and support through School of Computer Science and Information Systems, in enabling future value with technology |

In my experience, the factors in Table 2 facilitate meaningful learning about service for the students and meaningful technology value for the disadvantaged clients and the staff of nonprofit organizations. I believe strongly that the interactions of disadvantaged clients, organization staff, and students in the process of service is more critical to positive outcomes than the languages, tools and utilities of technology. It is important to let students and faculty know that people are more important than technology. It is critical that all parties—the faculty, nonprofit staff members, students, and clients—value the university-community partnership, whether they work on short-term or long-term projects.

To demonstrate this point, below I will analyze service-learning partnerships between SSCSIS and three medium-sized nonprofit organizations (i.e., >$10 million< in revenue in 2009) since 2003. The resulting projects have enabled the nonprofit organizations to help disadvantaged clients and offered organization staff real technology solutions for their challenges. The findings from the analysis will benefit instructors, as little relevant literature exists in the arenas of service-learning and technology education (Citurs, 2009). The nonprofit organizations are defined in Table 3.

## ANALYSIS OF PARTNERSHIPS

### Issues, Controversies, Problems

*"Not every course [in technology] ... can [enable you to] tell other students how proud you are of what you have done (for the community) as much as this course." – J.S. (Junior Student in Web Design for Nonprofit Organizations, Spring Semester 2004)*

The critical success factors of collaboration, pedagogy, project management, strategy and technology enable implementation of service-learning technology projects and ensure fruitful partnering practices between nonprofit organizations and SSCSIS. Below I analyze each of the courses – Community Empowerment through Information Systems and Technology, Social Networking Systems on the Web, and Web Design for Nonprofit Organizations – and each of the nonprofit

*Table 3. Courses, nonprofit organizations, clients and service-learning technology projects at the Seidenberg School of Computer Science and Information Systems of Pace University*

| Semesters | Course | Nonprofit Organizations* | Clients | Projects of Technology |
|---|---|---|---|---|
| Spring 2010 – Fall 2007 | Community Empowerment through Information Systems and Technology | A | Individuals with developmental and intellectual disabilities | -Assistive communication devices<br>-Digital art galleries<br>-Intranet portals<br>-Multimedia profiles<br>-Search systems |
| Spring 2005 | Social Networking Systems on the Web | B | Individuals with HIV / AIDS | Intranet social media networking systems |
| Spring 2004 – Fall 2003 | Web Design for Nonprofit Organizations | C | Individuals with drug and alcohol problems | -e-Commerce greeting cards on Internet<br>-Internet Site<br>-Virtual Tours on World Wide Web |

*Names of the nonprofit organizations are confidential in this chapter, due to the comparative evaluations of their partnership practices with Pace University.

organizations partnered with for the courses – A, B, and C. I analyze these partnerships in terms of the detailed sub-factors of each of the factors in Table 2 to determine the extent of project enablement and fruitfulness of partnering practices. I evaluate the sub-factors based on my personal perception of the collaboration experiences during the duration of the partnerships, using an overall three point scale in the detailed analysis of the sub-factors in Table 4, with a measurement of three (3) indicat-

ing high, two (2) indicating intermediate and one (1) indicating low impact or incident. I average the findings in Table 4 in the summary analysis of the factors in Table 5. The focus of the evaluations is more on the process of service-learning than on the output of the technology. At the end of this section I offer lessons learned through the service-learning technology project.

*Table 4. Critical success factors of courses, nonprofit organizations and technology projects at the Seidenberg School of Computer Science and Information Systems at Pace University: Detailed analysis*

| Critical Success Factors | Nonprofit Organizations | | |
|---|---|---|---|
| | A | B | C |
| **Collaboration** | | | |
| **Commitment of Institution of Higher Education**<br>-Institution of Higher Education<br>-School of Computer Science and Information Systems<br>-Department of Information Systems | 3.00 | 3.00 | 3.00 |
| **Commitment of Nonprofit Organization** | 3.00 | 1.00 | 2.00 |
| **Commitment of Center for Community Action and Research**<br>-Liaison<br>-Services | 3.00 | 3.00 | 3.00 |
| **Engagement and Mentoring of Disadvantaged Clients**<br>-"One-on-One" Relationship | 2.00 | 1.00 | 2.00 |
| **Perception of Project Urgency**<br>-"Skin in the Game" | 3.00 | 1.00 | 2.00 |
| **Pedagogy** | | | |
| **Customization of Course** | 3.00 | 2.00 | 1.00 |
| **Education of Students on Nonprofit Organization Problems** | 3.00 | 2.00 | 1.00 |
| **Flexibility and Innovation in Pedagogy**<br>-Learning vs. Service<br>-Service vs. Technology | 3.00 | 1.00 | 2.00 |
| **Maturity and Orientation of Students**<br>-Information Systems Students vs. Non-Information Systems Students | 2.00 | 2.00 | 3.00 |
| **Reflection of Students** | 3.00 | 2.00 | 3.00 |
| **Project Management** | | | |
| **Communication Forums**<br>-Currency of 21$^{st}$ Century Messaging | 3.00 | 1.00 | 2.00 |
| **Course as a Project**<br>-Project Manager in Nonprofit Organization<br>-Project Staff in Nonprofit Organization | 3.00 | 1.00 | 2.00 |

*continued on the following page*

*Table 4. continued*

| | | | |
|---|---|---|---|
| **Flexibility in Scheduling**<br>-Instructor<br>-Students<br>-Staff | 2.00 | 2.00 | 2.00 |
| **Meaningfulness of Projects** | 3.00 | 1.00 | 2.00 |
| **Ownership of Projects**<br>-Tasks | 3.00 | 1.00 | 2.00 |
| **Strategy** | | | |
| **Planned Program before Semester**<br>-Projects<br>-Syllabus | 3.00 | 2.00 | 1.00 |
| **Planned Programs after Semester**<br>-Projects | 2.00 | 1.00 | 2.00 |
| **Programs for Students**<br>-Internships Part-Time<br>-Positions in Summer | 1.00 | 1.00 | 1.00 |
| **Public Relations** | 3.00 | 1.00 | 3.00 |
| **Recognition of Students** | 3.00 | 3.00 | 3.00 |
| **Technology** | | | |
| **Productivity Technology for Nonprofit Organization Staff**<br>-Intranet Technology<br>-Internet Technology | 3.00 | 3.00 | 3.00 |
| **Self-Development Technology for Disadvantaged Clients**<br>-Internet Technology<br>-Mobile Technology<br>-Multimedia Technology | 3.00 | 1.00 | 3.00 |
| **Technology Training of Organization Staff**<br>-Productivity Tools | 2.00 | 1.00 | 2.00 |
| **Support through Nonprofit Organization Technology Department** | 1.00 | 3.00 | 1.00 |
| **Support through School of Institution of Higher Education Technology Department** | 1.00 | 2.00 | 1.00 |

*Table 5. Critical success factors of courses, nonprofit organizations and projects of technology at the Seidenberg School of Computer Science and Information Systems at Pace University: Summary analysis*

| Critical Success Factors | Nonprofit Organizations | | |
|---|---|---|---|
| | A | B | C |
| **Collaboration** | 2.80 | 1.80 | 2.40 |
| **Pedagogy** | 2.80 | 1.80 | 2.00 |
| **Project Management** | 2.80 | 1.20 | 2.00 |
| **Strategy** | 2.40 | 1.60 | 2.00 |
| **Technology** | 2.00 | 2.00 | 2.00 |

Legend: (3) – high, (2) – intermediate and (1) – low impact or incident on the groups of projects of service-learning and technology of the nonprofit organizations and SSCSIS.

**Pace University**
**Seidenberg School of Computer Science and Information Systems**
**Overview of Fall 2003 – Spring 2010 Semesters**
**Fall 2007 – Spring 2010 Semesters**
*Course: Community Empowerment through Information Systems and Technology*
*Nonprofit Organization: A*
*Clients of Nonprofit Organization A: Individuals with Developmental and Intellectual Disabilities*
*Technology Projects: Assistive Communication Devices, Digital Art Galleries on the Internet, Intranet Portals, Multimedia Profiles, and Search Systems*

## Project Snapshot

Nonprofit organization A contacted SSCSIS in spring 2007. The focus of interaction in the fall 2007 to fall 2008 semesters was the organization's need for internal intranet portals and search systems to help organization staff to schedule and search plans for self-development programs for clients with developmental and intellectual disabilities. From the spring 2008 through the spring 2010 semesters the organization expressed two other needs: first, for assistive communication devices – gadgets like iPhones – and customization of device menus, and second, for multimedia profiles for the clients with disabilities, which would allow the clients to present "My Story" person-centered planning resumes and support plans. The plans presented the dreams and hopes of the clients to engage with others in society and were not mere resumes to find jobs in industry. They were powerful tools that projected the personalities of the clients as human beings, and as though they were without disabilities. The clients were proud of their "My Story" plans that took advantage of multimedia technology. Later in the semester the focus shifted to a need for digital art galleries, in order for the clients to share their personal art

collections on the Internet. The projects were completed with external and internal off-the-shelf software, open source tools and grant-purchased tools and utilities. The Pace University Center for Community Action and Research was helpful as the initial liaison between organization A and SSCSIS. There were 107 undergraduate students in the course from the fall 2007 to spring 2010.

## Analysis of Critical Success Factors: Detail

(Measurement of the critical success factors is an average of the relevant sub-factors in the detailed analysis in Table 4 and is summarized in Table 5.)

## Collaboration

From the beginning of the fall 2007 semester, the commitment of nonprofit organization A was complete, including frequent and almost high (2.80 / 3.00) interaction between managerial and organization staff and the instructor and the students. Though the students were not engaged in mentoring individuals with developmental and intellectual disabilities until the spring 2008 semester, they were engaged in partnering with organization staff every semester. Throughout the partnership, the perception of project urgency was evident to SSCSIS.

## Pedagogy

The pedagogy was customized to address the exact needs of organization A through discussion with managerial staff. The organization educated students on problems that might be solved through technology projects but was flexible in considering solutions recommended by the students. The focus of the pedagogy, however, was more on service than technology. Though most of the students were not information systems majors, they researched and were substantially successful in using the technology through quick learning of open source tools and utilities on the Web. Student reflections on mid-term and final reports on the results of the relationship revealed an average score of 2.80 (nearly a high rating) in learning impact across the semesters.

## Project Management

I rated the management of the organization A project as almost high (2.80) in impact. Project managers and project staff were identified to serve as points of contact for the instructor and the students to ensure the meaningfulness of projects and tasks, were included on student teams, and interfaced through instant short messaging systems (SMS) – texting and tweeting – or mobile tools. These tools helped to minimize the impacts of scheduling problems that typically emerge when nonprofits work with students.

## Strategy

I evaluated the program strategy as generally intermediate (2.40) in impact for organization A. Throughout the latter period of the relationship, in the spring 2009 to spring 2010 semesters, management in the organization initiated long-term plans for other technology projects to be integrated in the fall 2010 to spring 2012 semesters. The collaboration began to include a public relations plan during the spring 2008 semester to promote the relationship among the organization, school, and students.

## Technology

The technology projects were evaluated to have an intermediate (2.00) impact in organization A. Individuals with intellectual disabilities leveraged the assistive communication devices and multimedia profiles in order to share their perspectives with other clients, their families, and staff. Organization staff leveraged the intranet portals, the open source content management systems

and the search systems on the web in order to share information about programs for the clients with staff at other sites. Plans were in progress to provide the staff with office productivity tool training. Though the technology projects were implemented to operate at the organization A site, the internal technology department would be needed to support the technology, as the school was proceeding on other projects with the staff. Plans were subsequently made for the department to support this technology in 2011.

## Lessons Learned from Service-Learning Technology Projects with Organization A

- Collaboration between organization A and SSCSIS to carefully define project parameters enabled a durable partnership of six semesters that is planned into 2012;
- Deliberative engagement of individuals with developmental and intellectual disabilities as partners with the students enabled learning experiences related to service that were more memorable than the technology projects themselves; and
- Effective project management by organization A enabled a flow of productive technology solutions.

**Spring 2005 Semester**
*Course: Social Networking Systems on the Web*
*Nonprofit Organization: B*
*Clients of Nonprofit Organization B: Individuals with HIV / AIDS*
*Technology Projects: Social Media Networking Systems*

## Project Snapshot

Nonprofit organization B contacted SSCSIS in fall 2004. The focus of interaction in the spring 2005 semester was a need for an intranet social media networking system, which would allow organization staff to share information about plans and programs with other staff members and with families of teenagers with HIV / AIDS. The project was completed with external off-the-shelf software that integrated with an existing external host service. The Center for Community Action and Research of the university was instrumental in connecting organization B with SSCSIS. There were 27 undergraduate students in the course in the spring 2005 semester.

## Analysis of Critical Success Factors: Detail

### Collaboration

I rated the collaboration commitment of nonprofit organization B as barely intermediate (1.80) based on the interactions between managerial and organization staff with the instructor and the students. The students were not engaged in the mentoring of the individual teens with HIV / AIDS, as they were isolated from them due to privacy requirements for teenagers. Throughout the relationship, the perception of project urgency was not evident to SSCSIS, as the organization staff seemed to consistently place priority on projects unrelated to those requested of the Pace students.

### Pedagogy

The pedagogy was customized to address the limited articulated needs of organization B in discussion with organization staff, including consideration of challenges that might be solved through social media networking technology projects. The pedagogy for this project was more focused on the technology than on the service; service to the individuals with HIV/AIDS was secondary to service to the staff. Inevitably, the reflection of the students on final reports on the results of the service was barely intermediate (1.80) in impact during the semester.

### Project Management

The project management of the organization B program was generally low (1.20) in impact. Project staff members were identified to work with the students, but the ownership of the project tasks was unclear in some periods of the semester, because the staff did not identify a project manager to the instructor or the students. Furthermore, the general manager of the organization was not on the project site with the student teams. Throughout the semester, the staff faced limitations in scheduling, so the students spent a great deal of time in suspense about where their projects were going.

### Strategy

The program strategy was indicated to be generally low (1.60) in incident for organization B, due to the limited relationship during the semester, though the organization recognized students for their service.

### Technology

The technology projects were indicated to be intermediate (2.00) in impact in organization B. Organization staff leveraged the social media networking systems to share programs and proposals with the families of the teenagers with HIV/ AIDS and with other staff, saving investment in a new system. SSCSIS supported the system into the subsequent semester, and the organization's hosting service supported the social networking technology thereafter.

## Lessons Learned from Service-Learning Technology Projects with Organization B

- It is possible to have a reasonably successful technology project with little obvious service-learning value for students, and it is important for faculty members to carefully weigh the usefulness of such projects based on course objectives;

• Despite the obvious importance of protecting client privacy, it may be worthwhile to give service-learning students some opportunity to interact with the people served by the organization in order to help them connect with the service aspect of the assignment;

• It is critical to have a clearly identified staff liaison who is responsible for interacting with students and faculty, rather than a group of staff members responsible for separate elements of the project; and

• Interaction between the organization and students might be improved through the use of mobile messaging tools (MMT) favored by Net Generation students rather than e-mail or the telephone.

**Fall 2003 and Spring 2004 Semesters:**
*Course: Web Design for Nonprofit Organizations*
*Nonprofit Organization: C*
*Clients of Nonprofit Organization C: Individuals with Drug and Alcohol Problems*
*Technology Projects: e-Commerce Greeting Cards on Internet, Internet Site, and Virtual Tours on World Wide Web*

**Project Snapshot**

Organization C contacted SSCSIS in summer 2003. The focus of interaction in the fall 2003 semester was a need for an Internet Web site and virtual tours on the World Wide Web, in order for organization staff to share information about drug and alcohol rehabilitation programs with the general public. The interaction was increased in the spring 2004 semester with a request for an e-Commerce marketing system to allow rehabilitation clients to sell greeting card products to the public. The projects required a hosting service to support the new web site, and

were completed with external off-the-shelf web site software and several open source utilities. The Center for Community Action and Research of the university was instrumental as the liaison between the organization and the school. There were 43 undergraduate students in the course in the fall 2003—spring 2004 semesters.

**Analysis of Critical Success Factors: Detail**

## Collaboration

The commitment of nonprofit organization C was generally limited and rated intermediate (2.40) in terms of interaction and intervention of organization staff with the students. The students were engaged with only a few of the rehabilitation program clients who worked with them on the projects. The perception of project urgency was evident to the school, but it was difficult to maintain this sense because the organization staff was frequently involved in other tasks and unable to engage with the instructor and students.

## Pedagogy

The pedagogy design for this project was customized based on the challenges facing organization C. The focus of the pedagogy was on the technology projects, inasmuch as most of the students were information systems students keenly interested in developing technology solutions. Student reflection indicated that the service was intermediate (2.00) in impact, in that they interfaced to some extent with individuals with drug and alcohol problems as they implemented technology projects together.

## Project Management

The project management of organization C project was rated at an intermediate (2.00) impact. Project managers were identified and matched to the student teams, but the ownership of the projects and of the systems was unclear during the semesters, as infighting between clients and staff impacted the tasks. Throughout the semesters, the staff was pulled away by routine tasks that impacted the scheduling of service-learning project work, so turnaround of feedback to the students was not timely.

## Strategy

The program strategy was evaluated as intermediate (2.00) in incident in organization C. Throughout the fall 2003 and spring 2004 semesters, the organization staff proposed other technology projects on the web that were pursued by another instructor in SSCSIS in the fall 2004 and spring 2005 semesters. Students received recognition for their service, and several of the students volunteered for other service with the organization in subsequent semesters.

## Technology

The impact of technology projects with organization C was indicated to be intermediate (2.00). Individuals with drug and alcohol problems leveraged the systems on the web to sell products profitably to the public. Organization staff leveraged the new site on the web to share information about rehabilitation programs. Organization staff was provided with office productivity tool training by an instructor from the school in a subsequent semester. The Seidenberg Scholars Program, a program of 4.00 GPA students, supported the new site and the systems on the web near the end of the fall 2003 semester, until the organization's hosting service began supporting it in the spring 2004 semester and beyond.

## Lessons Learned from Service-Learning Technology Projects with Organization C

- Student motivations are relevant to project outcomes. Students who are especially interested in technology will have a different sense of the service impact of a project than those who are primarily enrolled to engage in service;
- Politics among organization staff can significantly impact a project's progress, though they may not be obvious to students; and
- It is critical to have a long-term strategy in place for supporting the technology elements of a service-learning project.

## Summary of Factors Analysis

The critical success factors of collaboration, pedagogy, project management, strategy and technology enabled the implementation of service-learning technology projects in nonprofit organizations A, B and C. Organization A was enabled in impact (2.80, 2.80, 2.80, 2.40 and 2.00) more than organizations B (1.80, 1.80, 1.20, 1.60 and 2.00) and C (2.40, 2.00, 2.00, 2.00 and 2.00), as displayed in Table 5. Though organization A was in a long-term partnership more mature than the short-term partnerships of organizations B and C, the other organizations might have had equivalent enablement in impact if staff members had been able to dedicate more time and commitment to the projects during the semesters. Organization C and B, especially organization C, were in generally positive relationships that might have become even stronger if they had engaged more actively with SSCSIS. For the most part, the process of service-learning was more important than the output of the technology in the study.

Solutions and recommendations from the analysis of the critical success factors on service-learning technology projects are featured in the next section of this chapter.

## Solutions and Recommendations

*"I learned not to be frightened of [individuals with developmental and intellectual disabilities] because they are like you and I." - C.A. (Sophomore Student in Web Design for Nonprofit Organizations, Fall Semester 2003)*

The critical success factors model offers a solid model for planning and assessing technology-based service-learning projects. Effective collaboration establishes a commitment between nonprofit organizations and schools of computer science and information systems on the selection of appropriate projects and on shared evaluation standards. Customization and flexibility of pedagogy and project management attuned to the needs of nonprofit organizations (Sandy & Holland, 2006) maximize opportunities (McCallister, 2008) for successful projects. Effective project strategy ensures that the technology will be useful and will have necessary ongoing support and thus enables technology solutions that proceed seamlessly in subsequent semesters of study. These elements furnish a framework for partnerships between nonprofit organizations and schools of computer science and information systems that are beyond the nuances of technology.

These practices offer a good model for service-learning projects that encompass agile methodology on technology projects. Agile methodology is an iterative process for incremental technology projects (Beck, 2000). Factors in this methodology are acting on change, instead of following a detailed plan; collaborating, instead of negotiating a contract; doing the projects, instead of documenting detailed and fixed requirements; and focusing on interactions of people, instead of processes (Boehm, 1986). Clearly these ele-

ments informed the analysis in this case study. This flexible iterative model might be ideal for selecting and guiding service-learning technology projects (Wicox & Zigurs, 2004), instead of a rigid methodology that might prescribe solutions insensitive to the problems of nonprofit organizations. This methodology offers new ways to think about not only technology projects, but also service-learning overall.

Service-learning projects should allow university students to collaborate with clients of collaborating organizations, particularly individuals with disabilities. Such partnerships can be instrumental in refuting unfair perceptions of such individuals (Erickson & O'Connor, 2000), which was evident in projects A and C described here. Collaboration with organization staff also is instrumental in mutual problem resolution (Riley & Wofford, 2000). The integration of individuals with disabilities and organization staff into student teams ensures positive outcomes of the partnership, the responsive service, and the technology, which was especially evident in projects A and C. This process furnishes a meaningful model to demonstrate that people and service (Wade, 1997), are more important than the output of technology.

Technology projects offer a service-learning solution that entices media savvy Net Generation students with engaging and cutting edge learning opportunities. Projects involving mobile speech synthesis systems, multimedia technology and social media networking technology, and other Net neutral open source tools, enabled if not excited interest and ownership in the mix of information systems students and non-information systems students (Toncar, Reid & Anderson, 2004). The students favored mobile messaging tools (MMT) for asynchronous interfacing with project staff, which was evident in the organization A technology projects. Table 6 shows sample reflections on service-learning technology projects posted in the university Blackboard Learning and Community Portal System by students in my courses (Basinger & Bartholomew, 2006).

*Table 6. Sample reflections on courses, nonprofit organizations and technology projects at the Seidenberg School of Computer Science and Information Systems of Pace University*

| Reflections | Students |
|---|---|
| *"The course had an effect on me through the project[s] … I would not have known of [nonprofit organization A] … I feel that the portal [systems] will be important for the organization."* | A.M. (Sophomore Student in Community Empowerment through Information Systems and Technology, Fall 2007 Semester) |
| *"I learned about technology in a [manner] that I would not have learned about in my other [liberal arts] courses … I would like to learn of other [service-learning] courses like [these] project[s] where I would learn more technology … because I love to help others, and [technology] seems a very good way to do it."* | M.O. (Freshman Student in Community Empowerment through Information Systems and Technology, Fall 2007 Semester) |
| *"I was hesitant about the project[s] because I was informed that it would be too technical, but it was not … I will be thinking about taking other courses [of service-learning] that are technical … I would love to do something similar to this, [and I would] volunteer my time."* | L.S. (Freshman Student in Community Empowerment through Information Systems and Technology, Spring Semester 2008) |
| *"It was great to see how pleased [the individuals with disabilities] were with the [systems] that we [developed] for them … they were really impressed by what we [did] for them … Knowing I helped them is an experience I will never forget."* | D.S. (Senior Student in Community Empowerment through Information Systems and Technology, Spring Semester 2008) |
| *"I refined my project management skills on the [systems] … Response is we did highly functioning and friendly [systems] that will simplify [the organization staff] tasks … we did a rewarding thing with 21st century technology … thankful that I was on a great team."* | M.S. (Junior Student in Community Empowerment through Information Systems and Technology, Fall Semester 2009) |

Moreover, the instructor learned to be a mentor, rather than a "sage on the stage" (Mill, 2004), as the students learned about organization problems and the challenges and potential of technology. This learning gave all of us pride in the potential societal value of 21st century technology.

Finally, the relationship-based approach to service-learning I have outlined here offers a powerful model for partnerships between nonprofit organizations and schools of computer science and information systems on technology projects. Long-term relationships between these entities are a major goal of service-learning, as indicated in the literature. Institutionalization of service-learning in schools of computer science and information systems is a requirement (Chadwick & Pawlowski, 2007), as integration of service-learning technology projects is a requirement in nonprofit organizations, in order to migrate to a relationship of transformation (Enos & Morton, 2003). Projects need to be strategic to nonprofit organizations so that they are perceived by the organizations to be of value. This was evident and key in the case of

organization A described here. The relationship strategy of organization A and SSCSIS suggests the value of pursuing long-term relationships with medium-sized if not large-sized nonprofit organizations. These long-term relationship strategies furnish stronger and sustained value.

## FUTURE RESEARCH DIRECTIONS

The findings of this chapter on digital technology service-learning projects led by one instructor at one school of computer science and information systems at one institution may not be empirically generalizable to other institutions of higher education. However, given the experiences of SSCSIS in pioneering service-learning since 2003, the recommendations and solutions offered here may be cautiously extendable to other universities. Literature on nonprofit organization partnerships in service-learning is favorable to the solutions used by Pace University (Gurjathi & McQuade, 2002). Moreover, the promise associated with these technology solutions may be the future of service-learning in universities. Inasmuch as the solutions and recommendations benefited the organizations, school, and university involved in these projects, I am initiating research on this tool's use with other universities in order to improve the generalizability of the model.

Service-learning continues to grow in importance to institutions of higher education. The mission of Pace University includes publicized service-learning statements that inform nonprofit organizations of university outreach goals. Nonprofit organizations interact with the Center for Community Action and Research, in the Dyson College of the university, which serves as a liaison to SSCSIS and other schools of the university, to determine which technology-based and other projects might yield fruitful collaborations. The center also funds innovative technology-based projects for faculty through a relationship with the Eugene M. Lang Foundation (Barefoot, 2008). Institutionalized outreach departments are instrumental in integrating service-learning throughout universities (Prentice, 2004). They are connecting more and more with other organizations serving society, as was evident when the Center for Community Action and Research engaged Pace University students and faculty in international service projects supporting Haiti in 2010 and Indonesia in 2004. The positive relationship between Centers for Community Action and Research and schools, including schools of computer science and information systems, is indicative of a prevalent trend.

Partnerships between nonprofit organizations and schools of computer science and information systems, as practiced by SSCSIS, reveal a powerful relationship trend. The school is now piloting programs in which clients of some of the partner organizations in this study join matriculating Pace students in regularly scheduled technology training sessions and self-improvement workshops, socializing with the students as though they were classmates at the university. The school is further pioneering programs in which organization staff join Pace students in productivity training workshops. These programs are funded jointly by the nonprofit organizations and the university. Other programs include luncheons, open houses and summits on technology at the university geared toward nonprofit organizations. These events have been so successful that nonprofit organizations throughout New York City frequently inquire about creating partnerships with the university. This pattern of relationships is not a simple transactional trend but a substantial transformational one.

## CONCLUSION

The case study in this chapter analyzed critical success factors of technology-based service-learning projects included in courses at SSCSIS. Factors of collaboration, pedagogy, project management, strategy and technology, and inter-related subfactors, were demonstrated to be foundational to enabling successful implementation of the projects. Commitment to collaboration by both the leaders of the nonprofit organizations and the staff of SSCSIS was critical to the partnerships. Flexibility of pedagogy and project approach was important in maximization of opportunities to pursue powerful technology solutions, and strategy was important for the incremental pursuit of technology solutions in subsequent semesters of study. The chapter furnished a framework for ensuring long-term partnerships between nonprofit organizations and schools of computer science and information systems on technology solutions.

The engagement of individuals with disabilities or disadvantages in the bulk of the projects of the courses in the case study distinguished the ideal partnership. The integration of people – individuals with disabilities or disadvantages, managerial and organization staff and students – is critical to ensuring positive outcomes of the service and of the outputs of the technology. The processes of service-learning were more important than the technology solutions. In reflections on the services and on the solutions of technology, the students were proud of the societal utility of the technology. Through technology, they were rewarded with the satisfaction of serving those less fortunate than themselves – a satisfaction that they would not have had in any other courses at the university.

## REFERENCES

Barefoot, B. O. (2008). Institutional structures and strategies for embedding civic engagement in the first college year. In M. J. LaBare (Ed.), *First-year civic engagement: Sound foundations for college, citizenship and democracy* (p. 23). New York, NY: The New York Times.

Basinger, N., & Bartholomew, K. (2006). Service-learning in nonprofit organizations: Motivations, expectations, and outcomes. *Michigan Journal of Community Service Learning, 12*(2), 15–26.

Beck, K. (2000). *Extreme programming explained: Embrace change.* Reading, MA: Addison Wesley Longman.

Benson, L., & Harkavy, I. (2000). Higher education's third revolution: The emergence of the democratic cosmopolitan civic university. *Cityscape: A Journal of Policy Development Research, 5*(1), 47-57.

Boehm, B. (1986). A spiral model of software development and enhancement. *IEEE Computer, 21*(5), 61–72.

Chadwick, S. A., & Pawlowski, D. R. (2007). Assessing institutional support for service-learning: A case study of organizational sense-making. *Michigan Journal of Community Service Learning, 33.*

Citurs, A. (2009). An integrative pre-capstone course approach to service-learning - creating a win, win, win information systems – liberal arts. In D. Colton (Ed.), *Proceedings of the Information Systems Education Conference* (p. 43-54). Washington, DC: Educators Special Interest Group (EDSIG).

Coppola, J. F., Daniels, C., Gannon, S.-F., Hale, N.-L., Hayes, D., & Kline, R., & Pennachio, L. (2008). Civic engagement through computing technology. In M. J. LaBare (Ed.), *First-year civic engagement: Sound foundations for college, citizenship and democracy* (pp. 76-78). New York, NY: The New York Times.

Creighton, S. (2007). Significant findings in campus-community engagement: Community partner perspective. *The Journal for Civic Commitment, 10,* 4.

Daynes, G., & Longo, N. (2004). Jane Addams and the origins of service-learning practice in the United States. *Michigan Journal of Community Service Learning, 10*(3), 5–13.

Draper, A. J. (2004). Integrating project-based service-learning into an advanced environmental chemistry course. *Journal of Chemical Education, 81*(2), 221–224. doi:10.1021/ed081p221

Dunlap, J. C. (2006). Using guided reflective journaling activities to capture students' changing perceptions. *TechTrends, 50*(6), 26. doi:10.1007/s11528-006-7614-x

Ehrlich, T. (2000). *Civic responsibility and higher education.* Phoenix, AZ: Oryx Press.

Enos, S., & Morton, K. (2003). Developing a theory and practice of campus-community partnerships. In B. Jacoby (Ed.), *Building partnerships for service-learning* (pp. 20–41). San Francisco, CA: Jossey-Bass.

Erickson, J. A., & O'Connor, S. E. (2000). Service-learning: Does it promote or reduce prejudice? In C. O'Grady (Ed.), *Integrating service-learning and multicultural education in colleges and universities* (pp. 63, 65–66). Mahwah, NJ: Lawrence Erlbaum Associates.

Freire, P. (1985). *The politics of education* (p. 93). New York, NY: Bergin and Garvey.

Gurjathi, M. R., & McQuade, R. J. (2002). Service-learning in business schools: A case study in an intermediate accounting course. *Journal of Education for Business*, 144–150.

Hunter, S., & Brisbin, R. A. (2000). The impact of service-learning on democratic and civic values. *Political Science & Politics, 33*, 623–626. doi:10.2307/420868

Jacoby, B. (1996). *Service-learning in higher education: Concepts and practices.* San Francisco, CA: Jossey-Bass.

Kenworthy-U'Ren. A. L. (2000). Management students as consultants: A strategy of service-learning in management education, working for the common good. In P. Godfrey & E. Grasso (Eds.), *Concepts and models for service-learning in management* (pp. 55-68). American Association for Higher Education.

Kolb, D. A. (1984). *Experiential learning* (p. 110). Englewood Cliffs, NJ: Prentice Hall.

Lazar, J., & Norcio, A. (2000). Service-research: Community partnerships for research and training. *Journal of Informatics Education and Research, 2*(3), 21–25.

Liazos, A., & Liss, J. R. (2009). *Civic engagement in the classroom: Strategies for incorporating education for civic and social responsibility in the undergraduate curriculum.* A Project Pericles White Paper, August, 4.

McCallister, L. A. (2008) Lessons learned while developing a community-based learning initiative. *National Service-Learning Clearinghouse*, 10.

Mihalynuk, T. V., & Seifer, S. D. (2004). Partnerships for higher education service-learning. *Service-Learning*, September.

Mill, R. C. (2004). Integrating the student into the business curriculum. In R. Clute (Ed.), *Proceedings of the 2004 International Applied Business Research Conference* (p. 1). San Juan, PR: The Clute Institute for Academic Research.

Mitchell, T. D. (2008). Traditional vs. critical service-learning: Engaging the literature to differentiate two models. *Michigan Journal of Community Service Learning*, 51.

Petkus, J. (2000). A theoretical and practical framework for service-learning in marketing. *Journal of Marketing Education, 22*, 64–70. doi:10.1177/0273475300221008

Pompa, L. (2002). Service-learning as crucible: Reflections on immersion, context, power, and transformation. *Michigan Journal of Community Service Learning, 9*(1), 67–76.

Prentice, M. (2004). Twenty-first century learning: How institutionalized is service-learning? *The Journal for Civic Commitment, 4*, 1, 2, 5.

Riley, R. W., & Wofford, H. (2000). The reaffirmation of the declaration of principles. *Phi Delta Kappan, 81*(9), 670–672.

Sandy, M., & Holland, B. A. (2006). Different worlds and common ground: Community partner perspectives on campus-community partnerships. *Michigan Journal of Community Service Learning*, 39.

Saulnier, B. M. (2004). Service-learning in Information Systems: Significant learning for tomorrow's computer professionals. In D. Colton (Ed.), *Proceedings of the Information Systems Education Conference* (p. 2255). Newport, RI: Educators Special Interest Group (EDSIG).

Toncar, M., Reid, J., & Anderson, C. (2004). Student perceptions of service-learning projects: Exploring the impact of project ownership, project difficulty and class difficulty. In R. Clute (Ed.), *Proceedings of the 2004 International Applied Business Research Conference* (pp. 2-8). San Juan, PR: The Clute Institute for Academic Research.

Tryon, E., Stoecker, R., Martin, A., Seblonka, K., Hilgendorf, A., & Nellis, M. (2008). The challenge of short-term service-learning. *Michigan Journal of Community Service Learning*, 20.

Wade, R. C. (1997). *Community service-learning: A guide to including service in the public school curriculum* (p. 64). Albany, NY: State University of New York Press.

Waxer, C. (2008). Techies volunteering to save the world: How to enhance your high-tech career with new skills – and meaning. *Computerworld*, December 17, 1.

Wei, K., Siow, J., & Burley, D. L. (2007). Implementing service-learning to the Information Systems and technology management program: A study of an undergraduate capstone course. *Journal of Information Systems Education, 18*(1), 125–126.

Wilcox, E., & Zigurs, I. (2004). A method for enhancing the success of service-learning projects in Information Systems curricula. In D. Colton (Ed.), *Proceedings of the Information Systems Education Conference* (p. 3431). San Diego, CA: Educators Special Interest Group (EDSIG).

## KEY TERMS AND DEFINITIONS

**Agile Methodology:** A process for incremental and iterative implementation of service-learning technology solutions.

**Assistive Communication Devices:** Hand-held mobile technology that empowers disabled individuals in dialogue and interaction in the community and in society.

**Civic Engagement:** A form of community service that empowers or enables a difference in the civic life of disadvantaged individuals of a community and improves the quality of life in the community.

**Critical Success Factors:** A process for evaluating collaboration, pedagogy, project management, strategy and technology in the implementation of service-learning solutions of technology.

**Nonprofit Organization:** An organization that helps disadvantaged individuals in the community in potential partnership with schools of computer science and information systems that might implement service-learning technology solutions.

**Person-Centered Planning:** A process for inclusion of disadvantaged individuals of a community in the preparation of personal resumes through multimedia and social media networking technology.

**Service-Learning:** A form of experiential learning in which courses in the curricula of computer science and information systems are enhanced by community service that engages students in experiencing life at nonprofit organizations that help disadvantaged individuals of a community.

**Social Networking:** Interactive technology on the Internet that might engage disadvantaged individuals and staff of nonprofit organizations.

# Chapter 11
# "How Do We Know What They Need?"
## An Analysis of How ConnectRichmond Changed Service-Learning at the University of Richmond

**Theresa Dolson**
*University of Richmond, USA*

## ABSTRACT

*The University of Richmond, a mid-size liberal arts institution, had a longstanding institutional commitment to civic engagement. Campus location and curricular issues once made the popular model of service-learning, direct service to fellow citizens in need, too restrictive, and not a good fit for many of the university's courses. Campus leaders wanted to create community partnerships that would accommodate the wide range of pedagogical needs on campus, connect to every discipline, and still maintain healthy and sustainable partnerships in the community. This case study describes their collaboration with community leaders to launch ConnectRichmond, a network hub with many Web 2.0 features. This innovation has created a large online community that facilitates a variety of course models and has helped to support the development of a major program for community-based learning. ConnectRichmond allows UR to move beyond talking about meeting community needs to working in true reciprocity with fellow Richmonders.*

DOI: 10.4018/978-1-60960-623-7.ch011

## INTRODUCTION

*"When public intellectuals not only reach outside the university, but actually interact with the public beyond its walls, they overcome the ivory tower isolation that marks so much current intellectual work. They create knowledge with those whom the knowledge serves." (Cushman, 1999)*

While an essential element of service-learning as it is generally understood in the U.S. is that the work done by students should respond to a community-identified need, often "finding the right fit between student, agency and institution is like a huge, 3-D jigsaw puzzle. When it works, luck is as important as planning" (Stoeker and Tryon, 2009). This case study describes how the creation of a network hub helped streamline the process of identifying opportunities for community-university collaboration.

At the University of Richmond (UR), the path to learning about those community-identified needs was not obvious before the year 2000. In some ways our campus embodied the proverbial ivory tower Ellen Cushman describes in the epigraph above. As a residential, suburban campus, UR is physically separated from much of metropolitan Richmond, Virginia, and surrounded instead by affluent suburbs where needs are not always apparent. Cushman (1999) envisions academics as "public intellectuals" who "combine their research, teaching and service efforts in order to address social issues important to community members in under-served neighborhoods" (329). If geography is destiny, then our faculty and students seemed destined to be removed from many of the city's under-served communities. At the primarily undergraduate, liberal arts university, the work of most faculty did not have obvious service-learning implications, at least as service-learning is popularly conceived in the U.S., as direct service by university students on behalf of citizens in their communities. Prior to the launch of the project

described in this case study, only a few classes at UR included this model of service-learning. Two programs at UR, The Jepson School of Leadership Studies and the Bonner Scholars program, provided the impetus for the university to seek broader community connections.

In 2000, several faculty members who recognized this campus-community disconnection sponsored a meeting with leaders of about 50 local nonprofit agencies to learn more about their needs and to facilitate communication among them and campus offices. During that meeting, the nonprofits expressed a need for a tool to facilitate local communication. These nonprofit agencies identified the "fragmentation" of resources and communication among nonprofits, public agencies, and citizens as a problem for groups working to address community needs in the Greater Richmond area (Stutts, 2003). Faculty members Nancy Stutts, then a professor in the Jepson School, and Richard Couto, a UR professor and a designer of the Jepson School curriculum, worked with UR technology staff to create a simple e-mail listserv and Web site. By November of 2002, the ConnectRichmond site was on the Web, providing a repository for materials useful to nonprofit organizations and a link to join the listserv. The concept succeeded. Stutts, now at Virginia Commonwealth University, heads ConnectNetwork which is funded by The Community Foundation Serving Richmond and Central Virginia and the John S. and James L. Knight Foundation, and includes ConnectRichmond, ConnectRappahannock and ConnectSouthside.

ConnectRichmond was created as a network hub and a resource "designed for citizens who want to strengthen our community. We provide information, resources and instant access to nonprofits, civic leaders, volunteers and others interested in improving metro Richmond - the rest is up to you" (ConnectRichmond, 2007). Many citizens have answered the call to engage through this network hub. As of January 2010, the site's main listserv reached 4,000 e-mail addresses. As of that date, more than 1,400 member organizations were registered at the site, where they post opportunities for volunteers, note events on a common calendar, access data and reports, join and post to issue-specific e-mail lists, and find out about social networking opportunities. ConnectRichmond provided the online "infrastructure" to address the fragmentation of resources that had kept these groups from connecting for the greater good (Stutts, 2003).

Another program at UR had a mission that tied it to the Richmond community: the Bonner Scholars program, which linked scholarship money to community service. The Bonner Center for Civic Engagement (CCE) was established at UR in 2004 to support civic engagement efforts at the university, including the Bonner Scholars program. The center created sustained partnerships through a place-based initiative in the Highland Park neighborhood of Richmond, and an issue-based program, the Richmond Families Initiative. Both of these programs helped the Jepson School and the Bonner Scholars to place students with community partners where deep relationships formed and the student work could respond to needs identified by the community. But there was a large gap: the CCE is an academic unit, reporting to the provost. We were ready to help faculty to connect their courses to community needs, as long as their courses fit with the needs of one of our dedicated partners. The community partnerships were growing, but partners were connecting to only a few classes. Faculty were the missing link.

A turning point came when Dr. Amy Howard of the CCE made the connection between ConnectRichmond and faculty interests. A UR business professor, Dr. Lewis A. "Andy" Litteral, was attending a speaker series sponsored by the CCE and asked where he might find real data to use in teaching his business statistics class. This query provided a new venue for engaging UR faculty. Howard suggested local nonprofits might like to have some help with data, and she knew that many nonprofits subscribed to ConnectRichmond.

Together she and Litteral posted an e-mail to ConnectRichmond's listserv, and the response was sufficient to provide the projects needed for Litteral's class. Litteral has continued to develop projects in the local community every semester since then via ConnectRichmond's listserv. His students' work has now benefitted over 50 different area groups. Assessment indicates that students learn statistics, but also learn that in the real world, data is messy and incomplete. They also meet members of the community they would not have otherwise met, and they learn about the ways in which a variety of organizations work to make the community stronger. Some students develop an interest in careers in the nonprofit sector or develop a passion for an issue that a nonprofit addresses, and the exposure to statistical data on the issue gives them new perspective.

This project-based model of civic engagement is different from the more common model of service-learning in which students give direct service for a certain number of hours per week or throughout the semester, that our campus started with, and yet it fulfills the goals of connecting learning to the real world while filling a community need. The Bonner Center for Civic Engagement made a conscious decision to support all kinds of community-based learning, and developed a list of strategies or "modes" of community-based learning. Our community-based learning model accomplishes the same academic and community goals, but through a broader range of course types. The definition, posted on our program website, invites professors from any discipline to see a way that their own course could connect to the community:

Classes that connect students to the Greater Richmond community and beyond for meaningful experiential learning opportunities tied to course content are considered community-based learning classes. Community-based learning integrates theoretical texts and principles with practical experience. Community-based learning can take a variety of forms that help students and faculty meet a course's learning objectives, including:

- Service-learning (mentoring, tutoring, interpreting, etc.)
- Performing data analysis, research, or organizational studies for partner agencies
- Bringing community leaders into the classroom
- Participant observation & "shadowing"
- Teaching course material in schools
- Producing documentaries and performances about or for the community
- Study or service trips
- Clinical education

ConnectRichmond helps instructors find opportunities in all of these categories. As the manager of the community-based learning program, I work with faculty to identify the learning goals of the course, and we discuss what experiential learning might add to the class. Discussions center on two primary questions: 1) What skills are students learning that they might practice for the benefit of the community? 2) What assumptions do students hold about the course content that might be effectively upended by contact with reality? We brainstorm ideas, but we often can't get beyond basics until we look at ConnectRichmond. Sometimes the faculty and I will join a specialized "affinity e-mail list" to learn more about what is going on in our community with respect to a specific issue or population. For instance, to look for opportunities for a biochemistry class I joined the "Health Issues" list. I also search the site and encourage faculty to explore the list of nonprofits and issue areas. If faculty are leaning toward a service-learning model, we look first to our sustained program partners, but if there isn't a good match there, we look to ConnectRichmond to find other volunteer opportunities in the area that would be a better match for their course goals.

Some might question the quality and sustainability of partnerships formed through a "virtual community." When I first became manager of the community-based learning program, I wanted to work only with our sustained program partners. It quickly became apparent, however, that sometimes the course content or the kinds of projects to be accomplished were not good matches with the partners in those programs. Community-based learning (CBL) is first and foremost an academic endeavor, and the success of the course depends on how well the projects and partners fit with the course goals, so we never try to coerce a professor to work with a particular community partner. ConnectRichmond allows us to open up to more of the greater Richmond community.

We also have found that ConnectRichmond provides a vehicle for bringing community leaders into UR classrooms. Community leaders are happy to have the opportunity to share their knowledge with UR students, and, in turn, students' interests can be piqued so that they begin working with the organizations on their own. Members of the Richmond community have expressed to us that they love the opportunity to speak to classes or participate in panel discussions. Research confirms that community partners have a deeper interest in the educational mission of CBL than we might expect (Sandy & Holland, 2006). Inviting a speaker has proven to be an easy way for a faculty member to begin a relationship with a person and their organization that can develop in later semesters into other kinds of CBL.

Even a project that gets students out to sites in the community only a couple of times can have far-reaching effects. An example from Litteral's statistics class is a student who worked on a data project for a nonprofit that dealt with housing problems for the elderly. The student subsequently resurrected the campus Habitat for Humanity chapter, and in spring of 2010, the UR Habitat chapter partnered with the CCE and Habitat for Humanity to build a house in the Highland Park neighborhood. The many strands of our commitment to civic engagement seem separate, but they come together to create a rich fabric of involvement bonding the university to the surrounding metro area.

Organizations also appreciate that, through the calls we put on ConnectRichmond listservs, they know more about what is going on at UR, and how they can plug in and even benefit. And they appreciate that it is their choice; they frequently initiate the contact and propose the specific project they have in mind that fits the call for proposals. As Sandy and Holland (2006) discovered in a recent study of community partner perspectives on service-learning, one important trait they desired in a partnership was "flexibility and the ability to say 'no'" (34). When an organization responds to a listserv announcement or RFP, the professor and the community organization become partners in a reciprocal relationship, shaping a project that will meet both the learning goals of the class and the needs of the community.

When we enter into this virtual community as one of many members, we have a wider reach and we gain greater insight into our community. We operate as one organization among many who care about the Greater Richmond community, and that makes it easier for others to see us as partners rather than isolated or arrogant academics. At the same time, this interface opens up new ways for faculty to learn about community needs, foster new relationships, and imagine new ways for students to learn and for faculty to teach. We have gone beyond "luck," beyond locating a community need that we can fill, to mutual and reciprocal relationships where everyone gives and everyone receives.

I believe that the success of ConnectRichmond is not that it uses the latest tools, but that it uses the simplest, best tools for the purposes at hand. Because it is free for citizens and organizations to use, it allows for the parts of the community

with greatest need to participate; the site levels the playing field for many. Our experiences with ConnectRichmond members are changing our models for how to participate in our community and improve student learning through experiential opportunities.

## REFERENCES

ConnectRichmond. (2007). *What we do*. Retrieved on Nov. 4, 2010, from http://www.connectrichmond.org/About/WhatWeDo/tabid/393/Default.aspx

Cushman, E. (1999). The public intellectual, service learning, and activist research. *College English, 61*(3), 328–336..doi:10.2307/379072

Cushman, E. (2002). Sustainable service learning programs. *College Composition and Communication, 54*(1), 40-65. doi:10.2307/

Sandy, M., & Holland, B. A. (2006). Different worlds and common ground: Community partner perspectives on campus-community partnerships. *Michigan Journal of Community Service Learning, 13*(1), 30–43.

Smartt, R. (2007). *ConnectRichmond*. Retrieved from http://www.connectrichmond.org/

Stoeker, R., & Tryon, E. A. (Eds.). (2009). *The unheard voices: Community organizations and service learning*. Philadelphia, PA: Temple University Press.

Stutts, N. (2003). ConnectRichmond: Collecting and sharing information to build a stronger community. *Community Technology Review*, Spring 2003. Retrieved on Nov. 9, 2010, from http://www.comtechreview.org/spring-2003/000038.html.

# Chapter 12
# Service–Learning, Technology, Nonprofits, and Institutional Limitations

**Katherine Loving**
*University of Wisconsin-Madison, USA*

**Randy Stoecker**
*University of Wisconsin-Madison, USA*

**Molly Reddy**
*University of Wisconsin-Madison, USA*

## ABSTRACT

*This chapter develops a model of service-learning that focuses on serving the information and communication technology (ICT) needs of community organizations, and contrasts it with the traditional service-learning model used in universities, questioning if it is a more effective way of meeting nonprofits' ICT needs. The authors evaluate their model's utility from the perspective of a technology empowerment "stepstool" where nonprofit organizations can move from simply using existing technology better, to shaping the technology, to creating their own technology. The chapter then goes on to discuss attempts to implement versions of this model at the University of Wisconsin, discussing their strengths and weaknesses, and paying particular attention to the limitations of doing this work within an institutional framework. The current service-learning project has found working on social media projects to be more beneficial to the students and the nonprofits than more complex projects, but doing so goes against the community-identified need and request for more mission-critical assistance. To fully serve communities, the higher education context of service learning must change to make community outcomes the main priority, build courses around community projects rather than vice versa, provide students with the necessary professional skills preparation to do high quality service-learning, and design community projects around the community calendar, not the higher education calendar.*

DOI: 10.4018/978-1-60960-623-7.ch012

## INTRODUCTION: NONPROFITS AND THE INFORMATION/ COMMUNICATION GAP

Among the challenges facing the small to medium size nonprofit organization is the challenge of managing information. Groups providing services to individuals and families face the problem of managing all those files. The groups mobilizing volunteers must continually recruit and schedule those volunteers. The groups engaging in advocacy require in-depth research and the ability to get the word out to supporters. All groups must respond to the reporting requirements of their funders, of various government agencies, and of auditors. This involves collecting information that is often of little use in furthering the organization's mission, but must be done to avoid risking the organization's survival (Stoecker, 2007).

Given that the small to medium size nonprofit may have few or no staff, such information and communication challenges can be daunting. Many of these organizations lack staff trained in managing information (Stoecker, 2007). Technology skills can, of course, help to meet these challenges, but small and medium size nonprofits also wind up on the short end of the digital divide (Cravens, 2006; Kanayama, 2003). There is still no shortage of small nonprofits whose staff squint at 15-inch CRT monitors, or suffer the finger-drumming frustration of waiting for a Web page to load over a dial-up connection, particularly in rural areas (Stenberg et al., 2009).

Now, to make things even more challenging, from all corners comes the call for nonprofits to get on the Internet—to raise money, recruit volunteers, get the word out, and make themselves look beautiful. The good old days (which, in Internet time, means a few years ago) of simply putting up a Web page for your organization have been supplanted by the new focus on *Web 2.0* or *social media* applications. With its conceptual origins attributed to a conference in 2004, this new focus emphasizes the importance of Internet-based social interaction, collective information development, and end user-participation (O'Reilly, 2005). There are legions of Web sites purporting to advise the poor nonprofit on the best online fundraising strategy, the best software, and especially the best way to use the new social media applications like Facebook, YouTube, Twitter, and others (Ukura, 2010).

So the smaller nonprofit is in a bind in this newest brave new world of information and communication technologies, or ICTs. It must not only do its work on the ground, but also develop the capacity to operate in cyberspace to support its work—without skilled staff or the time to sift through the burgeoning array of online choices.

## SERVICE-LEARNING, NONPROFITS, AND ICTS

Here is where higher education community engagement comes in. As ICTs have become a focus of service-learning, new terms have arisen. One term that has recently emerged is *service-eLearning*. Its promoters put the "e" before the learning rather than before the service because they emphasize the role of ICTs in pedagogy rather than in the actual service projects, though in fact ICTs also show up in the service activities themselves (Dailey-Hebert, Donnelli, & DiPadova-Stocks, 2008). Another term is *e-service-learning*. While one might expect the placement of this e to signify an emphasis on ICTs in the actual service, this term seems just as likely to emphasize the use of ICTs as pedagogy (Malvey, Hamby, & Fottler, 2006; Strait & Sauer, 2004). Overall, this method includes students engaging in distance service-learning—designing a Web site for a far-away organization (Bjork & Schwartz, 2005) or using ICTs to facilitate a local service-learning project (Stoecker, Hilgendorf, & Tryon, 2008), and sometimes it is a combination of all those things, as we will describe.

Whichever term one uses, when the focus is on ICTs as the community issue rather than the pedagogy, the practice is new in a few important ways. First, it draws more from a project-based service-learning model (Chamberlain, 2003; Draper 2004), than traditional service-learning. Much service-learning sends students into the community to volunteer for a certain number of hours, but for no particular purpose (Stoecker & Tryon, 2009). Project-based service-learning has the advantage of focusing the students' involvement on creating an actual product. It also focuses on projects that require a fairly high knowledge and skill base to produce useful outcomes, compared to traditional service-learning.

These benefits come with their own costs, however. Because of the skill involved in developing and deploying an online strategy, the skill gap between the student who builds the Web site or constructs the database-driven e-mail list, and the nonprofit staff who use it, could be quite wide. In such circumstances ICT-focused service-learning has the same weakness as all service-learning—that it is an unsustainable model that may be serving the students more than the community (Stoecker & Tryon, 2009).

Service-learning's image has been showing signs of tarnishing recently as multiple studies have documented significant community concerns with how projects are designed and carried out. The absence of direct faculty communication with community groups in designing and monitoring service-learning, the lack of preparation of students, the short duration of most commitments, and other problems have shown service-learning often gets redefined in practice as community organizations serving the educational needs of students (Blouin & Perry, 2009; Sandy & Holland, 2006; Stoecker & Tryon, 2009).

Such problems, coupled with complex ICT projects, risk the possibility of students creating complex systems, and then leaving the organization without knowledge of how to maintain them. An organization that can't update or modify its own Web site or repair its own database is worse-off than when it started. This can be even more problematic than the average service-learning project, where the service has little visible impact to begin with and thus little risk of producing a negative public image.

## TOWARD A MODEL OF HIGH-IMPACT ICT-FOCUSED SERVICE-LEARNING

How do we ensure that service-learning will produce the best possible outcomes in the community, particularly when the focus of the service-learning is on ICTs? Technology, like many of the things that make up the infrastructure of our world, can be analyzed according to a ladder, or perhaps stepstool, of control. On the lowest rung of the stepstool is ability of an end-user to put technology into practice. Being able to use a piece of software provides one with some control over daily work that didn't occur before. But that control may be mythical, because the use of the software also occurs in a social context. The story goes that, before the mass production of the wringer washer, women washed clothing much less frequently because the task was so much more labor intensive. But, as washing clothes became easier, there was pressure to wash more clothes more often. Thus, women's work was actually made harder rather than easier by technology (Lupton, 1993). This can also be the case with computer technology. The errant paragraph that would have taken a couple of hours of extra typing to delete in the typewriter era can now be deleted in a keystroke, but the pressure to revise and revise can also increase with word processing software. The software itself sets the expectations for people's productivity. Such is the case with the pressures on nonprofits to use social media, where there is concern that all the time invested in setting up Facebook pages, Twitter accounts, and the like may not be producing the return hoped for (LaCasse, Quinn, & Bernard,

2010). So simply being a skilled end-user offers very little real power or control.

The next rung up on the stepstool of control is the ability to not just use technology but to shape it. Being able to adjust and repair the wringer washer means that you can limit down-time and cost when it breaks, and you can make it work better and easier. Likewise, being able to code an original widget for your Web site, or write your own database structure, allows one to custom-design technology to better fit what the user wants. This is significantly more control. Anyone who has ever shelled out $75 an hour only to watch the repair person fix the problem by tightening a screw knows the feeling of powerlessness that comes with not understanding your own technology. Those organizations that can move from having a Facebook page to developing their own interactive site using a highly customizable content management system such as Drupal (Buytaert, 2010) are much less limited in their social media possibilities.

The top of the stepstool of control is the ability to build the tools to maintain the system. Anyone who has searched in vain for a specialty screwdriver to get through a small hole around a corner and into a tight space knows the problem. Likewise, with ICTs and social media, the programmer is on the top of the stepstool. Now, true, few of us aspire to be programmers. But to the extent to which we do not have such aspirations, we are giving up significant control over our ability to control our management of ICTs. The organization that has its own programmer can build custom-designed accounting software, membership databases, project tracking software, and all manner of other applications fitted to the organization rather than the reverse. In fact, one of the principles of Web 2.0 is that the end-user becomes a co-developer (O'Reilly, 2005).

It is clear that moving up the rungs brings with it increasing requirements of time and expertise on the part of both the nonprofit organization and the service-learning support. Helping an organiza-tion simply learn how to tweet requires a lot less than helping them write, from scratch, their own membership database software. While the former can be accomplished in a few hours at most with the assistance of the average teenager, the latter could require a few semesters of support from a team of computer science majors.

The question facing service-learning, then, is how far up the stepstool can it help nonprofits move? The further up they can move, the more sustainable the products will be that service-learning can produce. But are our universities and colleges equipped to provide upper-rung service-learning? Or are we limited to simply creating smarter end-users? If so, what would it take to move from lower-rung to higher-rung service-learning?

The odds are against us. Service-learning of any variety in higher education has grown from a training tool used by professional schools to a peda-gogy broadly applied in undergraduate education. The focus has always been on the education of the student (Stoecker & Tryon, 2009). In professional programs, community partners presumably have a stake in the provision of services by the student or educating the next generation of profession-als, or both. In undergraduate service-learning, however, that shared sense of mission may not characterize student placements. Organizations that serve as placement sites are not likely to have a relationship to the curriculum or the learning goals for the course, and often find themselves reacting to student requests for service-learning placements rather than requesting students to help meet organization needs. Service-learning's proliferation and popularity in the academy has allowed it to thrive in an environment uninformed by community interests and priorities. We adhere to traditional structures and constructs—16-week semesters and a positivist theory of knowledge, for example—that render us unable to recognize community expertise or address the complex and enduring social issues whose solutions demand sustained, interdisciplinary engagement. Service-learning driven by student learning needs forces community partners into an existing, inadequate structure, and if a relationship can be characterized as mutually beneficial, it's a happy accident.

The case study we will explore next shows the challenges involved in providing top-rung service-learning and the compromises that necessarily result. Our recent attempts to develop service-learning programs at the University of Wisconsin-Madison illustrate how, despite being rich in ICT resources, our educational philosophies, structures and traditions prevent us from mobilizing our assets to address the significant ICT needs of nonprofit organizations.

## A CASE STUDY OF ICT-FOCUSED SERVICE-LEARNING

### 1. The ePICS Program

The problematic structure and culture of service-learning prevailed at the University of Wisconsin-Madison in 2003, when an Engineering professor adapted the EPICS model from Purdue University and created the e-Projects in Community Service (ePICS) course. Interdisciplinary teams of 8-10 students worked with nonprofit organizations to provide business and information technology solutions in areas such as marketing, communications, Web design and programming. The elective course offered sought-after "real world" experiences and applied problem-solving opportunities that were tremendously popular with students across campus. The ePICS philosophy favored the student learning experience over organizational capacity building and, as such, required nonprofit partners to fit their projects and participation into the unique course design. For example, in order to facilitate interdisciplinary learning and collaboration among students, nonprofit partners had to offer a set of integrated business and technology projects that would engage the entire team yet could be accomplished in one semester.

Community organizations were eager for the services provided, and in later semesters, applications from nonprofit organizations exceeded course capacity by at least half. Students and nonprofits alike were seduced by the array of slick new products an ePICS team could produce in a semester, like sophisticated applications for PDAs, glossy brochures, bold branding graphics, and attention-getting e-newsletters. Indeed, some of the projects were well-executed, providing organizations with capacity-building knowledge and materials. Other projects, however, left nonprofit partners with clever, yet highly complex, solutions that solved the presenting problems but created new challenges as nonprofit staff struggled to use and manage them, like the attractive new Web site with a fatal security flaw that left it vulnerable to attack.

The student-focused ePICS model could not overcome two important elements that, at times, interfered with successful community outcomes: nonprofit partners lacked information on how to move from goals to tools, and students, rather than trying to help their partners up the stepstool, raced to identify a solution and implement it. As we would find, this was less a program flaw than it was evidence of a deep digital divide and an educational system producing students ill-prepared to apply their knowledge in the real world. The student who selects a technology based not on its appropriateness for the task, but on his or her familiarity with it, demonstrates a low tolerance for the complexity and ambiguity of real-world problem solving, as well as the strong bias of his or her educational training toward product over process. In the world of ICT consulting, that is a fatally-flawed approach.

### 2. The Transition from ePICS

When the lead professor retired, the ePICS course ended, finding no institutional department willing to take on responsibility for a broadly interdisciplinary course populated primarily by non-majors.

The lack of a departmental home and the stability and credibility that come with it would also plague the subsequent course that was developed post-ePICS in an attempt to meet community needs for ICT services. Even worse, while ePICS was able to offer credits in several departments, the next incarnation of service-learning would not even have a course "on the books" and resorted to awarding directed study credits to participating students.

Professor Randy Stoecker agreed to take on some of the ePICS students who had already registered for the next semester when the course was cancelled. Eric Howland, former ePICS collaborator and executive director of DANEnet, a local nonprofit organization serving the information technology needs of other nonprofits in the county, joined Stoecker in a pilot project designed to have students conduct ICT assessments for nonprofit organizations. One of the challenges of the ePICS model was that it underestimated the importance of assessing the organization's ICT goals. Student teams, and sometimes even their nonprofit partners, then rushed to tool selection and implementation in order to produce deliverables by the end of the semester. In this pilot course, the emphasis was on doing a careful assessment of the organization's ICT resources and needs in order to develop goals that fit organizational priorities and existing resources. This focus had the opposite problem of ePICS. While the participating students had the skills to conduct and write up the assessments, they did not have the technical knowledge or time in the semester to provide the ICT interventions they recommended to their nonprofit partner organizations. As a result of the course, the ICT needs in nonprofit organizations were even better documented, and the emphasis on process over product was established. Yet, the question of how to deliver the information technology services so desperately needed by nonprofit organizations using the extensive resources available through the university, including students, remained.

Stoecker, Howland, and Katherine Loving, another ePICS collaborator and civic engagement coordinator at UW-Madison's University Health Services, remained committed to the question of how university resources could best be applied to meet the ICT needs of nonprofit organizations. With a grant from the Corporation for National and Community Service through Princeton University's National Community-Based Research Networking Initiative, we initiated a community-based research project to answer that question. At the time, we believed that if we had good research data, we could construct the most effective program possible.

The initial team of three assembled a group of campus and community representatives with a stake in the research. This collaborative steering committee designed a survey and sent it to 450 representatives of nonprofit organizations asking how they currently received ICT support and how they would ideally like to receive such support in the future.

With survey results from 65 organizations giving us basic information, we next wanted to know details about the concerns expressed in the survey and to identify the organizations most likely to participate with us in designing a more effective service-learning program. We organized a "flash seminar" (Stoecker, 2008) that attracted 15 students. The seminar's task was to conduct in-depth interviews with as many of the original 65 organizational representatives as were willing, and to study different models of providing ICT support to nonprofit organizations. The students ended up interviewing 30 nonprofits and studying two ICT support programs. They brought the results of their work to a half-day community event attended by many of the organization representatives interviewed for the research. One purpose of the event was to plan an outline for a new service-learning program to fill the organizations' identified ICT needs. The steering committee met subsequently to finalize program design, and

TechShop Madison, a student service-learning program, was born.

## 3. TechShop Madison

While the community-based research approach to designing the program ensured community support and buy-in, it did not garner institutional support from the university. No departments agreed to rearrange their curriculum to accommodate a new course responding to community needs. Individual faculty members are discouraged from embracing community-based scholarship; tenure and promotion guidelines do not reward community engagement. So, in order to run the course, Stoecker agreed to offer independent study credits through his department, even though the program involved all the work—and more—of a traditional course.

We also attempted to operate out of a science shop model, where student projects were determined by organization proposals. Prior to the start of the fall 2008 semester we sent a request for proposals to the organizations that had participated in the research, promising them a single student for 20 hours of service in one semester. What we received from them were second-rung, and one highly complex third-rung, proposals. The responding organizations were interested in new Web sites running off of content management systems (CMS), and the third-rung proposal was looking for a custom-designed database system. While in the end we had only four projects that semester, three of them were failures. In one case the student and organization built a sophisticated CMS-based Web site but had neglected to check with the nonprofit's national sponsor (who hosted the site), to see if they would support it. In another case the student created a database-driven site demanding maintenance far beyond the capability of the organization's skill level. And in the case of the third-rung custom-designed database system, there were simply too many problems within the

organization's existing server platform to make the new system work.

At the end of the first semester, it was clear that upper-rung projects building databases and designing Web sites were not realistic, despite being high-priority projects identified by the organizations themselves. The reemergence of the ePICS challenges—where students pursue their own learning over meeting organization needs, the semester schedule prevents the follow-through necessary for successful completion, and a lack of institutional support thwarts effective mentoring of students—demonstrated that even our new model could not overcome the institutional limitations. While these types of projects were high-need, high-impact improvements for the organizations, they confirmed for us the danger of students being allowed to apply their full range of technology power when organizational staff remained at a lower rung on the use-adapt-build stepstool. They also presented significant challenges to the student schedule and skill set. We expected approximately 40 hours of work from each student to earn one credit. TechShop students received approximately 20 hours of training and supervision and worked directly with their nonprofit partner for 20 hours during the semester. Essentially, the students were functioning as consultants, requiring a broad skill set that included communicating across difference, assessment, problem-solving, collaboration, negotiation, research, evaluation, applied practice and information technology. For such sophisticated projects, the traditional one-semester service-learning model proved inadequate.

Given that applied courses are not widely available at UW-Madison, and that the institution requires disciplinary specialization, twenty hours was hardly enough to train students with this broad skill set. But we couldn't adjust the allotment of time because at least twenty hours of direct service was required to complete most projects. Without adequate training and preparation, students required close supervision to ensure that organizational goals were adequately articulated and understood, that appropriate tools had been researched and evaluated, and that nonprofit partners were engaged in learning to implement and manage the chosen technologies. A two-semester model would allow for more extensive training as well as time to engage more deeply with nonprofit partners. However, rigid curricular structures and student requirements are currently incompatible with a multi-semester model.

The next semester, when we sent out the request for proposals, again the most important expressed needs were Web sites and databases. But we were now reluctant to take on these projects. So we looked at the proposals more closely and noticed a number of nonprofit needs that could be addressed through the use of social media tools. Given the challenges we had faced with the more sophisticated ICT projects, including attracting students with adequate ICT training to a course outside their disciplinary requirements, the shift to social media tools, which have a unique demographic fit with a college-student population, was appealing. With the course unattached to a department that would provide academic content or credit in related majors, students with advanced technology skills had little incentive to enroll in the course. Selecting social media as our focus compensated for the program's marginalized status, which was preventing it from taking hold as an option for skilled technology students to apply their knowledge in community settings.

The confines of the semester that define traditional service-learning required more manageable projects appropriate for the generalist skill sets of our student participants and more realistic learning goals for our nonprofit partners. But this meant diverting students from the high-priority projects identified by nonprofits, like Web sites and databases. Nonprofits did not rank social media applications as their top ICT needs. However, since making the shift, we can point to a much higher project success rate. Nonprofits achieve their social media goals, and highly rate their ability to sustain their achievements.

In making this shift, we conceded that our institutional limitations prevented us from meeting the most pressing higher-rung ICT needs of our partners. This is particularly concerning because, as we've noted, it is unclear that social media tools can significantly increase the capacity of small to medium size nonprofit organizations.

## DISCUSSION

While we have found a way to focus service-learning on community-based needs, we have not found a way to deliver more than a tiny fraction of the available university resources required to get the job done. Programs like TechShop that evolve independently of the curriculum require extensive adaptation to be offered as a course. In order for students to get credit for the course, Stoecker provides independent study credits because the interdisciplinary, applied course content does not fit neatly within the curriculum of any department. Similarly, we face the challenge of providing course content and project skill training without being able to rely on some common foundational set of knowledge that students bring to the course.

As a result of functioning independently of typical departmental and curricular supports, TechShop is an extremely labor-intensive course to teach and supervise. Achieving desired community outcomes—TechShop's measure of success—requires an additional layer of monitoring that exceeds the usual student-generated outcome measurements like exams and the staple of service-learning—reflection essays. Our management team, which consists of Loving, Stoecker, Howland, a tech volunteer, and two student employees, spends approximately four hours coordinating the program for every service hour. That is partly because our emphasis is on making sure that the community organization's goals are met and that they can sustain the result after the student is gone from the scene.

Attention to the community impact of service-learning is uncommon, for reasons attributable to its origins as already described, but also because of a feature unique to UW-Madison that influences the lack of congruity between student learning and service-learning that truly benefits the community. The celebrated outreach mission of the university—the Wisconsin Idea—has its roots in early 20th century progressivism and sets forth a challenge to the university community to extend its knowledge beyond the boundaries of the university to benefit the entire state. This call for the university to have community impact is disconnected from the current fervor over student-centered service-learning. While the Wisconsin Idea's traditional, unidirectional approach to outreach is slowly evolving into an engaged, collaborative model, the motivation to serve the community has remained constant. Service-learning, however, as it has spread to the general undergraduate education, is applied as an instrument of student learning rather than a tool for supporting community change. Without the ethic of the Wisconsin Idea shaping the practice of service-learning, institutional inertia allows it to remain outside of the university's outreach enterprise.

So, we experience the institutional barriers that hamper service-learning's effectiveness for community groups at both micro and macro levels. The semester is too short, the curriculum too inflexible, and the resulting training and supervision requirements are too unmanageable. Tenure and promotion requirements are a disincentive to faculty involvement in the community, and traditional educational models interfere with student abilities to learn new ways to solve technology problems. Departments cannot justify accommodating interdisciplinary programming, and without an institutional ethic of equity in service-learning relationships, are not inclined to devote resources to applied programs that are community-driven. As a result, even the best efforts to craft new, community-based models are not sufficient for service-learning to overcome the powerful institutional barriers to success and sustainability.

The result is that we trade off impact for practical realities. We have reduced our expectations to only move nonprofits to the first rung of the stepstool—to become effective end users of social media tools. We have wondered if this is enough. If we can only get organizations to the first rung, does it nonetheless provide a necessary stepping stone for them to then get to the second rung and, left to their own devices, will they find the support they need to achieve the next step? But it is interesting that, as we impose first-rung limitations on what we will promise from one student in one semester, the organizations themselves seem to chafe at it. They push the students to go beyond learning a social media tool to try and build a customized interactive dataset within that tool. The organization that starts out expressing an interest in blogging tries to then get a member-generated advice column on plant health complete with photo upload capability. We support the students in politely resisting such pressure, sometimes even against our own desires to want more for both students and organizations.

What is needed to fulfill the ultimate potential of the Wisconsin Idea and bring nonprofits to the third rung of the ICT stepstool? First, we have to establish community outcomes as the priority goal of all service-learning. A community development service-learning model that can support a focus on community outcomes is beginning to emerge (Stoecker & Beckman, 2010), but it is still in its infancy.

Second, we must consequently build the course around the project rather than build the project around the course. That means leveraging space in curricula across the disciplines for community-based projects. Stoecker organized the independent study work-around as an overload on top of his teaching obligations. It is only because he also has a University of Wisconsin-Extension appointment that reduces his regular teaching load that he is able to do so, since such project-based teaching also serves the Extension mission. Faculty already teaching a full load cannot be expected to facilitate community-engaged courses as an add-on.

Third, we need to bring into all service-learning the same field-placement ethic practiced by professional programs from architecture to social work. That means we need to provide the same level of professional preparation that those programs provide, whether the student is a literature major, a history major, botany major, or whatever other major. Courses in nonprofits, professional culture and practice, and the specific technical aspects of a service-learning project should be prerequisites before any student is placed in the community.

Fourth, the term-limited credit system has to go. We need to instill the same culture for campus-community partnership work that we instill for graduate education—we award credit when the student finishes the work at an acceptable level of quality, not when the semester ends. This means developing an expectation that students will commit their time beyond the confines of a specific term.

Even when we reach for the cutting edge of technology, we are brought back to the crucial reality that the world is built upon, or crumbles from the absence of, a firm foundation of ethics, commitment, and practice that are both deeply personal and necessarily interpersonal. Our higher education institutions must do better in that foundational work.

## REFERENCES

Bjork, O., & Schwartz, J. P. (2005). *E-service-learning: Web writing as community service.* Retrieved February 10, 2007, from http://kairosnews.org/e-service-learning-web-writing-as-community-service

Blouin, D. D., & Perry, E. M. (2009). Whom does service-learning really serve? Community-based organizations' perspectives on service-learning. *Teaching Sociology, 37,* 120–135. doi:10.1177/0092055X0903700201

Buytaert, D. (2010). *Drupal.* Retrieved March 6, 2010, from http://drupal.org/

Chamberlain, C. (2003). Teaching teamwork: Project-based service-learning course LINCs students with nonprofits. *Inside Illinois,* January 23. Retrieved July 20, 2009 from http://www.news.uiuc.edu/II/03/0123/linc.html

Cravens, J. (2006). *The growing digital divide among nonprofit organizations/civil society in the USA (and maybe it's not just digital).* Retrieved March 6, 2010, from http://www.coyotecommunications.com/volunteer/divide.html

Dailey-Hebert, A., Donnelli, E., & DiPadova-Stocks, L. (Eds.). (2008). *Service-e-learning: Educating for citizenship.* Charlotte, NC: Information Age Publishing.

Draper, A. J. (2004). Integrating project-based service-learning into an advanced environmental chemistry course. *Journal of Chemical Education, 81,* 221–224. doi:10.1021/ed081p221

Kanayama, T. (2003). *An organizational digital divide: Web adoption and use among nonprofit organizations in Appalachian Ohio.* Paper presented at the annual meeting of the International Communication Association, San Diego, CA. Retrieved March 6, 2010, from http://www.allacademic.com/meta/p111817_index.html

LaCasse, K., Quinn, L. S., & Bernard, C. (2010). *Using social media to meet nonprofit goals: The results of a survey.* idealware. Retrieved March 6, 2010, from http://www.idealware.org/sm_survey/

Lupton, E. (1993). *Mechanical brides: Women and machines from home to office.* New York, NY: Cooper-Hewitt National Museum of Design.

Malvey, D. M., Hamby, E. F., & Fottler, M. D. (2006). E-service-learning: A pedagogic innovation for healthcare management education. *The Journal of Health Administration Education*, *23*(2), 181–198.

O'Reilly, T. (2005). What is Web 2.0: Design patterns and business models for the next generation of software. Retrieved March 6, 2010, from http://oreilly.com/web2/archive/what-is-web-20.html

Sandy, M., & Holland, B. (2006). Different worlds and common ground: community partner perspectives on campus-community partnerships. *Michigan Journal of Community Service-Learning*, *13*, 30–43.

Stenberg, P., Morehart, M., Vogel, S., Cromartie, J., Breneman, V., & Brown, D. (2009). Broadband Internet's value for rural America. *Economic Research Report Number, 78*. United States Department of Agriculture. Retrieved March 6, 2010, from http://www.ers.usda.gov/Publications/ERR78/ERR78.pdf

Stoecker, R. (2007). The data and research practices and needs of non-profit organizations. *Journal of Sociology and Social Welfare*, *34*, 97–119.

Stoecker, R. (2008). Challenging institutional barriers to community-based research. *Action Research*, *6*, 49–67. doi:10.1177/1476750307083721

Stoecker, R., & Beckman, M. (2010). Making higher education civic engagement matter in the community. *Campus Compact*. Retrieved March 6, 2010, from http://www.compact.org/wp-content/uploads/2010/02/engagementproof-1.pdf

Stoecker, R., Hilgendorf, A., & Tryon, E. (2008). Information and communication technology in service-learning: A case study of appropriate use. In A. Dailey-Hebert, E. Donnelli, & L. DiPadova-Stocks (Eds.), *Service-e-learning: Educating for citizenship*. Charlotte, NC: Information Age Publishing.

Stoecker, R., & Tryon, E. (2009). *The unheard voices: Community organizations and service-learning*. Philadelphia, PA: Temple University Press.

Strait, J., & Sauer, T. (2004). Constructing experiential learning for online courses: The birth of e-service-learning. *Educause Quarterly, 1*, 62-65. Retrieved March 13, 2010, from http://net.educause.edu/ir/library/pdf/eqm04110.pdf

Ukura, K. (2010). *The COMM-ORG Web advice series*. Retrieved March 6, 2010, from http://comm-org.wisc.edu/node/18.

# Section 3
# Online Learning and Professional Development

# Chapter 13
# Preparing 21st–Century Faculty to Engage 21st–Century Learners:
## The Incentives and Rewards for Online Pedagogies

**Kristine Blair**
*Bowling Green State University, USA*

## ABSTRACT

*This chapter provides a constructive critique of the gap between the institutional rhetoric of technology and the academic reality of delivering curriculum digitally. As part of the analysis of the material conditions within the academy that inhibit the development of engaged online pedagogies, including ones with the potential for service-learning and community literacy components, this chapter establishes benchmarks for both institutions and units, not only to assess and sustain the success of such initiatives, but also to foster the professional development training of current and facilitate faculty to foster online learning as an important example of the scholarship of teaching, learning, and engagement. Ultimately, 21st-century colleges and universities need to develop ways to align technology with both pedagogy and policy to bridge the divide between the academy and the community to maintain relevance in both realms in the digital age.*

DOI: 10.4018/978-1-60960-623-7.ch013

## INTRODUCTION

I recently received the following email:

Dear Educator
Last chance! You only have 5 more days to register for this 60-minute webinar that will provide you with vital strategies to utilize Facebook, Twitter, and other social networks to recruit students to your college.

Companies like higheredhero.com aggressively market audio conferences to higher education professionals to help them "keep up to date with changes in their fields, and learn valuable insights that boost their performance" (higheredhero.com email, 2010). In addition to the topic area listed above, webinars include "YouTube on Campus: Marketing Strategies to Drive Student Recruitment," The Wiki Workshop: Tools & Tips to Build Enhanced College Courses" and "Alumni Newsletters: Keys to Transitioning from Print to Digital." Clearly, in the digital era, universities understand the need to move away from print-based recruitment methods to instead rely upon the technologies students commonly use in their literate lives outside the academy. Despite this emphasis, however, universities give far less attention to the impact of these same technologies on the academic labor and material conditions of faculty as scholar-teachers. Ironically, just as student affairs administrators, the primary audience for many of the higheredhero webinars, are encouraged in one session to engage faculty in the recruitment process, academic affairs administrators often overlook the need to provide faculty with appropriate support and reward structures for developing online pedagogies that may aid in both the recruitment and retention of non-traditional learners across the disciplines represented throughout this volume.

Despite Boyer's (1990) call to embrace a "scholarship of teaching" paradigm in the preparation and evaluation of current and future faculty,

all too often tenure and promotion processes privilege traditional definitions of both research and teaching and, as a result, limit institutional recognition of pedagogies—from distance education to service-learning—that engage external communities whose access to both educational and technological opportunities has been limited. As Hull and Schultz (2002) note:

*There is worry about a growing digital divide, one associated with schools (where access to technology and its meaningful use is unequal), with disparate technology and other resources, and also with workplaces in which low-income people of color are shut out of high-tech, well-paying jobs. How can teachers, researchers, and other educators join forces to bridge such divides? (p. 41)*

Such research has stressed the existence of varying types of digital divides among diverse cultural groups; yet I shall also contend that university faculty continue to represent what Prensky (2001) has termed "digital immigrants," personifying a type of divide that hinders their ability to develop online outreach initiatives, despite the strong evidence within this section of *Higher Education, Emerging Technologies, and Community Partnerships*, that advanced training in the form of certificates, degrees, and other professional development models are needed.

Thus, the purpose of this chapter is to provide a constructive critique of the gap between the institutional rhetoric of technology (Hawisher & Selfe, 1991) and the academic reality of delivering curriculum digitally. As part of my analysis of the material conditions within the academy that inhibit the development of engaged online pedagogies, including ones with the potential for service-learning and community literacy components, I establish a series of benchmarks for both institutions and units not only to assess and sustain the success of such initiatives, but also to facilitate the professional development training of current and future faculty to foster online learning as an important example of the scholarship of teaching, learning and engagement.

## FACULTY WORKLOAD AND THE LANGUAGE OF ONLINE EDUCATION

Elsewhere (Blair & Hoy, 2006; Blair & Monske, 2003) I have noted the impact of online teaching on faculty workload. While the rhetorics of online education stress convenience, immediacy and educational equity for students, the benefits to faculty teaching online courses are not as immediately transparent. Faculty within my own unit of English Studies have expressed concerns about the potential to migrate humanities curriculum online and argue that the labor to foster comparable quality dialogue in online settings takes its toll not only on teaching but upon the balance between teaching and other allocations of faculty effort, notably research. And whether it is a classroom discussion, a faculty lecture, or a final exam, the lack of technological savvy constrains faculty. Presumably, course management systems such as Blackboard help to alleviate the workload of online teaching in terms of its ease of use; indeed, in his book *Teaching Writing Online*, Scott Warnock (2009) contends that "because I assume you are new to online instruction, I think the best way for you to progress is to use an already available CMS probably provided and supported at some level by your institution" (p. xviii). As I have stressed in previous work (Blair, 2007), the course management system may indeed be convenient for faculty but may in fact function as a "gated community" to student populations whose online literacy practices involve tools all too often dismissed as less relevant to traditional academic discourse. Nevertheless, Warnock's text inevitably speaks the language that many faculty want to hear: "I'll assume that you want to lower the technology barrier as much as you can, and for teachers new to the online environment, that means

using a prepackaged CMS" (p. xviii). Ironically, platforms such as Blackboard, with its limits on customization may actually create a technology barrier between faculty and a range of student audiences whose learning styles require a broader range of multimodal teaching tools.

As Michael Wesch's (2007) video "Digital Ethnography: A Vision of Students Today" chronicles, many of today's students read volumes more web-based texts than they do print books and write equally voluminous numbers of e-mail as opposed to academic papers, spending a third of the day online. Wesch's student-generated data is confirmed by other more systematic studies such as the Pew Studies on the Internet and American Life or the Frontline PBS Series "Digital Nation." Ironically, Wesch's video concludes with an 1841 quote from Josiah Bunstead on the benefits of the chalkboard, e.g., the centenarian plus technology that metaphorically serves as the model for "Blackboard." As of this writing, Wesch's collaborative work with students at Kansas State has generated 3,609,276 hits on YouTube, a five-year old technology that is itself a testament to the power of Web 2.0 tools to counter the rhetorics of access and convenience with the realities of those attributes. While Warnock's message to faculty may emphasize a way to decrease workload through the logistical convenience of the course "shell," he inadvertently reinscribes a relationship between students as "digital natives," and faculty as "digital immigrants," the latter group defined by Prensky (2001) as contributing to the "biggest problem facing education today…that our Digital Immigrant instructors, who speak an outdated language (that of the pre-dated digital age), are struggling to teach a population that speaks an entirely new language" (p. 2). Prensky may be overstating the case when he argues that "faculty need to stop grousing" and just, as the Nike slogan suggests, "do it," yet workload issues affect faculty members' ability to experiment with tools such as blogs, wikis, podcasting, and the like that may actually enhance teaching and learning and better engage both traditional and non-traditional learners in terms of learning styles and community-based education. But perhaps the most problematic aspect of teaching online in today's Web 2.0 is, as J. Elizabeth Clark (2010) notes, that it is constantly "in flux," and "that there will always be new technologies… challenging our notions of the boundaries of the classroom and our pedagogical assumptions about learning" (p. 28).

Prensky doesn't lay the gauntlet only at the feet of the faculty; he ultimately concludes that faculty success "will come much sooner if their administrators support them" (p. 6). This is especially important given that in a number of disciplines, including English, a large percentage of entry-level courses in both composition and literature are taught by non-tenure track faculty or graduate students. As the Modern Language Association concludes in its Desk Reference for Department Chairs (2009), such numbers call for consistent commitment to supporting online teachers in the same manner as face-to-face teachers, ensuring access to clerical, technical, and general academic assistance. Similar to the higheredhero.com webinars, another online service titled "Faculty Focus" recently offered an audio seminar aimed at chairs, deans, and provosts, "Engagement Strategies for Online Adjuncts" (online) designed to not only develop shared expectations of faculty performance in online settings, but also establish opportunities for professional development and involvement in setting the institutional agenda with regard to online education. As I shall stress in the next section, such strategies must apply to tenure-track faculty as well in order to secure consistent buy-in across the curriculum.

## TWITTERING OUR WAY TOWARD TENURE?

As Lawrence Ragan (1999) notes in his well-cited "Good Teaching is Good Teaching,"

*As changing demographics and new technologies and methodologies cause educational institutions to reconsider the value of a general education within our society, these forces also force us to re-evaluate our concept of an "educational event." Time, location, and pace of study are becoming less important as indicators of quality instruction. The delivery system is secondary to the type of interactions and intellectual engagement that the system provides both the learner and the teacher.*

Ragan's commentary suggests that perhaps what constrains faculty and students is not the technical aptitude for online teaching and learning but educational attitude, a presumption that education is delivered face to face in semester or quarter intervals. Perhaps the biggest challenge is getting faculty to reflect on how and why they teach the way they do and how those methods—from the chalkboard to the overhead projector to the LCD—are all forms of technological delivery, with the migration to fully online delivery representing a particular point on a continuum of making content accessible to more diverse students. As with any technological choice, faculty must ask what is gained and what is lost in selecting one tool over another rather than presume that the shift to fully online delivery represents a loss. Just as with face-to-face teaching, faculty must have the opportunity to document the successes and challenges of online teaching in order to educate peer and administrative evaluators about how these approaches contribute to student success in achieving discipline-specific learning outcomes. Ironically, the common way to document those successes and challenges is through the print dossier, the behemoth compilation of teaching, research, and service roles.

The Modern Language Association's Taskforce on Tenure and Promotion recently reported that both tenure and promotion committees and department chairs have little knowledge of how to evaluate digital scholarship, and while the Taskforce report focuses primarily on research, there are clear implications for those whose works meshes with Boyer's original concept of the scholarship of teaching in that the tenure and promotion processes common to the academy don't sufficiently recognize or reward faculty for the labor and innovation of migrating curriculum online and don't provide documentation procedures that allow faculty to best showcase their work.

Nevertheless, many faculty, particularly those newer to the academy, are experimenting with digital tools not only in classroom practice but also in reflecting upon that practice. For instance, James Schirmer, an assistant professor of English at the University of Michigan Flint and better known as "betajames" on Twitter, drafted and shared his most recent annual review in blog form (2010), explaining the importance of social networking tools in his professional life as a teacher-scholar:

*Overall, I view teaching and learning as forms of public action; online communicative technologies like Posterous, a simple blogging service, and Twitter, a social networking service, illuminate both. Furthermore, the implementation of particular online communicative technologies (like Posterous and Twitter) facilitate and coordinate greater attention, encourage meaningful interaction and participation, promote better collaboration, help students develop narratives of their own learning as well as hone the critical consumption and crafting of academic (and nonacademic) work.*

Even as new faculty such as Schirmer rely upon technology to reflect on its role in their teaching and research, little has changed for faculty preparing tenure and promotion dossiers, although as early as 1998, the Conference on College Composition and Communication published their position statement on Promotion and Tenure Guidelines for Work with Technology that advocated for "viewing candidates' work in the medium in which it was produced," including web-based syllabi and other curricular materials. So often the develop-ment of online materials represents an invisible labor that includes learning software, migrating print materials, and designing appealing and accessible spaces that reflect not only pedagogical innovation but also design savvy.

A noteworthy alternative to the print portfolio model is the example of Cheryl Ball, a recently tenured faculty member at Illinois State University specializing in digital media who submitted a digital tenure dossier to her external reviewers, her departmental committee, and her upper administration. Organized in a manner similar to a print portfolio in its emphasis on teaching, research, and service, Ball's tenure portfolio is one of a kind, for as she points out, while a number of institutions have specifically acknowledged digital scholarship in their tenure and promotion documents, there are far fewer faculty who have actually designed a digital tenure dossier as more than mere supplement to the print portfolio process and who have had faculty colleagues actually review tenure candidates' credentials online. What makes Ball's dossier so compelling is its ability to showcase not only the work she does as a new media teacher and researcher but also the work her students do in a range of courses, including audio and video. Although Ball's portfolio does not showcase fully online courses, there is clear potential to showcase the labor of online teaching through such digital documentation processes.

In its application of the AAUP Statement on Distance Education to language and literature faculty, the MLA "continues to assert that institutions and departments bear a responsibility for making explicit the rewards and ramifications of creating online instructional materials" (2009, p. 127). Inevitably, relying on print versions of web-based syllabi and other curricular materials is a poor substitute for experiencing online courses as the students themselves do, which includes, as I will stress in the section on benchmarks, opportunities for online peer observations similar to those common to face-to-face courses. As Ball (2009) herself notes, "Making one's digital work supplemental—especially when digital work is the center of one's research and teaching—is often not the choice a tenure applicant would make; instead it is regulation of the tenure guidelines at one's school, and so the choice becomes trying to institute change or ensuring one's job. It's not surprising that most tenure-track scholars choose the latter" (online). In response to the concerns of pre-tenure faculty such as Ball, Western Carolina University has recently implemented a "scholarship of teaching" model that acknowledges that some tenure candidates may do work that does not fit within traditional concepts of research, such as the development of online resources for both students and teachers, including those outside the institution itself. According to the online forum *Inside Higher Ed* (Jaschik, 2007), Western Carolina's Chancellor stated "many emerging needs of society call for universities to be more actively involved in the community. Those local communities…need to rely on their public universities for direct help, not just basic research."

## PREPARING FUTURE FACULTY TO BE ONLINE EDUCATORS

In the Spring 2010 Newsletter of the Modern Language Association, MLA president Sidonie Smith offers powerful commentary on graduate student professionalization:

*Our students will be disadvantaged if they do not graduate from doctoral programs as skilled teachers, adept at engaging classes of various sizes and different mixes of students and versed in scholarship on student literacies and learning environments. Furthermore, they will need facility in digital composing, melding words, images, moving images, and sound. Many of them will produce digital scholarship that doubles as teaching tools, requiring sophisticated pedagogical approaches to concept design and platform use.*

Indeed, this is especially important in light of current academic job market constraints for students in literary studies, a dilemma extensively documented by the MLA, and something the organization has more recently addressed with regard to master's candidates (Steward, 2004). As community colleges and increasing numbers of four-year universities heed the call to provide more fully online courses to meet changing undergraduate populations requiring a range of entry points into higher education, the ability of graduate students to deliver courses in hybrid and fully online formats will be not only crucial to their marketability but also vital to the sustainability of the curriculum in the 21st century.

Inevitably, technology specialists, program directors, and department chairs must stress the role of technology in both the undergraduate and graduate curricula within their disciplines. In English studies, for example, a positive step in such a direction is recently evident through the MLA collection *Teaching Language and Literature Online*, which provides a range of case studies and best practices in literature, linguistics, English as a second language, foreign languages, and composition. With a range of institutions represented in the collection, there is ample evidence that digital pedagogies can foster the curricular agenda of both programs and individual courses. However, the question remains as to how such integration can be more widespread within programs, especially graduate programs, which seem to receive little attention even in what is an innovative collection for the MLA.

A related issue is the type of training current and future faculty receive. Typically, technology support privileges the institutional course management system, be it Blackboard, Angel, or Desire-2Learn, that faculty and graduate students may utilize in face-to-face courses. But how often do these same faculty and graduate students receive training to actual teach fully online courses with a wider range of presentation and communication tools? Granted, many disciplines have been critiqued for not foregrounding teacher training as part of the graduate student professionalization process. But even in those disciplines where teacher training is a significant portion of the graduate experience, much less attention is devoted to the role of technology in fostering teaching excellence.

At my own institution, I have been fortunate to develop two technological training courses that address these issues for graduate students in rhetoric and composition. The first, "Computer-Mediated Writing Theory and Practice," is designed to introduce students to a range of social networking tools that have strong potential as teaching and learning tools, including blogs, wikis, and Google groups. In addition, the course includes training in web-authoring, visual imaging and audio/video editing tools that allows graduate students to both theorize the impact of technology on literate practice and to align such theory with the development of pedagogical practices and curricular materials that are showcases in an electronic portfolio. The second course, "Online Learning for English Educators," is specifically focused on teaching teachers to teach fully online, introducing research in distance education, faculty development, adult learning, and assessment and aligning those scholarly conversations with projects that include virtual class facilitations, software reviews, and fully online teaching units.

Although these courses fulfill the needs of a particular graduate student population in English studies, there is an equal need to train graduate students across disciplines as well as public school teachers who are seeking additional certification and who play a vital role in introducing communication technologies to students in ways that prepare them for the use of technology within college-level classrooms both online and face to face. In order to meet the needs of such internal and external populations, I have recently developed a third course for our University's Summer Teaching Academy titled "Digital Writing Across the Curriculum," which introduces participants to a range of digital assignment contexts that foster writing, literacy, and communication. Similar to the Computer-Mediated Writing course, this two-day, one-credit hour workshop (a format that often suits non-traditional populations better than the traditional semester or quarter-long course) places emphasis on aligning writing technologies, including blogs, image and video storage sites, discussion forums, and wikis, with curricular objectives and pedagogical practices within the humanities, arts, social sciences, and sciences.

While graduate education is an ideal place to begin professional development related to teaching and learning with technology, the reality is that far too often both tenure-track and non-tenure track faculty receive little guidance in developing online pedagogies that meet the needs of adult learners from the institutions that encourage them to teach in virtual environments. This is not to suggest, however, that good models do not exist; for instance, Bowling Green State University's Center for Online and Blended Learning (COBL) has developed a short online training course that, similar to Online Learning for English Educators, introduces faculty to the theories behind online learning and the best practices in online pedagogies. In such instances, faculty have the opportunity to experience online learning just as their students would and to develop a sense of empathy for the logistical challenges for students who, in many cases, have not only never taken an online course, but are returning to their studies after several years, or in some cases, decades. BGSU's Center has frequently partnered with the University Center for Teaching and Learning to sponsor workshops on various tools such as blogging and podcasting applications but also has created consulting models in which faculty can work with instructional design specialist to develop and user-test online course interfaces.

## BENCHMARKS

An adage I often rely upon is that technologies all too often advance more rapidly than either pedagogies or policies that support their successful implementation, and some of the greatest challenges for online educators include a lack of clarity about the incentives and rewards for developing and delivering curriculum online. Based on some of the best practices outlined in this collection and experiences at my own institution, the following guidelines serve as helpful reminders that successfully engaging online learners requires careful triangulation of academic and technology infrastructures that support the tenured and tenure-track faculty who teach them.

## Workload

**Class and Cohort Size:** Although courses in English Studies, for instance, are typically capped lower than courses in other parts of the curriculum, the standard enrollments of 20-25 for writing intensive courses and 35 for more survey-based lecture-discussion courses are enough of a challenge that department chairs must advocate for lower enrollments to counteract the volume of e-mail traffic, discussion board moderation, and other forms of virtual classroom management that increase faculty workload above and beyond face-to-face classes. While at my own institution online courses other than first-year writing are capped at 30 students, this number can prove overwhelming for both novice and experienced online instructors across disciplines. A related problem occurs when in the rush to admit a cohort of online students, there may be more students enrolled than there are course sections or course seats, particularly at the graduate level, where seminars are limited in class size both online and face to face.

**Technical Support:** One of the most common concerns about online teaching is the extent to which faculty will assume technical troubleshooting roles for which they are not prepared. Such

roles are especially challenging given the diverse populations taking online courses and the multiple modes of computing access, including reliance on public library systems, workplace stations, and home systems that may not always have the minimum technical specifications to access various aspects of online delivery, such as current browser versions, media players, flash plugins, and javascripts. For these reasons, information technology and faculty development units should collaborate to establish a clear communication chain for students and faculty to secure online assistance, including websites and help-lines.

**Technological Tool Selection:** Although the ability to align curricular objectives with appropriate digital tools is a result of faculty development and training, it is a workload issue as well. Indeed, faculty are often concerned about the frequent recommendation to employ multiple tools to achieve the pedagogical goal of accommodating multiple learning styles among the diverse learners enrolling in online courses. Nevertheless, faculty need encouragement to explore digital tools in a progressive way, beginning with one or two tools that can mesh with pedagogical approaches they already employ to present content, foster teacher-student and student-student interaction, and assess how well students master course objectives. For instance, a blog may prove an excellent tool for meeting a number of curricular goals. Blogs allow students to individually respond to course material in the form of note taking or journaling is consistent with study habits in a range of disciplines. In addition to their ease of access (as a free Web 2.0 tool) and use, blogs can foster dialogue among students and between students and teachers, and can involve students in the assessment process by relying on students' self-reflections about their own learning.

## Tenure

**Aligning Promotion Policies with Educational Initiatives:** Tenure and promotion documents often include vague references to teaching excellence without much concrete detail about not only the curricular innovation but also the academic labor surrounding online course development and delivery. It is the shared responsibility of tenure candidates, departmental promotion committees, and senior administrators to review and revise unit-level tenuring documents. Such revisions should explicitly articulate the importance of rewarding faculty for aligning their teaching with the mission so many institutions now have to engage new student audiences through online learning and for recognizing that this institutional priority may impact other areas of faculty performance, including an stronger emphasis on the scholarship of teaching. Both candidates and departmental committees should look to existing guidelines in their disciplines; in English studies these would include the Modern Language Association, the Conference on College Composition and Communication, and the National Council of Teachers of English.

**Peer and Student Evaluation Guidelines:** Very often faculty peers have had little experience conducting peer observations of fully online classes; as a result, my own English department adopted guidelines from Maryland's Quality Matters Program, a rubric designed to assess online learning objectives, learner engagement, course technology, and several other items. Other considerations include the amount of time the observer should spend "in" the online course and the types of interactions directly observed or reviewed in archive form, including discussion boards, chats, and podcasts. Equally important, as several of the chapters in this section imply, is the need to develop student evaluation instruments that allow students to provide specific feedback on various tools and their impact on content delivery and learning outcomes rather than rely upon the generic student ratings form that doesn't account for varied learning objects.

**Electronic Portfolios:** E-portfolios and other genres such as blogs allow teachers to showcase digital pedagogies and reflect on their successes and challenges. Such efforts have a pragmatic element as well, for the more opportunity a faculty member has to read and write online the more likely that same instructor is to utilize these tools in his or her own classroom, whether fully online or hybrid. In addition, faculty members can actually showcase online work their students produce in similar forums, providing a richer picture of what actually happens in online settings than is visible through the traditional print portfolio, educational philosophy, or teaching narrative. While implementing an e-portfolio process for tenure and promotion processes is a longitudinal initiative, short-term strategies can include granting course access (such as Blackboard) to departmental and college review committees and submitting online pedagogical materials on CD or via URL for review, though as Ball's work suggest, such documentation should not be regarded as supplemental but as integral to the case for teaching excellence.

## Training

**Team-Development Models:** Collaborative models for migrating curriculum online are common to faculty development, with teachers typically receiving instructional design assistance from the campus center for teaching excellence but still maintaining ownership over the course material and a significant role in determining what tools will best mesh with curricular objectives and pedagogical approaches. This is especially important given that many technological training models rely too heavily on the one-time workshop that often doesn't translate to actual curricular and pedagogical innovation once a faculty member is back in his or her office working in isolation. Sharing responsibility and expertise, and relying on partnerships within and outside the academy is key to sustaining engaged online pedagogies.

**Discipline-Specific Workshops:** Prensky (2001) refutes the common lament of faculty that while it may be possible for some disciplines to easily migrate course content, in our field it just won't work. While clearly such views about the viability of online pedagogies are as much attitudinal as they are curricular, one way to begin to counter the belief that online learning isn't for me is to develop forums that allow early adopters to share best practices of what does work in terms of migrating pedagogical practices standard to the discipline, whether it's the arts, humanities, sciences, or social sciences, to allow colleagues to hear firsthand that it can and does work and that online delivery is vital to meeting the needs of increasingly diverse working adult student populations.

**Professional Development Plans:** Scott Warnock (2009) advocates that faculty consider a technological self assessment of 1) pedagogical need; 2) technology for that purpose; 3) availability of technology; and 4) required training. Similarly, I advocate a professional development plan, a narrative that asks faculty to reflect on where they are in terms of their technological and pedagogical knowledge, where they feel they need to be to achieve their instructional goals through technology, and finally, how they will get there. What professional development training exists in the form of courses, workshops, etc., and what readings/research might they begin to undertake to achieve their goals?

## CONCLUSION: MOVING FROM RECRUITMENT TO RELEVANCE

In *The Marketplace of Ideas*, Louis Menand (2009) asserts that "A lot has changed in higher education in the last fifty years. What has not changed is the delicate and somewhat paradoxical relations in which the university stands to the general culture. It is important for teaching and research to be relevant, for the university to engage with the public culture" (p. 158). Although Menand does not discuss technology, one powerful mode of

engagement is through the delivery of college-level curricula online to foster educational access to students from diverse cultural backgrounds. Menand asserts that engagement with the public in all forms requires training that most graduate students, as the future of the professoriate, do not receive. Clearly, the chapters in this collection document that curricular innovation through online pedagogies is enabled and constrained through a number of cultural and material conditions, and that training, support, and reward systems should begin early in one's academic career and be consistent throughout.

Thus, the access to and acquisition of digital literacies should be a collective concern of faculty across the disciplines as we prepare graduate students to enter the academic job market and to assume responsibilities as professors in the 21st century, including helping graduate students transition from pre-professional to technology-aware faculty. As graduate students become more comfortable with these technologies in both personal and academic contexts, there is a chance to bridge the gap that Prensky (2001) has identified between digital natives (students) and digital immigrants (teachers) so that we might consider what role the digital tools universities are providing as recruitment incentives can actually play in our classrooms. For Clark (2010), today's teachers are faced with a "digital imperative" that "asks how we can reshape our pedagogy with new uses of technology that are changing our personal and professional lives" (p. 28).

Even as we ask these questions, however, we must continue to address our assumptions about the learning needs of 21st-century students and the extent to which online learning fulfills the promise of making higher education more accessible, something the Sloan Foundation (Lorenzo, 2008) demonstrated in its "Sloan Semester," a national consortium of free online courses available to displaced students after Hurricane Katrina in 2005. Such an example also suggests that Boyer's powerful concept of the "scholarship of teaching," particularly when applied to online settings, has the potential to mesh with an equally powerful concept, "the scholarship of engagement." Inevitably, many of the material conditions that warrant developing engaged online pedagogies to serve 21st-century learners are the same conditions that may hinder their success. In order to both develop and sustain engaged online pedagogies, appropriate institutional infrastructures must be in place and in synch to ensure that faculty, as Menand concludes, can "look to the world to see what kind of teaching and research need to be done, and how they might better train and organize themselves to do it" (p. 158). Ultimately, today's colleges and universities need to look for ways to align technology with both pedagogy and policy to bridge the gap between what's happening outside the academy and what's happening inside to maintain our relevance in both realms and support both current faculty and the future faculty who hope to join our ranks.

## REFERENCES

Ball, C. (2009). *About this portfolio*. Retrieved March 23, 2010, from http://www.ceball.com/tenure/welcome-to-my-portfolio/about/

Blair, K. (2007). Course management systems as gated communities: Expanding the potential of distance learning spaces through multimodal spaces. In E. Bailey (Ed.), *Focus on distance education developments* (pp. 41–53). NJ: Nova Science Publishers.

Blair, K., & Hoy, C. (2006). Paying attention to adult learners online: The pedagogy and politics of community. *Computers and Composition*, *23*(1), 32–48. doi:10.1016/j.compcom.2005.12.006

Blair, K., & Monske, E. (2003). Cui bono?: Revisiting the promises and perils of online learning. *Computers and Composition*, *20*(4), 441–453. doi:10.1016/j.compcom.2003.08.016

Boyer, E. (1990). *Scholarship reconsidered: Priorities of the professoriate*. Princeton, NJ: Carnegie Foundation for the Advancement of Teaching.

Clark, J. E. (2010). The digital imperative: Making the case for a 21$^{st}$ century pedagogy. *Computers and Composition*, *27*(1), 27–35. doi:10.1016/j.compcom.2009.12.004

Conference on College Composition and Communication. (1998). *Position statement: CCCC promotion and tenure guidelines for work with technology*. Retrieved March 23, 2010, from http://www.ncte.org/cccc/resources/positions/promotionandtenure

Faculty Focus. (2010). *Engagement strategies for online adjuncts*. Retrieved March 23, 2010, from http://www.facultyfocus.com/online-seminars/engagement-strategies-for-online-adjuncts

Hawisher, G., & Selfe, C. (1991). The rhetoric of technology and the electronic writing class. *College Composition and Communication*, *42*(1), 55–65. doi:10.2307/357539

Higheredhero.com (2010). *Last chance! Facebook, twitter & blogs: Recruitment tips for prospective students*. Private email.

Hull, G., & Shultz, K. (2002). *Schools out! Bridging out-of-school literacies with classroom practice*. New York, NY: Teachers College Press.

Jaschik, S. (2007). Scholarship reconsidered as tenure policy. *Inside Higher Ed*, October 2, 2007. Retrieved March 23, 2010 from http://www.insidehighered.com/news/2007/10/02/wcu

Lancashire, I. (2009). *Teaching literature and language online*. New York, NY: Modern Language Association.

Lorenzo, G. (2008). The Sloan semester. *Journal of Asynchronous Learning Networks*, *12*(2), 5–40.

Maryland Online. (2006). *Quality matters*. Retrieved March 23, 2010, from http://qualitymatters.com

Menand, L. (2009). *The marketplace of ideas: Reform and resistance in the American university*. New York, NY: W.W. Norton.

Modern Language Association. (2007). *Report of the MLA taskforce on evaluating scholarship for tenure and promotion*. Retrieved March 23, 2010, from http://www.mla.org/tenure_promotion

Modern Language Association. (2009). The AAUP statement on distance education: Special considerations for language and literature. *ADE Bulletin, 147-48*, 127–128.

Prensky, M. (2001). Digital natives, digital immigrants. *Horizon, 9*(5), 1–6. doi:10.1108/10748120110424816

Ragan, J. (1999). Good teaching is good teaching: An emerging set of guiding principles and practices for the design and development of distance education. *CAUSE/EFFECT, 22*(1). Retrieved March 23, 2010, from http://net.educause.edu/ir/library/html/cem/cem99/cem9915.html

Schirmer, J. (2010, February 10). *Two-year review research summary* (draft). Retrieved March 23, 2010, from http://betajames.posterous.com/two-year-review-research-summary-draft

Smith, S. (2010). Beyond the dissertation monograph. *MLA Newsletter*. New York, NY: Modern Language Association.

Steward, D. (2004). The master's degree in modern languages since 1966. *ADE Bulletin, 136*, 50–68.

Warnock, S. (2009). *Teaching writing online: How and why?* Urbana, IL: National Council of Teachers of English.

Wesch, M. (2007). *A vision of students today*. Retrieved March 23, 2010, from http://www.youtube.com/watch?v=dGCJ46vyR9o

## KEY TERMS AND DEFINITIONS

**Adult Learner:** A student outside the traditional 18-22 year-old age range who is typically returning to their studies while working.

**Faculty Development:** Training programs designed to improve faculty performance, particularly in the area the teaching.

**Online Learning:** The development and delivery of academic curriculum or professional training via the Internet.

**Preparing Future Faculty:** Initiatives designed to provide graduate students with training programs to help them successfully transition into the professoriate.

**Scholarship of Engagement:** An emphasis on community outreach and civic engagement that attempts to establish a recursive relationship between university and community partners and impacts faculty efforts in teaching, research, and service roles.

**Scholarship of Teaching and Learning:** An inquiry into the relationship between teaching and learning that results in pedagogical research results that are formally disseminated within scholarly communities.

**Web 2.0:** Refers to most current online information sharing sites, such as weblogs and social networking sites that foster collaboration and interactivity to balance the relationship between user consumption of information and user production of information.

# Chapter 14
# Digital Partnerships for Professional Development:
## Rethinking University–Public School Collaborations

**William P. Banks**
*East Carolina University, USA*

**Terri Van Sickle**
*Tar River Writing Project, USA*

## ABSTRACT

*The following case study explores the impact of a university-school-community partnership developed in an online environment in order to address the immediate need of high school teachers in North Carolina to become more knowledgeable about responding to student writing in online and digital environments. Using a grassroots, teachers-teaching-teachers model fostered by the National Writing Project, members of the Tar River Writing Project, in partnership with a university faculty member and an administrator from a local public school district, developed and implemented an online professional development workshop to improve teacher response practices. This study demonstrates one method for using online technologies to engage community and university partners in the collaborative work of improving writing instruction and suggests a series of benefits inherent in such partnerships.*

## INTRODUCTION: MOVING TEACHER PROFESSIONAL DEVELOPMENT ONLINE

The recent economic recession in the United States has had numerous ripple effects beyond the Wall Street bailouts, car company woes and other stories

DOI: 10.4018/978-1-60960-623-7.ch014

that have occupied significant space in the national headlines. While experience suggests that district- and school-level support for public school teachers to attend conferences and other professional development events has dwindled over the last decade generally, the recent economic downturn has caused that support to dry up almost completely in our area of eastern North Carolina. This shift has caused the Tar River Writing Project (http://

www.trwp.org), a university-school-community partnership for teacher development in eastern North Carolina, to rethink the sort of standard, face-to-face teacher seminars, workshops, and institutes that it has traditionally conducted in area schools and districts. Increasingly, schools in TRWP's service region (23 counties between I-95 and the NC coast) have been struggling to fund substitute teacher pay and travel costs that arise when classroom teachers leave school for a day or more to participate in their own professional development (PD) with other educators. While such continued professional development is key to better teachers, schools, and student learning, the cost for such work in time, space, and money has come to feel increasingly prohibitive to many principals and district-level administrators.

This case study outlines one of TRWP's recent attempts to provide high-quality PD events by using Moodle, an online content management system (CMS), and thus work to reduce those peripheral costs of teacher training previously absorbed by schools and districts. Despite some difficulties, this experience has been largely productive and successful, allowing TRWP to meet some of the key outcomes of its mission: 1) increased collaboration between K-12 teachers and university researchers in a variety of environments; 2) improved teacher development through effective engagement with high-quality professional development materials; 3) increased integration of digital technologies in teacher development projects; and, 4) greater opportunities for developing teacher leadership capacity throughout the TRWP service region.

## HISTORY AND CONTEXT OF RESPONDING TO STUDENT WRITING ONLINE (RSWO)

In the fall of 2009, the state of North Carolina was beginning the process of implementing a statewide Graduation Project[1] for high school seniors, one that would involve a rich portfolio of different

kinds of writing, including a major researched paper. But as often happens with top-down, large-scale approaches, the NC Department of Public Instruction (NCDPI) and the NC Department of Education (NCDOE) had not allocated sufficient funding or time to provide detailed professional development for NC teachers who would be responsible for guiding students through the new Graduation Project process. As state-level discussions progressed, one local school district, NRMPS, was considering a move that would have their students' researched essays, a core component of the new NC Graduation Project (NCGP), responded to/evaluated by external constituencies. Some district administrators in the NRMPS system were concerned that students in their schools were not getting sufficiently rigorous responses to their writing; they worried that their own teachers would be tempted to "go easy" on their own students' work; central office wanted some outside (read "objective") evaluators to make sure that the students would receive valuable feedback that would inspire revision prior to the end-of-year Graduation Project assessments. NRMPS knew the qualities they sought in evaluators (e.g., teaching experience, knowledge of research writing, experience with assessing writing), but they were not necessarily sure who those evaluators should be or how NRMPS could ensure the evaluators would provide the services they sought.

This is where the Tar River Writing Project came into the picture. As with other sites of the National Writing Project (http://www.nwp.org), TRWP is built on a "teachers-teaching-teachers" model, one which values the contributions that classroom teachers can make when they are given the chance to wed experience with published research in order to become teacher-educators. TRWP's Teacher Consultants (TCs) are certified teachers who have been through an application-based, highly competitive Invitational Summer Institute (ISI) in which they read current research on the teaching of writing and reflect on the connections between their personal experiences and concepts from published research assigned in the course. When those teachers finish the ISI, they participate in their own classroom-based research projects and become part of collaborative groups that support each other in building in-service and other types of professional development activities for teachers in their own schools and those in TRWP's service region of eastern North Carolina. These groups are simultaneously supported by university research faculty. These professional development workshops/events tend to be extremely successful, in large part because they are developed and implemented by local teachers who work to combine current research and best practices in writing instruction with the opportunities and constraints at work in local school districts. Because TCs are themselves schoolteachers in the same or nearby districts, they have a degree of credibility *with other teachers* that is sometimes lacking in the trainers who come in from outside the state to present similar workshops. Likewise, in developing customized professional development workshops for teachers and schools, TCs create spaces in which local concerns can be directly, rather than obliquely, addressed. In the case of NRMPS, TRWP already had two TCs in the district who had communicated to the county office the value of writing project-styled professional development. When it came time for NRMPS to think about how to support their students and teachers in implementing the new Graduation Project, and given the shortage in funding available, a partnership among NRMPS, ECU, and TRWP seemed an obvious and economically viable choice. Likewise, since TRWP is part of the National Writing Project, it is approved as a professional development provider under the No Child Left Behind (NCLB) Act; therefore, NRMPS could use federal monies to pay for the professional development workshop with TRWP as its contracting partner.

Based on conversations with NRMPS administrators, members of the TRWP developed the online module "Responding to Student Writing in Online Environments" (RSWO), a module that represents a significant departure from traditional, after-school professional development workshop or expensive multi-day institutes. Normally, a school might pay for its own teachers to attend a workshop or conference, learn about some new research or teaching methods, and return to their home school/district to implement that work (Penuel et al., 2007). More recently, those workshops have begun to focus on showcasing a splashy new piece of software or technology; these look exciting in the polished PowerPoint presentations, but teachers may not have a chance to experiment/play with them in order to gain hands-on experience that will help them implement the technologies in their classrooms (Huber, 2010). In the case of RSWO, because the school district wanted well-trained *external* readers for their district-wide research projects, TRWP was contracted to train those external constituents, but the district and TRWP worked together to plan the most effective method for reaching those teachers. Given that this training would be for individuals who would eventually respond to the writing of actual high school students, NRMPS suggested that we recruit and train certified teachers from *other* North Carolina school districts; they would already know much about working with NC students, the reasoning went, and RSWO would help them to learn the complexities of responding to writing in digital/online environments while using the Graduation Project rubric, a new assessment instrument in North Carolina. Because NRMPS, TRWP, and ECU were working in a partnership model, we were able to customize the project from the ground up; we could easily choose who participated in planning, developing, and implementing the workshop, as well as how teachers were trained and how the whole process was evaluated at the end. Likewise, because the teachers would be using digital technologies to respond to student writing, we were able to agree together that conducting the training in an online environment would both provide new knowledge to the teachers *and* demonstrate how online technologies impact writing and responses to writing. After the training workshop, the teachers from across the state would then be contracted with individually by NRMPS to serve as responders to the research projects generated by students in Nash County.

Based on early discussions among the members of our partnership, the RSWO project was designed to consist of five separate modules that would move participants progressively through an understanding of best practices when responding to student writing, methods of effective communication in virtual environments, the North Carolina Graduation Project (NCGP) itself, as well as a discussion space that remained active throughout RSWO:

- *Module 1:Understanding the NCGP Research Paper* helped participants become more familiar with the NCGP Research Paper rubric and the contents of the rubric, which was crucial because evaluators would be using the rubric to determine whether students met the requirements necessary to graduate high school. The subsections of this rubric included the following: Understanding the Graduation Project Resource, Review of Informational Writing Features, North Carolina Graduation Project Research Paper Rubric (both of which are PDF documents from the North Carolina Department of Public Instruction and can be found at http://www.ncpublicschools.org/docs/acre/writing/rubrics/features.pdf and http://www.ncpublicschools.org/graduationproject/resources/rubrics/, respectively), and a subsection that engaged participants in Applying the Rubric.

- *Module 2: Writing in Digital Environments* offered suggestions on how to effect an online response persona that encourages writers to think critically about the comments

and to revise their work productively. It included components such as "Etiquette of Constructing Digital Responses" as well as reflections on choice of tone and vocabulary when responding to writing online.

- *Module 3: Responding to Inspire Revision* helped participants provide feedback that would prompt students into revision rather than merely commenting on the level of performance. As we noted in that module, "our goal as E-responders is *not* to edit or proofread student writing, nor to do their reading/researching or thinking for them, but to teach the student writers to do these things for themselves so they can become better and more confident writers. We want to focus on higher-order (or global) concerns in the pieces of student writing we read rather than focusing on lower-order (or sentence level) concerns." To that end, this module included sections that helped participants think about what type of feedback is most useful to student writers, and asked them to connect higher-order concerns to the NCGP rubric and to share examples of their commentary on their own student writing and reflect upon those commentaries after reading excerpts from Knoblauch and Brannon's "Teacher Commentary on Student Writing—The State of the Art," Lunsford and Straub's "Twelve Readers Reading," and Anson's "Reflective Reading: Developing Thoughtful Ways to Respond to Students' Writing."

- *Module 4: Working with Online Resources* provided links and resources divided into categories to align with the "Five Features of Writing" and the NCGP assessment rubric in order to help participants quickly and easily find resources most relevant to the feature of writing with which the student writers struggled most.

- In *Module 5: Practice Responding to Student Projects*, participants found sample research papers for use in practicing responding with comments and tracking changes, as well as forums for discussing each others' responses. These papers also served as anchor papers of sorts, calibrating participants' implementation of the NCGP Paper Rubric as they responded to NRMPS student papers during their contractual period with NRMPS the following semester.

After the online training period ended, we realized that the participants would need one more brief online workshop, *Logistics of Responding to NRMS Students*, so that they would have a better understanding of the students themselves and the contexts in which their research essays were constructed. Throughout the project, facilitators maintained *The Coffee Shop*, a discussion forum where participants were encouraged to post comments related to their expectations for the Moodle experience before they began it, as well as a space where, throughout the professional development, they could post random thoughts or ask for help. Office hours for the facilitators were also listed in this module.

It is worth noting here that our NRMPS partner had been extensively involved at the state level in developing the NCGP, so her insights into the project from both a development and an implementation standpoint were invaluable as we negotiated our partnership and built the online PD module. The five "content" modules involved summaries of current research on their respective topics, as well as connections among that research, the North Carolina Standard Course of Study (our state's standards document), and our facilitators' own experience as expert teachers. RSWO participants were able to read through the materials at their own pace and connect to the hyperlinked research or examples, and were then required to write reflective journal-styled entries wherein they made their own connections between the research and their practices as teachers. Facilitators helped

to synthesize those reflections and used them to engage the participants in further synchronous and asynchronous discussions. After the five "content" modules were completed, the participants worked on responding to a common set of sample student essays; this component gave them practice with the digital tools for response (primarily Microsoft Word's comment feature, but also the practice of narrative/holistic response) and provided a space to norm response practices.

Participants' self-evaluations suggested that they valued the flexibility that the online PD model provided. They did not need to attempt all six modules in the same session; they could return as frequently as they wanted or needed to complete their training. This provided for more reflective time throughout the PD event, a kind of time that can be rushed in single-session, after-school PD events (Penuel et al, 2007, pp. 924 – 925). Two TRWP teacher consultants, one ECU faculty member, and one NRMPS instructional coach were actively involved in constructing and facilitating the RSWO modules. Although participants completed the modules over the course of one month, the facilitators were available for follow-up consultation through the end of the school year.

## TECHNOLOGY-AS-CATALYST IN RSWO

While our experience so far has not suggested that all professional development for K-12 teachers should move into digital environments, it has suggested that certain types of PD can work effectively in large part *because of* the technological environment. Organizations like TRWP, which is a grassroots collection of teachers and scholars from different schools and different levels of education, often run into the problem of technological mismatch. On the TRWP leadership team alone, for example, are two Mac users and three PC users; some use Microsoft Word, while others use Mac's Pages program for word processing. Across such diffuse networks, having common server-based collaboration tools can be key to erasing the headaches of various formatting issues and cross-OS compatibility. Building RSWO in Moodle, an online content management system (CMS), provided a way around these and other issues and even allowed the facilitators to bring some of the best parts of face-to-face interaction (e.g., synchronous conversation) into the digital training environment.

Building and facilitating RSWO in a digital space also made more sense than traditional face-to-face interaction because the teacher participants trained in RSWO would use digital tools and networks for communicating with the student writers in Nash County. We believed at the time, and our assessment data has affirmed, that training the teachers in an environment similar to the one they would eventually use for responding to student writers would allow the technology itself to be a less cumbersome distraction later as the participants worked as online responders. We knew from our own experience that Moodle could be a fairly straightforward interface for inexperienced users, and we knew that we could customize the interface so that any functions that might distract users could be eliminated from view. The ability of the trainers to customize and control the design and functionality of the CMS allowed for the technology to not direct the teaching – which is often the case in proprietary platforms like Blackboard; instead, the technology functioned more to facilitate the vision of the trainers and allowed for the partnership stakeholders to see their needs met more precisely. As teachers, when we use proprietary systems like Blackboard, we have little space for customizing the interface, modifying the layout/theme, or adding plug-ins to augment the learning environment. CMSes, like Moodle, allow facilitators just that sort of functionality. In fact, as we were building the RSWO components, we quickly realized that some of the built-in feedback tools would not be robust enough

to capture the type of assessments we sought both during the PD event and after its completion. The university partner began to search for additional Moodle plug-ins that would assist that work, and we found that the new plug-ins allowed us to better understand when, where, and why the participants were struggling or experiencing frustration either with the RSWO content or the technology itself. Beyond that, we also knew that the NCDPI was beginning to use Moodle for some of its online professional development modules, so many of the participants would already have been somewhat familiar with the interface, and this experience would better prepare those who were not for future NCDPI professional development delivered via Moodle.

From traditional face-to-face PD models, TRWP facilitators knew the importance of interaction, of providing a space for informal conversations, questions, resource sharing, and peer coaching. In many of our previous PD projects, those interactive moments have been seen as the most effective (or at least most "memorable") elements of professional development for teachers in our region whose evaluations of our PD events suggest that they feel increasingly walled off from their colleagues, even in their own schools, where planning periods and cross-class collaboration have been increasingly pushed to the side in favor of "efficiency" and "one-size-fits-all" professional development models. In the planning stages, the Moodle provided a common space for the facilitators to interact with the contracting partner in the local school district, as well as the university faculty member, and eventually for all three to interact with the participants. The online platform provided both synchronous and asynchronous communication experiences and was flexible enough that the facilitators could access information such as time spent on each task, numbers of posts made by each participant in each discussion forum, types of posts (voicing an "aha" moment or a moment of frustration) in order to track participants' progress through the modules; these tools also allowed facilitators to assess the work of the larger partnership by quickly responding to questions or posing new questions, clarifying objectives, and articulating and responding to the various needs of the participants. While there are similar ways to "track" work in face-to-face environments, they often seem obtrusive and stop the flow of the work. These assessment tools could more effectively fade into the background in a digital environment like Moodle.

## FORMING COMMUNITY PARTNERSHIPS

On one level, TRWP already "works" as an effective, alternative professional development project for K-12 schools in large part because it is built on a partnership model that teachers have found valuable for over 30 years in National Writing Project sites around the country. While traditional PD tends to be offered to administrators and teachers as "top-down," prepackaged, and "user-proof," face-to-face PD offered by TRWP engages administrators, teachers, and university researchers in a collaboration that customizes PD in ways meant to best meet the unique needs of each group. Projects like RSWO expand upon such collaboration by creating a virtual space where teachers from various school districts across the state can work together on their own professional development, sharing knowledge related to their local contexts with other teachers across a broader network, and where university partners are viewed less as "experts" who cannot be communicated with and more as accessible partners (and collaborators) in education.

RSWO ultimately showed us that a partnership or collaborative model of professional development could continue to work in our socially networked, Web 2.0 world. Certainly, there were parts of our F2F model that the TCs missed; TCs are themselves teachers who work in traditional blackboard-and-desk classrooms, and there's a productive synergy that often occurs when people who share common goals come together in the same physical space. For years, educational research has valued small group collaboration (Atwell, 1987; Bruffee, 1984; Calkins, 1994; Estrada, 2005; Hull, 2003; McCann et al, 2004), which doesn't necessarily happen in the same ways in digital PD, although collaboration certainly occurs. Likewise, any training pedagogy that involves some sort of individual writing/sharing/reflection process will necessarily have to change in asynchronous environments.

What we gave up in moving PD to an online, modular environment, seems balanced by the gains: more teachers had access to high-quality, research-based professional development, greater cross-educational collaboration was able to occur, and more authentic training occurred in large part because the context for the training represented the values of the training itself (e.g., teachers learned about responding in online environments while also responding, and receiving responses themselves, in an online environment).

## COMMUNITY IMPACT ON RSWO

Because RSWO was able to move beyond a single-school, face-to-face (F2F) model of professional development, the RSWO builders/facilitators also gained a great deal from the experience. Key to various Writing Project models is the constructivist belief that all partners bring experience and knowledge/expertise to an activity; one goal of facilitating such partnerships is to convince all those members present that they have valuable contributions to make in the collective knowledge generated in that space. As facilitators, we found that our own knowledge of writing and responding to writing was frequently challenged in productive ways, and because we were involved as partners in this particular enterprise, we were able to revise and rethink the modules that had been prepared as part of the RSWO project. In this way, such partnerships allow for the two- and three-way flow of knowledge and information that works to continually restructure the "modular" approach embodied in the RSWO Moodle, and likewise works to build leadership capacity throughout our own TRWP/NWP network.

Perhaps the most significant impact that community partners had on RSWO came in the form of building teacher leaders. In the National Writing Project model, "capacity" is a direct function of quality teacher leaders; local NWP sites like TRWP can continue primarily because of successful teacher consultants who finish the ISI and go on to build and facilitate high-quality professional development for/in area schools. TRWP's success rests on how effectively it mentors teacher consultants and helps them to become educational leaders in their schools, districts, and region. Projects like RSWO, which involved teachers from multiple school districts across the state, not only provide a space for TRWP teacher consultants to develop their "teachers-teaching-teachers" practices and to grow as educational leaders, but also allowed them to develop their professional reputations and credibility across the state. Practice and validation go a long way in transforming teachers from mere cogs in a system to change agents in that same system.

## EDUCATIONAL IMPACT: VALUING RSWO

The primary educational impact of the RSWO project was on the teachers who participated in the training modules, as they were the focus of this partnership. TRWP's goal of engaging various teachers from across the state was achieved: 29 teachers from 21 different cities, 27 different schools, and 13 distinct school districts from across NC participated in the month-long training module. The online space allowed for a more geographically diverse and complex pool of participants than any of TRWP's previous PD events.

Likewise, these teachers' work in the RSWO project was immediately put to use in responding to the writings of high school students in our partner school system. As teachers who have, ourselves, participated in various PD events over the years, we know how often, with traditional, F2F professional development, teachers can struggle to integrate the ideas they receive because these ideas may have no direct connection to the curriculum of the school, or these ideas may just not be received at a timely moment when the teacher can put them to use. We recognize these as key issues with F2F teacher development, but we also felt confident that the RSWO would work against that as the teachers would, immediately after finishing the training, be responding to student writing from our partner school.

Increasingly, universities are being accused of ignoring their "town-gown" relationship as research practices and discourses seem to remove university faculty further and further from the "practical" concerns of their local communities (Eble and Gaillet, 2004; Deans, 2000). The RSWO project worked to build the "town-gown" connection in a reciprocal fashion. What the RSWO facilitators (all of whom had worked with TRWP in different settings) brought to the teacher participants was research on responding to writing effectively, as well as practice with doing so in digital environments. The contracting partner from NRMPS helped educate the university faculty member and TRWP TCs about the North Carolina Graduate Project, helping us to clarify its goals and intentions and to construct modules that would communicate that work to teacher participants. That shared knowledge then influenced TRWP's other PD work as we integrated more knowledge about the NCGP into our other activities. Similarly, teacher participants in the Moodle often spoke of their own experiences in K-12 classrooms, experiences that helped remind the university partners about the complexities of teaching and responding to writing in K-12 environments.

## STRATEGIES FOR EFFECTIVE PARTNERSHIPS: COLLEGE, K-12, COMMUNITY

Our partnership model is multi-layered and capitalizes on at least four unique partnerships: the TRWP/ECU/NRMPS partnership, the TRWP/ECU/teacher relationship, the teacher-to-teacher relationship, and the over-arching NWP/ECU/K-12 partnership.

Too often, teachers are taught a specific professional development activity and do not have a way to use that knowledge beyond the immediate task, while research continues to demonstrate that embedded, context-specific activities are more useful to teachers and more productive for improving teacher (and student) performance (Huber, 2010, pp. 41-42; Darling-Hammond and Richardson, 2009, p. 49). The partnerships created through the RSWO venture can truly be defined as unique partnerships in the context of public education, standing against the normal communication that obtains between professional development "givers" and teacher "receivers," because the partners involved all found uses for the work beyond the RSWO context itself, experienced the knowledge creation as reciprocal, and ultimately found the relationships that were built to be on-going. We believe this to be a powerful argument for both fully online and hybrid face-to-face/online PD models because digital environments like Moodle provide space for different types of feedback and discussion that remain grounded in the specific writings, thoughts, and experiences of the participants and facilitators. Those involved have the chance to return to these sorts of partnership spaces to resolve conflicts and pose questions (e.g., "The 'best practices' do not seem to be working for me; what am I doing wrong?") in ways that might not be available in more traditional models. Once the workshop facilitators have left their schools, there may be no space for follow-up.

It is worth noting, as well, that our local partnership may have been as successful as it was because it grew out of the partnership model inherent in the National Writing Project. As part of the community base of experts, teachers serve as experts in the development and implementation of PD work at the TRWP. Utilizing our vibrant network of teacher consultants who are themselves K-12 teachers in eastern NC, and thus experts in their field, creates a dialogue among peers that is often sought but infrequently attainable in the day-to-day work of teachers. This model of peer partnership is valuable and long-lasting, well beyond the parameters of our particular project. We find that this type of partnership is more sustainable than the majority of top-down models we frequently see and experience at work in local school systems. RSWO extends that model to an online space, and of course, parts of the partnership do not stop once the module itself has been completed by the teacher participants. During the following summer and fall, as module developers, we returned to the Web site and the feedback from participants in order to process what had worked well and what had not. Also, we debriefed the project with our public school partner, who provided feedback on where we might reshape the modules, which aspects of responding to student writing the participants struggled with, and how we might improve the modules to better address those gaps. Since then, we have made use of TRWP-sponsored writing retreats to revise our thinking and to share our experiences with other members of our network as they considered developing similar online PD projects for schools.

As for the partnership between the school system and the university, we found it to be rhetorically sound because the professional development provided was tailor-made for the school system, was based upon their expressed needs, and was evaluated by the contracting school partner for effectiveness. We realize, of course, that successful replications are necessary to lend validity to our findings.

## PROBLEMIZATION AND CONCLUSION

As in any teaching situation, there are some inherent issues that must be addressed when planning and adapting instruction to meet the needs of all learners. In our online professional development model, we experienced many of the same concerns as we would in a face-to-face professional development environment, such as the need for differentiated instruction for multiple learning styles and varying degrees of investment or ability to fulfill commitments among learners (Gardner, 1999; Dunn, 2001). There are the cruise-through learners and the lingerers, those who complete all parts of every task, and those who always seem to run out of time. What we noticed is that when participants are working in an asynchronous setting, not only is there the positive effect of having time to work when it is more convenient to the learner, but also the negative effect of having so much, virtually unlimited time, to complete each task (so long as the final deadline is met), that some participants spent much more time than the Moodle creators intended on each task. As is true too frequently in instructional planning, some tasks were overly detailed and belabored the point of the activity, leaving some participants frustrated. Without face-to-face interaction, it was difficult to judge that level of hyper-processing and to intervene *at the moment*, but, through the message board postings of participants, facilitators could surmise that frustration and were able to respond to and lessen the participants' concerns. This is a benefit of online instruction—each learner's voice is distinct and may be heard; whereas, in a traditional face-to-face setting, many learners choose not to participate verbally or their voices blend together, leaving quieter participants vocally overshadowed by stronger voices.

Beyond the teacher participants, there were also struggles among the Teacher Consultants and the other facilitators. Varying levels of expertise with Moodle creation among the partnership team

was an obstacle that slowed our preparation phase somewhat. Only the university partner had expertise with Moodle and thus he found it necessary to devote much of the time scheduled for content building to the task of training Teacher Consultants and the NRMPS partner in how to create and manipulate content in Moodle. While not a daunting task, this did slow the content-building phase of the project. The upside of that situation is that the formerly inexperienced partners walked away with new knowledge in the area of digital content management systems; one facilitator went on to create a Moodle for his own high school students as a result of working on this project.

A similar problem was that some members of the group participating in the professional development came to the scenario seriously lacking what the partnership team considered standard technical abilities. Some training in posting and locating message board comments and posting photos as avatars was unforeseen, but necessary. Again, in the end, participants took away new technical abilities that would be useful as they responded to NRMPS students, but which would also be useful to their own classrooms and future teaching. On some level, because these teachers were not in a training session required by their own schools/administrators, the technology-based training was low-stakes; we think this may have contributed to their ability to push on even in moments of frustration or when there were technological glitches. In the future, we plan to investigate this idea, comparing the low-stakes/high-stakes environments and their respective impacts on participant engagement.

Ultimately, our partnership among the university, the Tar River Writing Project, and the K-12 school system met the needs of the contracting partner (NRMPS), was a positive learning and leadership experience for writing project Teacher Consultants, and helped put a community partner face on the university, bringing the "ivory tower" and "the trenches" to a common ground. As a bonus, teacher participants across the state of

North Carolina benefitted from a quality online professional development experience in which they learned more about the NCGP rubric as well as online response to writing, which they could take back to their own classrooms, and students in NRMPS received revision-inspiring responses to their NCGP papers from highly-trained respondents. Based on this positive partnership, we feel confident that digitally mediated partnerships will become an increasingly important part of TRWP's professional development work.

## REFERENCES

Atwell, N. (1987). *In the middle: Writing, reading, and learning with adolescents*. Portsmouth, NH: Heinemann.

Bruffee, K. A. (1984). Collaborative learning and the conversation of mankind. *College English, 46*(7), 635–652. doi:10.2307/376924

Calkins, L. M. (1994). *The art of teaching writing*. Portsmouth, NH: Heinemann.

Cushman, E. (1996). The rhetorician as an agent of social change. *College Composition and Communication, 47*(1), 7–28. doi:10.2307/358271

Darling-Hammond, L., & Richardson, N. (2009). Teacher learning: What matters? *Educational Leadership, 66*(5), 46–53.

Deans, T. (2000). *Writing partnerships: Service learning in composition*. Urbana, IL: National Council of Teachers of English.

Dunn, P. A. (2001). *Talking, sketching, moving: Multiple literacies in the teaching of writing*. Portsmouth, NH: Boynton/Cook.

Eble, M., & Gaillet, L. L. (2004). Educating community intellectuals: Rhetoric, moral philosophy, and civic engagement. *Technical Communication Quarterly, 13*(3), 341–354. doi:10.1207/s15427625tcq1303_7

Estrada, P. (2005). The courage to grow: A researcher and teacher linking professional development with small-group reading instruction and student achievement. *Research in the Teaching of English, 39*(4), 320–364.

Gardner, H. (1999). *Intelligence reframed: Multiple intelligences for the 21st century*. New York, NY: Basic Books.

Huber, C. (2010). Professional learning 2.0. *Educational Leadership, 67*(8), 41–46.

Hull, G. A. (2003). At last: Youth culture and digital media: New literacies for new times. *Research in the Teaching of English, 38*(2), 229–233.

McCann, T. M., Johannesen, L. R., Kahn, E., Smagorinsky, P., & Smith, M. W. (Eds.). (2005). *Reflective teaching, reflective learning: How to develop critically engaged readers, writers, and speakers*. Portsmouth, NH: Heinemann.

Penuel, W. R., Fishman, B. J., Yamaguchi, R., & Gallagher, L. P. (2007). What makes professional development effective? Strategies that foster curriculum implementation. *American Educational Research Journal, 44*(4), 921–958. doi:10.3102/0002831207308221

## ENDNOTE

[1] The NC Public Schools Web site provides additional information about the NCGP, including rubrics and samples (http://www.ncpublicschools.org/graduationproject/).

# Chapter 15
# Web–Based Information Science Education:
## Leveraging the Power of the Network to Re-Define the Global Classroom

**Kathleen Schisa**
*Syracuse University, USA*

**Anne McKinney**
*University of Illinois at Urbana-Champaign, USA*

**Debbie Faires**
*San Jose State University, USA*

**Bruce Kingma**
*Syracuse University, USA*

**Rae Anne Montague**
*University of Illinois at Urbana-Champaign, USA*

**Linda C. Smith**
*University of Illinois at Urbana-Champaign, USA*

**Marianne Sterna**
*San Jose State University, USA*

## ABSTRACT

*Web-based Information Science Education (WISE) is a collaborative distance education model that increases the quality, access and diversity of online education opportunities. The WISE Consortium is a group of graduate Library and Information Science (LIS) programs founded on three pillars: quality, pedagogy, and collaborations (Montague & Pluzhenskaia, 2007). This chapter outlines the approach to achieving these three pillars and the assessment mechanisms used to measure the consortium's success. Highlights include WISE Pedagogy, the administrative division of WISE dedicated to providing faculty development resources for online education, and WISE+, an initiative that supports partnerships enabling WISE schools and LIS associations to develop courses together suitable for graduate credit and continuing education. While the WISE consortium is specific to LIS education, the model could be applied more broadly to other disciplines.*

DOI: 10.4018/978-1-60960-623-7.ch015

# INTRODUCTION

Web-based Information Science Education (WISE) is a distance education model that aims to increase the quality, access, and diversity of online learning opportunities in Library and Information Science (LIS) education. Established in 2004, The WISE consortium is a group of LIS programs that work together to define standards and metrics for online education, to provide a collaborative marketplace for online LIS courses, and to share faculty development resources. While WISE is specific to LIS education, the core model and principles could be applied to online education across a broad array of disciplines.

This chapter discusses the core model and activities of WISE and special initiatives including WISE Pedagogy, the administrative division of WISE dedicated to providing faculty development resources for online education, and WISE+, an initiative which supports partnerships that enable WISE schools and professional organizations to collaboratively offer courses suitable for graduate credit and continuing education.

## History of WISE

WISE was conceptualized in 2002 during a conversation on quality and access in online LIS education between colleagues Linda C. Smith (University of Illinois at Urbana-Champaign) and Bruce Kingma (Syracuse University). Over the subsequent two years, Kingma and Smith collaborated to define quality metrics in online education. During that time, Syracuse and Illinois began sharing online courses, allowing students matriculated at one school to enroll in electives hosted by the other with minimal administrative burden (e.g., no need to transfer credits; tuition paid to the home institution).

In 2004, Kingma and Smith received a Laura Bush 21st Century Librarian grant from the Institute of Museum and Library Services (IMLS) to establish WISE. This enabled the co-founders to bring additional schools on board. The consortium has since grown to 15 member schools and, as of fall 2010, 595 courses have been offered through WISE, and 917 students have enrolled through the consortium. WISE Pedagogy has served numerous faculty from WISE schools and the greater LIS community through online and face-to-face workshops and on-demand Web resources.

# THE WISE PILLARS

The vision of WISE is based on three pillars of online education identified by the founding schools:

1. Quality: the need for quality metrics for online courses and programs,
2. Pedagogy: the demand for pedagogical training for faculty teaching online, and
3. Collaboration: the value of collaboration between academic programs for the benefit of their students (Montague & Pluzhenskaia, 2007).

## Quality

One of WISE's core goals is definition and dissemination of quality metrics for online courses and programs. To reach this goal, the consortium developed a working quality metrics document titled *WISE: A model for quality online education in library and information science* (WISE, 2009). The document includes principles and metrics related to administrative and technical support for faculty and students, learning effectiveness, and student services, with core concepts including a commitment to emerging technologies, faculty and student support for teaching and learning online, access to library resources, support of the learning community. It is used in the WISE membership application process, and has also been used by non-member schools as a reference for developing or evaluating their own online courses and programs. Table 1 provides a summary of

*Table 1. Summary of WISE metrics*

| WISE: A model for quality online education in library and information science Summary of Metrics and Principles | | |
|---|---|---|
| | **Course-level Metrics** | **Program-level Metrics** |
| **Administrative and Technical Support** | • Learning management system (LMS) or host environment and supplemental technology are accessible, intelligible, reliable, stable, and authenticated.<br>• Schools have a technology plan and provide students and faculty with adequate technical support.<br>• Students are provided with information about course expectations and prerequisites prior to the start of the course.<br>• Students and faculty have access to appropriate course-related information resources (e.g., digitized library materials).<br>• There is a clear policy on ownership of materials developed for online courses. | • Schools provide administrative resources for the online program, including clear admission, registration, and advising processes, and a process to ensure quality in online courses.<br>• Online programs are accredited by a professional organization.<br>• Schools promote faculty and staff participation in organizations related to online education. |
| **Faculty** | • Faculty are well prepared and have access to support and resources for online teaching.<br>• Faculty are able to meet the diverse needs of online students.<br>• Faculty have opportunities to consider the online experience (e.g. through self-evaluation).<br>• Faculty provide students with opportunities for assessment which accurately measures achievement of learning outcomes<br>• Faculty provide prompt feedback. | |
| **Learning Effectiveness** | • Course design promotes learning effectiveness.<br>• Course objectives and outcomes are clear, evident, and regularly reviewed.<br>• Course materials support objectives and outcomes.<br>• Collaborative learning experiences support learning communities, which enhance learning outcomes.<br>• Course activities foster community and technology is used to enhance communication.<br>• Faculty and staff pay attention to factors that can enhance the quality of the learning experience for the student. | |
| **Students** | • Students are comfortable with the pace and style of the online course.<br>• Students actively contribute to the learning community, and receive feedback. | • Online students have opportunities for advising, internships, and orientations.<br>• Students are satisfied with administration of online programs.<br>• Availability of online courses allows students to complete degrees in a timely fashion.<br>• The school fosters a learning community that extends beyond the online classroom.<br>• Online students have access to student groups, special events (e.g. webcasts of campus lectures), and awards and scholarships. |

the metrics; the full version is available online at www.wiseeducation.org (WISE, 2009).

The WISE principles and metrics were developed by faculty and administrators from member schools with extensive collective expertise and practical experience in online education. They are revised periodically with consideration to new developments in the field. Members of the administrative leadership team have also been en-

gaged in research on quality in online education, impact of collaboration, and economic implications of consortial models like WISE on online education (Keefe & Kingma, 2006; Montague & Pluzhenskaia, 2007; Kingma & Schisa, 2010).

The work of the consortium has been guided and informed not only by WISE members, but also by the excellent work of many other organizations dedicated to online education including the Sloan

Consortium (Sloan-C), the American Distance Education Consortium (ADEC), WCET, Society for Applied Learning Technology (SALT) and the United States Distance Learning Association (USDLA), each of which promotes quality online education through means such as the definition of quality metrics, and discussion, publication, and dissemination of best practices and research findings (Moore, 2005; ADEC, 2003; WCET, 2010; SALT, 2010; USDLA, 2010.). Two resources of note are the Sloan Consortium Five Pillars of Quality in Online Programs, which address principles for quality asynchronous online education at the program level, and the American Distance Education Consortium guidelines for individual course quality, which address ideal characteristics not only for providers of online education, but also for learner engagement (Moore, 2005; ADEC, 2003).

**Assessment of quality:** Assessment of quality begins when prospective member schools submit a checklist documenting how their institutions fit the expectations outlined in the WISE quality metrics document. Existing members review the submission and identify areas in need of attention or explanation. Upon admission to the consortium, each school signs a Memorandum of Understanding (MOU) defining the responsibilities associated with membership. Items include adherence to the WISE quality metrics, provision of adequate administrative support to participate in the course exchange, and permission for WISE to survey students participating in WISE courses for assessment purposes.

The consortium also assesses quality by collecting student feedback and best practices from faculty recipients of the annual Excellence in Online Education Award. This information provides an overview of the strengths and weaknesses of the consortium's course-sharing activities, and provides insight into individual institutions' adherence to the quality metrics.

*Evaluations*: WISE surveys students enrolled through the consortium using a confidential electronic evaluation that assesses the following:

- Course quality
- Instructor effectiveness
- Satisfaction with technical support and access to resources
- Clarity of syllabus and course expectations
- Timeliness of instructor feedback
- Satisfaction with the level of personal interaction with faculty and students
- Achievement of course expectations
- Value of course in enhancing the student's program
- Suggestions for improvements to the course and WISE process

Response rate is typically 55 -75%. Due to the low number of WISE students typically enrolled in a course (2-3) or at an institution (5-10) each semester, the consortium cannot provide individualized feedback to each school every semester without compromising confidentiality. Instead WISE periodically provides a summary to each school, which includes feedback from a sufficient number of students across a sufficient number of courses to ensure confidentiality. While this may not be as beneficial to schools as individual course data, it is the best confidentiality-sensitive solution we have identified.

*Faculty awards*: Annually students are invited to nominate outstanding WISE instructors for the Excellence in Online Teaching Award. A unique aspect of the award is that students may only nominate instructors from institutions other than their own institution of matriculation. Statements from the students and tips contributed by the award recipients are combined to create a best practices publication, which is featured on the WISE and WISE Pedagogy Web sites (WISE Pedagogy, 2009b). Nomination themes typically include engagement and responsiveness, ability to create community online, and effective use of technology to enhance learning. The award gives WISE the opportunity to honor outstanding faculty while working toward achieving our goal of recognizing and sharing best practices in online education.

WISE also distributes best practices and quality metrics through our newsletter and annual report, the WISE Admin listserv, and presentations at various conferences. Representatives from the WISE schools also meet each year to discuss quality in online education. Meetings take place during LIS conferences or online using synchronous web-conferencing software, and periodically WISE hosts a multi-day mini-summit for the member schools.

## Pedagogy

One of the foremost goals of WISE is to increase the preparedness of instructors who wish to teach in the online environment. Through online and face-to-face workshops and resources, WISE Pedagogy seeks to provide LIS instructors with successful strategies to develop sound pedagogical practices for online instruction. By better preparing instructors to teach online, we can help to improve the overall quality of online education.

From July 2007 to September 2008, WISE offered eight sessions of an online workshop, *Introduction to Online Pedagogy*. This course was taught using the Moodle system through the University of Illinois at Urbana-Champaign. 137 individuals from WISE and non-WISE institutions throughout the United States, Canada, and Australia participated.

A self-paced on-demand course Web site was launched in 2009 in response to participant feedback and demand from individuals who were not able to participate in the workshop due to schedule limitation. The site is a wiki-based tutorial covering lessons and topics from the Moodle-based workshop, formatted into seven modules:

1.   Introduction & Overview

2.   Course Website Basics
3.   Communicating With Your Students
4.   Developing Reciprocity and Cooperation Among Students
5.   Planning the Path to Learning
6.   Achieving High Expectations
7.   Wrapping Up (2009)

The modules each contain a series of pages on topics relevant to online instruction, grafting Chickering and Gamson's *Seven Principles for Good Practice* (1987) to suit a graduate-level online learning environment:

1.   Good practice encourages student-faculty contact.
2.   Good practice encourages cooperation among students.
3.   Good practice encourages active learning.
4.   Good practice gives prompt feedback.
5.   Good practice emphasizes time on task.
6.   Good practice communicates high expectations.
7.   Good practice respects diverse talents and ways of learning.

Materials are delivered asynchronously and learners participate in interactive discussion and learning exercises through an online discussion board. The workshop incorporates other multimedia and web 2.0 technologies such as YouTube, Google Docs, podcasts, StripGenerator comic strips, and Creative Commons-licensed photos (http://introductiononlinepedagogy.pbworks.com/) (Figure 1).

Each of the workshop's modules includes an exercise designed to help students practice the information covered and interact with other learners. Participants who complete all the exercises are eligible to receive a certificate of completion. By obtaining this certificate, online instructors may demonstrate that they have taken measures to learn basic tenets of effective online teaching practices. The certificate does not equate to course

*Figure 1. Screenshot from the Introduction to Online Pedagogy on-demand workshop page, "Facilitating Group Work" (http://introductiononlinepedagogy.pbworks.com/Facilitating-Group-Work)*

credit toward a degree in online pedagogy, or certification that requires a similar depth of study. Its purpose is to indicate that the individual has been introduced to important concepts in online pedagogy and has engaged with a community of WISE scholars and instructors (Figure 2).

WISE has also offered six face-to-face pedagogy workshops at the annual conference of the Association for Library & Information Science Education (ALISE).These workshops have addressed effective practices for online teaching and learning through highly participatory panel pre-

sentations and breakout discussions led by successful WISE instructors. Technologies useful to instruction have also been addressed, including web 2.0 products, learning management systems, and social media networks.

WISE Pedagogy has also utilized social media resources including Twitter (http://twitter.com/wisepedagogy), a blog (http://www.wisepedagogy.com/blog/), and a Delicious link collection (http://delicious.com/annemck/bundle:OnlinePedagogy%2FeLearning) to continue dialogue on new developments in online pedagogy and teaching technologies throughout the year.

**Assessment of pedagogy:** Using statistics, feedback from participants and WISE Administrators (via face-to-face meetings, e-mail) and the checklist of WISE Quality Metrics, WISE Pedagogy has been able to adapt its workshops and resources to suit the needs of learners and instructors.

The on-demand workshop was created in response to evaluation forms and other feedback from the Moodle-based online workshop. Participants requested a way to learn without a set schedule that competed with their other responsibilities. There was also a need for a workshop that would not be limited to a specific number of registered participants on a first-come, first-served

*Figure 2. Screenshot from the Introduction to Online Pedagogy on-demand workshop page, "Learning Objectives" showing the student exercise prompt (http://introductiononlinepedagogy.pbworks.com/Learning-Objectives)*

basis. As a result, the on-demand workshop is publicly available to anyone without registration or a set schedule.

Feedback from the face-to-face workshops held at ALISE has also influenced future workshops and pedagogical resources. Evaluation feedback from face-to-face participants has allowed WISE to incorporate positive changes in the next year's workshop, selecting topics and formats requested by popular demand. The evaluations have also offered inspiration for other resources, such as the blog and Twitter feed (2009).

WISE Pedagogy's resources are freely available online and much of the material is broad enough in scope that online instructors across cultures and disciplines have found valuable information and effective practices within the resources. The asynchronous design has also made the resources more accessible to people located in different time zones: participants in the on-demand workshop have joined from all over the world. The same is true for the other social media resources. The blog is featured in two different directories of e-learning blogs: The International Edubloggers Directory and eLearning Learning (http://www.wisepedagogy.com/blog/).

## Collaboration

WISE is built on a solid foundation of collaboration among our members. This section details the course exchange model, technologies used for administration and instruction, and WISE+, the initiative which funds course development partnerships among member schools and associations.

**Course exchange:** The WISE course exchange model is based on the premise that even with a cap of 25 students there will be excess capacity in some online courses, especially those that deal with specialized topics of interest to a limited population. Using the consortium exchange, host schools invite students from other WISE schools to fill virtual seats, which would otherwise remain empty.

## Offering Courses through WISE

Before each enrollment period, members choose courses to offer through the consortium and post the details to the central WISE Web site. Hosting criteria include

- The course is likely to have excess capacity when capped at 25 students,
- The instructor has taught online successfully and will accept WISE students, and
- The course technology has been used successfully in past semesters as it will be used in the present course.

## Selecting Courses Available Through WISE

Members select WISE courses that complement their own curriculum. Selection criteria include:

- The course is likely to be of interest to the school's students,
- Course content does not overlap with a regular course offered by the school, and
- The course format (e.g. synchronous sessions) is likely to appeal to the students.

## Requesting Enrollment

- Each school has a dedicated student login.
- Students log in to view courses that are pre-selected by their home school.
- Students request enrollment through the WISE Web site.
- Central WISE administration confirms that each student has his or her home school's permission to enroll, notifies students of their enrollment status, and sends each member school a list of incoming and outgoing WISE students. Host faculty also receive lists of WISE students in their classes (Figure 3).

*Figure 3. Screenshot of WISE website*

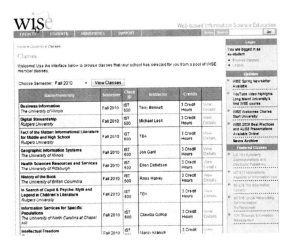

*Figure 4. Hosting a WISE course*

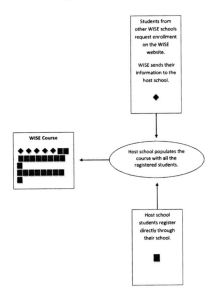

## Registration and Course Completion

- After acceptance into a WISE course, the student is registered for an independent study or special topics course at their home school.
- The student participates in the course using the host school's learning management system.
- Upon completion, grades are processed through WISE, and the student receives a grade and credit from their home school.

The primary challenge of the exchange is excess demand for limited capacity, which can result in students being shut out from their first choice course. To address this, WISE implemented a ranking system in the Web form that allows students to enter multiple course requests. If a student cannot be accommodated in their first choice they are enrolled in an alternative choice if available.

**Collaborative Technology:** Several administrative and instructional technologies are used to facilitate WISE collaboration. While the features and functionalities of the technologies may vary, students, faculty and staff consistently agree that stability, reliability and access are valued more

highly than innovation and the "cool factor." The foundational technical elements of the course should be seamless and user-friendly. Once this foundation is in place, both students and instructors should have the opportunity to experiment with innovative or elaborative technologies, but if these new technologies fail the core technology must still be sufficient to facilitate interaction, transfer of information, and achievement of learning outcomes.

***Instructional technologies***: WISE schools use a variety of learning management systems and supplemental instructional technologies. This poses a challenge to students who must adapt to new technologies when participating in WISE courses, but it provides a rich opportunity for members to share experiences with these technologies. Table 2 provides examples of some of the core and supplemental instructional technologies used by WISE member schools.

While most schools have established seamless procedures to provide hosted students with access to required instructional technology, occasionally issues arise. The issues often do not lie with the technology, but with a breakdown in communication among instructors, WISE administra-

*Table 2. Instructional technologies used*

| Instructional Technologies Used by WISE Schools | |
| --- | --- |
| **Learning Management Systems used include:** | **Supplemental technologies used include:** |
| • Blackboard<br>• ANGEL<br>• Desire2Learn<br>• eCollege<br>• Moodle<br>• Course wikis | • Elluminate Live<br>• Adobe Connect web conferencing<br>• Panopto lecture capture<br>• SharePoint<br>• Skype<br>• Second Life<br>• YouTube<br>• Twitter |

tors, technologists, and students. Problems are typically solved with an e-mail clarifying the situation. Students use support at the host school for any technology issues unrelated to general access. This local service model works well as long as students are provided with clear contact information and appropriate host school staff are well-versed in policies and processes for WISE students.

***Administrative technologies:*** Posting and registration for the course exchange is facilitated by a central website with a secure custom-built database. Phone, e-mail, face-to-face, and Skype communication and collaborative tools such as GoogleDocs are also used regularly. Other emerging applications (e.g. Twitter, FaceTime) are used periodically on request. As practices develop which regularly utilize these applications (e.g. use of Twitter to send out enrollment deadline reminders), several will likely be adopted for more consistent use.

While the exchange process is aided by technology, the human resources of the WISE Director and WISE school administrators are critical to the functionality of the system. At the current scale (serving 50-90 students each semester), personal communication with students and administrators is possible, and adds to the service level and value of the WISE experience. If substantial growth occurs the consortium may have to add administrative resources to maintain comparable quality of service.

Both for administrative and instructional technology, there is room for evolution. It is likely that an increasing number of WISE member schools will transition toward mobile access to online learning objects and administrative services at some point in the future if they have not yet done so. To remain user-friendly, WISE will need to adapt, not only considering mobile access for the administrative Web site, but also considering how the existing quality metrics should be revised to more completely address the impact of mobile learning.

**Assessment of collaboration:** In addition to assessment of individual courses, WISE assesses collaboration among members using institutional activity reports. Members periodically receive reports detailing their level of activity in the consortium, as well as popularity across all courses offered through the consortium. These reports provide an opportunity for the school to evaluate these factors:

- Number of students participating in the course exchange and effectiveness of internal efforts to market WISE courses,
- Retention of students participating in the course exchange (drop rates),
- Ability to contribute seats in courses of interest to WISE students from other schools.

**WISE+ course development sub-grants.** In 2006, WISE received a second IMLS grant to expand the consortium to include professional organizations. The WISE+ grant provided funding for WISE members to partner with organizations to develop and offer courses related to the specialty of the organization and suitable both for graduate and continuing education. The result is a dynamic classroom where LIS students and professionals learn together, network and share ideas. Course topics reflect current issues in the field and many WISE+ instructors are practicing librarians with

*Table 3. WISE+ instructor selection*

| WISE+ Instructor Selection | | |
|---|---|---|
| | **Benefits** | **Challenges** |
| **Existing host-school instructor teaches the course** | • Instructor is familiar with the course technology, resources available, and administrative processes such as grading and other deadlines.<br>• Well-known instructors may attract students from the host school based on reputation.<br>• May increase the potential for a new course to be offered regularly due to instructor support and availability. | • May be challenging to find a host school instructor who is already actively engaged with the organization.<br>• If the organization is not involved in instruction, it may be less likely to market the course to members and contribute to content. |
| **Organization member teaches the course** | • The instructor is fully immersed in the organization and is likely to have current practical experience in the course topic.<br>• The organization may feel a greater stake in the partnership<br>• Organization members may enroll based on instructor reputation.<br>• The instructor is well-positioned to utilize the organization's resources. | • The school risks losing access to the instructor for future semesters.<br>• The instructor may not have adequate online teaching experience; this must be carefully evaluated before the instructor is approved.<br>• The instructor must be familiarized with the host school course technology, support and resources, and administrative processes |

extensive experience in their subject area. As of spring 2010, seventeen WISE+ courses have been developed and several are now offered regularly by the host school. Several models of WISE+ partnerships emerged over the course of the WISE+ grant. This section provides examples of these models. Tables 3 and 4 summarize some of the benefits and challenges of instructor selection and use of new or existing courses for the various WISE+ partnership models.

***Model 1: An existing course is opened to organization members; an existing host school instructor teaches the course.*** Music Librarianship and Bibliography, a course offered by the University of Illinois at Urbana-Champaign (UIUC) in partnership with the Music Library Association, is an example of Model 1. The course

*Table 4. WISE+ course options: New vs. existing*

| New vs. Existing Courses | | |
|---|---|---|
| | **Benefits** | **Challenges** |
| **Existing course is opened to organization members and modified to meet the organization's needs if necessary** | • Less development effort is needed, but the course content will still be refreshed with input from the partner organization.<br>• An existing course may have a consistent following and guaranteed enrollment at the host school due to reputation.<br>• Trouble-spots will have been identified and resolved in previous iterations of the course. | • Demand can be a challenge; if the course is filled by host school students, it may be necessary to open an additional section to accommodate WISE and the organization. This is not always feasible due to instructor availability, or funding, as some of the participating students do not pay tuition to the host school.<br>• The instructor may hesitate to make significant changes proposed by the partner organization. |
| **New course is developed with input from the organization** | • Subject experts from the organization have the opportunity to help develop curriculum which will shape the future workforce.<br>• Course is very likely to meet the needs of the organization.<br>• The School has the opportunity to interface with practitioners to enrich curriculum and stay at the forefront of the specialty. | • There may be kinks in a new course the first time it is offered.<br>• When offering a new course through WISE+, trouble-spots are exposed not only to the host school students, but also to WISE students and members of the professional organization. |

has been offered annually on-campus for decades. The instructor John Wagstaff, UIUC Music Librarian initiated discussions with the Music Library Association's Education Committee to gain their support for an online offering. Based on feedback, he made some adjustments in the syllabus and received their endorsement. Organization members officially registered for community credit at UIUC, rather than through enrollment coordination through the association. All students participated in weekly synchronous sessions using web-conferencing software such as Elluminate supplemented with asynchronous activity using forums and other features of the Moodle course management system. Technical support is provided by staff at the host school.

This partnership benefited from having an existing course that could be presented for review by MLA, and an instructor who is a recognized and active member in MLA as well as a member of the host school community. His enthusiasm for teaching online and reaching more students was also key to the success of the course.

In the future, in addition to offering the Music Librarianship course annually, UIUC will explore possibilities for partnering with MLA to develop additional credit and non-credit online offerings on more specialized topics. This is of interest to UIUC, given the school's longtime strength in preparing music librarians and the potential audience for such offerings beyond Illinois.

***Model 2: A host school instructor teaches an existing course as with model 1; in this case the school partners with multiple organizations.*** An example of model 2 is Services to Racially and Ethnically Diverse Communities, a course offered by San Jose State University with the American Indian Library Association, REFORMA: Orange County CA Chapter, and REFORMA: Bibliotecas para la Gente Chapter. San Jose State saw potential interest in this existing course among LIS associations located in their richly diverse region. The course had also been offered successfully to

WISE in previous semesters, and was taught by an existing SJSU faculty member.

Communication with the organizations, including enrollment of organization members, took place primarily via e-mail, phone, and Web and print forms. WISE students enrolled through the WISE website, and host school students enrolled as usual through the online SJSU registration system. Students interfaced asynchronously with the instructor and with each other utilizing SJSU's learning management system, Angel.

This was a unique WISE+ partnership in that multiple associations were involved. Seats were evenly divided among three partners, WISE, and the host school. Organization members did not enroll for credit or pay tuition, but did complete an online form outlining prerequisite skills and technical requirements. This multi-organization partnership could form the basis for a sustainable method of offering WISE+ courses. Demand and cost could theoretically be distributed among the institution and organizations involved (assuming organizations or their members were willing and able to pay tuition), making delivery feasible in the absence of grant support.

One partner requested a Memorandum of Understanding (MOU), which the host school replicated with the other two partner organizations. The host school found the MOU to be a helpful way to articulate the conditions of the partnership. This is a good precedent for future partnerships, particularly if funding comes into consideration. If further WISE-related course partnerships are developed, a general MOU should be signed by the host institution, organizations, and lead consortium administrators.

***Model 3: A new course is developed by the host school to fit the needs of the organization and the school; an existing host school instructor teaches the course.*** Gaming in Libraries is an example of model 3. The course was developed by Scott Nicholson, a faculty member at Syracuse University, in partnership with the American Library Association (ALA). The month-long,

1-credit course was delivered via daily video lecture available to the public and the entire partner organization on YouTube and archive.org. Registered students were required to post public video responses to lectures on YouTube, and to participate in activities in the school's Blackboard LMS. ALA also established a forum dedicated to the course where members could view and discuss the material.

The course has had a broad reach due to the instructor's use of the Open Educational Resources model; thousands of people from the library and gaming communities have viewed it and many have participated in online discussions related to the content. The open access format has proven to be a great marketing tool for gaming in libraries as well as for librarianship as a field, and is also extremely valuable to librarians working in organizations with little funding for continuing professional development.

The true impact of free lectures is difficult to measure. In terms of sheer volume, however, the first lecture, which was released early in June 2008, has been viewed over 2,300 times. According to a survey conducted by the instructor, roughly 35% of the viewers were not formally engaged in the field of library and information science and would not have had access to the content had it only been shared in an LIS classroom setting (Kingma et al., 2010).

Though the course ended in June 2009, the instructor continues to post brief videos periodically, and all the lectures are still available on YouTube and at http://www.gamesinlibraries. org/course/. Nicholson also produces a Games in Libraries Podcast that is freely available and provides interested individuals with a continued source of information on the course topic.

The free lectures served the association and the public, and increased interest in the course topic. However, this combined with the intensity of the lecture-per-day format may have detracted from paid enrollment. To be sustainable without grant funding in the future there must be a mechanism in place to ensure that enough students or graduates seeking continuing education are paying for the credit-bearing aspects of the course (e.g., discussion, assignments, etc.) to make the production and sharing of the free course content viable.

*Model 4: A new course is developed and taught by an organization member for graduate and continuing education credit, with input and approval from the host school.* One example of model 4 is Theological Librarianship offered by the University of Illinois at Urbana-Champaign (UIUC) in partnership with the American Theological Library Association (ATLA). In 2006 the executive director of ATLA asked UIUC to partner with ATLA to develop and offer an online course on Theological Librarianship. The ATLA Professional Development Committee had already developed a course outline and the organization was able to recruit a member with experience teaching online. UIUC worked with the instructor to review the syllabus and ensure its suitability for a graduate credit course at Illinois. As with Music Librarianship (described in model 1), organization members officially registered for community credit at UIUC and all participants joined weekly online synchronous Web conferences, which were supplemented with asynchronous activity in Moodle.

The course is offered annually because it meets an identified need (there are no other regularly-offered full-semester courses on theological librarianship) and is well suited to the pedagogical model of weekly synchronous sessions, which enables the instructor to involve expert guest speakers from the theological librarianship community. Students are also encouraged to attend the annual ATLA conference following the conclusion of the course. The instructor has been effective not only in teaching the course but also in mentoring students through their job searches. The division of effort has worked well: ATLA is responsible for course development, instructor selection and course marketing while UIUC is responsible for student registration and course delivery.

Having had a successful initial experience in partnering with UIUC on this course, ATLA has actively sought ways to build on this success. They have made scholarships available to members in developing countries to participate in the course. They have collaborated to develop a non-credit course, Scholarly Writing for the LIS Profession, identified as a continuing education need by several ATLA members. Discussion has begun about offering a version of Theological Librarianship in Spanish to expand its international reach.

**Best practices.** Several useful practices for course development partnerships identified through the activities of the WISE+ grant were alluded to in the previous section. Below is a summary of the most useful

- *Start Early:* Start navigating organizational and institutional processes early. Course materials often must undergo review and approval by multiple boards or committees in each stage of revision, especially when developing new courses.
- *Identify Point People:* Identify an individual contact person both at the institution and within the partner organization(s) that has a full understanding of the steps needed to bring the course to fruition (e.g., course proposal, review and approval process, marketing channels, knowledge of organization's administrative capacity). These point people will serve as liaisons between the organization and institution, decreasing the confusion that may arise when multiple closed channels of communication related to the partnership exist simultaneously.
- *Sign an MOU:* Use a Memorandum of Understanding (MOU) to clarify the rights and responsibilities of each partner. The MOU provides a clear outline so that all stakeholders are aware of each others' expectations and intentions. It also provides a written record to refer to if a misunderstanding or issue arises.

- *Be Sensitive to Cost:* Be aware of reasonable rates for continuing education in a specialty when setting cost for association members. If formal enrollment through the host school is necessary, provide lower cost options such as community credit or audit rate tuition whenever possible.
- *Look for Support:* Find a faculty champion for the course (either internal to the host school or involved with the organization) who is a subject expert and has some relevant experience with or existing connections within the partner organization to help foster the collaboration.
- *Collaborate...more:* Consider involving multiple partners, particularly if cost must be distributed across institutions and organizations (e.g., grant funding is not available). Partners may be other schools, not just organizations.
- *Capitalize on the benefits offered by the partnership by:*
  ○ Inviting organization members to join the course as guest lecturers
  ○ Using organization publications, standards, or other content as required or suggested
  ○ Organizing attendance (or participation) in organization meetings and conferences
  ○ Promoting student membership in the organization (if available)
  ○ Promoting other courses or programs available through the host school (e.g., Certificates of Advanced Study) that may be of interest to association members

## Notes from the User Perspective

This section gives a voice to two of the most essential components of consortium operations: a student and a local WISE administrator.

**The WISE administrator's perspective.** San Jose State University's School of Library and Information Science (SJSU SLIS) joined WISE in 2007. Since joining, SJSU has enjoyed benefits in each of the three pillar areas: quality, pedagogy, and collaboration. SJSU SLIS Assistant Director of Distance Learning and WISE Administrator Debbie Faires contributed the following comments on participation in WISE:

*The quality metrics were important as SJSU determined guidelines for online courses. Policies such as maximum course size and pedagogical training for new faculty were instituted based on these well-researched benchmarks. In preparation for program re-accreditation, these strategies strengthened the school's successful proposal. When budget pressures threaten cutbacks, these metrics help the school hold the line on important issues. WISE has influenced the pedagogy of the instructors at SJSU. Not only have several faculty members directly benefited from participating in WISE Pedagogy workshops, but a portion of the school's required training for new faculty is based on the WISE model. This indirect influence has helped to shape the teaching philosophy throughout the SJSU SLIS program.*

*One of the biggest benefits of WISE membership is the opportunity it provides for SJSU students to take courses on subjects they would not otherwise be able to study at San Jose State. These classes have filled specific curricular needs for some students. Those who have participated report that they appreciate the chance to broaden their experience and take a class from another university while being spared the challenges of formally registering at the other institution and subsequently transferring the credits. SJSU faculty members have also reported that they enjoy having the WISE students in their classes. The visiting students bring new perspectives that enrich class discussion.*

*One of the challenges of administering participation is the selection of classes to be offered to WISE students. Ideally, SJSU makes available a few seats in a class that would otherwise be unfilled. However, it is difficult to accurately predict enrollment. Some classes fill and have wait lists while others do not draw sufficient numbers and are subject to cancellation. However, if WISE students are enrolled, the school feels obligated to honor the promised spots in these classes. Dealing with the varying schedules of participating universities is another challenge. Students need to clearly understand the implications such as early start dates or late notification of grades. However, these issues are generally dealt with quite easily with clear communication.*

*San Jose State has been pleased to participate in WISE and has enjoyed the benefits that come through this collaboration.*

**The WISE+ student perspective.** San Jose State University MSLIS student Marianne Sterna has completed two WISE+ courses, Theological Librarianship and Legal Information: Resources and Services (offered by Syracuse University and the American Association of Law Libraries). Sterna credits the knowledge and unique experience gained through each of these courses as extremely valuable to her education. In an interview with the author, Sterna elaborated on why her WISE+ experience was both useful and enjoyable.

A key concept Sterna took away from both courses is the importance of a working knowledge of the core resources in one's area of expertise. By visiting law and theological libraries to work on assignments, she began to develop a foundational awareness of the core resources for each field, including how and when to use them. Her WISE+ instructors challenged her to work hands-on with resources, and to develop an understanding of how people in different fields carry out research and treat information in different ways. This knowledge will help Sterna to excel in her chosen specialty and to actively demonstrate the value of information professionals with subject expertise.

Another benefit of Sterna's WISE+ experience was the networking opportunity inherent to mixing graduate students and professionals seeking continuing education in the same environment. In Theological Librarianship, Sterna found that the ATLA practitioners in the course "handled inexperience gently," serving both as resources and academic peers by contributing to course-wide discussions and one-on-one "side chats" without becoming an intimidating presence. Several guest lecturers were also invited to present during the course, providing a very enriching opportunity to make online connections with theological librarians from around the country. Sterna came away from her WISE+ courses with great contacts and the knowledge that if you have intent, purpose, and a plan, professionals in the LIS field will be there to help foster your interest and talents (personal communication, August 2009).

## THE FUTURE OF WISE

### Financial Sustainability

Member schools contribute $3,000 annually to cover core operational costs including staff (the central director) and administrative overhead (space, meetings, travel, supplies, and technology). Staffing costs are offset by funding in exchange for service from the school hosting the central administrative office (currently Syracuse University).

Membership is an investment. One major return is greater access to a broad range of courses with no additional production or delivery costs. Each semester students at member institutions typically have access to 10-30 additional courses on diverse topics including Theological Librarianship, Medical Informatics, and Information Security. This may increase program marketability and student satisfaction with their elective options. The students' home schools collect tuition on enrollment in WISE courses. The seats taken up by WISE students would not generate revenue for the host school if they remained empty, so the school is not taking a loss by offering the seats to WISE. To balance the exchange of students, schools receive $100 per student hosted from WISE. This cost is recaptured by charging home schools $100 per student sent into the consortium.

## Next Steps

WISE will continue most of its core functions into the foreseeable future. The collective effort and dedication of the WISE members provides the foundational energy needed to sustain elements such as the discussion and dissemination of quality metrics and the course exchange. In April 2009 the WISE schools met to discuss goals for the consortium, resulting in an effort to engage international LIS programs in WISE. We are currently focused on international growth to continue to increase the diversity of the member schools and courses available through WISE and to learn from the practices of high-quality LIS programs around the world. We are also dedicated to providing a global forum for dialogue on best practices in online LIS education. Currently this effort is centered on identifying international providers of online LIS education, increasing awareness of WISE among international schools, and recruiting international members. The consortium is also exploring how to better serve the professional LIS population by continuing to provide options for online learning through our member schools beyond the scope of the WISE+ course development partnerships.

WISE Pedagogy and the WISE+ initiative were funded by a grant, which ended in summer 2010. Select services of WISE Pedagogy, including the annual face-to-face workshop, will continue, however the consortium no longer provides funding for WISE+ course development partnerships.

## CONCLUSION

This chapter provided an overview of the mission and model of the WISE consortium, including the course exchange and promotion of quality online LIS education, framed by the three pillars of quality, pedagogy and collaboration. Special initiatives of the consortium dedicated to professional development including WISE Pedagogy and the WISE+ course development partnership project were also discussed. The perspectives of WISE administrative leaders, a member school administrator, and WISE+ student were represented in order to provide a well-rounded picture of what WISE is and how we contribute to the field of online LIS education.

Students, staff, and faculty and professionals from LIS programs and organizations around the world have taken part in the activities of the WISE Consortium. At the time of publication, WISE has fifteen members located across the United States, Canada, New Zealand, Australia, and the UK. Individually, many of the member schools have diverse populations with distance learners distributed across the globe, multiplying the reach of WISE. It is not uncommon to have students and faculty who reside on three or more different continents interacting in a single WISE class setting. Over 490 online instructors from locations as diverse as Saudia Arabia, Australia and the United States have benefited from resources provided by WISE Pedagogy, including the face-to-face workshop and Web-based materials. It is our hope that the efforts of WISE Pedagogy have had an indirect positive impact on the students we serve by better preparing their instructors to teach and to innovate in the online classroom.

Nineteen professional organizations ranging in specializations from theological librarianship (ATLA) to music librarianship (MLA) to literacy (ProLiteracy Worldwide) have been engaged with the WISE+ initiative, opening the doors for recip- rocal impact between and among constituents of the organizations, WISE, and the member schools (Appendix – WISE+ Partnerships). While the WISE+ grant has ended and funding for additional courses is no longer available, several schools have normalized courses initially developed for WISE+, meaning that the courses and associated partnerships will continue into the foreseeable future.

The consortium thrives on its membership, including the individuals at each member school that assist in coordination. The energy contributed by each member is what makes WISE what it is; it is truly a collaborative effort which would not be possible without the contributions of our students, faculty, and administrators. Another reason WISE works is the common understanding among our schools; we speak the same academic language, aspire to similar program outcomes for LIS education, and come from schools dedicated to advancing the library profession. The model could have broad application across disciplines if interested schools came together to share their resources around other subjects. Technology plays a large role in administrative and instructional processes of WISE, but at its core the consortium succeeds because of dedicated people and effective communication.

## REFERENCES

American Distance Education Consortium (ADEC). (2003). *ADEC guiding principles for distance teaching and learning*. Retrieved from http://www.adec.edu/admin/papers/distance-teaching_principles.html

Chickering, A. W., & Gamson, Z. F. (1987). Seven principles for good practice in undergraduate education. *AAHE Bulletin, 39*(7), 3-7. Retrieved from http://www.cord.edu/dept/assessment/sevenprin.htm

Keefe, S., & Kingma, B. (2006). An analysis of the virtual classroom: Does size matter? Do residencies make a difference? Should you hire that instructional designer? *Journal of Education for Library and Information Science, 47*(2), 127–143. doi:10.2307/40324327

Kingma, B., Nicholson, S., Schisa, K., & Smith, L. (2010). WISE+ course development partnerships: Collaboration, innovation, & sustainability. *Proceedings of the IFLA-ALISE-Euclid preconference, Cooperation and Collaboration in Teaching and Research: Trends in Library and Information Studies Education.* Borås, Sweden.

Kingma, B., & Schisa, K. (2010). WISE Economics: ROI of Quality and Consortiums. *Journal of Education for Library and Information Science, 51*(1), 43–52.

McKinney, A. (2009). *WISE pedagogy on-demand: Free training for LIS instructors.* Poster Presentation at the American Library Association Annual Conference, Chicago, IL.

Montague, R., & Pluzhenskaia, M. (2007). Web-based information science education (WISE): Collaboration to explore and expand quality in LIS online education. *Journal of Education for Library and Information Science, 48*(1), 36–51.

Moore, J. (2005). *The Sloan Consortium quality framework and the five pillars.* Retrieved from http://www.sloan-c.org/publications/books/qualityframework.pdf

Pedagogy, W. I. S. E. (2009a). *Introduction to online pedagogy.* Retrieved from http://introductiononlinepedagogy.pbworks.com/

Pedagogy, W. I. S. E. (2009b). *WISE excellence in online teaching award recipients: Best practices 2009.* Retrieved from http://wisepedagogy.com/bestpractices2009.shtml

Pedagogy, W. I. S. E. (2009c). *WISE pedagogy website.* Retrieved from http://www.wisepedagogy.com

Pedagogy, W. I. S. E. (2010a). *Annemck's bookmarks on delicious: Online pedagogy/e-learning bundle.* Retrieved from http://delicious.com/annemck/bundle:OnlinePedagogy%2FeLearning

Pedagogy, W. I. S. E. (2010b). *WISE pedagogy blog.* Retrieved from http://www.wisepedagogy.com/blog/

Pedagogy, W. I. S. E. (2010c). *WISE pedagogy Twitter feed.* Retrieved from http://twitter.com/wisepedagogy

Schisa, K., & McKinney, A. (2008). *Web-based Information Science education.* Presentation at the American Distance Education Consortium Annual Conference, Minneapolis, MN.

Society for Applied Learning Technology [SALT]. (2010). *SALT website.* Retrieved from http://www.salt.org/salt.asp?ss=1

United States Distance Learning Association (USDLA). (2010). *USDLA website.* Retrieved from http://www.usdla.org/

WCET. (2010). *WCET website.* Retrieved from http://www.wcet.info/2.0/

Web-based Information Science Education Consortium (WISE). (2009). *A model for quality online education in library and information science.* Retrieved from http://www.wiseeducation.org/media/documents/2009/2/principles_of_Quality_Online_Courses_2006.pdf

# APPENDIX

*WISE partnerships chart*

| Course | Host School | Partner Organization (s) |
|---|---|---|
| Theological Librarianship | University of Illinois | ATLA (American Theological Library Association) |
| WISE Libraries: Designing the Public Library of the Future | Syracuse University | ALC (Americans for Libraries Council) |
| Digital Libraries | Syracuse University | INASP |
| Librarianship for Latin American, Iberian and Latina Studies | University of Illinois | SALALM (Seminar on the Acquisition of Latin American Library Materials) |
| Building Literate Communities in the 21st Century | Syracuse University | Proliteracy Worldwide |
| Music Librarianship & Bibliography | University of Illinois | MLA (Music Library Association) |
| Civic Entrepreneurship and Public Institutions | University of Illinois | ULC (Urban Libraries Council) |
| Information Resources, Services and Technology for an Aging World | University of Pittsburgh | MLA (Medical Library Association) |
| Museum Archives | University of Pittsburgh | Palinet |
| Introduction to Information Science | University of Pittsburgh | ASIS&T (American Society for Information Science and Technology) |
| Contemporary Academic Librarianship | Syracuse University | ACRL (Association of College and Research Libraries) |
| Legal Information Resources and Services | Syracuse University | AALL (American Association of Law Libraries) |
| Gaming in Libraries | Syracuse University | ALA (American Library Association) |
| Geographic Information Systems (GIS) for Librarians | University of Pittsburgh | MAGERT (Map and Geography Round Table - ALA) |
| Copyright and Fair Use in the Digital Age | University of Pittsburgh | ALA OITP (Office of Information Technology Policy) |
| Developing Leadership Potential | Victoria University of Wellington | LIANZA (Library and Information Association of New Zealand Aotearoa) |
| Services to Racially and Ethnically Diverse Communities | San Jose State University | American Indian Library Association, REFORMA: Orange County CA Chapter, REFORMA: Bibliotecas para la Gente Chapter |
| Law Librarianship | University of Illinois | AALL (American Association of Law Libraries) |

# Chapter 16
# Teachers in Action:
## High–Tech, High–Touch Service–Learning with Special Populations

**Trae Stewart**
*University of Central Florida, USA*

**Rebecca A. Hines**
*University of Central Florida, USA*

**Marcey Kinney**
*Bethune-Cookman University, USA*

## ABSTRACT

*Teachers are increasingly expected to work with children with varying disabilities in the least restrictive environment—most commonly, the general education classroom. Yet, teachers who did not major in special education remain unprepared to meet the needs of children with disabilities in the classroom because they received no relevant formal field experiences during their pre-service years. As a result, unknowledgeable teachers may retain damaging stereotypes of persons with disabilities, hold a reduced sense of teacher efficacy to include all learners, and in the end, be less willing to work with exceptional students in their classes. This chapter provides an overview of a Florida-based project that aims to connect communities, nonprofit organizations, university pre-service teachers, and persons with disabilities using high-tech, high-touch service-learning.*

## CONTEXT OF *TEACHERS IN ACTION*

According to the U.S. Census Bureau (2000) more than 3.2 million Floridiansover the age of five have an identified disability, and nonprofits serving this population are experiencing grave reductions in operating revenue. In 2008, United Cerebral Palsy of Central Florida (UCP) was struggling to fully serve persons with disabilities (e.g., cerebral palsy, Down syndrome, autism, speech and developmental delays, vision and hearing impairments) after experiencing a 30% reduction in contributions and state-leveraged cuts at its six charter school sites. Just prior to the economic

DOI: 10.4018/978-1-60960-623-7.ch016

downturn, UCP acquired a community center in downtown Orlando to hold social and cultural events, job training workshops, computer classes, fitness classes, family recreation leagues, summer camps, drama/arts workshops, and holiday events. Now, the 11,000 square foot building sits unused over 70% of the time due to a lack of personnel.

Meanwhile, Florida's teachers are expected to be prepared to work with children with varying disabilities, yet most receive no relevant formal field experiences during their pre-service years. Individuals with Disabilities Education Act (IDEA) (Title I (B) Sec. 612 (a)(5)(A), 2004) mandates that students with disabilities are served in the least restrictive environment, which is commonly the general education classroom. As schools continue to become more inclusive, however, teachers remain unprepared to meet the needs of children with disabilities. Teachers who feel negatively toward students with disabilities or have not been trained in appropriate strategies for their successful inclusion are less likely to be willing to work with these students in their classrooms (Cook, Cameron, & Tankersly, 2007; Engelbrecht, Oswald, Swart, & Eloff, 2003). In contrast, individuals who have shared personal, intimate, and rewarding contact with persons with disabilities demonstrate more positive attitudes toward others with differences (Yucker, 1994). Furthermore, teachers who work collaboratively on a service-learning project are better able to plan, implement, and evaluate instruction to meet the needs of students with disabilities and their families, and to identify and analyze the community needs and incorporate these needs as the focus for a meaningful school curriculum for students with special needs (Davis, Miller, & Corbet, 1998; Muscott, 2001). Root, Callahan, and Sepanski (2002) found, working with ill or disabled adults appeared to have been an especially powerful experience, with candidates emerging from it more aware of the need for teachers to be interested in social problems and to involve their students in community service (p. 58).

## TEACHERS IN ACTION

The project emerged based on a need recognized by faculty attempting to integrate service-learning projects into an online elementary education course, Teaching Students with Disabilities in the General Education Classroom (EEX 4070). Specifically, two faculty members teaching the course required a "Make a Difference" assignment that called for students to complete a service project in their respective communities. The original projects were ad hoc and largely based on volunteerism on the part of students rather than goals of civic leadership and service-learning best practices. The feedback from students about the experience was so positive in terms of shaping dispositions about disability that faculty in exceptional education teamed with faculty specializing in service-learning to develop a more systematic, service-learning based project that would be easy for all faculty to use. Although the University does have an office of service-learning and community engagement, the number of staff necessary to systematically accommodate the placement of the large number of pre-service teacher participants (approximately 700 per semester) was not available. Hiring freezes within the College of Education were also a hindrance in hiring sufficient instructional staff to meaningfully oversee students' experiential activities, and even traditional internship programs were being cut due to budget constraints. Faculty teamed up to write a federal service-learning grant to create a structure for weaving service-learning into all sections of the EEX 4070 course, ensuring that over 1,000 elementary education majors per year would have an experience with persons with disabilities.

In addition to meeting the educational needs of pre-service teachers, *Teachers in Action* intentionally partnered with UCP of Central Florida to meet the needs of UCP's educational centers and programs for persons with disabilities throughout Central Florida. For example, one need identified by UCP was help in renovating the play area at one of its more remote preschool locations. Located on a busy street corner, a simple chain link fence at the site kept the children inside the existing dismal playground that consisted of bare concrete and one small plastic picnic table. No shelter covered the area. After the need was posted to the *Teachers in Action* site by one of the facilitators, five students from the area met at the preschool to survey the needs and develop a plan of action. They decided to weave bright-colored slats into the fencing to block out the traffic, paint a mural on the building wall, and paint games on the concrete as a start. As their efforts began to build, another UCP center offered extra playground equipment they were not using. Hearing of the project, a private UCP supporter offered $4,000 to have awnings added to the area to provide shade and other supplies. The students independently raised $200 to buy toys to contribute to the new playground to round out the collaborative effort. This is one of hundreds of efforts from *Teachers in Action* participants, and it was all initiated and planned online.

## TECHNOLOGY AS PROJECT CATALYST

In higher education, online enrollments have been growing at a rate substantially greater than overall higher education enrollments, and are showing no signs of slowing. Over 25 percent of students in higher education have taken at least one online course as a part of their studies (Allen & Seaman, 2010). Based on this realization and the difficulties of covering the large geographic area served by the university in person, the *Teachers in Action* model employs myriad technologies for marketing and content delivery including a Website, e-mails, videocasts, social networking sites, classroom management systems such as Blackboard's Webcourses, and Adobe Connect, a Web conferencing platform.

The College of Education at UCF has committed to including the *Teachers in Action* project as a requirement for every student taking EEX 4070 or EEX 4242. These courses provide an overview of teaching children with disabilities for pre-service elementary and secondary education majors. Because the *Teachers in Action* modules are designed as a stand-alone project, project directors made the modules available to any faculty at UCF who wish for students to complete a *Teachers in Action* 15-hour service-learning project with persons with disabilities as co-partners. The primary activity for *Teachers in Action* takes place in a Blackboard-based online environment that includes asynchronous discussion opportunities, tutorials, resources, and seamless links out to "real time" discussions hosted on Adobe Connect. Upon faculty consent, students are enrolled in the *Teachers in Action* Blackboard Webcourse where they view five video-based modules that introduce and are narrated by project personnel. The five modules that comprise the "Service-Learning

*Figure 1. Screen shot of "Teachers in Action" blackboard webcourse*

*Figure 2. Screen shot of asynchronous student discussion board*

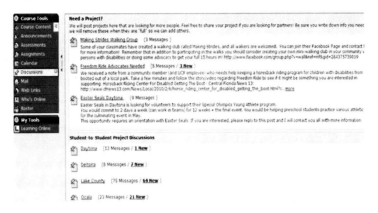

with Special Populations" content include: 1) Introduction 2) What is Service-Learning?, 3) Understanding Differences, 4) Getting Started, and 5) Reporting Results.

The "Introduction" module is a video introduction to the project and shapes initial understanding of service-learning and persons with disabilities. Next, "What is Service-Learning?" introduces the philosophical and practical foundations of service-learning. The "Understanding Differences" module provides students with an overview of communicating with persons with differences and understanding how perceptions shape our actions. Fourth, "Getting Started" shows the specifics of engaging in the service-learning activity, and links students to service-learning resources such as the National Service Inclusion Project and National Service-Learning Clearinghouse. The last module, "Reporting Results," provides a template for students to submit their project in digital format to a Web-based server.

In designing the course layout and components, knowledge and experience in best practices of online teaching were combined with consideration of student comments from previous "Make a Difference" projects. Since university students were spread across five counties, locating community service opportunities and identifying other students with whom they could partner had consistently been a problem for students. By establishing a more systematic way for students to connect with other students in their own community and by partnering with a specific agency, both of these issues were largely alleviated.

To eliminate the isolation often experienced by the distance learner (Abbey, 2000; Beard & Harper, 2002; Charp, 2002; Lynch, 2002) and encourage "high-tech, high-touch" student-instructor and student-student communication, students have the opportunity to participate in synchronous virtual reflective discussions with project personnel, instructors, and facilitators. Students interact with facilitators and other students via webcam and sidebar chats. Students simply click a designated time on an interactive calendar to join a "real time" discussion with project facilitators conducted using Adobe Connect. The Blackboard course format also allows students to engage in asynchronous discussions and plan with persons in their geographic region. Students use these spaces to establish service teams or announce volunteer opportunities. Young adults with disabilities from the community concurrently participate in and lead online discussions and community service activities.

Students use a project-planning template to conduct a community needs assessment that guides their design of an appropriate service project with persons with disabilities. Projects range from creating special events for persons with disabili-

*Figure 3. Module delivered through Adobe Connect*

*Figure 4. Synchronous web discussions with facilitators*

ties such as a Fitness with Friends Fair, providing after school opportunities for children with disabilities at the downtown community center, and increasing disability awareness by screening movies such as *Shooting Beauty*, a documentary about persons with severe disabilities, at their faith-based organizations or in community centers.

After completing service-learning projects, students create multimedia presentations displaying various aspects of the project as well as their thoughts and reflections on service-learning and working with people with disabilities. Final projects are uploaded to Slideshare, YouTube, DimDim, Slideboom, Authorstream, and various other sites that house multimedia projects. All final projects are expected to include images and a narration of the project.

## COMMUNITY IMPACT

The community is strengthened through increased program offerings at nonprofit agencies and through increased independence for Floridians with disabilities participating as co-providers of service. By engaging in collaborative service projects and developmentally appropriate programming by their same-aged peers, clients with disabilities develop interpersonal and job skills that are essential to their acceptance and self-actualization as contributing members of society.

UCF and UCP partner on a College Transition Program for young adults with cognitive disabilities, and participants are part of the online and service-learning community with *Teachers in Action*. Together they plan and carry out projects such as supporting area food banks, donation projects, and beautification efforts. For example, Susan, a young woman with cognitive disabilities who is highly social and interested in working with her community, leads a Thursday night group online to plan a series of workshops to collect donations and then prepare care packages for military personnel from families who are economically disadvantaged. To prepare for these events, Susan co-moderates group discussions through webcam chats with university students.

## TEACHERS IN ACTION
## EDUCATIONAL IMPACT

By supporting collaboration with persons with disabilities through service-learning, *Teachers in Action* first enables future educators to practice project management and organizational skills that will transfer to their classrooms. This project places students in a position to work in teams to create events specific to and appropriate for their immediate community. Service-learners must communicate effectively, schedule time, report ideas, and determine goals and how to achieve them. Collaboration skills, content knowledge, project development/implementation skills, and assessment design skills are enhanced. In addition to service activities, students have the opportunity to plan for the use of a metropolitan facility and become familiar with the use of numerous technologies for learning. In the latter case, this exposure may increase pre-service teachers' confidence to use or try technologies in their future classrooms.

Second, pre-service teachers develop a clearer and richer understanding of course content through contextualized experiences. What they learn in their courses is inextricably linked to real-life issues and human realities. Out of this experiential approach, students overcome the "inert knowledge problem" (Eyler, 2002, p. 517) by witnessing an immediate application of their learning. In their service projects, pre-service teachers increase their pedagogical knowledge by having to design, implement, and assess varying instructional strategies/techniques and management styles. This impact is particularly important considering that classrooms are becoming more inclusive and future teachers must feel efficacious to work with disabled learners. By working with persons with disabilities, pre-service teachers will develop more respectful attitudes and caring toward diverse groups (Hoover & Webster, 2004; Terry & Bohnenberger, 2003; Yates & Youniss, 1996) and have an enhanced ability to connect academic learning to societal issues and concerns (Eyler, Giles, Stenson, & Gray, 2000). One student's discussion board posting captures this sentiment:

*I think, subconsciously, I used to put distance between myself and another person who was different. I didn't avoid anyone, I just didn't make an effort to include anyone... It's amazing how a person's perception changes when you see the person, not the disability.*

## VALUE FOR THE EDUCATIONAL INSTITUTION

The University of Central Florida has a stated goal to "Be America's leading partnership university." With this in mind, the value of the *Teachers in Action* project is clear and is paramount to UCF's reinvigoration of the social charter of higher education by acculturating university students into engagement, service, change, and opportunity.

The higher education community is also strengthened through the availability of a replicable program infrastructure and management system to infuse service-learning into any course. This project systematizes service-learning in teacher education programs at UCF and reduces pressure on faculty to individually develop service-learning requirements. Partnerships created through this project will be sustainable, long-term, continuous programming rather than just a drop-in and serve approach. Activities are fully infused into course syllabi and used after the project period has ended. Just as online courses at the university can be copied and used in subsequent semesters through the Blackboard system, the *Teachers in Action* site can be copied and used by other programs at UCF. Before the pilot period had even ended, two other program areas at the university and various individual faculty had requested to copy the structure, and the course was transformed to a Community Connections site for exceptional education majors. Operating in the same general fashion as *Teachers in Action*, the site provides a structure for any faculty in exceptional education to easily post and manage service-learning opportunities, and to allow students to view the introductory videos for a full understanding of service-learning.

Specific to technology, UCF already has an international reputation for its use of online pedagogies, simulation and training technologies, and faculty training and support. The *Teachers in Action* project further deepens this reputation and adds to the university-supported toolbox of replicable models, especially ones that are facilitated partially by students and the community and utilize a range of technologies simultaneously.

## BEST PRACTICES/STRATEGIES FOR FORMING PARTNERSHIPS

Various practices and strategies have enabled *Teachers in Action* to form partnerships with community nonprofits, and began with personal connections. Sustained partnerships provided a solid foundation on which to base novel approaches that were technology-based and often virtual. Face-to-face meetings were conducted first and for specific purposes, but familiarity with each other's mission and working style allowed quick asynchronous communications. The interagency collaboration most often used e-mail as the primary technology, while *Teachers in Action* project team members most often correspond using Adobe Connect with webcams.

Students also offered considerable formative coaching and mentoring of one another and invited participation of peers in work with nonprofits they already serve. Media attention attracted other nonprofits to participate, and many communicated that they desired ongoing placement of students. By the end of the pilot semester, the students from *Teachers in Action* partnered with approximately 55 organizations. These organizations included public schools, individual disability specific organizations (e.g., Cystic Fibrosis Foundation, Down Syndrome Association of Central Florida, Autistic Society of Greater Orlando), therapeutic organizations (e.g., Freedom Ride, Marion Therapeutic Riding Association), as well as programs to develop community involvement and social skills (e.g., Special Olympics and Best Buddies UCF).

A continuous theme through our development and maintenance of healthy partnerships, regardless of the medium of communication, is the power and appreciation of constant, proactive, and honest feedback. This approach reduces the time needed in the future to deal with problems, respects partners' time by using the "straight to the point" approach, and transparently demonstrates *Teachers in Action's* dedication to addressing the needs of our non-profit partners as well as its celebration of our partners as valid co-instructors. Such reflexivity is paramount in sustaining these partnerships over time, and reflects the project's development based on effective practices in service-learning.

## CONCLUDING THOUGHTS

By combining a model for online delivery and service-learning, this project has created a replicable model that puts interaction with faculty and the community at the forefront of online learning while addressing the needs of persons with disabilities. Maximizing the use of technology for course delivery, research and mentored coaching will dramatically reduce overhead costs, while increasing instructional opportunities and personalized learning opportunities and feedback to students. In the pilot semester, 520 pre-service teachers engaged in service-learning activities through *Teachers in Action*. It is expected that more than 1,000 students per year will participate in service-learning in their respective communities at the University of Central Florida. Faculty in the Sport and Fitness program and in the College of Nursing have also asked for support in replicating the *Teachers in Action* structure so that they can likewise engage learners in service-learning activities.

In the end, *Teachers in Action* has enabled future educators to practice project management and organizational skills that will transfer to their classrooms. Further, they gain collaboration skills, content knowledge, project development/implementation skills, and awareness of the needs of persons with disabilities. Nonprofit partners benefit through increased programming opportunities and a more empowered, independent cohort of volunteer individuals with disabilities.

# REFERENCES

Abbey, B. (2000). *Instructional and cognitive impacts of Web-based education.* Hershey, PA: Idea Group Publishing.

Aksamit, D. (1990). Practicing teachers' perceptions of their preservice preparation for mainstreaming. *Teacher Education and Special Education, 13*(1), 21–29. doi:10.1177/088840649001300104

Allen, I. E., & Seaman, J. (2010). *Learning on demand: Online learning in the United States, 2009.* Babson Survey Research Group. Retrieved online from http://www.sloan-c.org/publications/survey/pdf/learningondemand.pdf

Beard, L. A., & Harper, C. (2002). Student perceptions of online versus on campus instruction. *Education, 122*(4), 658–663.

Charp, S. (2002). Online learning. *T.H.E. Journal, 29*(8), 8–10.

Cook, B., Cameron, D., & Tankersley, M. (2007). Inclusive teachers' attitudinal ratings of their students with disabilities. *The Journal of Special Education, 40*(4), 230–238. doi:10.1177/00224669070400040401

Cook, M. (2002). Outcomes: Where are we now? The efficacy of differential placement and the effectiveness of current practices. *Preventing School Failure, 46*(2), 54–56. doi:10.1080/10459880209603345

Davis, K. M., Miller, D. M., & Corbet, W. (1998). *Methods of evaluating student performance through service-learning.* Tallahassee, FL: Florida State University Center for Civic Education and Service.

Dede, C., & Kremer, A. (1999). Increasing students' participation via multiple interactive media. *Invention, 1*, 1. Retrieved from http://www.doiiit.gmu.edu/Archives/feb98/dede_1.htm

Engelbrecht, P., Oswald, M., Swart, E., & Eloff, I. (2003). Including learners with intellectual disabilities: Stressful for teachers? *International Journal of Disability Development and Education, 50*(3), 293–308. doi:10.1080/1034912032000120462

Eyler, J. (2002). Reflection: Linking service and learning – linking students and communities. *The Journal of Social Issues, 58*(3), 517–534. doi:10.1111/1540-4560.00274

Eyler, J., Giles, D., Stenson, C., & Gray, C. (2000). *At a glance: What we know about the effects of service-learning on college students, faculty, institutions and communities, 1993-2000* (3rd ed.). Nashville, TN: Vanderbilt University.

Hoover, T. S., & Webster, N. (2004). Modeling service-learning for future leaders of youth organizations. *Journal of Leadership Education, 3*(3), 58–62.

King, G., Law, M., King, S., Rosenbaum, P., Kertoy, M. K., & Young, N. L. (2003). A conceptual model of the factors affecting the recreation and leisure participation of children with disabilities. *Physical & Occupational Therapy in Pediatrics, 23*(1), 63–90.

Lynch, D. (2002). Professors should embrace technology in courses. *The Chronicle of Higher Education, 48*(19), 15–16.

Murphy, N. A., & Carbone, P. S. (2008). Promoting the participation of children with disabilities in sports, recreation, and physical activities. *Pediatrics, 121*(5), 1057–1061. doi:10.1542/peds.2008-0566

Muscott, H. S. (2001). Service-learning and character education as antidotes for children with egos that cannot perform. *Reclaiming Children and Youth, 10*(2), 91–99.

Root, S., Callahan, J., & Sepanski, J. (2002). Building teaching dispositions and service-learning practice: A multi-site study. *Michigan Journal of Community Service-Learning, 8*(2), 50–60.

Terry, A., & Bohnenberger, J. (2003). Fostering a cycle of caring in our gifted youth. *Journal of Secondary Gifted Education, 15*(1), 23–32.

U.S. Census Bureau. (2000). *State and county quick facts*. Retrieved from http://quickfacts. census.gov/qfd/states/12000.html

Yates, M., & Youniss, J. (1996). Community service and political-moral identity in adolescents. *Journal of Research on Adolescence, 6*(3), 271–284.

Yuker, H. (1994). Variables that influence attitudes toward people with disabilities. *Journal of Social Behavior and Personality, 9*(5), 3–22.

# Chapter 17
# Leveraging the Technology-Enhanced Community (TEC) Partnership Model to Enrich Higher Education

**Amy Garrett Dikkers**
*University of North Carolina at Wilmington, USA*

**Aimee L. Whiteside**
*University of Tampa, USA*

## ABSTRACT

*This chapter provides the Technology-Enhanced Community (TEC) Partnership Model to enrich higher education. The TEC Partnership Model addresses the incorporation of community resource professionals into coursework to provide authentic learning experiences for students. The model is situated in a case study of an online Human Rights Education course, designed to serve the needs and academic interests of K-12 practitioners, community practitioners, and students in a variety of disciplines. This chapter describes the experiences and impact from both perspectives of the partnership and provides examples from the Human Rights Education course to show the model in practice. The final section also provides an overview of the strategies others can use to incorporate similar partnerships and collaborations among instructors, students, student-practitioners, and practitioners in the field.*

## INTRODUCTION

Two rising forces in higher education around the world have shifted the work we do—the com-

DOI: 10.4018/978-1-60960-623-7.ch017

modification of higher education with the accompanying need to compete and an increased focus on technology-enhanced learning. The former often brings a focus on authentic learning and the latter often is elaborated through a focus on online and blended learning. The challenge is to bring authentic learning into an online or blended classroom in ways to enhance student participation and motivation in a course, especially when many of our online students are practitioners themselves.

This chapter introduces a model for integrating community partnerships and practitioners into higher education through technology, the *Technology-Enhanced Community (TEC) Partnership Model*. The explanation of the model is based around an online *Human Rights Education* course. We describe the experiences and impact from the perspectives of the partnership, and we provide examples from the *Human Rights Education* course to show the model in practice. The final section also provides an overview of the strategies others can use to incorporate similar partnerships and collaborations among students, student-practitioners, and practitioners in the field.

## ABOUT THE CASE

The *Human Rights Education* course is a partnership itself between the practitioners of the University of Minnesota's Human Rights Center and an instructor in the Department of Organizational Leadership, Policy, and Development. The course was originally designed for practitioners in K-12 education and community-based organizations who wish to learn about human rights, human rights education, and how to become advocates for human rights in their professions. In practice, the course appeals to a wide audience of students, ranging from K-12 teachers, higher education professionals, nurse educators, community practitioners, and undergraduate and graduate students from a variety of disciplines.

One of the main tenets of human rights education is that it is participant-guided and context-driven. As such, the instructors create an authentic human rights education (HRE) experience for students by bringing in as many real-life experiences of HRE advocates and practitioners from around the world as possible. They use many different technologies to do so. The instructors of the course call these practitioners "community resource professionals" and include the following statement on the course syllabus that explains their participation.

*Human Rights Education practitioners will join the class throughout the semester, offering their insights, experiences, research, and feedback. As a core component of this course, we believe that these individuals can help us have a deeper understanding of effective human rights advocacy and education strategies, methods, and impacts. Our reason for integrating Community Resource Professionals is to expand our learning community to ensure a global perspective and different experiences in the field.*

One stated course outcome also directly connects with the community resource professionals: The *Human Rights Education* course "introduces students to and facilitates conversations with human rights practitioners and scholars in the field." The involvement of the community resource professionals in the *Human Rights Education* course provides the examples for the incorporation of the Technology-Enhanced Community (TEC) Partnership Model.

## THEORETICAL CONTEXT

Helping students learn and discover by connecting to a community of practice is certainly not a new concept in education. The apprenticeship model was a common method dating back to the Middle Ages to help young children acquire a particular craft or skill. As the importance of learning of a particular proficiency ebbed toward a need for a more broad-based, general knowledge over centuries, John Dewey (1916) still stressed the role of education as "a fostering, a nurturing, a cultivating, process" to help students discover how connected we are to each other in our "social environment."

Then, in the late 1980s and the early 1990s the importance of cognitive apprenticeships emerged. Experts Lave and Wenger (1992) stressed the importance of situated learning as a process whereby novice learners integrate by establishing "legitimate peripheral participation" through learning from the experts within that community (Brown, Collins, & Duguid, 1989; Lave & Wenger, 1992). Another milestone in this movement occurred when the National and Community Service Act of 1990 authorized the Learn and Serve America grant program, which introduced the concept of service-learning.

Administrators often stress the importance of faculty integrating service-learning into academic coursework as means of higher education giving back to the community. Though seemingly the Deweyan ideal, the risk is that the community needs do not always align with the course learning outcomes, and unfortunately, course outcomes may be sacrificed to achieve the service outreach. To ease this tension, other experts have proposed moving toward a PBL (problem-based learning) or authentic learning model where students resolve a problem faced in industry (Barron, 1998; Herrington & Oliver, 2000; Herrington, Oliver, & Reeves, 2003). Today, we promote a unique model of integrating practitioners into technology-rich academic course communities where the focus is on learning with the community members, rather than doing something for them (Ward & Wolf-Wendel, 2000).

In our TEC Partnership Model, we merge the concepts of service-learning with authentic learning (Lave & Wenger, 1992; Wenger, 1998; Barab, Squire, & Dueber, 2000; Lombardi, 2007) in a technology-rich environment to show how different levels of engagement with community experts can both contribute to and extend course objectives and learning outcomes as well as students' levels of engagement and intrinsic motivation (Deci & Ryan, 1985). As Lombardi (2007) notes, "Only in the past few years have educational researchers begun to propose project after project aimed

at moving these class-bound exercises into the immersive, online realm, where students can try on varying perspectives and work in tandem with peers, mentors, and potential employers who may live continents away" (p. 15). We greatly value the intersection between Lombardi's learner-centered authentic approach and meaningful, technical-enhanced learning.

## THE TECHNOLOGY-ENHANCED COMMUNITY (TEC) PARTNERSHIP MODEL

Our Technology-Enhanced Community (TEC) Partnership Model rests on this rich theoretical history to provide structure to the integration of practitioners into technology-rich academic course communities. There are three levels of interaction between community practitioners and students in the TEC Partnership Model: Sharing of Content, Interaction with Students, and Partnership in Course Community. (See Figure 1). Each level is described in this section with examples from the *Human Rights Education* course, which illustrates how technology can enhance the connections and collaboration among community practitioners and students. At the end of this chapter, we also provide factors and strategies to consider when incorporating these levels and various technologies into course and other types of learning environments.

The next sections describe each level of the TEC Partnership Model, integrate student and practitioner feedback, and indicate how each level of the model can build on the previous level.

### Level One: Sharing of Content

At the Sharing of Content level, students typically have access to content from experts in the field, practitioners and scholars in the form of articles, books, chapters or other text-based readings, most often chosen by the instructor of the course.

*Figure 1. The technology-enhanced community (TEC) partnership model*

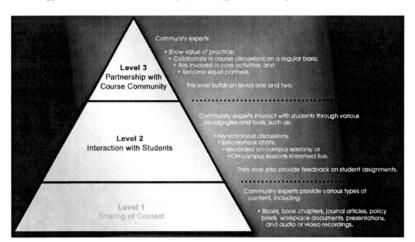

Hybrid and online courses lend themselves easily to the provision of content that is multi-media or Internet-based. In the *Human Rights Education* course, content from the experts was similarly text-based as discussed above, with additional websites and videos as required or additional resources.

Even today, a significant amount of content in most higher education courses is instructor-created, often in the form of lectures. One method of recreating this content-based interaction in a hybrid or online class is through the creation of PowerPoints narrated by the instructor. Students can view these online, as often as needed, in order to familiarize themselves with important aspects of the content and feel more connected with their instructor. Instructors can use the narration functions in PowerPoint itself, or use various third-party or other plug-in tools, such as Adobe Presenter that allows for greater functionality with editing their narrations. These technology tools can help ensure students are exposed to key concepts or other important aspects from their readings.

Student feedback regarding this aspect of the *Human Rights Education* course has been extremely positive. One student explains: "I loved these [narrated multimedia presentations]. I wish there were more." He goes on to suggest another technology-rich enhancement in the course, "Could the text or the transcripts of the text that is read during the PowerPoint accompany the viewing of an audio PowerPoint? Sometimes the audio component moves too fast." This request can typically be accommodated with ease since instructors have found working from a script is often the easiest way to record the PowerPoint narrations. It is a simple matter to upload the text to the same location in the course management system as the PowerPoint.

Community resource professionals can also record themselves narrating a PowerPoint at their own computers, with the appropriate software plug-ins, which provide a layer of authenticity to the course content as the practitioners themselves can connect the knowledge in the class to skills needed in the real world of practice. Students value this authentic voice.

Typically in face-to-face learning, students also interact with community resource professionals as guest speakers and panelists, or on their own, outside of class time, to complete an assigned activity. Technology enables instructors to enhance these interactions in several ways, through audio- or video-recording technologies and classroom lecture-capture software programs. First of all, in a face-to-face class meeting, a guest speaker can be recorded to capture the real-time presentation and archive it for future use by students in the specific class and other classes. At the very basic level, instructors can use a simple audio voice recorder to record a presentation and then upload it as a podcast or to a course website. There are many different types of digital voice recorders available for purchase; those that record as MP3s are some of the easiest to use for instructors at all levels of technological skill. More complex options (requiring time and resources) are to video-record a guest speaker session with a camcorder or webcam. If the guest speaker is using a PowerPoint presentation or other files on a computer to aid their presentation, instructors can use classroom capture software, such as Camtasia Relay, to record the audio and computer screen for later dissemination in multiple video derivatives.

As we move to level two, community resource professionals' direct interaction with students, we demonstrate how online learning technologies, synchronous and asynchronous, paired with the sharing of content can further enhance those interactions.

## Level Two: Interaction with Students

In the online *Human Rights Education* class, the instructors used several different methods of interaction between students and community resource professionals. They included asynchronous responses by the community resource professionals in discussion forums and recorded guest speakers as described above, with guest speakers on and off campus and synchronous and asynchronous options for students, and provision of substantive feedback on students' final course projects. The following scenarios speak to that interaction between students and community resource professionals.

Scenario One: The instructor approaches a scholar with a request for one or two articles as content in the course. Since the content of the articles aligns perfectly with a course-level learning outcome (in the instance of the *Human Rights Education* course, for example, becoming an advocate for human rights), the instructor invites the scholar to participate in an asynchronous discussion forum where students are asked several content-based questions regarding his or her article(s).

Scenario Two: Two on-campus community experts are asked to serve as a panel around a topic in the course. They meet in a technology-enhanced learning space at a predetermined time and provide their content as described in Level One, above. The classroom space can be enabled with a laptop and webcam to record the panel discussion, perhaps using Camtasia Relay as discussed above. In the *Human Rights Education* course, on-campus experts participated in a panel in a courtroom in the law school building on campus. This room is enabled with video cameras, microphones and a production booth. The community members' participation in the course does not end with content-based sharing, however. Instead, the community members join the class online in the following weeks' discussions, drawing connections between their presentation and the responses of students in the online forums. In this case, students are able to reflect on the panel and still have the opportunity to follow up with the experts in the course management system as questions arise. One affordance of online learning is this potential for deeper reflection on the part of students and instructors.

The benefits of this type of session for the guests are that guest participation for presenters is just like that of a typical face-to-face guest speaker. There are no specific technology skills needed. Technology skills are needed, however, for the extension of the interaction from the one-time, stand-alone presentation to the discussion forums online in the course management system. Another benefit of these types of sessions for students is that it can help build community if they are able to attend the face-to-face session. One student in the *Human Rights Education* course explains the benefit of these opportunities for her own learning: "[In the online class,] I missed the in-person interactions, and the gestures, the tone of voice, the impressions, the judgments that come along with them. To overcome that gap, I attended one of the video conferences held at the Law School. There I met a few classmates and our instructors. Very helpful, and I am glad it was offered."

Scenario Three: An alternative version of this type of interaction involves a community resource person who cannot come to campus. The guest speaker can connect virtually at a scheduled time when students are face-to-face in a scheduled place and synchronously present their topic. Again, the session is recorded for dissemination asynchronously. This recorded presentation can then be used in future face-to-face class sessions when a speaker is unable to physically come to campus. One disadvantage for guests is that this technique does require some tech savviness, access to high-speed Internet and webcam, and a comfort level with talking to students through a webcam. However, the instructors of the *Human Rights Education* course have found many advantages for this technique for students and the instructors, as it allows experts who are not able to come to campus to still share their knowledge and builds connections with the field of practice.

Scenario Four: These recorded guest sessions can be paired with discussion forum participation or synchronous chat sessions to greater enhance the collaboration between the students and the community practitioners. For example, students can reflect upon the presentation, view all or part of it again through the recording, and then engage with the community expert in an online forum asking more probing questions about the issues raised in his/her presentation. Often this follow-up is what is missed in a typical face-to-face guest speaker session where a presenter comes to class one week, presents on his or her topic, and then goes back into the community where he/she works without further interaction with students. In practice, the instructor of the class often ends

up fielding questions from students the next week regarding the guest's presentation and can be unable to answer those questions sufficiently. One student in the second iteration of the course stated, "[The community resource professionals] added great feedback and depth to many of the topics. At times … I felt they were more challenging with their response than the instructors were."

Scenario Five: Additionally, community partners can interact with students by providing feedback to students on their assignments. This participation is especially helpful when the community resource professionals have valuable practitioner experience and knowledge of best practice to be able to provide students authentic feedback regarding whether their projects are feasible in the "real world."

For example, one major goal of the *Human Rights Education* course is to create educators of and leaders for human rights and human rights education. Therefore, the final activity of the course is the creation of a curricular unit that incorporates human rights education or a community action plan around human rights. This project is situated in individual students' personal, academic, or professional environments. To ensure as much as possible that the students' projects are feasible and authentic, the instructors ask well-known human rights advocates or human rights educators to participate in an online discussion forum specifically geared toward the students' final projects. The human rights advocates and educators read summaries of the students' projects in progress, answer questions related to their feasibility and design, and read and respond to students' final projects. Students have expressed that this feedback from the experts is an extremely valuable addition to the feedback from their instructors. One student from the Spring 2009 class explains: "What a pleasure [it was] to get email responses from [the community experts]. [It was very] motivating to be speaking from (*sic*) people that are leaders in the field."

## Level Three: Partnership with Course Community

The Partnership with Course Community level represents the greatest involvement by community professionals. They participate in the online course community as equal partners. It follows Ward and Wolf-Wendel's (2000) assertion that the greatest rewards and collaborations may not derive from a traditional service-learning project aimed at "doing for the community," but from a more transformative, technology-enhanced experience where instructors, students, and community partners share and learn with each other.

This level requires building and nurturing ongoing relationships with community partners. At this level, instructors encourage an open dialogue with community partners to learn about the extent to which they would like to be involved in the course as well as what value they would like to get from this experience. The level is sustainable by connecting with community partners before the course begins and at agreed upon, regular intervals (e.g., monthly, three times per term), which are dependent upon the length of the course (e.g., full semester, three-week, summer session).

The *Human Rights Education* class embodies the Partnership with Course Community level because the community professionals have a genuine, intrinsic desire to connect with the students. Many times, they also feel a responsibility to help novice learners by bringing their authentic learning experiences into the classroom. In the three iterations of the course, there is one specific community resource person, Kyle, who has clearly partnered with the instructors and students in the course community. Kyle has advanced to the Partnership with Course Community level over time; he is now central to one required activity in the third iteration of the course. The following section introduces Kyle, describes the scaffolding of his experiences over time, and illustrates how he has become an equal partner in the third iteration of the *Human Rights Education* course.

## Introducing One Community Partner

Kyle is a Ph.D. Candidate in a Canadian university, focusing his research efforts on the field of human rights education, with a specific emphasis on educators' personal beliefs and professional practices in both formal and non-formal educational contexts. He is also interested in how experiential resources, in the form of personal stories, influence the emerging identities of human rights educators.

In year one, Kyle shared an article he had written regarding the importance of telling one's own human rights story, especially for educators (TEC Level One), responded to students in a discussion forum, and was online for a total of two weeks (TEC Level Two). In year two, he returned for the same content, met with students in a recorded Adobe Connect session, and also came back again later in the semester to facilitate dialogue on a different topic that was initially brought up in his presentation (enhanced interaction in TEC Level Two). The Adobe Connect space allows for meeting presenters to share their computer screens and PowerPoint presentations, as well as collaborate with participants through interactive chat and whiteboard features. There are multiple other videoconferencing tools available, such as Dimdim, Skype, and Windows Messenger. Each has a different price structure, often depending on the functionalities desired and the number of participants able to connect to one meeting.

In year three, where the true experience of Kyle is at the Partner in Course Community level (TEC Level Three), the instructors of the course have expanded his participation. His digital storytelling work that students discussed briefly in year two has become one of three major assignments the students complete and one block or unit of the course is specifically dedicated to the theme, "Stories for Making Change." Students watch Kyle's recorded AdobeConnect session from year two, read some of his scholarly works, see him in a new Adobe Connect session, and create digital stories of their own. Kyle then provides feedback to the students throughout the unit, especially regarding their own digital stories, and engages with them around the unit's theme through his participation in presentations and discussion forums.

Kyle has become increasingly more engaged in developing content and advising around the structure of the course in its third iteration. He shares his motivation around involvement in the course and his expectations in the following excerpt from an interview conducted mid-course in year three:

*After having been involved last year, I was very flattered to be invited again. The initial motivation for me was to have the opportunity to share some research ideas with a sympathetic audience. [The instructors were] very enthusiastic, and I was really happy with getting into the discussion fora and responding to some of the student postings. It really allowed me to reconnect with HRE on a very meaningful level, with people who were new to the field in some ways, and were curious about learning more. I wasn't sure what to expect, but it all went very well in the end. Contrasting last year to this year, I think it's changed in terms of my invited involvement, i.e., my feedback regarding some of the structuring of the weeks. I totally offered to help out, but what I find kind of challenging is to collaborate at a distance through e-mail or Skype.*

Other community resource professionals in the human rights education course have included human rights lawyers, professionals working in advocacy organizations across the world, educators incorporating human rights education into their instruction, and practitioners from non-governmental organizations. They have had a wide range of technical skills and a variety of technology available to them. For example, one advocate in Latin America was unable to access the Internet at regular intervals in order to communicate synchronously with the students; therefore, although

he was a partner in the course, his participation was less tech-intensive than Kyle's. He shared content (Level One) and engaged with students in asynchronous discussion forums (Level Two), also providing feedback to students on their advocacy projects (moving toward Level Three).

Overall, students have responded positively to the involvement of community resource professionals in the course, at all levels of the TEC Partnership Model. When explicitly asked about their thoughts regarding the impact of the community resource professionals on their learning in the course, the comments are highly supportive. For example, comments from students who responded to that inquiry at the end of year two are provided below:

- "I appreciated and benefited from their feedback to my postings and final project ideas."
- "We were connected I felt."
- "It was good to hear feedback from many people about my post."
- "I got a sense that they really cared. They were there the whole time with us."
- "Very interesting, especially since they participated actively and engaged us in discussion."

Community resource professionals can be a great asset to any course, especially courses with students who are practitioners or courses where students are preparing to work in a specific field of practice. Students in these courses often expect and demand authentic activities and content relevant to their immediate needs of practice. Utilizing the three levels of the TEC Partnership Model can help instructors in a strategic incorporation of the community resource professionals into the course. The next section moves from description of the model to suggestions for strategies to support these types of collaborations in courses.

*Table 1. Strategies for incorporating community collaborations and partnerships*

|  | Best when... | Not ideal when... |
|---|---|---|
| Level One: Sharing of Content | Instructors are new to online learning. Just as we scaffold our students in the learning process, it is best not to try to do too much at one time. Instead, carefully plan the addition of technologies and cultivating community relationships into the academic course setting. | Most learners are highly skilled practitioners who require or need a community of learners. Or Community partners have higher expectations of their participation. |
| Level Two: Interaction with Students | Instructors have excellent technical support so they can focus on the pedagogical, social, and evaluative aspects of the course. Or Community partners are knowledgeable in the technology or are excited to have the opportunity to use it. | Instructor(s), community partners and students are not comfortable with the technology tool, which could result in the tool, rather than the content and relationships, becoming the focus of the course. Or The technology tools are not stable or not well supported. |
| Level Three: Partnership in Course Community | Most participants are highly skilled practitioners demanding more of a community of learners. Or Community partners expect to commit a large amount of their time and they are excited to do so. | Instructors are new to online learning. It is best to take small steps when learning to create engaging learning environments. |

## STRATEGIES TO INCORPORATE COMMUNITY COLLABORATIONS AND PARTNERSHIPS

This final section provides five strategies to help online facilitators to incorporate partnerships and collaborations into academic courses or other online learning environments.

### Strategy One: Select a TEC Level Appropriate for Your Unique Situation

We fully recognize that a TEC Level Three partnership is not the ideal in all situations and contexts. Certainly, there are a number of factors to consider before determining the appropriate level of community collaboration or partnership, including the different levels of instructor, student, and community partner content expertise, online readiness, and technical aptitude. Table 1. Strategies for Incorporating Community Collaborations and Partnerships provides some helpful guidance

in understanding what level to integrate into your course(s).

As Table 1 illustrates, a key part of understanding each unique situation requires gaining a clear sense of the roles and responsibilities in the course, which leads us to our second strategy.

### Strategy Two: Provide Clear Expectations of Community Participation

When asked *"What suggestions do you have for the course instructors to optimize this experience for community experts, like yourself, who are graciously volunteering their time to be a part of this community of learners?"* one community resource professional, Kyle, noted, "I would suggest having more structure in place. I am not sure how others feel, but I was fine with the leeway that was extended to me....It may be good to have some suggested topics for the community people to address."

Interestingly, while instructors may see themselves as protecting the time of these vital volunteers and may feel a bit uncomfortable asking anything specific of them, community practitioners can easily view this practice as providing too much leeway and not enough structure. As a result, community practitioners can become overwhelmed, underwhelmed, or simply just confused and frustrated regarding the roles and responsibilities in the course, and it could affect the overall experience for everyone involved.

Therefore, it is important for the course instructor to have initial face-to-face, telephone, or video-based discussions with community partners so that everyone understands and agrees upon the roles and responsibilities in the course as soon as possible. And, while a legal document defining the partnership is perhaps not necessary, we do recommend a written document or e-mail correspondence to help everyone understand their respective roles and responsibilities and to help promote open communication about the course logistics.

Particularly in an online learning environment, it is imperative to address what technological support, if any, community practitioners can expect to ease any anxieties that they may have in terms of tools, technologies, and the specific content management system or learning environment. As Kyle suggests, instructors or technical support coordinators could "offer to put together PowerPoint presentations or something like that. I can imagine that support is key to getting this course to work well."

## Strategy Three: Promote this Unique Opportunity to the Students

Once you have cultivated a firm agreement with the community collaborators and partners as discussed above, let your students know early on and throughout the course how fortunate they are to have this level of expertise at their disposal. The *Human Rights Education* instructors noted that a number of students indicated in the end-of-term survey the extreme value that they received in hav-

ing community resource professionals as partners in their learning community. Thus, it is important to promote this value to them as soon as possible in the course. In an online course with students from a vast array of backgrounds and expertise levels themselves, integrating community resource professionals can be a great source of comfort and may improve your retention rates in the course.

## Strategy Four: Evaluate the Process Continually

We recommend an iterative, ongoing evaluation process that requires no more than 5-10 minutes of the community members' time and no more than 10-15 minutes of the students' time at regular intervals during the course. If possible, we suggest involving an independent researcher to conduct ongoing interviews, surveys, and/or focus groups to learn more about what is working well, what needs work, and what suggestion they have to improve these types of TEC learning opportunities.

## Strategy Five: Extend the Learning Community beyond the Academic Course Term

Finally, we suggest investigating some means of extending this learning community beyond the academic course term. That said, we also understand and empathize with the multifaceted, fast-paced life of academic professionals that face the endless strain of research, teaching, and service pressures, and we suggest that course instructors need not assume the responsibility for the learning community. Course instructors may seek out an enthusiastic or well-situated student or community partner to take on this role, or they simply offer all participants in the course the option of leading the learning community at the conclusion of the course. Alternatively, in the case of the *Human Rights Education* course, since the course is offered each spring term, students that have "graduated" from the course could be invited into the next iteration of the course as community collaborators and partners in the next term. Ultimately, it is important that (a) the learning community is not forced to halt when the academic course term ends and (b) the course instructor makes a concerted effort to extend it.

## CONCLUSION

This chapter introduces the Technology-Enhanced Community (TEC) Partnership Model, which provides a framework for the incorporation of community resource professionals into higher education courses. The levels of collaboration outlined in the model and described in this chapter present a multitude of options for the incorporation of community resource professionals into coursework, potentially leading to a partnership in the course community. With this model and the strategies we offer, you can identify ways in which you may also collaborate with community resource professionals in the courses you offer. We welcome and encourage research and application of the TEC Partnership Model and description of other cases that have found success with using the levels of the model in the development of collaborations between higher education and community professionals.

In this way, we extend the concept of learning in a community of practice to include the authentic voices of practitioners in the field through technology-enhanced learning. As one of the students in the *Human Rights Education* course reflected at the end of the course, "The course was an excellent blend of 'learning' in the … sense of just taking in new information and actually thinking about and beginning to apply what [Human Rights Education] can look like in our real lives." These authentic learning experiences are ones more and more in demand in higher education today, and the TEC Partnership Model provides guidance to instructors looking for ways in which to combine authentic practice with learning technologies and online and hybrid course offerings.

## REFERENCES

Barab, S. A., Squire, K. D., & Dueber, W. (2000). A co-evolutionary model for supporting the emergence of authenticity. *Educational Technology Research and Development*, *48*(2), 37–62. doi:10.1007/BF02313400

Barron, B., Schwartz, D. L., Vye, N. J., Moore, A., Petrosino, A., Zech, L., & Bransford, J. D. (1998). Doing with understanding: Lessons from research on problem- and project-based learning. *Journal of the Learning Sciences*, *7*(3&4), 271–311. doi:10.1207/s15327809jls0703&4_2

Brown, J. S., Collins, A., & Duguid, P. (1989). Situated cognition and the culture of learning. *Educational Researcher*, *18*(1), 32–42.

Deci, E. L., & Ryan, R. M. (1985). *Intrinsic motivation and self-determination in human behavior*. New York, NY: Plenum.

Dewey, J. (1916). *Democracy and education: An introduction to the philosophy of education*. New York, NY: Free Press.

Herrington, J., & Oliver, R. (2000). An instructional design framework for authentic learning environments. *Educational Technology Research and Development*, *48*(3), 23–48. doi:10.1007/BF02319856

Herrington, J., Oliver, R., & Reeves, T. C. (2003). Patterns of engagement in authentic online learning environments. *Australian Journal of Educational Technology, 19*(1), 59–71. Retrieved December 23, 2009, from http://www.ascilite.org.au/ajet/ajet19/herrington.html

Lave, J., & Wenger, E. (1991). *Situated learning: Legitimate peripheral participation*. New York, NY: Cambridge University Press.

Lombardi, M. M. (2007). Approaches that work: How authentic learning is transforming higher education. *EDUCAUSE*. Retrieved February 22, 2010 from http://net.educause.edu/ir/library/pdf/ELI3013.pdf

Ward, K., & Wolf-Wendel, L. (2000). Community-centered service learning: Moving from doing for to doing with. *The American Behavioral Scientist, 43*(5), 767–780. doi:10.1177/00027640021955586

Wenger, E. (1998). *Communities of practice: Learning, meaning, and identity.* New York, NY: Cambridge University Press.

## ADDITIONAL READING

Bransford, J., & Cocking, R. R. (2000). *How people learn: Brain, mind, experience, and school.* Washington, DC: National Research Council.

Burge, Z., & Collins, M. (1995). *Computer mediated communications and the online classroom.* Cresskill, NJ: Hampton Press.

Carswell, L., Thomas, P., Petre, M., Price, B., & Richards, M. (2000). Distance education via the Internet: The student experience. *British Journal of Educational Technology, 31*(1), 29–46. doi:10.1111/1467-8535.00133

Chickering, A., & Ehrmann, S. C. (1996). Implementing the seven principles: Technology as lever. *AAHE Bulletin, 49*(2), 3–6.

Chickering, A. W., & Gamson, Z. F. (1987). Seven principles for good practice in undergraduate education. *AAHE Bulletin, 39*(7), 3–7.

Collison, G., Elbaum, B., Haavind, S., & Tinker, R. (2000). *Facilitating online learning: Effective strategies for moderators.* Madison, WI: Atwood Publishing.

Conrad, R., & Donaldson, A. (2004). *Engaging the online learner: Activities and resources for creative Instruction.* San Francisco, CA: Jossey-Bass.

Dede, C. (1996). The evolution of distance education: Emerging Technologies and Distributed Learning. *American Journal of Distance Education, 10*(2), 4–36. doi:10.1080/08923649609526919

Dewey, J. (1910). *How we think.* Boston: D. C. Heath. doi:10.1037/10903-000

Dewey, J. (1997). *Experience and education.* New York, NY: Touchstone (Original work published 1938).

Fink, L. D. (2003). *Creating significant learning experiences: An integrated approach to designing college courses.* San Francisco: Jossey-Bass.

Garrison, D. R., & Kanuka, H. (2004). Blended learning: Uncovering its transformative potential in higher education. *The Internet and Higher Education, 7*(2), 95–105. doi:10.1016/j.iheduc.2004.02.001

Hooper, S. (1992). Cooperative learning and computer-based instruction. *Educational Technology Research and Development, 40*(3), 21–38. doi:10.1007/BF02296840

Lipson Lawrence, R. (2002). A small circle of friends: Cohort groups as learning communities. *New Directions for Adult and Continuing Education, 95*, 83–92. doi:10.1002/ace.71

Merriam, S. (1989). *Case study research in education: Qualitative approach.* San Francisco: Jossey-Bass Publishers.

Muilenburg, L. Y., & Berge, Z. L. (2005). Student barriers to online learning: A factor analytic study. *Distance Education, 26*(1), 29–48. doi:10.1080/01587910500081269

Neuhauser, C. (2002). Learning style and effectiveness of online and face-to-face instruction. *American Journal of Distance Education, 16*(2), 99–113. doi:10.1207/S15389286AJDE1602_4

Palloff, R., & Pratt, K. (1999). *Building learning communities in cyberspace: Effective strategies for the online classroom.* San Francisco: Jossey-Bass.

Palloff, R., & Pratt, K. (2001). *Lessons from the cyberspace classroom: The realities of online teaching.* San Francisco: Jossey-Bass.

Palloff, R., & Pratt, K. (2003). *The virtual student: A profile and guide to working with online Learners.* San Francisco: Jossey-Bass.

Palloff, R., & Pratt, K. (2005). *Collaborating online: Learning together in community.* San Francisco: Jossey-Bass.

Pea, R. D. (1994). Seeing what we build together: Distributed multimedia learning environments for transformative communications. *Journal of the Learning Sciences, 3*(3), 285–299. doi:10.1207/s15327809jls0303_4

Picciano, A. G. (2002). Beyond student perceptions: issues of interaction, presence, and performance in an online course. *Journal of Asynchronous Learning Networks, 6*(1), 21–40.

Salomon, G., & Perkins, D. N. (1998). Individual and social aspects of learning. *Review of Research in Education, 23,* 1–24.

Smith, S. J., & Robinson, S. (2003). Technology integration through collaborative cohorts: Preparing future teachers to use technology. *Remedial and Special Education, 24*(3), 154–161. doi:10.1177/07419325030240030401

Swan, K. (2002). Building learning communities in online courses: The importance of interaction. *Education Communication and Information, 2*(1), 23–49. doi:10.1080/1463631022000005016

Twigg, C. (2001). *Innovations in Online Learning: Moving Beyond No Significant Difference. The Pew Learning and Technology Program.* Rensselaer Polytechnic Institute.

Vygotsky, L. S. (1978). *Mind in society: the development of higher psychological processes.* Cambridge: Harvard University Press.

Vygotsky, L. S. (1986). *Thought and language.* Cambridge: MIT Press.

## KEY TERMS AND DEFINITIONS

**Asynchronous Learning:** Learning that occurs at a time independent of the participation of others. In online and blended learning, this often is through participation in discussion forums.

**Authentic Learning:** Incorporation of activities, professionals, issues, and contexts of the field into educational environments.

**Blended Learning:** Also called hybrid learning, describes a learning experience that takes place in a combination of online and face-to-face environments.

**Community Resource Professionals:** Community practitioners, scholars, or experts who share content, interact with students, or partner in the course community.

**Online Learning:** Learning experiences conducted solely through the Internet.

**Synchronous Learning:** Learning that occurs at a time in connection with others. In online and blended learning, this is often through real-time chat, or synchronous video or audio sessions.

**Technology-Enhanced Community (TEC) Partnership Model:** A model for integrating community partnerships and practitioners into higher education through technology. The model has three levels: Sharing of content; Interaction with students; and Partnership with course community.

**Technology-Enhanced Learning:** Learning supported, supplemented, and/or reinforced by technologies. Includes technology use in face-to-face, blended, and online learning environments.

# Chapter 18

# The Tennessee Public Health Workforce Development Consortium:
## A Multi-Campus Model of Online Learning for the Public Good

**Aleshia Hall-Campbell**
*University of Tennessee Health Science Center, USA*

**Pamela Connor**
*University of Tennessee Health Science Center, USA*

**Nathan Tipton**
*University of Tennessee Health Science Center, USA*

**David Mirvis**
*University of Tennessee Health Science Center, USA*

## ABSTRACT

*From 2003 to 2009, the Tennessee Public Health Workforce Development Consortium (The Consortium) served as a multi-institutional collaborative effort to develop and implement academic continuing professional education programs for public health professionals in Tennessee. The Consortium included the Tennessee Department of Health (DOH), East Tennessee State University (ETSU), the University of Tennessee at Knoxville (UTK), and the University of Tennessee Health Science Center in Memphis (UTHSC). Utilizing online, distance education techniques and technologies to provide graduate level certificate programs in epidemiology, health system leadership and health care management, as well as a Master of Public Health (MPH) degree to meet the specific needs of DOH's professional staff, the Consortium successfully implemented an innovative, cross-institutional model for the provision of public health education. The online technology not only facilitated the use of active learning approaches appropriate for older adult learners who are returning to academic work, but also helped students and faculty meet the challenges of learning and teaching across multiple, geographically distant sites. This*

DOI: 10.4018/978-1-60960-623-7.ch018

*chapter describes the central role technology played in the project in terms of fostering inter-organizational cooperation and collaboration and providing measurable educational impact. The chapter also illustrates the project's role in forming community partnerships, as well as explaining the best practices/ strategies learned from this project.*

## HISTORY OF THE TENNESSEE PUBLIC HEALTH WORKFORCE DEVELOPMENT CONSORTIUM

Prior to 2003, when the Tennessee DOH launched the Tennessee Public Health Workforce, no school of public health existed in the state, creating a significant education gap that limited capacity for the state to address health disparity issues. Complicating this educational shortfall was the high percentage of Tennessee DOH's upper-to-middle level managers who were eligible for retirement, resulting in a large workforce with no formal training in public health. Tennessee's unfortunate situation has been repeated across the nation (e.g., Honoré, Graham, Garcia, & Morris, 2008; Draper, Hurley, & Lauer, 2008; Lichtveld & Cioffi, 2003; Turnock, 2003; Morse, 2003), and has been made further challenging due to Tennessee residents who continue to exhibit and report poor health status. These combined public health related issues—along with the events of September 11, 2001—prompted the Tennessee DOH to create the Consortium as a joint curricular venture that would recognize and meet the challenges of potential threats posed by newly emerging diseases and bioterrorism, as well as enhance the capabilities of Tennessee DOH staff to meet current and future public health challenges.

The Tennessee DOH approached these challenges by joining with three academic campuses across the state to form the Consortium in 2003 to develop and implement advanced professional education programs specifically for Tennessee DOH professional employees. This Consortium concept became the first collaboration between the DOH and universities in Tennessee, bringing together for the first time the complementary skills of a state government agency (DOH) and three universities within two independent systems: the Tennessee Board of Regents (ETSU) and the University of Tennessee system (UTK and UTHSC) located across the state. The graduate educational programs, including student tuition, fees and course development support, were funded by a contract from the Tennessee DOH with the academic units. The first class was enrolled in January 2004.

Central to the success of the Consortium was the use of online technology, which was important for both educational and practical reasons. For example, for older students who were returning to academia and resuming their studies, the online format promoted active-learning approaches. These approaches also included the cross-institutional discussion board function within the BlackBoard system, which was used to provide prompt assessment and feedback interactions among students and faculty. In addition, given the geography of Tennessee and the location of the partnering institutions in Memphis, Knoxville, and Johnson City (see Figure 1), the use of technology also allowed DOH employees from across the state to participate without the travel required for convening trainings in a traditional classroom setting. Furthermore, the use of predominantly asynchronous teaching methods that did not require faculty/student coordination allowed flexibility in learning times and allowed students to continue with their full-time positions. Finally, the technology expanded the opportunities for students to interact with faculties with complementary expertise from the three universities.

*Figure 1. Map of Tennessee*

## OVERVIEW OF THE PROJECT'S USE OF TECHNOLOGY AS A CATALYST

Through the use of the common educational software management system BlackBoard, faculty from the three university partners designed courses with a uniform format that was subsequently adopted by all partnering institutions. Course instructors were distributed across the three university partners, and course materials were loaded onto the BlackBoard system of the instructor's campus. Students were then able to access the materials and interact with the instructor and classmates through that campus's BlackBoard system regardless of their location. Toward the end of the project, ETSU made a campus-wide decision to transition to the Desire2Learn (D2L) course management system but, because of the many similarities between D2L and BlackBoard, this transition did not affect the ongoing provision of course materials across institutions.

One particular challenge for the project involved acclimating students—many of whom had not been to school in years—to graduate school generally while also specifically acclimatizing them to a graduate program taught using distance learning techniques and technologies. Indeed, prior to course enrollment, numerous participants had no or very limited experience with technology. In response, the Consortium hosted a new student orientation using video and teleconferencing capabilities, which gave students a first look into distance learning and eased their transition in to new technologies by providing expectations and

explaining differences between online and traditional classroom settings. An additional benefit was discovered early on with regard to orienting students to the distance-learning platform, when it was found that if faculty invested the first week in class sessions to technology concerns, many technical issues that could potentially arise throughout the semester could be alleviated. As a result, the start-up phase for new students was significantly shortened.

Because courses were taught by faculty across multiple institutions and many of the courses were taught in conjunction with their traditional courses, the executive governing committee decided that all courses would be maintained on the BlackBoard site of the lead instructor's respective campus. It was therefore essential to work directly with Information Technology staff on each campus and get them involved in the initial planning phase, an involvement that generated much of the program's success with regard to technology. As part of the Consortium's admission requirements, students were also required to sign a "Student Acknowledgement Form" that granted the student's "home campus" permission to share student information with partnering institutions so that courses could be accessed outside their "home campus." BlackBoard usernames were generated by the "home campus" and shared with the partnering campuses' BlackBoard support staff, who created profiles for students not officially enrolled on their respective campuses but who were taking a course through the BlackBoard system on their campus. This allowed students to use the same username across multiple campuses and to access all of their courses while enrolled in the Consortium, thus eliminating having to sign in to multiple systems with multiple usernames. Although the process of creating a standard username for each participant as they matriculated through the Consortium was simple to do, it did require the active involvement of IT personnel from all participating campuses on the front to end to understand their role and impact in this collaborative.

In order to further reduce confusion, the executive governing committee along with cross-institutional faculty established a general course focused on the Consortium that was offered through the BlackBoard system. This course served as a common informational and networking center for students and faculty, not only allowing students to create individual profiles, but also serving as a communication tool that provided general announcements, administered course registration and evaluations, and provided general discussion forums. Due to the complexities of the Consortium such as multiple course listings with various course numbers and faculty, this general course was also used as a reference guide to aid students in identifying to which BlackBoard system they needed to log on in order to access their respective courses.

## EDUCATIONAL IMPACT ON STUDENTS AND FACULTY

The Consortium served as a graduate-level educational pipeline for DOH professional staff. Once participants successfully completed one of the graduate certificate programs, they were able to further pursue their education through the online MPH program. Successful completion of an online graduate certificate program would also provide the preparation necessary to advance their educational training through a degree program. Through the Consortium, 132 participants—most of whom otherwise would not have had the opportunity because of the out-of-pocket costs of tuition and lack of access to programs and courses—enrolled in at least one semester of graduate course work through this program. Sixty-nine (69) participants received a graduate certificate, and 27 went on to further pursue an MPH degree.

An alumni follow-up survey was administered in October 2009 to assess students' perceived benefits of participating in the program. Overall, participant feedback regarding the program and its impact on their careers has been valuable. Due to DOH's recent lay-offs and buy-outs, as well as the agency's e-mail domain change, we received a response from 36 (52%) participants. Of these 36 respondents, more than 60% felt their participation in the program improved their level of competency to perform their current job. Sixty-four percent (64%) of respondents reported their participation in the program enhanced formal networking opportunities with other participants, faculty, and staff, and 83% of participants said that participation in the program enhanced their ability to collect, summarize, and interpret information relevant to a public health issue.

Furthermore, course offerings consistently received high satisfaction ratings from students. Through the history of the program, there have been 90 course offerings in three certificate programs and the online MPH program. Of these 90 courses, only five course offerings received unfavorable reviews from students in standardized surveys (including faculty feedback, course delivery, and timing of mandated synchronized course activities). The Executive and Academic Affairs Committees of the Consortium were charged with reviewing and addressing concerns, as well as implementing changes promptly, all of which resulted in substantial improvements in student satisfaction.

## LOGISTICS OF MULTI-CAMPUS ENROLLMENT MANAGEMENT

The Consortium successfully advanced the educational missions of the participating universities while also supporting the educational needs of the Tennessee DOH. In addition, it promoted the use of educational technologies both on and off campus through the implementation and facilitation of additional educational and training opportunities for communities and participants that lay outside the programmatic scope and specific needs set out by the Consortium. Moreover, through the use of technology, partnering institutions were able to provide courses and programs that might not have normally existed on their respective campuses. Consequently, development of the Consortium's infrastructure has had a long-term impact on partnering institutions, which provided resources and staff for the development, expansion and conversion of courses and programs to online format. Other online certificate programs have now been initiated on several of the campuses using formats and materials developed initially from the Consortium.

The need for the Consortium to function across institutions also led to the development of new administrative approaches to inter-organizational collaboration. For example, the different finance systems (e.g., tuition rates, faculty payments, etc.) and organizational alignment (i.e., graduate schools, School of Public Health and departments) among institutional partners required the development of a financial model that would benefit all partnering institutions. Each student would enroll at one of the partnering institutions, known as their "home campus," and DOH's contract would pay tuition and fees for each course to the "home campus" at the rate normally charged by that campus for in-state graduate students. When a student took a course taught by faculty on another campus, the student's "home campus" transferred an Internal Tuition Transfer Rate (ITTR), based on the lowest tuition rate of the partnering campuses, to the institution providing the primary instructor. The remaining tuition and fees charged for the course remained on the student's "home campus" to cover expenses related to the operation of the program on that campus. However, if a student

registered for a course taught from their "home campus," the full tuition and fees remained on the "home campus."

In addition to creating a cross-institutional financial model, the Consortium also addressed the different organizational structures and faculty expectations (i.e., teaching loads, faculty reporting locally but expected to work in collaboration with faculty from other institutions). For example, the location of faculty for the different courses—as well as varying student populations in the different universities—mandated the development of novel approaches to academic functions such as teaching assignments, registration, and grading. Cross-institutional faculty created courses based on the identified need of DOH employees as well as on the collective educational capabilities of the participating institutions. The program provided tuition to the educational institutions for students enrolled in the program. The Consortium's impact also increased student enrollment for each respective campus department in which the certificate program was housed. The integration of Consortium courses with traditional courses within university programs proved to be challenging due to specific student requirements mandated by the Tennessee DOH. As a result, partnering institutions created separate course sections specifically designed for Consortium participants.

Each course offered through the Consortium was reviewed, approved and listed in the catalog of each participating campus regardless of which campus had developed and implemented the course. Thus, a course developed on one campus and taught by an instructor on that campus was also listed and assigned a course number in the catalog of the other partnering institutions. In the example below (Figure 2), the Biostatistics I (BIOE 720) course was taught through UTHSC, and was cross-listed at ETSU as Biostatistics I (PUBH 5310-504) and at UTK at Biostatistics I (PH 530-98750). A shadow instructor from each campus was assigned to the course, although the instructor from the implementing campus had

*Figure 2. Diagram of collaborative course offering*

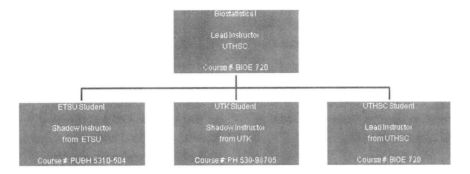

primary teaching responsibility. The courses' primary instructor assigned and transmitted grades to the shadow instructor at the student's "home campus" for inclusion in the official transcript. The course mechanism for this model enabled faculty members to cross-teach courses while maintaining autonomy through their respective campuses.

## BEST PRACTICES/STRATEGIES FOR FORMING COLLABORATIVE PARTNERSHIPS

Overall, the best practices/strategies learned in the formation of the Tennessee Public Health Workforce Development program included:

1.  Developing a set of operating procedures to guide the collaborative program that were developed and approved by all Consortium members;

Part of the Consortium's infrastructure development included the formation of an Executive Committee, composed of senior faculty and administrators from each academic campus and one senior staff person from the Tennessee Department of Health, to oversee the performance of the Consortium. As an effort to formalize the governing process, the Consortium's Executive Committee developed and adopted a set of policies

and procedures that governed all aspects of the multi-institutional collaborative. In addition, the key committees held frequent conference calls as well as face-to-face meetings at least once per year.

2.  Involving executive level administrators in the development phase to obtain buy-in from partnering agencies;

The development and implementation of the Consortium programs on multiple campuses required an extensive amount of planning and coordination of efforts. Therefore, by involving executive level administrators in the developmental planning phase, it created a commitment among committee members to handle and resolve all logistical issues on their respective campuses to ensure the Consortium was fully operational. Senior administration personnel on each campus and the DOH were kept informed of the programs and challenges on a regular basis.

3.  Maximizing the autonomy of the partnering institutions while assuring coordination of the educational and administrative functions of the programs;

While the Consortium involved extensive coordination of educational and administrative functions between the multiple campuses, it was also important that each institution was able to maintain a level of control in regards to their respective students, courses and staff. This was achieved through a structured set of operational policies as well as through open communication among the members.

4. Identifying a common educational course management system to reduce the level of confusion among students;

By providing a common educational course management system with similar formatting for all program courses regardless of which institution the courses were housed eliminated some of the confusion among students. This was one task assigned to the Academic Affairs Committee, which was composed of members from each academic partner.

5. Involving various university and departmental staff in the initial planning phase to work out logistical issues;

The complexity of the student and programmatic logistical issues (e.g., cross course and faculty listings, student enrollment on multiple campuses, and tuition transfers) of the Consortium were, in most cases, innovative concepts for the partnering institutions that it required coordination of efforts among and between various departmental staff among and between universities. The governing structure, composed of representatives from each academic partner, helped coordinate these cross-institutional issues.

6. Creating a financial model that benefited all partnering institutions; and

Due to the various financial arrangements of each campus, the Consortium's Executive Committee created a financial model that benefited all partnering institutions. The development of the Internal Tuition Transfer Rate "ITTR" based

on the lowest tuition rate was the core element to the success of this program.

7. Assuring open and honest communication with all stakeholders and participants.

Due to the collaborative efforts and innovation of the Consortium's concept, it was essential to provide open and honest communication with all stakeholders and participants.

Although the Consortium was discontinued in June 2009 due to state budget cuts, we consider the five years of its operation as highly successful. The Consortium attained its goal of enhancing the capabilities of the state's public health workforce by establishing graduate certificate programs in critical areas of public health disciplines identified by DOH, such as epidemiology, public health leadership, and health care management. Courses were designed to be accepted as full graduate credit by the partnering universities' MPH programs, and were provided through an innovative, cross-institutional, online distance-learning platform. The Consortium's programs not only provided graduate educational opportunities, but they also enabled other professional development and training opportunities that extended beyond DOH's professional staff.

Indeed, focusing on the needs of students within the various public health disciplines further aided the multi-institutional collaborative concept, as did the incorporation of advanced cross-campus technology. The Consortium's extensive use of distance education technology and tools also spurred greater interest from partnering institutions in their use of other educational programs on their respective campuses. In addition, while the concept of awarding academic certificates (rather than full degrees) was new on some campuses, the success of this program led to the development of other certificate programs.

The Tennessee Public Health Workforce Development Consortium was also effective in creating a partnership among a state government agency and three academic institutions based on the utilization of this advanced educational technology. For instance, the Consortium hosted a series of Grand Rounds seminars that utilized videoconferencing capabilities made available to public health and community professionals throughout Tennessee. Furthermore, the manner in which the Consortium's contract and program model were established provided additional educational trainings which included online conferences, public health training exercises, and courses for communities and participants outside the scope set forth by the program.

We believe that if the Consortium had continued to receive state funding allowing it to remain in existence, the competency level of Tennessee's public health workforce would continue improving. This in turn would result in enhanced job performance necessary for meeting current and future public health challenges. In addition, state monies would have allowed the Consortium's technology-based system of providing online distance education to continue, enabling even more far-reaching networking opportunities among and between participants and faculty. Yet while funding for this project has been terminated, the Consortium has nevertheless demonstrated itself as a successful model for fostering multi-institutional cooperation and providing cross-institutional public health education.

# REFERENCES

Draper, D. A., Hurley, R. E., & Lauer, J. (2008). *Public health workforce shortages imperil nation's health.* Center for Studying Health System Change, Research Brief no. 4. Retrieved on June 14, 2010, from http://www.hschange.org/CONTENT/979/979.pdf

Honoré, P. A., Graham, G. N., Garcia, J., & Morris, W. (2008). A call to action: Public health and community college partnerships to educate the workforce and promote health equity. *Journal of Public Health Management and Practice, 14*(6), S82–S84.

Lichtveld, M. Y., & Cioffi, J. P. (2003). Public health workforce development: Progress, challenges, and opportunities. *Journal of Public Health Management and Practice, 9*(6), 443–450.

Morse, S. S. (2003). Building academic-practice partnerships: The Center for Public Health Preparedness at the Columbia University Mailman School of Public Health, before and after 9/11. *Journal of Public Health Management and Practice, 9*(5), 427–432.

Turnock, B. J. (2003). Roadmap for public health workforce preparedness. *Journal of Public Health Management and Practice, 9*(6), 471–480.

# Chapter 19
# Enhancing a Rural School–University Teacher Education Partnership through an E-Mentoring Program for Beginning Teachers

**Janice Holt**
*Western Carolina University, USA*

**Lori Unruh**
*Western Carolina University, USA*

**A. Michael Dougherty**
*Western Carolina University, USA*

## ABSTRACT

*This case study describes an innovative and effective e-mentoring program for beginning teachers that has enhanced Western Carolina University's (WCU) school-university teacher education partnership. With national data indicating that nearly one-half of beginning teachers leave the classroom within five years, schools and universities are faced with the challenges of providing the support needed to keep new teachers in the classroom and developing them into effective professionals. Like those nationally, the schools in the university's rural service region were facing new teacher retention issues. The authors of this chapter and their school partners believed that technology-mediated mentoring had the potential to extend the benefits of face-to-face mentoring by providing professional development that engaged new teachers in an external community of learners, was connected to and driven by teachers' work, and was sustained, intensive, and respectful of teachers' demanding schedules. The School University Teacher Education Partnership (SUTEP) then developed and implemented this technology-based project.*

DOI: 10.4018/978-1-60960-623-7.ch019

## HISTORY OF THE PROJECT

School-university partnerships have become an important educational phenomenon in recent years, especially as they relate to school reform and teacher quality. School-university partnerships attempt to achieve beneficial change in the partner organizations through constructive initiatives (Calabrese, 2006). Although such partnerships have existed since the late 1800s (Clark, 1988), they started receiving significant attention in the early 1980s (Goodlad, 1988). These partnerships take on a variety of forms but typically have as their goal the improvement in the quality of some aspect of P-16 education (Handler & Ravid, 2001a). Our partnership, formally known as the School University Teacher Education Partnership (SUTEP), was created in 1997. SUTEP is housed in the College of Education and Allied Professions (CEAP) at WCU. SUTEP provides an umbrella for the majority of initiatives between the university and the public schools. The central mission of SUTEP is to support a seamless continuum for the ongoing development of professional educators. This mission is met through the work of four standing committees, one each dealing with recruitment, preparation, induction, and professional development. In order to provide maximum impact, all academic departments and centers in the College of Education and Allied Professions collaborate with SUTEP and have in their mission provision of services related to these initiatives. The university has signed partnerships with 108 schools in its region.

One goal of SUTEP is to assist school systems in meeting the North Carolina State Board of Education requirement to develop and provide a Beginning Teacher Support Program Plan (N.C. BOE, 2003). Implementing this plan can be a challenge to rural schools, like those in our region, where resources are limited. The SUTEP Induction Committee provides support by collaborating with beginning teacher coordinators to design

comprehensive services for teachers during their first three years of service.

Conversations within our partnership focusing on technology began in 2005. SUTEP and five partner school systems received grant funding in 2006 from the Z. Smith Reynolds Foundation to develop and pilot an online support program to enhance beginning teacher support. The pilot, Project START (Supporting, Training, And Retaining Teachers) Phase I, demonstrated that many benefits to first-year teachers are related to their opportunity to share new ideas and similar experiences. Technology was recognized as a viable format for this exchange. With the online support program housed on WCU's server, beginning teachers were able to talk with colleagues who were struggling with similar problems. Career master teachers and university faculty from CEAP and the College of Arts and Sciences (otherwise known as e-mentors) facilitated discussions and answered questions, providing the knowledge and skills that come from the wisdom of experience.

The first phase of this project was successful, as documented in the educational impact section of this chapter and led to Project START Phase II. This phase resulted in an expanded partnership between WCU and eleven WNC school systems in 2008. The purpose of this project was to increase the current support for first-year teachers established through the initial program to include teachers in years two and three of their careers. Building on the e-mentoring model, the program expanded to include synchronous online chats and the option of sharing classroom video clips. These new features better met the needs of technologically savvy teachers, providing opportunities for them to seek support through the virtual world in addition to the face-to-face school-based mentoring available in their schools. Technology was also used to differentiate professional learning among new teachers by providing a variety of support opportunities. For example, a primary concern for many new teachers is getting ready for the first days of school. Teachers participating in Project START Phase II had options to learn how seasoned teachers prepare for the opening of school through group discussions. They could also view sample room arrangements, access virtual resources, and download podcasts of e-mentors giving a video tour of their classrooms.

The 2009-2010 academic year marks the fifth year WCU has provided online support for new teachers. The program has been revised and refined using feedback and survey responses from all stakeholders: new teachers, mentors, principals, and beginning teacher coordinators. This year, the platform changed to another format that is modeled after current social networking sites (Elgg). The new platform provides an automatic email notification when a comment or resource is posted and provides just-in-time support allowing new teachers to access discussions and resources they want and need at any time. Conversations are organized by grade level, content area, or by topic. Other features include blog space and podcasts.

## USE OF TECHNOLOGY AS A CATALYST OF THE PROJECT

It is not surprising, given the growing reliance on technology, that people have turned to technology-mediated communications for social networking (Sproull & Kiesler, 1991). As early as 1991, projects have been identified that reported beginning teachers' feelings of isolation were lessened when they participated in a virtual network (Merseth, 1991). It is promising that this new method of induction support, delivered via the Internet, will provide experiences that address the needs of new teachers, increase teacher retention, and improve teacher quality (Gareis & Nussbaum-Beach, 2008).

But using technology as a means to provide support to new teachers is more than sending email or surfing the Web. Online mentoring, or e-mentoring as defined in this project, is a devel-opmental relationship in which an experienced teacher provides guidance to a new teacher using technology-mediated communications. Gareis and Nussbaum-Beach (2008) report that e-mentoring has the promise of overcoming limitations of face-to-face mentoring models, such as the mismatch between mentors and new teachers that too often occurs in schools. With online mentoring, new teachers can communicate with e-mentors teaching the same grade or subject, conversations often missing when there is a mismatch between them and their face-to-face school-based mentor. Due to the asynchronous nature of e-mentoring, every participant has an opportunity to contribute, has time to reflect on discussions, and can interact thoughtfully to solve classroom problems as recommended by Janasz, Ensher and Heun (2008). In addition, e-mentoring has no geographic boundaries, so support is not limited to the teacher across the hall. It is time and place independent—synchronous or asynchronous. This flexibility makes online support, as part of an induction program, an exciting possibility and provides easy access to resources—all just a click away (Price & Chen, 2003).

The SUTEP online support portal was developed using Plone open source software in the summer of 2006. The portal provided space for grade-level and content-specific discussion boards and a collection of resources. Lesson plans, instructional strategies and classroom management tips could be shared with colleagues from other systems. Teachers were also able to view video-streamed lesson clips that provided examples of best practice. In addition, teachers had opportunities to design units of study, collaboratively develop assessments, and examine student work. Career teachers in the region were recruited to apply as e-mentors for the program and were required to attend training in how to become effective mentors in an online environment.

First-year teachers from participating rural partnership systems were informed of the project by district-level administrators, enrolled in the program, and placed in groups matching their teaching assignment. Online face-to-face orientation took place in early August. The goals of the orientation were to familiarize participants with the site, provide an opportunity for them to meet their e-mentors, and begin to establish collaborative, trusting relationships among their colleagues.

Two formal online mentoring sessions of six weeks each were offered throughout the year. During these sessions, teachers participated in a variety of discussions. Not surprisingly, many focused on establishing rules and procedures, parent conferences and planning. Each discussion began with a prompt posing a question about a specific teaching issue, such as preparing for a parent conference or working with students who are chronically late or absent. Everyone in the group responded by sharing ideas, strategies and solutions. The project was based on the notion that professional learning experiences grow through online dialogue, therefore teachers were encouraged to read and post each week during these sessions. E-mentors were available to answer questions on an as-needed basis in addition to the formal six-week support sessions.

However, the online program was impacted by problems with technology that negatively affected the level of participation. Some first-year teachers reported that they did not have access to the Internet at home. Their only option was to use classroom computers during or at the end of the school day, limiting possible participation time. In addition, two school systems experienced a great deal of difficulty with firewalls. These teachers had intermittent problems accessing the site at school for much of the fall semester. Firewall issues were eventually resolved, but opportunities to benefit from the networking program for a good portion of the year were missed. As noted by Bishop, Giles, and Bryant (2005), limited time impacts the frequency of responses and engagement with the program.

## VALUE OF THE PROJECT IN FORMING COMMUNITY PARTNERSHIPS

Project START enhanced WCU's partnership in a variety of ways. The project helped our partners realize that working together on technology-related issues will continue to be an important aspect of the partnership. For example, the annual goal setting process now includes the inclusion of technology. In addition, several new projects are being developed collaboratively to incorporate the use of technology in supporting beginning teachers.

One project evolved into a much larger initiative that focuses on supporting our region's beginning teachers. WCU is currently working with the Western Regional Education Service Alliance (WRESA), an alliance of the 18 westernmost school systems in North Carolina. This expanded partnership between WRESA and WCU has led to the development of online professional development modules for second- and third-year teachers, which are currently being piloted. Public school teachers and WCU faculty have contributed to the design of these modules, which will be available to teachers throughout the region.

The WNC Educational Network, or WNC EdNET, is another newly developed partnership among the seven westernmost counties in North Carolina, WCU and two community colleges. The purpose of EdNET is to collaboratively assist the schools and school systems to procure and use upgradeable high capacity broadband technology configurations and services to enhance learning, professional development, and organization administration, and to open up learning opportunities not currently available or imagined. One of the objectives of the project is to establish a collaborative of partners for the purpose of enhancing the development and use of technology as a tool for improving learning opportunities such as our e-mentoring beginning teacher program.

## EDUCATIONAL IMPACT OF THE PROJECT (STUDENTS AND FACULTY)

Research has clearly shown that incorporating a variety of components into beginning teacher induction programs increases the retention of those teachers in the field (Reiman, Corbell, & Thomas, 2007). While strong school-based mentoring is considered the foundation, other support options that include additional resources and networking opportunities are important as well. In 2006 SUTEP and participating school systems expanded their offerings to include an online support program. The online component seemed to be especially important considering the challenges of providing services in a large rural area. Technology and resources have changed over time in direct response to information provided by teacher and e-mentor participants in the program.

Following the first year of implementation, the 2007 survey demonstrated that 91% of the teachers reported participating in the online resource program. However, the level of involvement from the teachers varied greatly across grade levels, subject area taught, entry level (lateral vs. traditional), and whether the teachers were hired before school or after school started. The majority of teachers who participated reported that they benefited from online services because it provided skills in the areas of Planning Lessons (54%), Classroom Management Strategies (69%), Setting Goals and Reflections on Teaching (66%), and Gaining Knowledge of Subject Matter/Teaching Strategies (69%). In addition, a significant correlation was found between reported levels of participation in the online program and skill development in the area of Planning Lessons ($r=-0.260$, $p<.05$) and in the area of Gaining Knowledge of Subject Matter/Teaching Strategies ($r=-0.254$, $p<.05$). In response to open-ended questions, teachers indicated that the primary benefit they received was in sharing new ideas and similar experiences with their colleagues from school systems across the region. However, there were new teachers who indicated that they did not benefit from this form of support. Technical problems appeared to affect their perceptions of the program. E-mentors included both experienced teachers and university personnel. On their surveys, e-mentors also indicated that the network of support and sense of community provided through the online program was very positive.

For the 2007-2008 school year, changes were made in the format of the e-mentoring program based on the feedback provided from the previous year. The beginning teacher survey completed in 2008 indicated that only 5% of the teachers reported having no participation in the online program, which was a slight improvement from the previous year. Many teachers reported more involvement in discussions held during the spring semester of the school year as opposed to the fall. In this survey, new teachers were asked to indicate the most helpful thing about participating in the online support group vs. the on-site mentoring program. The responses clearly indicated that the online support groups provided much-needed advice in helping to solve a wide range of problems while the school-based mentors were important because of their accessibility and emotional support. Another important factor identified through the 2008 e-mentor and school-based mentor surveys was the ability of the online mentoring programs to connect beginning teachers with others who were teaching at the same grade level/subject area. While only 49% of the school-based mentors reported that they had worked with teachers who were teaching at the same grade level/subject area, 93% of the e-mentors indicated such a match. This is an especially important consideration in rural areas where it is often very difficult to find school-based mentors who match with their beginning teachers.

The 2008 survey also included questions related to the attitudes of beginning teachers and administrators toward technology. The responses to these questions provided a clear picture that most teachers and administrators have a positive attitude toward technology. When asked if the use of technology improved their ability to do their job, 80% of teachers and 84% of administrators agreed. Likewise when asked if the use of technology improved their ability to learn, 84% of the teachers and 78% of the administrators agreed. These results provided additional incentive to continue to explore how technology could be used in the induction of beginning teachers.

In 2009, a three-year analysis of the survey results was completed. Results indicated that both school-based mentors and e-mentors consistently reported the ability to positively impact the development of beginning teachers' skills. E-mentors in particular indicated a positive impact in the areas of managing stress, planning lessons, and expanding the repertoire of teaching strategies. In addition, beginning teachers consistently indicated that the support provided to them, including both school-based mentoring and e-mentoring, was beneficial (see Table 1). The fact that the percentage of teachers reporting positive results has grown each year is significant and parallels the increased number of technological services provided during that time as described above.

The impact of virtual support is also reflected in the fact that teachers who participate in these programs have had a higher retention rate when compared to data collected on teachers from other parts of North Carolina. For those teachers who participated in the 2006-2007 beginning

*Table 1. Percent of beginning teachers indicating agree/strongly agree*

| Survey Item | 2007 | 2008 | 2009 |
|---|---|---|---|
| Support enhanced my teaching practices and made me a better teacher | 82% | 86% | 95% |
| | | | |
| Support increased likelihood of continuing my teaching career | 71% | 74% | 79% |
| | | | |
| I am overall satisfied with the support received | 85% | 89% | 90% |

teacher support program provided by SUTEP, 88% were still teaching after two years compared to only 74% of teachers from across all of North Carolina who started at the same time. The addition of the online support program is considered to be an important factor in these results as it provided a way for the beginning teachers in geographically remote areas to connect with and learn from each other in a way that would not have been possible otherwise.

## VALUE OF THE PROJECT FOR THE EDUCATIONAL INSTITUTION

The e-mentoring project has demonstrated to university faculty that computer-mediated technology is a viable method for delivering professional development. To that end, the College of Education and Allied Professions has developed new strategies for using technology to provide professional development opportunities for our faculty and school partners. For example, professional development services are expanding through Operation Ended. Operation Ended has facilitated a dialogue among our college, the Office of the Chief Information Officer, and public schools in the region about issues surrounding the implementation of technologically driven programs. These discussions have led to greater familiarity and awareness among personnel resulting in more effective collaboration and consultation on the part of our department of Instructional Technology (IT). In effect, IT is now a project partner. One initiative to address our geographic remoteness was to pilot Apple iChat to facilitate video conferencing. While that project was not continued due to issues with public school firewalls, university IT personnel are currently assisting the members of the partnership in identifying alternative software programs that would be supported in the schools.

University faculty members have also benefited due to their involvement with the online mentoring program. They now have a better understanding of the knowledge and skills required of their graduates during those critical first years in the classroom. Faculty revised their courses to better prepare pre-service teachers for the realities they will face. Participating faculty also gained insight from the interaction with graduates from their own programs to identify strengths and gaps in teacher education preparation programs.

Another outcome is that public schools receive valuable data about their induction program from the SUTEP partnership. Using the findings of program evaluation, they are able to make informed decisions to improve support for new teachers and retain them in their system. This information can help alleviate the growing concerns regarding classroom and school instability, teacher quality and supply, and the costs associated with recruiting, hiring, and inducting beginning teachers.

## LESSONS LEARNED

WCU and our public school partners learned a great deal about technology as we implemented Phase I and II of Project START. We learned that technology could be effectively used in geographically challenged regions to strengthen the development of new teachers. However, as previously reported, low or inconsistent teacher usage was reported. Researchers suggest that participation may be low in online support networks due to the additional commitment of time—time over and above the long days required of teachers new to the profession (Bishop, Giles, & Bryant, 2005; Rogan, 1997). In fact Hawkes (2001) found that as much as 82% of teachers reported lack of time as the main reason they did not post frequently, especially if their only option was to respond during the school day because internet access was not accessible in their homes. It is critical, therefore, that school-based technology coordinators work closely with the university's IT division to ensure

these problems are resolved before the start of the project.

Additional lessons learned in this project are really lessons that the partners "re-learned." Our project corroborated the literature (e.g., Borthwick, Stirling, Nauman, & Cook, 2003; Handler and Ravid, 2001b; Reaves and Narvaez, 2006) about best practices in developing and maintaining a school-university partnership. Project START reemphasized the importance of setting goals together, ensuring commitment of the partners, having on-going communication related to those goals during all aspects of the project, and having high-energy members in key positions within the partnership to ensure funding and other necessary resources. These elements lead to a properly structured and effectively managed partnership.

Our project built upon very strong exiting partnerships. The College of Education and Allied Professions and SUTEP had won two prestigious national awards, one in 2006 (Distinguished Program in Teacher Education) and one in 2007 (Christa McAuliffe Award for Excellence in Teacher Education). We received these recognitions in part due to the close, collaborative relationships among the partners. The dean of the College of Education, for example, annually visits each of the seventeen superintendents of the schools districts in the partnership. The meeting focuses on mutual needs and concerns. The resultant ongoing and systematic communication at the administrative levels of the partnership has resulted in long-standing relationships built on trust as well as an annual renewal of the commitment to the partnership by the partners through conscientious and systematic nurturing. Consequently, we agree with Reaves and Narvaez (2006) that partnerships need to blend the goals, structures and cultures of the partners and agree with Borthwick, Stirling, Nauman and Cook (2003) that effective communication and interaction within the partnership is essential in designing and maintaining partnerships.

Handler and Ravid (2001b) point out the importance of equal and mutually beneficial relationships in successful partnerships. Representatives from the schools and university planned the project together from the beginning, not only enhancing commitment, but also ensuring a non-hierarchical and equal relationship among the partners. The mutually beneficial nature of the project was emphasized so that it was clear from the outset that each partner would benefit. The university, for example, would partially meet its mission of serving the region, in this case serving its public school partners. School systems would benefit most by reduced attrition of beginning teachers.

Finally, we have learned that annual goal setting among the partners is essential for sustainability. Those interested in developing or reinventing partnerships may want to review the research conducted by Borthwick, Stirling, Nauman, and Cook (2003) that supports the notion of developing relatively short-term goals given that the goals in a partnership will change as the partnership evolves. Quality goal setting may well contribute to the long-term effectiveness and even the survival of a partnership.

## REFERENCES

Bishop, D., Giles, S., & Bryant, K. (2005). Teacher receptiveness toward Web-based training and support. *Teaching and Teacher Education, 21*(1), 3–14. doi:10.1016/j.tate.2004.11.002

Borthwick, A. C., Stirling, T., Nauman, A. D., & Cook, D. L. (2003). Achieving successful school-university collaboration. *Urban Education, 38*(3), 330–371. doi:10.1177/0042085903038003003

Calabrese, R. (2006). Building social capital through the use of an appreciative inquiry theoretical perspective in a school and university partnership. *International Journal of Educational Management, 20*(3), 173–182. doi:10.1108/09513540610654146

Clark, R. W. (1988). School-university relationships: An interpretative review. In K. Sirotnik, & J. I. Goodlad (Eds.), *School-university partnerships in action: Concepts, cases, and concerns* (pp. 32–65). New York, NY: Teachers College Press.

Gareis, C. R., & Nussbaum-Beach, S. (2007). Electronically mentoring to develop accomplished professional teachers. *Journal of Personnel Evaluation in Education, 20*(3), 227–246..doi:10.1007/s11092-008-9060-0

Goodlad, J. (1988). School-university partnerships for school renewal: Rationale and concepts. In K. A. Sirotnik, & J. I. Goodlad (Eds.), *School-university partnerships in action: Concepts, cases, and concerns* (pp. 3–31). New York, NY: Teachers College Press.

Handler, M. G., & Ravid, R. (2001a). Models of school-university collaboration. In R. Ravid, & M. G. Handler (Eds.), *The many faces of school-university collaboration: Characteristics of successful partnerships* (pp. 3–10). Englewood, CO: Greenwood Publishing Group.

Handler, M. G., & Ravid, R. (2001b). The center for collaborative research at National-Louis University. In R. Ravid, & M. G. Handler (Eds.), *The many faces of school-university collaboration: Characteristics of successful partnerships* (pp. 237–246). Englewood, CO: Greenwood Publishing Group.

Merseth, K. (1991). Supporting beginning teachers with computer networks. *Journal of Teacher Education, 42*(2), 140–147. doi:10.1177/002248719104200207

N.C. State Board of Education. (2003). *Improving student achievement through professional development: Final report to the state board of education and the state superintendent.* Raleigh, NC: NC Professional Development Committee. Retrieved from http://www.ncpublicschools.org/docs/profdev/reports/studentachievement.pdf

Price, M., & Chen, H. (2003). Promises and challenges: Exploring a collaborative telementoring program in a pre-service teacher education program. *Mentoring & Tutoring, 11*(1), 105–117. doi:10.1080/1361126032000054844

Reaves, W. E., & Narvaez, J. G. (2006). Managing and resolving organizational conflict in school-university partnerships through sound planning and design. *Journal of School Public Relations, 27*(2), 196–210.

Reiman, A., Corbell, K., & Thomas, E. (2007). *New teacher support. UNC Dean's Council on Teacher Education: Summary Evaluation Report.* UNC University School Programs.

Sproull, L., & Kiesler, S. (1991). Computers, networks, and work. *Scientific American, 265*(3), 116–123. doi:10.1038/scientificamerican0991-116

# Chapter 20
# Leveraging Online University Education to Improve K–12 Science Education:
## The ScienceMaster Case Study

**Thomas B. Cavanagh**
*University of Central Florida, USA*

## ABSTRACT

*While many K-12 teachers, especially those in elementary education, have extensive academic training and work experience in effective pedagogy, there is a concern that their discipline-specific knowledge may not be as robust as is necessary to address the needs of today's students in a competitive, global environment. This is especially true in the STEM fields of science, technology, engineering, and math. To address this need, Florida's Manatee County School District partnered with Embry-Riddle Aeronautical University (ERAU) and Nova Southeastern University (NSU) to develop the ScienceMaster program. The ScienceMaster program leveraged existing university expertise in science-related online education to provide in-service professional development for teachers, especially teachers in low-performing elementary schools. The ScienceMaster program offered full scholarships for online Master's degrees from ERAU or NSU to competitively-selected K-12 teachers, ad hoc graduate and undergraduate courses for those teachers not selected for full scholarships but who could benefit from an individual course, and just-in-time self-paced Web tutorials on a variety of science subjects. Teachers selected to receive full scholarships were required to commit to completing accelerated programs and serving as mentors in their schools, thus enabling a multiplier effect as a return on the scholarship investment.*

DOI: 10.4018/978-1-60960-623-7.ch020

## INTRODUCTION

Like numerous other states, Florida faces a challenge with many of its K-12 teachers teaching "out of field," or teaching subjects for which they have no formal academic training. This situation is especially acute in the STEM disciplines of Science, Technology, Engineering, and Mathematics. Exacerbating the situation is the fact that many elementary school teachers specialize in Elementary Education as a discipline without a deep exposure to the content of the individual subjects. As the state's Florida Comprehensive Assessment Test (FCAT) becomes more and more influential in measuring student achievement and rewarding schools and districts with resources, student success in these specific content areas has become an even higher-stakes enterprise than ever before.[1] Unfortunately, in 2006, the year before the program described in this chapter was proposed, the FCAT Statewide Science Scores (SSS) were unacceptably low (Florida Department of Education, 2006). If the five science achievement levels were classified as "grades":

- Only 8% of 5th graders earned an A or B while 65% earned a D or F.
- Only 6% of 8th graders earned an A or B while 68% earned a D or F.
- Only 4% of 11th graders earned an A or B while 65% earned a D or F.

Recognizing this clear need in their own district, science curriculum administrators in Manatee County led a coalition of partners to design a multi-pronged approach to improve science education through content knowledge. The science curriculum administration team partnered with the Florida Learning Alliance (FLA), a consortium of the state's rural K-12 school districts whose needs were the same but whose numbers, individually, were smaller. With Manatee County in the lead and

FLA supporting, a professional development program was collaboratively designed with several of the state's leading private colleges and universities, including Embry-Riddle Aeronautical University in Daytona Beach, Nova Southeastern University in Davie, and Eckerd College in St. Petersburg. The central characteristic of ScienceMaster was the fact that it would be designed and delivered completely online. With the intended program population of K-12 teachers being employed full-time, many with family and other commitments, the flexibility and convenience of online learning was a program requirement.

The ScienceMaster program targeted various district populations, with low-performing elementary schools being the priority. The program was structured into tiers of online offerings, designed to serve the maximum number of participants. All program offerings were made available to selected participants at no cost (including tuition, books, fees, and other expenses).

- Tier 1: Fully online master's degrees in science disciplines
- Tier 2: Individual online courses in selected science subjects
- Tier 3: Self-paced online learning tutorials in various science subjects

In addition to the professional development tiers, a commercial educational product called Gizmos™ was made available to teachers for hands-on lab activities. Furthermore, an online self-evaluation instrument called the Teaching Skills Assessment Program (TSAP: http://www.eckerd.edu/act/register/index.php) offered participants the opportunity to gauge their teaching knowledge and competencies as related to the state's twelve accomplished educator practices (Florida Department of Education, n.d.) and included a prescriptive action plan for personal professional development based upon the results.

## BACKGROUND

Manatee County is located along Florida's west coast, south of Tampa. The district includes 71 schools and a diverse student population of 42,353 (60% Caucasian, 15% African-American, and 20% Hispanic). Nearly 19,000 of the district's students are eligible for the federal free and reduced lunch program. The district's needs and challenges are reflective of the wider educational issues facing Florida as a high-growth, diverse state.

Among these issues is the problem of teachers teaching out-of-field. Manatee's concerns are no different from those at the national level (National Science Board, 2004). Educational research has shown that when students are taught by teachers without a proper background in the assigned subject, there is a negative effect on student achievement (Darling-Hammond, 2000; Goldhaber and Brewer, 1997; Monk and King, 1994). In fact, the literature related to this area of study indicates that teachers' subject matter knowledge may, in fact, be the most important aspect of teacher quality and that students in the higher grades benefit most from a teacher's deep understanding of the subject (Goldhaber and Brewer, 1997 and 2000; Monk and King, 1994; and Rowan, Chiang, and Miller, 1997).

Yet, according to a 1996 report from the National Center for Education Statistics (NCES), thirty-nine percent of U.S. public school students in grades 7-12 enrolled in life science or biology classes and fifty-six percent in physical science classes were taught by teachers without at least a minor in related subjects (NCES, 1996). While the situation has improved in recent years, it still has far to go, especially for students in high-poverty public high schools (National Science Board, 2004). It is against both these national and local backdrops that Manatee County and its partners designed the ScienceMaster program.

## THE SCIENCEMASTER PROGRAM

The ScienceMaster professional development program was designed to be both wide and deep, with the potential to reach all teachers across the district, and FLA partner districts, at some level, and significantly impact a targeted cohort of participants (Figure 1). A special emphasis was placed on improving the subject knowledge at low-performing schools, particularly elementary schools. The entire program was funded with a $2,000,000 grant from the Florida Department of Education.

At the highest and deepest level, one of several completely online master's degrees was offered to accepted participants. The grant funding paid for all tuition, fees, books, and materials required. While this portion of the program design focused on a relatively small number of teachers, it was intended to have the most dramatic impact and had a commensurate budget allocation. However, the disbursement of grant funds presented a unique challenge to program participants and partner universities of Embry-Riddle Aeronautical University (ERAU) and Nova Southeastern University (NSU). In order to conclude the program and receive funding for expenses, participants were required to complete their degrees in an accelerated 18-month schedule. With full-time jobs and other family commitments, completing a rigorous, accelerated graduate degree program proved to be challenging for many participants.

The next level of program design was slightly less deep but wider. For participants who were not accepted into or were unable to complete one of the full master's degree programs, several individual online courses in various science subjects were offered. As with the full degree programs, the grant funds covered all tuition, fees, and materials costs for participants enrolled in individual online courses.

*Figure 1. ScienceMaster program's tiered design*

At the widest level of professional development were the online self-paced tutorials. Addressing a broad range of granular science (and supporting) subjects, the 122 tutorials were all available at no cost to participants. The tutorials were designed for each to be completed in a single sitting, ranging in duration from twenty minutes to an hour. With the exception of one ScienceMaster Mentoring tutorial, none of the online tutorials were actually produced with grant funds. Rather, the tutorials were part of a legacy professional development program managed by Embry-Riddle Aeronautical University and were made available at no cost to the Manatee County and FLA district participants (however, some grant funds were used to convert selected tutorials for cross-platform delivery). These tutorials existed in a web-based learning management system that allowed participants to select their own topics of interest and maintain a transcript of completion and performance.

In addition to the tiered levels of the program design, Eckerd College made its online Teaching Skills Assessment Program (TSAP) available for program participants. Furthermore, grant funds allowed the distribution of classroom-based Gizmo™ lab subscriptions for follow-on reinforcement within the school environment.

## Online Master's Degrees

To participate in a master's degree program, a candidate had to commit to the rigorous demands of an accelerated schedule, agree to serve as a local mentor for other science teachers at the conclusion of the program, and meet the admission requirements of the partner university. The agreement to become a mentor was critical because it allowed the deeper investment in a relatively small number of educators to have a wider return by impacting many more teachers within the participants' local spheres of their own and nearby schools. A custom, self-paced online tutorial about mentoring expectations, procedures, and resources was produced specifically for the ScienceMaster graduates. This tutorial was added to the list of all tutorials available across the Manatee and FLA districts. Mentoring elements included classroom management modeling, sharing lesson plans, providing workshops, facilitating study groups, and other activities.

Three different degree programs were made available to participants, two from Embry-Riddle and one from Nova Southeastern. Embry-Riddle offered both a Master of Science in Aviation/Aerospace Education Technology and a Master of Science in Space Education. Nova Southeastern offered a Master of Science in Education, Science Specialty Track. These degrees were chosen because they both focused significant coursework on hard science subjects while also devoting some attention to how that subject knowledge could be applied in a grade-appropriate educational setting. Embry-Riddle's Master of Science in Space Education was actually a collaborative degree that included 15 hours of coursework from Nova Southeastern. The degree programs and the requisite courses are detailed below.

## Master of Aeronautical Science in Aviation/Aerospace Education Technology (Embry-Riddle)

- ASCI 602 The Air Transportation System
- ASCI 603 Aircraft and Spacecraft Development
- ASCI 604 Human Factors in the Aviation/Aerospace Technology

- ASCI 654 Adult Teaching and Learning Techniques
- ASCI 610 Instructional System Design Project
- ASCI 550 Aviation Education Foundations
- ASCI 663 Memory and Cognition
- GCCP 605 Methods and Procedures for the Graduate Capstone Project
- ASCI 514 Computer-Based Instruction
- ASCI 614 Advanced Aviation/Aerospace Curriculum Development
- ASCI 690 Graduate Capstone Project
- ASCI 615 Aviation/Aerospace Accident Investigation and Analysis **or**
- ASCI 660 Sensation and Perception

## Master of Science in Education, Science Specialty Track (Nova Southeastern)

- CUR 526 Educational Research for Practitioners
- EDU 5000 Orientation to the Graduate Teacher Education Program
- EDU 601 Professional Seminar I
- SCI 523 Methods in Science Education
- SCI 602 Teaching Comprehensive Ocean Science
- SCI 600 Foundations of Physical Science for Teachers
- SCI 603 Teaching Inquiry-based Life Science
- SCI 601 Inquiry-based Space Science
- SCI 604 Teaching Chemistry: An Activity-based Study of Matter and Energy
- SCI 605 Interdisciplinary Earth Science for Teachers
- SCI 511 The Solar System
- SCI 699 Applied Professional Experience in Science Education
- SCI 515 The Ocean System: Integrated Science
- EDU 602 Professional Seminar II
- SCI 519 Earth: Inside and Out

## Master of Science, Space Education (ERAU/NSU Collaboration)

- SCI 523 Methods in Science Education (NSU)
- ASCI 511 Earth Observation and Remote Sensing (ERAU)
- SCI 600 Foundations of Physical Science for Teachers (NSU)
- ASCI 512 Space Mission and Launch Operations (ERAU)
- ASCI 513 Space Habitation and Life Support Systems (ERAU)
- ASCI 603 Aircraft and Spacecraft Development (ERAU)
- SCI 601 Inquiry-Based Space Science (NSU)
- SCI 605 Interdisciplinary Earth Science for Teachers (NSU)
- SCI 602 Teaching Comprehensive Ocean Science (NSU)
- ASCI 604 Human Factors in the Aviation/Aerospace Industry (ERAU)
- ASCI 514 Computer-Based Instruction (ERAU)
- ASCI 601 Applications in Space: Commerce, Defense, and Exploration (ERAU)

Approximately 70% of the program participants chose the Nova Southeastern degree and 30% chose the Embry-Riddle degrees, mostly the Master of Science in Space Education. While the accelerated schedules did prove to be a challenge for many participants, there was minimal attrition and the program was able to exceed its targeted number of completers. Details are described in the Results section of this chapter.

## Individual Online Courses

A number of teachers in Manatee County and the FLA districts applied to receive the grant-funded scholarships for master's degrees but were not selected. Many of these candidates were deserving, but, ultimately, due to resource constraints, the grant administration team had to make difficult decisions based upon a variety of factors that included school performance (low performing schools were given preference), the team's assessment of each candidate's ability to be successful, and the candidate's level of commitment to share knowledge learned with others in a mentoring role. However, the grant administration team wanted to make as many resources available as the budget would allow for both those teachers in the Manatee and FLA districts who were not selected to receive master's degrees and those who self-selected out of applying for a master's degree scholarship. These latter teachers typically knew that they would not have the time to devote to a rigorous, accelerated program, yet they had the same need for professional development as their peers.

In order to reach as many teachers and have as great an impact as possible, a number of individual graduate and undergraduate online courses were offered to program participants. The original program plan proposed up to 240 individual seats in these courses for Manatee County and FLA teachers (although, as will be discussed in the Results section below, this proved to be an overly ambitious target). The partner universities, Nova Southeastern and Embry-Riddle, made these undergraduate and graduate online courses available to program participants in the same manner as the master's degree courses were offered. However, the participants were enrolled as non-degree seeking students on an ad hoc, course-by-course basis. The offered courses covered a variety of science subjects and the participants were able to choose the subjects in which they were most interested or felt they needed for professional development/ remediation.

## Online Learning Objects

At the widest level of the support plan were a series of 122 self-paced, online tutorials that covered a variety of professional development "in-service" topics (Table 1). The tutorials were designed for each to be completed in a single sitting, ranging from 20 to 60 minutes of student contact time, with the average being approximately 30 minutes. The tutorials were developed so that they could be taken at an individual pace with no instructor intervention.

Each tutorial included many opportunities for practice in the form of exercises and practical applications with instant feedback. A variety of media were incorporated into each tutorial and may have included graphics, text, animations, video, audio, and interactive games/exercises (Figure 2). Each tutorial also contained a pretest and a posttest. Some tutorials included separate practice exercises in addition to the practice presented within the primary content.

In addition to the many multimedia tutorials resident in the curricula were mentoring tools, a comprehensive list of books about space that can be used thematically to encourage reading, and information about how the space science tutorials directly related to national science standards and Florida's Sunshine State Standards (Figure 3). Furthermore, the tutorial environment included a library of interactive instructional visual aids that could be used by experienced teachers to support traditional, classroom-based lectures in space science subjects.

## RESULTS

As required by the state funding authority, the program administrators contracted with an external evaluation team to determine the project's

*Table 1. Self-paced tutorials included in ScienceMaster program offerings*

| Space Science: History and Fundamentals | Space Science/Physics: Propulsion Theory and Application |
|---|---|
| • History of Rocketry<br>• Space Flight-The Early Years<br>• Early Launch Complexes<br>• Orbital Science | • Introduction to Propulsion<br>• Newton's Laws of Motion<br>• The Forces of Propulsion<br>• Solid Propellant Rockets<br>• Liquid Propellant Rockets |
| **Space Science: Current and Future Space Applications** | **Hydrogen Familiarization** |
| • Space Flight-The Shuttle Program<br>• The International Space Station<br>• Military Space Programs<br>• Weather & Navigational Satellites<br>• U.S. Space Operations<br>• Current Launch Complexes<br>• International Aspects of Space Technology and Commerce<br>• Living and Working in Space<br>• Unmanned Exploratory Spacecraft: Planetary and Lunar Exploration<br>• Future Space Exploration<br>• Introduction to Cleanrooms<br>• --- Virtual Cleanroom Walkdown-Payload Changeout Room<br>• --- Virtual Cleanroom Walkdown-Space Station Processing Facility | • The Basics<br>• Liquid Hydrogen<br>• Manufacturing Processes<br>• Storage Methods<br>• Into the 21st Century |
| **Mathematics - Basic** | **Mathematics - Advanced** |
| • Algebra: Basic Concepts<br>• Decimal Fractions<br>• Fractions<br>• Geometry<br>• Percentage<br>• Powers and Roots<br>• Ratio and Proportion<br>• Signed Numbers<br>• Solving Equations<br>• Units and Measurements<br>• Whole Numbers | • Binary, Octal, and Hexadecimal Number Systems<br>• Boolean Algebra<br>• More Powers and Roots: Logarithms<br>• Simultaneous Equations<br>• Trigonometry<br>• Vectors |
| **General Science** | **Other Math and Science Education** |
| • Aerodynamic Terms<br>• Basic Aerodynamics<br>• Basic Electricity Part 1<br>• Basic Electricity Part 2<br>• Electrical DC Theory<br>• Life Science<br>• Marine Biology Part 1<br>• Marine Biology Part 2<br>• Science Education<br>• The Brain: Anatomy and Diseases | • Drug Abuse Awareness: Ecstasy<br>• Health Education<br>• Math and Science for Special Populations<br>• Math Education: Elementary<br>• Math Education: Middle and High<br>• Math Toolkit<br>• Mentoring<br>• Mentoring Toolkit Overview<br>• Oncology Overview<br>• Parent Homework Helper<br>• Reading with Math and Science<br>• Tobacco Awareness<br>• Shaping Tomorrow<br>• Women's Health: Breast Cancer Awareness |

*continued on following page*

*Table 1. Continued*

| Cryogenics Engineering | Digital Electronics |
|---|---|
| • Intro to Cryogenics<br>• What is Cryogenics?<br>• Thermodynamic States<br>• L02 Tanker Off-Load Operation Preparations<br>• --- Tanker Support Preparations<br>• --- Tanker Safety Preparations<br>• --- Tanker LOX Storage Preparations<br>• LO2 Tanker Off-Load Operation Procedures<br>• --- LO2 Tanker Off-Load: Pre-fill<br>• --- LO2 Tanker Off-Load: Fill<br>• --- LO2 Tanker Off-Load: Post-fill | • Introduction to Digital Electronics<br>• Introduction to Boolean Algebra<br>• Characteristics of Logic Circuits<br>• 'AND' Logic<br>• 'OR' Logic<br>• Buffer and Inverter Amplifiers<br>• 'NAND' Logic<br>• 'NOR' Logic<br>• Exclusive 'OR' Logic |
| **Fundamentals of Instrumentation I** | **Fundamentals of Instrumentation II** |
| • Definitions<br>• Fundamentals of Control<br>• Understanding Instrument Symbols<br>• Instrument Calibration<br>• Understanding Instrument Calibration Procedures<br>• Flow<br>• Pressure<br>• Level<br>• Temperature<br>• Control Valves<br>• Pneumatics<br>• Controllers | • Control (Part 1)<br>• Control (Part 2)<br>• Smart Instrument Calibration<br>• Smart Instrument Calibrators<br>• Instrument Installation (Part 1)<br>• Instrument Installation (Part 2)<br>• Instrument Maintenance<br>• Control Valve Maintenance<br>• Instrument Tubing<br>• Documentation<br>• Application |
| **Teaching Skills for the 21st Century (YesTeach!)** | |
| • Introduction<br>• Student Assessment<br>• Communication<br>• Continuous Improvement<br>• Critical Thinking<br>• Diversity<br>• Ethics<br>• Human Growth & Development<br>• Knowledge of Subject Matter<br>• Learning Environment<br>• Planning<br>• Role of the Teacher<br>• Technology<br>• Classroom Readiness<br>• Conclusion | |

*Figure 2. ScienceMaster self-paced tutorial (courseware and image are public domain)*

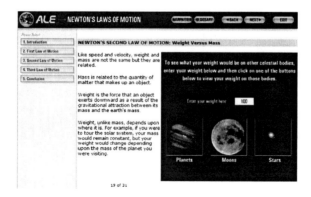

*Figure 3. Excerpt of matrix aligning space science instructional tutorials with NASA student activities, national science standards, and Florida sunshine state standards*

| ALE Lesson | NASA Activity | Location of Activity | Sunshine State Standards | National Science Standards |
|---|---|---|---|---|
| Rocketry | Antacid Tablet Race | Rockets pdf p. 64-67 http://www.spacelink.nasa.gov/products/Rockets | SC.A.1..4.3-4 | Unifying Concepts & Processes, Science as Inquiry, Physical Sciences |
| Rocketry/Propulsion/ Newton's Laws | Bottle Rocket Launcher & Bottle Rocket | Rockets pdf p. 94-101 http://www.spacelink.nasa.gov/products/Rockets | SC.A.1..4.3-4  SC.C.1.4.1-2 SC.C.2.4.1.6  SC.H.3.4.1 | Unifying Concepts & Processes, Science as Inquiry, Physical Sciences |
| Rocketry/Propulsion/ Newton's Laws | (non-NASA source of Estes Model Rocket Kit) | Craft, toy, general merchandise store, or http://www.estesrocketry.com/ | SC.A.1..4.3-4  SC.C.1.4.1-2 SC.C.2.4.1.6  SC.H.3.4.1 | Unifying Concepts & Processes, Science as Inquiry, Physical Sciences |
| Rocketry/Propulsion/ Newton's Laws | Altitude Tracking | Rockets pdf p. 86-93 http://www.spacelink.nasa.gov/products/Rockets | SC.C.1.4.1-2; SC.C.2.4.1 | Unifying Concepts & Processes, Science as Inquiry, Physical Sciences |
| The Space Race: Space Flight - The Early Years | Satellite Communications - A Short Course | http://ctc.grc.nasa.gov/rleonard/regs2.html#part1 | SC.C.1.4.1;  SC.C.2.4.1; SC.E.1.4.2;  SC.E.2.4.6 | Science as Inquiry, Physical Science, Science & Technology, Science in Personal & Social Perspectives, History & Nature of Science |
| The Space Race: Space Flight - The Early Years | Exploring the Moon Activity Guide | http://spacelink.nasa.gov/Instructional.Materials/NASA.Educational.Products/Exploring.the.Moon/Exploring.The.Moon.pdf | SC.E.1.4.2; SC.E.1.4.3; SC.H.1.4.1-7  SC.H.2.4.1.2; SC.H.3.4.1-6 | Science as Inquiry, Physical Science, Science & Technology, Science in Personal & Social Perspectives, History & Nature of Science |
| Orbital Science | Orbital Velocity & Period Calculator | http://liftoff.msfc.nasa.gov/academy/rocket_sci/orbmech/vel_calc.html | SC.C.1.4.1  SC.C.2.4.1; SC.H.3.4.1  SC.H.3.4.6 | Science as Inquiry, Physical Science, Science & Technology, Science in Personal & Social Perspectives, History & Nature of Science |
| Orbital Science: Newton's Laws | Solving for the Mass of Cyg X-1 | http://imagine.gsfc.nasa.gov/YBA/cyg-X1-mass/newton.html | SC.C.1.4.1  SC.C.2.4.1; SC.H.3.4.1  SC.H.3.4.6 | Science as Inquiry, Physical Science, Science & Technology, Science in Personal & Social Perspectives, History & Nature of Science |

success and impact. This evaluation team consisted of representatives from the University of South Florida's Coalition for Science Literacy and Florida State University's Florida Center for Research in Science, Technology, Engineering, and Mathematics (FCR-STEM). The program results, as reported by the external evaluation team, were extremely positive. Especially notable is the fact that the project planned to serve fifty participants in the master's degree programs, yet was able to enroll sixty-two and retain fifty-eight through completion, thus significantly exceeding its target. Of these fifty-eight completers, forty-six were from Manatee County and twelve were from the rural Florida Learning Alliance districts. A total of twenty-two university faculty were involved between the partner institutions (NSU and ERAU).

The initiative was able to demonstrate a positive impact on the participating teachers' science subject expertise. According to the final evaluation data:

*A 41-item content assessment covering all strands of the former Sunshine State Standards was given at the beginning and the end of the project period. A total of 48 participants (37 elementary, 8 middle, and 3 high school teachers) took the pre assessment with an average of 75% correct answers. A total of 45 participants (35 elementary, 7 middle and 3 high school teachers) took the post test with an average of 84% correct answers. A paired samples t-test indicates that the gain in science content knowledge was significant (p <.0001). (Science-Master Final Evaluation Report, 2008, p. 2)*

In addition, the participants in the online university courses were generally satisfied with their subject area courses (74% satisfied or very satisfied, 10% mixed feelings, and 16% with no response). A research-focused course did not fare as well with only 56% claiming to be satisfied or very satisfied. Just as important, where teachers felt hesitant or lacked confidence in using inquiry-based teaching methods or technology to enhance instruction before entering the program, after completing the program the survey data indicated that they had become much more comfortable incorporating reformed teaching strategies and technology into their daily work. In its final remarks, the external evaluation team unequivocally declared the partnership a successful one.

However, the individual courses were less successful than the degree programs at making an impact. Only fifteen teachers enrolled in individual online university courses. While there was no formal assessment of the reasons for the low participation, speculation within the team included reasons such as a perceived lower value for an individual course than a full degree program for their own professional development and time commitments in already busy lives. Furthermore, prerequisites were an obstacle for many. Graduate level science courses typically require extensive undergraduate course completions and even other graduate prerequisites. Many of the target population simply did not have the prior coursework to be enrolled or, if enrolled, to be successful. As a result, most of the individual course options were limited to freshman and sophomore level science offerings that did not have prerequisites. The team further speculated that potential participants already had completed such coursework in their own postsecondary studies and/or did not want to invest the significant time and effort in a course that could not be applied towards an eventual graduate degree. One benefit of the lower participation was that budget resources could be diverted to the master's degree scholarships, thus allowing the project to exceed its target in that category.

The self-paced tutorials registered 116 unique ScienceMaster users into the online learning management system. Each participant constructed his/her own unique curriculum based on his/her individual professional development needs and interests. The number of recorded registrants is likely lower than the actual participation for two reasons: (1) the system that housed the Science-Master tutorials pre-dated the project and some of the teachers, especially in the FLA districts, may have already had accounts under different organizations, so they were not captured in the ScienceMaster reporting and (2) the Science-Master administration team created a static Web page that contained links to most of the tutorials for users who were on Macs or other systems that may have experienced issues with some of the presentation and data tracking technologies used in the system—as a result, users of the static links were not captured for reporting purposes.

## CONCLUSION

This project would not have existed without partners committed to real collaboration. Beginning with the Manatee County School District, the assembled team needed to work together to handle curricular, logistical, and student hand-offs. For example, once the county selected candidates for a degree program, the candidates' application information had to be provided to the university, who had to accept them and register them for the appropriate courses. The university cooperated with the county to provide ongoing advising services to ensure that the program could be successfully completed during the accelerated timeline. Within the joint degree programs, the universities had to collaborate on curriculum, student services, and integration with the ScienceMaster program at large. County subject matter experts worked with online developers managed by a university partner to prepare the mentoring tutorial. The project's partnership landscape could be described as a networked web of interconnected relationships. Each partner intersected with others at different points and on multiple occasions.

The long-term expectation of the program is that the presence of engaged mentors who have completed master's degrees will have a positive effect on the performance of their schools in science measures. At this time of this writing it is too soon to measure if this expectation has been realized. Following up with program participants related to this expected impact is an area for recommended future research.

On balance, however, the ScienceMaster program was extremely successful as measured against the project requirements. It accomplished its goal to improve science subject matter expertise in the Manatee and FLA districts. It provided opportunities for K-12 teachers at all levels, in both broad (individual tutorials) and deep (master's degrees) ways. However, while the awarding of full master's degree scholarships was popular and effective, as a model for replication it remains problematic. Even with tuition discounts and fee waivers, such a strategy is expensive and difficult to scale. Since the project's completion, the absence of continuation funding has prevented the project from expanding. Yet, the full master's degrees were clearly the most popular components of the project and provided the deepest engagement with the subject matter. It may be that there really is no substitute for the slow, hard work associated with the acquisition of true expertise.

## REFERENCES

Darling-Hammond, L. (2000). Teacher quality and student achievement: A review of state policy evidence. *Education Policy Analysis Archives, 8*(1).

Florida Department of Education. (2006). *Florida comprehensive assessment test (FCAT) sunshine state standards state report of district results: Grade 05 science.* Florida Department of Education website. Retrieved February 12, 2010, from http://fcat.fldoe.org/scinfopg.asp

Florida Department of Education. (n.d.). *Educator accomplished practices: Competencies for teachers of the twenty-first century.* Florida Department of Education. Retrieved February 12, 2010 from http://www.fldoe.org/dpe/publications/accomplished4-99.pdf

Goldhaber, D. D., & Brewer, D. J. (1997). Evaluating the effect of teacher degree level on educational performance. In W. Fowler (Ed.), *Developments in school finance,* 1996, (pp. 197–210). (NCES 97-535). Washington, DC: U.S. Department of Education, National Center for Education Statistics.

Goldhaber, D. D., & Brewer, D. J. (2000). Does teacher certification matter? High school teacher certification status and student achievement. *Educational Evaluation and Policy Analysis, 22*(2), 129–145.

Monk, D. H., & King, J. (1994). Multi-level teacher resource effects on pupil performance in secondary mathematics and science: The role of teacher subject matter preparation. In R. Ehrenberg (Ed.), *Contemporary policy issues: Choices and consequences in education.* Ithaca, NY: ILR Press.

National Center for Education Statistics (NCES). (1996). *Statistical analysis report: Out-of-field teaching and educational quality.* National Center of Education Statistics, U.S. Department of Education Institute of Education Sciences. Retrieved March 1, 2010 from http://nces.ed.gov/pubs/web/96040.asp

National Science Board. (2004). *Science and engineering indicators 2004.* Two volumes. Arlington, VA: National Science Foundation (volume 1, NSB 04-1; volume 2, NSB 04-1A).

Rowan, B., Chiang, F., & Miller, R. J. (1997). Using research on employees' performance to study the effects of teachers on students' achievement. *Sociology of Education, 70*(4), 256–284. doi:10.2307/2673267

ScienceMaster Final Evaluation Report. (2008). *Internal program evaluation document provided to the project team that summarized final outcomes.*

## ENDNOTE

[1] In fact, the ScienceMaster program described in this chapter turned out to be decidedly anticipatory. In Spring 2010 the Florida legislature passed a law requiring that students take tougher math and science classes and pass end-of-course exams in order to graduate from high school.

# APPENDIX

*2006 Manatee County Grade 5 Florida Comprehensive Assessment Test (FCAT) Science Scores*

| School Name | Number of Students | Mean Scale Score (100-500) | Total Test Scores | | | | | % AL3+ | Mean Points Earned | | | |
|---|---|---|---|---|---|---|---|---|---|---|---|---|
| | | | % in each Achievement Level | | | | | | By Content Area | | | |
| | | | 1 | 2 | 3 | 4 | 5 | Percent in Achievement Levels 3 and Above | Physical and Chemical | Earth and Space | Life and Environmental | Scientific Thinking |
| Number of Points Possible | | | | | | | | | 12 | 14 | 13 | 12 |
| Statewide Totals | 195,877 | 299 | 29 | 36 | 27 | 6 | 2 | 35 | 7 | 7 | 7 | 7 |
| ANNA MARIA EL | 42 | 351 | 2 | 29 | 36 | 26 | 7 | 69 | 8 | 9 | 9 | 9 |
| BALLARD ELEM | 75 | 290 | 31 | 47 | 20 | 1 | 1 | 23 | 7 | 6 | 6 | 6 |
| BAYSHORE ELEM | 119 | 287 | 33 | 45 | 18 | 3 | 1 | 22 | 6 | 6 | 6 | 6 |
| DUETTE ELEM | 2 | * | * | * | * | * | * | * | * | * | * | * |
| MANATEE ELEM | 56 | 272 | 54 | 25 | 20 | 2 | 0 | 21 | 6 | 6 | 6 | 5 |
| JESSIE P MIL | 85 | 299 | 27 | 38 | 32 | 4 | 0 | 35 | 7 | 6 | 7 | 7 |
| MYAKKA CITY E | 57 | 277 | 40 | 46 | 12 | 2 | 0 | 14 | 6 | 5 | 6 | 6 |
| ONECO ELEM | 96 | 278 | 41 | 41 | 13 | 6 | 0 | 19 | 6 | 6 | 6 | 6 |
| ORANGE RIDGE | 99 | 263 | 55 | 34 | 9 | 2 | 0 | 11 | 5 | 5 | 6 | 5 |
| PALM VIEW ELE | 102 | 285 | 39 | 37 | 21 | 3 | 0 | 24 | 6 | 6 | 6 | 6 |
| PALMA SOLA EL | 113 | 319 | 12 | 38 | 42 | 5 | 2 | 50 | 7 | 7 | 8 | 7 |
| PALMETTO ELEM | 111 | 280 | 40 | 43 | 14 | 2 | 1 | 17 | 6 | 6 | 6 | 6 |
| ROBERT H PRI | 114 | 298 | 28 | 46 | 20 | 4 | 1 | 25 | 6 | 7 | 7 | 6 |
| BLANCHE H DA | 85 | 269 | 44 | 45 | 12 | 0 | 0 | 12 | 6 | 5 | 6 | 5 |
| SAMOSET ELEM | 77 | 260 | 57 | 30 | 12 | 0 | 1 | 13 | 5 | 5 | 5 | 5 |
| JAMES TILLMAN | 65 | 286 | 38 | 43 | 15 | 3 | 0 | 18 | 6 | 6 | 7 | 6 |
| BLACKBURN ELE | 86 | 293 | 26 | 40 | 33 | 2 | 0 | 35 | 6 | 7 | 7 | 6 |
| FRANCES WAKEL | 69 | 266 | 57 | 32 | 9 | 3 | 0 | 12 | 6 | 6 | 5 | 5 |
| SARA SCOTT HA | 1 | * | * | * | * | * | * | * | * | * | * | * |
| H S MOODY ELE | 114 | 299 | 25 | 45 | 25 | 5 | 0 | 31 | 7 | 7 | 7 | 6 |
| ABEL ELEM | 109 | 304 | 24 | 41 | 30 | 4 | 1 | 35 | 6 | 7 | 7 | 7 |
| STEWART ELEM | 97 | 292 | 30 | 34 | 32 | 3 | 1 | 36 | 7 | 6 | 7 | 6 |
| WILLIAM H BA | 114 | 311 | 17 | 45 | 29 | 8 | 2 | 39 | 7 | 7 | 7 | 7 |
| BRADEN RVR EL | 118 | 329 | 12 | 37 | 31 | 14 | 5 | 51 | 8 | 8 | 8 | 8 |
| SEA BREEZE EL | 118 | 299 | 23 | 52 | 22 | 3 | 1 | 25 | 6 | 6 | 6 | 7 |
| TARA ELEM | 145 | 302 | 24 | 39 | 33 | 4 | 0 | 37 | 7 | 7 | 7 | 7 |
| GENE WITT ELE | 164 | 327 | 10 | 33 | 43 | 10 | 4 | 57 | 8 | 9 | 8 | 7 |
| KINNAN ELEM | 115 | 285 | 36 | 33 | 29 | 3 | 0 | 31 | 6 | 6 | 6 | 7 |

*continued on following page*

*Appendix. Continued*

| School Name | Number of Students | Mean Scale Score (100-500) | Total Test Scores | | | | | | Mean Points Earned | | | |
|---|---|---|---|---|---|---|---|---|---|---|---|---|
| | | | % in each Achievement Level | | | | | % AL3+ | By Content Area | | | |
| | | | 1 | 2 | 3 | 4 | 5 | Percent in Achievement Levels 3 and Above | Physical and Chemical | Earth and Space | Life and Environmental | Scientific Thinking |
| ROWLETT ELEM | 113 | 302 | 27 | 36 | 27 | 7 | 2 | 36 | 7 | 7 | 7 | 7 |
| MCNEAL EL | 149 | 330 | 10 | 31 | 45 | 12 | 2 | 59 | 8 | 8 | 8 | 8 |
| FREEDOM EL | 91 | 318 | 16 | 30 | 44 | 8 | 2 | 54 | 8 | 7 | 8 | 8 |
| MILLS ELEMENT | 145 | 297 | 28 | 38 | 28 | 6 | 0 | 34 | 7 | 6 | 7 | 7 |
| WILLIS | 23 | 304 | 17 | 52 | 22 | 9 | 0 | 30 | 7 | 6 | 7 | 7 |
| HOSPITAL HOME | 2 | * | * | * | * | * | * | * | * | * | * | * |
| MANATEE GLEN | 2 | * | * | * | * | * | * | * | * | * | * | * |
| MANTEE PALMS | 2 | * | * | * | * | * | * | * | * | * | * | * |
| MANATEE SCH A | 26 | 307 | 23 | 38 | 35 | 4 | 0 | 38 | 7 | 7 | 7 | 7 |
| PAL ACADEMIC | 24 | 225 | 92 | 8 | 0 | 0 | 0 | 0 | 4 | 4 | 4 | 4 |
| CENTER ACADEM | 17 | 268 | 47 | 41 | 12 | 0 | 0 | 12 | 6 | 5 | 5 | 6 |

Source: Florida Department of Education: http://fcat.fldoe.org/scinfopg.asp

# Section 4
# Transcending Boundaries of Technologies and Using Technologies to Transcend Boundaries in Partnerships

# Chapter 21
# Rearticulating Web 2.0 Technologies:
## Strategies to Redefine Social Media in Community Projects

**Amy C. Kimme Hea**
*University of Arizona, USA*

## ABSTRACT

*This chapter argues that to align social media with community partnership building, all participants must develop a critical sensibility about these media. This sensibility must rearticulate social media to leverage their use toward the goals of the community action. A more thoughtful understanding of social media and their potentials and constraints can help to foment stronger, sustainable partnerships between higher education and community partners. This discussion is situated in a specific service-learning professional writing course and offers strategies to rearticulate personal use toward more critical deployments of social media.*

## INTRODUCTION

*Two out of three incoming freshmen spent more than one hour per week on social networking sites during their senior year of high school. 85 percent of U.S. college students use Facebook. One in four Americans have [sic] a MySpace account. 94 percent of U.S. teenagers send emails over the Internet; nearly three out of four teenagers use social networking sites and go online at least once a day. At least 136 U.S. universities have an education channel on YouTube. One in every three videos viewed in the United States in January 2008 was a YouTube video. Global enterprises will spend U.S. $4.6B on Web 2.0 technologies by 2013.*

*(Wilen-Daugenti, 2008, para. 1)*

DOI: 10.4018/978-1-60960-623-7.ch021

MySpace, Facebook, YouTube, Blogger, Digg. com, Twitter, Reddit: by now most of us have heard of, if not used, one or more of these social media. Often defined as interactive media that allow us to extend our personal and professional connections and cultivate shared interests, social media exploit Web 2.0 technologies to create community, exchange ideas, and foster relationships. In the most ideal of digital worlds, social media are a means to connect and engage. While social media continue to gain popularity, we users need to resist the temptation, however, to adopt an uncritical perspective that touts only the benefits of such media. As scholars have suggested, uncritical views on media and technology can unwittingly replicate power imbalances (in the classroom and beyond), reinscribe social inequities, and even perpetuate assumptions that media are self-generating forces outside our cultural domain (Hawisher & Selfe, 1991; Selber, 2004; Selfe, 1999a & 1999b). To deploy social media for the betterment of our communities, instructors, students, and community partners should strive toward critical understandings of social media, ones that both rearticulate[1] social media against assumptions that they are merely *personal* tools and help students to see the personal as always already politically and culturally inscribed.

In this chapter, I argue that to align social media with community partnership building, all participants must develop a critical media sensibility—or a conscious way of examining, grappling with, and understanding the roles of social media in our lives. This sensibility must rearticulate social media to leverage their use toward the goals of the community action. I situate my discussion in relationship to my own teaching of a newly offered upper-division professional and technical writing course (English 313: Introduction to Technical and Professional Writing) at the University of Arizona where a rearticulated understanding of personal use helped to move class members toward more critical deployments of social media in our work with community partners. This essay starts, then,

with an overview of both the programmatic and class-specific aspects of service-learning in my local context. After situating my work, I turn toward social networking and filesharing and the ways in which these two social media practices are constructed around personal use. After offering this articulation, I discuss the ways in which students, community partners, and I worked toward a more critical understanding of social media, and I suggest some strategies to rearticulate social media for the betterment of community projects.

## LOCAL TEACHING CONTEXT

Noted scholars in the field of professional and technical writing have long argued for the ways service-learning projects provide students with real-world audiences and purposes (Crabtree & Sapp, 2002), a means for civic engagement (Dubinsky, 2002), and opportunities to connect classroom and community (Huckin, 1997). Dedication to teaching service-learning projects also must take into account the range of complications that can come from unchallenged notions of charity (Bowdon & Scott, 2003; Scott, 2004), need to learn problem solving strategies (Matthews & Zimmerman, 1999), and instructor and student understandings of the political, economic, and social factors related to service-learning projects (Kastman Breuch, 2001; Scott, 2008). This theoretical grounding is particularly important at the University of Arizona where service-learning projects are integrated into the curricula of all of our professional and technical writing courses.

As the Associate Director of the Writing Program, I am accountable for creating and supervising service-learning curricula that are grounded in sound praxis. Among other responsibilities, I work for programmatic continuity in both the philosophy and teaching of our professional and technical writing courses. English 307: Business Writing and English 308: Technical Writing are long-standing courses in our department, and they are largely populated by majors from across the campus with less than 1% of students coming from the College of Humanities where the English Department is housed. To provide opportunities for English majors to learn more about professional and technical writing, I proposed two new courses for the English major: English 313: Introduction to Professional and Technical Writing and English 340: Special Topics in Professional and Technical Writing. Capped at 25 students, English 313 rolled out in fall 2009, and it was well received with a healthy demand from students. The structure of the course provides students with real-world audiences for all the course projects, offers them guidance and support to select audiences and purposes within the guidelines of those course projects, encourages students to write and edit collaboratively, and assists them in developing rhetorical research, writing, and editing practices that can be applied across different professional and technical writing contexts.

One of the central components of 313 is a service-learning project where students identify a particular community partner (non-profit, university organization, or small local business) and propose the creation of a business or technical writing project to benefit the organization. Students are also given the option to work individually or collaboratively with other class members. In our other courses' service-learning projects, students are usually restricted to working with only non-profit or university partners, but in English 313, I widened our partnership pool to include small local businesses. With the dire economic conditions of the city of Tucson and the state of Arizona, providing students this option was another means to extend our pedagogical usefulness to members of our local community.

To situate student community work, I frame service-learning using stakeholder theory (Donaldson & Preston, 1995; Freeman, 1984; Jones, 1995). Critical stakeholder theory argues for understanding the affects and interactions of all parties involved in service-learning projects,

from the students to the non-profits to members of the community, and for promoting dialogues and interactions with all parties to guard against universalizing assumptions about what is "good," "right," or "just" for others (Calton & Kurland, 1996; Freeman & Gilbert, 1992; Kimme Hea, 2005). The work in a service-learning project is always a negotiated understanding, one where participants are not forced to adopt the same value system but are encouraged to understand one another's. In other words, the application of this theory is that it asks students to think critically about their roles in relationship to their service-learning partner as well as that partner's constituencies and the community at large. This analysis also provides students with a starting point to think through issues of investment. Technological investment is just one of those categories for consideration as students map out field research practices that provide significant information about their client organization, its needs, and its resources. As M. Turnley (2007) argued, "[i]ncorporating critical reflection on the rhetorical and social dimensions of technology throughout students' collaborations with clients can help to situate their practice within larger public contexts" (p. 105). Agreeing with Turnley's stance, I strive to open up dialogue on the ways technologies impact student and partner decisions about the very purposes of certain projects. This integrated approach can illuminate technological constraints and work against inequities.

## OVERVIEW OF ROLE OF TECHNOLOGY IN THE PROJECT

Because English 313 is taught in a networked computer lab, students have access to a range of popular word processing, desktop publishing, image editing, and Web development programs. In recent years, service-learning students in our professional and technical writing courses have used these programs to produce more traditional print-based media forms such a brochures, hand-books, event materials, and press kits. In fall 2009, however, some 313 students engaged social media to develop their service-learning projects including the production of e-newsletters, Facebook cause pages and event notifications, and YouTube videos. Two social media practices that came to the forefront were social networking and filesharing. Through the service-learning projects, students and their partners confronted social media in relationship to larger concerns about advocacy, representation, and ownership. I discuss here the two specific cases of social networking and filesharing and their articulation, and then I turn to rearticulation strategies that proved useful in asserting a revised view of social media.

## Social Networking

In particular, one student addressed the role of social media in her work with a Tucson nonprofit dedicated to banking cord blood. This nonprofit wanted to explicitly deploy social media to help create more awareness of its organization. Although an avid user of Facebook, the student initially struggled with ways to leverage social media on behalf of her client organization. From my discussions with the student and her community partner, it became clear to me that assumptions about social media were articulated around its benefits as a *personal* social networking resource, not as a means to advocate for community work or activism. In other words, the nonprofit assumed that the student's personal use of social media made her "savvy" about social networking resources and that she could provide the organization with innovative suggestions for social media use. Similarly, the student assumed that social media were aligned with her own personal use, but her personal use was dominated by assumptions about fostering closer local friendships, staying in touch with geographically distant relatives and friends, playing games, and participating in online polls and quizzes. The student had trouble seeing her

personal social media activities as cultural or political choices. The uncritical articulation of social media as personal media is not unfounded. For this student and client, Facebook—the selected social media under investigation—is defined by the metaphor of "friendship," and it is strongly aligned with personal interaction. A corollary assumption about students as media savvy is not baseless as the largest percentage of social media users are those in the "m-generation" or the "millennials" (Vie, 2008). Their frequent and heavy use of social media, however, does not guarantee that they are expert users of these media beyond their own personal practices. These assumptions about personal use, then, needed to be complicated in order for the student and community partner to thoughtfully integrate Facebook as part of the organization's development strategy.

## Filesharing

Another technological context that is also defined along personal social media use is filesharing. As one of my students was working with a small local cupcakery to create a YouTube video, he was confronted with issues of ownership and representation. The student had created many videos in the past, especially spoofs and other humorous videos that he enjoyed sharing with friends and family. This student, however, had not confronted issues of copyright or permission for the music and images he had integrated into these past projects. Now, as he worked with this recently opened cupcakery, the student and his client had to negotiate these issues. For many of us, social media are an ideal means to share photos, songs, videos, documents, website bookmarks, and other content. With use of sites like Flickr, Pandora, YouTube, Box.net, Blogger, Ning, and Delicious, we can easily upload, download, tag, and share different media forms across social media accounts. While users may understand that certain forms of file sharing are illegal, it may not inhibit their use of social media in this way. For some being caught is a risk they are willing to take. In other words, filesharing practices may be defined as a zero-sum game where the assumed unlikelihood of being *the* one caught is the only consideration that drives personal sharing practices. These assumptions are supported by the relative technological ease of uploading, downloading, tagging, archiving, and distributing files. In their discussion of filesharing and its relationship to the composition classroom, D. DeVoss and J. Porter (2006) asserted that "[t]he attitudes and expectations students have learned in digital filesharing environments enter our classrooms, influence students' production and understanding of print texts (not to mention electronic texts), and affect their conception of the rhetorical situation" (p. 179). In the case of this student, his community partner, and me, we had to consider the full relationship of filesharing in the classroom against its dominant construction as a personal practice outside of the classroom.

## OVERVIEW OF THE BEST PRACTICES: RE-ARTICULATING THE PERSONAL TO THE POLITICAL

Instructors and students can work together to re-articulate social media. By complicating un-critical assumptions about personal use—making the personal both critical and political—they can understand social media as networks that can be leveraged for community partnerships. Likewise, community partners can come to realize that student use of social media does not necessarily encourage them to be critical producers. As suggested, community partners may not understand that students' frequent use of social media for personal reasons does not automatically translate to a sophisticated understanding of social media for other purposes.

To re-articulate social media, I offer four strategies: 1) inventory of personal use of social media, 2) social media log, 3) research on social media issues directly related to their own client

partnership, and 4) open dialogue with client partners about social media understanding. These practices can begin the process of rearticulating social media as part of the larger, complex cultural network of technologies and relationships. Rather than assuming social media are merely personal, instructors, students and their community partners can redefine social media as politically and culturally constructed.

## Social Media Inventory

To begin the critical process of rearticulating social media, students can be encouraged to inventory their own social media use. From this inventory, students in the class can discuss the ways their uses are certainly personal, as well as social, cultural, and political. Hosting a broader class discussion among students, the instructor can prompt them to consider cause memberships; invitations to nonprofit events; political Web sites; RSS local, national, and international news feeds; and other community practices as part of social media. In this way, then, the personal can be redefined as cultural and political.

## Social Media Log

In addition to whole group discussions about the personal, cultural, and political, instructors can encourage students to keep a data log, for at least one week, of social media and cultural practice. Individually or collaboratively, students can be assigned a specific social media technology (the artifact) as well as one or two media outlets (news sites, blogs, or other online sources). During the specified time, students can keep a record detailing any news item covering social media by their outlets. After they compile their list of news and events, students can relate their own specific social media artifact to the stories they have tracked.

By way of example, the January 12, 2010, earthquake in Haiti would have been an event that students could have tracked, recording the use of

- citizen journalism and Twitter to report the status of Haitians in the aftermath of the tragedy (Savageau, 2010);
- M-Give, Facebook, Twitter, and other social media to gain relief support (Wortham, 2010);
- the WWW (among other broadcasting sites) to host Hope for Haiti Now billed as an "international, multi-networked telethon" to gain global financial support for survivors (Associated Press, 2010).

Regardless of whether students' specific social media artifact was named in these reports, they could be asked to relate their artifact to these media stories. For example, students could consider, if their artifact was Facebook, did any members of their own Facebook community or friends of friends discuss the tragedy in Haiti? Did any of them donate to the relief efforts through Facebook? Did any of their friends or friends of friends watch Hope for Haiti? While these questions are still related to personal use, it rearticulates their personal understanding of social media as politically and culturally situated.

## Research into Social Media and Dialogue with Community Partners

With a renewed sense of the personal as social, political, and cultural, students can be moved to think of their work with the community partners in a new light. More specifically, then, students can seek out social media research directly related to their own clients' concerns. How do nonprofits, for example, leverage Facebook and other social media for social change and political advocacy? What copyright and permission issues must be attended to in relationship to organizational use, either nonprofit or local business? Finally, this important grounding work in the classroom can be the starting point to create dialogue among instructor, students, and community partners.

Such analytical activities can help both students and community partners come together to leverage social media in important ways. To illustrate, I want to return to the two particular cases from my own classroom. After going through analytical processes to rearticulate the personal dimension of social media, the two students came to new understandings and enactments of social media.[2]

In the case of the student working with the cord blood organization, she challenged her own understanding of social networking and began to see it as part of a larger system of community support. Her reconfigured understanding was negotiated through questions on her personal use, discussions with peers and her client that complicated those notions, and readings on nonprofit integration of social networking. Having challenged her own assumptions about Facebook as about friends and games and having a good working relationship with her client where she discussed the organization's needs, the student produced two important projects for the cord blood nonprofit: one was a traditional print document of a SWOT (Strengths, Weaknesses, Opportunities, and Threats) analysis and another was an event invitation to the organization's upcoming fundraiser. The student's SWOT analysis—which the student proposed to the client after completing her research—provided a broad view of the ways in which this particular organization might advance its work through social networking connections on Facebook. This larger context for engaging in social networking assumes that any nonprofit entering into social media use must have short- and long-term goals related to their deployment.

The student working with a small local business in need of a YouTube video also started to reconfigure his own social media development in relationship to larger issues of copyright, writing on behalf of an organization, and including video footage of employees and clients of the business. The student connected his own personal assessment of new media use to stories in the media about abuse of copyright. He also considered, however, the complicated assumptions about copyright in educational settings, and the ways that if his project were for the course, he may have been able to claim fair use, but because the project was going to move into the larger public domain as a product for potential profit, the student needed to consider consequences for his community client. To attend to these issues, the student first provided his client with a range of recommendations in relationship to the video coverage of employees and patrons. Assuming that some employees may not be comfortable being in the video but being equally uncomfortable saying no to the owner of the business, the student proposed three options—which he suggested were not mutually exclusive: shooting the video without displaying the employees' faces (a creative shooting approach); offering the employees, patrons, and even friends and family options to be in the video for small compensation (either in pay or free products); and having the employees, patrons, or other actors sign consent forms. These recommendations allowed the owner to discuss issues of representation and compensation with his employees, and the resolution was creative shooting, pay, and signed consent forms. The situation also instantiated the respect that the student and owner had for the cupcakery's employees, providing an immeasurable benefit of the student's and owner's negotiated approach. For the video, the student recommended that the owner seek the guidance of his lawyer about copyrighted material, and then either purchase the rights to use a song or find music already in the public domain. This aspect of the project provided me, the student, and owner with insights into the difficult negotiation process of copyright for service-learning projects. While such class projects are often argued to fall under fair use or supported through the use of creative commons works (Lessig, 2004), their life outside the classroom and for different types of clients, nonprofit, university or small business means that intellectual property issues are not always easily discernable.

## CONCLUDING REMARKS: FROM PERSONAL TO SOCIAL AND POLITICAL

Instructors, students, and community partners can create opportunities for more thoughtful negotiations of social media as part of service-learning projects. The suggestions provide here are only a starting point for a broader, more engaged understanding of the ways in which social media can support community activism and social change. My recommendations, then, should be adapted to particular local contexts with key stakeholders determining specific ways to integrate critical understandings of social media throughout their projects. I can see, for example, great potential in asking the community partners, if available, to be part of discussions—in and outside the classroom—about trends in social media around their spheres of interest. I also can imagine the addition of analytical activities and research practices through a student-initiated survey of community members. That targeted research could be incorporated into not just the course service-learning project but also a culminating series of university-community educational mixers where others in the community—even those not directly engaged in the service-learning projects during that semester—could come and learn more about critical deployments of social media. It is my hope that through instructor, student, and community member collaborations, we can come together in support of critical deployment of social media for community action.

## ACKNOWLEDGMENT

Special thanks to Melody Bowdon, Russell Carpenter, and the collection's blind reviewers for their thoughtful comments on this essay. I also want to thank Melinda Turnley for her input on an early draft of the project.

## REFERENCES

Associated Press. (2010, January 23). Haiti telethon haul put at $57 million so far: Celebrities unite in support of Haitian people with two hours of pleas. *MSNBC*. Retrieved from http://www.msnbc.msn.com/id/35023278/ns/entertainment-celebrities/

Bowdon, M., & Scott, J. B. (2003). *Service-learning in technical and professional communication*. San Francisco, CA: Addison Wesley Longman.

Calton, J. M., & Kurland, N. B. (1996). A theory of stakeholder enabling: Giving voice to an emerging postmodern praxis of organizational discourse. In D. M. Boje, R. P. Gephart, & T. J. Thatchenkery (Eds.), *Postmodern management and organization* (pp. 154–177). Thousand Oaks, CA: Sage Publications.

Crabtree, R. D., & Sapp, D. A. (2002). A laboratory in citizenship: Service learning in the technical communication classroom. *Technical Communication Quarterly, 11*(4), 411–432. doi:10.1207/s15427625tcq1104_3

DeVoss, D., & Porter, J. E. (2006). Why napster matters to writing: Filesharing as a new ethic of digital delivery. *Computers and Composition, 23*(2), 178–210. doi:10.1016/j.compcom.2006.02.001

Donaldson, T., & Preston, L. E. (1995). The stakeholder theory of the corporation: Concepts, evidence, and implications. *Academy of Management Review, 20*(1), 65–91. doi:10.2307/258887

Dubinsky, J. M. (2002). Service-learning as a path to virtue: The ideal orator in professional communication. *Michigan Journal of Community Service Learning, 8*(2), 61–74.

Freeman, R. E. (1984). *Strategic management: A stakeholder approach*. Boston, MA: Pitman.

Freeman, R. E., & Gilbert, D. Jr. (1992). Business, ethics and society: A critical agenda. *Business & Society, 31*(1), 9–17. doi:10.1177/000765039203100102

Hawisher, G. E., & Selfe, C. L. (1991). The rhetoric of technology and the electronic writing class. *College Composition and Communication, 42*(1), 55–65. doi:10.2307/357539

Huckin, T. (1997). Technical writing and community service. *Journal of Business and Technical Communication, 11*(1), 49–59. doi:10.1177/1050651997011001003

Johnson-Eilola, J. (1997). *Nostalgic angels: Rearticulating hypertext writing*. Norwood, NJ: Ablex Publishing Company.

Jones, T. M. (1995). Instrumental stakeholder theory: A synthesis of ethics and economics. *Academy of Management Review, 20*(2), 404–437. doi:10.2307/258852

Kastman Breuch, L. (2001). The overruled dust mite: Preparing technical communication students to interact with clients. *Technical Communication Quarterly, 10*(2), 193–210. doi:10.1207/s15427625tcq1002_5

Kimme Hea, A. C. (2005). What's at stake? Strategies for developing stakeholder relationships in service-learning projects. *Reflections: A Journal of Writing, Service-Learning, and Community Literacy, 4*, 54–76.

Kimme Hea, A. C. (2007). Riding the wave: Articulating a critical methodology for WWW research practices in computers & composition. In D. DeVoss, & H. McKee (Eds.), *Digital writing research: Technologies, methodologies, and ethical issues* (pp. 269–286). Cresskill, NJ: Hampton Press.

Lessig, L. (2004). *Free culture: The nature and future of creativity.* New York, NY: Penguin Books. *Composition* 11 (1991): 57-72.

Matthews, C., & Zimmerman, B. B. (1999). Integrating service learning and technical communication: Benefits and challenges. *Technical Communication Quarterly, 8*(4), 383–404.

Savageau, J. (2010, January 14). Citizen journalism and tweets bring Haiti's horror to the world. *Web 2.0 Journal.* Retrieved from http://web2.sys-con.com/node/1248590

Scott, J. B. (2004). Rearticulating civic engagement through cultural studies and service-learning. *Technical Communication Quarterly, 13*(3), 289–306. doi:10.1207/s15427625tcq1303_4

Scott, J. B. (2008). The practice of usability: Teaching user engagement through service-learning. *Technical Communication Quarterly, 17*(4), 381–412. doi:10.1080/10572250802324929

Selber, S. A. (2004). *Multiliteracies for a digital age.* Carbondale: Southern Illinois University Press.

Selfe, C. L. (1999a). Technology and literacy: A story about the perils of not paying attention. *College Composition and Communication, 50*(3), 411–436. doi:10.2307/358859

Selfe, C. L. (1999b). *Technology and literacy in the twenty-first century: The importance of paying attention.* Carbondale, IL: Southern Illinois University Press.

Slack, J. D. (1996). The theory and method of articulation in cultural studies. In D. Morley, & K.-H. Chen (Eds.), *Stuart Hall: Critical dialogues in cultural studies* (pp. 112–130). London, UK: Routledge.

Turnley, M. (2007). The importance of critical approaches to technology in service learning projects. *Technical Communication Quarterly, 16*(1), 103–123. doi:10.1207/s15427625tcq1601_6

Vie, S. (2008). Digital divide 2.0: Generation m and online social networking sites in the composition classroom. *Computers and Composition, 25*, 9–23. doi:10.1016/j.compcom.2007.09.004

Wilen-Daugenti, T. (2008). *Cisco higher education trends & statistics.* Retrieved from http://www.cisco.com/web/about/ac79/edu/trends/issue01.html

Wortham, J. (2010, January 13). $2 million in donations for Haiti, via text message. *The New York Times.* Retrieved from http://bits.blogs.nytimes.com/2010/01/13/1-million-in-donations-for-haiti-via-text-message/

## ENDNOTES

[1]  For a fuller discussion on the role of articulation theory as a practice/methodology to challenge dominant cultural narratives and their deleterious effects, please see Johnson-Eilola, 1997; Kimme Hea, 2007; Slack, 1996.

[2]  In the case of the two students, I had directed conversations with them asking them to articulate their personal use as political and cultural, discuss their use with peers in a guided class discussion, and talk extensively with clients, but I had not yet integrated the log project. It is important to note that a much more systematic installation of these recommendations can lead all students, regardless of their specific project, to a more critical perspective on the role of social media in their lives.

# Chapter 22
# Mobile Phones and Cultural Connections:
## Designing a Mutual World Between the DR Congo and United States

**Bernadette Longo**
*University of Minnesota, USA*

## ABSTRACT

*When people in the United States seek to collaborate with partners in the Democratic Republic of Congo (DRC), even good intentions cannot overcome differing expectations for how people use technologies to facilitate communication – both interpersonal and among social groups. This case study looks at an ongoing collaboration between a faculty member at the University of Minnesota and two NGOs working in the DRC: First Step Initiative, providing microloans to women entrepreneurs, and Pact, an international development organization. In the course of this collaboration, it has become clear that differing expectations for communication channels to support the NGOs have resulted in complications for collaborators both in the U.S. and the DRC. This study explores whether social networking tools and cell phones can be used to establish new channels for communication that meet interpersonal expectations for participants in both the U.S. and the DRC.*

## INTRODUCTION

When students and teachers share knowledge with people outside their classroom, the world becomes the classroom. With this enlarged classroom come opportunities for learning from untraditional sources, for instance from community partners in countries outside the U.S. This enlarged classroom also brings challenges to both teachers and students for understanding and communicating with people from other backgrounds and cultures. For partners in such a world classroom, good intentions

DOI: 10.4018/978-1-60960-623-7.ch022

alone cannot overcome differing expectations for how people relate socially and use technologies to facilitate communication. Partners on all sides of this world classroom are challenged to learn new ways of working together across oceans and cultures.

This study stems from a collaboration between my information design classes at the University of Minnesota (UMN) and two NGOs in the Democratic Republic of Congo (DRC): First Step Initiative (FSI), a nonprofit, microfinance organization working with woman entrepreneurs in DRC, and Pact, an international development organization based in Washington, D.C., and working in the DRC. Throughout this three-year collaboration, partners explored opportunities and barriers for communication and knowledge making across cultures. At the beginning of this work, it became clear that differing expectations for communication channels to support FSI's work resulted in sub-optimal participation in the organization from potential collaborators both in the U.S. and DRC. As it evolved, this study explored whether social networking tools and cell phones could be used to establish new channels for communication that could more effectively meet interpersonal expectations for participants in both countries. We learned that although individual entrepreneurs in the DRC wanted to use their cell phones to connect more readily to other people in Katanga Province, social and economic conditions made this goal more difficult than it initially appeared to those of us working at the University of Minnesota.

In spring 2008, I initially worked with FSI and my graduate information design students on a communication audit for FSI. This audit revealed differing expectations between the collaborators in the U.S. and DRC for using computer technologies to access Web-based information supporting FSI operations. In spring 2009, my graduate students explored whether social networking tools and cell phones could help to establish stable and robust communication channels between participants in the U.S. and DRC to facilitate fuller participation

in FSI programs. In Spring 2010, my graduate students explored a more specific question of connecting small farmers and artisanal miners in Katanga Province, working with Pact to implement a text messaging system to share pricing information for maize, cobalt, and copper. In order to progress toward this goal, however, the collaborators in Minnesota and Katanga Province first needed to build a common ground of understanding and communication. My students and I first needed to understand the context in which NGOs work in Katanga Province.

## BACKGROUND

Our initial partner, First Step Initiative, is a nonprofit microfinance organization with the mission of enabling women entrepreneurs in Katanga Province to start small businesses through microloans of US$50-150. FSI was established in 2006 by Chingwell Mutombu, whose family is from the DRC, but who has lived in the U.S. since her high school years. I first met Ms. Mutombu at a church we both attended and I learned about FSI's operations through our friendship. In 2007, when I began thinking about a project to work on in my information design class, I asked Ms. Mutombu if there was an FSI project that we could collaborate on in the Spring 2008 class. We decided to conduct an audit of the organization's communication tools and methods, and I started learning about life in Katanga Province.

The DRC is a developing central African country with very limited public infrastructure and governmental services. Katanga, a province in the southeast with over four million people, has an unemployment rate as high as 90% and few business opportunities for hopeful entrepreneurs. Because the DRC has not yet developed a comprehensive public sector that empowers private businesses, many NGOs are filling in some gaps within both its public and private sectors. Education is not free and families must pay for their children to attend school; most children do not have the opportunity to get an education even though their families aspire to send them to school.

Realities of life in Katanga Province are much different than in Minnesota. The graduate students in my information design class have the opportunity for education, even if they must take out large loans to finance it. At the University of Minnesota, virtually all my graduate students have access to a computer, enjoy ubiquitous wireless connectivity, and expect to use their computers to support many routine aspects of their lives. In addition, most of my graduate students have cell phones with many functions beyond voice and text messaging: i.e., taking still photos and video, running all kinds of applications, providing maps and GPS information, storing and retrieving data, playing games, accessing the Internet, and more. My graduate students and I generally assume that we will have easy access to a lot of online information and tools – and we have come to depend on this access to make our lives run smoothly.

During our information design class in Spring 2008, my students, Ms. Mutombu, and I focused on FSI's Web site and how information could be presented in a more compelling way to "tell the FSI story." We recommended narrative, navigational, and aesthetic changes to the Web site. One of that semester's students, Bethany Iverson, described her reaction to the challenges of the class:

*We became very close and personally involved in the work we did. Meeting Ms. Mutombu and hearing her stories was an unforgettable experience. I think we were all wowed by the fact that this soft spoken young woman was so fearless and driven, and it was all we could do to jump on the FSI train, which was obviously going to power ahead with or without us. We realized that our work over the course of the semester could have a potentially profound impact on many peoples' lives – an unexpected wildcard that pushed us from merely discussing ideas about information design in theory to actually putting it into practice. We*

*found ourselves solving real life problems in real time for someone who very much needed and deserved our help. It was powerful and motivational to say the least.*

After the semester ended, three students continued working with Ms. Mutombu on various aspects of FSI communications, including a redesigned Web site, with design work and hosting donated by a firm recommended by one of the students. This was clearly a successful course outcome, yet I began to realize that our expectations for the website were targeted to U.S. users. Although I had assumed that FSI staff and entrepreneurs in the DRC were using the Web site to support their activities, I was mistaken. Information on the Web site was geared toward potential donors to persuade them to become involved with FSI through monetary contributions. Internet access and computer availability for the DRC staff and entrepreneurs were difficult at best, and mostly non-existent. I wondered what technologies were available to our DRC colleagues so we might begin to design communication systems using those available technologies. The answer was cell phones.

## GETTING BEYOND THE WEBSITE TO CONNECT

After our experiences in spring 2008, I began to think about how FSI could add cell phones to its communication mix to accomplish its goals for supporting women entrepreneurs in Katanga Province. There were a number of groups who would potentially benefit from an expanded, cell phone-based information system: DRC entrepreneurs working in urban and rural areas, FSI staff in the U.S. and DRC, potential and current donors. This need for connecting a number of disparate groups to support FSI operations suggested that a social networking model would be appropriate for establishing and supporting communication channels among these groups. Even with this technological support structure, however, differing cultural expectations for interpersonal and social group communication also needed to be analyzed and accommodated in the final communication system.

In order to understand differing cultural expectations for the communication system we might establish, I posed four research questions to shed light on at least some assumptions about social networks and technology use:

- How do students at the University of Minnesota, FSI staff, and FSI entrepreneurs describe their social network?
- How do students at the University of Minnesota, FSI staff, and FSI entrepreneurs currently communicate with others in their social network?
- For what functions do students at the University of Minnesota, FSI staff, and FSI entrepreneurs currently use their cell phones?
- What expectations to students at the University of Minnesota, FSI staff, and FSI entrepreneurs have for using their cell phones to keep in contact with their social network?

Ms. Mutombu and I planned a Skype interview with FSI staff and entrepreneurs in Lubumbashi. We began by reviewing the interview questions we would ask to address the four research questions. Even in this phase of designing questions for two different groups of respondents – 1) the FSI staff and entrepreneurs and 2) the students – it became apparent that we had significant differences in worldview and background experiences to accommodate. In trying to craft phone interview questions for the FSI group and e-mail questionnaire questions for the student group, I initially wrote questions for everyone that looked very much like these four that we ultimately asked the graduate students:[1]

1. What part of your social interactions is most important for you in your closest social circle? You can choose to describe what you value most about your life and relationships with the people who are close to you, such as your business circle, family, friends, or other social group.
2. How do you currently stay in touch with the people in your closest social circle, such as your business circle, family, friends, or other social group? How do you communicate with the people in your closest social circle?
3. Please let us know how you currently use your cell phone.
4. Please let us know two ways you would like to use your cell phone to do things you do not currently do with your cell phone.

When I asked Ms. Mutombu to review these questions for our FSI colleagues, she quickly replied that the first two questions would not be answerable for this interview group because the concept of "social circle" was too abstract and unfamiliar. She explained that for Congolese people, their lives are so intimately intertwined within their web of social connections that to separate these connections from the rest of their lives is not something that makes any sense. Already I knew that I was learning about intercultural dialogue and why misunderstandings happen at such fundamental levels of expectation and worldview. After some give-and-take, we developed two different sets of questions. In order to connect to the FSI group's experiences, we asked these questions that focused on their "lending circles" rather than their "social circles":

1. What does your lending circle mean to you? How would you describe your lending circle to someone who didn't know about First Step Initiative?
2. How do you stay in touch with the people in your lending circle? Do you talk with them

every day? Do you use your cell phone to stay in touch?

3. Please tell me how you currently use your cell phone.

4. How would you like to use your cell phone?

5. Please describe how you connect to people in rural areas now and how you would like to improve those connections.

The result of this exercise in intercultural dialogue was that I would not be able to craft one set of questions to ask all of the interview and questionnaire participants, as would be an ideal research design. So my ideas about "good" research design changed as I struggled to adjust my methods to this situation while still gathering data relevant to my research questions. I wondered briefly about the universality of the scientific method, but pragmatically needed to move along and complete my data gathering.

In March 2009, we conducted interviews with FSI staff and entrepreneurs via a 90-minute, three-way Skype call. In Lubumbashi, we talked with one FSI loan officer and two entrepreneurs; Ms. Mutombu called in from her home in Minneapolis; I called from my university office with a graduate student from the Spring 2008 class, Marc Hannum, who recorded our conversation and later produced a podcast of the recording to share with our students and potentially our FSI colleagues.

During the interview, our FSI colleagues stated that they felt their lending circles helped women work together to fight poverty. They stayed in touch via weekly face-to-face meetings. Women connected with each other via cell phone only rarely and for urgent reasons, because the cost of the minutes is high and they cannot afford to use the cell phones very often. They generally keep an eye on how long they talk and rarely talk more than five minutes. If the women were able to afford more minutes, they would like to stay in contact more via their cell phones, which would help them do their work better. They could talk by phone, make arrangements, and not have to travel so far. Women mentioned that they would like to use text messaging, take photos and videos, and connect to the Internet. They would also like to share video with people in the U.S. and with their colleagues in rural DRC.

I also distributed questionnaires via e-mail to the 12 students in the Spring 2009 information design class; all 12 were returned with responses. For keeping in touch with people in their social network, students strongly preferred face-to-face interactions, with electronic communications coming in a close second. Trust, loyalty, two-way dialogue, and dependability were mentioned as being important to these interactions with people in students' closest social circles. Although students reported preferring to stay in contact with their closest social connections via face-to-face interactions, they also reported that they most frequently stayed in contact via telephone. Face-to-face contacts and social networking came in as close seconds for staying in contact. E-mail, text messaging, and chat were used by some students; gaming was also mentioned as a way to stay in touch.

All respondents indicated that they used their phones to talk with people in their social circles; for 11 respondents this was the most frequent use of their phones. Most sent text messages, used their phones to talk with people about business, or took photographs with their phones. Connecting to the Internet, sending multimedia messages, playing games, connecting to Facebook and Twitter, recording or viewing video, and listening to music were also mentioned as ways that students currently used their phones. In response to the question addressing what they would like to do with their phones that they were not currently doing, students most frequently reported that they would like to connect to the Internet. Viewing or recording video, sending multimedia messages, and connecting to Facebook were also frequently mentioned as additional ways that students would like to use their phones.

The three-way Skype conversation demonstrated that intercultural dialogue is difficult to accomplish even with technological assistance. Although we all shared at least some fluency in English, the stress of using Skype to connect people who had never met in person challenged all of our communication skills, and the Lubumbashi group preferred to speak in a language that was more comfortable for them (French or Swahili). Our first possible source of misunderstanding was also the tool that enabled our connection: the Internet with Skype voice-over protocol. Whereas we would have had a richer communication experience face to face, in practical reality we would not have been able to come together in person because of travel costs. If we had met face to face, we could have taken time to get to know each other before launching into the study questions. This relationship building might also have allowed us to form some kind of pidgin language and non-verbal understanding through which we could have communicated more directly without relying so heavily on Ms. Mutombu's interpreting. Although the data from the telephone interview was gathered under circumstances that increased the probability of misunderstanding, I believe that we gathered comments from this interview that added to our mutual understanding of the issues raised in the four research questions.

*How do students at the University of Minnesota, FSI staff, and FSI entrepreneurs describe their social network?*

In talking about their lending and social circles, the most striking similarity between both groups was a shared value for face-to-face interactions. The FSI groups met weekly to support each other's work. The students also expressed a strong preference for interacting with their social circle in face-to-face situations. They expressed their value for two-way dialogue and exploring different ideas with family and friends they could trust and depend on.

*How do students at the University of Minnesota, FSI staff, and FSI entrepreneurs currently communicate with others in their social network?*

Both groups indicated that they valued face-to-face communication with the people in their social circles. For the FSI group, this was by far their most frequent method of communication, although they did communicate by telephone in urgent situations. They further expressed a desire for more frequent telephone communication, but were currently held back from realizing that desire because they were not able to afford as many cell phone minutes as they would like to use.

The students reported that they connected with their social circles via the telephone slightly more often than via face-to-face communication. What was striking about this group's responses was that they reported using Internet social networking (Facebook, Twitter, instant messaging) to communicate with their social circle almost as frequently as face-to-face communication. They also reported using e-mail and text messaging frequently to keep in touch. Students' responses presented a picture of people who value face-to-face communication with their social circle, but use an array of technological devices to keep in touch probably more than they meet face-to-face. Even though people in social circles presumably have face-to-face relationships to build on, the fact that technology-based communications strip so much non-verbal information and cues from the situation leads me to question whether misunderstandings are more frequent in these situations vs. face-to-face situations. On the other hand, technology-based communications allow people to connect more readily than they could with only face-to-face communications.

*For what functions do students at the University of Minnesota, FSI staff, and FSI entrepreneurs currently use their cell phones?*

Both groups reported that they primarily use their cell phones for voice transmission vs. data transmission. The FSI group said they use their phones mostly in urgent situations and they keep track of the minutes they use because the minutes are very expensive for them to purchase (US$2.00 for 50 minutes). They talk with family and sometimes with others about business. For people in the DRC, the ability to own a phone is a relatively new experience. Vodacom, currently the largest provider of cell phone service in DRC, began business in that country in 2001; by 2005 they had 1.2 million subscribers. Before this boom in cell phone coverage, DRC had approximately 5,000 landlines and probably only 2,000 of them were operational at any one time, according to Vodacom Congo Chairman Alieu Conteh (2009). For most people in DRC, being able to talk with people at a distance is a new and welcomed opportunity. Cell phones used in DRC are mostly basic models with voice and text messaging (SMS) capabilities.

By contrast, the U.S. cell phone system was established by Motorola in 1984 (Motorola, Inc., 2009) and many of the UMN students have grown up with these devices. Minutes are affordable for most people, although not everyone in the country. However, most university students can afford cell phone minutes and would not consider them a luxury. Although some students have basic models of cell phones, many have models that are capable of taking photographs and video, connecting to the Internet, listening to music, and viewing videos.

Since the students in this study grew up with telephones and were very familiar with cell phones, they reported using their phones in many more ways than their FSI counterparts. Although they, too, primarily used their phones to talk with others, they also used their phones to send text messages nearly as often as they talked with the people in their social circles. They often used their phones for business. Many students used their phones for taking photographs and a few recorded video. Some connected to the Internet, used Facebook or Twitter, and played games on their phones.

This great difference in experience with cell phone technologies creates a divide between what the students and our FSI partners expect to be available via the phones. For the students, it is almost unimaginable that people would not have ready access to a wide array of cell phone services. If they are not aware that a divide exists between their expectations and those of their DRC colleagues, misunderstandings are certain to develop quickly. Without an awareness of the divide between groups with ready access to technologies and groups without such ready access, the group with access will tend to make decisions and choices that do not adequately meet the needs of groups with worldviews and expectations other than their own.

*What expectations do students at the University of Minnesota, FSI staff, and FSI entrepreneurs have for using their cell phones to keep in contact with their social network?*

The greatest divergence in the two groups' responses resulted from the question about how they would like to use their cell phones in the future. The FSI group responded that they would like to be able to afford more minutes so they could talk with people more frequently on their phones. For example, they would like to be able to connect with food growers in rural areas in order to coordinate transportation of their products into the city for sale. This expanded communication network would also allow people in rural areas greater access to the resources from the city, such as health care and other services or goods, which their urban partners could help to facilitate. This ability to widen their communication network via cell phones would allow entrepreneurs to conduct business more efficiently, and support their friends and family more robustly. They see cell phones as a tool for building social and business capacities, which is closely tied to better family life, better education, better health, and better government. (See Conteh video.)

By contrast, none of the students expressed interest in expanding the use of their cell phones for talking with people in their social group, for doing business, or sending text messages. For this group, their needs in these areas were satisfied and they wanted primarily to connect to the Internet with their phones. They also wanted to view or record video, send multimedia messages, listen to music, play games, and take photographs. One respondent in this group noted that the current uses of the phone were enough and this person did not want to add any more functions. This group primarily wanted to expand their data transmission uses and capabilities with their phones.

Comparing both groups' responses, the FSI loan officer expressed expectations for cell phone use that bridged the divide between new users of cell phone technologies in the DRC and more experienced users in the U.S. He indicated that he would like to connect to the Internet, get e-mail through his phone, and connect to the MSN.com for news and other information. Individuals like this loan officer who can understand different worldviews and possibilities show us a model for finding a common ground for collaboration.

## SOLUTIONS AND RECOMMENDATIONS

**Lesson 1:** Be skeptical of a technology's power to persuade people to adopt instrumental social and interpersonal relationships.

In my own study of intercultural dialogue between people in the U.S. and DRC, I want to be aware of the power of technologies to surmount intercultural differences in a totalizing way; I want to strive to maintain a space for the knowledge of interpersonal relations shared by my colleagues in the DRC and the knowledge of instrumental relationships shared by my colleagues at UMN without the power of technology overcoming

less instrumental human relationships. Graduate assistant Marc Hannum commented on this tendency of a technology – in this case cell phones – to impose an instrumental worldview on the people who use it:

*I was struck by the whole text messaging communication environment. If someone can only afford to send a single text, what decisions do they need to make when communicating? Does the technology favor certain decisions about communication? Does the Western engineering nature of the system coerce one's decisions within these systems of communication? It was rapidly apparent that yes, these rhetorical/coercive systems guide or even* push *communication decisions toward and into the limitations of a particular technological architecture. And this interaction produces an environment in which communication exists* separately *from the social environment. It was interesting to see this dynamic play out in our attempts to understand how our colleagues in the DR Congo communicate, and also how the technology communicates with them. Some interesting problems became visible when we began looking at these interactions.*

**Lesson 2:** Be open to learning about the world from colleagues whose ways of knowing do not conform to traditional academic logic.

From the perspective of a technical communication professor, I know first-hand how rationalized, science-based discourse overcomes non-scientific ways of making knowledge, even though these other ways of making knowledge can teach me things about human relations that will never be articulated in my technical textbooks. For example, I suspect that my colleagues in the DRC share ways of knowing the world based on their strong interpersonal connections that can teach me new things about how people live together. And I will learn about their culture through their discourse as well as their practices. Yet I know that in the interactions we have in this project about mobile technologies, there is a danger of the dominant technological discourse overcoming the more humane discourse of human relations.

Foucault (1980) and de Certeau (1980) argued that the project of technology is to standardize knowledge-making practices and discourses by educating unruly practices into science. De Certeau (1980) held that while scientists (or technical communicators) "acknowledge in these [erudite] practices a kind of knowledge preceding that of the scientists, they have to release it from its 'improper' language and invert [it] into a 'proper' discourse...Science will make princesses out of all these Cinderellas" (p. 67). As we proceed with this project, I am reminded that every coin has two sides: cell phone technology offers a tool for capacity building and community building; it also threatens to instrumentalize human relations.

**Lesson 3:** Share stories about our lives to bridge cultures and make new knowledge together.

So how will intercultural dialogue proceed in this case? We have decided to start sharing stories – narratives that can help us build a micro-culture spanning Katanga and Minnesota. In this culture building, we are like the "child or immigrant" that Lyotard (1992) described "enter[ing] a culture through an apprenticeship in proper names... lodged in little stories" (p. 31). One of the FSI entrepreneurs mentioned that she would like to be able to record her stories on video to share with us and with the world. When I visited my FSI colleagues in Lubumbashi, I took them a small video camera so they could join the dialogue more completely through the visual images they chose to record. And we in the U.S. can record and e-mail our stories to the DRC, becoming video pen pals and creating over time a shared culture to learn from each other.

## FUTURE RESEARCH DIRECTIONS

In Spring 2009, my graduate students in the information design class again worked with FSI to explore whether social networking tools and cell phones can be used to establish new channels for communication that meet interpersonal expectations for participants in both the U.S. and DRC. As Ms. Mutombu and I planned our collaboration with that year's class, we chose to focus on the problem of connecting urban and rural entrepreneurs via cell phones.

The project for connecting urban and rural entrepreneurs arose from needs communicated by the FSI staff and entrepreneurs in DRC. All too often, a businesswoman in the urban area of Lubumbashi, for example, might want to find tomatoes to sell. Right now, she arranges for transportation to a rural area and takes the chance that she will find someone who has grown tomatoes that are ready to harvest. If she does not find those tomatoes, she goes back to Lubumbashi empty-handed, having wasted her time and resources. Conversely, someone in a rural area who has harvested tomatoes might pack them up and transport them to Lubumbashi, which is most often a difficult, 100 km trip by bicycle. If the grower does not find someone to buy the tomatoes, the food will spoil and again the trip will result in wasted time and resources. Being able to communicate between urban sellers and rural growers would improve the chances of these efforts being successful and profitable.

In Spring 2009, we found that designing a text messaging system to connect urban and rural entrepreneurs was far more difficult than it first appeared. We needed to understand technical specifications, such as cell phone network capabilities and what kinds of cell phones most people had. Although the students' first impulse was to recommend that we find someone to donate some smartphones, we came to understand that introducing an entirely new technology into the system was not feasible technologically, and not appropriate socially. We needed to work with the simple devices and mobile networks already in place in Katanga Province. We did not make much evident progress that semester, but we learned a great deal about challenges of re-thinking our expectations and assumptions within the social context of Katanga Province.

In January 2010, I traveled with Ms. Mutombu to the FSI operations in Lubumbashi to conduct interviews in preparation for designing a text messaging system to support the entrepreneurs and staff operations. While I was there, I met Francois Philippart from Pact and saw their business development operations in Katanga Province. In Spring 2010, my class and I worked with two engineering professors at University of Minnesota to start designing a text messaging system to communicate pricing information for small farmers and artisanal miners that would be implemented with our Pact colleagues. And even though I had been working on this project for three years, I continued to learn new things about how we consider cell phone technology as "second nature" here in my neighborhood of the world. I shared one of these learning moments with Clayton Benjamin, a Spring 2010 student:

*I believe the biggest "aha" moment came when our first engineering partner visited our class. He started by presenting an idea to create an intricate menu selection system for basic phones, which would allow the user to select what type of information they would like to receive and to enroll in the program. His approach was very technology-driven and didn't appear to keep our user in mind. The information architecture he created would require training and lots of texts being sent from the people to the text messaging hub. In turn this would cost the organization a lot of money for training and it would also cost the users money to be sending multiple texts. It appeared that who he considered was the end user was vastly different than the end user we had developed. Therefore, during that class session, it was time for the big*

*aha: we must create a very simple system that can communicate a lot of information with a low cost of generation and participation. Together we collaborated and decided that we could create a system that relied not only on the technology, but also used paper handouts to teach the system pictorially and through a numbered code. Through this multimodal form of communication it would be possible to communicate a large amount of information in short text messages. Additionally, it would reduce costs because there wouldn't be a lot of training necessary for the system. Overall, for this communication deliverable to be successful, we had to scale everything back to its very technological minimum, and that meant even relying upon a paper source.*

## CONCLUSION AND LESSONS LEARNED

In the journey I have been on for the last three years with my classes of graduate students and engineers at the University of Minnesota, and colleagues at First Step Initiative and Pact, we have made incorrect assumptions, overlooked questions that needed to be asked, and struggled to explain our ideas to people at the university and around the world. Our efforts have brought us connections across cultures, offers of help, expressions of gratitude, and new avenues for our journey. In a way, our misunderstandings have opened up opportunities for dialogues that have brought people closer together in a paradoxical cycle. And one thing is certain: there will be more misunderstandings.

Christopher Cocchiarella, a student in the Spring 2010 class, summed up our dilemma as we ended this latest phase of the design for an SMS text messaging system for pricing information:

*We drew upon linguistic disciplines to understand Swahili grammar and linguistic translation. We worked out a standardized syntactic format that could communicate pricing information. We brainstormed on language forms and illustrations that would mitigate the DRC's limited rates of literacy. We even devised a business model that would allow Congolese miners and farmers to subscribe to periodic messages offered by an SMS system. Working out such facts and business propositions accordingly, we assumed that a precise information design would allow miners and farmers in the DRC to easily access pricing facts about commodities and crops. Theoretically, this pricing information should give Congolese workers opportunities to negotiate fair and competitive sales with buyers.*

*Nevertheless, in the midst of working out technical and theoretical details of the SMS system, we realized a number of problematic scenarios that revolved around one simple question: what would be the source of pricing information? An SMS system calls for a trustful source of pricing information before it actually can circulate this content among users. This is a concern in the DRC is because the country does not have an adequate legal infrastructure to counter dishonest business activity among buyers and sellers. For example, if the source of pricing information were to come from foreign buyers, then the prices might merely replicate one-sided offers, which would likely represent the lowest common denominators. With the buyers providing pricing information, an SMS system would give them dominance over Congolese sellers in pricing negotiations and dealings. Buyers could then control how much or how little they desired to pay for commodities and crops, hindering sellers and exposing Congolese farmers and miners to potential abuses and scams. The result may be the opposite of what an SMS system should do, which is to empower Congolese sellers with pricing information so they have a better chance of not getting cheated.*

As we look ahead with this project, my conclusion has to be that nothing is as simple as it seems, at least not when it comes to designing engaged learning experiences in a classroom that is open to the world. As the teacher in such a world classroom, I must be prepared to learn along with my students and collaborators as we take our journey together along paths that turn out to be unfamiliar for everyone concerned. But as we encounter unexpected experiences, both hopeful and disturbing, we can know that they all help to bring us closer together in a space of common understanding.

## ACKNOWLEDGMENT

Information Design graduate students Clayton Benjamin, Christopher Cocchiarella, Marc Hannum and Bethany Iverson contributed their good work to this project and their valuable insights to this chapter. This case study was supported from 2008-2009 by the Faculty Fellowship Program of the University of Minnesota Office of Information Technology and Digital Media Center.

## REFERENCES

Conteh, A. (2009). *DR Congo: Open for business.* Retrieved February 20, 2010, from http://www.businessactionforafrica.org/

de Certeau, M. (1984). *The practice of everyday life.* Berkeley, CA: University of California Press.

*First Step Initiative website.* (2010). Retrieved July 10, 2010, from http://www.firststepinitiative.net

Foucault, M. (1980). *Power/knowledge: Selected interviews and other writings 1972-77.* New York, NY: Pantheon.

Lyotard, J.-F. (1992). *The postmodern explained: Correspondence, 1982-1985.* Minneapolis, MN: University of Minnesota Press.

Motorola, Inc. (2009). Making history: Developing the portable cellular system. Retrieved February 20, 2010, from http://www.motorola.com/content.jsp?globalObjectId=7662-10813

*Pact website*. (2010). Retrieved July 10, 2010 from http://www.pactworld.org/

Pineau, C. (Director). (2006). *Africa: Open for business*. Available from http://www.africaopenforbusiness.com/

## ADDITIONAL READING

Clifford, J. (1992). Traveling cultures. In Grossberg, L., Nelson, C., & Treichler, P. (Eds.), *Cultural Studies* (pp. 96–117). London: Routledge.

Comaroff, J. (1991). *Of revelation and revolution: Vol. 1. Christianity, colonialism, and consciousness in South Africa*. Chicago, IL: University of Chicago Press.

Dunn, K. C. (2003). *Imagining the Congo: The international relations of identity*. New York, NY: Palgrave Macmillan.

Fabian, J. (1996). *Remembering the present: Painting and popular history in Zaire*. Berkeley, CA: University of California Press.

Fabian, J. (2003). Forgetful remembering: A colonial life in the Congo. *Africa*, *73*(4), 489–504. doi:10.3366/afr.2003.73.4.489

Hall, S. (1997). *Representation: Cultural representations and signifying practices*. London: Sage.

Hayes, K., & Burge, R. (2003). *Coltan mining in the Democratic Republic of Congo: How tantalum-using industries can commit to the reconstruction of the DRC*. Cambridge, UK: Fauna & Flora International.

Henry, F. (2004). Concepts of race and racism and implications for OHRC policy. Ontario Human Rights Commission, 2004. Retrieved February 20, 2010, from http://www.ohrc.on.ca/en/issues/racism/racepolicydialogue/fh?page=fh.html

Horst, H., & Miller, D. (2005). From kinship to link-up: Cell phones and social networking in Jamaica. *Current Anthropology*, *46*(5), 755–778. doi:10.1086/432650

Jameson, F. (1991). *Postmodernism, or, the cultural logic of late capitalism*. Durham, NC: Duke University Press.

Katz, S. B. (1992). The ethic of expediency: Classical rhetoric, technology, and the Holocaust. *College English*, *54*(3), 255–275. doi:10.2307/378062

Kreiswirth, M. (2000, Summer). Merely telling stories? Narrative and knowledge in the human sciences. *Poetics Today*, *21*(2), 293–318. doi:10.1215/03335372-21-2-293

Lagae, J. (2008). From 'Patrimoine Partagé' to 'Whose Heritage'? Critical reflections on colonial built heritage in the City of Lubumbashi, Democratic Republic of the Congo. *Afrika Focus*, *21*(1), 11–30.

Likaka, O. (2009). *Naming colonialism: History and collective memory in the Congo, 1870-1960*. Madison, WI: University of Wisconsin Press.

Longo, B. (1998, Winter). An approach for applying cultural study theory to technical writing research. *Technical Communication Quarterly*, *7*(1), 53–73.

Longo, B. (2000). *Spurious coin: A history of science, management, and technical writing*. Albany, NY: SUNY Press.

Longo, B. (2002). Growing through community: Opportunities for ongoing collaborations. In C. Benson, & S. Christianson (Eds.), *Writing to make a difference: Classroom projects for community change* (pp. 23–36). New York, NY: Teachers College Press.

Longo, B. (2009). Human+computer culture: Where we work. In R. Spilka (Ed.), *Digital literacy for technical communication: 21st century theory and practice* (147-168). New York, NY: Routledge.

Longo, B., Reiss, D., Selfe, C., & Young, A. (2003). The poetics of computers: Composing relationships with technology. *Computers and Composition, 20*(1), 97–118. doi:10.1016/S8755-4615(02)00172-X

Pels, P. (1997). The anthropology of colonialism: Culture, history, and the emergence of western governmentality. *Annual Review of Anthropology, 26*, 163–183. doi:10.1146/annurev.anthro.26.1.163

Petit, P., & Mutambwa, G. M. (2005). 'La Crise': Lexicon and ethos of the second economy in Lubumbashi. *Africa, 75*(4), 467–487. doi:10.3366/afr.2005.75.4.467

Pickering, M. (2001). *Stereotyping: The politics of representation.* New York, NY: Palgrave.

Plaisant, C., Schneiderman, B., & Mushlin, R. (1998). An information architecture to support the visualization of personal histories. *Information Processing & Management, 34*(5), 581–597. doi:10.1016/S0306-4573(98)00024-7

Scott, B., Longo, B., & Wills, K. (2006). *Critical power tools: Technical communication and cultural studies.* Albany, NY: State University of New York Press.

Wainaina. B. The ethics of aid. *Speaking of faith.* Retrieved February 20, 2010, from http://speakingoffaith.publicradio.org/programs/2008/ethics_of_aid-kenya/

Wood, A. F., & Smith, M. J. (2004). *Online communication: Linking technology, identity, and culture* (2nd ed.). Mahwah, NJ: Lawrence Erlbaum.

## KEY TERMS AND DEFINITIONS

**Artisanal Miners:** Small-scale or subsistence miners, not officially employed by a mining company, but working independently using their own resources.

**Cell Phones:** Hand-held devices for voice and data transmission.

**Culture:** Network of related belief systems, values, expectations, worldview that is shared by a group of individuals and viewed as "common sense".

**Democratic Republic of Congo:** Large country in central Africa.

**Information Design:** Preparing and displaying information so that people can use it efficiently and effectively in a particular medium.

**Katanga Province:** Mineral-rich area in southeast Democratic Republic of Congo.

**Microfinance:** Providing small business loans to people who are not able to secure financing through conventional financial institutions.

**Simple Message System (SMS):** Delivered over cell phones.

**Social Network:** Structure of inter-related individuals, often supported by Web 2.0-based tools such as Facebook or MySpace.

## ENDNOTE

[1] This study was reviewed and approved by the Institutional Review Board (IRB) at the University of Minnesota. There was no review board available in Katanga Province to review the study.

# Chapter 23
# Incarcerated Students and the Unintended Consequences of a Technology–Driven Higher Education System

**Patricia A. Aceves**
*Stony Brook University, State University of New York, USA*

**Robert I. Aceves**
*The City University of New York, Aviation Institute at York College, USA*

**Shannon Watson**
*Anoka Ramsey Community College, USA*

## ABSTRACT

*This case study outlines the partnership between the Minnesota Department of Corrections and St. Cloud State University. As higher education underwent significant changes in technology and distance education delivery during the 1990s, the print-based correspondence course was rapidly being converted to online delivery, leaving offender students without higher education access or options. The university-corrections partnership created an innovative and unique program through reverse-engineering online general education courses into print-based materials. The inability to use technology to provide cost effective education to many geographically dispersed students indicates that as a society, available technologies cannot yet be trusted to provide offender access to family, education and jobs while providing safety and security for citizens. What will make programs and partnerships like this successful in the future is the openness of corrections, education, and innovative technology partners to reexamine technology's role and allow for changes in operational procedures that can satisfy the needs of all societal stakeholders.*

DOI: 10.4018/978-1-60960-623-7.ch023

## INTRODUCTION

In 2005, 44 states were offering some form of post-secondary education to offenders, from vocational programs and certificates to full baccalaureate degrees. The impact of these partnerships, while small in scope, benefits citizens in the form of safer communities and a reduced tax burden (Erisman and Contardo, 2005). Research has consistently documented that offenders taking postsecondary college courses leading to an associate's degree or higher are significantly less likely to re-offend after release; on average, recidivism rates are reported to be up to 46% lower than for those who had not enrolled in college courses (Chappell, 2004).

This chapter is a case study of an interagency partnership between a state department of corrections and a state university and the role that technology played in furthering their commitment to providing postsecondary correctional education to offenders. Technology played a two-fold role in this partnership; on one hand, the increase of online learning decreased the accessibility of college courses that had formerly been provided through correspondence study. Conversely, technology facilitated the development of quality print-based courses and provided timely, cost effective delivery and communications between physical institutions, which ultimately made the educational process work.

## Background on Postsecondary Correctional Education

To the layperson—the average, tax-paying, law-abiding citizen—correctional ideology is not of major concern. United States citizens are accustomed to the concept "commit the crime, do the time." Correctional ideology, however, is like a pendulum that swings between rehabilitation and retribution, depending on the political climate of the time. An historical overview of correctional ideology will provide perspective on the context of this case study.

In the 1930s, prisons operated under the ideology of the medical model, which prescribed that crime was the result of illness that could be cured. For 30 years, corrections practiced the medical model, whereby criminal behavior could be effectively treated through behavior modification, medication, group counseling, individual psychotherapy and work therapy (MacNamara, 1977). By the late 1960s, however, a new theory surfaced: the opportunity (or justice) model, supporting the claim that people committed crimes not because they were sick, but because they lacked opportunities to acquire resources in a legitimate manner (McCarty, 2006; Page, 2004). Criminal justice practitioners and lawmakers began to devise ways to work the concept of rehabilitation into institutional programming, including the creation of educational programs within correctional facilities. Offenders now had access to higher education andPell grants to pay for classes; therefore, correctional education programs flourished (Page, 2004). By 1976, 237 prisons offered degree programs compared to the 12 that were available just eleven years earlier under the medical model (McCarty, 2006).

One of the first studies that assessed educational programming's impact on criminality was Project Newgate, which provided male inmates the opportunity to participate in college programming while incarcerated. In addition, upon release they were given the opportunity to continue their college coursework at the university. Post-release success for these students was determined by two criteria: educational achievement and reinstitutionalization (remaining incarceration-free for five years post-release). Of the 145 participants, 73% of program participants did not recidivate for at least five years (27% recidivism), compared with a national recidivism rate over 60% (Clendenen, Ellingston, & Severson, 1979). Large, longitudinal studies began to confirm that within three years of release, on average, 68% of all prisoners were being rearrested for a new offense (Langan& Levin, 2002). "The analysis of postrelease recidivism yielded evidence of a consistently negative association between postsecondary education participation and recidivism" (Winterfield, Coggeshall, Burke-Storer, Correa &Tidd, 2009, p.V). Meta-analysis of the education-recidivism studies conducted throughout the 1990s again showed a positive correlation between education and reduced recidivism (Chappell, 2004).

Although postsecondary correctional education was yielding successful offenders,by the early 1990s, inmate access to federal money for college came under attack. With "tough on crime" politicians in power, the ideology of corrections turned from rehabilitative to retributive, and in 1994, the Violent Crime Control and Law Enforcement Act became law and inmate access to Pell Grant money was officially terminated (Page, 2004; McCarty, 2006; Ubah & Robinson, 2003). With the main source of funding revoked, many college-in-prison programs closed and programming decreased 28% in just four years (McCarty, 2006). By this point, higher education access was eliminated for all but a few who had the means to pay for independent study courses, which were still proliferating in the mid-1990s. Ten years later, the correspondence course had gone the way of the dinosaur as higher education ushered in a new era of technology-supported access and opportunity through online education.

## The Digital Divide on the Prison Campus

Correspondence (independent, self-paced) study, the earliest form of distance education in the U.S. is defined as:

*A course provided by an institution under which the institution provides instructional materials, by mail or electronic transmission, including examinations on the materials, to students who are separated from the instructor. Interaction between the instructor and the student is limited, is not regular and substantive, and is primarily initiated by the student. Correspondence courses are typically self-paced. (Higher Education Opportunity Act, 2008, sec 600.2)*

This form of education was ideally suited to students who lived in rural areas, homemakers and the incarcerated. Correspondence study had limitations, however, and was viewed by most institutions as second-class education and only suited to those who were not serious students. Most colleges and universities had restrictions on how many credits by correspondence they would accept toward a degree, and while many institutions offered correspondence courses, few institutions offered entire degrees in this format. As e-learning emerged in the late 1990s, federal student aid would not pay for more than six credits per semester through distance delivery, creating disincentives to schools wanting to offer full degrees by distance and even more difficult for students seeking to achieve a degree by distance (Higher Education Reauthorization Act, 1998).

By the late 1990s, federal student aid restrictions eased and online learning began to move further into the mainstream of higher education, gaining credibility as a vehicle for delivering degrees anytime, anywhere. Where some students struggled academically within the correspondence model, online learning offered multimedia resources and interaction between faculty and students, opening the door to accommodate many more students. Technology's growth in higher education helped close the gap between educational haves and have-nots, creating access for students who could not have otherwise earned a college education. Online education had all but transformed distance learning into a respected and sought-after delivery mode and instructional strategy, but several significant populations were left out of the educational technology boom. The digital divide in the U.S. remained the greatest between Caucasians and African Americans, Hispanics and Native Americans (Anderson,1999). Caucasians outnumber minorities on our college campuses and continue to have the highest usage of broadband Internet access (Rainie, 2010; Knapp, Kelly-Reid, & Ginder, 2009).

While there have been significant efforts to eliminate this gap in technology access to underserved populations, incarcerated individuals have fewer educational options than ever before. More often than not, offenders have had little experience with technology prior to incarceration and once within the penal system there is no ability to access online education. The growth in technology-mediated higher education has further exacerbated the challenges for an already disenfranchised population and further marginalizes this group of potential students. Ineligible for federal financial aid, the incarcerated see educational opportunities all but disappear and with the elimination of most correspondence programs in favor of online delivery, even offenders with the ability to pay cannot connect with quality educational opportunities. With the no-Internet policies of state and federal prisons, offenders are at a disadvantage in many ways, being cut off from educational access, communication with family, and up-to-date legal materials. Imagine running a business where you cannot allow your employees to use any technology—your operating costs would be higher and less efficient. This is the situation where corrections finds itself, wanting to find ways to use more efficient technologies that are not only safe, but fail-safe. However, some state correctional systems are attempting to use secure technologies to allow for offenders to communicate and learn in a more cost effective way.

The Michigan State Department of Corrections (DOC) has recently started offering an inbound e-mail service for family members and others to send emails to offenders in state facilities. According to the Michigan DOC:

*The customer (family member or other) will have to purchase "stamps" or a subscription through JPay in order to send electronic messages. All mail is electronically scanned by JPay for security issues and then sent to the Michigan Department of Corrections where it is reviewed again prior to being released to the prisoner. Prisoners will receive a printed copy of the electronic message (Michigan State Department of Corrections, 2010).*

Similarly, a proof-of-concept project using an offender intranet has been tested in the United Kingdom allowing offenders to use a secure IT network to access online learning and job-hunting resources using Internet technology (Offender Information Services, 2008). Technologies are available that can provide a greater degree of opportunity for connection with family and educational resources, but critics remain skeptical about security and the perception that offenders would have "free access" to the Internet on the taxpayer dollar.

## Evolution of the Pathways Program for Incarcerated Students

St. Cloud State University began offering correspondence courses in the early 1960s as part of Project Newgate, and for over 40 years offered correspondence courses with approximately one-fourth of its enrollment coming from offenders at the medium security St. Cloud Correctional Facility. In addition to self-paced correspondence study, the university provided courses on-site at the prison and throughout the 1980s and 1990s provided a full-time university staff member to manage the higher education program at the facility (with funding from a state grant). By 2000, state funding cuts eliminated the grant and the staff position, and left the DOC scrambling to locate funds to continue the program. Education officials at the DOC reallocated phone commission monies (the fee offenders pay to the prison to make a phone call) and drew upon funding from the Federal Incarcerated Youthful Offender (IYO) grants to continue the educational programming, albeit on a smaller scale.[1] This funding model persisted for another six years, providing four on-site courses a year and offering hundreds of offenders a pathway to college and the chance for a brighter future upon release.

In 2004, with a change in state governance and a tough-on-crime administration, all funding for postsecondary correctional education was suddenly withdrawn. The university was determined to continue serving this population and redirected its focus to the self-paced correspondence courses that could be made available to students who could pay for them. In order to expand the program and create visibility to potential students throughout the state corrections system and across the country, the program was formalized into the Pathways Program for Incarcerated Students. A brochure was created, a promotional video was planned and faculty were recruited to reverse-engineer their courses from online to print-based. All told, the newly minted Pathways Program added nearly 10 new courses to its docket—not enough to offer an associates degree, but well on its way to being academically viable.

Throughout this time, the DOC remained in contact with its two most committed education partners, the state university and a private liberal arts college, forming the Correctional Higher Education Consortium. Meeting semi-annually, the Consortium worked to find alternative funding options and brainstormed ideas to continue higher education programming within the facilities. Four years later, the members' patience paid off when the state commissioner of corrections once again allowed Incarcerated Youthful Offender (IYO) grants to fund college courses for youthful offenders. The challenge for the DOC was to provide as much bang for the buck as possible, and while on-site instruction was part of the plan, they wanted to reach as many offenders as cost effectively as possible, which led to offering print-based courses to cohorts of students in six facilities across the state. For the university, it cost significantly less to pay a professor to teach 20 students in a print-based format than in a traditional classroom. The goal of serving 100 students per semester and

guaranteeing courses leading to a degree ensured a monumental undertaking for all involved and an even greater commitment to success.

## Controversies over Postsecondary Correctional Education

Postsecondary correctional education provides fodder for critics who oppose providing convicted criminals with free (or low-cost) college courses and degrees, and with a promising new program in the works, the Consortium had to answer the question: Hard working, law-abiding citizens do not get handed a free college education, why should criminals? While this argument may be hard to refute, the bottom line does not come down to fairness or who should get the government handouts. The bottom line comes down to the true cost of crime for our citizens, communities, legal system and corrections system that cannot accurately be computed.

The Correctional Higher Education Consortium struggled with that question and decided that the answer lies at the heart of the partnership; the DOC's mission to "hold offenders accountable and offer opportunities for change while restoring justice for victims and contributing to a safer Minnesota," along with the university's motto of "Excellence and Opportunity." Through many months of discussions, the Consortium changed its name to better fit what it ultimately aims to create: The Partnership for Safer Communities. With a new name and restored sense of purpose, the partners were ready to launch their next educational initiative.

As part of this initiative, offenders were required to make a financial commitment to their own education, and while small, it helped to create a sense of accountability among the participants. The DOC required a $5.00 contribution from each eligible offender to enroll in a print-based course (with remaining costs covered by the IYO federal grant). To offenders, $5.00 could be a week's worth of wages, as they typically earn fifty cents an hour for work assignments and time spent in rehabilitative programming (Minnesota Department of Corrections, 2010).In addition to their $5.00 contribution, offender students pay for all of their own incidentals, including all school supplies. While the offender contribution is small, it is part of the larger goal of making correctional postsecondary education more palatable to the taxpayers and meeting the partnership's goal of reducing recidivism through education and creating safer communities. While the pieces of this new program were being orchestrated, the larger issue of lack of technology resources for the students and the coursework created new challenges.

## Technology and Student Obstacles

One difficulty with not being able to use the Internet to deliver education is that many of our higher education resources are computer-based, from library search engines and research articles to quizzes and tests, not to mention entire courses and degrees. In designing a program that does not rely on technology, the burden was on the university to provide the same rigorous courses that were offered on campus and online, and convince more faculty to participate. In addition to converting courses from online to print, faculty were asked to provide greater flexibility to offender students than they provide to their traditional students.

The special needs of incarcerated students require services and options not available through traditional campus operations. These requirements include:

1. Open-ended semesters (usually up to 9 months) to complete a print-based course;
2. Options for hand-written assignments when computers are not available;
3. Flexibility in meeting deadlines for assignments and exams;
4. Intensive advising and follow-through during admissions and matriculation processes;

5. Signed permission from the offenders providing facility and university staff permission to share FERPA-protected information, including student progress, and individual academic information with family and/or outside advocates;
6. Special matriculation letters to offender students;
7. Campus assistance to navigate university administration from behind bars.

While the perception that offenders have "time on their hands" is true for the most part, their available time is not theirs to do with as they please. Their every movement is dictated for them—when they wake, eat, shower, exercise, work and sleep—and if that schedule is interrupted, they may not be able to complete course assignments or take a proctored exam when it is due. Interruptions to the offenders' daily schedules include unexpected headcounts when offenders stop what they are doing, return to their cells and stand to be counted—until everyone in the facility is accounted for—which in a large facility can sometimes take hours. They may be interrupted by a lock-in, requiring all offenders to stop what they are doing and return to their cells where they must stay for an indefinite period of time until the event has been resolved. During this time, each individual cell is inventoried for contraband items and offenders are allowed out only to shower on a strict schedule. During a lock-in, all educational activity ceases. In order to enroll in a course or keep course materials in their cells, permission is needed from the facility. Offender students must be certain that their course materials are on the list of acceptable items they can maintain in their cells and that they are kept to a minimum. Faculty offering courses through this program were, for the most part, willing and able to accommodate the students' special needs. In a 10-year period, only one course was dropped from the program due to inflexibility of the professor.

## Developing a Low-Tech, High Quality Program

Developing programs that meet university, corrections and accreditation standards require staff and faculty to maintain quality in the curriculum and service to students. Correspondence programs are generally considered to be substandard academic programs and no longer qualify for financial aid under federal student loan guidelines (Higher Education Reauthorization, 2008). Quality online, Internet-based courses and programs, however, have gained credibility by meeting rigorous academic and accreditation standards and are being offered through most universities, including the top research universities like Harvard, MIT, Yale and Stanford. Research on teaching and learning with technology has generated new knowledge and best practices, including the Quality Matters™ Inter-Institutional Quality Assurance in Online Learning.

In order to overcome the perception that the university's correspondence courses would be substandard quality, the partnership focused on developing print-based courses that met quality criteria, as established by the online education community.

Utilizing distance education best-practices and the Quality Matters™ Inter-Institutional Quality Assurance for Online Education rubric, the university staff reverse-engineered online courses into print-based courses. In doing so, they coordinated efforts with DOC education staff to ensure that students had a sound introduction to getting started in their courses and had consistent, quality print-based course materials, textbooks and access to adequate research and reference materials. DOC education staff within the participating facilities created scheduled study hall periods, provided access to inmate and volunteer tutors, and allowed faculty to visit the cohorts throughout the semester to meet students face-to-face, answer questions, and provide assistance with writing projects.

As a subscriber to the Quality Matters program, the university provides training in best practices to faculty in the development of online courses. As a result of this process, students are provided consistent design and delivery of courses. To translate these practices to the print-based model, faculty and staff worked to reverse-engineer online general education courses, attempting to retain the sense of "community" that the professors sought to achieve within the online environment. The result was creation of robust courses that fit the needed delivery model, *sans* technology, with both faculty and students finding greater satisfaction with the results of the reverse-engineering than originally anticipated. A few examples of how the best practices were translated to print courses include:

a.  Faculty included a welcome introduction to the course, including bios of themselves, and asked the students to respond with their own introductions, just as they would in online courses. Many of the faculty teaching in the print-based program visited the cohorts at their facilities during the semester, helping to create connections between the student and faculty and between the student and institution.

b.  Faculty included threaded discussion posts (anonymous) culled from the online composition courses, into the print course. Offender students would respond to the professor's questions as well as to what other students had written in past postings. This approach provided the offender student with a sense of what other students thought and how they had responded to the professor's questions, helping to create a sense of belonging and community.

c.  Online resources and Web pages were printed and videos were played at the facilities (by education staff) in a group setting. Staff, faculty and volunteers would facilitate discussions on the materials during study hall time, creating group discussion opportunities.

d.  Research materials and other student resources were forwarded to the facility library where students could check them out. The correctional facility libraries also participated in the interlibrary loan system with local libraries to provide additional access.

e.  To provide assessment and accountability for the program, student assessment data, progress and achievement was tracked each semester in order to meet programmatic outcomes.

f.  Having students work in cohorts provided opportunity for group projects that had been developed for the online and traditional classroom.

## Institutional Accommodations

The support needed to provide this level of service to students, faculty and the facilities required the hiring of a one halftime graduate assistant to serve as the day-to-day point person. Each correctional facility that participated in the program devoted staff time to assisting students in the cohorts and providing needed coordination with the university.

Considerations and accommodations required of both partners (the university and the correctional facilities) were to use digital tools, including e-mail, scanned PDF documents, and the campus course management system, as frequently as possible to facilitate communication and speed the sending and receiving of assignments and exams. Daily and weekly e-mail communication between facility education directors and the university helped to clarify questions on assignments and exams. Offenders would submit a question or problem they had with a course on a "kite" (a form used by offenders for paper communications within the facilities) and the education office personnel would e-mail the question from the offender to the Pathways graduate assistant, who would either respond to the question or pass it along to

the professor. While it may seem more efficient to have the facility personnel contact the professor directly, having the single point-of-contact at the university actually saved time, as faculty are not always available to answer e-mails in a timely fashion. The university's support staff could triage the problems and determine whether they were of an administrative nature or academic nature. Having the course syllabi and exams at hand, this person was familiar with the course material and could answer, or track down the professor to get an answer quickly.

Test proctoring was an additional point of concern within the facilities and for the faculty members. The DOC determined that given the increasing number of students in the print-based program, the staff requirements for proctoring tests was becoming unmanageable. As a solution, they set up regular group testing times during the week and students who had prepared to take an exam could test during scheduled periods. Permission was given for some courses to provide the facility education staff with the scoring key to score exams immediately, thereby reducing time for the exam to be returned to the university by mail to be scored and returned. At one point in time, staff discussed the idea of allowing offenders to take the online version of an exam within the security of the course management system under close supervision of a corrections officer, but the DOC was unable to allow even supervised access to the Internet, out of security concerns.

## FUTURE RESEARCH DIRECTIONS

The role that corrections plays in community will always be of concern to our neighborhoods, cities, states, nation—and, particularly, to our politicians. But what is missing from this equation is the role that technology can and should play in the management and rehabilitation of offenders. Technologies have been developed to track sex offenders nationally and across state borders, but it took tragedy and the effort of committed individuals to make the technology and funding happen. There is no driving force behind making education accessible to convicted felons, and there is even less money being put into developing the technologies that would make it a safe and affordable product. Education would not be the only beneficiary of these advances; workforce development could play an important role in allowing offenders to search for and connect with potential employers before they are even released. The potential for innovative technology in prisoner re-entry and rehabilitation efforts could make tremendous strides in advancing the mission of our corrections systems. Additionally, secure and affordable synchronous technologies could provide desperately needed services to connect children with their incarcerated parents. "In addition to lowering the likelihood of recidivism among incarcerated parents, there is evidence that maintaining contact with one's incarcerated parent improves a child's emotional response to the incarceration and supports parent-child attachment" (Family and Corrections Network, 2010, n.p.).

Many states recognize that offering youthful offenders behavioral treatment combined with education results in offenders who are better behaved while incarcerated, creating safer and more manageable prisons, and with increased employability upon release leads to lower recidivism rates. Ideally, these measures save taxpayer money and create safer communities. This outcome is not something that correctional institutions can create in a vacuum; it takes a common belief and a common goal working with community and state organizations to make these programs effective on the outside. This community support includes local workforce centers, prisoner re-entry programs, and housing initiatives with landlords and educational institutions willing to look beyond what has been to what could be.

The sustainability of the Pathways Program for Incarcerated Students partnership with the DOC has always been vulnerable to outside forces, including state lawmakers, the federal government, and the state college and university system. And while much of the success of this partnership has been built on the passion and commitment of individual staff members, the foundation of the partnership has changed the culture of both institutions, helping to maintain its viability after individual members of the original partnership have moved on. Infrastructures built on efficiency and economies are well documented within both institutions that support its longevity and sustainability.

## CONCLUSION

This partnership has weathered budget cuts and changes in political climate for over 40 years while continuing to provide incarcerated students access to higher education. Working toward the ultimate goal of creating safer communities through reduced recidivism, it will take the efforts of individuals at all levels to educate our citizens and politicians on the benefits to our communities from this type of programming. While the efforts of individuals within these two organizations were successful, the bureaucratic workarounds and creativity required were monumental. The inability to use technology to provide cost-effective education to many geographically dispersed students indicates that as a society, we cannot yet trust available technologies to provide offender access to family, education and jobs while providing safety and security for our citizens. What will make programs and partnerships like this successful in the future is the openness of corrections, education and innovative technology partners to reexamine technology's role and allow for changes in operational procedures that can satisfy the needs of all our societal stakeholders.

# REFERENCES

Anderson, R. (1999, October 14). Native Americans and the digital divide. *The Digital Beat, 1*, 1.

Batiluk, M. E., Moke, P., & Wilcox Rountree, P. (1997). Crime and rehabilitation: Correctional education as an agent of change - a research note. *Justice Quarterly, 14*(1), 167–180. doi:10.1080/07418829700093261

Chappell, C. A. (2004). Post-secondary correctional education and recidivism: A meta-analysis of research conducted 1990-1999. *Journal of Correctional Education, 55*(2), 148–169.

Clendenen, R. J., Ellingston, J. R., & Severson, R. J. (1979). Project newgate: The first five years. *Crime and Delinquency, 25*(1), 55–64. doi:10.1177/001112877902500104

Cullen, F., & Gendreau, P. (2000). Assessing correctional rehabilitation: Policy, practice, and prospects. In J. Horney (Ed.), *Criminal justice 2000, vol. 3: Policies, processes, and decisions of the criminal justice system* (pp. 109-175). Washington, DC: National Institute of Justice, U.S. Department of Justice.

Erisman, W., & Contardo, J. B. (2005). *Learning to reduce recidivism: A 50-state analysis of post-secondary correctional education policy.* Institute for Higher Education Policy report.

Family and Corrections Network. (2010). *Children and families of the incarcerated fact sheet.* The National Resource Center on Children and Families of the Incarcerated, Family and Corrections Network. Retrieved July 7, 2010, from http://fcnetwork.org/wp/wp-content/uploads/fact-sheet.pdf

Gladieux, L. E. (2000). Global on-line learning: Hope or hype? *Higher Education in Europe, 25*(3), 351–353. doi:10.1080/03797720020015953

Knapp, L. G., Kelly-Reid, J. E., & Ginder, S. A. (2009). *Enrollment in postsecondary institutions, Fall 2007, graduation rates, 2001 &2004 cohorts, and financial statistics, fiscal year 2007 (NCES 2009-155). National Center for Education Statistics, Institute of Education Sciences, U.* Washington, DC: S. Department of Education.

MacNamara, D. E. (1977). Medical models in corrections–requiescat in pace. *Criminology, 14*(4), 439–448. doi:10.1111/j.1745-9125.1977.tb00036.x

McCarty, H. J. (2006). Educating felons: Reflections on higher education in prison. *Radical History Review, 96*, 87–94. doi:10.1215/01636545-2006-005

Michigan Department of Corrections. (2010). Retrieved July 5, 2010, from http://www.michigan.gov/corrections/0,1607,7-119--201925--,00.html

Minnesota Department of Corrections. (2010). *Offender assignment and compensation plan.* Directive 204.010. Retrieved February 20, 2010, from http://www.doc.state.mn.us/DocPolicy2/Document/204.010.htm

Offender Information Services. (2008). *The programme for offender learning and resettlement information services is being installed in pilot prisons.* British National Management of Offender Services, Ministry of Justice. Retrieved July 5, 2010, from http://estep.iscavision.com/uploads/polaris.pdf?PHPSESSID=01e5f3fe3058ac39e5b88edbdc903e8f Page, J. (2004). Eliminating the enemy: The import of denying prisoners access to higher education in Clinton's America. *Punishment and Society, 6*(4), 357-378.

Rainie, L. (2010, January 5). *Internet, broadband and cell phone statistics.* Pew Internet & American Life Project, (p. 4). Retrieved February 15, 2010, from http://www.pewinternet.org/Reports/2010/Internet-broadband-and-cell-phone-statistics.aspx?r=1

Ubah, C. B., & Robinson, R. L. (2003). A grounded look at the debate over prison-based education: Optimistic theory versus pessimistic worldview. *The Prison Journal, 83*(2), 115–129. doi:10.1177/0032885503083002001

University of Chicago Library, Special Collections Research Center. (2010). William Rainey Harper, the University of Chicago faculty, a centennial view. Retrieved July 7, 2010, from http://www.lib. uchicago.edu/e/spcl/centcat/fac/facch01_01.html

U.S. Department of Education. (2010). *Grants to states for workplace and community transition training for incarcerated youth offenders.* Retrieved February 25, 2010, from http://www2. ed.gov/programs/transitiontraining/ index.html

West, H. C., & Sabol, W. J. (2009). *Prison inmates at midyear 2008, statistical tables.* U.S. Department of Justice, Office of Justice Programs, National Prisoner Statistics. Retrieved February 20, 2010, from http://bjs.ojp.usdoj.gov/content/ pub/pdf/pim08st.pdf

## ENDNOTE

[1]   The federal IYO funds provide "grants to state correctional education agencies to assist and encourage incarcerated youths [aged 25 years of age and younger and within 5 years of release] to acquire functional literacy, life, and job skills through the pursuit of postsecondary education certificates, associate of arts degrees, and bachelor's degrees" (U.S. Department of Education, 2010).

# Chapter 24
# Using Photovoice with NGO Workers in Sierra Leone:
## A Case for Community–Based Research

**Ashley Walker**
*Georgia Southern University, USA*

**Jody Oomen-Early**
*Walden University, USA*

## ABSTRACT

*Sierra Leone currently has one of the highest child mortality rates in the world. Among those children who have the greatest chance of survival are those who have access to life's basic needs. Because the government of Sierra Leone does not provide child welfare programming, non-governmental organizations (NGOs) are often lifelines for millions of children. Few studies have explored the barriers facing these NGOs or have used participatory action research methods to do so. This case study serves agencies working to address barriers to individual and community health in war-torn and developing countries. This research also makes a case for using technology as a tool for community engagement and empowerment. This chapter will highlight the findings of a participatory action research study and describe how Photovoice can be used to build community capacity and mobilize communities, organizations, and governments to bring about social change.*

## PROJECT HISTORY AND CONTEXT

Sierra Leone, a West African country, is one of the world's least developed countries and has one of the highest child mortality rates in the world

DOI: 10.4018/978-1-60960-623-7.ch024

(United Nations Development Programme, 2007). Sierra Leone is recovering from a decade long civil war which resulted in thousands of fatalities and orphaned and abandoned children (United Nations International Children's Emergency Fund [UNICEF], n.d.). Despite the poor health indicators reported by Sierra Leone, there is a paucity of research that explores the barriers and impacts to child health and development for the millions of orphaned and abandoned children living there. It is necessary to examine the barriers to child health from an ecological standpoint, which includes the sociological, economic, environmental, political, and cultural aspects of society.

The Sierra Leonean government does not provide support for child welfare programming; therefore, care provided by non-governmental organizations (NGOs) is vital to child survival. Recommendations in the literature support the need for action-based research to evaluate services provided by organizations that provide care to children, but prior to this project no known research of this kind was completed (De Jong & Kleber, 2007; Denov & Maclure, 2006). Because of the role these agencies play in child survival, NGOs should be willing to engage in participatory action research to improve upon these services. The purpose of this research was multi-fold: first, to examine factors that impede and promote the health and well-being of orphaned and abandoned children in Sierra Leone; second, to facilitate Photovoice, a participatory action research method, among NGO workers to identify barriers to care giving for orphaned and abandoned children; and third, to use digital technology to build organizational and community capacity to bring about social change. The researchers became acquainted with an international NGO in Freetown, Sierra Leone, during the summer of 2007. After discussions with the executive director about the barriers and challenges of caring for abandoned and orphaned children in a war-torn country and the global community's lack of awareness of these issues, the idea of participatory research emerged as a mechanism to explore these problems further and develop a plan to address the barriers. Participatory research emerged as a way to assess the needs of the community and build academic alliances within and outside of the country. The researchers and executive director agreed upon the plan to complete a Photovoice project in 2008.

Photovoice is a method developed by Dr. Caroline Wang and Mary Ann Burris, and was first used with the Yunnan Women's Reproductive Health and Development Program (Wang & Burris, 1997). Historically, this technique has been used to organize communities to address specific health issues among diverse and often vulnerable populations. Photovoice is emerging as a significant research tool in global health and it supports the objectives of Participatory Action Research (PAR) because individuals come together to identify factors contributing to social problems and organize to initiate change (Wang, Morrel-Samuels, Hutchinson, Bell, & Pestronk, 2004).

Wang and Burris present a nine-step methodology to help carry out the goals of Photovoice. These steps include: recruiting participants, selecting a target audience of community members, obtaining informed consent, conducting a training session, brainstorming with participants, distributing cameras, allowing time to take photographs, meeting to discuss photographs, and creating a plan for change (Wang & Burris, 1997). To complete this research project, we followed the methodology steps highlighted by Drs. Wang and Burris.

According to Wang (2006), Photovoice projects should include a sample of six to ten participants. To follow this recommendation, the researchers recruited ten caregivers employed by the NGO in Freetown. The participants were all natives of Sierra Leone, English-speaking, and included the two administrative directors, teachers, nurses, a security guard, childcare workers and childcare support staff at the Center.

In the spring of 2008, one of the researchers traveled to Freetown, Sierra Leone, to facilitate the project. Upon arrival, the researcher led a four-hour training session with the ten participants. During this session, the participants learned about Photovoice and signed informed consent forms. They were instructed to obtain verbal and written consent prior to taking an individual's photograph. The participants maintain ownership of their photographs; therefore, the researcher obtained consent to publish their photographs. This protocol aligns with consent protocol followed in other studies employing Photovoice (Wang & Pies, 2004). This project was approved by the researchers' institutional review board and by the executive director of the NGO.

## The Use of Technology as a Catalyst

Photovoice methodology is supported by three goals: (1) to record everyday realities through the use of photography, (2) to promote dialogue about a community's weaknesses and strengths, and (3) to reach policy makers (Wang & Burris, 1997). Photovoice is grounded in Paulo Freire's Empowerment Theory, as it allows participants to listen, to dialogue, and to engage others living the experience (Freire, 1970). Empowerment changes communities not only by influencing its members to examine the changes needed at the community level, but also by providing members the tools to create change within their own lives (Wallerstein & Bernstein, 1988).

The researchers raised funds to purchase the digital cameras used to complete the Photovoice project and disseminated them to the participants at the training session. Each of the ten caregivers was given a Nikon Coolpix battery-operated camera. The researcher trained the caregivers to operate the Nikons. The caregivers were given seven days to take photographs to address these primary research questions: (1) what factors impede the health and well-being of orphaned and abandoned children in Sierra Leone?, (2) what role/s do NGOs play in the care of the children?, and (3) how can NGOs work together to improve upon the care provided to these children? After seven days, the caregivers returned the cameras to the researcher and the researcher downloaded the digital images to her laptop. The photographs were projected on the laptop screen as the participants and the researcher reviewed them.

After completing Wang's (2006) prescribed Photovoice methodology, the researcher then asked the participants to choose at least four photographs to discuss through in-depth interviews. Participants contextualized their photographs using the SHOWeD method (Wang & Pies, 2004). SHOWeD provides a question outline to improve the ability of the caregiver to illustrate each photograph's story. The questions include (a) What do you see here?, (b) What is really happening here?, (c) How does this relate to our lives?, (d) Why does this problem or strength exist?, and (e) What can we do about it (Wang & Burris, 1997)? The photographs were analyzed with help from the participants. The researcher used a digital audio recorder to record the follow-up interviews. During this portion of the study, each participant identified the common themes or theories that were found in his or her photographs (Wang, 2006; Wang & Burris, 1997). The photographs were organized into folders and stored on a 4 GB flashdrive. The researchers reviewed the interviews and themes identified by the caregivers. A final analysis was provided to the executive director of the NGO and was shared with the participants and the NGO board. After the executive director, board members, and participants reviewed the findings, the researchers, along with the director and NGO workers, developed an action plan to address some of the barriers identified and to strengthen the organization to bring about necessary social change.

Putting technology into the hands of the most vulnerable populations may seem counter to addressing their basic survival needs, but it is actually through technology that communities may benefit from increasing their social and economic capacity rather than further the "Digital Divide" (Vidyasagar, 2006). In this research study, the use of technology engaged community and organizational members in the process of social change and enabled participants to capture their lived experiences and perceived barriers to care giving for orphaned and abandoned children in Sierra Leone. Using technology brought academicians and community and organizational members together for a unifying purpose; digital photography as a medium provided caregivers and native Sierra Leoneans with a "voice" to share their worldview and highlight socio-ecological factors, which they perceived influenced the country's high infant and child mortality rates and served as roadblocks to caregivers. The idea to initiate social change through participatory methods and technology is not new to the field of global health. Rifkin (2003) further explained, "In a study undertaken by WHO and UNICEF in 1974, examples showed that both at national and 'grassroots' levels, a focus on the poor and community participation in healthcare also contributed to positive health outcomes" (p.168).

The caregivers were able to digitally photograph places and themes that reflected their voices and stories. The lived experiences as captured by the caregivers might not be heard otherwise. Because the researchers were not native to Sierra Leone, the photographs taken by the caregivers would be impossible for the researchers to capture. As Baker and Wang (2006) explain, "It [Photovoice] is structured as a mechanism to engage participants in group discussions about their images and to present these images in public forums" (p. 1408). The main goals of Photovoice are to engage people in active listening and dialogue. As Baker and Wang (2006) note, Photovoice creates a safe environment for introspection and critical reflection, and moves people toward action. Technology created a more immediate response to the research questions. The digital photographs provided visual representation of the information provided during the interview portion of Photovoice. By claiming a "voice" through photography, participants were empowered and engaged in generating both awareness and social change.

## Limitations of Technology and the Project

Though the use of digital technology allowed the caregivers to illustrate their story through photography, the project did not come without its limitations. First, most of the participants had never used a digital camera prior to this project; therefore, extra time was needed during the training session to demonstrate the use of the camera. Because of the complexity of the camera, the researcher was only able to teach the caregivers how to turn the camera on and off, and how to take a picture, view the picture using the review feature, and delete the picture if needed. Second, because most of the participants had never used a digital camera before, some pictures were discarded due to clarity and quality issues.

Third, digital technology is often dependent upon access to electricity and in Freetown electricity is still considered a luxury for many. The NGO is powered by the National Power Authority (NPA) of Sierra Leone; however, in an attempt to conserve energy NPA disconnects power when necessary. When NPA "cuts power" the NGO depends on its generators, which are dependent on fuel, and in Freetown fuel is expensive. To minimize the problems associated with the limited access to electricity, the researchers invested in battery operated digital cameras. This did limit problems associated with the digital cameras, but the researcher used a laptop to download pictures; therefore, she was still dependent upon access to electricity. During the photograph review session, the NGO lost power at the beginning of the day. The researcher relied on the laptop's internal battery and NGO's generator for electricity, but this did cause a slight delay in data collection.

Finally, taking photographs can be viewed as invasive to some cultures. Sensitive cultures both domestic and international exist and it is important for researchers to be aware of this. In this project, participants did not report any issues related to culture sensitivity; however, they did report being approached and questioned about why the photographs were taken. The acceptance of this project in this city was largely due to the participants being natives to Sierra Leone. If the researchers facilitating this project tried to capture the photographs taken by the caregivers, it is possible that community members would not have been as accepting.

## Example of Photographs

According to the interviews and photographs taken by the caregivers, extreme poverty lies at the heart of the impeding factors affecting the health of the orphaned and abandoned children in Sierra Leone. According to the caregivers, extreme poverty in Sierra Leone is linked to poor sanitation, overcrowding, limited access to education and medical services, limited access to life's most basic needs (including water, food, and shelter), child labor exploitation, and abandonment and neglect. See figures 1 and 2 for examples of photographs taken by the NGO caregivers representing limited access to water.

All ten participants discussed the shortage of clean, running water in Sierra Leone, as about half of the citizens of Freetown do not have access to clean drinking water (World Health Organization, 2006a). The limitation of clean drinking water contributes to dehydration and intestinal diseases such as diarrhea, cholera, and typhoid that are linked to 20% of infant and child mortality rates (World Health Organization, 2006b).

The inadequate dwellings seen in Freetown also contribute to child mortality because the homes are not safe and provide little security from airborne and vector-borne infections. Pneumonia and malaria cause 25% and 12% of child and infant deaths respectively (World Health Organization, 2006b). Figure 3 illustrates an example of inadequate shelter seen in Freetown.

The caregiver who took this photograph describes this picture in detail.

*Figure 1. Waiting for water*

*Figure 2. Fetching water from a well*

*Figure 3. A self-constructed home*

*This is a picture of a house I took at the bay. This place is normally not supposed to be a dwelling place for people. Due to the post-war effect in our country, due to the rebel war, [sic] so many people came down to our town, as a result so many of them do not have places to sleep. This is a self-construction of house they have made for themselves. As you can see these are empty bags of rice, and some with plastic for windows. This is Funkia Bay.*

## Value of Project in Forming Community Partnerships

Community development and community participation are advancing as effective techniques in public health interventions. A problem seen in global health is the implementation of strategies that reach only a small group of people. Community partnerships increase the likelihood that public health programming will be community-based, instead of 'placed' interventions. This project exemplified the qualities of action research because it allowed those living the experience an opportunity to tell their story through the use of digital photography. According to the interview responses, the caregivers see the importance of governmental support to improve the health and wellbeing of orphans in Sierra Leone, but support and motivation must also be well represented within the community for change to be successful. The comment below by one of the caregivers represents the discussion surrounding change at the grassroots level.

Participant F:

*. . . something really needs to be done, something fast. Because we are in the 21st century [sic] otherwise we are never going to catch up and we need to catch up. There needs to be the political will on the part of our leaders and maybe the people themselves living in these communities to think positive and wish to get ahead. It rests on us to want to do something better with our lives, our*

*leaders should provide the necessary environment so that we can do those things.*

## Community Impact of the Project

By using Photovoice, the researchers were able to open dialogue and encourage participants to reflect on current problems as well as suggest possible solutions for Sierra Leone. All ten participants discussed the need for more governmental accountability and interventions by international governments; however, all agreed that dependence on these agencies should not be as great as the dependence on each other in the community. The participants all agreed that change must happen at the grassroots level.

Prior to this study, the participating NGO was focused on educating and empowering the 60 children it could accommodate; the mission of the organization did not mention empowerment or see its reach beyond the center. Following participation in the study, however, the NGO was able to fully realize its potential and impact on the entire country—not just the local community. The organization changed its mission to expand services beyond just the children living at the center. Board members established plans to build a medical center, a larger school to include children in the outlying areas who were not living at the center, and an occupational component to help empower young women and mothers trying to care for their children. The executive director of the NGO was asked what she envisioned resulting from this project. She responded:

*I would love to reach people who can catch sight of the vision for changing the future for the country of Sierra Leone. I somehow want to reach the core group of people who can really understand that we must take action and that it is POSSIBLE. To me, we need Sierra Leoneans and people in other countries to really join together on this. Without Sierra Leoneans "buying into the dream," it will never be accomplished. So we need to continue educating and recruiting more Sierra Leoneans to the "cause" along with the international community coming along to support with funds and other resources to make change happen.*

## Educational Impact of the Project

The Institute of Medicine has identified community-based participatory research as one of the eight new content areas in which all schools of public health should offer training (Minkler & Wallerstein, 2008). Photovoice is an innovative method often applied to community-based participatory research; therefore, engaging both undergraduate and graduate students enrolled in a variety of programs in the process could empower them to share the technique within their own communities, open dialogue, instigate social change, and build community capacity.

## Value of the Project for the Educational Institution

Partnerships between educational institutions and communities can prove to be beneficial for both entities. When an educational institution shares resources with a community in need, it provides the necessary resources to address the critical issues assessed within the community (Bringle & Hatcher, 2002). An effective community partnership will move beyond data-driven initiatives to ignite a greater social and civic engagement to improve student-learning outcomes and improve the community's quality of life (Bringle & Hatcher, 2002). According to Benson, Harkavy, and Puckett (2000), campus-community relationships are typically one-dimensional where faculty are viewed as elitist. This Photovoice project exemplifies how community-based research can create successful partnerships that are more collaborative, constructing community-based public health interventions to improve the health and well-being of target audiences. It led to an awakening within the aca-

demic unit to promote more global, participatory research using technology.

## Best Practices for Forming Community Partnerships

Suggested best practices and strategies resulting from this research include:

- Universities and community agencies can establish social alliances with underdeveloped countries and diverse populations by providing individuals with the tools and technology necessary to bring about social change.
- Vulnerable populations are willing and able to use technology to bring about this change and to share their "voice."
- Community alliances and projects must offer real, long-lasting benefits to the community. Participatory action research involves working toward sustainable community-based solutions.
- Researchers must be willing to listen and to engage community members in dialogue. All stakeholders should have some ownership in the process and in the project.
- One-sided agendas are a disservice to the community. If the proposed project does not have value or buy-in from the community members, it is doomed to fail.
- Trust is essential. This takes time to build and sincerity and effort to maintain.
- Change does not happen overnight. All parties involved must understand that change takes time.

By participating in this Photovoice project, the NGO board members and staff were able to determine what they were doing well in comparison to other local NGOs. They were also able to realize their potential for impacting the entire country, not just the children in their care. The caregivers, along with the executive director, wanted to build upon the organization's strengths to continue improving services provided to orphaned and abandoned children in Sierra Leone. In addition, they were able to move forward with an affirmation that Sierra Leoneans were the solution: by increasing awareness and providing a platform for Sierra Leoneans to share and advocate, change for the entire country is possible. Since the project's completion, the center has taken these steps to improve the health and well-being of the children in Sierra Leone: (1) sought and obtained school accreditation, and (2) provided support to the center's nurse as she seeks her midwife certification. Both steps are important to creating lasting change in Freetown. By seeking and obtaining school accreditation, the center is now able to offer basic school education to children not living at the center. This effort will increase the number of children in Freetown who have access to basic education and it will decrease the illiteracy rate documented in Sierra Leone. When the center's nurse completes her midwifery certification, she will be able to provide emergency maternal care to the women of Sierra Leone. This effort will combat the high infant and maternal mortality rates that plague this country.

Creating social change not only "takes a village" but an engaged global community as well. Community health is about working together and empowering people to help themselves. Change is not a didactic process where professionals, who claim to know what is best, reign over those who are most in need. Everyone plays an important role in improving quality of life on a global scale. We challenge you to adopt this mind-set, and as you work with others toward this common goal, and lead in the spirit of unity, so eloquently described in this ancient Chinese text:

Tao of Leadership
Go to the people
Live with them
Love them
Learn from them

Start with what they have
Build on what they know.
But of the best leaders
When their task is accomplished
Their work is done
The people will all remark
We have done it ourselves.
—Lao Tzu, from *The Tao of Leadership* (ancient Chinese text)
(as cited in Doyle, Ward, & Oomen-Early, 2010, p. 359).

## REFERENCES

Baker, T., & Wang, C. (2006). Photovoice: Use of a participatory action research method to explore the chronic pain experience in older adults. *Qualitative Health Research, 16*(10), 1405–1413. doi:10.1177/1049732306294118

Benson, L., Harkavy, I., & Puckett, J. (2000). An implementation revolution as a strategy for fulfilling the democratic promise of university-community partnerships: Penn-West Philadelphia as an experiment in progress. *Nonprofit and Voluntary Sector Quarterly, 29*(1), 24–45. doi:10.1177/0899764000291003

Bringle, R., & Hatcher, J. (2002). Campus-community partnerships: The terms of engagement. *The Journal of Social Issues, 58*(3), 503–516. doi:10.1111/1540-4560.00273

De Jong, K., & Kleber, R. (2007). Emergency conflict-related psychosocial interventions in Sierra Leone and Uganda: Lessons from Médecins Sans Frontiéres. *Journal of Health Psychology, 12*(3), 485–497. doi:10.1177/1359105307076235

Denov, M., & Maclure, R. (2006). Engaging the voices of girls in the aftermath of Sierra Leone's conflict: Experiences and perspectives in a culture of violence. *Anthropologica, 48*(1), 73–85. doi:10.2307/25605298

Doyle, E., Ward, S., & Oomen-Early, J. (2010). *The process of community health education and promotion* (2nd ed.). Longgrove, IL: Waveland Press.

Freire, P. (1970). *Pedagogy of the oppressed.* New York, NY: Continuum.

Minkler, M., & Wallerstein, N. (2008). *Community-based participatory research for health: From process to outcomes* (2nd ed.). San Francisco, CA: Jossey-Bass Publishers.

Rifkin, S. B. (2003). A framework linking community empowerment and health equity: It is a matter of choice. *Journal of Health, Population, and Nutrition, 21*(3), 168–180.

United Nations Development Programme. (2007). *Measuring human development: A primer: Guidelines and tools for statistical research, analysis and advocacy.* Retrieved May 24, 2008, from http://hdr.undp.org/en/media/Primer_complete.pdf

United Nations International Children's Emergency Fund. (n.d.). *At a glance: Sierra Leone.* Retrieved September 17, 2007, from http://www.unicef.org/infobycountry/sierraleone.html

Vidyasagar, D. (2006). Digital divide and digital dividend in the age of information technology. *Journal of Perinatology, 26*(5), 313–315. doi:10.1038/sj.jp.7211494

Wallerstein, N., & Bernstein, E. (1988). Empowerment education: Freire's adapted to health education. *Health Education & Behavior, 15*(4), 379–394. doi:10.1177/109019818801500402

Wang, C. (2006). Youth participation in photovoice as a strategy for community change. *Journal of Community Practice, 14*(1-2), 147–161. doi:10.1300/J125v14n01_09

Wang, C., Morrel-Samuels, S., Hutchison, P., Bell, L., & Pestronk, R. (2004). Flint Photovoice: Community building among youths, adults, and policymakers. *American Journal of Public Health, 94*(6), 911–913. doi:10.2105/AJPH.94.6.911

Wang, C., & Pies, C. (2004). Family, maternal, and child health through photovoice. *Maternal and Child Health Journal, 8*(2), 95–102. doi:10.1023/B:MACI.0000025732.32293.4f

Wang, C. C., & Burris, M. (1997). Photovoice: Concept, methodology, and use for participatory needs assessment. *Health Education & Behavior, 24*(3), 369–387. doi:10.1177/109019819702400309

World Health Organization. (2006a). *Health action in crises.* Sierra Leone: Retrieved September 19, 2007, from http://www.who.int/hac/crises/sle/background/ 2004/SierraLeone_June06.pdf

World Health Organization. (2006b). *Mortality country fact sheet 2006: Sierra Leone.* Retrieved May 24, 2008, from http://www.who.int/whosis/mort/profiles/mort_afro_sle_sierraleone.pdf

# Chapter 25

# From Collision to Collaboration:
## An Expanded Role for Project Evaluators in the Development of Interactive Media

**Karla Saari Kitalong**
*Michigan Technological University, USA*

## ABSTRACT

*In traditional software, hardware, and program development processes, the project evaluator has been relegated to a peripheral role at the end of the process. Today's complex interactive media projects require a different evaluation model, one that situates the project evaluator firmly at the center. From this vantage point, the evaluator subtly guides a technologically sophisticated integration of people, institutions, technologies, and cultural assumptions. Instead of the summative role—verifying that milestones and objectives have been met—the 21st-century evaluator is cast in a formative role as a problem finder. From this vantage point he or she not only confirms that project goals and objectives have been met, but also evaluates collaborative processes and facilitates collaborations among the myriad stakeholders.*

## INTRODUCTION

### Scene

It's early December. About 20 people have assembled in Orlando for the annual two-day meeting of the *Water's Journey through the Everglades* (*WJE*) development team. *WJE* is a series of interactive learning experiences that, when complete, will help bring to life the biology, history, and geography of the Florida Everglades for visitors to a South Florida science center. The project is funded by the National Science Foundation.

DOI: 10.4018/978-1-60960-623-7.ch025

## Attendees

The development team is large and diverse. Twenty people are in the room at any given time; they include three co-principal investigators, the project's operations manager, an audio expert, and five representatives of the science center that will house the themed experiences (the director, educational advisors, and youth coordinators). The graduate research assistants who design and build the interactive experiences drift in and out as their class schedules allow. The group also includes three project evaluators: the author, a university faculty member charged with formative evaluation; and two professional evaluators charged with summative evaluation. Although not physically present at the table, the thousands of target audience members—middle school students, their parents, their teachers, and other potential visitors to the museum—are on everyone's minds. Counting these virtual stakeholders, it's standing room only in the double conference room at the Media Convergence Lab on the campus of the University of Central Florida.

## Agenda

Officially, the meeting was convened so the different groups could update one another on overall progress. Although information flows back and forth across the Internet throughout the year, this annual meeting brings the far-flung teams together for a face-to-face, two-day work session. The designers showcase the latest versions of the interactive kiosks and demonstrate new technologies that might be used. The museum personnel and principal investigators revisit the rhetorical situation—the audience, purpose, and context—for which the kiosks are being designed, as well as referring to the content requirements, examining the architectural plans and space constraints, and consulting the construction timetable. The evaluators cite relevant literature and interject with findings concerning middle school students'

expressed likes and dislikes to generate ideas for future assessment protocols.

The above description, while factually accurate, doesn't begin to capture the energetic and collaborative spirit of the meeting. In particular, it glosses over those generative moments when team members' different backgrounds and goals collide. This chapter examines several such moments of collision in two related realms—the technological and the interpersonal—to highlight the collaborative opportunities they open up for designers of complex virtual environments.

## CONTEXT: VIRTUAL ENVIRONMENTS FOR INFORMAL LEARNING

Two virtual environments are featured: *WJE* and an earlier interactive museum prototype, *Journey with Sea Creatures* (*JwSC*), designed in 2003 and 2004. Both environments employ mixed-reality technology (sometimes called augmented reality), in which virtual reality and real life come together through the medium of the computer screen to create an immersive experience for participants. (See Kitalong, Moody, Middlebrook, & Ancheta, 2009, for a full description of *JwSC*'s mixed reality elements.)

The completed *JwSC* prototype was pilot tested for about 10 days in October 2004 at the Orlando Science Center (OSC). Just before the prototype was installed at OSC, I was invited to design and carry out an on-site assessment, which I did. At the time, I knew very little about the assessment of informal learning, but my background in usability testing provided a starting point. Well-established methods exist for assessing both product usability and formal (school-based) learning; in contrast, few tried-and-true methods exist for evaluating museum-based technologies and the informal learning they facilitate (Falk & Dierking, 2000; Hooper-Greenhill, 1994b). Undaunted, I mobilized a team of undergraduate and graduate students, and we spent several days observing how museum visitors interacted with the *JwSC* prototype; the results of that study are published in Kitalong, Moody, Middlebrook, & Ancheta, 2009.

## THE AHA! MOMENT

Toward the end of the pilot-testing period, OSC advisory board members and other interested parties were invited to an afternoon focus group at the center to discuss their receptivity to *JwSC* and other similar exhibits. After watching and talking to visitors as they interacted with *JwSC* and other nearby exhibits, the focus group gathered in a conference room. Sometime during the meeting, I noted the following brief but enlightening conversation:

**Advisory Board Member**: "So, tell me about the learning objectives for this project."
**Lead Technical Guy**: "Hmmm, I don't think we had any learning objectives."

Of course, *JwSC* had learning objectives, which the project leader was quick to elaborate. But the technical developers had been so caught up with experimenting with the seductive technology that they virtually ignored their obvious role in sculpting what the visitors learned about Florida's prehistory.

When high-technology workers, including developers of interactive experiences, become mesmerized by the technologies they work with, they lose sight of the rhetorical context into which the technologies must fit. Museum personnel, on the other hand, care **primarily** about the rhetorical context, along with the content and the learning activated by the experience. This impending collision of goals, objectives, and values might have been noticed before the pilot testing phase, had the development process incorporated a systematic program of formative evaluation. Formative evalu-

ation consists of a series of interim evaluations designed to track how well a developing product adheres to key goals and objectives. In the ideal scenario, representatives of the target audience are recruited to assist with the interim evaluations, which can take many forms, from brainstorming and sketching to interacting with prototypes. In the case of *JwSC*, formative evaluations implemented as part of a comprehensive user-centered design process, would have exposed representative audience members to early prototypes—as early as the paper-and-pencil stage—to see how well they liked the product, could understand its interface, and could relate to and learn from its content. Unfortunately, the *JwSC* development team adhered to a more traditional model that relegated evaluation to a summative role at the end of the development process, thereby limiting what developers might learn from representative users along the way.

User-centered design and formative evaluation take time and are "messy," in that they can disrupt or even derail the development trajectory. On the other hand, traditional product development processes appear well organized, largely because they are centered on the controllable and predictable needs of the developers, rather than on the diverse and largely unpredictable preferences of the users. Projects employing a traditional (or formal) design process are divided into discrete components, with each component the responsibility of a semi-autonomous individual or team. In this type of assembly-line project management model, the teams work independently and in parallel, guided by a set of specifications, a schedule, and a work-flow diagram, with different teams' tasks carefully synchronized to begin and end as dictated by the schedule (Prasad, 1998). Yet this very organized structure places certain limitations on the developers. For example, reflection and rethinking are strongly discouraged lest they derail the coordinated schedule, which means that time for formative evaluation can seldom be allowed. Evaluation is something that happens late in the development cycle (if at all), and thus necessarily has a summative rather than a formative function. In other words, once the specs have been put into place, traditional development processes do not interrogate the user experience until the product is nearly market ready.

Formal process models rely on discrete teams working in parallel and adhering to preset milestones, in order to produce an on-time end product that meets rigid specifications. A manager coordinates the work by communicating with team leaders, who in turn supervise the teams. They work in a hierarchical manner that Panitz would define as cooperative rather than collaborative. Cooperative work is a "structure of interaction designed to facilitate the accomplishment of a specific end product or goal through people working together in groups" (Panitz, 1997). Cooperative design, Panitz adds, is "more directive than a collaborative system of governance and closely controlled" (Panitz, 1997). This sort of model is well established and works well in many cases, but it has one significant drawback: "[B]y imposing a structure that fixes a series of distinct steps in a project, formal process models of collaboration can isolate the knowledge and abilities of one team member from another" (Panitz, 1997). Indeed, a formal process model risks "becom[ing] a rigid template" (Wambeam & Kramer, 1996, p. 349) in which participants work in a "series of dissociated movements" (p. 350) that merely masquerade as collaboration.

## THE EVALUATOR AS RESEARCH COLLABORATOR

*JwSC* represented my first attempt to work as a project evaluator within an academic research group that designs large-scale, interactive environments—museum experiences and immersive virtual worlds—that encourage informal, leisure-based science learning. The technology for such experiences is constantly evolving and, as the scenario outlined at the outset of this chapter illustrates, the stakeholder groups tend to be large and diverse. Successful development of such innovative interactive experiences requires a rigorous user-centered design model that encourages participants to talk with one another at all times.

Collaboration is a philosophy of interaction where individuals are responsible for their actions…and respect the abilities and contributions of their peers. … In all situations where people come together in groups, it suggests a way of dealing with people which respects and highlights individual group members' abilities and contributions. There is a sharing of authority and acceptance of responsibility among group members for the group's actions. (Panitz, 1997)

*JwSC* succeeded as a pilot installation, but the summative evaluation revealed problems related to the usability of the kiosk interface, its accessibility to disabled museum visitors, the location in which it was deployed on the museum floor, the appropriateness of the learning objectives *vis-à-vis* the context of informal learning, and methods for delivering the key content. (See Kitalong et al. 2009, for details.) Everyone agreed that if the development team members had talked to one another, and if formative evaluations had been employed early on, the installation could have worked much better. Emerging best practices encourage design models that bring together developers, evaluators, end users, and content experts together in a collaborative rather than a cooperative approach; that is the approach adopted by the *WJE* team. Interestingly, new National Science Foundation (NSF) requirements and Institutional Research Board (IRB) expectations, often viewed as barriers or impediments, encourage such collaboration.

## GOVERNMENTAL AND INSTITUTIONAL MANDATES

NSF, in response to the U.S. government's Deficit Reduction Act of 2005, mandates that recipients of the foundation's funds conduct complex, highly structured formative and summative assessment (Friedman, 2008, p. 10; U.S. Department of Education, 2007), carefully planned in advance and submitted with the grant proposal. This assessment mandate, a technology in its own right, helps ensure government accountability. The work done by the project evaluator during the proposal stage can make or break a project's funding success, and, once the project has been funded, the evaluator's work helps to move the project along. But because the project evaluator cannot be a principal investigator, the role is not traditionally valued in academic institutions, despite its complexity and significance.

The NSF's insistence that each project they fund include significant and detailed formative and summative assessments can be viewed as an endorsement of collaborative design. For the *WJE* team, having learned from the forgotten learning objectives of *JwSC*, evaluation functions not only as funding agency mandate but also as a catalyst for collaboration. When technological and interpersonal collisions emerge during the annual team meetings, when the conservatism of a well-established and successful science museum partner collides with the R&D mentality of the developers, when the reality of informal learning contexts collides with traditional learning expectations such as those associated with schools, a quick formative evaluation can offer guidelines. The evaluator might say, "Why don't we add that question to the next round of evaluations?" Or, she might bring up a published study that addressed a similar question. These collisions illustrate that, although the developers do not know the evaluation world, the evaluators do, and can enhance the collaborative nature of project work.

The IRB is another institutional mandate that can be viewed as either a barrier to progress or as a catalyst for collaboration with the representative audience members. In the case of *WJE,* the target audience members are minors, a population considered to be vulnerable to the potential for researcher misconduct. As such, their participation entails a multi-level informed consent procedure that is subject to scrutiny by the IRBs of all participating institutions. Learning and complying with IRB rules—which, although mandated by government regulation, are nevertheless handled a little differently at each institution involved in the research—is challenging, to say the least.

Our target audience consists of middle-school-aged children. Research shows that children in this age group are often the sponsors of their families' museum visits (Hooper-Greenhill, 1994a, p. 9). They actively seek out new knowledge and especially enjoy immersive experiences. They catch on to new ideas quickly and have a near-intuitive grasp of complicated interactive technology (Prensky 2001a; Prensky 2001b). As well, they are often the sponsors of their families' technology success and strongly influence household technology purchases. Prensky calls these people "digital natives" (Prensky 2001a; Prensky 2001b). In contrast with older "digital immigrants," who learned digital technology as a second language, digital natives have grown up with computers, video games, and the Internet. As a result, their expectations for imagery, interactivity, and verisimilitude are high and their boredom thresholds low. When we evaluate their interactive exhibit experiences, we seek insight into what triggers and sustains their engagement. Some scholars find self-disclosed information to be of dubious value (Falk & Dierking, 2000), but youth in this age group tend to be forthcoming with their views and open to suggesting alternative strategies. Self-disclosure augmented by close observation works well in this context.

Evaluation methods for informal learning contexts are being developed, but few of these methods have been tested extensively nor have they been validated through repetition because of the myriad and highly individualized ways in which informal learning can play out. The situatedness of informal learning is both its strength and its challenge. Each visitor comes to the museum with a unique set of experiences, and each makes sense of the visit in his or her own unique way. For example, some of *WJE*'s future visitors will be native South Floridians with first-hand exposure to the Everglades. Others will hail from as far away as Northern Michigan, and may have limited—if any—knowledge of tropical wetlands. In fact, when I asked a small group of Michigan eighth graders to describe the Everglades, they all agreed that it must be a frozen place with snow and ice floes. Clearly, individual experiences affect the learning potential.

Therefore, the design of evaluation mechanisms for informal learning entails a great deal of research, invention, experimentation, hedging, and interpretation. While this is time-consuming and the results cannot always be generalized, it is especially interesting and challenging for a scholar.

## CONCLUSION AND RECOMMENDATIONS

To undertake the formative assessment of usability and engagement value is to find oneself at the nexus of colliding institutional, technological, social, demographic, cultural, and even economic forces, and at the mercy of many stakeholders. The highly technical developers who design virtual environments showcase exciting experimental ideas only to be squelched by a pragmatic and highly experienced museum director, who sees long lines and bottlenecks generated by the time-consuming nature of the compelling activity. Sometimes the developers' voices are even squelched by the evaluator's work, which may show that, although an environment is technologically "cool," no one understands it. Back to the drawing board!

Meanwhile, the pace of technological change—especially in emerging technological realms such as visual representation and display, mixed and augmented reality, and touch-screen interactivity—keeps accelerating. Although the developers remain fluid and keep abreast of innovations that could be applied to the project, obsolescence is a constant threat; some virtual worlds will undoubtedly be out of date before they are deployed.

In this chapter, I have illustrated the central role of formative evaluation to the software development process, and conveyed the importance of evaluators as members of the community and as catalysts to the development process. The key recommendation is to involve expert evaluators throughout the development cycle, whether the desired end result is a suite of software, a community program, or an interactive exhibit. Involving target users in the whole process is equally crucial. Here is how these recommendations have been enacted for *WJE*, now in its third year of development. As the range of evaluation mechanisms listed below suggests, a variety of contexts afford formative evaluation opportunities—some rigorously planned and others more *ad hoc*.

1. We reconceptualized the summative findings of the *JwSC* evaluation as interim/formative findings for *WJE*, in an effort to build on what was learned through that exciting but flawed project.

2. We conducted focus group sessions with sixth graders at an Orlando science magnet school. In this one-hour session, we asked the children to draw pictures and then explain them in order to capture their understanding of Florida's water story, to hear about their roles as their families' technology experts, and to learn what they liked and disliked about museums they had visited.

3. The developers attend an annual gaming exposition in Orlando to engage a large group of gamers in evaluating the playability and

engagement value of selected interactive experiences.

4. In conjunction with World Usability Day in Houghton, Michigan, 35 adults reviewed a series of animated artist's renditions of the finished museum exhibits and provided general impressions in response to targeted questions.

5. Two classroom sessions with eighth-grade science students helped us assess whether the text in pop-up windows was written at an appropriate reading and conceptual level.

6. A family-group evaluation session held in the Media Convergence Lab's spacious development facility allowed us to simulate how family groups might interact with the experiences at a science center.

7. A series of sessions at a Northern Michigan summer camp allowed us to simulate how middle-school children on a school field trip might interact with one or more kiosks.

Each of these formative evaluation sessions yielded insights about the emerging products and their development processes. In addition, viewed cumulatively, they reveal patterns of behavior that help us describe middle-school-aged children—digital natives—and to understand how this unique segment of our community interacts with technology.

Conventional wisdom suggests that project evaluators should be objective outsiders who carry out their work in isolation from the development and implementation of an exhibit or experience (Hein, 1994, p. 307). However, our research team has come to regard this view as somewhat misguided. Especially in the formative evaluation stages, project evaluators who are embedded within the research team—who are on board from the very start of the project—can help the team view sites of collision as generative rather than immobilizing. The project evaluator, who, in traditional development processes, has been relegated to a peripheral role at the end of

the process, is in this new model situated firmly at the center of the development universe, subtly guiding disparate forces to achieve a technologically sophisticated collaboration among people, institutions, technologies, and cultural contexts. Cast in the role of problem finder instead of the traditional end-of-cycle role of verifying that the project's milestones and objectives have been met, the 21st-century evaluator occupies a unique vantage point from which not only to assess the accomplishment of project goals and objectives, but also to critique collaborative processes and facilitate collaborations among the myriad stakeholders whose opinions matter in the development process.

## REFERENCES

Falk, J. H., & Dierking, L. (2000). *Learning from museums: Visitor experiences and the making of meaning*. Walnut Creek, CA: Altamira Press.

Friedman, A. (2008). *Framework for evaluating impacts of informal science education project.* Retrieved April 6, 2010, from http://insci.org/resources/Eval_Framework.pdf

Hein, G. (1994). Evaluation of museum programmes and exhibits. In E. Hooper-Greenhilll (Ed.), *The educational role of the museum* (2nd ed., pp. 305–311). London, UK: Routledge.

Hooper-Greenhill, E. (1994a). Education, communication, and interpretation: Towards a critical pedagogy in museums. In E. Hooper-Greenhill (Ed.), *The educational role of the museum* (2nd ed., pp. 3–27). London, UK: Routledge.

Hooper-Greenhill, E. (1994b). Learning from learning theory in museums. In E. Hooper-Greenhill (Ed.), *The educational role of the museum* (2nd ed., pp. 137–145). London, UK: Routledge.

Kitalong, K., Moody, J. E., Middlebrook, R. H., & Ancheta, G. S. (2009). Beyond the screen: Narrative mapping as a tool for evaluating a mixed-reality science museum exhibit. *Technical Communication Quarterly*, *18*(2), 142–165. doi:10.1080/10572250802706349

Panits, T. (1997). Collaborative versus cooperative learning: Comparing the two definitions helps understand the nature of interactive learning. *Cooperative Learning and College Teaching, 8*(2).

Prasad, B. (1998). Decentralized cooperation: A distributed approach to team design in a concurrent engineering organization. *Team Performance Management*, *4*(4), 138–165. doi:10.1108/13527599810224624

Prensky, M. (2001a). Digital natives, digital immigrants. *Horizon*, *9*(5). doi:10.1108/10748120110424816

Prensky, M. (2001b). Digital natives, digital immigrants, part II: Do they really think differently? *Horizon, 9*(6). doi:10.1108/10748120110424843

U.S. Department of Education. (2007). *Report of the academic competitiveness council.* Retrieved July 19, 2010, from http://www2.ed.gov/about/inits/ed/competitiveness/accmathscience/report.pdf

Wambeam, C., & Kramer, R. (1996). Design teams and the Web: A collaborative model for the workplace. *Technical Communication, 43*(4), 349–357.

# Chapter 26
# Here and Now or Coming in the Future?
## E-Learning in Higher Education in Africa

**James Kariuki Njenga**
*University of the Western Cape, Republic of South Africa*

**Louis Cyril Henry Fourie**
*University of the Western Cape, Republic of South Africa*

## ABSTRACT

*Phenomenal changes have occurred in higher education (HE) since the emergence of e-learning, thus necessitating change in teaching and learning approaches. The rate of change, demands, and pressures of the workplace brought by these ICTs, and the need for continual self improvement, job market competition, and job relevance have created an unprecedented demand for HE. There seem to be mythical ideas about the potential effects of e-learning and the proximal and contingent contextual factors that might affect its use, especially in Africa. Thus, e-learning's ability to reach non-traditional learners to offer the required alternative access to education or offer supplementary access to traditional learners is questioned, leading to the observation that its benefits may be achieved only in the future rather than in the present. Hence the focal question: Is e-learning coming in the future or is it a present engagement, and how do partnerships figure into this issue?*

## INTRODUCTION

The use and implementation of Information and Communication Technologies (ICTs) has led to changes within organizations, in particular it has

yielded revolutions in social, political, economic, educational and work environments (Gyamfi, 2005). ICTs are sometimes seen as a panacea, involving an information revolution "that presents a seeming cornucopia of opportunities" (Wilson III & Wong, 2003, p. 155). Many countries need to be assisted in managing these technologies

DOI: 10.4018/978-1-60960-623-7.ch026

and opportunities to avoid being marginalised or exploited (Commission for Africa, 2005; UNDP, 1997). ICT developments, and particularly the Internet, have created an important revolutionary wave in education with regard to interdependencies, connectedness, improved collaboration, and changes in the approach to service delivery (Friedman, 2007; Melville & Wallace, 2007).

The information revolution and globalization have led to a number of factors that shape the demand for e-learning: the reality that education is becoming a service that can be traded (e.g. see Sidhu, 2007); the need for constantly acquiring new skills to remain employable and competitive; the need for international and regional cooperation and collaboration amongst educational providers and experts to address the broad needs of higher education institutions; a rising need for higher education and higher enrolment rates; educational offerings that are flexible and easily customizable to fit the needs of a specific audience; and the creation of communities of practice or knowledge repositories that are easily accessible (Melville & Wallace, 2007). The aforementioned factors have led to the proliferation of a number of e-learning offerings worldwide—both in higher education and in the corporate word (Allan & Lewis, 2006). In this chapter, the benefits and reasons given for using e-learning as a means for teaching and learning delivery in higher education, and the barriers to its use with specific focus on Africa (South Africa in particular) are discussed. Although there are clearly differences among the many countries in Africa, and also among the different regions in some countries which might serve as a limitation to the discussions below, many of these arguments would and indeed do hold in almost all the countries in Africa. The Commission for Africa (2005), for instance, laments the status of many technologies and the vulnerability of most African countries to exploitation. Questions of access to essential amenities and quality education facilities seems inherent in African countries – only the scope or depth of the access differs among countries

or regions. Reports on brain drain in Africa cut across the continent (Teferra & Altbach, 2004). With this context in mind, the chapter concludes with a discussion aimed at answering the focal question, "Is e-learning *coming in the future* for higher education in Africa or is it a *here and now* engagement between the stakeholders in higher education that should already be in place?"

# THE BENEFITS OF E-LEARNING

## Creation of a Workforce that is Knowledge-Economy Ready

There is currently a substantial focus on the knowledge economy, which broadly stated is the requirement of specialised information-handling skills and knowledge expertise with the ability to add value to the information and skills (Williams, 2007; Melville & Wallace, 2007). With the global increasing demand for knowledge workers and e-skills in governments and organisations, the onus is now on institutions of higher learning to produce knowledge-economy-ready graduates. Viewed in this light, e-learning can assist students to acquire skills and familiarity with the tools of the knowledge economy as they learn. However, questions have arisen regarding the readiness of Africa for the knowledge economy, and much still needs to be done for it to become a reality, although there is slow progress towards such a model in some African countries (Britz, Lor, Coetzee, & Bester, 2006).

## Creation of Continental and International Networks and Partnerships

If effectively used, e-learning can lead to the creation of local, regional, continental and international networks and partnerships that can also deliver borderless education and knowledge (Huysman & Wulf, 2006; Painter-Morland, Fontrodona, Hoffman, & Rowe, 2003). Huysman and Wulf (2006) indicate that this is particularly important for businesses because of the changes in organizational boundaries and identities, coupled with the growth of virtual and geographically dispersed teams that limit the control of knowledge in organizations. These changes bring about diversity in perspectives and experiences that could alert learners to the contextual dynamics of their specific environments in relation to the rest of the world (Painter-Morland et al., 2003). The inference from this is that higher education institutions (HEI) need to be taking the lead by carefully studying and forecasting the needs of the emerging networks.

## Flexibility

E-learning provides flexibility in terms of content and delivery, pace, place and time of learning (Donnelly & Benson, 2008; Uys, Nleya, & Molelu, 2003). The availability of content in electronic standards makes its transformation to a variety of formats easy and quick. In addition, updating the content is easier in terms of accessibility cost, and distribution than, for example, updating printed content. In addition, the updated content can be available to the intended audience electronically without undue delays (Donnelly & Benson, 2008). The content can also be translated by electronic interpretors (though they are prone to errors) and be distributed in more than one language (Donnelly & Benson, 2008). The ease of updating, and by extension customization, is touted to improve learning speeds and understanding of the subject matter because the students suit the material to their own needs (Cantoni, Cellario, & Porta, 2004; Zhang & Nunamaker, 2003). The ease of customization leads to a self-paced approach to learning.

## Provision of Easy Learning and Learning Process Management

When assistive and enabling technology like learning management systems and electronic portfolios are used, it is not only easy for the university's administration to manage the students and their learning but also for the students to track their personal development (Black et al., 2007). In Learning and Course Management Systems (LCMS), most of the administration of the content, assignments and discussions is controlled and managed by a lecturer in each course while in the case of ePortfolios the students control and manage their work "across multiple courses throughout an academic career" (Greenberg, 2004, p. 31).

## Creation of Communities of Practice and Repositories of Educational Content

The creation of communities of practice (CoPs) consisting of valuable intellectual and human capital (Madoc-Jones & Parrott, 2005; Uys, Nleya, & Molelu, 2003) offers the advantage of transcending geographical boundaries and can lead to the formation of a critical mass of students and facilitators who offer educational and supportive content and services to each other (Madoc-Jones & Parrott, 2005). The main challenge of educational repositories lies in the ability of the audience to access and localise them to their contexts as well as getting content that is interoperable with their computer software. A number of interoperability standards have been drafted to cater for compatibility of the Open Educational Resources (OERs) and the users' software. The onus is on the educational system to train audiences on the localisation and adaptation of the OERs.

## Increase in Students' Motivation, Retention and Success Rates

Although there is little conclusive evidence, e-learning has been shown to increase students' motivation, retention of subject matter and success rate (Riffell & Sibley, 2005; Cameron, 2003). However, research indicates that the students who benefit the most from e-learning, and complete their courses with high grades, are the academically stronger students (those with higher academic performance at school and university; higher verbal reasoning capability, better discernment, and verbal IQ; higher intelligence and conscientiousness), who also score high in self-efficacy, goal commitment and learning efficiency (Clegg, Bradley, & Smith, 2006; Taylor & Bedford, 2004; Stanz & Fourie, 2002). This raises questions about the appropriateness of the modality for widespread use among all students.

## Increase Interactivity, Support and Communication

The core feature of the use of ICTs in education is their interactivity and communication capabilities. E-learning can increase interactivity, support and communication among teachers, learners and the learning content. Interactivity in this context is seen as both an activity and a property or an attribute inherent in the technology (Richards, 2006). These two views present the students' interactions with the learning materials and technologies on one side, and the social activity of exchanging and generating ideas on the other (Nunes & McPherson, 2007). The increased interactivity and communication in e-learning can facilitate student-centred learning that is in agreement with the constructivist view of education in which students actively create meaning and new knowledge based on their engagements during the learning process (Madoc-Jones & Parrott, 2005; Cameron, 2003).

## Addressing the Demand of Higher Education

Technology also has the potential of addressing the increase in demand for higher education by, amongst other things, allowing cross-border providers of education to offer distance-learning courses, as well as strengthening academic partnerships through the use of ICTs and encouraging lifelong learning (Harpur, 2006; Osborne & Oberski, 2004; Uys, Nleya, & Molelu, 2003; Fielden, 2001). These partnerships could ease the management challenges brought about by the technologies, and at the same time make the most of what these technologies offer (Fielden, 2001). Indeed, Harpur (2006, p. 145) sees e-learning as a revolutionary technology that is "uniquely situated to modern mass access to higher education." Therefore, it would be surprising if HEIs ignored the use of ICTs to cope with increasing demand.

In summary, the case for e-learning use in higher education in Africa would be to improve the efficiency and effectiveness, extend the reach, and maximise the impact of and respond to the demand for higher education. Effectiveness and efficiency can be realised in terms of costs and speed of delivery. Lower costs could be realised through lower investments in travel, physical infrastructure, resource management and development of learning materials (Aczel, Peake, & Hardy, 2008). The use of the current Internet and web-based technologies allows for quick delivery of these materials, and also quick and 24/7 access to expertise beyond geographical boundaries. With e-learning, higher education can offer a wide range of courses without barriers that are evidenced in *brick and mortar* courses: distance, time, inflexibility and inadaptability. The ease of adaptation and customization ensures that the learning content is well suited to an individual's learning style and preferences, hence increasing its impact and reach. In the cases where the demand for higher education outweighs the physical resources on campuses, e-learning could be used to cater to increased numbers of students and courses.

## THE CHALLENGES OF E-LEARNING IN AFRICA

Africa faces enormous challenges with regard to technology for teaching and learning.

### Bandwidth

The availability, quality, quantity and cost of bandwidth in Africa are still prohibitive and beyond the reach of many HEIs and individuals. According to a recent study, "an average university in Africa has no more bandwidth than the amount found in a residential connection in Europe or the United States"; they typical HEI pays on average 50 times more than a typical US university per Kbps; and the quality is low without firm commitments of policy from the Internet providers of guaranteed uptimes (Hawkins, 2007, pp. 92-93). In addition, lack of skills and policies on bandwidth management at the institutions contribute to the ineffective use of bandwidth (see also Steiner, Tirivayi, Jensen, & Gakio, 2004).

### Policies and Regulations

Most countries in Africa have conservative and restrictive ICT policies that often serve as a hindrance to the use of e-learning and related technologies (Yieke, 2005). In addition, there is a lag between both the diffusion and development of ICT-based processes and policies governing their operations in Africa. Indeed, there is a "mismatch between the techno-economic and the socio-institutional system, which makes the catching up process more difficult for large parts of the developing world" (Castellacci, 2006, p. 841). There still remain to be policy directions that seek to fully exploit the developments in ICTs both for educational and other socio-economic activities. These policy directions should cover institutions, national and international regimes as the lack of policies leads to unnecessary duplications of efforts, and uncoordinated and duplicated investments. This duplication and lack of coordination hinders the creation of institutional support strategies and mechanisms and acts as a hindrance to the use of e-learning. It has been reported that countries that have undergone regulatory reforms have had positive short-term impacts, especially in stimulating investments and lowering the costs of ICT products and services (Henten, Falch, & Anyimadu, 2004). Major policy implications for the region with regard to ICT development like changes in telecommunications and economic policies, and the incorporation of ICTs into educational and other institutional systems, have been advocated for some time (Oyelaran-Oyeyinka & Lal, 2005).

The need for higher education institutions in Africa to address policy issues by creating *proactive* and *reactive* policies (Cross & Adam, 2007), while managing issues to do with acceptance, pressure and pedagogical needs of their target (Cleg et al., 2003) in the *techno-economic* and *socio-systems paradigms* (Castellacci, 2006), are large challenges. The challenge is due to the fact that most HEIs rely on government funding or in some projects, donor funding. Donors usually need to see policies in place as a condition for funding, and there is generally a need for management to raise more funds through course offerings while at the same time reducing or lowering costs (Cross & Adam, 2007). These donors' requirements coupled with the pressures from the private sector have led collaborators, especially development partners, to allude to the need for inclusivity and wider participation in the policies in higher education, and by implication ICTs and e-learning (Lazarus et al., 2008; Cross & Adam, 2007; King, 2007; LaRocque & Michael, 2003). While there is some movement towards institutional e-learning policy formulation, much more needs to be done.

## Access

What constitutes access to technology is debatable, but it has been defined as the state of technology being within the reach of its intended users with reasonable limitations. Some countries define the limitations in terms of time, population or distance (Henten, Falch, & Anyimadu, 2004, p. 2) as is the case with telephone access. Access to communication technologies and information is a major concern in Africa. With access, there are a number of facets: access to the technology, access to resources to invest in the technology, access to training and expertise, and access to market information about the technology. With these facets in mind, potential access to or availability of technologies alone do not directly translate (or always lead) to their ownership or use (James & Versteeg, 2007) due to lack of or inadequate access to the other core components. Most African countries are lagging with regard to access to technology (see for example, United Nations, 2005).

## Power and Related Infrastructure

Linked to the communication infrastructure are the related issues of unreliability, unavailability and high cost of power in most African countries. Power remains one of the most expensive costs manufacturing firms bear in Africa, accounting for over 50% of the production costs in some countries (Eifert, Gelb, & Ramachandran, In Press). Furthermore, Africa has the lowest electrification rate in the world - 24% compared to the world average of 73%, with many rural areas still uncovered by the main grids. About 10% of the population covered is in urban and industrial centres (Wolde-Rufael, 2006). Although most universities in Africa are located in major urban centres, these challenges, as well as the intermittent availability of power, still concern them.

## University Management Buy-In

Higher education institutions have been described as resistant to change and largely bureaucratic with e-learning innovations often "implemented as an isolated, bottom–up initiative of academic staff for efficiency purposes" (Uys, Nleya, & Molelu, 2003, p. 69). While top management may disregard e-learning, top management commitments have significant influence on the use of e-learning in higher education (Leseure, Bauer, Birdi, Neely, & Denyer, 2004; Swanson & Ramiller, 2004; Sharma & Rai, 2003; Gallivan, 2001). Doubtlessly, top management within higher education institutions act as linkages between individuals and e-learning, and high level support is also one of the best predictors of continued use of an innovation like e-learning (Jeyaraj, Rottman, & Lacity, 2006). Where there is lack of public and explicit approval of e-learning by management within higher education, together with the allocation of resources, time and commitment toward the success of e-learning, any implementation of e-learning would be very difficult (Sharma & Rai, 2003; Greenhalgh, Robert, Macfarlane, Bate, & Kyriakidou, 2004; Gallivan, 2001).

## New Teaching and Learning Paradigms

The paradigmatic shifts called for in e-learning bring about challenges not only in quality, but also in delivery, accountability and skills required (see Pond, 2002). The new paradigm challenges facilitators to involve and engage students frequently to avert loneliness, low self-esteem, isolation, and low motivation to learn, which often lead to low achievements and/or eventual dropout (Rovai, 2002). The engagement and involvement of facilitators during the teaching and learning process, as well as the development of learning materials and contexts translate to increased workloads for facilitators (Connolly & Stansfield, 2007). This dual challenge and increased workload due to the use of e-learning in HE could lead to user resistance, and eventual failure of any e-learning initiative (Lippert & Davis, 2006; Saunders, Charlier, & Bonamy, 2005; Piderit, 2000; Gallivan, 2001).

## Human Capacity

Perhaps what compounds the paradigm shift challenges is the perceived and real shortage of skills in Africa, especially in e-learning and in ICT in general. The skill shortage has not only led to a lack of or poor research capacity but has also acted as a hindrance to the use of ICTs in HEIs. Further complicating the situation is the difficulty of keeping qualified personnel in Africa because of the renowned brain drain (Ndulu, Chakraborti, Lijane, Ramachandran, & Wolgin, 2007; Teferra & Altbach, 2004). The flight of skilled labour from Africa leads to a drag in investment, income and growth and adversely affects the development and adoption rates of inventions and innovations. The brain drain could also curtail the development of new networks and partnerships and the strengthening of existing ones. The brain drain contributes to the shortage of skilled labour to complement the semi-skilled and unskilled labour in the socio-economic development of African countries (Ndulu, 2004; Teferra & Altbach, 2004; Ndulu et al., 2004). Africa should therefore address the issue of brain drain, increase enrolment in higher education, especially the sciences; improve on staff retention programs; launch extensive and continuous staff training programs; and make the best use of available human capital (Ndulu et al., 2004; Ndulu, 2004). The challenge of inadequate human capacity has an adverse effect on the adoption of innovations like e-learning (Ndulu, 2004).

## Limited or Lack of Financial Resources

Teferra and Altbach (2004) indicate that most higher education institutions in Africa are facing financial crises, arising from, amongst other things,

expansionist and massification pressures, poor economic status in host countries, lack of external funding, students defaulting or an inability to pay, and misallocation and poor prioritization of available funds. This implies that a) higher education is limited to those who can afford to pay the higher fees, leaving the majority without affordable access to education; b) HEIs limit enrolment to be in line with the funds offered to them by the government or sponsors; c) HEIs are limited to low cost, low quality education programs that in the long run don't address the urgent and pertinent needs of the society in terms of socio-economic developments; and d) HEIs get involved in uncoordinated infrastructural development that ends up being too costly (TFHES, 2000). These issues have an adverse effect on investment in e-learning technologies. Proper coordination and formation of flexible funding models encouraging public participation in HE and coherent and rational national approaches should be used to optimise the financing and funding for higher education (TFHES, 2000).

## Socio-Cultural Paradoxes and Issues

Cultural barriers have been cited as preventing the use of new technology (Lichtenthaler & Ernst, 2008). Technopositivists and techno-centric leaders have advocated for the use of technologies with lots of promises and gusto that fall just short of demonising the culture of those who are hesitant to adopt these technologies. Cultural barriers in the adoption of technology, like e-learning, arise from the perceived threat of eroding the African culture with the Western media and culture; creation of new forms of identities that are incompatible with the African cultural identities; the inapplicability of *foreign* ideologies and intellectual knowledge to the African context and realities; the death of African languages and indigenous knowledge; and the inapplicability of *foreign* pedagogies in teaching and learning contrary to *time-tested* African pedagogies (Alzouma, 2005; Heath 2004;

Zhao, Massey, & Murphy, 2003; Wejnert, 2002; Ess & Sudweeks, 1998; Gray, 1982). The issues of Westernization, authenticity of *foreign* tools and processes in relation to the African context and cultural identity are briefly discussed below.

Cultural identity is strongly related to economic vulnerability, especially when used as a status symbol in emergent cultures, which makes developing countries more reliant on the West for economic reprieve and at particular high risk of its loss (Tomlinson, 2003). In HEIs, these vulnerabilities and this status symbolism can be seen in the production and consumption of knowledge using technology that would consequently define the competitiveness of the institutions, which consequently leads to the creation of an identity of its own. While e-learning, and indeed other technologies, can be a factor in defining competitiveness, competitiveness in HEIs is complex and technology or e-learning alone cannot be used as the gauge (Njenga & Fourie, 2008; Tomlinson, 2003).

## HERE AND NOW OR COMING IN THE FUTURE?

Without sounding pessimistic, the use of e-learning for higher education in Africa seems to be a mirage given the challenges discussed, despite its benefits and potential. There are still real unresolved issues blocking its use in Africa. Until these issues are resolved, e-learning will always be a "coming in the future" phenomenon rather than being a "here and now" kind of engagement. To address these issues, the next section lists some of the strategies that can be employed. The list is not exhaustive, and more things need to be done. Hopefully then, and as we resolve the issues, we will have a "here and now" approach to e-learning for HE in Africa.

## What are the Strategies for Moving into the Future?

- *Formation of networks and partnerships*: HEIs and other organizations should collaborate to form the networks and partnerships that create opportunities for not only sharing knowledge but also reaching new markets beyond their borders and at the same time creating a culture of collaboration and cooperation. HEIs should be leaders in defining what is required for the network by carefully studying and forecasting the needs of the emerging networks.

- *Fostering relationships between HEIs, students and their environments:* The understanding of these relationships will ensure that HE providers achieve flexibility as an objective and at the same time "identify the factors that serve to increase/reduce flexibility and to say something about the consequences of flexibility" (Rye, 2008).

- *Dealing with human resources*: Perhaps Africa should address the lack of sufficient human resources by increasing enrolment in higher education, especially in the sciences, attend to the brain drain, improve on staff retention programs, launch extensive and continuous staff training programs, and make the best use of available human capital (Ndulu et al., 2004; Ndulu, 2004 Adam, 2003).

- *Proper coordination and formation of flexible funding models*: This effort would encourage public participation in HE Coherent and rational national approaches should be used to optimise the financing and funding for higher education (TFHES, 2000).

## REFERENCES

Aczel, C. J., Peake, S. R., & Hardy, P. (2008). Designing capacity-building in e-learning expertise: Challenges and strategies. *Computers & Education, 50*, 499–510. doi:10.1016/j.compedu.2007.07.005

Allan, B., & Lewis, D. (2006). Virtual learning communities as a vehicle for workforce development: A case study. *Journal of Workplace Learning, 18*(6), 367–383. doi:10.1108/13665620610682099

Alzouma, G. (2005). Myths of digital technology in Africa: Leapfrogging development? *Global Media and Communication, 1*(3), 339–356. doi:10.1177/1742766505058128

Black, E. W., Beck, D., Dawson, K., Jinks, S., & DiPietro, M. (2007). The other side of the LMS: Considering implementation and use in the adoption of an LMS in online and blended learning environments. *TechTrends, 51*(2), 37–39, 53.

Britz, J. J., Lor, P. J., Coetzee, I. E., & Bester, B. C. (2006). Africa as a knowledge society: A reality check. *The International Information & Library Review, 38*(1), 25–40. doi:10.1016/j.iilr.2005.12.001

Cameron, B. (2003). The effectiveness of simulation in a hybrid and online networking course. *TechTrends, 47*(5), 18–21. doi:10.1007/BF02763200

Cantoni, V., Cellario, M., & Porta, M. (2004). Perspectives and challenges in e-learning: Towards natural interaction paradigms. *Journal of Visual Languages and Computing, 15*, 333–345. doi:10.1016/j.jvlc.2003.10.002

Castellacci, F. (2006). Innovation, diffusion and catching up in the fifth long wave. *Futures, 38*, 841–863. doi:10.1016/j.futures.2005.12.007

Clegg, S., Bradley, S., & Smith, K. (2006). I've had to swallow my pride: Help seeking and self esteem. *Higher Education Research & Development, 25*(2), 101–113. doi:10.1080/07294360600610354

Commission for Africa. (2005). *Our common interest: Report of the Commission for Africa.* Retrieved August 22, 2008, from http://www.commissionforafrica.org/english/report/thereport/english/11-03-05_cr_report.pdf

Connolly, T. M., & Stansfield, M. (2007). From e-learning to games-based e-learning: Using interactive technologies in teaching on IS course. *International Journal of Information Technology and Management, 6*(2/3/4), 188-207.

Cross, M., & Adam, F. (2007). ICT policies and strategies in higher education in South Africa: National and institutional pathways. *Higher Education Policy, 20*, 73–95. doi:10.1057/palgrave.hep.8300144

Donnelly, P., & Benson, J. (2008). Get the most from electronic learning. *Education for Primary Care, 19*, 100–102.

Eifert, B., Gelb, A., & Ramachandran, V. (2008). The cost of doing business in Africa: Evidence from enterprise survey data. *World Development, 36*(9), 1531–1546. doi:10.1016/j.worlddev.2007.09.007

Ess, C., & Sudweeks, F. (1998). Computer-mediated communication or culturally-mediated computing? Challenging assumptions of the electronic global village. *Electronic Journal of Communication/Revue Electronique de Communication, 8*. Retrieved on July 22, 2008, from http://www.cios.org/www/ejcmain.htm

Fielden, J. (2001). Markets for borderless education. *Minerva, 39*(1), 49–62. doi:10.1023/A:1010374319689

Friedman, T. (2007). *The world is flat* (3rd ed.). New York, NY: Picador USA.

Gallivan, M. J. (2001). Organizational adoption and assimilation of complex technological innovations: Development and application of a new framework. *The Data Base for Advances in Information Systems, 32*(3), 51–85.

Gray, R. (1982). Christianity, colonialism, and communications in sub-Saharan Africa. *Journal of Black Studies, 13*(1), 59–72. doi:10.1177/002193478201300105

Greenberg, G. (2004, July/August). The digital convergence: Extending the portfolio model. *EDUCAUSE Review, 4*, 28–36. Retrieved 17 July, 2008, from http://www.educause.edu/apps/er/erm04/erm0441.asp

Greenhalgh, T., Robert, G., Macfarlane, F., Bate, P., & Kyriakidou, O. (2004). Diffusion of innovations in service organizations: Systematic review and recommendations. *The Milbank Quarterly, 84*(4), 581–629. doi:10.1111/j.0887-378X.2004.00325.x

Gyamfi, A. (2005). Closing the digital divide in sub-Saharan Africa: Meeting the challenges of the information age. *Information Development, 21*(1), 22-30.

Harpur, J. (2006). Transformation in higher education: The inevitable union of alchemy and technology. *Higher Education Policy, 19*, 135–151. doi:10.1057/palgrave.hep.8300116

Hawkins, R. (2007). The persistent bandwidth divide in Africa: Findings for the African Tertiary Institution Connectivity study and lessons for developing knowledge infrastructure and networks in Africa. In *Integrating science & technology into development policies: An international perspective* (pp. 91–99). OECD Publishing. doi:10.1787/9789264032101-11-en

Heath, J. (2004). Liberalization, modernization, westernization. *Philosophy and Social Criticism, 30*(5/6), 665–690. doi:10.1177/0191453704045760

Henten, A., Falch, M., & Anyimadu, A. (2004). Telecommunications development in Africa: Filling the gap. *Telematics and Informatics, 21*, 1–9. doi:10.1016/S0736-5853(03)00019-4

Hofstede, G., Neuijen, B., Ohayv, D. D., & Sanders, G. (1990). Measuring organizational cultures: A qualitative and quantitative study across twenty cases. *Administrative Science Quarterly, 35*(2), 286–316. doi:10.2307/2393392

Huysman, M., & Wulf, V. (2006). IT to support knowledge sharing in communities, towards a social capital analysis. *Journal of Information Technology, 21*, 40–51. doi:10.1057/palgrave.jit.2000053

Internet World Stats. (2008). *Internet usage statistics for Africa*. Retrieved August 21, 2008, from http://www.internetworldstats.com/stats1.htm

James, J., & Versteeg, M. (2007). Mobile phones in Africa: How much do we really know? *Social Indicators Research, 84*, 117–126. doi:10.1007/s11205-006-9079-x

Jeyaraj, A., Rottman, J. W., & Lacity, M. C. (2006). A review of the predictors, linkages, and biases in IT innovation adoption research. *Journal of Information Technology, 21*, 1–23. doi:10.1057/palgrave.jit.2000056

King, K. (2007). Balancing basic and post-basic education in Kenya: National versus international policy agendas. *International Journal of Educational Development, 27*, 358–370. doi:10.1016/j.ijedudev.2006.10.001

LaRocque, N., & Michael, L. (2003). *The promise of e-learning in Africa: The potential for public-private partnerships*. IBM Endowment for the Business of Government.

Lazarus, J., Erasmus, M., Hendricks, D., Nduna, J., & Slamat, J. (2008). Embedding community engagement in South African higher education. *Education. Citizenship and Social Justice, 3*(1), 57–83. doi:10.1177/1746197907086719

Leseure, M. J., Bauer, J., Birdi, K., Neely, A., & Denyer, D. (2004). Adoption of promising practices: A systematic review of the evidence. *International Journal of Management Reviews, 5/6*(3/4), 169–190. doi:10.1111/j.1460-8545.2004.00102.x

Lichtenthaler, U., & Ernst, H. (2008). Innovation intermediaries: Why Internet marketplaces for technology have not yet met the expectations. *Creativity and Innovation Management, 17*(1), 14–25. doi:10.1111/j.1467-8691.2007.00461.x

Lippert, S. K., & Davis, M. (2006). A conceptual model integrating trust into planned change activities to enhance technology adoption behavior. *Journal of Information Science, 32*(5), 434–448. doi:10.1177/0165551506066042

Madoc-Jones, I., & Parrott, L. (2005). Virtual social work education—theory and experience. *Social Work Education, 24*(7), 755–768. doi:10.1080/02615470500238678

Melville, W., & Wallace, J. (2007). Workplace as community: Perspectives on science teachers professional learning. *Journal of Science Teacher Education, 18*, 543–558. doi:10.1007/s10972-007-9048-5

Ndulu, B., Chakraborti, L., Lijane, L., Ramachandran, V., & Wolgin, J. (2007). *Challenges of African growth: Opportunities, constraints and strategic directions*. Washington, DC: The World Bank.

Ndulu, B. J. (2004). Human capital flight: Stratification, globalization, and the challenges to tertiary education in Africa. *JHEA/RESA, 2*(1), 57–91.

Njenga, J. K., & Fourie, L. C. H. (2010). The myths about e-learning in higher education. *British Journal of Educational Technology, 41*(2), 199–212. doi:10.1111/j.1467-8535.2008.00910.x

Nunes, M. B., & McPherson, M. (2007). Why designers cannot be agnostic about pedagogy: The influence of constructivist thinking in design of e-learning for HE. [SCI]. *Studies in Computational Intelligence, 62*, 7–30. doi:10.1007/978-3-540-71974-8_2

Osborne, M., & Oberski, I. (2004). University continuing education: The role of communications and Information Technology. *Journal of European Industrial Training, 28*(5), 414–428. doi:10.1108/03090590410533099

Oyelaran-Oyeyinka, B., & Lal, K. (2005). Internet diffusion in sub-Saharan Africa: A cross-country analysis. *Telecommunications Policy, 29*(7), 507–527. doi:10.1016/j.telpol.2005.05.002

Painter-Morland, M., Fontrodona, J., Hoffman, W. M., & Rowe, M. (2003). Conversations across continents: Teaching business ethics online. *Journal of Business Ethics, 48*, 75–88. doi:10.1023/B:BUSI.0000004384.53153.97

Piderit, S. K. (2000). Rethinking resistance and recognizing ambivalence: A multidimensional view of attitudes toward an organizational change. *Academy of Management Review, 25*(4), 783–794. doi:10.2307/259206

Pond, W. K. (2002). Distributed education in the 21st century: Implication for quality assurance. *Online Journal of Distance Learning Administration, 5*(11). Retrieved on July 8, 2008, from www.westga.edu/~distance/ojdla/summer52/pond52.html

Richards, R. (2006). Users, interactivity generation. *New Media & Society, 8*(4), 531–550. doi:10.1177/1461444806064485

Riffell, S., & Sibley, D. (2005). Using Web-based instruction to improve large undergraduate biology courses: An evaluation of a hybrid course format. *Computers & Education, 44*(3), 217–235. doi:10.1016/j.compedu.2004.01.005

Rovai, A. (2002). Building sense of community at a distance. *International Review of Research in Open and Distance Learning, 3*(1), 1–16.

Rye, S. A. (2008). Dimensions of flexibility-students, communication technology and distributed education. *International Journal of Media, Technology and Lifelong Learning, 4*(1). Retrieved from http://www.seminar.net/images/stories/vol4-issue1/rye-dimensionsofflexibility.pdf

Saunders, M., Charlier, B., & Bonamy, J. (2005). Using evaluation to create provisional stabilities: Bridging innovation in higher education change processes. *Evaluation, 11*(1), 37–54. doi:10.1177/1356389005053188

Sharma, S., & Rai, A. (2003). An assessment of the relationship between ISD leadership characteristics and IS innovation adoption in organizations. *Information & Management, 40*(5), 391–401. doi:10.1016/S0378-7206(02)00049-6

Sidhu, R. (2007). GATS and the new developmentalism: Governing transnational education. *Comparative Education Review, 51*(2), 203–227. doi:10.1086/512020

Stanz, K., & Fourie, L. C. H. (2002). The need for online learning support. *Proceedings of the 5th Annual industrial psychology Conference,* Pretoria, 13-14 June.

Steiner, R., Tirivayi, N., Jensen, M., & Gakio, K. (2004). *Africa tertiary institution connectivity survey.* Retrieved on September 13, 2006, from http://www.worldbank.org/afr/teia/pdfs/ATICS_2004_Report.pdf

Swanson, B. E., & Ramiller, N. C. (2004). Innovating mindfully with Information Technology. *Management Information Systems Quarterly, 28*(4), 553–583.

Taylor, J. A., & Bedford, T. (2004). Staff perceptions of factors related to non-completion in higher education. *Studies in Higher Education, 29*(3), 375–394. doi:10.1080/0307507042000168237

Teferra, D., & Altbach, P. G. (2004). African higher education: Challenges for the 21st century. *Higher Education, 47,* 21–50. doi:10.1023/B:HIGH.0000009822.49980.30

TFHES. (2000). *Higher education in developing countries peril and promise.* Washington, DC: International Bank for Reconstruction and Development / The World Bank.

Tomlinson, J. (2003). Globalization and cultural identity. In D. Held, & A. McGrew (Eds.), *The global transformations reader: An introduction to the globalization debate* (2nd ed., pp. 269–277). Cambridge, MA: Polity Press.

UNDP. (1997). *Human development report 1997: Human development to eradicate poverty.* New York, NY: Oxford University Press.

United Nations. (2005). *Core ICT indicators. Partnership on Measuring ICT for Development.* Geneva, Switzerland: WSIS.

Uys, P. M., Nleya, P., & Molelu, G. B. (2003). Technological innovation and management strategies for higher education in Africa: Harmonizing reality and idealism. *Educational Media International, 40*(3/4), 67–80.

Wejnert, B. (2002). Integrating models of diffusion of innovations: A conceptual framework. *Annual Review of Sociology, 28,* 297–326. doi:10.1146/annurev.soc.28.110601.141051

Williams, P. J. (2007). Valid knowledge: The economy and the academy. *Higher Education, 54,* 511–523. doi:10.1007/s10734-007-9051-y

Wilson, E. J. III, & Wong, K. (2003). African information revolution: A balance sheet. *Telecommunications Policy*, *27*(1/2), 155–177. doi:10.1016/S0308-5961(02)00097-6

Wolde-Rufael, Y. (2006). Electricity consumption and economic growth: A time series experience for 17 African countries. *Energy Policy*, *34*, 1106–1114. doi:10.1016/j.enpol.2004.10.008

Yieke, F. A. (2005). Towards alternatives in higher education: The benefits and challenges of e-learning in Africa. *CODESRIA Bulletin*, *3/4*, 73–75.

Zhang, D., & F, N. J. (2003). Powering e-learning in the new millennium: An overview of e-learning and enabling technology. *Information Systems Frontiers*, *5*(2), 207–218. doi:10.1023/A:1022609809036

Zhao, W., Massey, B. L., & Murphy, J. F. (2003). Cultural dimensions of website design and content. *Prometheus*, *21*(1), 75–84. doi:10.1080/0810902032000051027

# Section 5
# Using Digital Technologies to Cross Generational and Cultural Divides

# Chapter 27
# The Tools at Hand:
## Agency, Industry, and Technological Innovation in a Distributed Learning Community

**Charles Underwood**
*University of California, USA*

**Leann Parker**
*University of California, USA*

## ABSTRACT

*This chapter presents an anthropological case study of the response to rapidly changing technologies by members of a distributed network of 35 technology-based afterschool programs throughout California. University-Community Links (UC Links) is a collaborative effort among university campuses and local communities to develop a network, both physical and virtual, of afterschool program sites for underserved youth in California. While each UC Links program is a physical setting with its own set of learning activities developed in response to the cultural, linguistic, and educational concerns of the local community, the UC Links network as a whole serves as a larger virtual context for defining and pursuing shared goals and objectives and communicating information about effective uses of new digital technologies for afterschool learning. Using a cultural historical perspective, the authors approach UC Links as a sociotechnical activity system engaged in joint activity, and examine and assess its long-term adaptability and the differential capabilities of its local member sites to innovate in response to successive transformations of emerging technologies.*

DOI: 10.4018/978-1-60960-623-7.ch027

## INTRODUCTION

Over the past three decades, new digital technologies have proliferated rapidly and transformed the character of both public and interpersonal communications. The use of these new technologies in educational settings has been both promising and problematic, especially in addressing issues of educational equity and providing sustainable innovative learning experiences for underserved youth (Cole, 1996, 2006; Parker, 2008; Underwood, 2000, 2003; Vasquez, 2003). This chapter looks at the use of diverse technologies by the University-Community Links (UC Links) network of afterschool program sites. The network is both physical and virtual. It includes 35 physical sites in schools or community organizations that offer afterschool activities for youth in urban communities throughout California; yet it also represents a network of partners who interact virtually to share ideas about implementing innovations and responding to challenges. Most of the work of providing engaging educational activities for underserved youth takes place in physical space, but the interaction of key UC Links partners across sites takes place in both physical and virtual space.

In this sense, this chapter represents a study of distributed cognition among dispersed university and community partners and the emergence of a sense of community out of their joint activity–their collective attempts to create and sustain innovative afterschool learning environments for underserved youth in low-income neighborhoods. This perspective on the development of UC Links shows that while local programs and the network, both jointly and individually, have developed innovative educational uses of differentially available technologies, the programs have been limited in their capability to take full advantage of the rapidly growing possibilities of new technologies for teaching, learning, and collaboration.

## University-Community Links

The UC Links network is a dispersed organization of local community-university collaborations operating afterschool programs for underserved youth in low-income communities throughout California. Each collaboration operates at least one physical afterschool site and involves university faculty, staff[1] and students working with community and school partners (teachers, parents, community leaders). These programs also collaborate with similar sites in other states and nations. University faculty affiliated with this network teach discipline-based university courses[2] that link theory with practice in real-world settings by placing their undergraduate students at local afterschool sites. At each physical site, university and community partners use available digital media and other hands-on resources to create face-to-face collaborative learning activities for local children and youth. Guided by undergraduates, these activities promote literacy and technology skills development, academic preparation and enrichment, and enthusiasm for higher learning among local youth. As a statewide network of programs active since 1996, UC Links has grown from 14 physical sites in 1996-97 to 35 sites in 2008-09. Led by 21 university faculty and their school and community partners, UC Links in 2008-09 served over 3,500 P-12 youth from low-income backgrounds and almost 1,100 college students. The university and community people involved in running local programs also constitute a virtual network of communicating partners working to maintain local and cross-site collaboration and coherence both within and among the programs. UC Links' assessments consistently indicate positive program impact of technology-based activities both on K-12 student participants' literacy and digital skills and knowledge, and on undergraduate students' attitudes, aspirations and learning (Underwood & Parker, 2010).

As a collaborative network of professionals and practitioners, UC Links pursues various approaches to afterschool teaching and learning. For example, at the Poetry Academy site in Santa Ana, California, Latino elementary students improve their English language proficiency in reading, writing, vocabulary and grammar through writing poetry; college undergraduates provide the students with guidance and feedback on their writing, both face to face and online. Two UC Links sites in Santa Cruz integrate digital literacy with writing, reading, multimedia art and problem solving in community action research projects carried out by youth with undergraduates' guidance. As these examples illustrate, each UC Links site offers instructional and enrichment activities that reflect both university and community interests, especially those related to local culture, language, and educational concerns.

A major goal of UC Links has been to extend access to digital technologies in ways that encourage and improve the academic preparation of underserved young people in low-income communities. Another explicit goal of UC Links has been to establish an extensive community of learners—a virtual network of scholars and practitioners focused on the productive educational uses of digital technologies. The emergence of this learning community and the local programs it operates is interesting, especially in its varied response over the years to the rapid evolution of new digital and multimedia technologies. These technologies have enabled UC Links partners both to carry out their local site activities for youth and to share ideas and experiences with colleagues using similar digital activities at other sites, thus contributing to shared understandings of effective learning activities for underserved youth from diverse backgrounds and to the sense of belonging to an ongoing distributed community of learning and practice. It is often assumed that educational programs make quick and productive use of new technologies. However, the achievement of a distributed learning community using cutting-edge technologies across program sites is by no means a foregone conclusion. This chapter

examines opportunities and challenges presented both by the emergence of new technologies for learning and by local differences in technology access at various program sites within the UC Links organization.

Early in UC Links history (during the mid 1990s), the goal of extending access for underserved youth to "new technologies" involved using computer hardware and software that would today be considered antiquated; early sites used Apple II computers or small-screen PCs and used software that was more text- than image-based. The use of technology for distance communication across the UC Links community involved e-mail using modems tenuously connected to a newly emerging Internet. In contrast, what we would call "new technologies" today includes a vast array of computers with high-speed processors, a vastly expanded Internet, digital cameras, audio- and image-based software, and Web resources–all, one might assume, at the service of campus-based university faculty and students and community-based youth taking part in local afterschool programs. In considering both the changes in technologies and programs over time and in the cultures within each physical program site, we can observe critically the limitations in programs' capacities to take full advantage of the rapidly evolving technologies for teaching, learning, and collaboration. We suggest that the reasons may be best understood in theoretical terms by taking a cultural-historical approach that connects sociotechnical systems theory with activity theory to elucidate the processes by which UC Links has adapted to constraints and opportunities at various levels.

## Theoretical Background

A *sociotechnical system* is an organizational system consisting of activities that constitute a functional whole encompassing both its social subsystem and its technical subsystem—that is, the interplay between people engaged in a work system and the technical resources they use (Trist & Bamforth, 1951; Trist & Murray, 1993). Because the social and technical subsystems are independent yet correlative, they must be seen as intricately linked for their joint optimization and for the optimization of the organizational system as a whole (Trist, 1981; Fox, 1995). While first envisioned as a tool for analyzing and optimizing work systems, the concept of the sociotechnical system has broader implications. In the afterschool arena, as well as other educational domains, it has clear implications for program impact and sustainability.

Sociotechnical systems function at three interconnected levels: as primary work systems, whole organization systems, and macrosocial systems (Trist, 1981). Primary work systems are relatively small face-to-face work units that collaboratively develop and implement set tasks and activities. Whole organization systems work collaboratively across individual primary work systems, coordinating their efforts in pursuit of common or complementary goals and objectives. Macrosocial systems encompass broader communities, social agencies, and institutions within a particular sector of industry (Trist, 1981). For the UC Links network of programs, each local program site constitutes a primary work system; the network of physical program sites represents the whole organization system; and the community, school district, statewide, and national sociopolitical contexts together represent the macrosocial system in which both site and network take place.

At the same time, a sociotechnical system like UC Links is at its heart an *activity system*. The link between sociotechnical systems theory and activity theory is a close but not always recognized fit. Activity theory approaches human experience as being shaped or mediated by the human use of tools and sign systems (Nardi, 1996). Individual human development and cognition takes place not simply as an internal psychological process, but in social context–that is, in the context of sociocultural activities in which human beings,

using the tools at hand, negotiate and pursue shared goals (Vygotsky, 1978). Following Lewin (1935), Vygotsky suggests that human cognition and action is shaped in the context of sociocultural activity and of the conditions in which activity takes place. In brief, human thought and work takes place in the context of an activity system, a coordinated system of related tasks and activities with complementary or cumulative objectives.

Cole (1996, 2006) has examined afterschool youth programs closely as activity systems in which individual and small-group learning takes place as a process of *distributed cognition*. In this context, he has studied the development of activities using *mediational tools*—e.g., computer games, new digital media, and other hands-on materials—as a cultural system that frames the collaborative engagement of young people and sets up multiple opportunities for "the zone of proximal development," in which youth can together accomplish tasks that they could not have completed individually (Vygotsky, 1978). This co-construction of the framework for cumulative zones of proximal development, linking novice and expert peers in constellations of informal collaborative tasks, constitutes a "fifth dimension" of human cognitive experience—the dimension in which individual and small-group learning, in the context of activity systems, becomes culturally mediated and institutionally sustained over time. Cole designed the Fifth Dimension afterschool program as a pragmatic implementation of his findings, and it has been adapted and implemented worldwide (Cole, 2006). UC Links grew out of this theoretical and practical work, as a means to institutionalize this activity system as a broad-based, long-term strategy for engaging universities and communities in the collaborative development of sustainable afterschool programming for underserved youth.

As a *sociotechnical activity system* in which existing technological artifacts and resources mediate human action and distributed cognition, UC Links offers an example of how technological practice and the capacity for innovation comes to be challenged by local conditions limiting technological access (the question of when which tools, new or old, are available to whom). The rapidity of the changes in digital technologies potentially available to programs like UC Links during the last two decades makes it possible to look historically at the systems facing this change—for instance, how they perceive their potential use of new technologies either to fit into or to transform their ways of engaging youth informally in learning. In our view, the historical process by which each UC Links site has adopted and adapted specific technologies and uses of technologies has established an agentive technical practice, a systemic technological stance, or industry. We approach the concept of *industry* anthropologically, not simply as the systematic production and distribution of goods and services but as an orienting stance toward and agentive implementation of particular tasks and activities, given the tools at hand. In other words, industry is a technological *habitus* (Bourdieu, 1990), in which technology is intricately tied to human relationships engendering meaning. That is, people do not simply *have* technology; they *enact* technology. Technology is not simply the tools we have at hand; it is also an orientation or stance toward the meaning and value of those tools for social life (Dobres, 2000, 127). This stance or selective orientation toward technology in a particular socio-technical system may represent either an adaptive opportunity for immediate innovation or an inhibition from innovation as successive technological advances take place.

These processes of adaptation may be further understood in terms of the law of evolutionary potential, which states, "the more specified and adapted a form in a given evolutionary stage, the smaller is its potential for passing to the next stage" (Sahlins & Service, 1997). In other words, as tool users, human beings act on their world by modifying and adapting material objects to extend their physical capacities to act on the world. From prehistory to the present, human groups have invested in technical systems, or tool kits, that represent their adaptive orientation to the world. Overinvestment in specific adaptations may limit the general adaptability of the social system for the long term. This general principle of biological and cultural evolution is directly applicable to our understanding of *sociotechnical activity systems* like UC Links and how they evolve over time. Local UC Links programs have been highly agentive in their use of available technologies and equipment, but in some cases, they have also been inhibited from taking on new technologies and uses of technologies as a result of their technical *industry*–i.e., their adaptive embrace of technologies that have quickly become either obsolete or limited in their capability to accommodate newly developed applications. Their industry, or technological *habitus*, is important as a stance which can be either an impetus or an inhibition in adaptations to successive technological advances. By looking closely at these processes, we can understand the relationship between industry and agency in the development of sociotechnical systems like UC Links.

## UC LINKS AS A SOCIOTECHNICAL ACTIVITY SYSTEM

As noted earlier, as a collaborative network of physical program sites and people, UC Links pursues a variety of approaches to afterschool teaching and learning. Each UC Links site explores effective uses of digital and hands-on resources in the development of instructional and enrichment activities. Collectively, UC Links sites have worked to establish a sustainable and scalable learning community focused on the innovative educational uses of digital technologies.

## Industry and Agency in the Primary Work System

In practice, as might be expected, this learning community has developed most intensely in the primary work system of the local program site. There, university faculty and their graduate students, key community representatives, and in some cases teachers, collaboratively develop learning activities using digital technologies or other resources. Built around key cultural, linguistic, and educational concerns that resonate in the local community, the activities and resources are developed interactively over time, and in many cases, participating youth are themselves active in determining the range of activities used. For example, based on local concerns, various sites have approached the activity of digital storytelling in distinctive ways; some have focused the activity on individual or family narratives, while others have focused on creating community narratives, including the creation of formal presentations such as community mapping projects that communicate to local public officials questions of pressing concern to the community in which the program exists.

In this way, each local program site constructs, in effect, an activity system in which both community and university collaborators feel intensely invested. This sense of shared investment includes the specific tools used at the site, such as the kinds of computers available at the school or community organization where the program site is located. In the initial stages of each program, these tools were often pre-established, depending on the specific time and place that the program began. For example, some sites built their activities around Mac computers while others built activities around PCs, the choice based solely on local circumstances—the equipment that was then available in the computer room at the school or community organization where the site was located. In this way, some sites often became wedded historically to the tools immediately at hand. In some cases, the equipment may change over time, as schools or community organizations upgrade their computers. In other cases, the UC Links collaboration has been the impetus for such upgrades. For example, when the UC Links afterschool program began in east Oakland, leaders were given access to the host school's computer lab; however, the room was initially unusable, because the school's existing electrical system would not accommodate the power that the computers in the lab demanded. Moreover, the computers themselves were relatively old and were not networked. To address these challenges, the collaborating partners pooled their resources. UC Links staff brought in professional technology staff from UC Berkeley, while school staff negotiated with the local school district to upgrade the lab's electronic capabilities. Together, they played a catalytic role in upgrading the school's electrical system and networking the computers in the host school's classrooms and computer lab.

Yet despite several similar cases, most programs have been limited for considerable periods of time to whatever equipment their host sites had in place when the program began. In the early years of UC Links, when the state of technology did not allow cross-platform uses of software, this factor meant that programs with access to Mac computers were limited in the range of educational software available for the students they served. Over time, it has become increasingly possible to use software on both Mac and PC platforms. Yet even with these advances, access to new and more advanced educational software has been limited at a number of sites because of the age of their computers. Because most UC Links sites are located at schools or community organizations in underserved communities, they had limited resources for acquiring digital technologies. Thus, the computers to which they had access were either provided by private donors who were essentially offloading old or outdated equipment or were acquired by higher level administrative offices whose purchasing guidelines focused more on frugality than quality of equipment. As a result, programs sites have often been limited, for years at a time, to using a relatively limited range of hardware and software for which their host computer systems have had the capacity. These specific adaptations to local conditions have limited programs' capabilities to adapt and innovate at a level in keeping with successive technological advances.

These limitations clearly have implications for the kinds of innovation—in both technical devices and programmatic activities—that local sites can incorporate and manage. For example, schools' firewalls and other restrictions on the use of e-mail and the Internet have made it very difficult for sites to engage in cross-site activities or Web-based inquiry projects for young people. In any case, there has been a highly varied response among program sites to the rapid development of new digital technologies. Different sites have had differential access to particular technologies, and with the often long-term investment in the digital resources locally available at the time of sites' creation, the result has been that lessons learned about the use of new tools at one site cannot always or easily be transferred for use at other sites.

This adaptational limit does not mean that the people working at individual sites have been passive in response to technological change. In fact, they have explicitly recognized the limitations of their local technical industry and have been highly agentive in using, and even leveraging, the technological tools they have had at hand to sustain high quality learning activities that engage the young people participating in their respective programs. At a UC Links site located in an under-resourced community organization in San Diego, university partners brought in personal computers and accessory equipment. These resources boosted the site's level of technical industry. As a result, they were able to engage the youth at the site in learning activities that included technical skills development, digital storytelling, stop action movie animation illustrating science concepts, and

a Virtual Ocean Project that helps youth improve their reading and science knowledge and skills through use of both a virtual world and traditional media (including books, poster boards, puppets). This turning to volunteered resources allowed for a significant leap in digital learning activities that, while highly laudable, is neither scalable nor sustainable for most programs.

The implementation of digital storytelling as an educational activity in UC Links afterschool programs represents a good example of UC Links sites' innovative use of limited digital resources. Digital storytelling, the use of digital multimedia technologies to create personal or community narratives, can be a compelling learning activity for youth who have become disengaged from schooling. With training from the Center for Digital Storytelling, UC Links began incorporating the activity into its programs in the 1990s. To encourage implementation across sites, the UC Links statewide office sponsored trainings for staff from UC Links sites statewide. Many sites embraced the idea of using the activity but encountered challenges in implementing it locally. One of the chief obstacles was technological. At that point in time, trainings in digital storytelling focused almost exclusively on the use of such software as Adobe Premier and Adobe Photoshop. During trainings, UC Links staff were excited about the capabilities of the Adobe tools, but when they returned to their sites, they soon found obstacles to using them. For some, the cost of the software was prohibitive. For others, it was a platform issue. At that time, Adobe software could not be used across platforms, and sites that had relatively old Mac computers could not use it. Before the development and broader availability of iMovie, and especially at sites equipped with PCs, site staff opted for other digital tools. At the East Oakland site, the host school had invested in relatively inexpensive, low-end computers several years earlier and lacked the resources to acquire new ones at that time (2000-2001). Recognizing this limitation in their local technical industry, the site director and her staff made use of a scaled-down version of digital storytelling, employing a combination of PC-friendly visual and audio tools, particularly PowerPoint and Audacity, and imaginatively adapted the idea of producing personal narratives with multi-media tools. Several years later (2005-06), through the collaboration of UC Links and local partners, the school lab procured new Macs, and since the new Macs were equipped with iMovie, the program was able to use it for this activity.

In short, limited access to upgraded or new technologies (e.g., personal digital assistants, e-readers, iPads, unfettered broadband Internet for research, problem-solving, communication, and collaboration) has required staff in local UC Links programs to build learning activities creatively around whatever limited technological tools are available; yet it also means that local program staff are limited in their ability to integrate newly emerging technological tools into the learning activities they offer at their sites. As a result, while UC Links program sites extend the opportunities for youth in underserved areas to utilize new technological tools for learning, their innovations are obviously limited by the inability to draw on new technological innovations as rapidly as they happen. We might say that their local industry or stance toward available technologies at the primary work systems limits their access to and agential use of rapidly emerging technologies.

This lag between availability of new technologies and their adaptive use in the UC Links community of afterschool programs is mirrored in the educational system at large. A recent CDW-G survey of high school students suggests that high school students are more likely to use a variety of new technologies (e.g., iPods, smartphones, online text, blogs, digital content, and podcasts) on their own time rather than as learning tools in school, owing primarily to limited adoption by teachers and limited refreshing of technology by schools (CDW-G, 2010). This disparity between the innovation and adoption of new technologies for both in-school and afterschool teaching and learning, especially in low-income communities, is underscored in a number of recent articles and reports (e.g., see Dickard & Schneider, 2002; Warschauer, Knobel, & Stone, 2004; Collier, 2008; Parker, 2008; Education Week, 2009; Gray, Thomas, & Lewis, 2010; Smith, 2010). It is clear that the agential use of successive new technologies by educational organizations is limited by their technical industry or investment in specific technologies.

## Industry and Agency in the Organization System

Digital technologies have enabled UC Links partners both to carry out their local site activities for youth and to share ideas and experiences across sites. Digital tools have been used to support continuing online discussions that contribute to shared understandings of effective learning activities for underserved youth from diverse backgrounds and that help build the sense of belonging to an ongoing distributed community of learning and practice. The tools that UC Links participants have primarily used have not changed a great deal over the life of the UC Links network. They were considered fairly innovative in the 1990s, when the program started up, but now would be considered rather *passé*. The use of and orientation to a common Web site and to two listservs that include key players from participating program sites in the statewide network have proven valuable for carrying out these functions. Interestingly, UC Links has not found successive innovations in distance communication and collaboration–e.g., blogs, Twitter, Facebook, Skype–to be broadly useful across the network, in part because key participants at various sites have had unequal access to and familiarity with those emerging tools. In practice, the participants who are most active at the organizational level are university faculty and program administrators and their students and staff, most of whom have become accustomed to using the listservs and email over time, and this *habitus* has continued. Large-scale videoconferencing has proven difficult to schedule and fragile to implement, especially because different locations have had very different capabilities to accommodate their respective videoconferencing tools without untimely glitches and interrupted service; technologies like Skype have had limited use, except in one-to-one or very small group communications linking undergraduate courses at different campuses, because until recently few UC Links participants have had equal access to or familiarity with the tools, and because so few people can be easily involved within the Skype focal range. For cross-site meetings with larger numbers of participants, older technologies like telephone conferencing simply work better.

Nonetheless, the UC Links Web site and listservs, as well as annual face-to-face conferences and meetings, have served as key means for pooling both theoretical and practical knowledge contributing to the productive use of new technologies for localized learning activities. Equally effective, though more difficult to sustain, have been instances of cross-site collaboration in the implementation of multi-site activities that engage young people from different sites in joint digital activities and practices. For example, a recent message on the UC Links listserv about combining narrative with digital photography as a way to promote the literacy and analysis skills of elementary and middle school students, resulted in a collaboration between two sites located in low-income communities in Sacramento and Santa Barbara. In this collaboration, students from the two sites engaged in collaborative storytelling. The students found the ongoing exchange and collaboration with distant partners exciting and engaging. However, the two sites were unable to send the stories back and forth digitally because one of the sites did not have computers with sufficient capacity to download the files sent by the other; instead, they made CDs of their stories and sent them back and forth by mail. Such cross-site

ventures effectively serve not only to connect children and youth from different communities in captivating digital activities adapted from distinctive models and approaches to teaching and learning; they also serve to engage site coordinators and practitioners in common tasks that build shared understandings about the productive use of emerging technologies. However, unequal resources limit their ability to make full use of the capabilities that contemporary technologies would in more privileged conditions make possible.

Such cross-site collaboration, while valued and indeed pursued to a limited degree by local sites in the UC Links system, remains problematic. Some programs have tried to capitalize on the digital expertise of graduate students and staff to develop protected social networking tools such as Ning, that provide opportunities for youth to post and share their digital products for their peers, both within and across sites. Other programs have discussed and initiated the pilot use of closed social networking websites for cross-site communications among young people. Most host schools and organizations, however, are wary of allowing their use. Moreover, funding and technical challenges for the university team developing and using the software, human subjects and privacy concerns, and the technical resources at other sites, have limited the use of the new software to a small cluster of sites, while more extensive cross-site investigation, development, and implementation of the tools have thus far proved impracticable.

The rather conservative use of distance communication tools within the UC Links network has perhaps served the function of leveling the playing field for a sociotechnical system that, at the primary work level, continues to experience unequal access to new digital resources. Reliance on the two listservs, for instance, while allowing for differential access to technology resources among key players at various sites, has both provided for the presence of diverse voices to deepen the dialogue and solidarity of key UC Links players across multiple sites and ensured the flow of funding and accountability information vital to the network at large. It has also been the most productive means for communicating the successes of UC Links, both locally and as a larger organization system so that those working at the primary site level do not lose sight of their collective accomplishments and cumulative achievements, while also getting recognition for their local accomplishments. The UC Links statewide office has served as the central point of communication for connecting the work of individual sites, clarifying externally mandated accountability and other reporting requirements, and sharing the outcomes of sites' reports. Through such oversight of the listservs and website, UC links sites have developed not only a sense of the connectedness of their joint obligations and responsibilities to each other (for instance, the importance of individual reporting to ensure the funding of all), but also a recognition and mutual appreciation for the collective fruits of their dispersed labors. In this way, the UC Links organization system feeds back into the work and identity of the individual sites as primary work systems.

## Industry and Agency in the Macrosocial System

Innovations and adaptations in the UC Links sociotechnical system are both limited and enabled by the macrosocial system in which they occur—namely, the local, state, and national sociopolitical contexts in which they take place. These larger contexts have historically set the boundaries of evolutionary potential for technological adaptations taking place both within local sites as primary work systems and in the UC Links network as a whole organizational system. For example, such macrosocial constraints as school district, state, and federal guidelines for funding and assessing education programs have increasingly been extended to afterschool. The strong mandate for test-driven instructional activities, even after school, has limited the ability to adapt both to

community concerns and to the opportunities that new technology innovations potentially represent. While many afterschool programs like UC Links have effectively responded to these accountability mandates (Underwood & Parker, 2010), doing so has entailed considerable transaction costs.[3]

The relationship between the macrosocial system and the primary work system is evident in the difficulty that local primary sites have in linking to the benefits of statewide initiatives like the partnership between the state-funded California K-12 High Speed Network and the university-based Corporation for Educational Network Initiatives in California (CENIC) and their collaborative attempts to extend broadband Internet access. The last-mile issues of extending broadband Internet remain prevalent, especially for underserved low-income communities such as those that UC Links serves. Many schools and community organizations that host UC Links programs still do not have access to broadband Internet. Yet even where access to broadband Internet exists the industry of primary work sites, their technical *habitus* toward relatively obsolete equipment, limits programs' adaptability to and innovation with new capabilities. Moreover, local partnerships' efforts to create innovative, stimulating learning activities using the capacities of broader bandwidth have at times been stymied by school or school district concerns about students' unmonitored use of the Internet. In short, the technology tools that sites have at hand are often a function of the host organization's technological *habitus*. In this way, programs, though by no means immobilized by the methodological strictures imposed by these macrosocial constraints, have had to adapt their approach to the educational uses of technology.

The role of the digital technologies industry (and here we refer to the commercial production and sale of digital goods) in this process has been important. While this industry has been assiduous in advancing a variety of new digital tools and applications, the distribution of these tools across socioeconomic divisions has been at best incidental and problematic. The connections between systemic efforts like UC Links and the digital industry have been equally problematic, with an implicit bias on each side that hinders communication. The result has generally been an impasse, a cultural divide, with neither side recognizing fully the knowledge and opportunities that the other has to offer. The continuing outcome of this impasse has been that the kinds of equipment and tools available at many of the community sites served by UC Links have often been antiquated by contemporary standards. The technological facilities in the schools and community organizations served have been set by state or school district policies or by commercial philanthropy. Once these technologies are physically established, especially in schools and organizations in underserved neighborhoods, upgrades to assimilate successive technological advances are difficult to accomplish.

The adaptive response to these macrosocial pressures has been proactive among UC Links sites. Local partners have been key players in securing more current equipment or in strategically assessing and collecting the best auxiliary accessories to the technical equipment available to them. In most cases, the specific equipment that has been donated or purchased for specific local sites is what each program site has had to work with in implementing the most effective instructional and enrichment activities possible. The strategic implementation of learning activities that are optimal, given the limited tools at hand, constitutes a major investment of time and personnel, as well as financial resources on the part of each program site as a primary work system. Here again, the statewide office along with the physical network of participating colleagues using e-mail and listservs has served a mediating role, providing a forum for discussing the range of optimal innovations that are possible, given the use of specific kinds of equipment. This mediation, however, does not mean that local sites can change

the technical conditions in which they operate; funding and other decision-making issues at the macrosocial level, in both the public and private sectors, limit the sociotechnical adaptability of local sites.

## CONCLUSION AND RECOMMENDATIONS

The UC Links experience shows that educational uses of technology in the afterschool arena in underserved areas are affected by multiple factors that come into play in and across the primary, whole organization, and macrosocial levels of a program like UC Links. Given both the emergence of new technologies and the local, organizational, and macrosocial limitations and constraints that local sites have faced in securing their use of those technologies, UC Links sites have experienced a diversification in their available technologies and in their approaches to using them. The initial investment made in the training and use of specific equipment has constituted a technological orientation or *habitus*, a local industry that is resilient but limited in its ability to adapt to successive technological changes.

Community-university partners, especially in underserved communities, necessarily have to work with the limited tools they have at hand. They can effectively create innovative learning activities around that industry or tool kit, even when it consists primarily of "older" technologies, as the UC Links experience has shown. Yet as the UC Links experience suggests, to take full advantage of new technological developments and innovations for the young people they serve, partners need to be explicitly aware of their technical industry and their specific adaptational stance toward their existing technology, especially within their primary work systems. Only when this local industry is explicitly defined, only when their enactment of technology is clear in their minds, can participants fully recognize and act upon both the limits and the opportunities that they have before them in attempting new adaptations and innovations. Part of this recognition involves the often implicit or unexamined constraints that obtain in the macrosocial context in which they conduct their activities locally.

Thus, a critical examination of the role of industry as the productive stance toward technology, and agency, as the adaptive enactment of technology, is crucial not only at the primary work system level but also at the whole organization and macrosocial levels because of the way all three levels interact with each other. At this latter level, federal, state, and local educational institutions, corporations of the technology industry, and philanthropic organizations need to work more closely together, not only to make new technologies more readily available to schools and community-based centers that serve youth across socioeconomic boundaries, but also to work to adjust policies to enable the more productive use of those technologies for teaching and learning by schools and afterschool programs. The university needs to step forward as a more active institutional partner in these collaborative efforts. Only in this way can school systems, local schools, and youth development programs take full advantage of the resources and opportunities that new technologies potentially offer for creating innovative activity systems for teaching and learning.

Viewing program networks like UC Links as sociotechnical activity systems helps clarify the dynamics of their social organizations in relation to their strategic use of technological resources. Viewing them as sociotechnical activity systems that evolve along predictable paths as cultural systems allows for a better understanding and potential optimization of the processes of adaptation and innovation in technological practice. In the afterschool arena, as well as other educational domains, it has clear implications for program impact and sustainability. It also enables us to anticipate predictable pitfalls and situate our efforts strategically to maximize the productivity

of our enactment of technology. It further helps us understand how, through both digital and face-to-face interactions, efforts like UC Links can establish the framework for sharing information about the educational use of technological tools and related multimedia pedagogical strategies for particular activities, in order to become an ever broader community of learners in the use of digital media for teaching and learning. Recognizing the implications of this approach is important for understanding both the dilemma and the promise of technological innovation for all students, not only for afterschool programs, but also for other educational and social institutions–indeed for any organization whose day-to-day and long-term functioning must answer to the demands of rapid technological change.

# REFERENCES

Bourdieu, P. (1990). *The logic of practice*. Stanford, CA: Stanford University Press.

CDW-G. (2010). *21st-century classroom report: Preparing students for the future or the past?* Retrieved from http://newsroom.cdw.com/features/feature-06-28-10.html

Cole, M. (1996). *Cultural psychology: A once and future discipline*. Cambridge, MA: Harvard University Press.

Cole, M., & Engeström, Y. (2007). Cultural-historical approaches to designing for development. In J. Valsiner, & A. Rosa (Eds.), *The Cambridge handbook of sociocultural psychology* (pp. 484–506). New York, NY: Cambridge University Press. doi:10.1017/CBO9780511611162.026

Cole, M.The Distributed Literacy Consortium. (2006). *The fifth dimension: An after-school program built on diversity*. New York, NY: Russell Sage Foundation.

Collier, L. (2008, November). The C's of change: Student—and teachers—learn 21st century skills. *National Council of Teachers of English Council Chronicle*, 6-9.

Dickard, N., & Schneider, D. (2002, July 1). The digital divide: Where we are. *Edutopia*. Retrieved from http://www.edutopia.org/digital-divide-where-we-are-today

Dobres, M. A. (2000). *Technology and social agency: Outlining a practice framework for archaeology*. Malden, MA: Blackwell.

Education Week. (2009, March 26). State technology grades and ranking tables. *Technology Counts 2009, 28*(26). Retrieved from http://www.edweek.org/ew/toc/2009/03/26/index.html

Fox, W. M. (1995). Sociotechnical system principles and guidelines: Past and present. *The Journal of Applied Behavioral Science, 31*(1), 91–105. doi:10.1177/0021886395311009

Geertz, C. (2000). *Local knowledge: Further essays in interpretive anthropology*. New York, NY: Basic Books.

Gray, L., Thomas, N., & Lewis, L. (2010). *Educational technology in U.S. public Schools: Fall 2008--first look*. (NCES Report 2010-034). National Center for Education Statistics, U.S. Department of Education. Retrieved from http://nces.ed.gov/pubsearch/pubsinfo.asp?pubid=2010034

Leontiev, A. N. (1978). *Activity, consciousness, and personality*. Englewood Cliffs, NJ: Prentice-Hall.

Lewin, K. (1935). *A dynamic theory of personality*. New York, NY: McGraw-Hill.

Luria, A. R. (1976). *Cognitive development: Its cultural and social foundations*. Cambridge, MA: Harvard University Press.

Parker, L. L. (2008). Technology in support of young English learners in and out of school. In L. L. Parker (Ed.), *Technology-mediated learning environments for young English learners: Connections in and out of school* (pp. 213–250). New York, NY: Erlbaum.

Sahlins, M. D., & Service, E. R. (1997). *Evolution and culture*. Ann Arbor, MI: University of Michigan Press.

Smith, A. (2010). *Mobile access 2010*. Pew Internet & American Life Project. Retrieved from http://www.pewinternet.org/Reports/2010/Mobile-Access-2010.aspx?r=1

Trist, E. L. (1981). *The evolution of socio-technical systems: A conceptual framework and an action research program*. Ontario Quality of Working Life Center, Occasional Paper no. 2.

Trist, E. L., & Bamforth, K. (1951). Some social and psychological consequences of longwall coal mining: An examination of the psychological situation and defenses of a work group in relation to the social structure and technological content of the work system. *Human Relations, 4*, 3–38. doi:10.1177/001872675100400101

Trist, E. L., & Murray, H. (1993). *The social engagement of social science: A Tavistock anthology* (*Vol. II*). Philadelphia, PA: University of Pennsylvania Press.

Underwood, C., Mahiri, J., Toloza, C., & Pranzetti, D. (2003). Beyond the mask of technology: Educational equity and the pedagogy of hope. In K. C. MacKinnon (Ed.). *Behind many masks: Gerald Berreman and Berkeley anthropology, 1959-2001*. (Kroeber Anthropological Society Papers, No. 89-90). Berkeley, CA: University of California, Berkeley, Department of Anthropology.

Underwood, C., & Parker, L. (2010). *University-community links to higher learning. Annual Report, 2008-09*. Berkeley, CA: University of California.

Underwood, C., Welsh, M., Gauvain, M., & Duffy, S. (2000). Learning at the edges: Challenges to the sustainability of service learning in higher education. *Journal of Language and Learning Across the Disciplines, 4*(3), 7–26.

Vasquez, O. A. (2003). *La clase magica: Imagining optimal possibilities in a bilingual community of learners.* Mahwah, NJ: Erlbaum.

Vygotsky, L. S. (1978). *Mind in society: The development of higher psychological processes.* Cambridge, MA: Harvard University Press.

Warschauer, M., Knobel, M., & Stone, L. (2004). Technology and equity in schooling: Deconstructing the digital divide. *Educational Policy, 18*(4), 562–588. doi:10.1177/0895904804266469

## KEY TERMS AND DEFINITIONS

**Activity System:** A coordinated system of complementary tasks and activities with common or cumulative objectives.

**Adaptation:** The strategic response to existing or perceived environmental conditions, pressures, resources and opportunities.

**Distributed Cognition:** The view that learning, thinking, and knowledge is not simply located or possessed inside the individual but is mediated through the use of human artifacts and accomplished through joint activity among individuals, groups, and activity systems.

**Habitus:** The historically emergent system of structure and structuring dispositions, or orienting stance, implicit or explicit, that informs practical activity.

**Industry:** The orientation or stance toward and agentive implementation of particular tasks and activities, given the tools at hand, including but not limited to the commercial production and distribution of goods and services.

**Mediating Tools:** Material resources modified to extend the capacities of the human body and mediate human beings' ability to act upon each other and the world around them.

**Socio-Technical Activity System:** An organizational system consisting of activities that constitute a functional whole encompassing both its social and technical subsystems.

**Technology:** The human use of tools—i.e., the modification, refinement, and use of material resources to meet or fulfill perceived needs.

**Technical Agency:** The active sociocultural engagement with or enactment of industry, including the productive development and use of tools, artifacts, and products.

## ENDNOTES

[1]    UC Links program staff include graduate students and upper-level undergraduates working with UC Links faculty leaders and/or site-based staff working or volunteering for the school or community organization hosting the site.

[2]    UC Links undergraduate courses have been taught in a variety of academic disciplines, including anthropology, communications, education, English, history, physics, psychology, sociology, and urban and regional planning.

[3]    Site data suggest that UC Links has consistently met its benchmark of over 70% of its K-8 participants performing at or above grade levels; moreover, UC Links assessments of literacy and technology skills suggest that the program is having a positive impact in these areas (see Appendices IV and V in Underwood & Parker, 2010).

# Chapter 28
# Partners in Storytelling:
## UMBC, Retirement Living TV, and the Charlestown Digital Story Project

**William Shewbridge**
*University of Maryland, Baltimore County, USA*

## ABSTRACT

*In 2006, the University of Maryland, Baltimore County (UMBC) entered into a unique partnership with Retirement Living Television (RLTV). Initially driven by the practicalities of bringing a new broadcast network to air, the relationship came to influence the role of new media technology in teaching and learning on the UMBC campus. The Charlestown Project brought university students and senior citizens together to create short digital movies. The project also became a catalyst for creating human connections beyond the campus and across generations. Along the way, students formed new attitudes towards aging and community, and the campus attained an increased awareness of the power of digital storytelling.*

## INTRODUCTION

Inspired by the workshop process pioneered by the Center for Digital Storytelling (CDS), UMBC's New Media Studio (NMS) has built a community of digital story practice through faculty workshops and support of visual assignments in the classroom. The CDS approach centers on a three-day workshop in which participants create short (3-4 minute) digital videos using ubiquitous desktop software such as Final Cut, iMovie and Windows MovieMaker. Participants construct a

personal narrative using photos and other media artifacts (Lambert, 2009). An idea central to digital storytelling is that the storyteller's sense of individuality and ownership is enhanced when people are allowed to tell their own stories in their own voices (ELI).

In the five years that NMS has facilitated digital storytelling activities at UMBC, faculty members have adapted the CDS methodology for use in a wide range of contexts. These projects have built on digital storytelling's ability to blend emerging and traditional literacies in ways that effectively engage students (Ohler, 2008, p. 11). At UMBC, history students have produced stories exploring

DOI: 10.4018/978-1-60960-623-7.ch028

samurai culture. Returning Peace Corp volunteers have used digital storytelling as a means of reflecting on their service. Students in Mass Communication Studies and American Studies have built media literacy skills while analyzing popular media in visual assignments (http://www.umbc.edu/stories).

## BACKGROUND

NMS's work in this area occurred at a time when a relationship was forming between UMBC and RLTV. Founded in 2006 by John Erickson of Erickson Retirement Communities, RLTV is a national cable network targeting an audience of 50 and older. As a start-up network, RLTV faced a number of formidable challenges, including the need to find production and master control facilities quickly. This was due in large part to an initial distribution opportunity with Comcast Cable, which required the network to be on the air in six months (E. Beimfohr, personal interview, February 4, 2010).

Erickson had an established relationship with UMBC, which is home to the Erickson School. In part because of this relationship, the campus was considered as a possible base of operations for the new network. After touring the campus's aging television production facility, which is managed by NMS, RLTV suggested that if it were upgraded, it would meet their immediate needs. An agreement was reached by which RLTV would fund a complete re-equipping and remodeling of the UMBC television production facility in exchange for use of the space for a period of 18 months. During this period, RLTV would build a permanent facility in UMBC's research park, including corporate headquarters, master control and production studios. RLTV planned to relocate to the new building, when it was completed, leaving UMBC with the updated facility. In addition, the presence of RLTV on campus promised to create internship and job opportunities for students.

These opportunities were of particular interest to UMBC's fledgling Media and Communication Studies program.

RLTV hired a former UMBC employee, Kathy Raab, as campus liaison. Raab was charged with coordinating the many details of the partnership, from arranging Studio tours and internships to securing parking on campus for RLTV employees. Raab's institutional knowledge of UMBC was invaluable in providing a conduit for communication and pulling the relationship together (E. Beimfohr, personal interview, February 4, 2010). NMS worked closely with Raab and others at RLTV to support the partnership.

Early in the process, RLTV asked the NMS to explore ideas for involving viewers in content creation. Drawing on its previous experience, the Studio proposed a project with the nearby Charlestown retirement community, partnering students with seniors to create digital stories. Out of subsequent discussions, the Charlestown Project was born. Former network vice president Ed Beimfohr remembers his initial impressions:

*I looked at this proposal and said, "This is fascinating." A chance to not only produce some unique programming that would fit nicely into our roster but also . . . enable [seniors] to capture some of their own history . . . and of course empowering them in the process. (E. Beimfohr, personal interview, February 4, 2010)*

RLTV agreed to fund an initial workshop during the summer of 2006. Six students were recruited and trained in the digital storytelling process. Recruiting participants from the Charlestown community came with its own challenges. There was an understandable caution on the part of community administrators concerned about potential exploitation of residents. After meeting with the Studio staff and learning about the project, the administration offered their full support to the project. Seven residents signed on to participate at a public information session held in the community and the workshop began the following week.

Over the course of the next two months, the seniors worked closely with student partners in an open lab environment to create their 300-400 word digital stories. This involved recording narration, scanning photos and brainstorming ways to visualize each story. During this period, there was much interplay among the production teams as they shared ideas and encouragement. The story teams continued to work independently until the stories were complete. After approximately a month, the group reconvened to view the completed works.

*When the resulting pieces came into RLTV I, of course, looked at them first and said "a couple of these are just killer, they're just knockouts." … As I rolled it out around RLTV, I got similar reactions. Everyone talked about it and was very pleased with the outcome. I would say it exceeded expectations by and large. (E. Beimfohr, personal interview, February 4, 2010)*

RLTV was pleased enough to fund an additional two rounds of workshops over the course of the following year. Eventually, 40 stories were produced. Participants appeared on the network to talk about digital storytelling and the project. RLTV also featured the stories on the network's Web site. A special showing of the stories at the 2007 Maryland Film Festival was arranged by RLTV's campus liaison. The most significant public recognition of the project came with a 2007 Telly Award. RLTV went to great lengths to publicize the award by hosting a ceremony at Charlestown where each participant received a bronze statuette. The award was a fitting capstone for the project, recognizing all participants and the entire body of work produced.

Following the success at Charlestown, NMS was asked to develop a plan to expand the project nationwide. The proposal submitted by NMS included initial workshops in Boston, Berkeley, and Denver, organized in partnership with CDS.

An online community where participants could share their stories and learn from each other was also included. RLTV initially funded development of the site (http://www.digitalstorynetwork.org) and a CDS-led workshop at Erickson's Wind Crest community in Denver, Colorado. While the resulting stories were well received by the network and the senior communities, funding for the project was discontinued due to budget reductions at RLTV in 2009.

## COMMUNITY AND EDUCATIONAL IMPACT

While the Charlestown Project thrived for only a relatively short time, it was successful on a number of levels. It is characteristic for digital storytelling to reveal universal themes in the everyday experiences of the storytellers (Thuman, 2008). The seniors who participated discovered that their personal stories resonated beyond their immediate families as they found an audience online and within their communities. For UMBC, the project served as a catalyst for promoting interest in digital storytelling within the campus community. The Telly award brought recognition from campus leadership who cited the project as an example of making human connections through technology (Educause, 2008). Publicity about the project helped stimulate faculty interest in the classroom applications of the technology, increasing demand for additional workshops and support of visual assignments. Today, UMBC's Digital Story Interest Group boasts 120 members with ongoing projects in a diversity of disciplines.

For those directly involved in the project, the greatest benefit was the experience itself. According to Jack Suess, UMBC Vice President for Information Technology, this was a case where "technology was an opening for having a conversation and that was really powerful."

*[The Charlestown Project] really changed the game . . . in terms of the way that some of the senior administrators on campus began to appreciate the power of digital stories. . . . We've been able to expose this more broadly on campus. We're seeing a heavy use in lots of different areas; increasing interest among faculty for trying to use it for reflective student performance. I don't think in the end we would have gotten to this point quite as quickly without the RLTV project helping to propel us forward in getting some visibility on the campus. (J. Suess, personal interview, February 2, 2010)*

The Charlestown Project also allowed RLTV to make a strong connection within the Erickson communities. The project gave seniors a chance to tell their stories to an audience beyond their families and immediate community. This was in keeping with RLTV's goal of giving seniors a voice. For Beimfohr, this was an issue of empowerment:

*Very simply, seniors are stereotyped as technophobic and that is true only to the extent that they have not been exposed to technology. Once they've been exposed ... and it's been demystified for them a bit, they take to it like ducks to water. ... Digital storytelling was a genius model not only because it was so productive but also because on a human level ... they learned so much from one another. (E. Beimfohr, personal interview, February 4, 2010)*

The rare opportunity for intergenerational dialogue created at Charlestown left a lasting impression on seniors and students alike. UMBC student participant Cathryna Brown reflected on the experience:

*The technology is a wonderful gift but I think the more important gift is that they are willing to open up their lives, their families, their memories, their most treasured tokens of life and to entrust us to*

*take these things that are so sacred to them and to create for them. ... We are inspired to live because we get to see the joy that they've experienced in living themselves and that's huge, especially for someone my age. (C. Brown, personal interview, January 3, 2007)*

## CONCLUSION

RLTV's presence on the UMBC campus has allowed both partners to move forward in important ways. Immediate benefits for each organization were realized with the renovation of UMBC's television production facility. The relationship that was formed in these early days laid the groundwork for the rich collaboration that resulted in the Charlestown Digital Story Project. Maintenance of strong communication channels at all levels of the organizations involved was a key element in keeping the process moving forward. This has led to an understanding of what each partner expects from the relationship and to a spirit of cooperation that continues today. Ed Beimfohr sees the approach taken by UMBC as an example for building strategic relationships beyond the campus:

*Historically academe has isolated itself; the ivory tower phenomenon . . . . That is something that will have to be overcome and that is something that UMBC has particularly excelled at. It has seen itself as of the community and has built very extensive relationships with the community, the various publics, widely defined stakeholders including businesses and business organizations. I think that's a really good model for the future and I think it is a healthy thing for all concerned. (E. Beimfohr, personal interview, February 4, 2010)*

For more information on digital storytelling at UMBC and to view the stories that were produced by the Charlestown Project, visit http://www.umbc.edu/stories.

## REFERENCES

Educause. (2008). *EDUCAUSE 2008 general session: Why IT matters: A president's perspective on technology and leadership.* Retrieved June 21, 2010, from http://hosted.mediasite.com/mediasite/Viewer/?peid=60706773509a468985f07cd6e23b2609

ELI. (2007). Seven things you should know about digital storytelling. *Educause.* Retrieved June 21, 2010, from http://net.educause.edu/ir/library/pdf/ELI7021.pdf

Lambert, J. (2009). *Digital storytelling: Capturing lives, creating community* (3rd ed.). Berkeley, CA: Digital Diner Press.

Ohler, J. (2008). *Digital storytelling in the classroom: New media pathways to literacy, learning and creativity.* Thousand Oaks, CA: Corwin Press.

Thumin, N. (2008). It's good for them to know my story: Cultural mediation as tension. In K. Lundby (Ed.), *Digital storytelling, mediatized: Self-representations in new media stories* (pp. 85–103). New York, NY: Peter Lang Publishing, Inc.

# Chapter 29

# Bridging the Gaps:
## Community–University Partnerships as a New Form of Social Policy

**Caroline Collins**
*Center for Academic and Social Advancement, USA*

**Olga. A. Vásquez**
*University of California San Diego, USA*

**James Bliesner**
*University of California San Diego, USA*

## ABSTRACT

*The following case study chronicles the activities of a community-university partnership that supports the University of California, San Diego's threefold mission of teaching, research, and service while directing educational resources to underrepresented communities. This partnership, instantiated in a research project widely known as La Clase Mágica, involves a broad spectrum of institutional units seeking to bridge the digital, cognitive, and employment gaps that exist between middle-class mainstream communities and those at the margins. The case study examines the project's history and philosophy, theoretical framework, commitment to collaboration, assessment, and impact over the past two decades.*

## INTRODUCTION

### The State of Education in California's Underserved Populations: Why Intervention is Necessary

Countless minority, language-minority and low-income youth encounter various systemic and independent barriers that impede the quality of their P-12 public educational experiences, and these circumstances hinder many of these children from continuing on to higher education. This differential access of minority and low-income youth to postsecondary education begins long before they come of age (Chavez & Arrendondo, 2006). The gap begins in early childhood with a lower number of Latino and language-minority youth attending pre-school (NCLR, 2009; Rumberger & Tran, 2006) and continues up the educational ladder (Vásquez, 2007). In 2004, for example,

DOI: 10.4018/978-1-60960-623-7.ch029

Latino, African-American, and American Indian students represented only 44% of the state's 343,484 graduating seniors; yet they constituted 74% of the 74,824 students who graduated from the state's lowest performing high schools—i.e., the bottom 10-30% (Chavez & Arrendondo, 2006). These schools bore higher enrollments of students from lower socioeconomic statuses, as 60% of their students were eligible for free or reduced lunch and only 18% represented families with at least one parent possessing a college or professional level education. Compounding this situation is the fact that fewer numbers of fully prepared teachers and levels of per-pupil funding exists in these schools as compared to higher performing campuses (Chavez & Arrendondo, 2006). In fact few, if any, of these schools are among the privileged 17% of California's high schools that offer the complete A-G course selection1, one of the most important means of achieving competiveness for admission to the University of California (UC) and other top-tier higher education institutions (Chavez & Arrendondo, 2006 and Vásquez, 2008).

Though there have been increases in the number of minorities entering higher education in recent decades, a gap remains in college matriculation rates (Cook & Códova, 2006). The likelihood that this disparity will continue to grow without intervention is evident in several developments. First, the diminishing funding to P-12 schools (EdSource, 2010) continues to impact an education system that is already bearing increasing dropout rates (Lansberg, 2008). Second, the 1996 dismantling of Affirmative Action, a policy that considers race, gender, or ethnicity as a benefit, has made it more difficult to admit talented minority youth who had the misfortune of attending under-resourced schools. Third, increased tuition and the importing of highly elevated number of paying out-of-state and foreign students into California's public universities will make it even harder for the state's low-income youth to gain access to affordable public higher education.

The University of California acknowledges these challenges and charges itself to "serve society as a center of higher learning, providing long-term societal benefits" (The University of California Academic Plan). In order to remit these long-term societal benefits to the largest degree possible, the UC system seeks to be accessible to diverse statewide populations. This distinct mission lends itself to a promising new form of intervention in which universities partner with underserved communities in order to meet the specific educational needs of under-represented populations while concurrently broadening the university's reach.

## CASE STUDY NARRATIVE

### The History of La Clase Mágica

Over the last two decades, our research and practice has focused on redressing this impending academic catastrophe by endeavoring to find the most effective learning conditions for non-mainstream youth. The driving force of our effort has been a community-university partnership that utilizes a technology-based pedagogy in order to benefit both entities. *La Clase Mágica,* an afterschool educational activity, connects UCSD with five underserved communities throughout San Diego County in community centers such a Head Start Program located at a local Catholic Mission, a community center located on the U.S./Mexico border, two affordable housing complexes, and the education complex of an American Indian Reservation. These community institutions provide their residents access to much needed computer labs. The nonprofit CASA (Center for Academic and Social Advancement) that grew out of the early work of *La Clase Mágica* furnishes some of these computers and at some sites even purchases the labs' wireless Internet service. Though these community centers may provide space for computer use, they often do not offer educational programming. This programming is provided by a UCSD research team that focuses on developing an optimal learning environment that meets the distinct needs of a given community through culturally relevant technology-based pedagogy.

In 1989, the fledging partnership between UCSD and a small Mexican-origin community gave birth to *La Clase Mágica*. At the time, it was a loosely coordinated arrangement of several institutional units including a Catholic Church, a federally funded Head Start Program, and UCSD's Laboratory of Comparative Human Cognition (LCHC) where principal investigator Vásquez had joined Michael Cole as a post-doctoral fellow. She was taken by the protean nature of LCHC's after-school project, the Fifth Dimension, and its ability to adapt to the institutional constraints of context and the particular needs of the target population. Vásquez entered the community with the idea of creating an ideal setting where Mexican origin bilingual children could excel intellectually. What began as a Fifth Dimension site immediately transformed to *La Clase Mágica* in response to the community's ethnic and linguistic composition as well as its specialized and complex educational needs. This new project built on the Fifth Dimension's theoretical and organizational foundation through strategies such as mixing play with education to also now address the importance of cultural, linguistic, and socioeconomic relevance in effective technology-based pedagogy.

Over the ensuing years, *La Clase Mágica* developed from a focus on elementary school age children to include three other developmental aged groups: *Mi Clase Mágica* (pre-school learners), *Wizard Assistants* (adolescent participants), and *La Gran Dimensión* (adult learners) each with an age-appropriate curriculum. It also extended to other locations across San Diego County and to another language group (Ipai) via an adaptation for the learners at the Kumeyaay American Indian Reservation of San Pasqual, called TACKLE (Technology and Culture Kumeyaay Literacy Education). In 1996, the Fifth Dimension/*La*

*Clase Mágica* model was adopted across the UC system in the form of the UC Links consortium of community-university partnerships (www. uclinks.org). This consortium's charge was to help prepare underserved youth for higher education after the dismantling of Affirmative Action. Today, 35 UC system after-school projects are linked across this statewide network. In 2000, after 11 years of project growth, *La Clase Mágica* began an effort to gain sustainability. Independently, the local effort produced the Center for Academic & Social Advancement (CASA). This not-for-profit organization supports *La Clase Mágica* and its adaptations by securing funding from The San Diego Foundation, California Virtual Campus, and numerous other local and national entities. In the fall of 2009, *La Clase Mágica* was adopted at two University of Texas campuses (Austin and San Antonio) to "enhance the academic achievement of underserved children by exposing them to the latest technological advancements, which can help them achieve success" (Rodríguez, 2010).

Today, San Diego youth participants in grades P-12 attend age-appropriate adaptations of *La Clase Mágica* two to three days a week. Undergraduate students enrolled in *La Clase Mágica* practicum courses at UCSD and Palomar Community College work under the direction of community site coordinators who have strong cultural and linguistic ties to the service area. The child participants and their undergraduate "amiga/os" select from a variety of computer-based learning multicultural2 "task card" activities designed by the UCSD Research Team. Working collaboratively, they bond via these culturally and linguistically relevant educational activities or life-skills games. Keeping with the program's emphasis on imaginative play, youth participants also chat online with "El Maga," the program's magical entity, who is ventriloquated by a member of the research team, (a well-kept secret to promote the aspect of fantasy). Though there is a set curriculum, participants have the option to choose among a variety of specially designed activities organized through a maze structure, affording them a valuable sense of ownership over their instructional activities and academic enrichment. These computer-based educational games and activities generate critical thinking and core academic skills as well as digital literacy, financial literacy, health, and civic community awareness. This optimal learning setting fosters a dialogic, collaborative, bilingual/bicultural environment that allows minority individuals to embrace their linguistic and cultural backgrounds as intellectual tools for the problem-solving process. The goal is to eventually prepare them academically and socially for 21st Century Global Citizenry.

The specific sets of pedagogical strategies (i.e., technology-based curriculum and pedagogy, cultural relevance, the mixture of play and education) embedded within the project did not develop in a vacuum. They represent the culmination of years of research honing and refining optimal learning environments to produce improved academic achievement. The following section illustrates how technology serves as the medium supporting this particular community-university curricular system of learning and development.

## Technology as the Project Catalyst

Technology, specifically information and communication technology (ICT), is the link across the various components of this educational process, practically and theoretically. It is the foundation of *La Clase Mágica's* pedagogy as it represents the means for expressing one's sense of self and the world. Importantly, it is also the mechanism for cultural exchange as it facilitates the circulation of newly acquired knowledge throughout the system. Two perspectives on the affordances of information and communication technology align closely with the project's theoretical bases: Jonassen's (1996) vision of the computer as a mindtool and Starr's (2008) ideas of infrastructure as both relational and ecological.

## The Computer as a "Mindtool"

Though many may be tempted to view information and communication technology solely as a technical tool, Jonassen's theories of computers as mindtools elevates the discussion of the potentialities of technology to support learning and development. On their own, technical tools are stagnant devices. However, Jonassen asserts that ICT can act as *cultural tools* that not only structure the ways individuals view themselves and the world around them, but can also promote actual change in the individual and their environment when properly harnessed as intercessory devices. Information and computer technology, like language, can actually help individuals successfully define themselves. For example, when individuals fail to obtain fluency in their culture's dominant language, they are effectively shut out from functioning at their society's highest level. ICT, at its highest use, has this same potential for societal impact. Information and communication technology, when managed as an educational device, can assist individuals as they express themselves and gain knowledge. It is not just a tool for inactive and numbing "skill and drill" (Cummins, 2008; Jonassen, 1996). It operates as a means for critical thinking and exploration: a "mindtool" for learners. This strategy is critical for 21st century global citizenship, which is increasingly reliant on technology for social, cultural, and economic viability. The driving force behind the *La Clase Mágica's* philosophy and pedagogy is founded on the ability of these technological cultural tools to promote participants' critical thinking and the exploration of knowledge about themselves and the world around them. The technology is not meant to replace children's thinking, but instead to promote it for social and individual benefit.

## Relational and Ecological Technological Infrastructure

Information and communication technology also provides a new relational and ecological infrastructure for expanded social interaction founded on ideals of self as learner, worker and citizen. As ICT links individuals in a community of learners, they process and gather new information about the community and the world at large. These linkages create new networks of knowledge as opposed to relying upon centric modes of institutional or top-down based information—i.e., from teachers and parents (Moll, Díaz, and Anderson, 1985). The content of this interaction and its manifestation facilitates social change when experienced in the context of a broader community of learners that seeks cultural, linguistic and global relevance. This concept of networks of knowledge is the catalyst for *La Clase Mágica's* newest initiative to digitally link each project site via a common online platform in which participants can globally disseminate their site's locally generated knowledge. It gives access to locally generated knowledge digitally repackaged for broader consumption. We expect that a close analysis of this process will provide us with findings on how this relationship to knowledge generation and consumption impacts the learner when compared to traditional top-down relationships, which exist in much of education today.

## Measuring La Clase Mágica's Success

Across our 21 years of operation, youth participants' progress has been charted via ethnographic field notes, pre- and post-surveys, and at times via CA state standardized test scores. The results of these measures show a positive impact of participation in this community-university sponsored program. For example, last year, during the 2009-2010 academic school year, our participants made significant gains in reading skills (UC Links Annual Report). At the end of the 2009-2010 school year, 74.1% of our program participants* read at or above their grade level. These findings are telling considering only 31% of economically disadvantaged African-American and Native American students, and 29% of economically disadvantaged Hispanic students, passed the 2008 CA STAR ELA (English Language Arts) Exam (Lansberg, 2008).

Additional findings show that *La Clase Mágica:*

- *Develops positive self-image.* More than 75% of a group of past participants interviewed declared that *La Clase Mágica* impacted in a significant way their self-esteem and confidence in their ability to express themselves in educational or professional settings (Mercado, 2007).

- *Promotes a college-going culture.* Ninety percent of a cross-section surveyed who had participated in *La Clase Mágica* for three or more years self-reported being enrolled in or already completing their college education (Martinez & Vásquez, 2006).

- *Validates new forms of pedagogy.* In a comparative study across three pre-school programs, the children in the pre-schools that partnered with the *La Clase Mágica* after-school program showed a greater developmental trajectory than the two control groups (Relaño and Vásquez, 2011).

- *Prepares undergraduate volunteers for more advanced studies.* Twenty undergraduate mentors involved in our programming interviewed years after revealed how their training and exposure to *La Clase Mágica* projects had led to graduate studies in which they had pursued research interests surrounding education, ethnic studies, language, and culture (Martinez & Vásquez, 2006). Additionally, according to our 2009-2010 UC Links Annual Report

70% of our participating program mentors who were graduating college seniors self-reported applying to graduate school.

## A BROADER VIEW OF COMMUNITY-UNIVERSITY PARTNERSHIPS

### Forming Community-University Partnerships

Multiple years of collaboration have shown that understanding and empathy are two of the most important tools needed when developing relationships with communities that have uneasy relationships with a university (Vásquez & Marcello, 2010). Just as the community comes to know and trust the university research team, partnerships must take proactive measures to ensure that representatives of the university also understand and respect the partner communities. In the case of *La Clase Mágica*, the project's ongoing practicum course sponsored by the UCSD Department of Communication/Human Development Program is an example of a proactive measure that ensures the university's sensitivity to the community. The course provides undergraduate students an opportunity to study, in real-life settings, the role of technology, communication and cultural phenomena in intellectual development of non-mainstream learners. It also mediates stereotypical conceptions of minority groups and helps students understand the complex social and cultural phenomena that shape the conditions of various communities.

### Challenges to Community-University Partnerships

While community collaboration presents the valuable opportunity for equitable cross-cultural exchange, over two decades of work reveals challenges to forming such community-university partnerships. One of the ongoing challenges of such a complex functional system is to maintain a sense of cohesiveness supported by clearly defined goals while at the same time encouraging and promoting individual sites' independence. These overall concerns have led to the following suggestions for other entities considering partnerships:

- Collaboration must be founded on mutual relations of exchange, making the integration of the community's intellectual and human resources on equal par with those of the university (i.e., Starr's findings on "relationship," 2008).
- Although technology maintains the flow of information and basically provides the infrastructure for change, there is no substitute for face-to-face contact (Vásquez, 2006).
- Partnerships need to be fluid and flexible in order to allow for change, adaptation, and evolution, when revolving around the ever-changing aspects of technology and cultures.
- Partnerships should bring together diverse communities, organizations, and populations representing various demographics, industries, and areas of emphasis in order to promote the most useful and dynamic dialogue and exchange (Montes, 2009).

### Sustainability, Adaptation and Replication of Community-University Partnerships

Sustaining these community-university partnerships often requires support by corporate and non-profit funding. In fact, the multi-dimensionality of these types of projects can actually make it possible to approach funding sources from multiple perspectives. For example, *La Clase Mágica* is sustained by both academic and industry-based partnership and sponsorship. *La Clase Mágica* has also established multiple adaptations for multiple ages and has been replicated or adapted in various education systems across California through the UC Links consortium and through two University of Texas campuses (San Antonio and Austin). *La Clase Mágica* also is spearheading research with similar projects in Spain and Columbia as one-third of a tri-national research initiative examining the role that technology plays in the acquisition of target language and argumentative skills (Vásquez, 2010). These growing collaborations led to the likely question: *Can and should these partnerships be disseminated broadly?* This case study asserts that these partnerships not only show promise for adaptation and replication, but that they can in fact be utilized as a new form of broad-based social policy (Vásquez et al., 2010).

## Community-University Partnerships as a New Form of Social Policy

Our mutual model suggests a new form of social policy that replaces top-down affirmative action policies with a cross-system collaborative effort (Martinez & Vásquez, 2006; Vásquez et al., 2010). In an effort to examine the broad impact of the possible implementation of these collaborations across the nation, we analyzed four community-university partnerships3 that sponsor similar technology-based afterschool programs. This process reveals several core similarities. Alongside the afterschool programming, these community-university partnerships all include a university research team, an affiliated undergraduate course, and one or more community-based research field sites. These common components establish an infrastructure of change that funnels the progression of underserved youth into higher education while simultaneously supporting the mission of the university.

Together, these four partnership projects emphasize three consistent broad-based social policy implications of community-university collaborations (Vásquez et al., 2010):

- The collaboration between university and community partners creates an institutional framework for sustainable and scalable after-school programming.
- A dynamic combination of instructional and enrichment activities helps build multiple "new" literacies, mathematics and technology skills, and academic knowledge.
- Consistent participation in afterschool programs transfers to students' school performance and aspirations to pursue higher education.

Research also indicates that these partnerships exhibit very specific impacts upon the communities they serve by:

- Providing educational resources and institutional support to help communities meet the educational and safety needs of their youth (Miller, 2003).
- Creating employment opportunities by hiring local community members as coordinators, typically women with children enrolled in the project (Vásquez, 2003 & Montes, 2009).
- Validating cultural norms and community-based knowledge as a springboard for learning via distinct "funds of knowledge" (Gonzáles, Moll & Amanti, 2005).
- Producing alternative methods of assessing learning beyond the more traditional methods by focusing on *how* students learn vs. *what* they learn (Barron, 2006).
- Utilizing educational resources as remittances for individual, family and community development (Sen, 1989), in much the same way that immigrant workers' monetary remittances sent home provide children and adults in those countries with the tools to succeed in school and the job market.

Additionally, these partnerships can benefit partnering universities by:

- Providing universities with dynamic and low-cost laboratory environments for testing new pedagogy and training prospective researchers, teachers, leaders at tremendous saving for the university (Vásquez, 2003).
- Establishing and maintaining a steady flow of eligible marginalized students prepared to enter higher education (Moll, Diaz, & Anderson, 1985).
- Supplying a replicable model for sustainable and scalable afterschool projects such as the UC Links initiative has demonstrated by serving thousands of students and numerous communities statewide.

## CONCLUSION

We are at the interstices of great cultural change that demands a detailed and earnest historical re-evaluation of structural inequality in the classroom and society. This case study has presented one example of how higher education and marginalized communities can together affect change in closing the technological, cognitive, and employment gaps that exist disproportionately among low-income populations. It is not the panacea, the least expensive nor the most short-term of solutions, but our research clearly shows that it helps learners take advantage of future opportunities (Sen, 1989), specifically in the familiarity and comfort in inter-group relations that it produces (Martinez & Vásquez, 2006), and the prompting of undergraduate students to re-evaluate their experiences and knowledge base vis-à-vis the new social, cultural and economic realities of the 21st century (Vásquez, Marcello, and Gomez, in preparation). Specifically, it sheds light on social action as a cross-system of collaborative effort, based on rigorous research, state-of-the art undergraduate education, relevant technology-based pedagogy and community service, which all function together to promote effectual and meaningful change.

## REFERENCES

Barron, B. (2006). Interest and self sustained learning as catalyst of development: A learning ecology perspective. *Human Development, 49*, 193–224. doi:10.1159/000094368

Chavez, L., & Arredondo, G. (2006). *Access to the University of California for graduates from low-API high schools*. Berkeley, CA: UC Berkeley Center for Latino Policy Research.

Cook, B., & Códova, D. I. (2006). *Minorities in higher education: Twenty-second annual status report*. Washington, DC: American Council on Education Press.

Cummins, J. (2008). Information and communication technologies: Considerations of current practice for teachers and teacher educators. In L. Smolin, K. Lawless, & N.C. Burbules (Eds.), *The 106th yearbook of the National Society for the Study of Education* (*Vol. 106*, pp. 182–206). Malden, MA: Blackwell Publishing.

EdSource. (2010). *School finance 2009 – 2010: Budget cataclysm and its aftermath*. CA: Mountain View.

Gonzáles, N., Moll, L. C., & Amanti, C. (2005). *Funds of knowledge: Theorizing practices in household, communities and classrooms*. New Jersey: Lawrence Erbaum.

Jonassen, D. H. (1996). *Computers in the classroom: Mindtools for critical thinking*. Columbus, OH: Merrill/Prentice Hall.

La Clase Mágica Research Initiative, University-Community Links (UC Links), Center for Mathematics Education for Latinos/as (CEMELA) and Academy for Teacher Excellence. (2010). *Laboratories for learning: Collaborative research-based after-school programs.*

Lansberg, M., & Blume, H. (2008, July 17). Data reveal greater student dropout rate across state. *Los Angeles Times.*

Martínez, M., & Vásquez, O. A. (2006). *Sustainability: La clase mágica beyond its boundaries.* Unpublished manuscript.

Mercado, A. (2007). Address to American Education Research Association. Chicago, IL.

Miller, B. (2003). *Critical hours: After school programs and educational success.* Brookline, MA: Nellie Mae Education Foundation.

Moll, L. C., Anderson, A., & Diaz, E. (1985). *Third college and CERRC: A university-community system for promoting academic excellence.* Paper presented at the University of California Linguistic Minority Conference, Lake Tahoe, CA.

Montes, M. (2009). *Latino youth in expanded learner time programs.* Washington, DC: National Council of La Raza.

National Council of La Raza. (2009). *Investing in our future: The status of Latino children and youth in the United States.* Washington, D.C.

Relaño Pastor, A. M., & Vásquez, O. A. (In press). Accountability of the informal: Challenges and new directions. In *Pedagogies: An International Journal.* Nanyang, Singapore.

Rodriguez, K. (2010, June 17). 'La clase magica' program helps children succeed by using technology. *UTSA Today.*

Rumberger, R., & Tran, L. (2006). *Preschool participation and the cognitive and social development of language minority students.* Washington, DC: National Center for Education Statistics.

Sen, A. (1989). Development as capability expansion. In *Readings in human development, concepts, measures and policies for a development paradigm. Human Development Report United Nations Development Program.* New York, NY: Oxford University Press.

Starr, L. (2008). The ethnography of infrastructure. *American Behavioral Scientist.* Retrieved from http://abs.sagepub.com

University – Community Links. La Clase Mágica. (2010). *End of the year report.* San Diego, CA: UCSD CREATE La Clase Mágica.

University of California. (2010). *About page.* Retrieved February 24, 2010, from http://www.universityofcalifornia.edu/aboutuc/mission.html

Vásquez, O. A. (2003). *La clase mágica: Imagining optimal possibilities in a bilingual learning community.* New Jersey: Lawrence Erlbaum.

Vásquez, O. A. (2006). Social action and the politics of collaboration. In P. Pedraza, & M. Rivera (Eds.), *Educating Latino youth: An agenda for transcending myths and unveiling possibilities.* New Jersey: Laurence Erbaum.

Vásquez, O. A. (2007). Latinos in the global context: Beneficiaries or irrelevants? *Journal of Latinos and Education, 6*(2), 119–138.

Vásquez, O. A. (2008). Reflection: Rules of engagement for achieving educational futures. In L. L. Parker (Ed.), *Technology-mediated learning environments for young English learners: Connections in and out of school.* New York, NY: Taylor & Francis Group.

Vásquez, O. A. (2010). *Keynote address: Alianzas de investigación sobre una pedagogía de lengua meta.* Congreso Internaciónal de Informática Educativa: Aulas virtuales, diseño pedagógico, simulaciones ciberculturas: RIBIE-Col, 20 Años. Popayan, Colombia, 14, 15, 16, July, 2010.

Vásquez, O. A. (under revision). Language and ICT and the making of a change infrastructure. In O. Erstad, & J. Stefton-Green (Eds.), *Learning lives: Literacy, place, technology and learner identity.* Cambridge, UK: Cambridge University Press.

Vásquez, O. A., & Marcello, A. (2010). *A situated view at scaling up in culturally and linguistically diverse communities: The need for mutual adaptation.*

# ENDNOTES

[1] The A-G courses are a series of high school level coursework required for admission to the University of California.

[2] In the context of our project, we use multi-cultural to indicate inclusion of 2 or more cultures in the system of artifacts that make up the learning environment and intercultural when we specify an interaction between two monolingual/monocultural interlocutors as it happens between the undergraduates and *La Clase Mágica* participants.

[3] Our own *La Clase Mágica*, The UC System's University Community Links programs, University of Texas at San Antonio's Center for Teacher Excellence's *La Clase Mágica*, and the Center for Mathematic Education for Latinos/as (CEMELA) projects.

# Chapter 30
# Developing the Role of 'Values' Within Information and Communication Technology:
## An Introduction to the Schools Intergenerational Nurturing and Learning Project (SIGNAL)

**John Patterson**
*Liverpool Hope University, UK*

## ABSTRACT

*This chapter investigates the Schools Intergenerational Nurturing and Learning (SIGNAL) project at Liverpool Hope University and its impact on communities of learning within some of the most deprived areas of the United Kingdom. Embracing the wide aims of Citizenship Education in England, SIGNAL encompasses intergenerational and partnership activities, volunteerism, values education, and entrepreneurial learning shaped to assist with the unique issues faced by diverse school communities. Central to the project is the engagement of service-learning (SL) focussed student teachers, and their use of Information and Communication Technology (ICT). Whereas the majority of research about SL investigates its value to participating students (Eyler & Giles, 1999, 2002), less documentation can be found demonstrating its value to recipients. This chapter will look at the reciprocal value of SL projects utilising ICT for school communities, drawing its research from past projects delivered across Liverpool since 1999 and celebrated at www.schoolsinteractive.co.uk.*

DOI: 10.4018/978-1-60960-623-7.ch030

## GOVERNMENT POLICY AND COMMUNITY PRACTICE

Coming to power in the United Kingdom in 1997, New Labour's journey into educational reform followed an exhaustive push to embed social capital theory into the school system. The party's vision for a complete "moral and social reconstruction" became linked to the willingness of extended families, networks of neighbourhoods, community groups, religious organisations, businesses, public services and parent-teacher associations to involve themselves in tackling economic underperformance, social division and the general malaise viewed by the Commission on Social Justice (1994) as the scourge of the United Kingdom. Governmental efforts to mend the social fabric were punctuated by a myriad of policies, initiatives and processes that at best were aimed at generating community cohesion and a new generation of multi-skilled and employable, entrepreneurial individuals. Outcomes from their interventions are now emerging and, at their worst, are viewed as having evolved into a "pragmatic mix or 'muesli' of moralism, care and control, universalism and selectivism" (Featherstone & Trinder, 2001). Within this "muesli," great efforts were made to enhance the central role of ICT in teaching and learning across communities, with much being expected from closing "the digital divide" for deprived areas in terms of new business developments and employment opportunities.

The new coalition government, although remaining focussed on ICT development, has strengthened a resolve initiated by New Labour through the Russell Commission (2005) to engage volunteerism across communities. The former government's vision of a network of youth engagement has been replaced with a new vision centred on "empowering communities." Launched to the media in Liverpool in July 2010, the coalition's "Big Society" initiative placed a strong emphasis on the perceived value of volunteerism. A clear agenda for how this priority will manifest in

education has yet to materialise. It has, however, placed pressure on higher education institutions (HEIs) to consider again their own participation in volunteering. This chapter suggests that what has been missing from the outset and what is needed in the future are projects of clear relevance to school communities that utilise ICT; projects that volunteer student teachers may shape for diverse school community settings; and, furthermore, projects that use activities to engage children and their parents in learning about the potential ICT has in shaping their futures.

In considering how volunteerism among student teachers (those training to become teachers) may be engaged, HEIs delivering teaching degrees must consider the New National Professional Standards Framework for Teaching and Supporting Learning in Higher Education (NPSF) (The Future of Higher Education, 2003). As a descriptor-based approach covering six areas of activity, core knowledge and professional values, the "standards" are a means through which to focus learning, teaching and assessments. Institutions are, however, free to determine their own criteria in the application. Furthermore, student teachers themselves must provide evidence of accomplishments to pass their Professional Attributes, Professional Skills, Professional Knowledge and Learning Standards to achieve a Qualified Teacher Status (QTS) degree. In practical terms, this places a requirement upon student teachers to provide evidence that is tracked by tutors to demonstrate their strength of understanding within such 'standards' as relationships with children and young people, communicating and working with others, personal professional development, assessment and monitoring, achievement and diversity, planning, teaching, team working and collaboration. Predictably, the controversy over the value of asking student teachers to volunteer in the community schools is connected with these standards. For QTS degrees, volunteering and service to community remain for the most part optional, which places pressure on tutors involved in running volunteer programmes to engage student participation by highlighting the opportunities it provides to secure narrow standards, rather than the wider values brought about by creative, school-based volunteering.

Aware that SL models in the United States tend to be active within course pathways, this chapter promotes the application of SL in a purely volunteer capacity (Patterson & Loomis, 2007; Patterson & Patterson, 2009). Where ICT sits within the new and exciting creative industries, education about its applications should be equally exciting and creative. This chapter aims to demonstrate how volunteer and SL-focussed student teachers, acting outside the formality of the "standards," can generate innovative learning experiences and enhance creativity in ICT.

## BALANCING SOCIAL CAPITAL AND ICT

To ensure that ICT training generates innovation and employable individuals, overlapping initiatives in education since the 1997 white paper "Excellence in Schools" were aimed at transforming underperformance in deprived areas of England via "...diversity of provision within a coherent framework" (National Foundation For Educational Research in England and Wales, 2002). Targeted educational provision was introduced within the seven-strand Excellence in Cities (EiC; http;//www.standards.dfes.gov.uk) programme covering "Gifted and Talented" children, Learning Mentors, Learning Support Units, City Learning Centres, EiC Action Zones, Specialist Schools and Beacon Schools. The use of ICT percolated through all strands and was highlighted within the City Learning Centres, where state of the art high specification equipment was provided for school cluster and community usage. Although research into the effectiveness of such provision has been debatable, the Office for Standards in Education (Ofsted) noted a rise in the *achievement*

of pupils but an inconsistent impact on *attainment* levels (Excellence Clusters, 2003). Studies by the University of Cardiff (Power, Rees and Taylor, 2005), however, reported the falling of attainment levels as a result of the intervention. In brief, EiC programmes focussed on short-term goals meeting few of their own targets and failing as "champions of innovation." The simple provision of ICT "kits" in communities was not enough. A failure to embed the technology in diverse communities through a curriculum of local relevance and the need for effective partnerships to assist in the delivery of such a curriculum began to emerge. Seeking to support their initiatives, the focus by New Labour on performativity, accountability, "standards" and procedures was at this time heavily influenced by quantitative "evidence based" research (Humes & Bryce, 2001, p. 332). Writing on the role of values in education, Kerr (2009) describes this pursuit of performance measures as the "innovation and standards agenda" (p. 17). Believing a pursuit of the "standards" alone has had an adverse effect on children's learning, he called for teachers to "innovate and experiment" (Kerr, 2009, p. 11). Although research collated by Higgins (2003) for the British Educational Research Association suggests that the use of ICT does make a difference to a student's learning, there is little evidence to help us understand how ICT may link achievement to the future attainment (and hopefully employment) of students. Where New Labour stressed the measurement of children's examination results (attainment levels), insufficient attention has been paid to where and how personal successes outside the "standards agenda" (achievement) can be nurtured and used to enhance a pupil's future prospects. What we do know as indicated in studies by Moseley, Higgins, Bramald, Hardman, Miller, Mraz, Tse, Newton, Thompson, Williamson, Halligan, Bramald, Newton, Tymms, Henderson and Stout (1999) is that the most effective schools use ICT resources at their disposal in innovative and creative ways. It could be argued that the importance lies in the way in which ICT is used by individual and creative teachers, and the partners they may draw upon to impact children's learning and their future prospects. The role of SL students as community partnership leaders, and as an under-utilised resource for schools, offers exciting food for thought.

Where New Labour pushed social capital theory as an intervention, this chapter suggests that there is little understanding of its forms or the barriers to learning that an incorrect balance within partnerships delivering ICT learning can generate. Putnam (1995) saw two forms of social capital: 1) bonding, where value is assigned to social networks between homogeneous groups of people; that is, the ties between people in similar circumstances and 2) bridging capital, where value is assigned to social networks between socially heterogeneous groups such as more distant ties of like persons, loose friendships and workmates. Woolcock (2001) added a further dimension in suggesting linking social capital, where the joining of a diversity of people in dissimilar situations from entirely outside a community can enable members to achieve wider goals than can be secured locally. In this sense, the space where a diversity of student teachers actively serve a learning community, drawing together a balance of partners to demonstrate the application of ICT, demands careful consideration.

## COMMUNITY PARTNERSHIPS

The real need for community partnerships in education was highlighted in the U.K. by the introduction of Every Child Matters (2003). As hotly debated as the U.S. version "No Child Left Behind" (2002), its "delivery arm" in the primary school sector was heralded by the introduction of the New Primary strategy, "Excellence and Enjoyment" (2003). A more creative emphasis was placed on the curriculum itself with music, art, dance, drama, sports, ICT and environmental lessons aimed at enhancing creativity and achievement.

As with previous interventions, it was expected for ICT usage to act as a "cross-cutting" theme through all lessons. Alongside the pace of change in education, the notion of cross-cutting themes became coupled with the developing importance of Citizenship Education (CE) and its three distinct strands: moral and social responsibility, community involvement and political literacy. Encouraged by the Evidence for Policy and Practice Information and Coordinating Centre (EPPI) to have a place in all taught lessons, and within the context of a "bigger picture" and "values" formula by the Organisation for Economic Cooperation and Development (OECD, 1998) and the then Department for Trade and Industry (DTI, 2000), the role of CE has developed far beyond its origins within the "hidden curriculum." The teaching of CE was encouraged to have a clear focus on "reconciling social cohesion with economic success" (OECD, 1998, p. 34) while generating "higher order critical and creative learning skills within the process of learning itself" (EPPI, 2004, p. 3) and within a local/global vision of learning and achievement seen from a more ". . . holistic perspective, where different kinds or categories of learning are viewed as complementary, not separate" (EPPI, 2005, p. 65). Are there opportunities to use CE and a values curriculum to enhance a focussed ICT usage where the "bigger picture" lies in the provision of creative experiences that may impact upon future employment? Can SL-focussed volunteers provide a new category of learning for school recipients through the developing picture of CE?

Ultimately, it is the children themselves who may answer this question as recent progressions in CE demonstrate a movement towards a need for children's participation in their learning. The final report and recommendations of the Cambridge Primary Review, *Children, their World, their Education*, calls for "children's voices" to be heard in shaping a curriculum for the future, yet provides evidence to suggest there is still ". . . a long way to go in re-conceptualising the school as a collaborative, inclusive community for learning" (Alexander, 2009, p. 362). Recommendations from the review include a consideration of how schools may function as communities, both locally and globally. Emphasis is placed on the need for educational experiences that may enable children to engage with the culture and life of their communities. Through such engagement, it is expected for them to develop meaningful relationships and participate as active members of their local and global communities. Education in the U.K. at the start of the 21st century is seen as needing new life breathed into it – a new life that would encourage reflection upon the value of education itself, community spirited action, civic pride and the role of "values" to embody the principle that "every child and community matter" (Alexander, 2009, p. 363). I would argue that the student teacher acting as a positive role model through volunteerism can have an important position in shaping new, inclusive communities for learning.

As changes in the community learning environment are called for, so too are changes to the current National Curriculum as detailed in *The Independent Review of the Primary Curriculum* (Rose, 2009). In considering what the "new" curriculum should contain and how its content and teaching may be shaped to develop diverse abilities, Rose suggested several changes to the structure of the curriculum. Recommendations include the retention of core (English, mathematics, science) and foundation subjects (music, art, dance, drama, sports, etc.), supported by a complementary provision of cross-curricular studies, progression in learning across the Key Stages, which establishes subjects taught in state schools, through the curriculum with a unifying statement of values, a focus on literacy, numeracy and the embedding of ICT with greater emphasis on personal development. Rose suggested a broader scope for teachers to shape how learning is delivered with more flexibility to plan a curriculum to meet national entitlements alongside "greater discretion to select curriculum content according to their local circumstances and resources" (Rose,

2009, p. 41). In essence, this approach may well provide the opportunity for schools to engage the student teacher and their individual subject specialization as part of cross-curricular provision. An understanding of the underlying principles of SL at the school level, and reports of successful projects underpinned by them, are needed, however, in order to encourage head teachers to invite this inclusion within their curricula.

## DEVELOPING SL TO ENHANCE CROSS-CURRICULAR ICT PROVISION

SIGNAL has three distinct stages: the *engagement* of children in their school setting through themed CE assemblies; the *education* of children through workshops devised by SL volunteers attached to the CE themes and underpinned by entrepreneurial learning; and, an end of project *celebration,* highlighting the children's work within a social enterprise. In the assemblies, Liverpool Football Club provide its "Truth for Youth"(TFY) messages: "show racism the red card"; "kick drugs into touch"; "more important than being a good footballer is being a good person"; "we is better than me"; "shoot goals not guns" and "fire your dreams." The SL volunteers undertake a range of activities in school such as generating a song, a play, a dance, or a story using a TFY theme that participating children identify as relevant to their particular school community. Once workshops commence, the element of entrepreneurial learning is introduced; the children are asked to consider how they could run an event to showcase all their work and make it financially profitable. In such workshops, previous school pupils have quickly suggested the selling of seats at their celebration event and refreshments programmes and CDs containing their expected performances. It is at this point that parents/guardians, local partners including community police officers, faith groups and businesses are invited to offer their time and ideas to make the celebration happen, thus embedding the project into the local community. In all SIGNAL celebrations, significant attendance has been recorded from across community partners. In providing the physical means by which a community may actually meet together in a shared experience, positive and locally valuable messages can be underlined. At this juncture participants are asked to provide suggestions as to which charities should benefit from any funds made during the celebration. Not only serving to reinforce the CE and social enterprise underpinnings, this part of the process has acted as a "pump prime" towards continued participation, and additional projects have developed in support of the chosen charities.

Developed in the context of numerous changes in education, SIGNAL would claim success in embedding "core value" messages into diverse communities through the use of local partnerships and student-teacher SL volunteers. Through this framework, head teachers (or school principals) may be encouraged to review as they plan their own local curricula. The SIGNAL framework allowed for a use of ICT whereby naturally occurring 'spin-off' ideas could be pursued in creative and innovative ways by volunteers and the children in their care. Technology became the medium through which engaged and reciprocally learning volunteers and children saw their ideas come to life within the delivery of a project that they "owned" and that was relevant to their community. Just as or possibly more exciting than the "bigger pictures" were those "golden" learning moments as individual children benefited from the personalised learning afforded by the presence of SL student teachers. These may be described as the immeasurable 'soft-outcomes,' not related to the attainment-driven interventions of government policy; their value to children's achievement linked to the provision of SL offers a timely research agenda. With roots in the philosophy of John Dewey where learning comes through action and reflection, the theoretical underpinnings of SL are evidenced in the experiential learning work of Kolb

(1984), where reflection on experience helps to connect the learner to abstract conceptualisation, and Moore (1990), where experience provides the opportunity to explore "shifting systems of meaning." SIGNAL would argue that this potent mix of reflective, values-focussed student SL volunteers alongside children in a local, project-based curriculum has an empowering impact on the teaching and learning of ICT. Additionally, where barriers to learning exist amongst parents whose negative experiences of schooling may impact their perceptions of "new" learning entwined within ICT, SL volunteers offer a less formal route for engagement in their children's and subsequently their own learning.

## THE PIVOTAL ROLE OF ICT

As we consider the three stages of SIGNAL (engage, educate, celebrate), it is the processes that revolve around the making, advertising, delivery and recording of the children's work as a themed cross-curricular micro-enterprise that provide the 'hooks' onto which ICT usage is creatively attached. For example, the creation of advertising posters for the community necessitates online research to decide on style, etc; making and costing programmes for the event requires software usage linked to mathematical problem solving lessons; recording and producing CDs for sale raises the need for digital recording and marketeering lessons; making a local newspaper to sell after the event generates similar teaching and learning experiences attached to the pivotal role of ICT. Determining who makes important decisions has generated significant interest amongst the SL volunteers. Past experience has demonstrated that groups of children engaged in the process often identify the skill sets of individual peers and invite them to make the choices. Where the children's personal esteem and self-worth is raised in this way, those barriers to learning that are unique and individual may be affected. Importantly, where

ICT is perceived as the medium through which children raise their self-worth, it places future engagement in a positive light. Where time has allowed in several SIGNAL projects, children have written their own job specifications and framed them within a structured "company" designed to deliver the project. Although under-researched, the link between children's personal strengths and the interaction between others in a "business venture" has its own intrinsic value. There is great potential in the possibility of helping student teachers to make explicit connections between skill sets needed in the work world and the learning outcomes of the ICT projects.

When considering the value of SIGNAL in forming community partnerships, the involvement of SL students may indeed present itself as the connective 'glue,' pulling together the often disparate aims and objectives of potential community partners. Although studies by Butcher, Howard, Labone, Bailey, Groundwater-Smith, McFadden, McMeniman, Malone, and Martinez (2003) point out that the diversity of student backgrounds calls for an increased understanding and widening of research agendas, this chapter sees widening diversity as a positive opportunity to advance the recipient value coming from SL participation. Individual students coming from unique communities in Liverpool have been able to engage most positively with the children whose local culture they understand. Additionally, their enhanced role in educating their volunteer peers around local issues has learning outcomes teacher training courses may well be advised to consider.

As a group of volunteers divorced from assignment or grading pressures, they were freed both to be creative and to work with or for a variety of project partners. Acting as conduits, the volunteer students provided access to the project for partners; having the knowledge, skills and understanding to 'package' their input in an educational wrapping these volunteer students often secured the outcomes participating partners wanted from their involvement. An example of student volunteers acting as such conduits is the ongoing partnership between Merseyside Police and SIGNAL. First, SL students perceived as not "fully fledged" teachers, presented parents with negative experiences of school and the police with a non-threatening route through which to engage their children. Second, SL students became positive role models for the children in their care. In many cases this enabled them to reinforce positive messages about the police in general, challenging "them and us" perceptions and directing them towards a more "people who help us" consideration. Held on the "old site" project area of the school's interactive Web site, the "Freewheelers" initiative delivered through the SIGNAL process serves as an excellent example. In an area of the city where motorcycle theft was amongst the highest in the U.K., children and their parents made a motorcycle from scratch and raffled it using the "we is better than me" TFY theme. Although motorcycle mechanics appeared as the primary aim, engaged children and parents designed a Web site, the ideas for it, and a range of learning resources. Importantly, this partnership enabled the SL students, assisted by police officers, to offer computer use lessons for the parents. Some community members speculated that this collaborative process may have even led to decrease in motorcycle theft in the neighbourhood. Post-project discussions with the police revealed that several of the most prolific motorcycle thieves attended the project. An engagement appeared to have diverted their negative interests, which was marked by a subsequent increase in motorcycle theft after the project ended. The mix of practical motorcycle building and ICT usage attached directly to the motorcycle project appears to have maintained a level of interest sufficient enough to replacing (at least for a time) the need to steal. An understanding of how similar scenarios unfolded may be gleaned from the school's interactive Web site, where TFY messages have been used as a catalyst to engage communities in local issues, and through a wide range of activities (from music and dance, to cricket matches and plant growing) with CE, entrepreneurial learning, and ICT as 'cross-cutting themes.'

## SHARING BEST PRACTICES

Liverpool Hope University is the only faith-based university in Europe. Clearly, the institutional value of the SIGNAL project on our campus is significant as it connects with the institution's own mission and vision. As debates heat up around the nature of volunteerism and the deeper engagement of students in their own course design and learning (Carini, Kuh & Klein 2006), this will influence community perceptions in the future. Where professional courses aim at promoting critically reflective, active and responsible citizens having the ability to transform their communities (Crowther, Galloway & Martin 2005), careful consideration should be given to the nature of QTS design, especially as to the nature of volunteering within those designs as it reaches into community education. This project helped the university to connect its mission with community concerns.

As a model of SL, SIGNAL would claim to provide the space where student teachers can learn about themselves and others in a non-threatening and productive manner, preparing themselves for a transformative role in education. At the same time, a 'win-win' situation can be generated with students practically serving surrounding communities through educational interventions, while undertaking action research for community benefit. Through this process, informed decisions on QTS course design alongside the integral use of ICT can be made.

Best practices in the SIGNAL process circulate around student-teacher SL volunteering. The student teachers' presence within a "values" formula appears to generate innovative and creative ideas. These ideas can be brought to fruition by the higher order ICT skills prevalent amongst students who have in essence grown up with their application. Additionally, student teachers' involvement in a "pure" SL initiative, free from formal assessments, allows them to 'spread their wings,' try ideas and become more creative within their experience of teacher training. Most models in the United States place SL within their curriculum, whereas this chapter argues that "pure" SL should remain totally in the voluntary sector. The space where students are free to give of themselves from the basis of their own strengths, seeing its impact in a service capacity amongst equally engaged children, deserves detailed analysis. When this space has been provided in SIGNAL projects, there appears to be an effect on partnership capacity building, with students acting as a bridge between communities and their concerns, and those seeking educational inputs and outcomes. As engaged partners use this student bridge, significant opportunities have emerged to help guide children and their parents towards employment possibilities, especially in the "creative industries."

Sharing SIGNAL experiences on the school's interactive Web site has generated a space where students have learned valuable lessons from their peers. The opportunity to critically reflect on initiatives in advance of formally assessed learning placements has emerged as significant in post-project evaluations. Encouraging students to become action researchers, investigating and evaluating local issues has been a best practice within the SIGNAL process. It holds great potential for development by the research community. Their non-threatening, active SL participation and research may assist in shaping curricula on both the public school and higher education levels. By assisting us to understand "what works" in diverse and unique communities, we may direct educational partnerships to effectively target their provision of "values based" ICT teaching and learning.

# REFERENCES

Alexander, R. (2009). *Children, their world, their education. Final report and recommendations of the Cambridge Primary Review*. New York, NY: Routledge.

Butcher, J., Howard, P., Labone, E. E., Bailey, M., Groundwater-Smith, S., & McFadden, M. (2003). Teacher education, community service learning and student efficacy for community engagement. *Asia-Pacific Journal of Teacher Education, 31*(2), 109–124. doi:10.1080/13598660301612

Carini, R. M., Kuh, G. D., & Klein, S. P. (2006). Student engagement and student learning: Testing the linkages. *Research in Higher Education, 47*(1), 1–32. doi:10.1007/s11162-005-8150-9

Clusters, E. *The first ten inspections.* (2003). Manchester, UK: Office for Standards in Education. Retrieved from http//: www.ofsted.co.uk

Commission on Social Justice. (1994). *Social justice: Strategies for national renewal*. New York, NY: Vintage.

Crowther, J., Galloway, V., & Martin, I. (2005). *Popular education: Engaging the academy: International perspectives*. Leicester, UK: Niace.

Deakin Crick, R., Coates, M., Taylor, M., & Ritchie, S. (2004). *A systematic review of the impact of citizenship education on the provision of schooling*. In Research Evidence in Education Library. London, UK: EPPI-Centre, Social Science Research Unit, Institute of Education, University of London. Retrieved from http://eppi.ioe.ac.uk/cms/Default.aspx?tabid=127

Deakin Crick, R., Taylor, M., Tew, M., Samuel, E., Durant, K., & Ritchie, S. (2005). *A systematic review of the impact of citizenship education on student learning and achievement*. In Research Evidence in Education Library. London, UK: EPPI-Centre, Social Science Research Unit, Institute of Education,University of London. Retrieved from http://eppi.ioe.ac.uk/cms/Default.aspx?tabid=129

Department for Trade and Industry (DTI)/ Department for Education and Employment. (DfEE). (2000). *Opportunity for all in a world of change. A white paper for enterprise*. London, UK: Her Majesty's Stationery Office.

Department of Education and Skills. (2003). *The future of higher education Whitepaper*. Her Majesty's Stationery Office.

Education Action Zones. *Tackling difficult issues in round two zones.* (2003). Manchester, UK: Office for Standards in Education. Retrieved from http//: www.ofsted.co.uk

Every, C. M.*Change for Children*. (2003). Nottingham, UK: Department for Education and Skills. Retrieved from http://nationalstrategies.standards.dcsf.gov.uk/node/85063

Excellence and Enjoyment. *A Strategy for Primary Schools.* (2003). Nottingham, UK: Department for Education and Skills. Retrieved from http://nationalstrategies.standards.dcsf.gov.uk/node/85063

*Excellence in Cities: City Learning Centres: An evaluation of the first year.* (2003). Manchester, UK: Office for Standards in Education. Retrieved from http//:www.ofsted.co.uk

Excellence in Schools. (1997). *Department of Education and Employment White paper*. London, UK: Her Majesty's Stationery Office.

Eyler, J. (2002). Reflection: Linking service and learning-linking students and communities. *The Journal of Social Issues, 58*(3), 517–534. doi:10.1111/1540-4560.00274

Eyler, J., & Giles, D. E. Jr. (1999). *Where's the learning in service-learning?* San Francisco, CA: Jossey-Bass.

Featherstone, B., & Trinder, L. (2001). New labour, families and fathers. *Critical Social Policy, 21*(4), 534–536. doi:10.1177/026101830102100418

Higgins, S. (2003). *Does ICT improve learning and teaching in schools. A professional user review of UK research undertaken for the British educational Research Association.* BERA, Southwell.

Humes, W., & Bryce, T. (2001). Scholarship, research and the evidential basis of policy development in education. *British Journal of Educational Studies, 49*(3), 329–352. doi:10.1111/1467-8527. t01-1-00179

Kerr, D. (2009). *Citizenship and values education to the rescue! Making the case for a call to action.* Full report from the Ninth Annual Conference National Foundation for Educational Research.

Kolb, D. A. (1984). *Experiential learning: Experience as the source of learning and development.* Englewood Cliffs, NJ: Prentice Hall.

Moore, D. T. (1990). Experiential education as a critical discourse. In M. H. Wasburn, K. Laskowitz-Weingart, & M. Summers (Eds.), Service-learning and civic engagement: Recommendations based on evaluations of a course. *Journal of Higher Education Outreach and Engagement, 9*(2), 59-75.

Moseley, D., Higgins, S., Bramald, R., Hardman, F., Miller, J., Mraz, M., et al. Stout, J. (1999). *Ways forward with ICT: Effective pedagogy using information and communications technology for literacy and numeracy in primary schools.* Newcastle Upon Tyne, UK: University of Newcastle Upon Tyne. Retrieved from http://www.ncl.ac.uk/ecls/research/project_ttaict/

Organisation for Economic Cooperation and Development. (1998). *The OECD jobs strategy: Fostering entrepreneurship.* OECD Publishing.

Patterson, J., & Loomis, C. (2007). Combining service learning and social enterprise in higher education to achieve academic learning, business skills development, citizenship education and volunteerism. In A. Campbell, & L. Norton (2007). *Learning, Teaching and Assessing in Higher Education: Developing Reflective Practice.* Exeter: Learning Matters, 120-129.

Patterson, J., & Patterson, A. (2009). A call to arms: Developing students with diverse backgrounds through service-learning. In R. Sage (2010). *Meeting the needs of students with diverse backgrounds.* (pp. 116-129). London, UK: Continuum.

Power, S., Rees, G., & Taylor, C. (2005). *The promise and perils of area-based initiatives: The UK experience.* (The Times Educational Supplement, 22nd April 2005).

Putnam, R. D. (1995). Bowling alone: America's declining social capital. *Journal of Democracy, 6*(1), 65–78. Retrieved from http://muse.jhu.edu/demo/journal_of_democracy/v006/putnam.html. doi:10.1353/jod.1995.0002

Rose, J. (2009). *Independent review of the primary curriculum: Final report.* Retrieved from http://publications.teachernet.gov.uk/default.aspx?PageFunction=productdetails&PageMode=publications&ProductId=DCSF-00499-2009&-

Russell, I. M. (2005). *A national framework for youth action and engagement: Executive summary to the Russell Commission.* London, UK: Her Majesty's Stationery Office.

Woolcock, M. (2001). The place of social capital in understanding social and economic outcomes. *Isuma: Canadian Journal of Policy Research, 2*(1), 1–17.

# Section 6
# Universities, Digital Technologies, and the Public Good

# Chapter 31

# You Can't Step Into the Same Network Twice:
## Community Literacy, Client–Based Communication, and the Evolution of Networked (Re)Publics

**Trey Conner**
*University of South Florida St. Petersburg, USA*

**Morgan Gresham**
*University of South Florida St. Petersburg, USA*

**Jill McCracken**
*University of South Florida St. Petersburg, USA*

## ABSTRACT

*Drawing on experiences of creating a partnership between the University of South Florida St. Petersburg and a social service organization, Mt. Zion Human Services, Inc., the authors of this chapter moved from a plan for installing and directing a program of networking technologies—refurbished computers scavenged by professors, servers built from components by students, operating systems and software coded by the open-source programming community, and communications technologies that enable an open-source "bazaar" or ecology of writing in the client-based classrooms—to a plan for participating in and responding to the dynamics of the social and cultural networks that emerge vis-à-vis technology. This chapter describes the change in metaphor from building a network, which suggests control over this entity and its role in a public space, to participating in evolving networks, where the environment in which these networks may grow is cultivated, participation in that growth occurs as it develops with other participants, advocates, and organizations it is observed. Finally, the authors continued to participate in the engendering of new projects and networks that are grounded in the programmatic and core values.*

DOI: 10.4018/978-1-60960-623-7.ch031

# INTRODUCTION

When the University of South Florida St. Petersburg's (USFSP) writing program began a partnership with Mt. Zion Human Services, Inc. (MZHS), our diverse interests and energies converged around meeting the critical needs of midtown St. Petersburg, FL, an area with the highest levels of illiteracy, education failure, crime, violence, poverty, and substance abuse in Pinellas County (FL). We chose to work with Mt. Zion, in part, because of its work on these areas and our own interest in social justice, advocacy, and equality that are foundations of our teaching and research. Open-source technology was one vehicle through which we worked toward these goals and values in the communities with which we collaborated. The USFSP-MZHS partnership, informed by the Stanford model of service-learning, reinforces and grounds our vision of a community-based professional communications program and highlights the most important challenges, lessons and possibilities that adhere to our growth of both computer networks and the rhetorical and socially patterned space of teaching, community partnering and program-building that coalesce as a social imaginary that we have named "networked (re)publics." According to Ito (2007), a "networked public" is "a linked set of social, cultural, and technological developments that have accompanied the growing engagement with digitally networked media" (p. 2). Ito argues

*"that technology does not stand apart as an external force that impacts society and culture. Rather, technologies are embodiments of social and cultural structures that in turn get taken up in new ways by existing social groups and cultural categories." (p. 3)*

As these cultural, social and technological embodiments inherent in the pre-existing entities (in our case, USFSP writing program and Mt. Zion)

co-develop, they redefine those convergences in unexpected ways. Drawing on Ito's "networked publics" and what Lawrence Lessig (2001) calls the physical and code layers of any given network, we added the "(re)" to this concept for two reasons. First, the network we envisioned was to be comprised of re-purposed computers and open-source operating systems or software and introduced by students experimenting with open-source ethics and learning strategies. Second, in order to enact this experiment, our inquiry and pedagogy required an amplified attention to computer technology as described by Chris Kelty's (2008) concept of a "recursive public" as a dynamic social, cultural, and technological scene that "includes not only the discourses of a public, but the ability to make, maintain, and manipulate the infrastructures of those discourses as well" (p. 40). Rather than subsume computer-based technologies as tools in the service of the productive forces of discursive rhetorical practice, on the one hand, or position computer code, software or hardware as the material and prime mover of the discursively elaborated public sphere, on the other, Kelty's recursive public category intervenes on "the dichotomy between ideas and material practice" by focusing on the ways that

*"geeks use technology as a kind of argument, for a specific kind of order: they argue about technology, but they also argue through it. They express ideas, but they also express infrastructures through which ideas can be expressed (and circulated) in new ways." (p. 29)*

Using Kelty's premise that technologies are means of argument, our case study reports on the obstacles we met in trying to enact and unhinge from the idea that we can guide convergences and that we can use computer technologies to provide guidelines for the convergence. We initially believed that computer technologies and computer networks could stand as a metaphor and a means for creating social networks that would create and enhance communities. In a sense, we believed if we "built it," they—the local community—would come. However, in this chapter we describe our own change in metaphor from *building* a network, which suggests that we have control over such convergences as an entity and its role in a public space, to participants in the *evolution of networks*, where we cultivate the environment in which networks may grow; participate in the growth that occurs; observe as it develops with other participants, advocates, and organizations; and then continue to participate in the engendering of new projects and networks that are grounded in our programmatic and individual core values. What we have discovered is that convergences are organic, and that in trying to control the growth of the system, we hastened its dissolution. However, despite the difficulties we encountered, student participants significantly benefitted from the process, and the dissolution of one partnership led to a greater system of convergence culture taking shape through a larger grant that involves many more students and nonprofit organizations.

## HISTORY AND CONTEXT

### The Development of a Program through Client-Based Communication

The University of South Florida St. Petersburg (USFSP) is a small, formerly regional junior-senior campus located in St. Petersburg. In 2006, our institution received separate accreditation, and shortly thereafter, three new tenure-track writing faculty arrived on the campus, responsible for the Professional and Technical Writing (PTW) track of the English major. That major consisted of a curriculum of five (5) writing classes—Technical, Expository, Advanced Composition, Advanced Technical, and Special Topics—alongside seven

(7) literature courses. With the configuration of the major we inherited, students could complete the courses required for the Professional and Technical Writing track without taking courses in a sequence or without completing a writing course from any of the tenure-track writing faculty. We wanted to reinvent the curriculum around a series of PTW classes that provide professionalization within the civic nature of writing. Further, as we agree that our students need complex, problem solving writing situations, we want to provide our students with client-based writing projects that challenge them to meet the sophisticated language practices Betsy A. Bowen (1994) suggests comes from such situated writing processes:

*"[S]tudies suggest that students develop sophisticated uses of language when they read and write to provide information that people need, solve shared problems, and reflect on what they know, and that these activities are most likely to happen when students can both learn and teach other students." (p. 119)*

Bowen's claims support our turn to service-learning and client-based writing classes, but despite our university's commitment to civic engagement, civic-minded practices are currently under-realized in our student body. For example, according to our institutional research, incoming USFSP first-year students are less likely to have performed community service as a part of a high-school class (39%) than have their counterparts nationally (52%), and during their first year in college, USFSP students have reported lower levels of community service or volunteer work (30%) than college first-year students nationally (40%). As we considered drawing together our teaching and research interests and the disparate sections of writing classes into a writing program, we wanted to establish a programmatic civic-engagement component for our Professional and Technical Writing major. We found ourselves program-building with limited departmental resources and we co-authored and received a small, university-sponsored New Investigator Research Grant to create an open-source computer network system that we could share with any interested Pinellas County schools that did not have full access to computers for all students.

The purpose of our project was to create and implement small, Linux-based networks at USFSP and in Pinellas County public schools that would provide an open-source alternative to existing computing technologies and create a transferable knowledge base and learning modules for USFSP PTW students. Our goals for the technology were clear—to use open-source alternatives and to duplicate these programs—creating computer network pods that would continue to be replicated at local schools. When we look at the terms from which we laid out this project for the New Investigator Research Grant and judge its success on those terms, we failed because we did not establish small, replicable Linux networks in Pinellas County schools. However, rather than simply trying to "spin" this failure into a success story, or even a "lessons learned" commentary, here we outline the projects that have developed from this initial grant and our interpretation of how networks, technologies, and community partnerships grow and evolve.

## From Open-Source Networks to Technology as Evolution and Growth

Our first efforts focused on bringing open-source computer networks to Pinellas County schools to foster students' early experiences with computer-mediated composition in multiple writing environments. Because we could obtain the recycled computers and the open-source operating software with little or no expense, we believed it would not be difficult to create a partnership that would quickly implement the open-source writing network we

envisioned. In order to create these networks at limited cost to our university and the schools (the New Investigator Research Grant was funded at $6,500), we began stockpiling outdated computers as we worked to create connections within the public schools. We were, however, stymied in these efforts both on our own campus and in the public school system. For our own campus, the greatest concern with open-source networks derived from its strength: as an open-source network, it would have been difficult to meet the security demands of our campus IT department. We could—and eventually did—create a network, but it needed to be a closed system "off the grid." Similarly, we struggled in our attempts to replicate our network pods in the school system because, although we made contacts with various schools, at no time were we able to acquire the permissions necessary to start building open-source networks in any of them. By chance, while we searched for schools, one of us connected with the executive director of MZHS at a gathering hosted on our campus by our Center for Civic Engagement. Mt. Zion, whose mission is "to strengthen individuals and families by providing social and economic services that emphasize a self-sufficient, drug-free, productive, and nurturing family environment" in midtown St. Petersburg, offers pre-school, before- and afterschool programs, adult education, life-skills preparation, literacy programs, tutoring, and an affordable housing program. Mt. Zion's mission echoed the priorities emphasized in the City of St. Petersburg Midtown Strategic Planning Initiative, April 4, 2002, that state:

*"Three main tenets of economic development for the participants were: employment opportunities that offer living wages and benefits, opportunities for entrepreneurship, and expansion/enhancement of existing businesses. Successful economic development in midtown, as envisioned by the*

*community, will help to resolve these and other quality of life issues." (RMPK et al., 2002, p.3)*

We quickly recognized the connection between Mt. Zion's mission and our own goals of a client-based, civic-engagement writing project. Ultimately, we were able to connect and form a partnership with MZHS not only because they were interested in the resources we could offer but also because they had greater autonomy and decision-making latitude and did not have to receive approval from a higher entity about their partnerships with organizations or the computing network infrastructure that could be used in their facilities.

The USFSP-MZHS partnership began as we created an initial computer network following the Linux Terminal Server Project (LTSP) model. Due to the small size of the Linux Operating System (OS), it is possible for "strong" PCs to orchestrate otherwise obsolete PCs as "thin clients," which were, in our case, discarded PCs, wiped clean of the larger (and out-of-date) proprietary operating systems, that boot and run applications from a network server running Ubuntu or Xubuntu (Linux-based operating systems). This type of network is cheaper and more reliable than stand-alone PCs because the whole network can be maintained by attending to the server unit. Also, the software installations and updates applied to the server are downloaded instantly to all the PCs (thin clients) on the network. This process saves time by significantly reducing the number of software installations and updates that must be managed and saves money because open-source software requires no site licensing fees. For MZHS, such a network meant that the youth and preschool programs could have reliable computer network access at little to no cost, and USFSP PTW students and instructors could have innumerable client-based writing projects such as how-to build, use, maintain, and incorporate the networked computers.

## CONTROL AND INNOVATION: WHAT COMMUNITY COLLABORATIONS CAN TEACH US

### Concerns and Drawbacks: Technological

Throughout this collaboration, the MZHS community, like us, struggled to understand the technical layers of the LTSP innovation. Because the "thin client" computer experience was different from computer experiences engendered by proprietary software and because computer access was new, MZHS was not establishing a culture of use in the LTSP labs on its own. Although we had intended to create a space of technological free play, users at MZHS were afraid of breaking the network and needed encouragement from university sources to experiment. Without the nourishment that the student-teacher-client guiding interactions provided, these social and cultural layers of network lay fallow. Without continual prompting from university students to encourage experimentation with the computers and network, Mt. Zion attempted to control—and ultimately, lock down—the network, and that control eventually led to disuse.

### Concerns and Drawbacks: Student Resources

Students were heavily invested in the process of finding and developing their own interests from the many opportunities for involvement with MZHS. After our initial outlay of computer technologies and networks at Mt. Zion, the project grew rapidly. Throughout academic year 2008-2009 USFSP students wrote grants, created brochures and technical manuals, designed a monthly newsletter, installed and maintained two thin client labs, researched and implemented a mentoring program, developed new curriculum materials and assessment protocols for an existing afterschool tutoring program, refurbished the creative/art studio, and documented the process along the way. The intensity of this work and partnership allowed the authors of this chapter to consider how the partnership could continue to grow as well as to cross class interactions in both projects and resources for MZHS. Culminating in spring 2009, our partnership had three Professional and Technical writing courses simultaneously working on projects for and with Mt. Zion.

Each of us, in differing ways, sought more control of the combined project. Ultimately less concerned with the computer network, we struggled to control access to students and the resources they represented. At times, we found ourselves as instructors struggling to manage the students' varied participation and discovered that on several occasions, students were so heavily invested in MZHS that they acted as agents of the partnership outside the realm of the classroom. In what ways did our project, including our way of teaching civic communication and rhetorically sound technical writing strategies, depend on technical layers of programming with code; with the acquisition, refurbishing, and networking of computer hardware; or with the technicalities and rules of daily operations at MZHS? Any definition functions as a filter, generally speaking, as operational and useful definitions work to control meaning and achieve clarity by leaving things out. In this case, for both the teachers and the community partner, understanding and defining a piece of network, at times, became synecdoche for controlling the network, even when control of the highly technical or "physical" layers of the network was not presumed by any party.

In a brief history of the Internet traced in *The Future of Ideas*, Lessig (2001) questions whether "control [of computer technologies and systems] is feasible" (p. 39), and our partnership with MZHS has taught us to take such concerns seriously: Is more control always better? Lessig's answer that "leaving the technology uncontrolled is a better way of . . . finding . . . innovation" offers us a possible revision of our metaphor and our initial choice to "build" networks (p. 39). Networked

writing depends on a real potential for "multiple and coordinated unplanned uses" and digital ecologies offer potential for learning and innovation only when the architecture/regulatory mechanism allows the freedom to respond to and dwell in uncertainty. We needed to inhabit the nexus between ideas and materiality in our nascent network, but without too much recursive reference to the means of creating and sustaining the network. When that spring 2009 semester ended, we had no way to nurture, develop, and interact as a networked (re) public. We may have met the technical needs of MZHS, but the rhetorical "software" for further recursion seemed to be beyond our capacities. As we directly confronted our community partner's exigencies for student work and tried to integrate them with our writing course goals and student needs, we found that we were no longer able to continue working on this project together.

However, as we shared our work with faculty colleagues and students on our campus, our partnership with MZHS gave way to those housed in Social Work and Education. And the students who were directly involved in these projects continue their own volunteer work with these organizations, which has led to the pollination of these projects in our community and in our students' lives. In addition to finding short-term success for our classes, students, and MZHS, our greater success came not from the computer technology and its replication in new pods throughout the community, but rather how this initial grant has mushroomed into different projects, one of which is a $395,000 Learn and Serve America (LSA) grant that continues to grow the seeds we planted within the local community (explained more fully below) and provides sustenance in yet unknowable ways as our students and the community continue to evolve through these networks.

## Positive Aspects and Innovations

In reflecting on her 1996 essay "The Rhetorician as an Agent of Social Change" in a collection of Braddock Award winners, Ellen Cushman writes, "Without risks—and the imagination and passion that infuse them—knowledge advances slowly indeed" (p. 388). Our initial partnership with Mt. Zion *was* infused with risk, imagination, and passion; not merely our own, but more significantly that of our students. Driven by student interest and based on community needs, the ideas, projects and experiences continued to develop even as students, instructors and civic partners cycled in and out of the partnerships. Our collaborators at MZHS were experienced community partners who had previously worked with client-based classrooms. In our classrooms, the executive director of MZHS generously offered time and guidance to our students working on service-learning projects that included allowing some of our students to interact with children in the day-care center, working closely with others researching mentoring and tutoring programs, and bringing wisdom and clarity to collaborative grant-writing sessions.

We were able to draw on these experiences with MZHS to create a foundation from which we could apply for a Learn and Serve America (LSA) grant. Although the partnership was not directly linked to the grant—despite the fact that a further partnership with MZHS was our initial intent when we learned of the LSA request for proposals—our work together served as a springboard for our client-based work in the community, and our partnership with MZHS brought our university's attention to our Professional and Technical Writing program, resulting in broad-based university support that we believe contributed to our successful application for the LSA grant.

Awarded in August 2009, this grant has blossomed into the next iteration of our networked (re) publics that combines our Composition Program and our Professional and Technical Writing major as well as campus-wide Leadership and Civic Engagement programs. As these various centers, along with our writing programs, converged

upon the LSA grant, a new resonance emerged between these constituencies, forming a larger network of scholars on our campus committed, in different ways, to the creation of real-world community-based learning experiences for our students. Therefore, for us, one of the benefits of forming community partnerships was to support the conditions by which new collaborative relationships on our campus could also be formed.

By expanding our focus from a set of networking technologies that embody the open-source ideals of access to code and freedom to recode (and therefore empowerment to control the values embodied in the technology) to cultural and social networks that partner around other understandings of technology, we learn to dwell in uncertainty and to keep open to the constant change axiomatic to the dynamic information ecologies where our students live and write. Inhabiting this space means we must be willing to be "wrong" and to let go of plans, including those programmatic plans that are the product of hard work and careful preparation. As Clay Shirky (2001) argues in an early analysis of the Napster effect, "if the Internet has taught technology watchers anything, it's that predictions of the future success of a particular software method or paradigm are of tenuous accuracy at best" (p. 26). In the course of our partnership with MZHS, we graduated from a technology-driven metaphor to an evolutionary one in our program development. We moved from a plan for installing and directing a program of networking technologies—refurbished computers scavenged by professors, servers built from components by students, operating systems and software coded by the open-source programming community, and communications technologies that enable an open-source "bazaar" or ecology of writing in our client-based classrooms—to a plan for participating in and responding to the dynamics of the social and cultural networks that emerge *vis-à-vis* technology.

## Morphing and Growth: Community and Educational Impact of Partnership Possibilities

In addition to the numbers of community members receiving services from Mt. Zion, and our students who learned about client-based projects, civic engagement, and communication, the impact of this collaboration is currently being realized in the LSA grant. Led by the Center for Civic Engagement, The Bishop Center for Leadership Studies, the Writing Program, and Academic and Student Affairs, the LSA grant will award approximately $200,000 in grants to local non-profit organizations. Over the course of three years (2009-2011), based in courses ranging from Technical Communication to Environmental Science to Anthropology, students will create Student Philanthropy Boards that each write a Request for Proposals directed toward all nonprofit organizations in Hillsborough and Pinellas Counties that focus on the critical needs in the community and then award $5,000 to their chosen community organization (40 total). One of the goals of this grant is to help students learn about the critical needs of local agencies and to help students become more involved in the local community. Because of the broad-based support and involvement in this grant throughout the university, the community impact continues to snowball in unforeseen directions.

The evolution of the collaboration with MZHS to the LSA grant has afforded us opportunities to create leadership-based first-year learning communities with a civic engagement component and the ability to track whether students are doing more with the community based on their involvement with either MZHS or other organizations. Furthermore, the LSA collaboration has created a sustainable base for stimulating further the student-driven interactions with community partners and will help ensure that our community partnering efforts produce value for a greater number of partners across a broader spectrum of the community (in particular, the non-profit community).

The LSA project also produces value for students and teachers. Now, our technical writing courses can harbor Student Philanthropy Boards, which, like the more unstructured technical writing collective that served MZHS, enact technical communication performances in the spirit of the service-learning tradition. The difference is a shift in the model of service and community engagement. Now, rather than merely performing work for a specific partner, student advocates function as "pollinators" capable of generating further meaningful connections between the university and a broader range of potential community partners, much in the manner of self-organization processes among bees and other social animals, as studied by systems scientists (Camazine, 2001; Deacon, 1998; De Waal, 2003). As teachers shepherd students through the LSA version of the client-based process—which sets a sharp envelope, with closure, beginning with researching problems in the non-profit sector, moving into composing an RFP, advocating for and assisting community applicants with their writing, and finally evaluating the proposals—writing-based engagements between the university and the nonprofit sector multiply. In this model, the "stigmergy" ethic of open-source culture "embedded" in the hardware component (refurbished computers running Linux and OSS) of the MZHS partnership blossoms into a different version of a network. By loosening our fix on Kelty's model of a "recursive public" and emphasizing a different kind of observation and participation for teachers, community partners, and students, we enable diverse styles of engagement.

In this "relaxed" but still critical lens on the recursive layers of ideas and material practices that technical writers, community partners, and teachers of writing share together in a network, classical principles of emergence can take root and create the conditions for reformulations that emerge in further opportunities, education, and collaborations.

## Lessons Learned: From Control to Evolution, or Looking Forward while Looking Back

*If you spend too much time on a college campus, all you think about and the only way you view the world is through these theories, but you actually have to get out and try to apply these theories to see if they work; so this is great, this getting students out of the ivory tower.*
    —Spring 2009 PTW student

Within our collaborations and opportunities, we look for the patterns. We expect certain kinds of processes will occur. And yet we cannot step in the same network twice—there are complex processes we cannot imagine. In some crucial ways, our vision did not manifest. And yet focusing too much on the inner activity of maintaining and controlling a network means we risk losing sight of the larger, dynamic, interlocking systems. Our metaphor and understanding of technology has changed in the course of this critical case. No longer focused on a single lab, network or pilot, our treatment of network technologies needed a broader ecological metaphor, which moved us from a control model to an evolutionary one. The ways in which the project met with obstacles or "failed" center around technology *qua* technology. At the same time, forming community partnerships on the terrain of writing requires direct work with technology *qua* technology. We often have a fear of being wrong. And yet computers teach us about the entropic process of technology practices. Failure, loss, even death—all occur in the learning process. We want to leverage the real phenomenon of technology (its unpredictable aspects), the law of unintended consequences, and of tinkering. As our project has continued to evolve, we continue to learn many lessons about the intersections of teaching writing and forming community partnerships. One lesson (re)learned: Technology is a powerful force, and, in certain conditions, technology can even assume a causal deterministic force. Technology, for the different participants in a partnership, creates different images of, and perspectives on, control. We learned to look anew at the ways technology and metaphor combine and recombine to write and rewrite the terms and conditions of a community partnership, in part simply by means of a capacity for compressing and embodying very different systems of ideas and cultural norms. We can now continue to work on emerging projects with an expanded understanding of these technologies and their place in our community networks. Our reflections provide space from which we can offer suggestions for practical approaches that could be integrated within courses, programs or departments that seek to increase community partnerships:

- Make connections with local organizations in terms of community needs and projects;
- Course projects
  - Ask students to interview and better understand community needs and then create a plan for achieving these needs within a project, course, or future course; share these project plans with community organizations;
  - Develop courses in which students can create technological networks in a community partner space that directly meets their needs;
    - Locate and stockpile discarded computers and parts for use in creating both technological and social networks (see History and Context);
    - Develop Linux OS strong PCs and thin clients (See History and Context);
  - Ask students to reflect on these course projects and this work. How does this work relate to the course goals? How does it relate to their understanding of communication? To their understanding of technology and networks?

- Showcase student work; discuss projects with colleagues; make connections across your own campus;
- Collaborate with colleagues, departments, and colleges in order to create and grow ideas and projects;
- Meet regularly with colleagues about these projects; discuss, write, talk, and think about plans, dreams, underlying values and goals for these projects;
- Examine the perceived successes and failures of these projects through student reflections, community partner feedback, and all collaborators' critiques. These reflections point to the ways in which we often over-determine the definitions of success or failure of a project because we are not in control of these technologies and their impact on the communities we hope to serve.

In our collaboration, we did not necessarily have an illusion of control, but we did have hopes and planned to achieve specific goals. Now the growth of networks grounded in our shared values of social justice, equality, and research with and for the communities in which we belong becomes an expanded understanding of technologies as we consider both "hard"ware and "soft"ware (including the bodies we all inhabit—race, class, ability, gender, sexuality, and positionality). We cannot control the technologies or the processes. We can create the conditions grounded in these values—and then watch them grow.

# REFERENCES

Bowen, B. A. (1994). Telecommunications networks: Expanding the contexts for literacy. In C. Selfe, & S. Hilligoss (Eds.), *Literacy and computers: The complications of teaching and learning with technology* (pp. 113–129). New York, NY: MLA.

Camazine, S., Deneubourg, J., Franks, N. R., Sneyd, J., Theraulaz, G., & Bonabeau, E. (Eds.). (2001). *Self-organization in biological systems*. Princeton, NJ: Princeton University Press.

Conner, T., Gresham, M., & McCracken, J. (2007). *Piloting pedagogies: Open-source solutions*. New Investigator Research Grant. University of South Florida St. Petersburg.

Cushman, E. (1999). Afterword. The rhetorician as an agent of social change. In L. Ede. (Ed.), *On writing research: The Braddock essays 1975-1998* (pp. 372–389). Boston, MA: Bedford St. Martin's.

De Waal, F. B. M., & Tyack, P. L. (Eds.). (2003). *Animal social complexity: Intelligence, culture, and individualized societies*. Cambridge, MA: Harvard University Press.

Deacon, T. W. (1998). *The symbolic species: The co-evolution of language and the brain*. New York, NY: W.W. Norton.

Ito, M. (2007). Introduction. In K. Varnelis (Ed.), *Networked publics* (pp. 1–13). Cambridge, MA: MIT Press.

Kelty, C. M. (2008). *Two bits: The cultural significance of free software*. Durham, NC: Duke University Press.

Lessig, L. (2001). *The future of ideas: The fate of the commons in a connected world*. New York, NY: Random House.

RMPK Group, Inc. A.A. Baker and Associates, & Strategic Planning Group, Inc. (2002). *The Midtown strategic planning initiative*. Retrieved from www.stpete.org/stpete/midtownsummary-master.pdf

Shirky, C. (2001). Listening to Napster. In A. Oram (Ed.), *Peer-to-peer: Harnessing the benefits of a disruptive technology* (pp. 21–37). Sebastopol, CA: O'Reilly.

Chapter 32

# Using Digital Technology to Enhance a Century Old Partnership Between University and Cooperative Education Employers

**Cheryl Cates**
*University of Cincinnati, USA*

**Kettil Cedercreutz**
*University of Cincinnati, USA*

**Anton C. Harfmann**
*University of Cincinnati, USA*

**Marianne W. Lewis**
*University of Cincinnati, USA*

**Richard Miller**
*University of Cincinnati, USA*

## ABSTRACT

*Cooperative Education (the systematic alternation of school and work) creates ongoing partnerships between institutions of higher education and their corporate partners. The beauty of co-op is that it allows feedback on student work performance while the student is enrolled in an academic program. The objective of this project was to use emerging digital technologies to capture partnership information and channel it back to faculty in charge of curriculum development for summative and formative purposes. The project was funded by the U.S. Department of Education's Fund for the Improvement*

DOI: 10.4018/978-1-60960-623-7.ch032

*of Postsecondary Education (FIPSE) through the grant Developing a Corporate Feedback System for Use in Curricular Reform. The project resulted in a system that captures the level and uniformity of student work performance and reports the data both numerically and graphically both separately and in combination. Performance uniformity as a measure is important, as it illustrates how well all students in a group absorb the instruction.*

## INTRODUCTION

The production of goods and services has, over the past 50 years, moved from a supply-oriented to a demand-oriented focus (Deming & Kilian, 1992). This evolution is reflected in outcomes-oriented assessment that, since the early 1990s, has been reflected in accreditation standards (Higher Learning Commission, 2003). Most of these criteria require that a methodology of continuous improvement be used. Effective assessment is further considered to be blind (instructor independent), direct (straight measurement of activity of interest), and contextual (measurement happens in the environment for which the student is being trained) (Banta, 2002; Suskie, 2004). Simultaneously, with the development of outcomes-oriented assessment, the world has seen the evolution of electronic networks that have no comparison in history. The project described in this case study integrates the latest assessment technologies with a Web-based delivery structure, resulting in a system that can be used for blind and direct measurement of student performance in the context of work. The system helps the university redesign programs to support the development of employable skills. The assessment methodology further measures the aggregate effect of changes pursued in a multitude of courses. The system further supports outcomes-oriented accreditation.

## BACKGROUND

The research project is set in an environment of Cooperative Education (co-op) at the University of Cincinnati. The co-op model was pioneered by Dean Herman Schneider in 1906 at the university (Park, 1943). This educational initiative has transcended time, disciplines, and programs. Schneider's cooperative system of education introduced the concept of linking theory with practice through the alternation of time spent in classroom instruction with time spent in work-based practical experience in the students' chosen fields. A century later (Cates & Cedercreutz, 2008), the design of the corporate feedback system sought to re-examine and build upon the original core principles of the cooperative system of education through the use of digital technology.

The University of Cincinnati combines high-impact research ($378 million research budget) (University of Cincinnati, 2009) with a strong professional profile (approximately 5,000 student placements per year) (Cedercreutz, 2007). The structure of the UC co-op program is based upon full-time, alternating quarters of study and co-op work experience beginning in the sophomore year and extending over three years. Figure 1 shows a typical alternating University of Cincinnati co-op curriculum. This alternation paces the development of the student frame of reference with the progression of the curriculum. Every co-op work quarter is evaluated through a three-party online assessment process: by the student, by the employer, and by the faculty member (Cates & Jones, 1999). Analyzing the employer assessment data while a student cohort is still enrolled allows the university to react swiftly to changes in the environment.

Co-op students are assigned to a Professional Practice (co-op) faculty adviser by discipline area.

*Figure 1. Typical UC co-op curriculum*

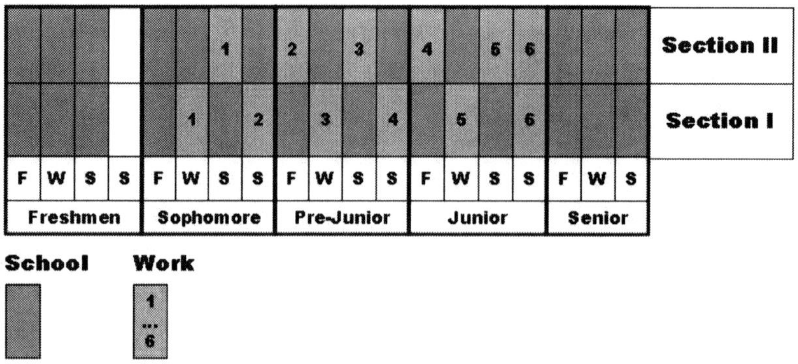

This faculty adviser is responsible for all aspects of the cooperative education program for their assigned disciplines (Cates & Jones, 1999). Faculty members in the academic departments provide classroom training that enables students to effectively work in industry prior to graduation (Cedercreutz et al., 2002).

## FEEDBACK SYSTEM DEVELOPMENT

### Initial Steps

In 2004, the University of Cincinnati received a total of $555,133 from the U.S. Department of Education. The matching contribution of the University of Cincinnati was $421,396, making the grand total almost one million dollars. The funded project was a collaborative effort to build a closed loop system that measures student performance while at work and directs this feedback into curricular development.

The Corporate Feedback loop presented in Figure 2 closes the loop between industry and academia through digital technology that quickly and efficiently gathers assessment data on student work performance and then reports that data in aggregate form as part of a continuous improvement process for pedagogic development.

Specific goals for the project included:

1. The creation of a process to systematically examine employer input gathered through online and individual evaluations of co-op students as an aggregate;
2. The development of additional online assessment instruments that would be used for a specific period of time and targeted toward a particular issue of importance; and
3. Complementary analysis of data gathered through the online assessment database through the use of employer focus groups.

A first crucial step to the development of a corporate feedback system was the creation of a vigorous online database that would capture work term assessment data. Historically, data had been captured in paper format, which made any significant analysis cost prohibitive.

The vigorous online database (based on using ASP language, using a Microsoft SQL server, and accessing the web through Internet Information Services) allowed employers to directly input assessment data into a database that could provide subsets of data based upon specified parameters. These data subsets would then be used to conduct further analysis related to student development. Next, the development of a statistically sound methodology to view co-op employer evaluations within the context of student learning would be critical to the success of the project. Multiple cycles of curricular reform would maximize

*Figure 2. Corporate Feedback System. The system allows the university to alter course delivery as a result of supervisor assessment of student work performance.*

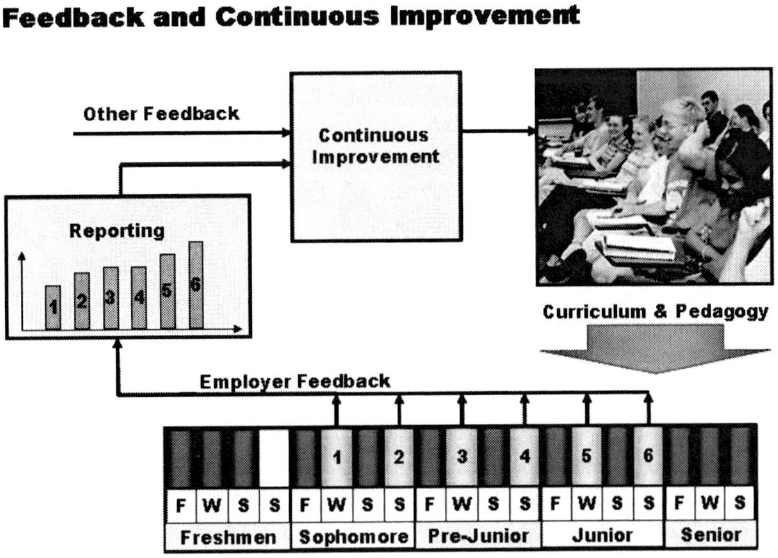

opportunities for success. In the final stages of the project, the creation of a reporting system to provide accessible reports for the departments would become the focus.

## Overview of Assessment Structure

The assessment principle of the FIPSE project was to rely on three layers of assessment as presented in Figure 3.

As Assessment Instruments I and II are primarily quantitative, they are easily delivered in a digital format; whereas Assessment Instrument III, for obvious reasons, relies on face-to-face contacts among faculty, students and employers. Assessment Instrument I uses 40 independent parameters to measure communication, conceptual and analytical ability, learning/theory and practice, professional qualities, teamwork, leadership, technology, design and experimental skills, work culture, organization planning and evaluation of work habits based on a 1-to-5 Likert scale. Assessment Instrument II can be freely defined by the user to measure ten distinct parameters.

## PROFESSIONAL ASSESSMENT AND LEARNING SYSTEM, PAL

The Professional Assessment and Learning System (PAL) was developed at the University of Cincinnati in parallel with the FIPSE project. The PAL system consists of five interconnected components: a student component, an employer component, a division component, an administration component and a college component. These five components feed data into one central assessment database.

*The **Student Component*** regulates student interaction with the system. The system gives the student the ability to review, save, edit and submit a complete assessment of the work term. The student component keeps a historical record, allowing students to revisit and modify (within specified time limits) their co-op placement record.

*The **Employer Component*** regulates employer interaction with the system. The system allows the supervisor to view and revisit a student's completed learning assignments and learning objectives and to complete all related employer assessments.

*Figure 3. Levels of assessment in the UC FIPSE Project Developing a Corporate Feedback Loop for Curricular Reform*

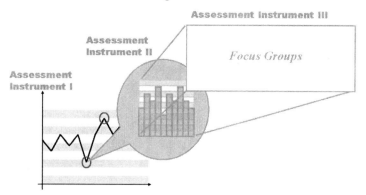

The Human Resource level contact can view the assessment provided by the supervisor, view their placement history, update job descriptions, and alert UC of impending employment needs.

*The **Division Component*** regulates co-op faculty advisor interaction with the system. This component allows co-op faculty to download assessment data and to view assessment data submitted by both students and employers. The system has a strong reporting capability that enables faculty members to view reports of aggregate student learning data.

*The **Administration Component*** allows a system administrator the ability to manipulate system data and add or modify student data, placement data, employer data, learning module and question data, and support data; and to send and edit emails automated by the system.

*The **College Component*** allows college-level administrators and faculty members to interact with the system. This component enables downloads of aggregate assessment data for further analysis.

PAL is a comprehensive system that not only incorporates Assessment Instrument I and II but also learning modules and communication functions.

## Reporting Tools

It is obvious that all reporting requires effective tools. After an extensive search of the literature, the research team found Mean/Standard Deviation Matrixes (MSM) and Delta Mean/Standard Deviation Matrixes ($\Delta$MSM) to be a very effective way to communicate outcome levels and process stability as schematically presented in Figure 4.

A low variation in student performance suggests a high stability of the educational process. High means are typically preferable. The matrix is visual and simple to read. Scores in the upper left-hand corner tend to indicate a quality process. Scores in the lower right-hand corner typically indicate a problem. In general, we found that the more care is given to the educational process, the more uniform the student performance becomes. As the system generates longitudinal data, the University will be able to monitor whether changes have a positive impact on student performance over time.

The MSM gives a good picture of where the educational process is stable and where further improvements are needed. Six Sigma and Lean Manufacturing literature typically encourage process developers to initially focus on limiting the standard deviation of a particular process

*Figure 4. Mean/Standard Deviation Matrix (MSM)*

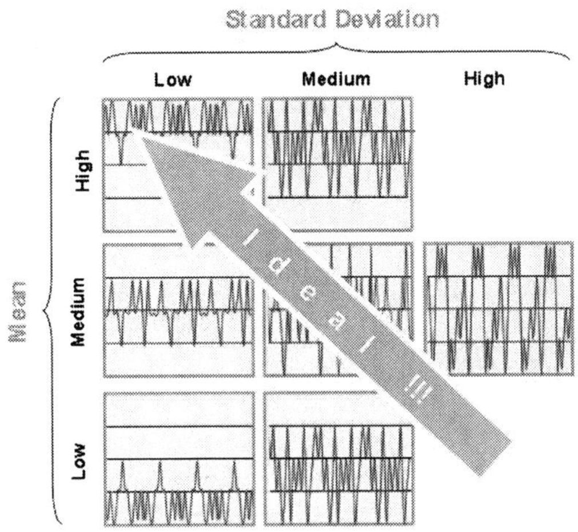

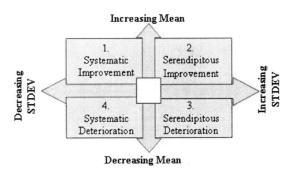

outcome. Only after the control of a process has been obtained can the means of process outcomes be enhanced.

MSMs describe a process in relation to the assessment of a specific group of assessors. They show a picture of a process at a specific state of development. ΔMSMs are used to compare the development of a specific student cohort over the course of the curriculum and are valuable instruments especially in before and after studies. Figure 5 shows the principle of a ΔMSM.

A ΔMSM gives valuable information about the effectiveness of an educational process. Whenever the mean of student performance increases and the standard deviation decreases as a function of curricular progression, the educational program is doing what it is supposed to do. Besides MSMs and ΔMSMs, conventional tables obviously have their niche to fill in data reporting, and the graphical representations should, in most cases, be complemented with tables detailing sample sizes, assessor numbers, means and standard deviations.

## FUTURE RESEARCH DIRECTIONS

The development of the system has opened an abundance of avenues for future research. The

*Figure 5. The principle of the Delta Mean Standard Deviation Matrix (ΔMSM)*

fact that the system produces 200,000 external assessment points annually alone illustrates the opportunities of the system. The system could be developed into an educational research laboratory that could compare different educational methodologies with one another. The system could further be used to compare various student populations based upon differentiating factors such as gender, grade point average or discipline. Virtually any educational hypothesis could be tested with careful differentiation of data into comparison groups.

## LESSONS LEARNED

While the University of Cincinnati has a 104-year tradition of cooperating with industry with regard to cooperative education, the value of the assessment system is best demonstrated through the enhancement of instructional match with employer needs, rather than in the attraction of new employers. The project has clearly initiated a cultural change at the university. While the implementation of a measurement system can be pursued in just a few years, the cultural change takes far longer. The list below summarizes the evolution to date:

- The project has resulted in a substantive improvement of the outcomes-based accreditation process administered by the Higher Learning Commission and ABET. The enhanced assessment process has prompted faculty to implement curricular changes to enhance student employable skills.
- The Provost Office has been impressed with the system and is using the principle to assess service-learning.
- Advisory committees are using the data to direct the evolution of specific academic departments.
- Employers have indicated the relevance of all measured parameters and have, at an employer symposium, expressed the value of aggregating the assessment data to foster a connection between employment and education.

As the cycle times for this methodology is relatively slow (one year), it is at this point too early to tell at what point all programs at the university will exhibit uniform and strong development of student performance. Accreditation reports, however, suggest that the assessment methodology is slowly changing the culture. Education of students for employment in the real world is by definition shooting at a moving target. To be successful one does, however, need to have a measurement instrument.

The research has further shown the boundary conditions for the methodology. The system gives quality results in the measurement of behavioral traits that are a) visible to the employer, b) understandable by the employer and c) frequent enough to form a basis for statistical analysis. Additionally, the research gives a hint to the fact that the more a student cohort is nurtured, the more uniform the performance results become.

The results of the research project *Developing a Corporate Feedback System for Use in Curricular Reform* has to date resulted in the implementation of a measurement system. The research has also revealed what the system is suitable for measuring. The system is at this point having a steady impact on the application orientation of the academic culture on partnerships between higher education and business.

## REFERENCES

Banta, T. W. (2002). Characteristics of effective outcomes assessment, foundations and examples. In T. W. Banta (Ed.), *Building a scholarship of assessment*. San Francisco, CA: Jossey-Bass.

Cates, C., & Cedercreutz, K. (2008). *Leveraging cooperative education to guide curricular innovation: The development of a corporate feedback system for continuous improvement*. Cincinnati, OH: The Center for Cooperative Education Research and Innovation. Retrieved from http://www.uc.edu/propractice/fipse/publications.asp

Cates, C., & Jones, P. (1999). *Learning outcomes, the educational value of cooperative education*. Columbia, MD: The Cooperative Education Association.

Cedercreutz, K. (2007). *Calibration of a work performance assessment instrument to support continuous improvement of cooperative education curricula.* ProQuest online publication, October 2007.

Cedercreutz, K., Cates, C., Eckart, R., & Trent, L. (2002). Impact of outcome based accreditation standards on the cooperation between the College of Engineering and the Division of Professional Practice at the University of Cincinnati. In *Proceedings for Accreditation Board for Engineering and Technology ABET Annual Meeting, 2nd National Conference on Outcomes Assessment for Program Improvement*, Baltimore, MD, Accreditation Board for Engineering and Technology.

Deming, W. E., & Kilian, C. S. (1992). *The world of W. Edwards Deming.* Knoxville, TN: SPC Press.

Park, C. W. (1943). *Ambassador to industry: The ideas and life of Herman Schneider.* Indianapolis, IN/ New York, NY: The Bobbs-Merrill Company.

Suskie, L. (2004). *Assessing student learning: A common sense guide.* Boston, MA: Anker Pub. Co.

The Higher Learning Commission. (2003). *Handbook of accreditation* (3rd ed.). Chicago, IL: The Higher Learning Commission.

University of Cincinnati. (2009). *Annual report on research.* (p. 12). Retrieved from http://www.uc.edu/ucresearch/documents/ucresearch_nov09.pdf

## ADDITIONAL READING

Accreditation Board for Engineering and Technology. (1999). *Conventional criteria: Criteria for accrediting engineering programs.* Baltimore, MD: Accreditation Board for Engineering and Technology.

Astin, A. (2002). *Assessment for excellence: the philosophy and practice of assessment and evaluation in higher education.* Westport, CT: Oryx Press.

Ayyub, B. M., & McCuen, R. H. (2003). *Probability, statistics, and reliability for engineers and scientists* (2nd ed.). Boca Raton, FL: Chapman & Hall/CRC.

Bhote, K. R. (2003). *The power of ultimate Six Sigma: Keki Bhote's proven system for moving beyond quality excellence to total business excellence.* New York, NY: AMACOM.

Boyce, M. E. (2003). Organizational learning is essential to achieving and sustaining change in higher education. *Innovative Higher Education, 28*(2), 119–136. doi:10.1023/B:IHIE.0000006287.69207.00

Brumm, T. J., Hanneman, L. F., & Mickelson, S. K. (2006). Assessing and developing program outcomes through workplace competencies. *International Journal of Engineering Education, 22*(1), 123–129.

Cardner, B., & Ragan, P. (2004). *Measurement matters: how effective assessment drives business and safety performance.* Milwaukee, WI: ASQ Quality Press.

Deming, W. E. (2000). *The new economics: For industry, government, education* (2nd ed.). Cambridge, MA: MIT Press.

Gitlow, H. S., & Levine, D. L. (2005). *Six Sigma for green belts and champions: foundations, DMAIC, tools, cases, and certification.* Upper Saddle River, NJ: Pearson/Prentice Hall.

Greenwood, R., Suddaby, R., & Hinings, C. (2002). Theorizing change: The role of professional associations in the transformation of institutionalized fields. *Academy of Management Journal, 45*(1), 58–80. doi:10.2307/3069285

Hanneman, L. F., Mickelson, S. K., Pringnitz, L. K., & Lehman, M. (2002). Constituted-Created, Competency Based ABET Aligned Assessment Tools for the Engineering Experiential Education Work Place. In *Proceedings for Accreditation Board for Engineering and Technology ABET Annual Meeting, 2nd National Conference on Outcomes Assessment for Program Improvement,* Baltimore, MD, Accreditation Board for Engineering and Technology.

Hoey, J., Marr, J., & Gardener, D. C. (2002). Multiple vantage points for employment related feedback: Some vantage points. *Proceedings for Accreditation Board for Engineering and Technology ABET Annual Meeting, 2nd National Conference on Outcomes Assessment for Program Improvement,* Baltimore, MD, Accreditation Board for Engineering and Technology.

Holbeche, L. (2006). *Understanding change: Theory, implementation and success.* Oxford, UK: Elseiver/Butterworth-Heinemann.

Jenkins, L. (2003). *Improving student learning: applying Deming's quality principles in classrooms* (2nd ed.). Milwaukee, WI: ASQ Quality Press.

McGregor, D. (2003). The human side of enterprise. In M. Handel (Ed.), *The sociology of organizations: Classic, contemporary and critical readings* (pp. 108–113). Thousand Oaks, CA: Sage.

Pfeffer, J., & Salancik, G. (2003). *The external control of organizations: A resource dependence perspective.* Stanford, CA: Stanford University Press.

Poole, M. S., & Van de Ven, A. H. (Eds.). (2004). *Handbook of organizational change and innovation.* New York: Oxford University Press.

Rhodes, F. H. (2001). *The creation of the future: The role of the American university.* Ithaca, NY: Cornell University Press.

Rowden, R. (2001). The learning organization and strategic change. *Society for the Advancement of Management Journal, 66*(3), 11–24.

Ruben, B. D. (2004). *Pursuing excellence in higher education: Eight fundamental challenges.* San Francisco: Jossey Bass.

Scott, W. R. (2001). *Institutions and organizations.* Thousand Oaks, CA: Sage.

Senge, P. M. (2000). The academy as learning community: Contradiction in terms or realizable future? In A. Lucas (Ed.), *Leading academic change: Essential roles for department chairs* (pp. 275–300). San Francisco: Jossey-Bass.

Senge, P. M. (2006). *The fifth discipline: The art and practice of the learning organization.* New York: Currency Doubleday.

Suskie, L. (2006). Accountability and quality improvement. In P. Hernon, R. E. Dugan, & C. Schwartz (Eds.), *Revisiting outcomes assessment in higher education.* Westport, CT: Libraries Unlimited.

Taylor, F. W. (2003). The principles of scientific management. In M. J. Handel (Ed.), *The sociology of organizations: Classic contemporary and critical readings* (pp. 24–33). Thousand Oaks, CA: Sage.

# Chapter 33

# An Open Network of Digital Production Centers:
## Empowering Schools, Teachers, NGOs, and Communities with Educational Multimedia Creation Capabilities

**Alfredo Alejandro Careaga**
*Ibero-American Network for Sustainable Development, Mexico*

**Alberto Ramirez-Martinell**
*Ibero-American Network for Sustainable Development, Mexico*

## ABSTRACT

*In this chapter, the authors present the Network of Digital Production Centers, a modular, scalable scheme for the development of educational and cultural content in schools and nongovernmental organizations (NGOs) in the state of Veracruz, Mexico. The chapter describes its goals, philosophy, its operations, and its growth plans, as well as the results achieved during the first phase of its implementation. The authors frame the project within the overall objectives of its funding institution, the Ibero-American Network for Sustainable Development, an NGO that began this project with the goal of transforming traditional content consumers into developers and producers of educational and cultural digital materials. The learning curve in the field of user multimedia production is steep, but the Network of Digital Production Centers and the Ibero-American Network for Sustainable Development are harvesting the first set of tangible benefits and usable knowledge.*

## HISTORY

The Ibero-American Network for Sustainable Development (known by its acronym in Spanish, REDDES) is a Mexican nongovernmental organization focused on developing appropriate technological platforms to foster sustainable development, "the interaction of society with nature through technology" (REDDES, 2010). We believe that the selection of the correct technological package and the implementation of the appropriate strategies for its deployment can lead

DOI: 10.4018/978-1-60960-623-7.ch033

to a sustainable and ethical model of development. In particular REDDES is advancing two modular, scalable and interconnected programs:

1. The network of centers for the digital production of educational and cultural content, which we briefly describe in this chapter.
2. A network of centers for the rescue, development and dissemination of biophilic technologies for housing, water, energy, food production, waste disposal and environmental management whose roots go back to 1978 in the Research Center of Quintana Roo (CIQRO) and Sian Ka'an projects (Careaga, 1984, p. 119).

## CONTEXT

The Network of Digital Production Centers was launched by REDDES in 2007 with the support of the Ministry of Education of the state of Veracruz (MEV). Veracruz is a region in Mexico where the delivery of educational services is particularly difficult for several reasons:

1. The geographical situation: The eastern Sierra Madre covers a large part of a territory characterized by peaks, canyons and ravines; thus access to the many small isolated communities is difficult.
2. The social situation: Veracruz has about 7.1 million inhabitants, 48.5% of whom live in rural areas. There are 22,000 communities, of which 63.8% have fewer than 50 inhabitants. Besides Spanish, fourteen other native languages are spoken by several ethnic communities, each with its own ancient culture and traditions.
3. Ecological, cultural and economical diversity: Diversity in these areas is the trademark of Veracruz. It has the highest mountain in Mexico, pine and cloud forests, desert,

savanna and rain forests. It is rich in oil and other natural resources and houses important academic, industrial, commercial and touristic centers. However, it is also one of Mexico's poorest states.

The Ministry of Education and the state government of Veracruz have realized that, in addition to the usual methods of instruction and delivery of educational services, digital technologies can offer innovative and interesting possibilities to overcome geographic, social and diversity limitations. Technology has been a catalyst for partnership creation among different state bodies, projects from the Ministry of Education, individuals and NGOs that have joined forces to improve the current ways in which education is being delivered to students of all levels. For instance, the itinerant Vasconcelos classrooms—a recipient project of the "2008 Access to Learning Award" from the Bill and Melinda Gates Foundation (2008 Access to Learning Award: Vasconcelos Program, 2008)—equipped with full information services and satellite connectivity, are installed on buses outfitted for all-terrain travel that reach the most isolated communities; the Clavijero Project, a consortium of higher education institutions that offers online education in formal and non-formal modes (http://www.clavijero.edu.mx/), and the Network of Digital Production Centers (http://www.rtpd.net) have been supported and projected to achieve goals that in other times were outside of government duties.

### Technology and Development

Providing relevant knowledge is the most effective means for empowering underprivileged communities that strive for self-sustained development and higher levels of quality of life. Improving the local capacities and promoting individual and collective skills raises the self-esteem of its members and facilitates their autonomous management of housing, nutrition, water supply, health, schooling, productivity, asset procurement, governance and environmental use. However, when analyzing the problems faced by developing countries, it is evident that one of the main causes of their limited growth is the effect of the imposition of exogenous models, inappropriate to local needs and characteristics, which increase communities' technological and economical dependence. The blind implementation of schemes like those once followed in the industrialized countries, far from helping to solve the country's basic problems, often aggravate them (Careaga, 1984). Digital technologies are seldom put in the hands of marginal communities despite their obvious potential for empowering the community to participate in the worldwide dialogue. The civil society, and in particular the marginal communities, must activate and participate in their own development. They need to appropriate suitable technologies and decide how they should use these technologies for their own benefit. The creation of a center oriented to attend to these matters seemed imminent, and the Ibero-American Network for Sustainable Development in partnership with the Ministry of Education of the State of Veracruz engaged in the Network of Digital Production Centers project as a strategy to facilitate the appropriation of information and communication technologies by these populations, convinced that the communities themselves will know best how to use them to promote their own development.

## The Network of Digital Production Centers

The Network of Digital Production Centers project is based on a modular architecture that can be implemented in the public, private, academic and social sectors, and therefore can be scaled and adapted to diverse local conditions. Central to the project is the philosophy of Open Access Culture (Berlin Declaration, 2003), whereby the content

produced in each Digital Production Center is freely available for use by anyone in or out of the network. The Network of Digital Production Centers relies on the use of 1) open source software; 2) international open data formats; and 3) the Creative Commons license.

- A Digital Production Center is composed of four elements: hardware, software, methodology and multimedia producers:
  - *Hardware*: A server, a workstation (powerful enough to edit video), input and output peripherals (still and video cameras, scanner, printer, etc.), and access to the Internet.
  - *Software*: Ubuntu is the main operating system and a complete suite of open source editors for multimedia production such as Audacity, Gimp, Inkscape, Stopmotion, Kdenlive and OpenOffice.
  - *Methodology*: A set of powerful methods for educational and cultural content production that cover instructional design, high-level architecture, low-level interactive design, multimedia element production, final integration and delivery as well as an online repository for hosting all multimedia products.
  - *Multimedia producers*: Two people belonging to the community or institution that hosts the Digital Production Center fully trained and in some cases even certified by the state in the use of production methodology, production hardware and digital tools.

The goal of the project is to provide educators, students and individuals of the civil society with standard digital multimedia production knowledge and equipment in order 1) to help them change a predominant passive information consumption attitude into an active content production mode; 2) to make the creation and open distribution of knowledge an everyday activity for many schools, NGOs and individuals; 3) to foster the production of derived works, shared creativity and amplified productivity and 4) to reach a "critical mass" that will promote sustainability and self sufficiency within the Network of Digital Production Centers and those who reach the content created by the Digital Production Center.

The transfer of technology, however, is not enough to assure that its use will be beneficial to the recipient communities while not harming the natural environment that surrounds them. As part of the distribution of knowledge and the transfer of technology for sustainable development, RED-DES provides a set of guidelines and values that includes a realistic perspective on whole systems as seen from the point of view of developing countries, as well as a philosophy of respect for the local ancient knowledge and values traditionally based on a profound reverence towards nature.

Transforming these goals and values into a sustainable project has been the job of a small interdisciplinary group of technologists, educators and designers that defined the platform on which the Network of Digital Production Centers is being built. This interdisciplinary group of individuals bootstrapped the process by creating and operating the first Digital Production Center within itself and then replicating it in other hosting institutions. Since its creation, the first Center has focused on 1) the definition of hardware specifications and selection of software for all the other Digital Production Centers; 2) the development of a general methodology that facilitates the production of educational content by the multimedia producers; 3) building, operating and maintaining a general repository for the content created by all the Digital Production Centers; and 4) providing just-in-time training to other multimedia producers.

## Growth and Operation of the Network of Digital Production Centers

The network started in late 2007. The first Digital Production Center, referred to as the Center of Innovation and Services in 2008, was the model to be replicated in the coming months in other hosting institutions. As of mid 2010, nine operating Digital Production Centers have been established in the state of Veracruz and a slow growth is projected to take place in the short term, but an increasing growing pace is expected on the long run.

The first two steps for setting up a Digital Production Center are 1) equipping the center with hardware and software; and 2) training the multimedia producer. Once these steps are complete, a dialogue begins among the multimedia producer, the people who have the interest of producing a tailor made digital educational object, and the content experts—who can be either the schoolteachers in K-12 institutions; the educators and researchers in higher education institutions; or the experts in the cultural or educational field of their particular interest in NGOs; and the elders and keepers of the ancient traditions in the remote indigenous communities. In this dialogue the multimedia producer uses the content and instructional techniques provided by the content expert to design a model of what the multimedia product is to be. The dialogue between a particular content expert and a multimedia producer is aided by a web-based question-and-answer system that delivers a pedagogical framework for the type of product that will be developed. By the end of this stage, the types of data, the educational models and the instructional strategies to be used in the final product have been defined. The later stages follow a standard multimedia production process until the learning object, courseware, class material or cultural product is finished. All the elements and final products developed in every center in the network are uploaded to a digital repository where they can be downloaded by any other Digital Production Center and used freely by other content experts to generate further educational or cultural products. Digital content living on the repository is free to use not only for the members of the Network but also for everyone who agrees to follow the Creative Commons licensing agreements.

## Partnerships with Distinct Communities

To manage the growth of the Network for Digital Production Center project, the Ibero-American Network for Sustainable Development must address several distinct communities. Besides the sponsors, such as the MEV, other government agencies or private donors, there are the teachers and students in the participant educational centers, the leaders and volunteers of educational NGOs and the urban and rural communities themselves with their families and individuals. Partnerships with these communities must be established, as their active support is a necessary condition for success. With only a few months' experience, only preliminary assessments can be made. Nevertheless, previous experiences in technology transfer to underprivileged and indigenous populations (See Careaga, 1984) allow us to be optimistic. Below, we will try to share some of the initial experiences collected in a project that, by design, will take time to mature and prove its worth. In mid 2010, the network was formed by nine Digital Production Centers in the state of Veracruz. The DPCs were hosted in a kindergarten, an elementary school, a secondary school, a teacher training college, Vasconcelos itinerant classrooms, in three indigenous communities, and in a research center. All DPCs are producing educational and cultural products; for example, the DPC at the kindergarten has produced video-rich interactive storybooks, illustrated and voiced by the children. The DPCs at the elementary and secondary school have worked in the production

of multimedia rich presentations and documentary videos where pollution problems within the community and in the local waterfall are addressed. The products developed by the teacher training college range from physical education dances for elementary school teachers to pedagogical foundations videos. Presenting the project to the leaders of the potential hosting institutions is a difficult task due to its complexity, depth and long-term orientation. School directors, teachers and NGO leaders tend to focus first on the immediate benefits that having a Digital Production Center on their premises will bring. The possibility of producing their own content is generally received with great interest, but interest becomes enthusiasm when these leaders look beyond the first benefits and realize the potential of being able to tap into the repository of educational and cultural content that the network provides. Other benefits of being part of the network have been identified by the particular needs of each Digital Production Center; for example, the teacher training college has seen the changes in the multimedia producers of their center and has even considered extending the multimedia production training program to students and teachers campus wide. Further, the people at the Vasconcelos itinerant classrooms have decided to start producing digital content in indigenous languages related and relevant to the local culture and tradition and thanks to the Network they can benefit at any time from the Digital Production Centers that are located in the indigenous communities. We expect the Network for Digital Production Center to keep growing within the state of Veracruz and even to expand into other states of Mexico. The modular, self-supporting and scalable structure of the network has the potential to become a model for community partnerships that, by appropriating the use of digital technologies, enables information consumers to become active producers and knowledge creators and empowers underprivileged people to use digital technologies for their own good.

## REFERENCES

Access to Learning Award. Vasconcelos Program. (2008). *Bill and Melinda Gates Foundation website*. Retrieved February 2010, from http://www.gatesfoundation.org/atla/Pages/2008-vasconcelos-program.aspx

Berlin Declaration. (2003). *Berlin Declaration on Open Access to Knowledge in the Sciences and Humanities*. Presented at the Conference on Open Access to Knowledge in the Science and Humanities. Retrieved June 2010, from http://oa.mpg.de/openaccess-berlin/berlindeclaration.html

Careaga, A. A. (1984). Sian ka'an: Una reserva de la biósfera en Quintana Roo. [Mexico: CONACyT.]. *Journal Ciencia y Desarrollo, 36*(5), 119–122.

REDDES. (2010). *REDDES' wiki*. Retrieved February 13, 2010, from http://www.rtpd.net/reddes/wiki

World Heritage Center. (No Date). *Sian Ka'an*. Retrieved June 2010 from http://whc.unesco.org/en/list/410

# Chapter 34
# Community–University Engagement in an Electronically-Defined Era

**Lois Gander**
*University of Alberta, Canada*

**Diane Rhyason**
*Legal Resource Centre of Alberta Ltd., Canada*

## ABSTRACT

*Universities can enhance the return on the public investment that they represent by collaborating with their natural allies in addressing pressing social issues. That work can be further enhanced by harnessing appropriate digital technologies. In this chapter, the authors profile a current example of a community-led, multi-layered partnership that was formed to strengthen the infrastructure of the charitable sector in Canada. In particular, the chapter demonstrates that the "habit of partnerships" combined with the "habit of technology" is a potent strategy for addressing community needs. The authors argue that no single partnership or technology will transform the academic enterprise, but rather that the widespread adoption of technologies among universities' allies, competitors, students, and faculty that characterizes the electronically-defined era will compel universities to adopt both the habit of partnerships and the habit of technology. That, in turn, will transform the way universities do their business and those with whom they do it.*

## INTRODUCTION

Universities are under pressure to show significant returns on the public investment they represent by demonstrating that they have a tangible impact on real problems. They recognize that critical social problems can only be addressed through approaches that require academics to collaborate not only within disciplines but across them and to form partnerships with a range of external stakeholders. At the same time, developments in electronic telecommunications technologies have radically changed who can communicate with whom, about what and why. Suddenly anyone can be a source of knowledge and have access to a global audience. Agencies, like universities,

DOI: 10.4018/978-1-60960-623-7.ch034

that were previously tasked with generating and legitimizing knowledge and mediating relations between knower and knowledge-seeker, now find their knowledge empires under attack. Emerging digital technologies also make forming and maintaining partnerships much more cost-effective.

The writing is on the wall: in the future, successful universities will collaborate with other knowers, value a variety of ways of knowing, and work with other formal and informal knowledge mediators to expand both access to, and the scope of, the knowledge domain. In challenging universities to renew themselves as transformational institutions, the Kellogg Commission may not have called on universities to do anything new, but emerging digital technologies certainly do (Kellogg Commission on the Future of Land-Grant Universities, 2001).

## THE HABIT OF PARTNERSHIPS

The University of Alberta in Canada was established along the lines of the American "Wisconsin model" in 1908 to serve the needs of the province. It established a Department of Extension in 1912 to share the university's answers to economic and social problems with everyone (Archer & Wright, 1999). Since then, Extension has been engaged in a wide variety of outreach activities contributing to the cultural and economic well-being of the province. The work of Extension continues to evolve in response to changing community needs and opportunities. It currently offers a range of informal (unorganized, unsystematic) and non-formal (organized, systematic, but not credentialed) learning opportunities, formal continuing education credentials, a post-baccalaureate certificate, an embedded graduate certificate, and a graduate degree. Faculty members engage in both community-based and discipline-based research, practice the scholarships of integration (making connections across disciplines) and application (generating knowledge through practice) (Boyer,

1990), and are active citizens of the university, professions, and communities of interest and practice.

In 1975, Extension (which was just about to be promoted from a department to a faculty) was approached by a charitable organization, the Legal Resource Centre of Alberta Ltd. (LRC), with a request to enter into a partnership. The LRC had been established to develop a program of educational resources and services that would assist the public to become more knowledgeable about the law and better equipped to engage in legal affairs individually and collectively. At the time, the notion of educating the public about the law was considered radical, even dangerous (Gander, 1999). In today's engagement terminology, Extension would become engaged with communities in discovering, sharing, translating, and mobilizing legal knowledge and competencies, particularly through the scholarships of integration (e.g., integrating legal, education, and library science knowledge) and application (practice in a variety of community and professional contexts).

The unit that carried out these activities was headed by a lawyer, drawn from a university-affiliated student-run legal service, who would, in time, become a tenured faculty member. Its multi-disciplinary staff included educators and librarians. Priorities were established within the unit. The operating costs of the unit and some projects were funded by the Alberta Law Foundation. Government departments and foundations were the principal sources of funding for other projects. The University and Extension provided in-kind support (furnishings, equipment, technical assistance, and sometimes space). The role of the board of the LRC varied throughout this period, at times taking full responsibility for obtaining funding for the program, giving direction in its overall development, and providing advice and assistance on specific activities.

In 2007, the program devolved out of the university to the LRC (Gander, 2009) and their roles reversed. The board of the LRC became fully responsible for the program. Extension now provides advice and assistance when requested or commissioned by the LRC. One of the authors and a founding member of the LRC continued in an academic position with Extension and provides advice and assistance to the LRC and to graduate students and visiting scholars interested in studying the theory and practice of public legal education in Canada. Extension continues to provide the LRC with access to the university's library, which contains one of the largest public legal education collections in the world.

The other author, also a founding member of the LRC, left the university to become the executive director of the newly-independent LRC. For its part, the LRC continues to collaborate with several faculty members at the university by providing opportunities for students to engage in community service-learning; in evaluating LRC program; by engaging academics as advisors on activities; and by supporting the public legal education research of academics, visiting scholars, and graduate students. The LRC's library complements the university's collection. The organization's extensive network throughout government, the not-for-profit sector, and the public legal education community is an invaluable research resource. A formal memorandum of understanding between Extension and the LRC is contemplated and other ways of acknowledging the ongoing collaboration are under discussion.

For ease of reading, the work done first by Extension and now by the independent LRC will be described in this chapter as being done by the LRC since the board was involved in some way throughout the entire period and has inherited much of the intellectual and experiential legacy of Extension.

From the beginning, the LRC's public legal education activities were developed in partnership with a range of stakeholders, including schools, libraries, community organizations, government agencies, police forces, law firms, legal and judicial organizations, correctional facilities, band

councils, métis settlements, private foundations, research centres, academics in other faculties in the university and elsewhere as well as countless individuals acting in the personal or professional capacities. Through these partnerships, the LRC addresses topics that have included domestic violence, residential tenancies, "mail-order brides," advanced care planning, offender reintegration into the community, and human trafficking as well as the day-to-day problems that people face in employment, recreational, and family settings and that not-for-profit organizations face in managing their affairs. These activities have had an impact on the lives of individuals, professional practices, the quality and availability of services, the governance of the voluntary sector, government policy, and legislation. The LRC played a major leadership role in establishing the provincial and national associations of public legal education providers and guides an informal international network of individuals and organizations that carry on similar work. Through its many activities, the LRC has also contributed significantly to defining and theoretically grounding the practice of public legal education in Canada. As a result of the varied contributions of stakeholders, access to legal information is an essential element of the Canadian justice system.

Throughout their histories, both Extension and the LRC have acquired the habit of partnerships—the purposeful selection of appropriate partners—in addressing contemporary community issues.

## THE HABIT OF TECHNOLOGY

Many of Extension's successes relate directly to the use of the educational and communications technologies of the day – magic lantern slides, 16 mm films, videocassettes, radio broadcasting, teleconferencing, and other media. In 1997, Extension hosted Academic Technologies for Learning, the unit in the University responsible for encouraging and supporting early adopters of emerging electronic telecommunications technologies. Today, Extension uses online and blended-learning approaches in its programming and supplements formal learning activities with online portals, newsletters, and podcasts; provides instructors with tips on using various digital technologies; and, maintains a faculty intranet to facilitate internal knowledge sharing. It continues to engage in informal and non-formal learning activities digitally, through print, and through face-to-face interactions.

An early traveler on the Internet highway, the LRC has become proficient in using digital technology in developing Web-based portals, interactive learning resources, and online services for various publics and in supporting the public legal education community in Canada. Using those technologies has made the LRC more socially relevant and financially viable.

The LRC selects technologies for use in its projects on the basis of a variety of factors including the cost of the particular technology to the LRC and to prospective users and its suitability in advancing project goals. The LRC uses technologies with which it and other partners are familiar as well as some with which the LRC, the university, and other partners have little or no direct experience—challenging all to become more technologically competent in the process. The LRC now takes this habit of technology— the purposeful selection of appropriate electronic telecommunications technologies—as one of its defining characteristics. It is a habit that requires the organization to keep pace with new developments in digital technology and to explore innovative applications of existing technologies. Understanding and applying new technologies as they emerge is a core organizational competency.

## THE CHARITY CENTRAL PROJECT

In 2006 the LRC became involved in a series of informal and non-formal educational activities

to strengthen the infrastructure that supports the 85,000 organizations that constitute the charitable sector in Canada. The project has been funded through the Charities Directorate, Canada Revenue Agency (CRA). The project described here was prompted by problems that charities were having in complying with their obligations under the federal *Income Tax Act,* sometimes resulting in their charitable status being revoked for reasons that could have been avoided if they had a better understanding of the regulations. Many of those charities were still active and so sought to be re-registered – an onerous process for themselves and a burden on the Directorate. The government's response to this situation was multi-pronged and included an explicit policy of working with the charitable sector to create an atmosphere of mutual respect and trust so they could collaborate in encouraging and supporting voluntary compliance with the regulations governing charities. Implementing the government's strategy required a nationwide, sector-wide education program. Staff and boards of charities, the resource people they turned to for assistance, sector associations, and sector educators all needed to know about changes in policy, forms, and regulatory requirements (Government of Canada, 2009).

To facilitate a partnership with the sector in carrying out that educational program, the CRA established the Charities Partnership and Outreach Program (CPOP). The purpose of CPOP is to fund selected registered charities to develop and deliver innovative education and training activities that would raise awareness among the charitable sector of those obligations, increase the capacity of the sector to comply in a sustainable fashion, and improve the capacity of the sector to develop and deliver sustainable compliance-based education programs (Government of Canada, 2009). The major groups targeted through CPOP are small and medium-sized charities.

The LRC has years of experience in working with the not-for-profit sector in general and the charitable sector in particular and has an extensive national network with links internationally. The LRC also has direct experience in working with the CRA, undertaking research, and providing advice on policies and services. Accordingly, the LRC responded to calls for proposals under the CPOP and, to date, three of the LRC's proposals have received funding totaling over $2 million CDN[1]. These funds are enabling the LRC to create a range of informational and educational resources and interactive services to help guide registered charities through complex regulations about such things as issuing official donation receipts, maintaining proper books and records, complying with the tax requirements of charitable fundraising and the importance of transparency and accountability in their operations if they are to maintain public confidence in the their organization and in the sector. Resources and services also help charities understand the role and services provided by the CRA.

For the purposes of this discussion, the activities funded under the LRC's successful proposals are collectively referred to as "the project."

## MULTILEVEL PARTNERSHIPS

Like others in the not-for-profit sector, the LRC has to leverage the funds it gets. It also subscribes to the proposition that knowledge is generated and enriched through the interaction and synthesis of the insights and experiences of a diverse group of individuals. Reach and, therefore, impact of its resources is multiplied many times over by working with intermediary agencies and through networks. Since one of the requirements of the CRA's funding is that activities have national impact, the LRC, as a simple matter of practicality, collaborates with other agencies and individuals in a variety of ways, and on a variety of terms. Accordingly it initiated and leads a multilevel, community-based partnership to achieve the project's goals. Not all the relationships that make up this partnership fit within a strict interpretation of the term "partner-

ship" and certainly not within its legal meaning as a type of business entity in which partners are owners and share profits and losses with each other. The term "partnership" is used here more in the sense of a relationship where people are engaging in a common activity, working together toward common or at least compatible goals, and sharing knowledge, expertise, and other types of resources. The relationships are described in descending order of formality.

- **Level one - Funder/grant recipient**: The LRC's primary relationship in this project was with the Government of Canada through the CRA. The principal terms of their partnership were documented through a formal agreement. It set forth the responsibilities of both partners for outputs and communication, content validation, ownership of results, and the conditions under which other partnerships could be entered into.
- **Level two - Subcontractor**: The LRC entered into several formal agreements with community organizations, other public legal education groups, and with Extension, which set out their responsibilities for specific activities within the project.
- **Level three - Advisor**: Less formal relationships were developed with organizations within the charitable sector (e.g., volunteer centres), professionals and professional associations (accountants and lawyers), and academics. These participants volunteered to provide advice and feedback through focus groups, online surveys, and evaluation sessions, and they disseminated resources through their own networks.
- **Level four - Resource and service users**: In this project, there were three types of users of resources and services: individual charities (through their staff or volunteers); those who support charities in some way (professionals, government agencies, sector associations, and the like); and organizations

with a broader information mandate (like libraries and multicultural organizations). Because the ultimate success of the project depends on the buy-in of all three types of users, they too are considered partners, and individual users were engaged with informally throughout the project and formally through formative and summative evaluation activities.

- **Level five - Liaison**: The LRC was not the only organization funded by the CPOP initiative. Approximately a dozen disparate organizations across the country including other post-secondary institutions, national volunteer organizations, provincial public legal education organizations, and economic development and social enterprise organizations were also funded to undertake similar work. In an effort to share expertise and resources and to avoid duplication, representatives of funded organizations have used both in-person and technology-supported approaches to solidify their relationships.

At least 35 agencies and organizations are now part of the project partnership and more yet are part of a growing international network of individuals and agencies concerned with the regulation of the charitable sector. Some of the partnerships within these layers, like that of the LRC and Extension, are themselves multi-layered, adding further to the complexities and reach of the relationships.

## MULTIPLE APPLICATIONS OF TECHNOLOGY

Technologies supported the project in two important ways: developing and sustaining relationships; and, developing, delivering, and maintaining resources and services.

## Developing and Sustaining Relationships

Teleconferencing, video conferencing, e-mail, shared online event calendars, online document sharing, forums, RSS feeds, Facebook, and Twitter have all been used to complement phone calls and in-person meetings that helped solidify project relationships.

## Developing, Delivering, and Maintaining Resources and Services

An interactive Web site, online tutorials, podcasts, webinars, CDs, and wikis have been used to generate and mobilize the knowledge to be shared among charities and their supporters. However, recognizing that not all its partners have high speed Internet access, the LRC also provides a toll-free long distance service and a variety of print-based resources. Technologies used to develop those resources include desktop publishing tools, an open source content management system, and presentation and animation software.

The project proposals did not assume that all these technologies would be called into play. The first technologies adopted included a project Web site, a telephone helpline, and some print resources. As the project progressed other technologies were adopted as appropriate. One of the latest innovations has been the creation of both a physical and a virtual "office in a box"—a start-up mini office kit for new, small charities.

## THE BENEFITS OF THE PROJECT

### Substantive Benefits

Both the LRC and the CRA are undertaking formative and summative evaluations which will provide more feedback on the nature and scale of the impacts of the CPOP overall and of specific projects funded through it. However, some immediate benefits of the project can be catalogued. Individuals, organizations, and others who need access to specific information are benefitting from resources and services. Of equal importance to charities is their ability to access resources and services according to their own needs. The CRA, the LRC, and level-five partners all have a much better understanding of the needs of the charitable sector and of effective ways of meeting them.

## Benefits of the Partnership

None of the partners in this project had the knowledge or capacity to undertake the project alone. Only by working collaboratively could they address the objectives of the CRA. As a result, all of them have established new and better working relationships with each other and the LRC has a more substantial relationship with the CRA in particular.

## Benefits of the Technology

The appropriate use of digital technology made this project possible both by enabling the partners to communicate more effectively with each other and by enabling them to produce resources and provide services that could be widely accessed by the charitable sector at little or no cost to users and maintained by the LRC at little on-going cost. The cost of relying solely on travel and teleconferencing to support partner communications and of relying solely on print, telephone, and face-to-face resources and services to reach the sector would have made the project prohibitively expensive.

Some of the relationships developed through this project have come into being specifically because of new technologies. Those technologies have also helped to reduce the demands on the partners, to clarify their expectations of each other, and to bring a blend of voices to bear in advancing the capacity of the charitable sector to focus on its public functions. Digital technologies

will play a continuing role in sustaining several of those relationships.

All the partners in this project gained more experience in using technologies to meet the needs of the charitable sector. Although the development of the technological capacity of partners is not an explicit objective of the project, it is a significant intended consequence.

## LESSONS LEARNED

## About Partnerships

Effective working relationships require a sufficient measure of mutual respect and a sufficient degree of commitment to the project to enable partners to overcome difficulties that might arise in the course of the project. Some relationships will be more equal, reciprocal, and sustainable than others, which is not only inevitable but sometimes desirable. As a result, judicious use needs to be made of formalizing partnership arrangements. It would have been prohibitively time-consuming to require all the partnerships in this project to have been formally documented. Certainly the arrangement between the CRA and the LRC needed to be clearly articulated and formally confirmed by both parties. Wherever the intention is to create legally enforceable obligations, formal contracts should be used. However, in many of the partnerships in this project, notably those at levels three, four, and five, a formal, legally binding relationship would be inappropriate, even counter-productive. Reserving the term "partnership" to describe only those relationships that can be formalized may result in the importance of the participation of key stakeholders being discounted and even overlooked.

## About Technology

As the LRC's experience demonstrates, advances in digital technology have made it possible for universities to partner with external organizations in mounting projects of a sufficient scale and complexity to have a meaningful impact on contemporary issues on community and social concern. But since both community-university engagement and the effective use of electronic telecommunications are context-specific, the lesson to be learned from that project is not how any specific technology was successfully applied and for what purpose, but rather the importance of developing the habit of technology.

That said, digital technologies were particularly useful in developing and delivering resources, services, and training. Key to the development of e-learning modules was the use of interactive software that enabled step-by-step learning, branched scenarios, and uploading of resources to other websites. These services were often backed up with downloadable print products. The Alberta SuperNet, a network of fiber optic cables and towers built to connect public institutions across the province, has been instrumental in providing province-wide access to Web-based resources and services. It also enables the LRC to conduct group training events. Project staff worked with two specific SuperNet services: Innovative Communities Connecting and Networking (ICANN provides video and audio training through local Adult Learning Councils) and Rural Information Services Initiative (RISE reaches 450,000 people in 89 communities through the public libraries) to provide over 75 people in 25 rural communities with video training sessions.

There was, however, one digital technology-based service that was not successful in supporting relationships. Despite the growing acceptance of social media as a primary communication tool, the attempt to use a forum as a method to connect charities with one another was not successful. Preliminary focus groups suggested that while there was an encouragingly high level of interest expressed in the idea, in practice there was very little participation in the forum that was set up. The follow-up evaluation indicated that most forum members planned to visit the forum only every few months, and that their major reason for doing so would be to seek information (Extension Learning Solutions, 2009). So the digital technology selected in this instance missed the mark.

## CONCLUSION

As the example of the LRC demonstrates, combining a habit of partnerships with a habit of technology can be a potent way of addressing community needs. Universities can enhance their ability to address the needs of the communities they serve by working in sometimes complex partnerships with a variety of external allies. Universities do not need to drive these initiatives nor even be a senior partner in them for their contribution to be meaningful. Relationships can be fluid and adjust to changing circumstances. But for universities to succeed in serving their communities, they must recognize and value the knowledge and competencies of individuals, organizations, government agencies, and corporations that make up those communities. It will need to become second nature for universities to form appropriate collaborations with their natural allies. In short, they will need to develop the habit of partnerships.

Universities also need to recognize that they exist in a digitally defined era. Allies, competitors, students and faculty are becoming increasingly competent in using digital technologies – competencies that include dealing with the rapid change in those technologies. Universities will soon acquire those same competencies, if only because they will soon be comprised of staff and students who posses them and for whom using those technologies has become second nature. So, whether by design or default, universities will acquire the habit of technology. That habit will necessarily take the university outside itself and into the wider digitally defined universe – a universe inhabited by a host of potential allies and partners that will, in turn, compel universities to develop the habit of partnerships.

Whether those inevitable changes are managed proactively by universities will determine the success they will experience in attracting and maintaining technologically savvy staff and students and in satisfying their mandates to serve the public good. It will also determine their success in being institutions of personal and social transformation.

## REFERENCES

Archer, W., & Wright, K. (1999). Back to the future: Adjusting university continuing education research to an emerging trend. *Canadian Journal of University Continuing Education, 25*(2), 61–83.

Boyer, E. L. (1990). *Scholarship reconsidered: Priorities of the professoriate*. San Francisco, CA/Princeton, NJ: The Carnegie Foundation for the Advancement of Teaching.

Extension Learning Solutions. (2009). *Interim evaluation: Charity central essentials*. Edmonton, Canada: University of Alberta, Faculty of Extension.

Gander, L. (1999). *The radical promise of public legal education in Canada. Unpublished LL.* Edmonton: M., University of Alberta.

Gander, L. (2009). The incubation model of university-community relationships: A case study in incubating new programs, new knowledge, and new fields of practice. *Canadian Journal of University Continuing Education, 35*(1), 25–44.

Government of Canada. (2009). *Charities partnership and outreach program funding guide and application*. Retrieved from http://www.cra-arc.gc.ca/E/pub/tg/rc4411/README.html

*Income Tax Act*, R.S., 1985, c. 1 (5th Supp.) as amended.

Kellogg Commission on the Future of Land-Grant Universities. (2001). *Returning to our roots: Executive summaries of the reports of the Kellogg Commission on the future of state and land-grant universities*. Washington, DC: National Association of State Universities and Land-Grant Colleges.

## ENDNOTE

[1]   T3010B Registered Charity Information Return available at www.cra-arc.gc.ca

# Chapter 35
# Encouraging Public Involvement in Public Policymaking Through University–Government Collaboration

**Marco Adria**
*University of Alberta, Canada*

**Yuping Mao**
*University of Alberta, Canada*

## ABSTRACT

*New methods of involving large numbers of citizens in public decision-making using information and communications technologies have spurred academic and professional interest. This chapter will describe the case of the Citizen Panel, a public-involvement project in which a municipal government and university combined their capacities to create a significant new opportunity for public involvement in public policymaking. Technology was used to broaden access to participation in, and awareness of, the Citizen Panel. Technology application included development of a video version of the information resources used by the Citizen Panel, posting key information on the website, hosting a Facebook group discussion, and live broadcast of panel sessions by Web streaming. The Citizen Panel provided a "proof of concept" for the subsequent establishment of the Centre for Public Involvement, which is a partnership between the municipal government and the university. The Centre for Public Involvement's purpose will be to engage in research and development in support of improved public-involvement practices and processes.*

## HISTORY AND CONTEXT

The Citizen Panel was a new approach to citizen involvement in Canada. The budgets for social housing in the city of Toronto and for family services in the city of nearby Guelph are decided, in part, through public deliberation. Neither city has taken the broad approach to budget priorities represented by the Citizen Panel project, in which large-scale budget priorities were considered. Outside of Canada, the city of Porto Alegre in Brazil provides an example of public participa-

DOI: 10.4018/978-1-60960-623-7.ch035

tion in civic budgeting that has been successfully operating since 1989 (Lerner, 2006). The purposes of similar citizen-involvement events for policy-making include developing budgets, designing rural and urban landscapes, making policy recommendations, posing public questions to politicians, and taking voluntary action (Levine, Fung, & Gastil, 2005). Success has been identified based on the following factors: realistic expectations of influence (e.g., government involved); inclusive, representative process; informal, substantive, conscientious discussion with the aim of reaching "common ground," not consensus; and neutral professional staff (Levine, Fung, & Gastil, 2005).

This case study of the Citizen Panel demonstrates how a university and municipal government collaborated on a deliberative democracy pilot project by engaging a diverse group of citizens on an important issue of public policy.

Edmonton is a city with a metropolitan population of about 780,000. It is the capital and seat of government in the Western Canadian province of Alberta. The population of Alberta is about 3.7 million. The Alberta context in Western Canada has historically provided a fertile reception for deliberative democracy, and the Faculty of Extension at the University of Alberta in Canada has been associated with the concept and practices of public deliberation since the time of E.A. Corbett (Corbett, 1957).

The Edmonton Citizen Panel pilot project was a response to an inquiry by a member of city council (an elected representative), who asked the city's administration to provide a report on participatory democracy. The report would describe the concept of participatory democracy, explain how participatory democracy relates to the objectives of the city's public involvement policy, and provide details on what potential opportunities there were to engage in participatory democracy. A report prepared by a team representing the university and the city was presented for information to city council. Several months later, the Citizen Panel pilot project was proposed to

and approved by city council. The Citizen Panel was organized collaboratively by the City of Edmonton and the University of Alberta, bringing together women and men of diverse ages, incomes, cultural backgrounds, and experience to learn about and discuss their city's budget priorities. It met for six Saturday sessions, beginning in February 2009, continuing throughout all of the Saturdays in March, and concluding on 25 April 2009. It was constituted by approximately 50 citizens selected to represent the city's ages and incomes, chosen through telephone invitation from a list created by random selection within selected demographic dimensions. The goal of the Citizen Panel was to gather informed citizen opinion for city council to consider seriously as input into the 2010-2011 budget process. The Panel was not limited or constrained to consider any part of the annual budget, which is approximately $CA1.5 billion per year. During the six full-day sessions that they met, panelists learned about the City of Edmonton's budgeting process and the processes and strategies underpinning that process. They also learned about the City Vision and the 10-year strategic plan. Information presentations were made to panelists by senior city managers as part of the learning stage of the Panel's deliberations. The Citizen Panel concluded its active stage of participation by presenting six recommendations to city council in July 2009.

## The Use of Technology as a Catalyst in the Project

There is a tradition of using new media (for example, radio broadcasting in the 1930s and 1940s) for enhancing democratic participation (Peers, 1969). Interest in new methods of aspiring to the democratic ideal has increased in tandem with widening access to the Internet (Citizens' Assembly 2008; Kelshaw & Gastil, 2008). Thompson (2005) states that a "new visibility" is a prominent feature of our social environment: "Since the advent of print, political rulers have found it impossible to control completely the new kind of visibility made possible by the media and to shape it entirely to their liking; now, with the rise of the Internet and other digital technologies, it is more difficult than ever" (38). Technology was used to broaden access to participation in, and awareness of, the Citizen Panel. First, a video version of the resources and topics used by the Citizen Panel was created collaboratively by the city and the university for use by members of the Citizen Panel, as an alternative to the text version. The use of the video ensured that panel members with lower literacy levels were able to grasp the key content of the major written materials for facilitating the discussions. Second, both the video and text versions of these resources were posted on the city's official Web site to help raise awareness of the Citizen Panel in the general public. Third, some 200 citizens joined a Facebook site for discussion about the topics that the Citizen Panel was addressing in its deliberations. To try to maintain the neutrality of the Facebook discussion, graduate students and a staff member of the university served as moderators. Fourth, the plenary sessions of the Citizen Panel, which were the first and last hours of each of the six Saturdays of the Citizen Panel meetings (12 hours in total), were broadcast live by web-streaming for viewing by anyone using the web. Recordings of the webcasts were posted on the city's Web site for viewing by the public during and after the Citizen Panel's work. The recordings were accessed later as an artefact of the Citizen Panel by public-involvement practitioners, researchers, Citizen Panel members, the media, and the general public.

## Value of the Project in Forming a Community Partnership

The Citizen Panel provided a basis for further collaboration between the City of Edmonton and the University of Alberta. Following the conclusion of the Citizen Panel, the city and university decided to extend and strengthen the nature of their partnership. A year after the completion of the Citizen Panel, the Centre for Public Involvement was approved by both partners. The mission and purpose of the Centre is to provide leadership in understanding and applying innovative practices and new technologies for citizen participation, engagement, and deliberation. The Centre's main areas of activity will be based on the University of Alberta's core activities of research, teaching and service and will include the following activities:

- Carry out research to enhance discovery and learning associated with public-involvement projects;
- Identify appropriate methods and practices for application in public-involvement activities;
- Assess innovative forms of public participation and involvement;
- Provide advice and expertise to organizations and institutions respecting state-of-the-art practices of public deliberation and public communication;
- Create opportunities for learning for undergraduate and graduate students in support of the value noted in the University of Alberta's *Dare to Discover* vision document of "enlightened service that builds citizenship";
- Provide national and international leadership through research, development, and innovation in the theory and practice of public communication.

The Centre will intentionally and continuously seek to provide a balance among best practices, research and consulting.

## Community Impact

Public involvement provides opportunities for individuals and stakeholders to make meaningful contributions to decision-making. Fostering public involvement increases the opportunities available and broadens the range of people who have access to those opportunities. The Citizen Panel found a place within the city's existing policy of involving citizens while exploring an area of public involvement that has not been widely practiced in Edmonton or elsewhere. It was situated on the continuum between consultation and active participation. In terms of consultation, the panel involved citizens in collaborating to develop solutions to build commitment, and its purpose was to involve citizens in the development of solutions. The panel also encouraged the active participation of citizens, although it was not fully a form of shared decision making or decision delegation. When the Citizen Panel pilot project was approved, city council agreed that the recommendations would be seriously considered. The Citizen Panel extended the City of Edmonton's commitment to involving people in setting budget priorities. Edmontonians could also continue to add their views and their voice to Edmonton's budget priorities through other means, such as the annual Citizen Satisfaction Survey, telephone calls, letters, and e-mails to the mayor and city councillors, and the public hearings on the budget.

## Educational Impact

As part of the Citizen Panel project, seven graduate students (one in a doctoral program and the other six in master's programs), two undergraduate students, and a recent master's graduate were involved in the Citizen Panel as facilitators in the panel proceedings, Facebook moderators, and recruiters. The areas of study of the 10 students included political science, communications and technology, psychology, and political philosophy. Some of the students were volunteers, providing support and assistance because of their interest in the project in relation to their studies and personal interests. Others completed a directed studies graduate course under the supervision of a faculty member as part of their participation in

the Citizen Panel, exploring and applying current developments in public involvement. One student was appointed as a research assistant to coordinate the recruitment of panelists.

In the proposal for the Centre for Public Involvement, five of the university's 20 faculties provided letters of support, indicating the interest generated by the Citizen Panel and Centre initiatives. Faculty members at the university will be encouraged to participate as Associate Members of the Centre for Public Involvement. They will also be asked to participate as members of the Academic Advisory Board. The Academic Advisory Board will review and advise on the major projects to be carried out under the auspices of the Centre. Among the Centre's expected activities will be to organize or provide training to students and public-involvement practitioners in such areas as moderation of small groups, recruiting and orientating participants in public-involvement events, and evaluation.

## Value of the Project for the Educational Institution

The University of Alberta's vision document, entitled *Dare to Discover*, expresses the strategic intention to provide a broad overview of the institution's educational and community engagement. The document includes the value of encouraging "excellence in teaching that promotes learning, outstanding research and creative activity that fuel discovery and advance knowledge, and enlightened service that builds citizenship." Both the Citizen Panel and the proposed Centre demonstrate that value. In addition, they aim to enhance and contribute to the Faculty of Extension's Strategic Academic Plan by providing opportunities for individuals and stakeholders to make meaningful contributions to decision-making about public policy. It will also support the faculty's mandate to foster public involvement and broaden the range of people who have access to opportunities for public involvement, through means such as the following:

- The university's External Relations Office exemplifies its commitment to engaging the public in its planning and activities. The Centre will assist the university in involving the public in such decisions as land use and green initiatives.
- The Faculty of Extension exemplifies the university's commitment to studying public involvement. The faculty has stated that it intends to pursue its strategic goal of enhancing its leadership and capacities in the scholarship of community engagement; that is, it seeks to take a systematic and reflective approach to documenting the practices and processes of community engagement through research and scholarship.
- The Centre will be a resource for use in developing and refining public consultation processes and tools. It will assist in the further development and implementation of public involvement processes, and their incorporation within the university's standard practices.
- The Centre will function as a resource for undergraduate and graduate students for development and learning—in emerging areas of study such as urban ecology and communicative design.

The Citizen Panel was a fully collaborative project between the university and the city. It represented an effort that enjoyed widespread support with the public and with administrators and elected representatives at the city because of the sharing of experience and expertise from the university. When the proposal was initially approved by city council, elected representatives were congratulatory regarding and supportive of the proposal. The mayor publicly mentioned his discussions with the university's president concerning the mutual benefits to the City of Edmonton and the

University of Alberta of continuing to develop a community-based university.

## Best Practices and Strategies for Forming Partnerships

An evaluation framework for the Citizen Panel was established as part of the Citizen Panel project. It includes a large-scale survey questionnaire of citizens about their knowledge and opinions about public-involvement activities, as well as interviews with and focus groups involving Citizen Panelists, university researchers, city administrators, and elected representatives.

A key best practice for public-involvement activities that are organized through university-government collaborations is following up with and seeking to understand citizen views after formal consultations have concluded. Citizens who participate in public-involvement activities such as the Citizen Panel have a primary concern to know not only that they are given an opportunity to "speak," but also that they will be "heard." The Citizen Panel received updates after their discussions ended about how city council was consulting and using the recommendations produced by the Citizen Panel. This has been done through email, follow-up meetings with panelists, and public discussions with city council. Through its design and management, the Citizen Panel project encouraged informed, values-based discussion by citizens through providing broad-based direction to city council, which can then be used to support, inform, correct, or shape policymaking decisions.

One of the best practices of the Citizen Panel is the recruitment of the panelists. The method for selecting panelists employed *random stratified selection within a purposive sampling framework.* This method was designed in order to ensure that social groups would not be left out of the Citizen Panel. The method helped to avoid putting together a group that would have more in common than the polity in the wider context could justify. Stratified sampling was used to appoint 35 of the participants, roughly two-thirds of the total. These panelists were contacted by the use of a computer-generated list of names and addresses drawn randomly from Edmonton's 411 ("White Pages") listings. Around one third of the panelists belonging to special social groups were selected through outreach. The panel members represented different age and income groups of citizens in Edmonton. In total, 57 citizens were appointed for participation in the event. The Panel included three more men than women. Aboriginal people, disabled people, and visible minorities were included. About 10 percent of panelists had been residents of the city for less than three years. All of the city's six wards were represented.

One of the lessons learned was that there was a clear sense that partnership between the city and the university was critical to the acceptance and implementation of the Citizen Panel. For many senior administrators at the city, the planning-team members, and panel members, the involvement of the university provided a sense of the involvement of a neutral third party. It also provided an enhanced sense of legitimacy and rigor to designing and learning from the project. Still, some citizens and city staff felt the process was very much a city initiative and questioned the value of marrying an academic exercise with the business of the city. Indeed, some panelists said that they did not welcome being part of what they saw as a "social experiment" or "research project." There was some concern among senior managers interviewed that the process did not allow for "ownership" by senior management. At the same time, these administrators stated that they did not want to be seen leading it. There was also some sense, on the part of administrators at the city, that the university team outweighed the city team in influencing the process, perhaps because the university researchers took primary responsibility for the original design of the process and development of the *Issue Book*, which was used to frame the questions considered by the Citizen Panel.

Members of the planning team described the Citizen Panel as a significant learning experience and a respectful partnership. They indicated that they saw deliberative dialogue in operation in their work together. There was a shared sense of purpose and recognition of a substantive opportunity to take forward the idea of citizen engagement, which is an important part of the mandate of both the university and the city. They felt the difference in culture between the city and the university was a real strength of the partnership and affirmed their desire and commitment to ongoing work together. Members of the planning team also emphasized the importance of the art of "balancing dance" between the university and the city. The differences between the two institutions also bring challenges in the collaboration. Communication is key in successful collaboration. Throughout the process of the Citizen Panel, members of both the university and the city tried to take the other side's perspective, appreciate each other's strengths, complement each other's weaknesses, and lay out a clear and detailed work plan with objectives, responsibilities, and actions. Differences and conflicts were addressed explicitly as part of the process of improving the collaborative relationship.

In terms of technology, two lessons were learned. The live web streaming was costly, and only a few hundred people viewed the Citizen Panel proceedings as they happened. Recording and posting the proceedings online would be much less expensive and less technologically complicated than live web streaming. Likewise, social media such as Facebook are interpreted and used by many citizens as a broadcast medium, but not as a method for increasing their interaction and engagement with governments, even when an invitation is offered to do so. Without the deliberation process that was characteristic of the Citizen Panel, the online discussion appeared to be superficial and less focused. As a consequence, the Facebook discussion did not appear to contribute to building informed opinion. Through the large-scale survey as part of the evaluation plan of the Citizen Panel, we found that the strategic use of mass media through newspaper advertisements, online ads in Facebook, and coverage on television and radio had no significant effect on public opinion about public deliberation or the issues being discussed within the public-deliberation event. However, the survey showed an increase in citizens' willingness to participate in future public-deliberation or public-involvement events, which could be a result of using different technologies to inform the general public of the Citizen Panel and invite them for the wide discussion around the topics discussed in the Panel.

The evaluation of the Citizen Panel was conducted as elected representatives, senior administrators, and members of the Citizen Panel participated in focus groups and interviews after city council approved the budget for 2010-11. The results showed that the Citizen Panel was perceived as a positive activity that has supported public involvement at the City. The recommendations of the Panel were welcomed and approved by city councillors and senior managers. The recommendations in the Citizen Panel's report affirmed the directions and strategies of the City's 2010-2011 budget. The lessons learned from the Citizen Panel in developing new partnerships between the university and the city will be used in the development of the Centre for Public Involvement.

# REFERENCES

*Citizens' Assembly on Electoral Reform.* (n.d.) Retrieved on March 12, 2008, from http://www.citizensassembly.bc.ca/public

Corbett, E. (1957). *We have with us tonight.* Toronto, Canada: Ryerson.

Kelshaw, T., & Gastil, J. (2008). When citizens and officeholders meet, part 2: A typology of face-to-face public meetings. *International Journal of Public Participation, 2*(1), 33–54.

Lerner, J. (2006). Let the people decide: Transformative community development through participatory budgeting in Canada. *Shelterforce Online, 146.* Retrieved from http://www.nhi.org/online/issues/146/canadianbudgeting.html

Levine, P., Fung, A., & Gastil, J. (2005). Future directions for public deliberation. In J. Gastil & P. Levine (Eds.), *The deliberative democracy handbook: Strategies for effective civic engagement in the twenty-first century* (271-288). San Francisco, CA: Jossey-Bass.

Peers, F. (1969). *The politics of Canadian broadcasting, 1920-1951.* Toronto, Canada: University of Toronto Press.

Thompson, J. (2005). The new visibility. *Theory, Culture & Society, 22*(6), 31–51. doi:10.1177/0263276405059413

# Chapter 36

# The Rise and Fall of Tobacco in the Lake City Market Area:
## A Case Study of Technology-Intensive Community-Based Research

**Cora M. Allard**
*Clemson University, USA*

**Debbie G. Whittington**
*Florence School District Three, USA*

**Barbara J. Speziale**
*Clemson University, USA*

## ABSTRACT

*In 2005, Clemson University's SC LIFE Project and South Carolina's Florence School District Three began a collaborative project to catalyze research among teachers and students in the rural community. This project piloted the concept of using Web-based videoconferencing to allow university faculty to facilitate research in a precollege setting. This technology removed the more than 200 miles distance between the partners as an impediment to the participation of district teachers and students in Clemson University programs. To prepare teachers for the research, an online course was developed and disseminated from Clemson University via Macromedia Breeze. Teachers and administrators from Florence District Three met with Clemson University faculty through videoconferencing and bulletin board technology. District personnel chose the theme, "The Rise and Fall of Tobacco in the Lake City Market Area." The school district personnel also gained proficiency in digital technology skills (e.g. Adobe Photoshop Elements, Adobe Premier Elements, Movie Maker) that they and their students used to collect information and create a final DVD.*

DOI: 10.4018/978-1-60960-623-7.ch036

## INTRODUCTION

This chapter will serve as a case study for using technology to facilitate university and school district interactions during a collaborative research project. This project was initiated in 2005 to test a method for engaging precollege students and teachers in research while simultaneously teaching them digital technology skills. From Fall 2005 through Summer 2006, university faculty worked with students and teachers in an entire small, rural school district to create a locally relevant, life sciences DVD product that would be used for instruction in local schools and the community. The collaboration between Clemson University and Florence School District Three in South Carolina arose through Clemson University's SC LIFE Project (SCLIFE), funded since 1998 by the Howard Hughes Medical Institute. This chapter presents the process, obstacles and outcomes of the year-long project. The overall objective is to explore the benefits of using technology to facilitate community-based research between geographically distant university and school district partners.

## BACKGROUND

SC LIFE offers life sciences education and research opportunities for college students and for precollege students and teachers, with a strong focus on exploring local natural history. Technology education is interspersed throughout SC LIFE programs, from creation of online "virtual field trips" to South Carolina natural areas (SCETV), to assisting teachers to create instructional DVDs for their classrooms using digital editing software. This collaborative project expanded these instructional techniques to involve students as young as elementary school age in a technology-intensive research project on a community-based topic. In order to motivate students to participate and to foster their vested interest in the project outcomes,

leaders chose tobacco farming, a theme of local relevance (Trexler, 2004). According to Lave (1988), developing relevant community-based themes for research projects should also enhance the learning experience for the students; learning occurs in a context and culture (situated learning). The theme of the project, "The Rise and Fall of Tobacco in the Lake City Market Area," was relevant to many individuals in the rural farming community that encompasses Florence School District Three. The main municipality in this district, Lake City, was once the site of one of the largest tobacco leaf markets in South Carolina (Chamber of Commerce). As tobacco farming declined in the region, most families quit the industry and the once iconic tobacco barns fell into ruin. This theme fostered exploration into the sociological, cultural and biological aspects of tobacco cultivation, negatives and positives, in the community.

Florence School District Three serves approximately 3550 students and is comprised of five elementary schools, two middle schools, an alternative school, a career school and a high school. The district is located in an area that was profiled in the 2005 video, *Corridor of Shame*, which exposed the poor conditions in rural school districts in South Carolina. District-wide, 87% of students receive free or reduced-price lunch. Prior to this project, Florence School District Three's interactions with Clemson University consisted of sending nine teachers and 45 students from three schools to the campus each year for the two-day Biology Merit Exam. By using technology, we were able to engage with 20 teachers and approximately 600 students from eight schools in the project over the course of a school year. In addition the project involved many families, businesses, agencies, farmers, local artists and museums.

## PROJECT DESCRIPTION

### Educational Impact and Impact on the Community

The project theme was suggested by the Florence School District Three superintendent and sanctioned by the local school board. In choosing this topic, all acknowledged the issues and controversies surrounding tobacco use and, by extension, tobacco farming. They also recognized that tobacco farming was intrinsic to their community's heritage and thus was an important topic for all ages to understand in the changing rural farming community. A second concern during project planning was the issue of equally incorporating cultural and ethnic diversity. Guest speakers, performers, and interviews were selected with a conscious effort towards balance. For example, one of the narrators was an African-American principal at one of the middle schools. As an African-American woman whose family grew tobacco during her childhood, she spoke to students about how income from farming paid for her education as well as what it was like growing up during that time period. Digital audio of her story was recorded and made a powerful contribution to the DVD record of the project.

The enthusiastic support and involvement of the superintendent and assignment of a key district administrator and the project liaison were essential to the success of this project. This support enabled teacher involvement throughout the district, field trips for the students and assistance from the district technology support staff. The district liaison also set up an open community meeting at which district teachers and Clemson University faculty co-presented the project plans and invited comments and collaborations. As a result of that meeting, the project gained the support of the four local municipalities, local farmers and personnel at a federal office within the study area.

### Technology Bridges Distance

Teacher recruitment is always an issue with extramural projects. The distance is too great to send a university professor to conduct a class for teachers and it is impractical to send teachers and students to Clemson University at anytime other than during the summer. By offering project support by means of a Saturday distance education class, the project attracted teachers who would ordinarily not participate in a university-sponsored initiative. To bridge the more than 200 miles separating Florence District Three from Clemson University, team members used a web-based communication mechanism, videoconferencing via Macromedia Breeze (now known as Adobe Connect) using synchronous IP connection to the Internet. This technology allowed mutual visual and auditory presence at all locations and allowed the school district personnel to see the PowerPoint presentations and other instructional materials during the exchange. At the time of this project, this technology was fairly new and Florence District Three had recently invested in computers and Internet capabilities for classrooms in the district. Problems during the first videoconference included poor video and sound quality. The problems were resolved through communications between dedicated technology staff in the school district and Clemson University. The ultimate success of the project is due, in great part, to the district's willingness to embed a technology staff member as a full participant within the project.

Clemson University faculty developed a series of reference "How to" video tutorials using Adobe Captivate that were readily available online. Clemson University's Blackboard course content management system was used to post and manage course materials and to share items developed by the student teams. School district teachers and students learned to use: 1) Adobe Photoshop Elements to manage photos (editing, resizing, enhancing, etc.); 2) Adobe Premier Elements for video editing; 3) Timeliner to create timeline posters; 4) PowerPoint 2003 to create posters; and 5) Microsoft MovieMaker to create project-specific video segments for eventual incorporation into the cumulative DVD. Teachers used video recorders and edited digital video to make movies with Microsoft Movie Maker. History classes used the Timeliner software program to create a timeline of tobacco agriculture including images they collected. Digital video and audio were recorded of guest speakers and field trips. Family home videos of tobacco farming were converted to digital format to be included in the project and preserved.

## Student Projects and Use of Technology

Using tobacco as the relevant central theme offered a connection to the entire rural farming community, making it possible to recruit teachers and to involve students and community members. Teachers volunteered their classes, each choosing a topic that was relevant to the course content and that involved learning new technology skills. The project was cross-curricular, with participation of students in grades 3 to 12, in diverse classes including biology, English language arts, and chorus. All of the projects are outlined in Appendix 1. Some classes focused on negative health aspects of tobacco. Other students digitally recorded interviews with parents and grandparents about the role tobacco played in their lives. Interview topics ranged from stories of games played around the tobacco barn as children to the income tobacco generated to pay for clothes, food and an education. Students conducted online literature research and visited a tobacco museum to design and make a quilt representing different aspects of tobacco farming. A middle school math class created scale models of tobacco barns while a high school art class created digital photography essays of the barns. A local gospel group visited the high school and sang spirituals from the tobacco fields with students. Chemistry students researched alternative crops

that are currently grown locally. They visited the local Clemson University agricultural research station to learn about the farming of muscadine grapes, which contain chemicals and antioxidants that may fight heart disease and cancer. An Advanced Placement environmental science class researched the impacts of agricultural practices on Carolina Bays, using Google Maps to locate and determine the current land usage of Carolina Bays. These projects resulted in involvement from the entire community.

The project purchased disposable (one-time use) video cameras for the students to use during interviews and filming in the community. The camera videos were downloaded to DVDs at a local drugstore. The teachers used mini-DVD Sony camcorders to record class activities related to the project. When all the projects were completed, a teacher, Debbie Whittington, combined all digital materials produced by the students and teachers using iDVD on a Macintosh computer to produce the final DVD.

## Outcomes

The final product was a DVD entitled, "The Rise and Fall of Tobacco in the Lake City Market Area," compiled by the teachers after editing the student projects they had digitally preserved, documented, and presented. The DVD was presented to the public during the region's annual Tobacco Festival (SCNOW.com) at the National Bean Market Museum (Discover South Carolina). Parents and community members expressed pleasure at having their children investigate their community's history while learning to utilize technology at the same time.

Clemson University provided a three-credit graduate level technology course to a core group of Florence District Three teachers who then relayed these skills to other teachers and their students. The teachers involved in the technology class collected digital evidence from all of the projects and each participated in creating a cumulative

DVD documenting the research. Still images and video were combined with oral personal stories to be used as a background soundtrack for the DVD. These teachers were each assessed on their contributions to the project and other work done during the class

## Assessment

Assessment of project impact is based upon teachers' perceptions of the project's value and the continued use of the DVD and other products in district classrooms. For example, the DVD "The Rise and Fall of Tobacco in the Lake City Market Area" is used with students in seventh grade South Carolina History, elementary level English language arts, seventh grade discussions of human diseases, and high school environmental science. Copies of the digital materials were donated to the local museum and are available to the public via an exhibit. The model tobacco barns made by middle school math students are used as exemplars and displayed at their schools. The quilt made by ninth grade English students is on display at the Florence School District Three office. But the most valuable benefits lingered with the teachers and students that participated in the projects and continues to resonate throughout the district. The teachers and students continue to use the technological skills that they learned. They are more confident in continuing to use them with future classes. Three of the teachers are now curriculum coordinators and one is the Director of Accountability for the district. The teachers and district administrators remain highly supportive of collaborations with Clemson University. The students continue to use their critical thinking skills and take pride in being part of this project.

## CONCLUSION

This project served to develop a procedural template that was employed in three subsequent community-based research projects. Each new project had as its goal to engage precollege students and teachers in research while simultaneously teaching them digital technology skills. The relationship between the school district and Clemson University has evolved from this initial project. Collaborations between the two entities continue via grants, courses and workshops for in-service teachers in Florence District Three, inclusion in the Biology Merit Exam (state-wide biology competition for middle and high school students held at Clemson) and development of biology curricula. Also, teachers who were part of the project continue to use Clemson as a resource when creating new digital media projects with their students. These collaborations with Florence District Three have opened a 'pipeline' and support network for the students that participate in these collaborations.

## ACKNOWLEDGMENT

This research was supported by an award to Clemson University from the Howard Hughes Medical Institute Undergraduate Science Education Program.

## REFERENCES

Chamber of Commerce, Greater Lake City. (2010). *History*. Retrieved on February 28, 2010, from http://www.lakecitysc.org/history.php

Clemson University. (2010). *Biology merit exam*. Retrieved on February 28, 2010, from http://biology.clemson.edu/bme/default.html

Discover South Carolina. (2010). *National bean market museum*. Retrieved on February 28, 2010, from http://www.discoversouthcarolina.com/products/25750.aspx

Ferillo, B. (2005). *Corridor of shame: The neglect of South Carolina's rural schools*. Ferillo and Associates. Retrieved on February 28, 2010, from http://www.youtube.com/watch?v=rjY69hO0fxk

Florence District Three. (2010). *About us*. Retrieved on February 28, 2010, from http://www.florence3.k12.sc.us/AboutUs.htm

Lave, J. (1988). *Cognition in practice: Mind, mathematics, and culture in everyday life*. Cambridge, UK: Cambridge University Press. doi:10.1017/CBO9780511609268

Life, S. C. (2010). *Natural history of South Carolina*. Retrieved on February 28, 2010, from http://www.clemson.edu/cafls/sclife/

SC Educational Television. (2010). *K-12 educational Web portal: SC LIFE virtual field trips*. Retrieved on February 28, 2010, from http://www.knowitall.org/sclife

SCNOW.com. (2008). *Tradition, heritage keep folks celebrating tobacco industry*. Retrieved on February 28, 2010, from http://www2.scnow.com/scp/news/local/article/tradition_heritage_keep_folks_celebrating_tobacco_industry/14814/

Trexler, C. (2004). Teacher researchers in agricultural education: Developing teacher leaders through action research. *The Agricultural Education Magazine, 76*(6), 12–14.

# Conclusion

# Remediating the Community–University Partnership:
## The Multiliteracy Space as a Model for Collaboration

**Russell G. Carpenter**
*Eastern Kentucky University, USA*

## ABSTRACT

*The concept of remediation, as outlined by Jay David Bolter and Richard Grusin, offers a lens through which 21st-century partnerships might be analyzed and reinvented. Accordingly, this chapter argues that looking to the future, community-university partnerships will gain momentum as centralizing educational venues, while emerging technologies will offer mediated spaces where academic, professional, and nonprofit institutions merge to provide learning opportunities that engage both sides. This chapter situates the multiliteracy space—in this case the Noel Studio for Academic Creativity at Eastern Kentucky University—as a model for community-university partnerships that employ emerging technologies to develop communication skills.*

## INNOVATION, COLLABORATION, AND COMMUNITY ENGAGEMENT

**Date:** Tuesday, October 26, 2010 12:30 p.m.
**Space:** Discovery Classroom, Noel Studio for Academic Creativity
**Campus:** Eastern Kentucky University, Richmond, KY, USA

The Noel Studio Advisory Committee convenes for a biweekly meeting in the Noel Studio's new Discovery Classroom, a space designed as a technologically sophisticated, adult-centered learning environment. The committee meeting commences with a brief video and some light discussion of the week's activities, including an open house, and briefly overviews the upcoming dedication ceremony for this cutting-edge new space. The meeting's primary focus is a brainstorming session about community partnerships that the Noel Studio might form for summer programming. The ideas generated are rich and varied, and the enthusiasm and commitment displayed for community engagement permeate this new space.

DOI: 10.4018/978-1-60960-623-7.ch037

The Noel Studio's Advisory Committee consists of leadership representing facets of writing, oral communication, research, and technology on campus, including the dean of libraries; dean of university programs, an interdisciplinary set of complementary programs intended to support liberal foundations in education; chair of the English department; chair of the communication department; information technology (IT) director; Quality Enhancement Programs (QEP) director; Noel Studio coordinators for Communication, Research, and Writing; coordinator for library instruction; and the Noel Studio's director, who serves as chair of the committee. The committee generates idea after idea, thinking innovatively and widely about possibilities for partnerships and engagement. Every committee member in attendance shares a thought, including possibilities for working with local journalists and journalism undergraduates and developing a relationship with the Richmond Chamber of Commerce. Most interesting, perhaps, is the potential for partnerships that span several areas on campus—the library, QEP, IT, department of communication, department of English, and office of service-learning—in addition to potential community collaborators. The energy surrounding this brainstorming session provides momentum for community-university partnerships involving the Noel Studio. Moreover, the technologically sophisticated space provides the ideal dynamic environment to engage the community in developing creative products that integrate multiple modes—written, oral, nonverbal, visual, and electronic communication—believing that literacy is multiple and that multiliteracy skills are key to developing effective communication in the 21st century. The space includes video equipment, monitors, and touch-screen technologies, all of which help its staff members provide support for developing multiliteracy skills while recognizing different learning styles.

**Date:** Wednesday, October 27, 2010 5:30 p.m.
**Space:** Conference Room, Noel Studio for Academic Creativity
**Campus:** Eastern Kentucky University, Richmond, KY, USA

A group of public relations students in the Department of Communication at Eastern Kentucky University (EKU) use Skype to interview industry leaders about communication in the workplace. The collaboration includes both video and audio, allowing students and members of the business community in another part of the country to see and communicate with each other in real time. The session engages students through video, which helps create a deeper connection between students and community leaders, giving the sensation of being (virtually) there.

**Date:** Summer 2015
**Space:** Invention Space, Noel Studio for Academic Creativity
**Campus:** Eastern Kentucky University, Richmond, KY, USA

Students from an area high school use colorful magnetic tiles and marker boards to map ideas for a video project that they will eventually upload to a web site as part of their college applications. The goal of the project is to create one-minute videos that showcase students' academic creativity. In collaborative fashion, students use the space to visualize ideas, to give thoughts life, and to bring communication products into a social forum in a supportive and energetic space. Students spend about an hour working one-on-one and in small groups with Noel Studio consultants who have experience with technology and training in multimodal rhetoric. Together, students and consultants use a combination of high- and low-tech invention tools to arrive at new understandings for composing electronic artifacts. Employing a think-with-your-hands approach, consultants

*Figure 1 Students Working with Video in the Noel Studio*

encourage students to focus on the process of developing multimodal pieces that are persuasive and to consider rhetorical conventions for that media. Through this approach, students also develop an understanding of new media composition as a process and not simply a product.

**Date:** Summer 2015
**Space:** Greenhouse, Noel Studio for Academic Creativity
**Campus:** Eastern Kentucky University, Richmond, KY, USA

Noel Studio consultants work interactively with students from a local high school in the Greenhouse, a large, open space dedicated to collaboration, creative thinking and the development of effective communication practices. Small pods of students and consultants construct and deconstruct visual poetry as a method for thinking about expression and the importance of creative compositions in the development of communication skills. Many of these students later apply for college, and these sessions yield creative and visual products for their electronic portfolios.

What has led to this key moment in the development of a new academic space? The Noel Studio's planning team began discussions over five years before the doors ever opened with a mission of

serving the EKU community as a collaborative, innovative learning experience dedicated to the improvement of communication and research skills (Noel Studio Mission). The university prides itself on community engagement. As a centralizing component to the academic mission at EKU, the Noel Studio also engages the community. Below, I pose several questions that guide my inquiry into emerging technologies and collaborative spaces and that might be of use to other scholars interested in developing engaged multiliteracy centers as they invent roles and envision collaborative relationships for their spaces: What will engagement look like in this new space? How will this new mission and vision engage the community through emerging technologies? What does remediation look like in community-university partnerships?

The Noel Studio is one example of an emerging and collaborative space in tune with the ways that students create and communicate in the 21st century through and with technology. A member of a small group of spaces that have developed an integrated model, the Noel Studio houses services in a technologically sophisticated environment, aligning itself with the multiliteracy centers that have developed similar missions and goals by foregrounding the need for communication practices that use more than words and include images, charts, graphs, music, voices, bodies, nonverbal cues, and multimedia.

## EMERGING TECHNOLOGY AND THE COMMUNITY-UNIVERSITY PARTNERSHIP

Community-university partnerships are gaining momentum throughout the United States and abroad. As these partnerships continue to develop, their roles also change, moving from place-based practices to complex networks that often transcend place and space. In recent years, the advent of emerging technologies has expanded opportunities for community-university partnerships; that is, mutually beneficial, engaging interactions between universities and the communities in which they are situated.

Steven Levy (2006) discusses the iPod's widespread adoption even among people who seem incongruous in digital movements. Levy writes:

*It paints a telling picture of how even the most cautious humans have been adjusting to the furious pace of the modern world. Ever since, say, electricity, society has had to endure a steady succession of disruptions in the name of progress. Forward-thinking folks have always embraced novelty and been quick to identify the virtues of an unexpected new technology. (p. 32)*

That is to say, technology has become central to many of us. Technology provides access to information, and many of us have become accustomed to immediately accessible information. The iPod, for example, is a cultural icon, an icon of coolness that merges visual, textual and audio communication elements in one space. Some colleges and universities have even decided to provide students and faculty members with mobile communication technologies such as iPads, Apple's tablet computer (Kolowich, 2010). Other institutions have provided laptops to students

for years, but the popularity of tablet devices on campuses suggests a move toward the most cutting-edge mobile devices. A move from laptops to tablets and smart phones is just one example of ways in which universities are trying to make information accessible to students through the emerging technologies that have contemporary appeal. But what does the increased presence of emerging technologies mean for community-university partnerships?

As the examples in *Higher Education, Emerging Technologies, and Community Partnerships* suggest, community-university partnerships are changing. The broad range of countries, institutions, partnerships and communities represented in this collection offer a rich and complex sampling of some of the most robust partnerships taking place in the world. The same emerging technologies our contributors have discussed as catalysts in their own partnership projects allowed us to assemble this very collection. In a global economy consisting of education partners located thousands of miles away, the chapters offered in this collection establish a number of threads that should serve as starting points for the development of new partnerships and the redevelopment or remediation of existing ones.

While emerging technology is highlighted throughout this collection, we should not lose sight of the partnership aspects of collaboration fostered between universities and communities. It is the culture of collaboration, the desire to share information and resources, a passion for teaching, and a willingness to explore opportunities beyond our institutions that drive the need for further experimentation with emerging technologies.

The wealth and breadth of partnerships between and among higher education institutions and community organizations highlighted in this collection only begin to depict the rich and complex nature of these collaborative practices. Moreover, the concepts, models, and applications with which scholars, students, and community members carry out these partnerships should provide a useful context and motivation for future endeavors. With the wide array of partnerships provided in this collection, it would be difficult to argue that they do not serve a substantial and meaningful role in the development and education of college students; however, different institutions and communities will have unique local, regional, national, and even international needs and expectations. The cases in this collection offer an international range of perspectives, including successes and challenges. It is our intention to also provide tangible details about these partnerships that make them replicable and adaptable to a variety of institutions and communities.

This chapter situates emerging technologies as collaborative spaces that facilitate partnerships between communities and higher education institutions. Below, I make the case that emerging technologies allow initiatives to be more sustainable and are critical to the success of new and developing community-university partnerships in the 21st century. Similarly, emerging technologies provide opportunities for creating sustainable relationships and transcending spatial boundaries that often and, unfortunately, serve to discourage community work across long distances or among multiple locations. I also urge community university partners to take an exploratory approach to integrating technology into their partnerships by testing new freeware, services and support while developing multiliteracy skills in college learners. I am constantly inspired by the academic creativity—the development of rhetorically compelling, novel, and useful pieces and practices—that emerges when we put technology in the hands of motivated and informed students. Flashes of academic creativity here in the Noel Studio have provided the necessary motivation to develop strong intellectual ties to the community.

The partnerships detailed through the case studies in this collection should prompt us to think about the past as well as the future. They allow us to study partnerships as models and practices in addition to technological spaces for sustainable,

innovative, and creative community-university partnerships.

This collection highlights best practices in developing community-university partnerships. Additionally, the critiques of technology are valuable to readers considering the development of new partnerships, redeveloping existing programs, or integrating technology into a current program. Emerging technological spaces, as seen through many of the cases in this collection and even the examples offered from the Noel Studio's mission, provide rich spaces for communication, connecting universities and communities in new and interesting ways.

The broad range of interesting partnerships taking place throughout the United States and internationally offers a prime example of the potential for emerging technology to serve a profound role in connecting the university and community. While many areas in the United States and abroad suffered challenging economic times, technology is helping many partnerships to thrive.

## HIGHER EDUCATION AND COMMUNITY PARTNERSHIPS

Partnerships exist at a variety of institutions throughout the country. Many institutions offer support for engaging the community. EKU's Office of Regional Stewardship supports developing community-university partnerships within the university's 22-county service region. Although the landscape of community-university partnerships includes a variety of efforts, including service-learning, participatory research, and other forms of engagement, EKU's Office of Regional Stewardship coordinates the delivery of educational resources to the community, increases the involvement within the university's service region, engages youth in the service region in stewardship initiatives, and increases faculty, staff, and student engagement in the community (Regional Stewardship).

Institutions of varying shapes and sizes display a great deal of creativity in the goals and missions of their partnerships. Likewise, the communities in which students and faculty engage practitioners, nonprofit leaders, and business people serve as unique learning spaces. Remarkably, these spaces are created not just in classrooms or even offices. Emerging technologies bridge geography and time, in many cases, providing opportunities for developing collaborative efforts that are sustainable even in difficult economic climates.

Implicit in the discussion of emerging technology's role in community-university partnerships are mutual goals and pre-determined expectations. The mere integration of technology will not enhance a partnership. Technology should encourage and facilitate collaboration, complement goals of the partnership, and support the mission of the program and university by aligning with strategic initiatives.

## EMERGING TECHNOLOGY AS SUSTAINABLE COLLABORATIVE SPACE

In the American Association of Colleges and Universities' (AAC&U) strategic plan for 2008-2012, titled *Aim High and Make Excellence Inclusive*, the organization notes several important broad trends confronting higher education today, including

- The rise of a knowledge economy, with U.S. prosperity dependent on continued global leadership in "high-end" innovation, science, technology, and creative industries; and

- The emergence of online and technology-enhanced curricula and pedagogies, which further blurs the traditional boundaries between institutions. (Broad Trends Confronting Higher Education, AAC&U Strategic Plan)

Furthermore, the AAC&U highlights trends related to liberal education, including

- The emergence of strong campus-led leadership for civic, ethical, intercultural and global learning—what AAC&U has termed the "Personal and Social Responsibility" outcomes—in the college years; these issues are already priorities for AAC&U. Nonetheless, all the research either done or consulted for AAC&U in the past few years reveals an *"also-ran status"* for these educational goals. They are widely espoused in principle, but largely left to individual initiative and choice in actual practice. Despite mission-level commitment to educating global citizens, there is at best faint national leadership for reclaiming the public and democratic purposes of college learning and liberal education. (Trends Related to Liberal Education, AAC&U Strategic Plan)

- An engaged campus offers opportunities for students in the community while providing community partners with a service. Most partnerships are built upon the idea that we all have something to give and something to gain (Holland & Gelman, 1998). While Holland and Gelman's point might seem simple enough on the surface, partnerships often involve collaboration among multiple institutions. Oftentimes, partnerships can offer great benefits for knowledge acquisition, learning opportunities, and the betterment of a region. Successful efforts focus on mutual benefits (Holland & Gelman, 1998), which can come in a variety of forms.

- Successful partnerships are sustainable. They persist in difficult economic times, promote collaboration and exchange between partners and among participants, and offer opportunities for participation and learning on both sides. The ubiquitous

*Table 1. Literacy Practices for Collaborating with Emerging Technologies*

| Strategy | Literacy Practice for Emerging Technology in Partnerships |
|---|---|
| Plan time to introduce and discuss technology. | Map technology within the brick-and-mortar space. Develop visual ideations and models for long-term use, including flow of traffic and information. |
| Set clear and realistic goals for communicating through technology. | Record where the partnership is currently and where it needs to go. Consider referring back to visual models, maps, and traffic flows. Approach technology goals with a clear plan that you can articulate individually and as a group. |
| Integrate technology into the intended outcomes of the partnership. | Consider specific, measurable, and attainable goals for integrating technology into the partnership as a platform and space. Consider technology literacy—as a language and text—for further development within the space of the collaboration. |
| Encourage students to explore technology in a low-risk environment. | Consider play as part of the discovery process with emerging technologies. Shift perception about uses of technology. |
| Provide suggestions for successful communication and collaboration. | Consider goals for successful communication among students and partnership facilitators. Make successes and challenges clear to collaborators. Potential uses and pedagogies for emerging technologies should become more fluid as collaboration and conversations intensify. |
| Plan time for reflection and response through technology. | Gain an objective perspective on emerging technology's role in the collaboration. Perform regular assessment and take a critical approach to the uses of emerging technology. |

nature of emerging technologies seems to offer a space for sustaining partnerships across great distances even during unstable economic times.

- Emerging technologies continue to be exploratory (Selfe, 2007). Mobile communication technologies, like laptops, portable video cameras, smart phones, tablets, and MP3 players have provided new avenues for communication. With access to these technologies, students, faculty, and community partners are able to compose texts, communicate information, expand thinking, express ideas, and explore passions in new ways. Furthermore, these technologies allow for new collaborative spaces to emerge. As technology has become more prevalent, researchers have explored potential uses in the classroom and beyond. Community and university partners will need to keep the evolving nature of these technologies in mind as they develop programs by considering communication goals for the technology, educational goals for students, course requirements (if necessary), and the needs of the community and its members.

As members of the Noel Studio planning group made arrangements for technology, conversations about its role and implementation increased in intensity and complexity. Technological needs became clearer as the small planning group refined discussions. Monthly meetings quickly turned into weekly meetings, with an engaged group sharing ideas, mapping plans on poster-sized schematic diagrams, and constructing and deconstructing a complex list of interrelated items. The group started with a simple wish list of devices, which quickly expanded to more complex interfacing technological systems. Members of the IT department were integral in the development of a technologically sophisticated collaborative space, while the Noel Studio advisory committee offered guidance and served as a sounding board. Toward the end of the planning process, as the group finalized a list for purchase, members understood the language of Noel Studio technology. A literacy developed that considered the vision and mission of the new space and its collaborative function through discussions of emerging technology. Throughout the year-long planning and implementation process, the group kept sustainability in mind by projecting far beyond the Noel Studio's first year. Discussions of scenarios, usability, and flow in the space guided the collaboration. This rather complex planning and implementation process reveals a model for creating sustainable social spaces through literacy practices for emerging technology.

## REMEDIATING THE COMMUNITY UNIVERSITY PARTNERSHIP

According to Bolter and Grusin (1999), we employ media as vehicles for defining personal and cultural identity. Emerging technologies provide spaces for collaboration. These technological spaces bridge universities and communities and provide a neutral setting for the development of productive and meaningful relationships.

Emerging technologies have attracted the interest of researchers for years now. Technological evolution acts as a factor of cultural and behavioral change in the mobile society. In this sense, the oral and written languages used in mobile communication, as well as other forms of expression, such as the 'smiley' reflect this transformation (Castells, Fernández-Ardèvol, Linchuan Qiu, & Sey, 2007).

Community partnerships have existed in many forms historically and have prompted new forms of expression. Some have found ways to thrive through face-to-face interactions, while others have incorporated technology as a catalyst for rethinking or even improving their partnerships. In this collection, Shewbridge describes a partnership between the University of Maryland, Baltimore County (UMBC) and Retirement Living Television through the Charlestown Digital Stories Project. In it, university students and senior citizens came together to produce digital movies. As we learned from Shewbridge's Charlestown Digital Stories Project at UMBC, digital technologies allow for new forms of expression among senior citizens. This project also explored new relationships between students and senior citizens. Increasingly, partnerships between the university and community will form in technological space as we have seen through online mentoring programs.

We will also continue to see creative artifacts of digital composition result from these relationships: digital movies, archives, repositories, interactive media and virtual worlds. Partnerships may move from offering services or outreach to engaging each other through emerging technologies that have permeated our communities. Participants might find themselves involved in creating artifacts and collections that archive important pieces of our culture, history or story. Through emerging technologies, partnership and collaboration take on new meaning—from engaging one another to engaging important pieces of our memory, oral culture and visual history. Through the many community partnerships offered in this collection, we see that forms of engagement do not end when the face-to-face contact of the program ends. Through technology, these programs have long-lasting and positive impacts on the people and communities involved. Technology presents students and community members with opportunities for new forms of expression that serve as a chance not only to learn but also to create and archive experiences and moments that are often lost. Thus, partners will find that they are not only communicating with digital technologies, they are communicating within digital technologies. The spaces that they use create and are created through these partnerships.

Communication practices within and with digital technologies are highly literate activities. While some partnerships focus on literacy in print-based media, others explore opportunities to compose with digital media and video, as staff members and students in the Noel Studio have done. Many partnerships between the community and university exist to support communication practices. Some offer opportunities for participants to consider the world around them through creative writing, while others document the history of at-risk communities through digital video or virtual worlds in place-based virtual reality installations (Freeman). Partnerships have changed as the culture of the institution has moved toward digital resources. Emerging technologies offer a number of advantages over print-based media. Access to information and sustainability in the archival process are chief among them. Digital archives are easy and cost-efficient to store and access (Cohen & Rosenzweig, 2006). Many of the partnerships discussed in this collection have made the move from print to digital resources and spaces as shown through numerous case studies (see DeBerg's SAGE, Adria and Mao's Citizen Panel, or Banks and Van Sickle's collaboration with the Tar River Writing Project). Each project is unique, of course, yet all employ emerging technologies as spaces for bringing the university and community in contact with one another.

## THE IMPORTANCE OF EMERGING TECHNOLOGY IN COMMUNITY-UNIVERSITY PARTNERSHIPS

Johndan Johnson-Eilola (1997) prompts us to rethink the role of commodity and construction in virtual environments, arguing that knowledge is spatial. If knowledge is spatial, the virtual environments that house this knowledge are critical to the success of future community-university partnerships. Williams & James (2009) discuss new technologies in their case study of Houston's Bureau of Air Quality Control. Cashman, Hale, Candib, Nimiroski, & Brookings (2004) highlight staffing and funding challenges faced by community-university health partnerships. I attempt to foreground technology's role in developing a better understanding of its effective uses and possibilities for sustaining partnerships. While many studies mention technology as a key aspect of their partnership, discussions of technology are often muted by organizational information, policies, and shrinking resources. The importance of selecting the most appropriate task cannot be overstated.

Selecting appropriate technology is no easy task, and should factor in carefully with the design of the partnership, goals of the project,

and resources available to participants. Sandy & Holland (2006) found that community partners are profoundly dedicated to educating college students—even when it is not an initial expectation of a project. Interestingly, Prensky (2001) argues that students have changed. Empowered with new technologies, students have grown up digital. Prensky coins the term "digital native" for students who have grown up with technology, claiming that they are native speakers of the digital language of computers, video games and the Internet. In many cases, students taking part in community-university partnerships will be digital natives, savvy with technology and familiar with communication practices (and habits) in a digital age. Prensky seems to offer words of encouragement for digital immigrants—those new to technology. Community-university partnerships can provide opportunities for an education in emerging technology. While participants might consider digital realms the students' turf, it is certainly an important and timely space for exploration, and the safe environment of the partnership can provide an excellent opportunity.

## SUSTAINING TECHNOLOGICAL PARTNERSHIPS THROUGH VIRTUAL SPACE

Sustainable partnerships foster participation. Emerging technologies should reduce barriers to participation between the university and community. As Jenkins, Clinton, Purushotma, Robison, & Weigel (2009) explain, the technologies employed in partnerships should create spaces with

1. Relatively low barriers to artistic expression and civic engagement,
2. Strong support for creating and sharing creations with others,
3. Some form of informal mentorship whereby what is known by the most experienced is passed along to novices,

4. Members who believe that their contributions matter, and

5. Members who feel some degree of social connection with one another. (pp. 5-6)

Emerging technologies reduce barriers to creativity, expression, and communication while supporting participants in their efforts to learn from one another. In many cases, sustainable partnerships may require mentorship with the technology and within the technology. With the appropriate guidance, technology can create a safe space where participants are free to make thoughtful contributions. Within a safe space that technology helps create, participants should adhere to ground rules that support academic creativity. A culture of support and tolerance should be central to any partnership. A lack of face-to-face contact can be supplemented by unique but complementary technologies.

Through this collection, we have seen a number of community-university partnerships that have developed out of technical communication programs. Although these partnerships will all vary in terms of scope and substance, they all require a certain level of collaboration that bring students or community partners together for a common goal. Whether the objective is to produce a product or a piece of user documentation, students have to collaborate with other students, students have to collaborate with community partners, and partners have to collaborate with students. A collaborative approach that originates in the classroom could go a long way toward extending effective communication, goals and visions in the community as well. As J. Katz Jameson, P. H. Clayton and R. G. Bringle explain, faculty need to have a collaborative approach to course and curriculum development, which may also run counter to typical academic values of independence and academic freedom (2008, p. 17). While effective collaboration can certainly be challenging as we have learned, it is worth it for the many benefits to students and members of the community. A successful partner-

*Table 2. Emerging Technologies, Concepts, and Models*

| Emerging Technology | Concepts and Models |
|---|---|
| Video Chats | Video chat services like Skype and Adobe Connect provide multimedia options that can augment synchronous or asynchronous online discussions. Participants can use video to interact with one another, capture features of their project, or explore avenues for expression. |
| Mobile Video Cameras | Mobile communication technologies, like handheld cameras and smart phones, provide students with a powerful means of communication. These technologies will require guidance and instruction to teach students how to capture interesting and usable footage. With the popularity and accessibility of social networking and web technology, video cameras provide opportunities for students to explore, express, and expand ideas in new ways. Students can tell stories and archive institutional and programmatic memory in creative, engaging, and inspiring ways. The composition process moves from the printed page to visually expressive video that also becomes portable for distribution. |
| Social Media | Colleges, nonprofit organizations, and businesses alike have used social media to push information to interested followers, often called "fans" or "friends." These spaces also allow partners to develop fan pages or feeds where participants can interact with one another. As social media spaces have developed, they have begun to include video options that allow users to capture images and post them within moments of the event, enhancing the sense of immediacy. Videos, images, and texts are immediately available and readable to all participants. |
| Immersive Virtual Worlds | Virtual worlds like Second Life offer opportunities for community-university partners to develop visual artifacts representative of current events, regional issues, and multimedia texts. In addition to providing a space to explore, virtual worlds often house collaborative events, demonstrations, and installations. In virtual worlds, community-university partners can explore concepts visually while repurposing printed texts into visual and interactive ones. |
| Video Games | Video games offer opportunities for play—creative expression and exploration without real consequences where partners are encouraged to let their guard down. Play is enhanced in the virtual space of the video game, which enhances playfulness in learning and literacy development. |

ship is also built to survive a variety of personnel and economic changes. Many of the keys to sustaining technological partnerships—collaborations between the institution and community for the purposes of this collection—are highlighted throughout the mix of case studies offered here. A collaborative spirit is critical to developing partnerships. This same spirit embodies the education that takes place among students and community partners. Furthermore, collaboration encourages an important interdisciplinary perspective—providing a lens for students to view their work. Technical communicators, for example, often find themselves at the center of interdisciplinary and collaborative conversations. Subject matter experts (SMEs) develop equipment, machines and content. They understand what makes the equipment work. The SMEs then communicate the information—often through the use of schematic diagrams, cut sheets, and other mechanical documents—to the technical communicators. The technical communicators then compile the necessary information, conduct tests and studies and collaborate with SMEs to ensure successful products and associated documentation. Without a truly collaborative process, technical communicators will not receive the information they need to develop successful documentation. Companies risk alienating frustrated customers who cannot learn to use products. Complicated machines—like airplanes, cars and other heavy equipment—even become dangerous without effective and accessible associated documentation. The relationship between SMEs and technical communicators, although depicted through an ideal relationship here, show just how critical collaboration can be to a community-university partnership. Successful partnerships are also flexible:

*Providing time and flexible scheduling is an important cultural norm and expectation that helps sustain service projects. Teachers need flexibility in the school day schedule to incorporate service-learning projects. Some students at the high school and middle school levels may need to miss other classes in order to have time for trips to community sites. (Krebs, 2008, p. 97)*

Emerging technologies open up new opportunities for communication and collaboration. Senders and receivers of messages are always at the heart of communication. The partners involved must also determine the technology and extent to which it is employed in the partnership. In other words, the people involved should guide technological choices that project administrators make when thinking through the design and goals of the program. After all, partnerships exist to bring people together who might not have had the chance to interact otherwise—for example, connecting diverse or at-risk communities with students to develop writing skills. Video archives facilitate partnerships that provide learning opportunities not only in the ways these resources can be used to capture ideas but also in the literacy of using technology for communication. In low-income communities, these partnerships could be the first contact students have with information communication technologies (ICTs). These same ICTs, for example, serve as important cultural artifacts signifying opportunities for learning.

## MEETING TECHNOLOGICAL CHALLENGES

What are the technological challenges that new partnerships will face? How can new community-university partnerships confront these challenges? All partnerships are unique, but readers can assemble best practices by modeling successful and even revising unsuccessful partnerships. At times, it is helpful to take an objective look at the technologies employed. Poor technology decisions also create frustration in communication, creativity and overall functionality of partnerships. The right technologies will facilitate collaboration. Here I offer best practices for confronting, managing and navigating the technological challenges that have surfaced in partnerships from around the country and internationally:

- Promoting ongoing education and communication between university and community partners;
- Including technology as part of the mission/vision of partnerships;
- Practicing technology pedagogy;
- Viewing technology as a space and not just a tool;
- Defining clear goals for engagement; and,
- Engaging partners and encouraging collaboration among IT, university, and community.

## EMERGING TECHNOLOGY AND 21ST-CENTURY PARTNERSHIPS

Community-university partnerships will continue to evolve, but in the future they may look significantly different from those we have come to know. Re-envisioned partnerships may involve multiple community partners and originate from collaborative campus spaces where participants will have access to resources that promote the integration of written, oral, visual, electronic and nonverbal communication. The popularity of emerging technologies that encourage literacy learning and creativity, such as video games, immersive worlds, and mobile communication devices, create new spaces for exploration through innovative partnerships.

### Games as Immersive Participatory Spaces

It is worth exploring video games as potential spaces for 21st-century partnerships in a collection about emerging technologies and community partnerships. By definition,

*A game is a rule-based system with a variable and quantifiable outcome, where different outcomes are assigned different values, the player exerts effort in order to influence the outcome, the player feels emotionally attached to the outcome, and the consequences of the activity are negotiable. (Juul, 2005, p. 36)*

Eric Zimmerman (2009) highlights the growing conversation about video games across universities, commercial game companies, classrooms and nonprofit foundations. Video games mark a cultural turn toward integrated electronic and visual literacies. Zimmerman documents important developments in game design. He also highlights the role of play and the significance of an emerging gaming literacy. While traditional literacy has centered on print-based practices such as reading books and writing papers, gaming helps to develop technological literacy. Furthermore, play has a profound role in games. Through quizzes, equations, and systems, participants learn about structures, images, and rules. Games, Zimmerman has argued, provide one of the best platforms for play by encouraging exploration and engaging students beyond standard tests, quizzes and other intellectual challenges. In his exploration of play and gaming, Zimmerman (2009) argues the following:

*As our lives become more networked, people are engaging more and more with structures. But they are not merely inhabiting these structures—they are playing with them. A social network like Wikipedia is not just a fixed construct like a circuit diagram. It is a fuzzy system, a dynamic system, a social system, a cultural system. Systems only become meaningful as they are inhabited, explored, and manipulated by people. In the coming century, what will become important will not be just systems, but human systems. (p. 27)*

The spirit of exploration and risk taking is evident in gaming and key to the development of partnerships remediated through emerging technology. A culture of play frees us of intellectual and academic constraints that often hamper participation. Play implies participation and engagement. It implies becoming a part of your environment and interacting with someone or something. Video games encourage active exploration and engagement with technology. Recently, video games have become increasingly interactive, requiring physical movements from players. Video games encourage players to think through a series of tests. The player will move from stage to stage or level to level in order to advance status or earn points. Players study moves within games; they learn and adapt to situations. Other games require players to build teams, change configurations and set levels. In other words, they require the player to think about the environment and intended outcomes. While community-university partnerships have grown through developing websites, blogs, and social media, video games offer even more potential for engagement through critical and creative thinking on both sides. Games offer potential to move from spaces consumed by participants to opportunities for production.

## Second Life as an Immersive Participatory Space

Immersive spaces, like Second Life, offer opportunities for community-university partners to develop embedded exercises, games, and collaborations that promote learning and literacy practices along with opportunities to explore important topics such as gender, culture, and race among many others.

Technology is produced (and consumed) within partnerships. As partnerships emerge within technological spaces, we should be concerned not only with unidirectional output—pure output can be alienating—but also input, a focus on reciprocity, if technological space is to facilitate communication between the university and community. Community-university partnerships will find that

technology-rich spaces will facilitate participation from both sides. Physical distances often prohibit spontaneous communication that encourages creativity among participants. The creative impulse is lost in structured times, planned meetings, and access to people and facilities. Technology can serve to break down those boundaries by providing a space for these conversations to emerge. These discussions can also allow participants to extend ideas by linking to supplemental materials; thus, participants become both producers and consumers of information. Video technologies allow students to develop their own resources that can be archived and explored by others.

Partnerships generating creative writing and literature will also find new homes online. N. Katherine Hayles (2008) describes literature in the 21st century as computational. Cloud document storage options, wikis, and other textual spaces make electronic composition collaborative. Community-university partnerships that once found homes in brick-and-mortar settings may now find that emerging technologies create spaces that also promote learning and literacy. Previous practices may be remediated with electronic tablet and stylus. Portable video cameras may push the edge of electronic literature by allowing for the creation of *visual* literature. Whereas community-university partnerships may have provided pens, pencils, and paper to participants, many 21st-century partnerships will provide video cameras or web cameras in the future. Community-universities partnerships will find collaborative spaces within digitally enhanced environments whether online or face-to-face.

To engage emerging technologies in community-university partnerships, we must also be prepared to teach technology pedagogy, as foregrounded through the Noel Studio discussion earlier in this chapter. Our partnership spaces need to be responsive to multiliteracies, as outlined by the New London Group. For academic spaces intent on engaging the community, like the Noel Studio, it is an opportunity to engage electronic, oral, written and visual communication. Community-university partners can prepare students and collaborators by providing intellectual, technical, and physical space to teach a pedagogy of technology (see Selfe, 2007)—a pedagogy for producing technology and (re)mediated texts, including resources for teachers and partners. Partnerships can foreground the communication and invention that occurs within the margins, a praxis of invention through and with emerging technology. This transitional space is where much of the cognitive activity takes place, the space of community-universities partnerships.

## NEXT STEPS FOR PARTNERSHIPS

Maurrasse (2002) argues that much work is to be done to enhance the effectiveness of partnerships between higher education institutions and the community. His work is mostly concerned with funding and assessment issues; however, it does raise valid questions that probe further the depths of partnership applications and models. Maurrasse prompts us to think deeply about the benefits of partnerships for higher education and communities, citing trust and communication as keys to effective programs. Furthermore, Maurrasse encourages us to think critically about current practices and assumptions about education-community partnerships, as he calls them. Maurrasse explains that the higher education-community partnerships movement is in its early stages despite its deep historical roots in teaching, research and service, making it an especially interesting time to explore these collaborations in more detail.

Through this chapter, I have attempted to build momentum for new academic spaces like the Noel Studio at EKU—innovative programs that have roots in multiliteracy pedagogies and push disciplinary boundaries by encouraging community-university partnerships that engage literacy learning and forge new collaborative environments. In many cases, our institutional pro-

grams can provide access to emerging technologies where access has not been available before. I call for other pioneers to join us not only in exploring new technological frontiers but re-envisioning and remediating the ways we collaborate.

## REFERENCES

American Association of Colleges and Universities. (2007). *Strategic plan 2008-2012: Aim high and make excellence inclusive*. Retrieved from http://www.aacu.org/About/strategic_plan.cfm

Bolter, J. D., & Grusin, R. (1999). *Remediation: Understanding new media*. Cambridge, MA: MIT Press.

Castells, M., Fernández-Ardèvol, M., Linchuan Qiu, J., & Sey, A. (2007). *Mobile communication and society: A global perspective*. Cambridge, MA: MIT.

Cohen, D. J., & Rosenzweig, R. (2006). *Digital history: A guide to gathering, preserving, and presenting the past on the Web*. Philadelphia, PA: Pennsylvania Press.

Freeman, J. C. (2010). *Imaging place: Place-based virtual reality*. Emerson College. Retrieved on, 29 July 2010, from http://institute.emerson.edu/ vma/faculty/john_craig_freeman/imaging_place/ imaging_place.html

Hayles, N. K. (2008). *Electronic literature: New horizons for the literary*. Notre Dame, IN: University of Notre Dame Press.

Holland, B., & Gelman, S. (1998). The state of the engaged campus: What have we learned about building and sustaining university and community partnerships. *AAHE Bulletin. American Association for Higher Education, 51*(1), 3–6.

Jameson, J. K., Clayton, P. H., & Bringle, R. G. (2008). Investigating student learning within and across linked service-learning courses. In M. A. Bowdon, S. H. Billig, & B. A. Holland (Eds.), *Scholarship for sustaining service-learning and civic engagement*. Charlotte, NC: Information Age Publishing.

Jenkins, H., Clinton, K., Purushotma, R., Robison, A. J., & Weigel, M. (2009). *Confronting the challenges of participatory culture: Media education for the 21st century*. Cambridge, MA: MIT.

Johnson-Eilola, J. (1997). *Nostalgic angels: Rearticulating hypertext writing*. Norwood, MA: Ablex.

Juul, J. (2005). *Half-real: Video games between real rules and fictional worlds*. Cambridge, MA: MIT.

Kolowich, S. (2010, April 5). Should colleges start giving Apple's iPad to students? *USA Today*. Retrieved from http://www.usatoday.com/news/education/2010-04-05-IHE-colleges-give-iPads-to-students05_N.htm

Krebs, M. M. (2008). Sustainability of service-learning: What do K-12 teachers say? In M. A. Bowdon, S. H. Billig, & B. A. Holland (Eds.), *Scholarship for sustaining service-learning and civic engagement*. Charlotte, NC: Information Age Publishing.

Levy, S. (2006). *The perfect thing: How the iPod shuffles commerce, culture, and coolness*. New York, NY: Simon & Schuster.

Maurrasse, D. J. (2002). Higher education-community partnerships: Assessing progress in the field. *Nonprofit and Voluntary Sector Quarterly, 31*, 131. doi:10.1177/0899764002311006

Noel Studio Mission. (2010). *Mission statement*. Retrieved on 13 November, 2010, from http://www.studio.eku.edu/mission_statement.pdf.

Prensky, M. (2001a). Digital natives, digital immigrants. *Horizon, 9*(5). doi:10.1108/10748120110424816

*Regional Stewardship*. (2010). Retrieved on 5 February 2011, from http://www.cedet.eku.edu/stewardship.php.

Sandy, M., & Holland B. A. (2006). Different worlds and common ground: Community partner perspectives on campus-community partnerships. *Michigan Journal of Community Service Learning*, 30-43.

Selfe, R. J. (2007). Sustaining multimodal composition. *Multimodal composition: Resources for teachers*. Cresskill, NK: Hampton.

Williams, M. F., & James, D. D. (2009). Embracing new policies, technologies, and community partnerships: A case study of the city of Houston's bureau of air quality control. *Technical Communication Quarterly, 18*(1), 82–98. doi:10.1080/10572250802437515

Zimmerman, E. (2009). Gaming literacy: Game design as a model for literacy in the twenty-first century. In B. Perron & M. J. P. Wolf (Eds.), *The video game theory reader 2*. New York, NY: Routledge.

# Compilation of References

Abbey, B. (2000). *Instructional and cognitive impacts of Web-based education*. Hershey, PA: Idea Group Publishing.

Access to Learning Award. Vasconcelos Program. (2008). *Bill and Melinda Gates Foundation website*. Retrieved February 2010, from http://www.gatesfoundation.org/atla/Pages/2008-vasconcelos-program.aspx

Aczel, C. J., Peake, S. R., & Hardy, P. (2008). Designing capacity-building in e-learning expertise: Challenges and strategies. *Computers & Education*, *50*, 499–510. doi:10.1016/j.compedu.2007.07.005

Aksamit, D. (1990). Practicing teachers' perceptions of their preservice preparation for mainstreaming. *Teacher Education and Special Education*, *13*(1), 21–29. doi:10.1177/088840649001300104

Alexander, R. (2009). *Children, their world, their education. Final report and recommendations of the Cambridge Primary Review*. New York, NY: Routledge.

Allan, B., & Lewis, D. (2006). Virtual learning communities as a vehicle for workforce development: A case study. *Journal of Workplace Learning*, *18*(6), 367–383. doi:10.1108/13665620610682099

Allen, I. E., & Seaman, J. (2010). *Learning on demand: Online learning in the United States, 2009*. Babson Survey Research Group. Retrieved online from http://www.sloan-c.org/publications/survey/pdf/learningondemand.pdf

Alzouma, G. (2005). Myths of digital technology in Africa: Leapfrogging development? *Global Media and Communication*, *1*(3), 339–356. doi:10.1177/1742766505058128

American Association of Colleges and Universities. (2007). *Strategic plan 2008-2012: Aim high and make excellence inclusive*. Retrieved from http://www.aacu.org/About/strategic_plan.cfm

American Distance Education Consortium (ADEC). (2003). *ADEC guiding principles for distance teaching and learning*. Retrieved from http://www.adec.edu/admin/papers/distance-teaching_principles.html

Anderson, R. (1999, October 14). Native Americans and the digital divide. *The Digital Beat*, *1*, 1.

Archer, W., & Wright, K. (1999). Back to the future: Adjusting university continuing education research to an emerging trend. *Canadian Journal of University Continuing Education*, *25*(2), 61–83.

Associated Press. (2010, January 23). Haiti telethon haul put at $57 million so far: Celebrities unite in support of Haitian people with two hours of pleas. *MSNBC*. Retrieved from http://www.msnbc.msn.com/id/35023278/ns/entertainment-celebrities/

Association to Advance Collegiate Schools of Business. (2006a). *A world of good: Business, business schools and peace*. Report of the AACSB International Peace through Commerce Task Force. Retrieved February 15, 2010, from http://www.aacsb.edu/publications/thoughtleadership/peace-english.pdf

Association to Advance Collegiate Schools of Business. (2006b). *Eligibility procedures and accreditation standards for business accreditation*. AACSB International, January 1, 2006.

Atwell, N. (1987). *In the middle: Writing, reading, and learning with adolescents*. Portsmouth, NH: Heinemann.

Baez, N. (2007). *E-mail sent to author*. October 20, 2007.

Baker, T., & Wang, C. (2006). Photovoice: Use of a participatory action research method to explore the chronic pain experience in older adults. *Qualitative Health Research, 16*(10), 1405–1413. doi:10.1177/1049732306294118

Ball, C. (2009). *About this portfolio.* Retrieved March 23, 2010, from http://www.ceball.com/tenure/welcome-to-my-portfolio/about/

Banta, T. W. (2002). Characteristics of effective outcomes assessment, foundations and examples. In T. W. Banta (Ed.), *Building a scholarship of assessment.* San Francisco, CA: Jossey-Bass.

Barab, S. A., Squire, K. D., & Dueber, W. (2000). A co-evolutionary model for supporting the emergence of authenticity. *Educational Technology Research and Development, 48*(2), 37–62. doi:10.1007/BF02313400

Barefoot, B. O. (2008). Institutional structures and strategies for embedding civic engagement in the first college year. In M. J. LaBare (Ed.), *First-year civic engagement: Sound foundations for college, citizenship and democracy* (p. 23). New York, NY: The New York Times.

Barron, B., Schwartz, D. L., Vye, N. J., Moore, A., Petrosino, A., Zech, L., & Bransford, J. D. (1998). Doing with understanding: Lessons from research on problem- and project-based learning. *Journal of the Learning Sciences, 7*(3&4), 271–311. doi:10.1207/s15327809jls0703&4_2

Barron, B. (2006). Interest and self sustained learning as catalyst of development: A learning ecology perspective. *Human Development, 49,* 193–224. doi:10.1159/000094368

Basinger, N., & Bartholomew, K. (2006). Service-learning in nonprofit organizations: Motivations, expectations, and outcomes. *Michigan Journal of Community Service Learning, 12*(2), 15–26.

Batiluk, M. E., Moke, P., & Wilcox Rountree, P. (1997). Crime and rehabilitation: Correctional education as an agent of change - a research note. *Justice Quarterly, 14*(1), 167–180. doi:10.1080/07418829700093261

Beard, L. A., & Harper, C. (2002). Student perceptions of online versus on campus instruction. *Education, 122*(4), 658–663.

Beck, K. (2000). *Extreme programming explained: Embrace change.* Reading, MA: Addison Wesley Longman.

Bell, S. M., & Carlson, R. (2009). Motivations of community organizations for service learning. In R. Stoecker, & E. A. Tryon (Eds.), *The unheard voices: Community organizations and service learning.* Philadelphia, PA: Temple University Press.

Benfield, M. P. J. (2003). *Determining the development of engineering teams.* Paper presented at the American Society for Engineering Management 2003 Conference, St. Louis, MO.

Benfield, M. P. J., & Turner, M. W. (2009). *Senior design concepts for a lunar exploration transportation system (LETS) for the NASA Marshall Space Flight Center.* Paper presented at the 47th AIAA Aerospace Sciences Meeting, Orlando, Florida. (AIAA-2009-568).

Benfield, M. P. J., & Utley, D. R. (2005). *Describing team development in science and engineering organizations.* Paper presented at the American Society for Engineering Management 2005 Conference, Norfolk, VA.

Benfield, M. P. J., & Utley, D. R. (2007). *The team phase change theory–a new team development theory.* Paper presented at the 2007 Industrial Engineering Research Conference, Nashville, TN.

Benfield, M. P. J., Turner, M. W., Runyon, C. J., & Hakkila, J. (2010). *The new frontiers academic AO experiment.* Paper presented at the Lunar and Planetary Institute's 41st Lunar and Planetary Science Conference, The Woodlands, TX.

Benson, L., Harkavy, I., & Puckett, J. (2000). An implementation revolution as a strategy for fulfilling the democratic promise of university-community partnerships: Penn-West Philadelphia as an experiment in progress. *Nonprofit and Voluntary Sector Quarterly, 29*(1), 24–45. doi:10.1177/0899764000291003

Benson, L., & Harkavy, I. (2000). Higher education's third revolution: The emergence of the democratic cosmopolitan civic university. *Cityscape: A Journal of Policy Development Research, 5*(1), 47-57.

Berlin Declaration. (2003). *Berlin Declaration on Open Access to Knowledge in the Sciences and Humanities.* Presented at the Conference on Open Access to Knowledge in the Science and Humanities. Retrieved June 2010, from http://oa.mpg.de/openaccess-berlin/berlin-declaration.html

Bishop, D., Giles, S., & Bryant, K. (2005). Teacher receptiveness toward Web-based training and support. *Teaching and Teacher Education, 21*(1), 3–14. doi:10.1016/j.tate.2004.11.002

Bjork, O., & Schwartz, J. P. (2005). *E-service-learning: Web writing as community service.* Retrieved February 10, 2007, from http://kairosnews.org/e-service-learning-web-writing-as-community-service

Black, E. W., Beck, D., Dawson, K., Jinks, S., & DiPietro, M. (2007). The other side of the LMS: Considering implementation and use in the adoption of an LMS in online and blended learning environments. *TechTrends, 51*(2), 37–39, 53.

Blair, K., & Hoy, C. (2006). Paying attention to adult learners online: The pedagogy and politics of community. *Computers and Composition, 23*(1), 32–48. doi:10.1016/j.compcom.2005.12.006

Blair, K., & Monske, E. (2003). Cui bono?: Revisiting the promises and perils of online learning. *Computers and Composition, 20*(4), 441–453. doi:10.1016/j.compcom.2003.08.016

Blair, K. (2007). Course management systems as gated communities: Expanding the potential of distance learning spaces through multimodal spaces. In E. Bailey (Ed.), *Focus on distance education developments* (pp. 41–53). NJ: Nova Science Publishers.

Blake, M. (2007). Formality and friendship: Research ethics review and participatory action research. *ACME: An International E-Journal for Critical Geographies, 6*(3), 411–421.

Bland, D. C., & Atweh, W. (2004). A critical approach to collaborating with students as researchers. In E. McWilliam, S. Danby, & J. Knight (Eds.), *Performing education research: Theories, methods, and practices* (pp. 331-344). Flaxton, Qld: Post Pressed.

Blouin, D. D., & Perry, E. M. (2009). Whom does service-learning really serve? Community-based organizations' perspectives on service-learning. *Teaching Sociology, 37,* 120–135. doi:10.1177/0092055X0903700201

Boehm, B. (1986). A spiral model of software development and enhancement. *IEEE Computer, 21*(5), 61–72.

Boland, J., & McIlrath, L. (2007). The process of localising pedagogies for civic engagement in Ireland: The significance of conceptions, culture and context. In L. McIlrath, & I. MacLabhrainn (Eds.), *Higher education and civic engagement: International perspectives.* Aldershot, UK: Ashgate.

Bolter, J. D., & Grusin, R. (1999). *Remediation: Understanding new media.* Cambridge, MA: MIT Press.

Bornstein, D. (2004). *How to change the world: Social entrepreneurs and the power of new ideas.* New York, NY: Oxford University Press.

Borthwick, A. C., Stirling, T., Nauman, A. D., & Cook, D. L. (2003). Achieving successful school-university collaboration. *Urban Education, 38*(3), 330–371. doi:10.1177/0042085903038003003

Bourdieu, P. (1990). *The logic of practice.* Stanford, CA: Stanford University Press.

Bowdon, M., & Scott, B. (2003). *Service-learning in technical and professional communication.* New York, NY: Addison Wesley Longman.

Bowdon, M. (2008). Introduction. In M. Bowdon, S. H. Billig, & B. A. Holland (Eds.), *Scholarship for sustaining service-learning and community engagement* (pp. xiii–xix). Charlotte, NC: Information Age Publishing.

Bowen, B. A. (1994). Telecommunications networks: Expanding the contexts for literacy. In C. Selfe, & S. Hilligoss (Eds.), *Literacy and computers: The complications of teaching and learning with technology* (pp. 113–129). New York, NY: MLA.

Boyer, E. L. (1990). *Scholarship reconsidered: Priorities of the professoriate.* San Francisco, CA/Princeton, NJ: The Carnegie Foundation for the Advancement of Teaching.

Brabeck, K. (2004). Testimonio: Bridging feminist and participatory action research principles to create new spaces for collectivity. In M. Brydon-Miller, P. Maguire, & A. McIntyre (Eds.), *Traveling companions: Feminism, teaching, and action research* (pp. 41–52). Westport, CT: Praeger Publishers.

Bredderman, T. (1982). What research says: Activity science—the evidence shows it matters. *Science and Children, 20*(1), 39–41.

Bringle, R., Phillips, M., & Hudson, M. (Eds.). (2003). *The measure of service learning: Research scales to assess student experiences.* Washington, DC: American Psychological Association.

Bringle, R. G., & Hatcher, J. A. (2009). Innovative practices in service-learning and curricular engagement. *New Directions for Higher Education, 147,* 37–46. doi:10.1002/he.356

Bringle, R. G., & Hatcher, J. A. (1996). Implementing service learning in higher education. *The Journal of Higher Education, 67*(2), 221–239. doi:10.2307/2943981

Bringle, R., & Hatcher, J. (2002). Campus-community partnerships: The terms of engagement. *The Journal of Social Issues, 58*(3), 503–516. doi:10.1111/1540-4560.00273

Brisolara, S. (1998). The history of participatory evaluation and current debates in the field. *New Directions for Evaluation, 80,* 25–41. doi:10.1002/ev.1115

Britz, J. J., Lor, P. J., Coetzee, I. E., & Bester, B. C. (2006). Africa as a knowledge society: A reality check. *The International Information & Library Review, 38*(1), 25–40. doi:10.1016/j.iilr.2005.12.001

Brown, J. S., Collins, A., & Duguid, P. (1989). Situated cognition and the culture of learning. *Educational Researcher, 18*(1), 32–42.

Bruffee, K. A. (1984). Collaborative learning and the conversation of mankind. *College English, 46*(7), 635–652. doi:10.2307/376924

Brunner, I., & Guzman, A. (1989). Participatory evaluation: A tool to assess projects and empower people. *New Directions for Program Evaluation, 42,* 9–18. doi:10.1002/ev.1509

Burgess, J. (2006). Hearing ordinary voices: Cultural studies, vernacular creativity and digital storytelling. *Continuum, 20*(2), 201–214. doi:10.1080/10304310600641737

Butcher, J., Howard, P., Labone, E. E., Bailey, M., Groundwater-Smith, S., & McFadden, M. (2003). Teacher education, community service learning and student efficacy for community engagement. *Asia-Pacific Journal of Teacher Education, 31*(2), 109–124. doi:10.1080/13598660301612

Buytaert, D. (2010). *Drupal.* Retrieved March 6, 2010, from http://drupal.org/

Cabrera, A. F., Colbeck, C. L., & Terenzini, P. T. (2001). Developing performance indicators for assessing classroom teaching practices and student learning. *Research in Higher Education, 42,* 327. doi:10.1023/A:1018874023323

Cahill, C., Rios-Moore, I., & Threats, T. (2008). Different eyes/Open eyes: Community-based participatory action research. In J. Cammarota & M. Fine (Eds.), *Revolutionizing education: Youth participatory action research in motion* (pp. 89–124). New York, NY: Routledge.

Calabrese, R. (2006). Building social capital through the use of an appreciative inquiry theoretical perspective in a school and university partnership. *International Journal of Educational Management, 20*(3), 173–182. doi:10.1108/09513540610654146

Calkins, L. M. (1994). *The art of teaching writing.* Portsmouth, NH: Heinemann.

Calton, J. M., & Kurland, N. B. (1996). A theory of stakeholder enabling: Giving voice to an emerging postmodern praxis of organizational discourse. In D. M. Boje, R. P. Gephart, & T. J. Thatchenkery (Eds.), *Postmodern management and organization* (pp. 154–177). Thousand Oaks, CA: Sage Publications.

Camazine, S., Deneubourg, J., Franks, N. R., Sneyd, J., Theraulaz, G., & Bonabeau, E. (Eds.). (2001). *Self-organization in biological systems.* Princeton, NJ: Princeton University Press.

Cameron, B. (2003). The effectiveness of simulation in a hybrid and online networking course. *TechTrends, 47*(5), 18–21. doi:10.1007/BF02763200

Cammarota, J., & Fine, M. (Eds.). (2008). *Revolutionizing education: Youth participatory action research in motion.* New York: Routledge.

Cano, J., & Bankston, J. (1992). Factors which influence participation and non-participation of ethnic minority youth in Ohio 4-H programs. *Journal of Agricultural Education, 33*(1), 23–29. doi:10.5032/jae.1992.01023

Cantoni, V., Cellario, M., & Porta, M. (2004). Perspectives and challenges in e-learning: Towards natural interaction paradigms. *Journal of Visual Languages and Computing, 15,* 333–345. doi:10.1016/j.jvlc.2003.10.002

Careaga, A. A. (1984). Sian ka'an: Una reserva de la biósfera en Quintana Roo. [Mexico: CONACyT.]. *Journal Ciencia y Desarrollo, 36*(5), 119–122.

Carini, R. M., Kuh, G. D., & Klein, S. P. (2006). Student engagement and student learning: Testing the linkages. *Research in Higher Education, 47*(1), 1–32. doi:10.1007/s11162-005-8150-9

Castellacci, F. (2006). Innovation, diffusion and catching up in the fifth long wave. *Futures, 38*, 841–863. doi:10.1016/j.futures.2005.12.007

Castells, M., Fernández-Ardèvol, M., Linchuan Qiu, J., & Sey, A. (2007). *Mobile communication and society: A global perspective.* Cambridge, MA: MIT.

Cates, C., & Jones, P. (1999). *Learning outcomes, the educational value of cooperative education.* Columbia, MD: The Cooperative Education Association.

Cates, C., & Cedercreutz, K. (2008). *Leveraging cooperative education to guide curricular innovation: The development of a corporate feedback system for continuous improvement.* Cincinnati, OH: The Center for Cooperative Education Research and Innovation. Retrieved from http://www.uc.edu/propractice/fipse/publications.asp

CDW-G. (2010). *21ˢᵗ-century classroom report: Preparing students for the future or the past?* Retrieved from http://newsroom.cdw.com/features/feature-06-28-10.html

Cedercreutz, K. (2007). *Calibration of a work performance assessment instrument to support continuous improvement of cooperative education curricula.* ProQuest online publication, October 2007.

Cedercreutz, K., Cates, C., Eckart, R., & Trent, L. (2002). Impact of outcome based accreditation standards on the cooperation between the College of Engineering and the Division of Professional Practice at the University of Cincinnati. In *Proceedings for Accreditation Board for Engineering and Technology ABET Annual Meeting, 2ⁿᵈ National Conference on Outcomes Assessment for Program Improvement,* Baltimore, MD, Accreditation Board for Engineering and Technology.

Chadwick, S. A., & Pawlowski, D. R. (2007). Assessing institutional support for service-learning: A case study of organizational sense-making. *Michigan Journal of Community Service Learning, 33.*

Chamber of Commerce, Greater Lake City. (2010). *History.* Retrieved on February 28, 2010, from http://www.lakecitysc.org/history.php

Chamberlain, C. (2003). Teaching teamwork: Project-based service-learning course LINCs students with non-profits. *Inside Illinois,* January 23. Retrieved July 20, 2009 from http://www.news.uiuc.edu/II/03/0123/linc.html

Chappell, C. A. (2004). Post-secondary correctional education and recidivism: A meta-analysis of research conducted 1990-1999. *Journal of Correctional Education, 55*(2), 148–169.

Charp, S. (2002). Online learning. *T.H.E. Journal, 29*(8), 8–10.

Chavez, L., & Arredondo, G. (2006). *Access to the University of California for graduates from low-API high schools.* Berkeley, CA: UC Berkeley Center for Latino Policy Research.

Chickering, A. W., & Gamson, Z. F. (1987). Seven principles for good practice in undergraduate education. *AAHE Bulletin, 39*(7), 3-7. Retrieved from http://www.cord.edu/dept/assessment/sevenprin.htm

*Citizens' Assembly on Electoral Reform.* (n.d.) Retrieved on March 12, 2008, from http://www.citizensassembly.bc.ca/public

Citurs, A. (2009). An integrative pre-capstone course approach to service-learning - creating a win, win, win information systems – liberal arts. In D. Colton (Ed.), *Proceedings of the Information Systems Education Conference* (p. 43-54). Washington, DC: Educators Special Interest Group (EDSIG).

Clark, D. (2004). Is professional writing relevant? A model for action research. *Technical Communication Quarterly, 13*(3), 307–323. doi:10.1207/s15427625tcq1303_5

Clark, J. E. (2010). The digital imperative: Making the case for a 21ˢᵗ century pedagogy. *Computers and Composition, 27*(1), 27–35. doi:10.1016/j.compcom.2009.12.004

Clark, R. W. (1988). School-university relationships: An interpretative review. In K. A. Sirotnik, & J. I. Goodlad (Eds.), *School-university partnerships in action: Concepts, cases, and concerns* (pp. 32–65). New York, NY: Teachers College Press.

Clegg, S., Bradley, S., & Smith, K. (2006). I've had to swallow my pride: Help seeking and self esteem. *Higher Education Research & Development, 25*(2), 101–113. doi:10.1080/07294360600610354

Clemson University. (2010). *Biology merit exam.* Retrieved on February 28, 2010, from http://biology.clemson.edu/bme/default.html

Clendenen, R. J., Ellingston, J. R., & Severson, R. J. (1979). Project newgate: The first five years. *Crime and Delinquency, 25*(1), 55–64. doi:10.1177/001112877902500104

Clusters, E. *The first ten inspections.* (2003). Manchester, UK: Office for Standards in Education. Retrieved from http//: www.ofsted.co.uk

Cohen, J., & Kinsey, D. (1994). Doing good and scholarship: A service-learning study. *Journalism Educator, 48*(4), 4–14.

Cohen, D. J., & Rosenzweig, R. (2006). *Digital history: A guide to gathering, preserving, and presenting the past on the Web.* Philadelphia, PA: Pennsylvania Press.

Cole, M. (1996). *Cultural psychology: A once and future discipline.* Cambridge, MA: Harvard University Press.

Cole, M.The Distributed Literacy Consortium. (2006). *The fifth dimension: An after-school program built on diversity.* New York, NY: Russell Sage Foundation.

Cole, M., & Engeström, Y. (2007). Cultural-historical approaches to designing for development. In J. Valsiner & A. Rosa (Eds.), *The Cambridge handbook of sociocultural psychology* (pp. 484–506). New York, NY: Cambridge University Press. doi:10.1017/CBO9780511611162.026

Collier, L. (2008, November). The C's of change: Student—and teachers—learn 21st century skills. *National Council of Teachers of English Council Chronicle,* 6-9.

Commission for Africa. (2005). *Our common interest: Report of the Commission for Africa.* Retrieved August 22, 2008, from http://www.commissionforafrica.org/english/report/thereport/english/11-03-05_cr_report.pdf

Commission on Social Justice. (1994). *Social justice: Strategies for national renewal.* New York, NY: Vintage.

Community Knowledge Initiative. (2001). *CKI strategic plan* 2002-2005. Galway, Ireland: National University of Ireland Galway.

Conference on College Composition and Communication. (1998). *Position statement: CCCC promotion and tenure guidelines for work with technology.* Retrieved

ConnectRichmond. (2007). *What we do.* Retrieved on Nov. 4, 2010, from http://www.connectrichmond.org/About/WhatWeDo/tabid/393/Default.aspx

Conner, T., Gresham, M., & McCracken, J. (2007). *Piloting pedagogies: Open-source solutions.* New Investigator Research Grant. University of South Florida St. Petersburg.

Connolly, T. M., & Stansfield, M. (2007). From e-learning to games-based e-learning: Using interactive technologies in teaching on IS course. *International Journal of Information Technology and Management, 6*(2/3/4), 188-207.

Conteh, A. (2009). *DR Congo: Open for business.* Retrieved February 20, 2010, from http://www.business-actionforafrica.org/

Cook, B., Cameron, D., & Tankersley, M. (2007). Inclusive teachers' attitudinal ratings of their students with disabilities. *The Journal of Special Education, 40*(4), 230–238. doi:10.1177/00224669070400040401

Cook, M. (2002). Outcomes: Where are we now? The efficacy of differential placement and the effectiveness of current practices. *Preventing School Failure, 46*(2), 54–56. doi:10.1080/10459880209603345

Cook, B., & Códova, D. I. (2006). *Minorities in higher education: Twenty-second annual status report.* Washington, DC: American Council on Education Press.

Coppola, J. F., Daniels, C., Gannon, S.-F., Hale, N.-L., Hayes, D., & Kline, R., & Pennachio, L. (2008). Civic engagement through computing technology. In M. J. LaBare (Ed.), *First-year civic engagement: Sound foundations for college, citizenship and democracy* (pp. 76-78). New York, NY: The New York Times.

Corbett, E. (1957). *We have with us tonight.* Toronto, Canada: Ryerson.

Cormode, G., & Krishnamurthy, B. (2008). Key differences between Web 1.0 and Web 2.0. *First Monday, 13*(6). Retrieved July 19, 2010, from http://www.uic.edu/htbin/cgiwrap/bin/ojs/index.php/fm/article/view/2125/1972

Crabtree, R. D., & Sapp, D. A. (2002). A laboratory in citizenship: Service learning in the technical communication classroom. *Technical Communication Quarterly, 11*(4), 411–432. doi:10.1207/s15427625tcq1104_3

Craig, E. M. (2007). Changing paradigms: Managed learning environments and Web 2.0. *Campus-Wide Information Systems, 24*(3), 152–161. doi:10.1108/10650740710762185

Cravens, J. (2006). *The growing digital divide among nonprofit organizations/civil society in the USA (and maybe it's not just digital)*. Retrieved March 6, 2010, from http://www.coyotecommunications.com/volunteer/divide.html

Creighton, S. (2007). Significant findings in campus-community engagement: Community partner perspective. *The Journal for Civic Commitment, 10*, 4.

Cross, M., & Adam, F. (2007). ICT policies and strategies in higher education in South Africa: National and institutional pathways. *Higher Education Policy, 20*, 73–95. doi:10.1057/palgrave.hep.8300144

Crowther, J., Galloway, V., & Martin, I. (2005). *Popular education: Engaging the academy: International perspectives*. Leicester, UK: Niace.

Cruz, N. I., & Giles, D. E. (2000). Where's the community in service-learning research? *Michigan Journal of Community Service Learning,* Special Issue, 28-34.

Cuban, L. (2004). *The blackboard and the bottom line: Why schools can't be businesses*. Cambridge, MA: Harvard University Press.

Cullen, F., & Gendreau, P. (2000). Assessing correctional rehabilitation: Policy, practice, and prospects. In J. Horney (Ed.), *Criminal justice 2000, vol. 3: Policies, processes, and decisions of the criminal justice system* (pp. 109-175). Washington, DC: National Institute of Justice, U.S. Department of Justice.

Cummins, J. (2008). Information and communication technologies: Considerations of current practice for teachers and teacher educators. In L. Smolin, K. Lawless, & N. C. Burbules (Eds.), *The 106th yearbook of the National Society for the Study of Education* (Vol. 106, pp. 182–206). Malden, MA: Blackwell Publishing.

Cushman, E. (1999). The public intellectual, service learning, and activist research. *College English, 61*(3), 328–336..doi:10.2307/379072

Cushman, E. (1996). The rhetorician as an agent of social change. *College Composition and Communication, 47*(1), 7–28. doi:10.2307/358271

Cushman, E. (1999). Afterword. The rhetorician as an agent of social change. In L. Ede (Ed.), *On writing research: The Braddock essays 1975-1998* (pp. 372–389). Boston, MA: Bedford St. Martin's.

Cushman, E. (2002). Sustainable service learning programs. *College Composition and Communication, 54*(1), 40-65. doi:10.2307/

Dailey-Hebert, A., Donnelli, E., & DiPadova-Stocks, L. (Eds.). (2008). *Service-e-learning: Educating for citizenship*. Charlotte, NC: Information Age Publishing.

Dalgarno, B., Bishop, A. G., Adlong, W., & Bedgood, D. R. Jr. (2009). Effectiveness of a virtual laboratory as a preparatory resource for distance education chemistry students. *Computers & Education, 53*, 853–865. doi:10.1016/j.compedu.2009.05.005

Darling-Hammond, L., & Richardson, N. (2009). Teacher learning: What matters? *Educational Leadership, 66*(5), 46–53.

Darling-Hammond, L. (2000). Teacher quality and student achievement: A review of state policy evidence. *Education Policy Analysis Archives, 8*(1).

Davis, K. M., Miller, D. M., & Corbet, W. (1998). *Methods of evaluating student performance through service-learning*. Tallahassee, FL: Florida State University Center for Civic Education and Service.

Davis, A. (2004). Co-authoring identity: Digital storytelling in an urban middle school. *Then Journal, 5*(1). Retrieved from http://thenjournal.org/feature/61/

Davis, E., & Hardy, S. (2003). Teaching writing in the space of Blackboard. *Computers and Composition Online.* Retrieved July 10, 2010, from http://www.bgsu.edu/cconline/DavisHardy/index.html

Daynes, G., & Longo, N. (2004). Jane Addams and the origins of service learning practice in the United States. *Michigan Journal of Community Service Learning, 11*(1), 5–13.

de Certeau, M. (1984). *The practice of everyday life.* Berkeley, CA: University of California Press.

De Jong, K., & Kleber, R. (2007). Emergency conflict-related psychosocial interventions in Sierra Leone and Uganda: Lessons from Médecins Sans Frontiéres. *Journal of Health Psychology, 12*(3), 485–497. doi:10.1177/1359105307076235

De Waal, F. B. M., & Tyack, P. L. (Eds.). (2003). *Animal social complexity: Intelligence, culture, and individualized societies.* Cambridge, MA: Harvard University Press.

Deacon, T. W. (1998). *The symbolic species: The co-evolution of language and the brain.* New York, NY: W.W. Norton.

Deakin Crick, R., Coates, M., Taylor, M., & Ritchie, S. (2004). *A systematic review of the impact of citizenship education on the provision of schooling.* In Research Evidence in Education Library. London, UK: EPPI-Centre, Social Science Research Unit, Institute of Education, University of London. Retrieved from http://eppi.ioe.ac.uk/cms/Default.aspx?tabid=127

Deakin Crick, R., Taylor, M., Tew, M., Samuel, E., Durant, K., & Ritchie, S. (2005). *A systematic review of the impact of citizenship education on student learning and achievement.* In Research Evidence in Education Library. London, UK: EPPI-Centre, Social Science Research Unit, Institute of Education, University of London. Retrieved from http://eppi.ioe.ac.uk/cms/Default.aspx?tabid=129

Deans, T. (2000). *Writing partnerships: Service-learning in composition.* Urbana, IL: NCTE.

Deci, E. L., & Ryan, R. M. (1985). *Intrinsic motivation and self-determination in human behavior.* New York, NY: Plenum.

Dede, C. (2008). A seismic shift in epistemology. *EDUCAUSE Review, 43*(3), 80–81.

Dede, C., & Kremer, A. (1999). Increasing students' participation via multiple interactive media. *Invention, 1,* 1. Retrieved from http://www.doiiit.gmu.edu/Archives/feb98/dede_1.htm

Dees, J. G. (2003). *Social entrepreneurship is about innovation and impact, not income.* Center for the Advancement of Social Entrepreneurship. Retrieved February 15, 2010, from http://www.caseatduke.org/articles/1004/corner.htm

Deming, W. E., & Kilian, C. S. (1992). *The world of W. Edwards Deming.* Knoxville, TN: SPC Press.

Denov, M., & Maclure, R. (2006). Engaging the voices of girls in the aftermath of Sierra Leone's conflict: Experiences and perspectives in a culture of violence. *Anthropologica, 48*(1), 73–85. doi:10.2307/25605298

Department for Trade and Industry (DTI)/ Department for Education and Employment. (DfEE). (2000). *Opportunity for all in a world of change. A white paper for enterprise.* London, UK: Her Majesty's Stationery Office.

Department of Education and Skills. (2003). *The future of higher education Whitepaper.* Her Majesty's Stationery Office.

DeVoss, D., & Porter, J. E. (2006). Why napster matters to writing: Filesharing as a new ethic of digital delivery. *Computers and Composition, 23*(2), 178–210. doi:10.1016/j.compcom.2006.02.001

Dewey, J. (1916). *Democracy and education: An introduction to the philosophy of education.* New York, NY: Free Press.

Dickard, N., & Schneider, D. (2002, July 1). The digital divide: Where we are. *Edutopia.* Retrieved from http://www.edutopia.org/digital-divide-where-we-are-today

Diehl, A. (2006, February 2). What is Web 2.0 and how will technical writers be impacted? *Content Matters, 1*(2). Retrieved July 11, 2010, from http://www.msu.edu/user/diehlamy/atw/ezine/

Discover South Carolina. (2010). *National bean market museum.* Retrieved on February 28, 2010, from http://www.discoversouthcarolina.com/products/25750.aspx

Dobres, M. A. (2000). *Technology and social agency: Outlining a practice framework for archaeology.* Malden, MA: Blackwell.

Donaldson, T., & Preston, L. E. (1995). The stakeholder theory of the corporation: Concepts, evidence, and implications. *Academy of Management Review, 20*(1), 65–91. doi:10.2307/258887

Donnelly, P., & Benson, J. (2008). Get the most from electronic learning. *Education for Primary Care, 19*, 100–102.

Doyle, E., Ward, S., & Oomen-Early, J. (2010). *The process of community health education and promotion* (2nd ed.). Longgrove, IL: Waveland Press.

Draper, A. J. (2004). Integrating project-based service-learning into an advanced environmental chemistry course. *Journal of Chemical Education, 81*(2), 221–224. doi:10.1021/ed081p221

Draper, D. A., Hurley, R. E., & Lauer, J. (2008). *Public health workforce shortages imperil nation's health.* Center for Studying Health System Change, Research Brief no. 4. Retrieved on June 14, 2010, from http://www.hschange.org/CONTENT/979/979.pdf

Driscoll, A., Holland, B., Gelmon, S., & Kerrigan, S. (1996). An assessment model for service-learning: Comprehensive case studies of impact on faculty, students, community, and institution. *Michigan Journal of Community Service Learning, 3*, 66–71.

Drucker, P. F. (1994). The age of social transformation. *Atlantic Monthly, 274*(5), 53–80.

Druin, A. (Ed.). (1999). *The design of children's technology.* San Francisco, CA: Morgan Kaufmann Publishers.

Dubinsky, J. M. (2002). Service-learning as a path to virtue: The ideal orator in professional communication. *Michigan Journal of Community Service Learning, 8*(2), 61–74.

Dunlap, J. C. (2006). Using guided reflective journaling activities to capture students' changing perceptions. *TechTrends, 50*(6), 26. doi:10.1007/s11528-006-7614-x

Dunn, P. A. (2001). *Talking, sketching, moving: Multiple literacies in the teaching of writing.* Portsmouth, NH: Boynton/Cook.

Eble, M., & Gaillet, L. L. (2004). Educating community intellectuals: Rhetoric, moral philosophy, and civic engagement. *Technical Communication Quarterly, 13*(3), 341–354. doi:10.1207/s15427625tcq1303_7

Ede, L., & Lunsford, A. (1990). *Singular texts/plural authors: Perspectives on collaborative writing.* Carbondale & Edwardsville, IL: Southern Illinois University Press.

EdSource. (2010). *School finance 2009 – 2010: Budget cataclysm and its aftermath.* CA: Mountain View.

Education Action Zones. *Tackling difficult issues in round two zones.* (2003). Manchester, UK: Office for Standards in Education. Retrieved from http//: www.ofsted.co.uk

Education Week. (2009, March 26). State technology grades and ranking tables. *Technology Counts 2009, 28* (26). Retrieved from http://www.edweek.org/ew/toc/2009/03/26/index.html

Educause. (2008). *EDUCAUSE 2008 general session: Why IT matters: A president's perspective on technology and leadership.* Retrieved June 21, 2010, from http://hosted.mediasite.com/mediasite/Viewer/?peid=607067 73509a468985f07cd6e23b2609

Ehrlich, T. (2000). *Civic responsibility and higher education.* Phoenix, AZ: Oryx Press.

Eifert, B., Gelb, A., & Ramachandran, V. (2008). The cost of doing business in Africa: Evidence from enterprise survey data. *World Development, 36*(9), 1531–1546. doi:10.1016/j.worlddev.2007.09.007

Eijkman, H. (2008). Web 2.0 as a non-foundational network-centric learning space. *Campus-Wide Information Systems, 25*(2), 93–104. doi:10.1108/10650740810866567

Eijkman, H. (2009). Using Web 2.0 to decolonise transcultural learning zones in higher education. *Campus-Wide Information Systems, 26*(3), 240–255. doi:10.1108/10650740910967401

ELI. (2007). Seven things you should know about digital storytelling. *Educause.* Retrieved June 21, 2010, from http://net.educause.edu/ir/library/pdf/ELI7021.pdf

Engelbrecht, P., Oswald, M., Swart, E., & Eloff, I. (2003). Including learners with intellectual disabilities: Stressful for teachers? *International Journal of Disability Development and Education, 50*(3), 293–308. doi:10.1080/1034912032000120462

Enos, S., & Morton, K. (2003). Developing a theory and practice of campus-community partnerships. In B. Jacoby (Ed.), *Building partnerships for service-learning* (pp. 20–41). San Francisco, CA: Jossey-Bass.

Erickson, J. A., & O'Connor, S. E. (2000). Service-learning: Does it promote or reduce prejudice? In C. O'Grady (Ed.), *Integrating service-learning and multicultural education in colleges and universities* (pp. 63, 65–66). Mahwah, NJ: Lawrence Erlbaum Associates.

Erisman, W., & Contardo, J. B. (2005). *Learning to reduce recidivism: A 50-state analysis of postsecondary correctional education policy.* Institute for Higher Education Policy report.

Ess, C., & Sudweeks, F. (1998). Computer-mediated communication or culturally-mediated computing? Challenging assumptions of the electronic global village. *Electronic Journal of Communication/Revue Electronique de Communication, 8.* Retrieved on July 22, 2008, from http://www.cios.org/www/ejcmain.htm

Esson, J. M., Stevens-Truss, R., & Thomas, A. (2005). Service-learning in introductory chemistry: Supplementing chemistry curriculum in elementary schools. *Journal of Chemical Education, 82*(8), 1168. doi:10.1021/ed082p1168

Estrada, P. (2005). The courage to grow: A researcher and teacher linking professional development with small-group reading instruction and student achievement. *Research in the Teaching of English, 39*(4), 320–364.

Every, C. M. *Change for Children.* (2003). Nottingham, UK: Department for Education and Skills. Retrieved from http://nationalstrategies.standards.dcsf.gov.uk/node/85063

Excellence and Enjoyment. *A Strategy for Primary Schools.* (2003). Nottingham, UK: Department for Education and Skills. Retrieved from http://nationalstrategies.standards.dcsf.gov.uk/node/85063

*Excellence in Cities: City Learning Centres: An evaluation of the first year.* (2003). Manchester, UK: Office for Standards in Education. Retrieved from http//:www.ofsted.co.uk

Excellence in Schools. (1997). *Department of Education and Employment White paper.* London, UK: Her Majesty's Stationery Office.

Extension Learning Solutions. (2009). *Interim evaluation: Charity central essentials.* Edmonton, Canada: University of Alberta, Faculty of Extension.

Eyler, J. (2002). Reflection: Linking service and learning – linking students and communities. *The Journal of Social Issues, 58*(3), 517–534. doi:10.1111/1540-4560.00274

Eyler, J., Giles, D., Stenson, C., & Gray, C. (2000). *At a glance: What we know about the effects of service-learning on college students, faculty, institutions and communities, 1993-2000* (3rd ed.). Nashville, TN: Vanderbilt University.

Eyler, J., & Giles, D. E. Jr. (1999). *Where's the learning in service-learning?* San Francisco, CA: Jossey-Bass.

Eyler, J., & Giles, D. (1997). The importance of program quality in service-learning. In A. Waterman (Ed.), *Service learning: Applications from the research* (pp. 57–76). Mahwah, NJ: Lawerence Erlbaum Associates, Publishers.

Faculty Focus. (2010). *Engagement strategies for online adjuncts.* Retrieved March 23, 2010, from http://www.facultyfocus.com/online-seminars/engagement-strategies-for-online-adjuncts

Falk, J. H., & Dierking, L. (2000). *Learning from museums: Visitor experiences and the making of meaning.* Walnut Creek, CA: Altamira Press.

Fals-Borda, O. (2001). Participatory (action) research in social theory: Origins and challenges. In P. Reason & H. Bradbury (Eds.), *Handbook of action research: Participative inquiry and practice* (pp. 27–37). Los Angeles, CA: SAGE Publications.

Family and Corrections Network. (2010). *Children and families of the incarcerated fact sheet.* The National Resource Center on Children and Families of the Incarcerated, Family and Corrections Network. Retrieved July 7, 2010, from http://fcnetwork.org/wp/wp-content/uploads/fact-sheet.pdf

Featherstone, B., & Trinder, L. (2001). New labour, families and fathers. *Critical Social Policy, 21*(4), 534–536. doi:10.1177/026101830102100418

Feenberg, A. (1991). *Critical theory of technology*. New York, NY: Oxford University Press.

Ferillo, B. (2005). *Corridor of shame: The neglect of South Carolina's rural schools*. Ferillo and Associates. Retrieved on February 28, 2010, from http://www.youtube.com/watch?v=rjY69hO0fxk

Ferman, B., & Hill, T. L. (2004). The challenges of agenda conflict in higher-education-community research partnerships: Views from the community side. *Journal of Urban Affairs*, *26*(2), 241–257. doi:10.1111/j.0735-2166.2004.00199.x

Fielden, J. (2001). Markets for borderless education. *Minerva*, *39*(1), 49–62. doi:10.1023/A:1010374319689

*First Step Initiative website*. (2010). Retrieved July 10, 2010, from http://www.firststepinitiative.net

Florence District Three. (2010). *About us*. Retrieved on February 28, 2010, from http://www.florence3.k12.sc.us/AboutUs.htm

Florida Department of Education. (2006). *Florida comprehensive assessment test (FCAT) sunshine state standards state report of district results: Grade 05 science*. Florida Department of Education website. Retrieved February 12, 2010, from http://fcat.fldoe.org/scinfopg.asp

Florida Department of Education. (n.d.). *Educator accomplished practices: Competencies for teachers of the twenty-first century*. Florida Department of Education. Retrieved February 12, 2010 from http://www.fldoe.org/dpe/publications/accomplished4-99.pdf

Fortune, J., Utley, D. R., & Benfield, M. P. (2005). *Modeling teams: An investigation into teaming theories and their application*. Paper presented at the American Society for Engineering Management 2005 Conference, Norfolk, VA.

Foucault, M. (1980). *Power/knowledge: Selected interviews and other writings 1972-77*. New York, NY: Pantheon.

Fox, W. M. (1995). Sociotechnical system principles and guidelines: Past and present. *The Journal of Applied Behavioral Science*, *31*(1), 91–105. doi:10.1177/0021886395311009

Frederick, R. A., Jr., Pawlak, M.-S., Utley, D. R., Corsetti, C. D., Wells, B. E., & Landrum, D. B. (2002). *International product teams for aerospace systems design*. Paper presented at the 38th AIAA/ ASME/ SAE/ ASEE Joint Propulsion Conference and Exhibit Indianapolis, Indiana. (AIAA 2002-4337).

Frederick, R. A., Jr., & Sanders, J. (1993). *The effective use of mentors in undergraduate design*. Paper presented at the 1993 ASME Winter Annual Meeting, AES Vol. 30/ HTD Vol. 226, Thermodynamics, Analysis, and Improvement of Energy Systems, (pp. 219-225). New Orleans, LA.

Freeman, R. E. (1984). *Strategic management: A stakeholder approach*. Boston, MA: Pitman.

Freeman, R. E., & Gilbert, D. Jr. (1992). Business, ethics and society: A critical agenda. *Business & Society*, *31*(1), 9–17. doi:10.1177/000765039203100102

Freeman, J. C. (2010). *Imaging place: Place-based virtual reality*. Emerson College. Retrieved on, 29 July 2010, from http://institute.emerson.edu/vma/faculty/john_craig_freeman/imaging_place/imaging_place.html

Freire, P. (1985). *The politics of education* (p. 93). New York, NY: Bergin and Garvey.

Freire, P. (1970). *Pedagogy of the oppressed*. New York, NY: Continuum.

Friedman, T. L. (2005). *The world is flat: A brief history of the twenty-first century*. New York, NY: Farrar, Straus and Giroux.

Friedman, A. (2008). *Framework for evaluating impacts of informal science education project*. Retrieved April 6, 2010, from http://insci.org/resources/Eval_Framework.pdf

Furco, A., & Holland, B. (2004). Institutionalizing service-learning in higher education: Strategy for chief academic officers. In M. Langseth, & W. M. Plater (Eds.), *Public work and the academy – an academic administrators guide to civic engagement and service-learning*. Boston, MA: Anker Publishing Company.

Gallivan, M. J. (2001). Organizational adoption and assimilation of complex technological innovations: Development and application of a new framework. *The Data Base for Advances in Information Systems*, *32*(3), 51–85.

Gander, L. (1999). *The radical promise of public legal education in Canada. Unpublished LL.* Edmonton: M., University of Alberta.

Gander, L. (2009). The incubation model of university-community relationships: A case study in incubating new programs, new knowledge, and new fields of practice. *Canadian Journal of University Continuing Education, 35*(1), 25–44.

Garcia, V. (2007). *E-mail sent to author.* October 26, 2007.

Gardner, H. (1999). *Intelligence reframed: Multiple intelligences for the 21ˢᵗ century.* New York, NY: Basic Books.

Gareis, C. R., & Nussbaum-Beach, S. (2007). Electronically mentoring to develop accomplished professional teachers. *Journal of Personnel Evaluation in Education, 20*(3), 227–246..doi:10.1007/s11092-008-9060-0

Gates, B. (2008, August 11). How to fix capitalism. *Time Magazine,* 40-45.

Geertz, C. (2000). *Local knowledge: Further essays in interpretive anthropology.* New York, NY: Basic Books.

Geisler, C. (2001). IText: Future directions for research on the relationship between information technology and writing. *Journal of Business and Technical Communication, 15*(3), 269–308. doi:10.1177/105065190101500302

Gelmon, S., Holland, B., Driscoll, A., Spring, A., & Kerrigan, S. (2001). *Assessing service-learning and civic engagement: Principles and techniques.* Providence, RI: Campus Compact.

Gelmon, S. (2000).Challenges in assessing service-learning. *Michigan Journal of Community Service Learning,* Special Issue, 84-90.

Gladieux, L. E. (2000). Global on-line learning: Hope or hype? *Higher Education in Europe, 25*(3), 351–353. doi:10.1080/03797720020015953

Goldhaber, D. D., & Brewer, D. J. (2000). Does teacher certification matter? High school teacher certification status and student achievement. *Educational Evaluation and Policy Analysis, 22*(2), 129–145.

Goldhaber, D. D., & Brewer, D. J. (1997). Evaluating the effect of teacher degree level on educational performance. In W. Fowler (Ed.), *Developments in school finance,* 1996, (pp. 197–210). (NCES 97-535). Washington, DC: U.S. Department of Education, National Center for Education Statistics.

Gonzáles, N., Moll, L. C., & Amanti, C. (2005). *Funds of knowledge: Theorizing practices in household, communities and classrooms.* New Jersey: Lawrence Erbaum.

Goodlad, J. (1988). School-university partnerships for school renewal: Rationale and concepts. In K. A. Sirotnik, & J. I. Goodlad (Eds.), *School-university partnerships in action: Concepts, cases, and concerns* (pp. 3–31). New York, NY: Teachers College Press.

Goodwin-Jones, R. (2008). Emerging technologies—Web-writing 2.0: Enabling, documenting, and assessing writing online. [Retrieved]. *Language Learning & Technology, 12*(2), 7–13.

Government of Canada. (2009). *Charities partnership and outreach program funding guide and application.* Retrieved from http://www.cra-arc.gc.ca/E/pub/tg/rc4411/README.html

Gray, R. (1982). Christianity, colonialism, and communications in sub-Saharan Africa. *Journal of Black Studies, 13*(1), 59–72. doi:10.1177/002193478201300105

Gray, L., Thomas, N., & Lewis, L. (2010). *Educational technology in U.S. public Schools: Fall 2008--first look.* (NCES Report 2010-034). National Center for Education Statistics, U.S. Department of Education. Retrieved from http://nces.ed.gov/pubsearch/pubsinfo.asp?pubid=2010034

Greenberg, G. (2004, July/August). The digital convergence: Extending the portfolio model. *EDUCAUSE Review, 4,* 28–36. Retrieved 17 July, 2008, from http://www.educause.edu/apps/er/erm04/erm0441.asp

Greenhalgh, T., Robert, G., Macfarlane, F., Bate, P., & Kyriakidou, O. (2004). Diffusion of innovations in service organizations: Systematic review and recommendations. *The Milbank Quarterly, 84*(4), 581–629. doi:10.1111/j.0887-378X.2004.00325.x

Greenhow, C., & Belbas, B. (2007). Using activity-oriented design methods to study collaborative knowledge-building in e-learning courses within higher education. *International Journal of Computer-Supported Collaborative Learning, 2*(4), 363–391. doi:10.1007/s11412-007-9023-3

Gurjathi, M. R., & McQuade, R. J. (2002). Service-learning in business schools: A case study in an intermediate accounting course. *Journal of Education for Business,* 144–150.

Gyamfi, A. (2005). Closing the digital divide in sub-Saharan Africa: Meeting the challenges of the information age. *Information Development, 21*(1), 22-30.

Handler, M. G., & Ravid, R. (2001a). Models of school-university collaboration. In R. Ravid, & M. G. Handler (Eds.), *The many faces of school-university collaboration: Characteristics of successful partnerships* (pp. 3–10). Englewood, CO: Greenwood Publishing Group.

Handler, M. G., & Ravid, R. (2001b). The center for collaborative research at National-Louis University. In R. Ravid, & M. G. Handler (Eds.), *The many faces of school-university collaboration: Characteristics of successful partnerships* (pp. 237–246). Englewood, CO: Greenwood Publishing Group.

Hanna, L., Risden, K., & Alexander, K. J. (1997). Guidelines for usability testing with children. *Interaction, 4*(5), 9–14. doi:10.1145/264044.264045

Haraway, D. (1988). Situated knowledges: The science question in feminism and the privilege of partial perspective. *Feminist Studies, 14*(3), 575–599. doi:10.2307/3178066

Harpur, J. (2006). Transformation in higher education: The inevitable union of alchemy and technology. *Higher Education Policy, 19,* 135–151. doi:10.1057/palgrave.hep.8300116

Harris, K. R., Santangelo, T., & Graham, S. (2010). Metacognition and strategies instruction in writing. In H. S. Waters, & W. Schneider (Eds.), *Metacognition, strategy use, & instruction* (pp. 226–256). New York, NY: Guilford.

Hatch, R. J. (2008). *Discovering differences in software designed by children versus software designed by adults.* Doctoral dissertation. Available from ProQuest Dissertations and Theses database. (UMI No. 3371427)

Hatcher-Skeers, M., & Aragon, E. (2002). Combining active learning with service learning: A student-driven demonstration project. *Journal of Chemical Education, 79*(4), 462. doi:10.1021/ed079p462

Hawisher, G., & Selfe, C. (1991). The rhetoric of technology and the electronic writing class. *College Composition and Communication, 42*(1), 55–65. doi:10.2307/357539

Hawkins, R. (2007). The persistent bandwidth divide in Africa: Findings for the African Tertiary Institution Connectivity study and lessons for developing knowledge infrastructure and networks in Africa. In *Integrating science & technology into development policies: An international perspective* (pp. 91–99). OECD Publishing. doi:10.1787/9789264032101-11-en

Hayles, N. K. (2008). *Electronic literature: New horizons for the literary.* Notre Dame, IN: University of Notre Dame Press.

Heath, J. (2004). Liberalization, modernization, westernization. *Philosophy and Social Criticism, 30*(5/6), 665–690. doi:10.1177/0191453704045760

Hein, G. (1994). Evaluation of museum programmes and exhibits. In E. Hooper-Greenhill (Ed.), *The educational role of the museum* (2nd ed., pp. 305–311). London, UK: Routledge.

Hembrooke, H., & Gay, G. (2003). The laptop and the lecture: The effects of multitasking in learning environments. *Journal of Computing in Higher Education, 15*(1), 46–64. doi:10.1007/BF02940852

Henry, J. (1995). Teaching technical authorship. *Technical Communication Quarterly, 4*(3), 261–282.

Henry, J. (1998). Documenting contributory expertise: The value added by technical communicators in collaborative writing situations. *Technical Communication, 45*(2), 207–220.

Henry, J. (2010). Greening the subject of/through technical writing. *Academic Exchange Quarterly, 14*(1), 140–146.

Henten, A., Falch, M., & Anyimadu, A. (2004). Telecommunications development in Africa: Filling the gap. *Telematics and Informatics, 21,* 1–9. doi:10.1016/S0736-5853(03)00019-4

Herrington, J., & Oliver, R. (2000). An instructional design framework for authentic learning environments. *Educational Technology Research and Development, 48*(3), 23–48. doi:10.1007/BF02319856

Herrington, J., Oliver, R., & Reeves, T. C. (2003). Patterns of engagement in authentic online learning environments. *Australian Journal of Educational Technology, 19*(1), 59–71. Retrieved December 23, 2009, from http://www.ascilite.org.au/ajet/ajet19/herrington.html

Herron, J. D., & Nurrenbern, S. C. (1999). Chemical education research: Improving chemistry learning. *Journal of Chemical Education, 76*(10), 1353. doi:10.1021/ed076p1353

Higgins, S. (2003). *Does ICT improve learning and teaching in schools. A professional user review of UK research undertaken for the British educational Research Association.* BERA, Southwell.

Higheredhero.com (2010). *Last chance! Facebook, twitter & blogs: Recruitment tips for prospective students.* Private email.

Hofstede, G., Neuijen, B., Ohayv, D. D., & Sanders, G. (1990). Measuring organizational cultures: A qualitative and quantitative study across twenty cases. *Administrative Science Quarterly, 35*(2), 286–316. doi:10.2307/2393392

Holland, B. (2001). A comprehensive model for assessing service-learning and community-university partnerships. *New Directions for Higher Education, 114*, 51–60. doi:10.1002/he.13.abs

Holland, B., & Gelman, S. (1998). The state of the engaged campus: What have we learned about building and sustaining university and community partnerships. *AAHE Bulletin. American Association for Higher Education, 51*(1), 3–6.

Honnet, E., & Poulen, S. (1989). *Principles of good practice for combining service and learning: A wingspread special report.* Racine, WI: The Johnson Foundation.

Honoré, P. A., Graham, G. N., Garcia, J., & Morris, W. (2008). A call to action: Public health and community college partnerships to educate the workforce and promote health equity. *Journal of Public Health Management and Practice, 14*(6), S82–S84.

Hooper-Greenhill, E. (1994a). Education, communication, and interpretation: Towards a critical pedagogy in museums. In E. Hooper-Greenhill (Ed.), *The educational role of the museum* (2nd ed., pp. 3–27). London, UK: Routledge.

Hooper-Greenhill, E. (1994b). Learning from learning theory in museums. In E. Hooper-Greenhill (Ed.), *The educational role of the museum* (2nd ed., pp. 137–145). London, UK: Routledge.

Hoover, T. S., & Webster, N. (2004). Modeling service-learning for future leaders of youth organizations. *Journal of Leadership Education, 3*(3), 58–62.

Howard, J. (2003b). Community service learning in the curriculum. In *Campus Compact's introduction to service-learning toolkit: Readings and resources for faculty* (2nd ed., pp. 101–104). Providence, RI: Brown University.

Howard, J. (1993). Community service-learning in the curriculum. In J. Howard (Ed.), *Praxis I: A faculty casebook on community service-learning* (pp. 3–12). Ann Arbor, MI: OCSL Press.

Huber, C. (2010). Professional learning 2.0. *Educational Leadership, 67*(8), 41–46.

Huckin, T. (1997). Technical writing and community service. *Journal of Business and Technical Communication, 11*(1), 49–59. doi:10.1177/1050651997011001003

Hull, G., & Katz, M. (2006). Crafting an agentive self: Case studies of digital storytelling. *Research in the Teaching of English, 41*(1), 43–81.

Hull, G., & Shultz, K. (2002). *Schools out! Bridging out-of-school literacies with classroom practice.* New York, NY: Teachers College Press.

Hull, G. A. (2003). At last: Youth culture and digital media: New literacies for new times. *Research in the Teaching of English, 38*(2), 229–233.

Humes, W., & Bryce, T. (2001). Scholarship, research and the evidential basis of policy development in education. *British Journal of Educational Studies, 49*(3), 329–352. doi:10.1111/1467-8527.t01-1-00179

Hungerford, H. A., & Volk, T. L. (1990). Changing learner behavior through environmental education. *The Journal of Environmental Education, 21*(3), 8–22.

Hunter, S., & Brisbin, R. A. (2000). The impact of service-learning on democratic and civic values. *Political Science & Politics, 33,* 623–626. doi:10.2307/420868

Huysman, M., & Wulf, V. (2006). IT to support knowledge sharing in communities, towards a social capital analysis. *Journal of Information Technology, 21,* 40–51. doi:10.1057/palgrave.jit.2000053

Ibeneme, E. (2009). *SAGE team of JSS Jikwoyi emerge winner of FCT SAGE exhibition* (pp. 32–34). TELL.

*Income Tax Act,* R.S., 1985, c. 1 (5th Supp.) as amended.

International Labor Organization. (2009). *Youth employment: Breaking gender barriers for young women and men.* Retrieved February 15, 2010, from http://www.ilo.org/wcmsp5/groups/public/dgreports/gender/documents/publication/wcms_097919.pdf

Internet World Stats. (2008). *Internet usage statistics for Africa.* Retrieved August 21, 2008, from http://www.internetworldstats.com/stats1.htm

Intrator, S. (2004). The engaged classroom. *Educational Leadership, 62*(1), 20–25.

Ito, M. (2007). Introduction. In K. Varnelis (Ed.), *Networked publics* (pp. 1–13). Cambridge, MA: MIT Press.

Jackson, K. (1996). Managing distributed documentation. *Society for Technical Communication Conference Proceedings.* Retrieved July 9, 2010, from http://www.stc.org/confproceed/1996/PDFs/PG6162.PDF

Jacoby, B. (1996). *Service-learning in higher education: Concepts and practices.* San Francisco, CA: Jossey-Bass.

James, J., & Versteeg, M. (2007). Mobile phones in Africa: How much do we really know? *Social Indicators Research, 84,* 117–126. doi:10.1007/s11205-006-9079-x

Jameson, J. K., Clayton, P. H., & Bringle, R. G. (2008). Investigating student learning within and across linked service-learning courses. In M. A. Bowdon, S. H. Billig, & B. A. Holland (Eds.), *Scholarship for sustaining service-learning and civic engagement.* Charlotte, NC: Information Age Publishing.

Jaschik, S. (2007). Scholarship reconsidered as tenure policy. *Inside Higher Ed,* October 2, 2007. Retrieved March 23, 2010 from http://www.insidehighered.com/news/2007/10/02/wcu

Jenkins, H., Clinton, K., Purushotma, R., Robison, A. J., & Weigel, M. (2009). *Confronting the challenges of participatory culture: Media education for the 21st century.* Cambridge, MA: MIT.

Jeyaraj, A., Rottman, J. W., & Lacity, M. C. (2006). A review of the predictors, linkages, and biases in IT innovation adoption research. *Journal of Information Technology, 21,* 1–23. doi:10.1057/palgrave.jit.2000056

Johnson-Eilola, J. (1997). *Nostalgic angels: Rearticulating hypertext writing.* Norwood, NJ: Ablex Publishing Company.

Jonassen, D. H. (1996). *Computers in the classroom: Mindtools for critical thinking.* Columbus, OH: Merrill/Prentice Hall.

Jones, T. M. (1995). Instrumental stakeholder theory: A synthesis of ethics and economics. *Academy of Management Review, 20*(2), 404–437. doi:10.2307/258852

Jones, T. (2009). *E-mail to author.* September 9, 2009.

Juul, J. (2005). *Half-real: Video games between real rules and fictional worlds.* Cambridge, MA: MIT.

Kalivas, J. H. (2008). A service-learning project based on a research supportive curriculum format in the general chemistry laboratory. *Journal of Chemical Education, 85*(10), 1410–1415. doi:10.1021/ed085p1410

Kanayama, T. (2003). *An organizational digital divide: Web adoption and use among nonprofit organizations in Appalachian Ohio.* Paper presented at the annual meeting of the International Communication Association, San Diego, CA. Retrieved March 6, 2010, from http://www.allacademic.com/meta/p111817_index.html

Kaplan, S. (2000). Human nature and environmentally responsible behavior. *The Journal of Social Issues, 56*(3), 491–508. doi:10.1111/0022-4537.00180

Kapor, M. (2006, April 23). Architecture is politics (and politics is architecture). *Mitch Kapor's blog.* Retrieved July 19, 2010, from http://blog.kapor.com/index9cd7.html?p=29

Kastman Breuch, L. (2001). The overruled dust mite: Preparing technical communication students to interact with clients. *Technical Communication Quarterly, 10*(2), 193–210. doi:10.1207/s15427625tcq1002_5

Katz, S. (1997). Presumed guilty: How schools criminalize Latino youth. *Social Justice (San Francisco, Calif.), 24*(4), 77–96.

Keefe, S., & Kingma, B. (2006). An analysis of the virtual classroom: Does size matter? Do residencies make a difference? Should you hire that instructional designer? *Journal of Education for Library and Information Science, 47*(2), 127–143. doi:10.2307/40324327

Kellogg Commission on the Future of Land-Grant Universities. (2001). *Returning to our roots: Executive summaries of the reports of the Kellogg Commission on the future of state and land-grant universities.* Washington, DC: National Association of State Universities and Land-Grant Colleges.

Kelly, D. M. (1993). Secondary power source: High school students as participatory researchers. *The American Sociologist, 24*(1), 8–26. doi:10.1007/BF02691942

Kelly, D. (2006). Frame work: Helping youth counter their misrepresentations in media. *Canadian Journal of Education, 29*(1), 27–48. doi:10.2307/20054145

Kelshaw, T., & Gastil, J. (2008). When citizens and officeholders meet, part 2: A typology of face-to-face public meetings. *International Journal of Public Participation, 2*(1), 33–54.

Kelty, C. M. (2008). *Two bits: The cultural significance of free software.* Durham, NC: Duke University Press.

Kenworthy-U'Ren. A. L. (2000). Management students as consultants: A strategy of service-learning in management education, working for the common good. In P. Godfrey & E. Grasso (Eds.), *Concepts and models for service-learning in management* (pp. 55-68). American Association for Higher Education.

Kerr, D. (2009). *Citizenship and values education to the rescue! Making the case for a call to action.* Full report from the Ninth Annual Conference National Foundation for Educational Research.

Kimme Hea, A. C. (2005). What's at stake? Strategies for developing stakeholder relationships in service-learning projects. *Reflections: A Journal of Writing, Service-Learning, and Community Literacy, 4,* 54–76.

Kimme Hea, A. C. (2007). Riding the wave: Articulating a critical methodology for WWW research practices in computers & composition. In D. DeVoss, & H. McKee (Eds.), *Digital writing research: Technologies, methodologies, and ethical issues* (pp. 269–286). Cresskill, NJ: Hampton Press.

King, G., Law, M., King, S., Rosenbaum, P., Kertoy, M. K., & Young, N. L. (2003). A conceptual model of the factors affecting the recreation and leisure participation of children with disabilities. *Physical & Occupational Therapy in Pediatrics, 23*(1), 63–90.

King, K. (2007). Balancing basic and post-basic education in Kenya: National versus international policy agendas. *International Journal of Educational Development, 27,* 358–370. doi:10.1016/j.ijedudev.2006.10.001

Kingma, B., & Schisa, K. (2010). WISE Economics: ROI of Quality and Consortiums. *Journal of Education for Library and Information Science, 51*(1), 43–52.

Kingma, B., Nicholson, S., Schisa, K., & Smith, L. (2010). WISE+ course development partnerships: Collaboration, innovation, & sustainability. *Proceedings of the IFLA-ALISE-Euclid preconference, Cooperation and Collaboration in Teaching and Research: Trends in Library and Information Studies Education.* Borås, Sweden.

Kinnevy, S. C., & Boddie, S. C. (2001). Developing community partnerships through service-learning: Universities, coalitions, and congregations. *Michigan Journal of Community Service Learning, 8*(1), 44–51.

Kitalong, K., Moody, J. E., Middlebrook, R. H., & Ancheta, G. S. (2009). Beyond the screen: Narrative mapping as a tool for evaluating a mixed-reality science museum exhibit. *Technical Communication Quarterly, 18*(2), 142–165. doi:10.1080/10572250802706349

Klaebe, H., Foth, M., Burgess, J., & Bilandzic, M. (2007). Digital storytelling and history lines: Community engagement in a master-planned development. In *Proceedings 13th International Conference on Virtual Systems and Multimedia,* Brisbane. Retrieved from http://eprints.qut.edu.au.

Kleimann, S. (1993). The reciprocal nature of workplace culture and review. In R. Spilka (Ed.), *Writing in the workplace: New research perspectives* (pp. 56-70). Carbondale & Edwardsville, IL: Southern Illinois University Press.

Knapp, L. G., Kelly-Reid, J. E., & Ginder, S. A. (2009). *Enrollment in postsecondary institutions, Fall 2007, graduation rates, 2001 &2004 cohorts, and financial statistics, fiscal year 2007 (NCES 2009-155).* National Center for Education Statistics, Institute of Education Sciences, U. Washington, DC: S. Department of Education.

Kolb, D. A. (1984). *Experiential learning: Experience as the source of learning and development.* Englewood Cliffs, NJ: Prentice Hall.

Kolowich, S. (2010, April 5). Should colleges start giving Apple's iPad to students? *USA Today.* Retrieved from http://www.usatoday.com/news/education/2010-04-05-IHE-colleges-give-iPads-to-students05_N.htm

Krebs, M. M. (2008). Sustainability of service-learning: What do K-12 teachers say? In M. A. Bowdon, S. H. Billig, & B. A. Holland (Eds.), *Scholarship for sustaining service-learning and civic engagement.* Charlotte, NC: Information Age Publishing.

La Clase Mágica Research Initiative, University-Community Links (UC Links), Center for Mathematics Education for Latinos/as (CEMELA) and Academy for Teacher Excellence. (2010). *Laboratories for learning: Collaborative research-based after-school programs.*

LaCasse, K., Quinn, L. S., & Bernard, C. (2010). *Using social media to meet nonprofit goals: The results of a survey.* idealware. Retrieved March 6, 2010, from http://www.idealware.org/sm_survey/

Ladson-Billings, G. (2004). New directions in multicultural education: Complexities, boundaries, and critical race theory. In J. A. Banks, & C. A. McGee Banks (Eds.), *Handbook of research on multicultural education* (2nd ed., pp. 50–65). San Francisco, CA: Jossey-Bass.

Lambert, J. (2007). *Digital storytelling cookbook.* Berkley, CA: Digital Diner Press.

Lambert, J. (2009). *Digital storytelling: Capturing lives, creating community* (3rd ed.). Berkeley, CA: Digital Diner Press.

Lancashire, I. (2009). *Teaching literature and language online.* New York, NY: Modern Language Association.

Lansberg, M., & Blume, H. (2008, July 17). Data reveal greater student dropout rate across state. *Los Angeles Times.*

LaRocque, N., & Michael, L. (2003). *The promise of e-learning in Africa: The potential for public-private partnerships.* IBM Endowment for the Business of Government.

Lave, J., & Wenger, E. (1991). *Situated learning: Legitimate peripheral participation.* New York, NY: Cambridge University Press.

Lave, J. (1988). *Cognition in practice: Mind, mathematics, and culture in everyday life.* Cambridge, UK: Cambridge University Press. doi:10.1017/CBO9780511609268

Lawler, J., Coppola, J., Feather-Gannon, S., Hill, J., Kline, R., Mosley, P., & Taylor, A. (2010). Community empowerment and service learning practices through computer science curricula of a major metropolitan university. *Journal of Computing Sciences in Colleges, 25*(3), 10.

Lay, M., Wahlstrom, B., Rude, C., Selfe, C., & Selzer, J. (2006). *Technical communication* (3rd ed.). New York, NY: McGraw Hill.

Lazar, J., & Norcio, A. (2000). Service-research: Community partnerships for research and training. *Journal of Informatics Education and Research, 2*(3), 21–25.

Lazarus, J., Erasmus, M., Hendricks, D., Nduna, J., & Slamat, J. (2008). Embedding community engagement in South African higher education. *Education. Citizenship and Social Justice, 3*(1), 57–83. doi:10.1177/1746197907086719

Leontiev, A. N. (1978). *Activity, consciousness, and personality.* Englewood Cliffs, NJ: Prentice-Hall.

Lerner, J. (2006). Let the people decide: Transformative community development through participatory budgeting in Canada. *Shelterforce Online, 146.* Retrieved from http://www.nhi.org/online/issues/146/canadianbudgeting.html

Leseure, M. J., Bauer, J., Birdi, K., Neely, A., & Denyer, D. (2004). Adoption of promising practices: A systematic review of the evidence. *International Journal of Management Reviews, 5/6*(3/4), 169–190. doi:10.1111/j.1460-8545.2004.00102.x

Lessig, L. (2001). *The future of ideas: The fate of the commons in a connected world.* New York, NY: Random House.

Lessig, L. (2004). *Free culture: The nature and future of creativity.* New York, NY: Penguin Books.*Composition* 11 (1991): 57-72.

Levine, P., Fung, A., & Gastil, J. (2005). Future directions for public deliberation. In J. Gastil & P. Levine (Eds.), *The deliberative democracy handbook: Strategies for effective civic engagement in the twenty-first century* (271-288). San Francisco, CA: Jossey-Bass.

Levy, S. (2006). *The perfect thing: How the iPod shuffles commerce, culture, and coolness.* New York, NY: Simon & Schuster.

Lewin, K. (1948). *Resolving social conflicts.* New York, NY: Harper and Row.

Lewin, K. (1935). *A dynamic theory of personality.* New York, NY: McGraw-Hill.

Liazos, A., & Liss, J. R. (2009). *Civic engagement in the classroom: Strategies for incorporating education for civic and social responsibility in the undergraduate curriculum.* A Project Pericles White Paper, August, 4.

Lichtenthaler, U., & Ernst, H. (2008). Innovation intermediaries: Why Internet marketplaces for technology have not yet met the expectations. *Creativity and Innovation Management, 17*(1), 14–25. doi:10.1111/j.1467-8691.2007.00461.x

Lichtveld, M. Y., & Cioffi, J. P. (2003). Public health workforce development: Progress, challenges, and opportunities. *Journal of Public Health Management and Practice, 9*(6), 443–450.

Life, S. C. (2010). *Natural history of South Carolina.* Retrieved on February 28, 2010, from http://www.clemson.edu/cafls/sclife/

Lippert, S. K., & Davis, M. (2006). A conceptual model integrating trust into planned change activities to enhance technology adoption behavior. *Journal of Information Science, 32*(5), 434–448. doi:10.1177/0165551506066042

Liu, C. C., & Kao, L. C. (2007). Do handheld devices facilitate face-to-face collaboration? Handheld devices with large shared display groupware to facilitate group interactions. *Journal of Computer Assisted Learning, 23*(4), 285–299. doi:10.1111/j.1365-2729.2007.00234.x

Lombardi, M. M. (2007). Approaches that work: How authentic learning is transforming higher education. *EDUCAUSE.* Retrieved February 22, 2010 from http://net.educause.edu/ir/library/pdf/ELI3013.pdf

Lorenzo, G. (2008). The Sloan semester. *Journal of Asynchronous Learning Networks, 12*(2), 5–40.

Louv, R. (2005). *Last child in the woods: Saving our children from nature-deficit disorder.* Chapel Hill, NC: Algonquin Books.

Lundby, K. (2008). Editorial: Mediatized stories: Mediation perspectives on digital storytelling. *New Media & Society, 10*(3), 363–371. doi:10.1177/1461444808089413

Lupton, E. (1993). *Mechanical brides: Women and machines from home to office.* New York, NY: Cooper-Hewitt National Museum of Design.

Luria, A. R. (1976). *Cognitive development: Its cultural and social foundations.* Cambridge, MA: Harvard University Press.

Lynch, D. (2002). Professors should embrace technology in courses. *The Chronicle of Higher Education, 48*(19), 15–16.

Lyotard, J.-F. (1992). *The postmodern explained: Correspondence, 1982-1985.* Minneapolis, MN: University of Minnesota Press.

MacNamara, D. E. (1977). Medical models in corrections–requiescat in pace. *Criminology, 14*(4), 439–448. doi:10.1111/j.1745-9125.1977.tb00036.x

Madoc-Jones, I., & Parrott, L. (2005). Virtual social work education—theory and experience. *Social Work Education, 24*(7), 755–768. doi:10.1080/02615470500238678

Malvey, D. M., Hamby, E. F., & Fottler, M. D. (2006). E-service-learning: A pedagogic innovation for healthcare management education. *The Journal of Health Administration Education, 23*(2), 181–198.

Martin, D. (2007). Bureacratizing ethics: Institutional review boards and participatory research. *ACME: An International E-Journal for Critical Geographies, 6*(3), 319–328.

Martin, A. SeBlonka, K., & Tryon, E. (2009). The challenge of short term service. In R. Stoecker & E. A. Tryon (Eds.), *The unheard voices: Community organizations and service learning.* Philadelphia, PA: Temple University Press.

Martínez, M., & Vásquez, O. A. (2006). *Sustainability: La clase mágica beyond its boundaries.* Unpublished manuscript.

Marullo, S., Cooke, D., Willis, J., Rollins, A., Burke, J., Bonilla, P., & Waldref, V. (2003). Community-based research assessments: Some principles and practices. *Michigan Journal of Community Service Learning, 9*(3), 57–68.

Maryland Online. (2006). *Quality matters.* Retrieved March 23, 2010, from http://qualitymatters.com

Matthews, C., & Zimmerman, B. B. (1999). Integrating service learning and technical communication: Benefits and challenges. *Technical Communication Quarterly, 8*(4), 383–404.

Maurrasse, D. J. (2002). Higher education-community partnerships: Assessing progress in the field. *Nonprofit and Voluntary Sector Quarterly, 31,* 131. doi:10.1177/0899764002311006

Mazzone, E., Xu, D., & Reed, J. (2007). Design in evaluation: Reflections on designing for children's technology. *British Computer Society: Proceedings of the 21st BCS HCI Group Conference.*

McCallister, L. A. (2008) Lessons learned while developing a community-based learning initiative. *National Service-Learning Clearinghouse, 10.*

McCann, C. (2009). *Let the great world spin.* London, UK: Bloomsbury.

McCann, T. M., Johannesen, L. R., Kahn, E., Smagorinsky, P., & Smith, M. W. (Eds.). (2005). *Reflective teaching, reflective learning: How to develop critically engaged readers, writers, and speakers.* Portsmouth, NH: Heinemann.

McCarty, H. J. (2006). Educating felons: Reflections on higher education in prison. *Radical History Review, 96,* 87–94. doi:10.1215/01636545-2006-005

McKinney, A. (2009). *WISE pedagogy on-demand: Free training for LIS instructors.* Poster Presentation at the American Library Association Annual Conference, Chicago, IL.

Meadows, D. (2003). Digital storytelling: Research-based practice in new media. *Visual Communication, 2*(2), 189–193. doi:10.1177/1470357203002002004

Melville, W., & Wallace, J. (2007). Workplace as community: Perspectives on science teachers professional learning. *Journal of Science Teacher Education, 18,* 543–558. doi:10.1007/s10972-007-9048-5

Menand, L. (2009). *The marketplace of ideas: Reform and resistance in the American university.* New York, NY: W.W. Norton.

Mercado, A. (2007). Address to American Education Research Association. Chicago, IL.

Merseth, K. (1991). Supporting beginning teachers with computer networks. *Journal of Teacher Education, 42*(2), 140–147. doi:10.1177/002248719104200207

Meyer, R. C. (2007). *A case study of one-to-one computing: The effects on teaching and learning.* Doctoral dissertation. Available from ProQuest Dissertations and Theses database. (UMI No. 3289413)

Michigan Department of Corrections. (2010). Retrieved July 5, 2010, from http://www.michigan.gov/corrections/0,1607,7-119--201925--,00.html

Middleton, R. L., Frederick, R. A., & Norman, R. L. (2000) *UAH network-based engineering classes for international design teams.* Paper presented at The Huntsville Simulation Conference, Simulation in the New Millennium, The Practice and the Effect, The Holiday Inn at Research Park, Huntsville, Alabama.

Mihalynuk, T. V., & Seifer, S. D. (2004). Partnerships for higher education service-learning. *Service-Learning*, September.

Mill, R. C. (2004). Integrating the student into the business curriculum. In R. Clute (Ed.), *Proceedings of the 2004 International Applied Business Research Conference* (p. 1). San Juan, PR: The Clute Institute for Academic Research.

Miller, B. (2003). *Critical hours: After school programs and educational success.* Brookline, MA: Nellie Mae Education Foundation.

Minkler, M., & Wallerstein, N. (2008). *Community-based participatory research for health: From process to outcomes* (2nd ed.). San Francisco, CA: Jossey-Bass Publishers.

Minnesota Department of Corrections. (2010). *Offender assignment and compensation plan.* Directive 204.010. Retrieved February 20, 2010, from http://www.doc.state.mn.us/DocPolicy2/Document/204.010.htm

Mitchell, T. D. (2008). Traditional vs. critical service-learning: Engaging the literature to differentiate two models. *Michigan Journal of Community Service Learning, 51.*

Modern Language Association. (2007). *Report of the MLA taskforce on evaluating scholarship for tenure and promotion.* Retrieved March 23, 2010, from http://www.mla.org/tenure_promotion

Modern Language Association. (2009). The AAUP statement on distance education: Special considerations for language and literature. *ADE Bulletin, 147-48,* 127–128.

Moll, L. C., Anderson, A., & Diaz, E. (1985). *Third college and CERRC: A university-community system for promoting academic excellence.* Paper presented at the University of California Linguistic Minority Conference, Lake Tahoe, CA.

Monk, D. H., & King, J. (1994). Multi-level teacher resource effects on pupil performance in secondary mathematics and science: The role of teacher subject matter preparation. In R. Ehrenberg (Ed.), *Contemporary policy issues: Choices and consequences in education.* Ithaca, NY: ILR Press.

Montague, R., & Pluzhenskaia, M. (2007). Web-based information science education (WISE): Collaboration to explore and expand quality in LIS online education. *Journal of Education for Library and Information Science, 48*(1), 36–51.

Montes, M. (2009). *Latino youth in expanded learner time programs.* Washington, DC: National Council of La Raza.

Moore, D. T. (1990). Experiential education as a critical discourse. In M. H. Wasburn, K. Laskowitz-Weingart, & M. Summers (Eds.), Service-learning and civic engagement: Recommendations based on evaluations of a course. *Journal of Higher Education Outreach and Engagement, 9*(2), 59-75.

Moore, J. (2005). *The Sloan Consortium quality framework and the five pillars.* Retrieved from http://www.sloan-c.org/publications/books/qualityframework.pdf

Morse, S. S. (2003). Building academic-practice partnerships: The Center for Public Health Preparedness at the Columbia University Mailman School of Public Health, before and after 9/11. *Journal of Public Health Management and Practice, 9*(5), 427–432.

Moseley, D., Higgins, S., Bramald, R., Hardman, F., Miller, J., Mraz, M., et al. Stout, J. (1999). *Ways forward with ICT: Effective pedagogy using information and communications technology for literacy and numeracy in primary schools.* Newcastle Upon Tyne, UK: University of Newcastle Upon Tyne. Retrieved from http://www.ncl.ac.uk/ecls/research/project_ttaict/

Motorola, Inc. (2009). Making history: Developing the portable cellular system. Retrieved February 20, 2010, from http://www.motorola.com/content.jsp?globalObjectId=7662-10813

Murphy, N. A., & Carbone, P. S. (2008). Promoting the participation of children with disabilities in sports, recreation, and physical activities. *Pediatrics, 121*(5), 1057–1061. doi:10.1542/peds.2008-0566

Muscott, H. S. (2001). Service-learning and character education as antidotes for children with egos that cannot perform. *Reclaiming Children and Youth, 10*(2), 91–99.

N.C. State Board of Education. (2003). *Improving student achievement through professional development: Final report to the state board of education and the state superintendent*. Raleigh, NC: NC Professional Development Committee. Retrieved from http://www.ncpublicschools.org/docs/profdev/reports/studentachievement.pdf

Nardi, B. A., & Whitaker, S. (2002). The place of face-to-face communication in distributed work. In P. Hinds, & S. Kiesler (Eds.), *Distributed work* (pp. 83–110). Cambridge, MA: MIT Press.

National Center for Education Statistics (NCES). (1996). *Statistical analysis report: Out-of-field teaching and educational quality*. National Center of Education Statistics, U.S. Department of Education Institute of Education Sciences. Retrieved March 1, 2010 from http://nces.ed.gov/pubs/web/96040.asp

National Council of La Raza. (2009). *Investing in our future: The status of Latino children and youth in the United States*. Washington, D.C.

National Science Board. (2004). *Science and engineering indicators 2004*. Two volumes. Arlington, VA: National Science Foundation (volume 1, NSB 04-1; volume 2, NSB 04-1A).

Ndulu, B., Chakraborti, L., Lijane, L., Ramachandran, V., & Wolgin, J. (2007). *Challenges of African growth: Opportunities, constraints and strategic directions*. Washington, DC: The World Bank.

Ndulu, B. J. (2004). Human capital flight: Stratification, globalization, and the challenges to tertiary education in Africa. *JHEA/RESA, 2*(1), 57–91.

Neathery, M. F. (1997). Elementary and secondary students' perceptions toward science and the correlation with gender, ethnicity, ability, grade, and science achievement. *Electronic Journal of Science Education, 2*(1), 11.

Newell, R. (2003). *Passion for learning: How project-based learning meets the needs of 21st century students*. Lanham, MD: The Scarecrow Press, Inc.

Njenga, J. K., & Fourie, L. C. H. (2010). The myths about e-learning in higher education. *British Journal of Educational Technology, 41*(2), 199–212. doi:10.1111/j.1467-8535.2008.00910.x

Noel Studio Mission. (2010). *Mission statement*. Retrieved on 13 November, 2010, from http://www.studio.eku.edu/mission_statement.pdf.

Noguera, P. A. (2004). Transforming high schools. *Educational Leadership, 61*(8), 26–31.

Norman, R., & Frederick, R. A. (2000). Integrating technical editing students into a multidisciplinary engineering project. *Technical Communication Quarterly, 9*(2), 163–189.

Nunes, M. B., & McPherson, M. (2007). Why designers cannot be agnostic about pedagogy: The influence of constructivist thinking in design of e-learning for HE. [SCI]. *Studies in Computational Intelligence, 62*, 7–30. doi:10.1007/978-3-540-71974-8_2

O'Reilly, T. (2005). What is Web 2.0: Design patterns and business models for the next generation of software. Retrieved March 6, 2010, from http://oreilly.com/web2/archive/what-is-web-20.html

Oates, K. K., & Leavitt, L. H. (2003). *Service-learning and learning communities: Tools for integration and assessment*. Washington, DC: Association of American Colleges and Universities.

OECD. (2001). The well-being of nations, the role of human and social capital. Centre for Educational Research and Innovation. Paris, France: Organisation for Economic Co-operation and Development.

Ohler, J. (2008). *Digital storytelling in the classroom: New media pathways to literacy, learning and creativity*. Thousand Oaks, CA: Corwin Press.

One Laptop per Child. (2009, December 22). *Deployment statistics*. Retrieved February 21, 2010 from http://wiki.laptop.org/go/Deployments

Organisation for Economic Cooperation and Development. (1998). *The OECD jobs strategy: Fostering entrepreneurship*. OECD Publishing.

Osborne, M., & Oberski, I. (2004). University continuing education: The role of communications and Information Technology. *Journal of European Industrial Training, 28*(5), 414–428. doi:10.1108/03090590410533099

Oyelaran-Oyeyinka, B., & Lal, K. (2005). Internet diffusion in sub-Saharan Africa: A cross-country analysis. *Telecommunications Policy*, *29*(7), 507–527. doi:10.1016/j.telpol.2005.05.002

*Pact website*. (2010). Retrieved July 10, 2010 from http://www.pactworld.org/

Painter-Morland, M., Fontrodona, J., Hoffman, W. M., & Rowe, M. (2003). Conversations across continents: Teaching business ethics online. *Journal of Business Ethics*, *48*, 75–88. doi:10.1023/B:BUSI.0000004384.53153.97

Panits, T. (1997). Collaborative versus cooperative learning: Comparing the two definitions helps understand the nature of interactive learning. *Cooperative Learning and College Teaching, 8*(2).

Paretti, M. C., McNair, L. D., & Holloway-Attaway, L. (2007). Teaching technical communication in an era of distributed work: A case study of collaboration between U.S. and Swedish students. *Technical Communication Quarterly*, *16*(3), 327–352.

Park, C. W. (1943). *Ambassador to industry: The ideas and life of Herman Schneider*. Indianapolis, IN/ New York, NY: The Bobbs-Merrill Company.

Parker, L. L. (2008). Technology in support of young English learners in and out of school. In L. L. Parker (Ed.), *Technology-mediated learning environments for young English learners: Connections in and out of school* (pp. 213–250). New York, NY: Erlbaum.

Patterson, J., & Loomis, C. (2007). Combining service learning and social enterprise in higher education to achieve academic learning, business skills development, citizenship education and volunteerism. In A. Campbell, & L. Norton (2007). *Learning, Teaching and Assessing in Higher Education: Developing Reflective Practice*. Exeter: Learning Matters, 120-129.

Patterson, J., & Patterson, A. (2009). A call to arms: Developing students with diverse backgrounds through service-learning. In R. Sage (2010). *Meeting the needs of students with diverse backgrounds.* (pp. 116-129). London, UK: Continuum.

Payne, D. A. (2000). *Evaluating service-learning activities and programs*. Lanham, MD: The Scarecrow Press.

Pedagogy, W. I. S. E. (2009a). *Introduction to online pedagogy*. Retrieved from http://introductiononlinepedagogy.pbworks.com/

Pedagogy, W. I. S. E. (2009b). *WISE excellence in online teaching award recipients: Best practices 2009*. Retrieved from http://wisepedagogy.com/bestpractices2009.shtml

Pedagogy, W. I. S. E. (2009c). *WISE pedagogy website*. Retrieved from http://www.wisepedagogy.com

Pedagogy, W. I. S. E. (2010a). *Annemck's bookmarks on delicious: Online pedagogy/e-learning bundle*. Retrieved from http://delicious.com/annemck/bundle:OnlinePedagogy%2FeLearning

Pedagogy, W. I. S. E. (2010b). *WISE pedagogy blog*. Retrieved from http://www.wisepedagogy.com/blog/

Pedagogy, W. I. S. E. (2010c). *WISE pedagogy Twitter feed*. Retrieved from http://twitter.com/wisepedagogy

Peers, F. (1969). *The politics of Canadian broadcasting, 1920-1951*. Toronto, Canada: University of Toronto Press.

Penuel, W. R. (2006). Implementation and effects of one-to-one computing initiatives: A research synthesis. *Journal of Research on Technology in Education*, *38*(3), 329–348.

Penuel, W. R., Fishman, B. J., Yamaguchi, R., & Gallagher, L. P. (2007). What makes professional development effective? Strategies that foster curriculum implementation. *American Educational Research Journal*, *44*(4), 921–958. doi:10.3102/0002831207308221

Petkus, J. (2000). A theoretical and practical framework for service-learning in marketing. *Journal of Marketing Education*, *22*, 64–70. doi:10.1177/0273475300221008

Piderit, S. K. (2000). Rethinking resistance and recognizing ambivalence: A multidimensional view of attitudes toward an organizational change. *Academy of Management Review*, *25*(4), 783–794. doi:10.2307/259206

Pineau, C. (Director). (2006). *Africa: Open for business*. Available from http://www.africaopenforbusiness.com/

Pompa, L. (2002). Service-learning as crucible: Reflections on immersion, context, power, and transformation. *Michigan Journal of Community Service Learning*, *9*(1), 67–76.

Pond, W. K. (2002). Distributed education in the 21st century: Implication for quality assurance. *Online Journal of Distance Learning Administration, 5*(11). Retrieved on July 8, 2008, from www.westga.edu/~distance/ojdla/summer52/pond52.html

Power, S., Rees, G., & Taylor, C. (2005). *The promise and perils of area-based initiatives: The UK experience.* (The Times Educational Supplement, 22nd April 2005).

Prasad, B. (1998). Decentralized cooperation: A distributed approach to team design in a concurrent engineering organization. *Team Performance Management, 4*(4), 138–165. doi:10.1108/13527599810224624

Pratt, M. L. (1991). Arts of the contact zone. *Profession, 91*, 33–40.

Prensky, M. (2001). Digital natives, digital immigrants. *Horizon, 9*(5), 1–6. doi:10.1108/10748120110424816

Prensky, M. (2001b). Digital natives, digital immigrants, part II: Do they really think differently? *Horizon, 9*(6). doi:10.1108/10748120110424843

Prentice, M. (2004). Twenty-first century learning: How institutionalized is service-learning? *The Journal for Civic Commitment, 4*, 1, 2, 5.

Price, M., & Chen, H. (2003). Promises and challenges: Exploring a collaborative telementoring program in a pre-service teacher education program. *Mentoring & Tutoring, 11*(1), 105–117. doi:10.1080/1361126032000054844

Putnam, R. D. (1995). Bowling alone: America's declining social capital. *Journal of Democracy, 6*(1), 65–78. Retrieved from http://muse.jhu.edu/demo/journal_of_democracy/v006/putnam.html. doi:10.1353/jod.1995.0002

Ragan, J. (1999). Good teaching is good teaching: An emerging set of guiding principles and practices for the design and development of distance education. *CAUSE/EFFECT, 22*(1). Retrieved March 23, 2010, from http://net.educause.edu/ir/library/html/cem/cem99/cem9915.html

Rainey, K., Turner, R., & Dayton, D. (2005). Do curricula correspond to managerial expectations? Core competencies for technical communicators. *Technical Communication, 52*(3), 323–352.

Rainie, L. (2010, January 5). *Internet, broadband and cell phone statistics.* Pew Internet & American Life Project, (p. 4). Retrieved February 15, 2010, from http://www.pewinternet.org/Reports/2010/ Internet-broadband-and-cell-phone-statistics.aspx?r=1

Ravitz, J., & Becker, H. J. (2000). *Evidence for computer use being related to more constructivist practices and to changes in practice in amore constructivist-compatible direction.* Paper presented at the annual meeting of the American Educational Research Association, New Orleans, LA.

Reardon, K. M. (1998). Participatory action research as service-learning. *New Directions for Teaching and Learning, 73*, 57–64. doi:10.1002/tl.7307

Reaves, W. E., & Narvaez, J. G. (2006). Managing and resolving organizational conflict in school-university partnerships through sound planning and design. *Journal of School Public Relations, 27*(2), 196–210.

Reblando, B. M. (2009, August 15). Sultan Kudarat students invent new cement block. *Manila Bulletin*, 2009. Retrieved February 15, 2010, from http://www.mb.com.ph/node/216005/

REDDES. (2010). *REDDES' wiki.* Retrieved February 13, 2010, from http://www.rtpd.net/reddes/wiki

*Regional Stewardship.* (2010). Retrieved on 5 February 2011, from http://www.cedet.eku.edu/stewardship.php.

Reid, N., & Shah, I. (2007). The role of laboratory work in university chemistry. *Chemistry Education and Research Practice, 8*(2), 172–185.

Reiman, A., Corbell, K., & Thomas, E. (2007). *New teacher support. UNC Dean's Council on Teacher Education: Summary Evaluation Report.* UNC University School Programs.

Relaño Pastor, A. M., & Vásquez, O. A. (In press). Accountability of the informal: Challenges and new directions. In *Pedagogies: An International Journal.* Nanyang, Singapore.

Richards, R. (2006). Users, interactivity generation. *New Media & Society, 8*(4), 531–550. doi:10.1177/1461444806064485

Riffell, S., & Sibley, D. (2005). Using Web-based instruction to improve large undergraduate biology courses: An evaluation of a hybrid course format. *Computers & Education, 44*(3), 217–235. doi:10.1016/j.compedu.2004.01.005

Rifkin, S. B. (2003). A framework linking community empowerment and health equity: It is a matter of choice. *Journal of Health, Population, and Nutrition, 21*(3), 168–180.

Riley, R. W., & Wofford, H. (2000). The reaffirmation of the declaration of principles. *Phi Delta Kappan, 81*(9), 670–672.

RMPK Group, Inc. A.A. Baker and Associates, & Strategic Planning Group, Inc. (2002). *The Midtown strategic planning initiative.* Retrieved from www.stpete.org/stpete/midtownsummarymaster.pdf

Rodriguez, K. (2010, June 17). 'La clase magica' program helps children succeed by using technology. *UTSA Today*.

Root, S., Callahan, J., & Sepanski, J. (2002). Building teaching dispositions and service-learning practice: A multi-site study. *Michigan Journal of Community Service-Learning, 8*(2), 50–60.

Rose, J. (2009). *Independent review of the primary curriculum: Final report.* Retrieved from http://publications.teachernet.gov.uk/default.aspx?PageFunction=productdetails&PageMode=publications&ProductId=DCSF-00499-2009&-

Rovai, A. (2002). Building sense of community at a distance. *International Review of Research in Open and Distance Learning, 3*(1), 1–16.

Rowan, B., Chiang, F., & Miller, R. J. (1997). Using research on employees' performance to study the effects of teachers on students' achievement. *Sociology of Education, 70*(4), 256–284. doi:10.2307/2673267

Rumberger, R., & Tran, L. (2006). *Preschool participation and the cognitive and social development of language minority students.* Washington, DC: National Center for Education Statistics.

Russell, M., Bebell, D., & Higgins, J. (2004). Laptop learning: A comparison of teaching and learning in upper elementary classrooms equipped with shared carts of laptops and permanent 1:1 laptops. *Journal of Educational Computing Research, 30*(4), 313–330. doi:10.2190/6E7K-F57M-6UY6-QAJJ

Russell, I. M. (2005). *A national framework for youth action and engagement: Executive summary to the Russell Commission.* London, UK: Her Majesty's Stationery Office.

Rye, S. A. (2008). Dimensions of flexibility-students, communication technology and distributed education. *International Journal of Media, Technology and Lifelong Learning, 4*(1). Retrieved from http://www.seminar.net/images/stories/vol4-issue1/rye-dimensionsofflexibility.pdf

Sabo Flores, K. (2008). *Youth participatory evaluation: Strategies for engaging young people.* San Francisco: Jossey-Bass.

Sahlins, M. D., & Service, E. R. (1997). *Evolution and culture.* Ann Arbor, MI: University of Michigan Press.

Sandholtz, J. H., Ringstaff, C., & Dwyer, D. C. (1997). *Teaching with technology: Creating student-centered classrooms.* New York, NY: Teachers College Press.

Sandy, M., & Holland, B. A. (2006). Different worlds and common ground: Community partner perspectives on campus-community relationships. *Michigan Journal of Community Service Learning, 13*(1), 30–43.

Saulnier, B. M. (2004). Service-learning in Information Systems: Significant learning for tomorrow's computer professionals. In D. Colton (Ed.), *Proceedings of the Information Systems Education Conference* (p. 2255). Newport, RI: Educators Special Interest Group (EDSIG).

Saunders, M., Charlier, B., & Bonamy, J. (2005). Using evaluation to create provisional stabilities: Bridging innovation in higher education change processes. *Evaluation, 11*(1), 37–54. doi:10.1177/1356389005053188

Savageau, J. (2010, January 14). Citizen journalism and tweets bring Haiti's horror to the world. *Web 2.0 Journal.* Retrieved from http://web2.sys-con.com/node/1248590

425

Savitz, A. W., & Weber, K. (2006). *The triple bottom line: How today's best-run companies are achieving economic, social and environmental success-and how you can too.* San Francisco, CA: John Wiley & Sons.

SC Educational Television. (2010). *K-12 educational Web portal: SC LIFE virtual field trips.* Retrieved on February 28, 2010, from http://www.knowitall.org/sclife

Schein, E. (1990). Organizational culture. *The American Psychologist, 45*(2), 109–119. doi:10.1037/0003-066X.45.2.109

Schirmer, J. (2010, February 10). *Two-year review research summary* (draft). Retrieved

Schisa, K., & McKinney, A. (2008). *Web-based Information Science education.* Presentation at the American Distance Education Consortium Annual Conference, Minneapolis, MN.

Schwartz-Bloom, R. D., & Halpin, M. J. (2003). Integrating pharmacology topics in high school biology and chemistry classes improves performance. *Journal of Research in Science Teaching, 40*(9), 922–938. doi:10.1002/tea.10116

ScienceMaster Final Evaluation Report. (2008). *Internal program evaluation document provided to the project team that summarized final outcomes.*

SCNOW.com. (2008). *Tradition, heritage keep folks celebrating tobacco industry.* Retrieved on February 28, 2010, from http://www2.scnow.com/scp/news/local/article/tradition_heritage_keep_folks_celebrating_tobacco_industry/14814/

Scorce, R. A. (2010). Perspectives concerning the utilization of service learning projects for a computer science course. *Journal of Computing Sciences in Colleges, 25*(3), 75–81.

Scott, J. B. (2004). Rearticulating civic engagement through cultural studies and service-learning. *Technical Communication Quarterly, 13*(3), 289–306. doi:10.1207/s15427625tcq1303_4

Scott, J. B. (2008). The practice of usability: Teaching user engagement through service-learning. *Technical Communication Quarterly, 17*(4), 381–412. doi:10.1080/10572250802324929

Selber, S. A. (2004). *Multiliteracies for a digital age.* Carbondale, IL: Southern Illinois University Press.

Selfe, C. L., & Selfe, R. J. (1994). The politics of the interface: Power and its exercise in electronic contact zones. *College Composition and Communication, 45*(4), 480–504. doi:10.2307/358761

Selfe, C. L. (1999a). Technology and literacy: A story about the perils of not paying attention. *College Composition and Communication, 50*(3), 411–436. doi:10.2307/358859

Selfe, C. L. (1999b). *Technology and literacy in the twenty-first century: The importance of paying attention.* Carbondale, IL: Southern Illinois University Press.

Selfe, R. J. (2007). Sustaining multimodal composition. *Multimodal composition: Resources for teachers.* Cresskill, NK: Hampton.

Sen, A. (1989). Development as capability expansion. In *Readings in human development, concepts, measures and policies for a development paradigm. Human Development Report United Nations Development Program.* New York, NY: Oxford University Press.

Senge, P. M., & Scharmer, C. O. (2001). Community action research: Learning as a community of practitioners, consultants, and researchers. In P. Reason & H. Bradbury (Eds.), *Handbook of action research* (pp. 195–206). Los Angeles, CA: SAGE Publications.

Sharma, S., & Rai, A. (2003). An assessment of the relationship between ISD leadership characteristics and IS innovation adoption in organizations. *Information & Management, 40*(5), 391–401. doi:10.1016/S0378-7206(02)00049-6

Shirky, C. (2001). Listening to Napster. In A. Oram (Ed.), *Peer-to-peer: Harnessing the benefits of a disruptive technology* (pp. 21–37). Sebastopol, CA: O'Reilly.

Sidhu, R. (2007). GATS and the new developmentalism: Governing transnational education. *Comparative Education Review, 51*(2), 203–227. doi:10.1086/512020

Slack, J. D. (1996). The theory and method of articulation in cultural studies. In D. Morley, & K.-H. Chen (Eds.), *Stuart Hall: Critical dialogues in cultural studies* (pp. 112–130). London, UK: Routledge.

Smartt, R. (2007). *ConnectRichmond*. Retrieved from http://www.connectrichmond.org/

Smith, J. (2001). Global civil society? Transnational social movement organizations and social capital. In B. Edwards, M. W. Foley, & M. Diani (Eds.), *Beyond Tocqueville: Civil society and the social capital debate in comparative perspective* (pp. 194–206). Hanover, NH: University Press of New England.

Smith, A. (2010). *Mobile access 2010*. Pew Internet & American Life Project. Retrieved from http://www.pewinternet.org/Reports/2010/Mobile-Access-2010.aspx?r=1

Smith, S. (2010). Beyond the dissertation monograph. *MLA Newsletter*. New York, NY: Modern Language Association.

Society for Applied Learning Technology [SALT]. (2010). *SALT website*. Retrieved from http://www.salt.org/salt.asp?ss=1

Solorzano, D. G., & Yosso, T. J. (2001). Critical race and latcrit theory and method: Counter storytelling. *International Journal of Qualitative Studies in Education*, *14*(4), 471–495. doi:10.1080/09518390110063365

Spinuzzi, C. (2007). Guest editor's introduction: Technical communication in the age of distributed work. *Technical Communication Quarterly*, *16*(3), 265–277.

Sproull, L., & Kiesler, S. (1991). Computers, networks, and work. *Scientific American*, *265*(3), 116–123. doi:10.1038/scientificamerican0991-116

Stanz, K., & Fourie, L. C. H. (2002). The need for online learning support. *Proceedings of the 5th Annual industrial psychology Conference*, Pretoria, 13-14 June.

Starr, L. (2008). The ethnography of infrastructure. *American Behavioral Scientist*. Retrieved from http://abs.sagepub.com

Steiner, R., Tirivayi, N., Jensen, M., & Gakio, K. (2004). *Africa tertiary institution connectivity survey*. Retrieved on September 13, 2006, from http://www.worldbank.org/afr/teia/pdfs/ATICS_2004_Report.pdf

Stenberg, P., Morehart, M., Vogel, S., Cromartie, J., Breneman, V., & Brown, D. (2009). Broadband Internet's value for rural America. *Economic Research Report Number, 78*. United States Department of Agriculture. Retrieved March 6, 2010, from http://www.ers.usda.gov/Publications/ERR78/ERR78.pdf

Steward, D. (2004). The master's degree in modern languages since 1966. *ADE Bulletin*, *136*, 50–68.

Stoecker, R., Tryon, E. A., & Hilgendorf, A. (Eds.). (2009). *The unheard voices: Community organizations and service learning*. Philadelphia, PA: Temple University Press.

Stoecker, R. (2002). Practices and challenges of community-based research. *Journal of Public Affairs*, *6*(1), 219–239.

Stoecker, R. (2007). The data and research practices and needs of non-profit organizations. *Journal of Sociology and Social Welfare*, *34*, 97–119.

Stoecker, R. (2008). Challenging institutional barriers to community-based research. *Action Research*, *6*, 49–67. doi:10.1177/1476750307083721

Stoecker, R., & Beckman, M. (2010). Making higher education civic engagement matter in the community. *Campus Compact*. Retrieved March 6, 2010, from http://www.compact.org/wp-content/uploads/2010/02/engagementproof-1.pdf

Strait, J., & Sauer, T. (2004). Constructing experiential learning for online courses: The birth of e-service-learning. *Educause Quarterly, 1*, 62-65. Retrieved March 13, 2010, from http://net.educause.edu/ir/library/pdf/eqm04110.pdf

Strand, K., Marullo, S., Cutforth, N., Stoecker, R., & Donohue, P. (2003). Principles of best practice for community-based research. *Michigan Journal of Community Service Learning*, *9*(3), 5–15.

Stutts, N. (2003). ConnectRichmond: Collecting and sharing information to build a stronger community. *Community Technology Review*, Spring 2003. Retrieved on Nov. 9, 2010, from http://www.comtechreview.org/spring-2003/000038.html.

Sullivan, P., & Porter, J. (1997). *Opening spaces: Writing technologies and critical research practices*. Greenwich, CT: Ablex Publishing Corporation.

Suskie, L. (2004). *Assessing student learning: A common sense guide*. Boston, MA: Anker Pub. Co.

Swanson, B. E., & Ramiller, N. C. (2004). Innovating mindfully with Information Technology. *Management Information Systems Quarterly, 28*(4), 553–583.

Tan, J., & Phillips, J. (2005). Incorporating service learning into computer science courses. *Journal of Computing Sciences in Colleges, 20*(4), 57–62.

Taskforce on Active Citizenship. (2007). *Report of the Taskforce on Active Citizenship*. Dublin, Ireland: Secretariat of the Taskforce on Active Citizenship. Retrieved July 20, 2010, from http://www.activecitizen.ie/UP-LOADEDFILES/Mar07/Taskforce%20Report%20to%20Government%20%28Mar%2007%29.pdf

Taylor, J. A., & Bedford, T. (2004). Staff perceptions of factors related to non-completion in higher education. *Studies in Higher Education, 29*(3), 375–394. doi:10.1080/0307507042000168263 7

Teferra, D., & Altbach, P. G. (2004). African higher education: Challenges for the 21st century. *Higher Education, 47*, 21–50. doi:10.1023/B:HIGH.0000009822.49980.30

Terry, A., & Bohnenberger, J. (2003). Fostering a cycle of caring in our gifted youth. *Journal of Secondary Gifted Education, 15*(1), 23–32.

TFHES. (2000). *Higher education in developing countries peril and promise*. Washington, DC: International Bank for Reconstruction and Development / The World Bank.

110th United States Congress. (2008). *H.R. 3036: No Child Left Inside Act of 2008*. Civic Impulse LLC. Retrieved November 27, 2009, from http://www.govtrack.us/congress/bill.xpd?bill=h110-3036&tab=summary

The Higher Learning Commission. (2003). *Handbook of accreditation* (3rd ed.). Chicago, IL: The Higher Learning Commission.

Thompson, J. (2005). The new visibility. *Theory, Culture & Society, 22*(6), 31–51. doi:10.1177/0263276405059413

Thumin, N. (2008). It's good for them to know my story: Cultural mediation as tension. In K. Lundby (Ed.), *Digital storytelling, mediatized: Self-representations in new media stories* (pp. 85–103). New York, NY: Peter Lang Publishing, Inc.

Tiamiyu, M. F., & Bailey, L. (2001). Human services for the elderly and the role of university-community collaboration: Perceptions of human service agency workers. *Educational Gerontology, 27*(6), 479–492. doi:10.1080/036012701316894171

Tomlinson, J. (2003). Globalization and cultural identity. In D. Held, & A. McGrew (Eds.), *The global transformations reader: An introduction to the globalization debate* (2nd ed., pp. 269–277). Cambridge, MA: Polity Press.

Toncar, M. F., Reid, J. S., Burns, D. J., Anderson, C. E., & Nguyen, H. P. (2006). Uniform assessment of the benefits of service learning: The development, evaluation, and implementation of the Seleb Scale. *Journal of Marketing Theory and Practice, 14*(3), 223–238. doi:10.2753/MTP1069-6679140304

Toncar, M., Reid, J., & Anderson, C. (2004). Student perceptions of service-learning projects: Exploring the impact of project ownership, project difficulty and class difficulty. In R. Clute (Ed.), *Proceedings of the 2004 International Applied Business Research Conference* (pp. 2-8). San Juan, PR: The Clute Institute for Academic Research.

Toupin, L., & Plews, B. (2007). Exploring the looming leadership deficit in the voluntary and nonprofit sector. *The Philanthropist, 21*(2), 128–137.

Trexler, C. (2004). Teacher researchers in agricultural education: Developing teacher leaders through action research. *The Agricultural Education Magazine, 76*(6), 12–14.

Trist, E. L., & Bamforth, K. (1951). Some social and psychological consequences of longwall coal mining: An examination of the psychological situation and defenses of a work group in relation to the social structure and technological content of the work system. *Human Relations, 4*, 3–38. doi:10.1177/001872675100400101

Trist, E. L., & Murray, H. (1993). *The social engagement of social science: A Tavistock anthology (Vol. II)*. Philadelphia, PA: University of Pennsylvania Press.

Trist, E. L. (1981). *The evolution of socio-technical systems: A conceptual framework and an action research program*. Ontario Quality of Working Life Center, Occasional Paper no. 2.

Tryon, E., Stoecker, R., Martin, A., Seblonka, K., Hilgendorf, A., & Nellis, M. (2008). The challenge of short-term service-learning. *Michigan Journal of Community Service Learning, 20.*

Turner, M. W., Benfield, M. P. J., Runyon, C. J., & Hakkila, J. (2010). *The Mars sample return integrated product team academic experiment.* Paper presented at the Lunar and Planetary Institute's 41st Lunar and Planetary Science Conference, The Woodlands, TX.

Turnley, M. (2007). Integrating critical approaches to technology and service-learning projects. *Technical Communication Quarterly, 16*(1), 103–123. doi:10.1207/s15427625tcq1601_6

Turnley, M. (2007). The importance of critical approaches to technology in service learning projects. *Technical Communication Quarterly, 16*(1), 103–123. doi:10.1207/s15427625tcq1601_6

Turnock, B. J. (2003). Roadmap for public health workforce preparedness. *Journal of Public Health Management and Practice, 9*(6), 471–480.

U.S. Census Bureau. (2009). *Computers for student instruction in elementary and secondary schools.* Retrieved February 21, 2010, from http://www.census.gov/compendia/statab/cats/education.html

U.S. Census Bureau. (2000). *State and county quick facts.* Retrieved from http://quickfacts.census.gov/qfd/states/12000.html

U.S. Department of Education. (2010). *Grants to states for workplace and community transition training for incarcerated youth offenders.* Retrieved February 25, 2010, from http://www2.ed.gov/programs/transitiontraining/ index.html

U.S. Department of Education. (2007). *Report of the academic competitiveness council.* Retrieved July 19, 2010, from http://www2.ed.gov/about/inits/ed/competitiveness/accmathscience/report.pdf

Ubah, C. B., & Robinson, R. L. (2003). A grounded look at the debate over prison-based education: Optimistic theory versus pessimistic worldview. *The Prison Journal, 83*(2), 115–129. doi:10.1177/0032885503083002001

Ukura, K. (2010). *The COMM-ORG Web advice series.* Retrieved March 6, 2010, from http://comm-org.wisc.edu/node/18.

Underwood, C., & Parker, L. (2010). *University-community links to higher learning. Annual Report, 2008-09.* Berkeley, CA: University of California.

Underwood, C., Welsh, M., Gauvain, M., & Duffy, S. (2000). Learning at the edges: Challenges to the sustainability of service learning in higher education. *Journal of Language and Learning Across the Disciplines, 4*(3), 7–26.

Underwood, C., Mahiri, J., Toloza, C., & Pranzetti, D. (2003). Beyond the mask of technology: Educational equity and the pedagogy of hope. In K. C. MacKinnon (Ed.). *Behind many masks: Gerald Berreman and Berkeley anthropology, 1959-2001.* (Kroeber Anthropological Society Papers, No. 89-90). Berkeley, CA: University of California, Berkeley, Department of Anthropology.

UNDP. (1997). *Human development report 1997: Human development to eradicate poverty.* New York, NY: Oxford University Press.

United Nations. (2005). *Core ICT indicators. Partnership on Measuring ICT for Development.* Geneva, Switzerland: WSIS.

United Nations Development Programme. (2007). *Measuring human development: A primer: Guidelines and tools for statistical research, analysis and advocacy.* Retrieved May 24, 2008, from http://hdr.undp.org/en/media/Primer_complete.pdf

United Nations International Children's Emergency Fund. (n.d.). *At a glance: Sierra Leone.* Retrieved September 17, 2007, from http://www.unicef.org/infobycountry/sierraleone.html

United States Distance Learning Association (USDLA). (2010). *USDLA website.* Retrieved from http://www.usdla.org/

University – Community Links. La Clase Mágica. (2010). *End of the year report.* San Diego, CA: UCSD CREATE La Clase Mágica.

University of California. (2010). *About page.* Retrieved February 24, 2010, from http://www.universityofcalifornia.edu/aboutuc/mission.html

University of Chicago Library, Special Collections Research Center. (2010). William Rainey Harper, the University of Chicago faculty, a centennial view. Retrieved July 7, 2010, from http://www.lib.uchicago.edu/e/spcl/centcat/fac/facch01_01.html

University of Cincinnati. (2009). *Annual report on research.* (p. 12). Retrieved from http://www.uc.edu/ucresearch/documents/ucresearch_nov09.pdf

Utley, D. M., Farrington, P. A., & Frederick, R. A. (2002). *Using an undergraduate design course as an experimental environment for team development research.* Proceedings from the 2002 American Society for Engineering Management National Conference, Oct. 2002, (pp. 88-92).

Uys, P. M., Nleya, P., & Molelu, G. B. (2003). Technological innovation and management strategies for higher education in Africa: Harmonizing reality and idealism. *Educational Media International, 40*(3/4), 67–80.

Vasquez, O. A. (2003). *La clase magica: Imagining optimal possibilities in a bilingual community of learners.* Mahwah, NJ: Erlbaum.

Vásquez, O. A. (2006). Social action and the politics of collaboration. In P. Pedraza, & M. Rivera (Eds.), *Educating Latino youth: An agenda for transcending myths and unveiling possibilities.* New Jersey: Laurence Erbaum.

Vásquez, O. A. (2007). Latinos in the global context: Beneficiaries or irrelevants? *Journal of Latinos and Education, 6*(2), 119–138.

Vásquez, O. A. (2008). Reflection: Rules of engagement for achieving educational futures. In L. L. Parker (Ed.), *Technology-mediated learning environments for young English learners: Connections in and out of school.* New York, NY: Taylor & Francis Group.

Vásquez, O. A. (2010). *Keynote address: Alianzas de investigación sobre una pedagogía de lengua meta.* Congreso Internaciónal de Informática Educativa: Aulas virtuales, diseño pedagógico, simulaciones ciberculturas: RIBIE-Col, 20 Años. Popayan, Colombia, 14, 15, 16, July, 2010.

Vásquez, O. A.(under revision). Language and ICT and the making of a change infrastructure. In O. Erstad, & J. Stefton-Green (Eds.), *Learning lives: Literacy, place, technology and learner identity.* Cambridge, UK: Cambridge University Press.

Vásquez, O. A., & Marcello, A. (2010). *A situated view at scaling up in culturally and linguistically diverse communities: The need for mutual adaptation.*

Vidyasagar, D. (2006). Digital divide and digital dividend in the age of information technology. *Journal of Perinatology, 26*(5), 313–315. doi:10.1038/sj.jp.7211494

Vie, S. (2008). Digital divide 2.0: Generation m and online social networking sites in the composition classroom. *Computers and Composition, 25*, 9–23. doi:10.1016/j.compcom.2007.09.004

Vinogradova, P. (2008). Digital stories in an ESL classroom: Giving voice to cultural identity. *Language, Literacy, and Cultural Review.* Retrieved on December 16, 2009 from http://www.umbc.edu/llc/llcreview/2008/2008_digital_stories.pdf.

Vygotsky, L. S. (1978). *Mind in society: The development of higher psychological processes.* Cambridge, MA: Harvard University Press.

Wade, R. C. (1997). *Community service-learning: A guide to including service in the public school curriculum* (p. 64). Albany, NY: State University of New York Press.

Wallace, J. (2000). The problem of time: Enabling students to make long-term commitments to community-based learning. *Michigan Journal of Community Service Learning, 7*, 133–141.

Wallerstein, N., & Bernstein, E. (1988). Empowerment education: Freire's adapted to health education. *Health Education & Behavior, 15*(4), 379–394. doi:10.1177/109019818801500402

Walters, M., Hunter, S., & Giddens, E. (2007). Qualitative research on what leads to success in professional writing. *International Journal on the Scholarship of Teaching and Learning, 1*(2). Retrieved July 11, 2010, from http://academics.georgiasouthern.edu/ijsotl/v1n2/articles/walters/media/

Wambeam, C., & Kramer, R. (1996). Design teams and the Web: A collaborative model for the workplace. *Technical Communication, 43*(4), 349–357.

Wang, C. (2006). Youth participation in photovoice as a strategy for community change. *Journal of Community Practice, 14*(1-2), 147–161. doi:10.1300/J125v14n01_09

Wang, C., Morrel-Samuels, S., Hutchison, P., Bell, L., & Pestronk, R. (2004). Flint Photovoice: Community building among youths, adults, and policymakers. *American Journal of Public Health, 94*(6), 911–913. doi:10.2105/AJPH.94.6.911

Wang, C., & Pies, C. (2004). Family, maternal, and child health through photovoice. *Maternal and Child Health Journal, 8*(2), 95–102. doi:10.1023/B:MACI.0000025732.32293.4f

Wang, C. C., & Burris, M. (1997). Photovoice: Concept, methodology, and use for participatory needs assessment. *Health Education & Behavior, 24*(3), 369–387. doi:10.1177/109019819702400309

Ward, K., & Wolf-Wendel, L. (2000). Community-centered service learning: Moving from doing for to doing with. *The American Behavioral Scientist, 43*(5), 767–780. doi:10.1177/00027640021955586

Ware, P. (2008). Language learners and multimedia literacy in and after school. *Pedagogies: An International Journal, 3*(1), 37–51.

Warnock, S. (2009). *Teaching writing online: How and why?* Urbana, IL: National Council of Teachers of English.

Warschauer, M., Knobel, M., & Stone, L. (2004). Technology and equity in schooling: Deconstructing the digital divide. *Educational Policy, 18*(4), 562–588. doi:10.1177/0895904804266469

Waxer, C. (2008). Techies volunteering to save the world: How to enhance your high-tech career with new skills – and meaning. *Computerworld*, December 17, 1.

WCET. (2010). *WCET website*. Retrieved from http://www.wcet.info/2.0/

Web-based Information Science Education Consortium (WISE). (2009). *A model for quality online education in library and information science*. Retrieved from http://www.wiseeducation.org/media/documents/2009/2/principles_of_Quality_Online_Courses_2006.pdf

Webster, L. D., & Mirielli, E. J. (2007). *Student reflections on an academic service learning experience in a computer science classroom*. Paper presented at the 8th ACM SIGITE Conference on Information Technology Education, Destin, Florida, USA.

Wei, K., Siow, J., & Burley, D. L. (2007). Implementing service-learning to the Information Systems and technology management program: A study of an undergraduate capstone course. *Journal of Information Systems Education, 18*(1), 125–126.

Weick, K. (1984). Small wins: Redefining the scale of social problems. *The American Psychologist, 39*(1), 40–49. doi:10.1037/0003-066X.39.1.40

Weis, T., Benmayor, R., O'Leary, C., & Eynon, B. (2002). Digital technologies and pedagogies. *Journal of Social Justice, 29*(4), 153–167.

Weiser, M. (1996). *Ubiquitous computing*. Retrieved February 21, 2010, from http://www.ubiq.com/hypertext/weiser/UbiHome.html

Wei-Skillern, J., & Marciano, S. (2008). The networked nonprofit. *Stanford Social Innovation Review, 6*(2), 38–43.

Wejnert, B. (2002). Integrating models of diffusion of innovations: A conceptual framework. *Annual Review of Sociology, 28*, 297–326. doi:10.1146/annurev.soc.28.110601.141051

Wenger, E. (1998). *Communities of practice: Learning, meaning, and identity*. New York, NY: Cambridge University Press.

Wesch, M. (2007). *A vision of students today*. Retrieved March 23, 2010, from http://www.youtube.com/watch?v=dGCJ46vyR9o

West, H. C., & Sabol, W. J. (2009). *Prison inmates at midyear 2008, statistical tables*. U.S. Department of Justice, Office of Justice Programs, National Prisoner Statistics. Retrieved February 20, 2010, from http://bjs.ojp.usdoj.gov/content/pub/pdf/pim08st.pdf

Wilcox, E., & Zigurs, I. (2004). A method for enhancing the success of service-learning projects in Information Systems curricula. In D. Colton (Ed.), *Proceedings of the Information Systems Education Conference* (p. 3431). San Diego, CA: Educators Special Interest Group (EDSIG).

Wilen-Daugenti, T. (2008). *Cisco higher education trends & statistics*. Retrieved from http://www.cisco.com/web/about/ac79/edu/trends/issue01.html

Williams, P. J. (2007). Valid knowledge: The economy and the academy. *Higher Education, 54*, 511–523. doi:10.1007/s10734-007-9051-y

Williams, M. F., & James, D. D. (2009). Embracing new policies, technologies, and community partnerships: A case study of the city of Houston's bureau of air quality control. *Technical Communication Quarterly, 18*(1), 82–98. doi:10.1080/10572250802437515

Wilson, E. J. III, & Wong, K. (2003). African information revolution: A balance sheet. *Telecommunications Policy, 27*(1/2), 155–177. doi:10.1016/S0308-5961(02)00097-6

Wolde-Rufael, Y. (2006). Electricity consumption and economic growth: A time series experience for 17 African countries. *Energy Policy, 34*, 1106–1114. doi:10.1016/j.enpol.2004.10.008

Woolcock, M. (2001). The place of social capital in understanding social and economic outcomes. *Isuma: Canadian Journal of Policy Research, 2*(1), 1–17.

World Health Organization. (2006a). *Health action in crises*. Sierra Leone: Retrieved September 19, 2007, from http://www.who.int/hac/crises/sle/background/2004/SierraLeone_June06.pdf

World Health Organization. (2006b). *Mortality country fact sheet 2006: Sierra Leone*. Retrieved May 24, 2008, from http://www.who.int/whosis/mort/profiles/mort_afro_sle_sierraleone.pdf

World Heritage Center. (No Date). *Sian Ka'an*. Retrieved June 2010 from http://whc.unesco.org/en/list/410

Wortham, J. (2010, January 13). $2 million in donations for Haiti, via text message. *The New York Times*. Retrieved from http://bits.blogs.nytimes.com/2010/01/13/1-million-in-donations-for-haiti-via-text-message/

Yates, M., & Youniss, J. (1996). Community service and political-moral identity in adolescents. *Journal of Research on Adolescence, 6*(3), 271–284.

Yieke, F. A. (2005). Towards alternatives in higher education: The benefits and challenges of e-learning in Africa. *CODESRIA Bulletin, 3/4*, 73–75.

Yuker, H. (1994). Variables that influence attitudes toward people with disabilities. *Journal of Social Behavior and Personality, 9*(5), 3–22.

Zhang, D., & F, N. J. (2003). Powering e-learning in the new millennium: An overview of e-learning and enabling technology. *Information Systems Frontiers, 5*(2), 207–218. doi:10.1023/A:1022609809036

Zhao, W., Massey, B. L., & Murphy, J. F. (2003). Cultural dimensions of website design and content. *Prometheus, 21*(1), 75–84. doi:10.1080/0810902032000051027

Zimmerman, E. (2009). Gaming literacy: Game design as a model for literacy in the twenty-first century. In B. Perron & M. J. P. Wolf (Eds.), *The video game theory reader 2*. New York, NY: Routledge.

Zlotkowski, E. (2007). The case for service learning. In L. McIlrath, & I. MacLabhrainn (Eds.), *Higher education and civic engagement: International perspectives*. Aldershot, UK: Ashgate.

Zucker, A. A., & McGhee, R. (2005). *A study of one-to-one computer use in mathematics and science instruction at the secondary level in Henrico County Public Schools*. Arlington, VA: SRI International.

# About the Contributors

**Melody A. Bowdon,** Ph.D., is Director of the Karen L. Smith Faculty Center for Teaching and Learning and Associate Professor of Writing and Rhetoric at the University of Central Florida. She has served as Senior Research Fellow for Florida Campus Compact since 2005 and has published widely on the subjects of service-learning and teaching with technology, including articles in national journals and essay collections. She is co-author of *Service-Learning in Technical and Professional Communication* with Blake Scott and co-editor of *Scholarship for Sustaining Service-Learning and Civic Engagement* with Shelley Billig and Barbara Holland. Melody is a member of the editorial board of *Reflections on Community-Based Writing,* a journal that focuses on service-learning in composition studies, and co-edited a special issue of that journal on professional writing and service-learning in 2003. She also serves as a founding member of the editorial board for the journal *Community Literacy* and is co-editing a Fall 2011 issue of that journal focusing on digital technologies and community literacy partnerships with Russell Carpenter. Melody received her Ph.D. in rhetoric, composition, and the teaching of English from the University of Arizona and her BA in English literature and secondary education from Oklahoma City University. Since 1992, Melody has taught 57 service-learning courses at three universities and has been awarded several teaching and community service awards, including the 2005 Gulf South Summit Award for Outstanding Faculty Contributions to Service-Learning in Higher Education. Melody and her students have worked with over 110 nonprofit organizations in Central Florida. Melody has served as a Guardian ad Litem in her community and volunteers regularly in local public schools.

**Russell G. Carpenter,** Ph.D., is the founding Director of the Noel Studio for Academic Creativity and Assistant Professor of English at Eastern Kentucky University in Richmond, KY. The Noel Studio at EKU is a nationally unique mission and vision that emphasizes collaborative and creative approaches to developing student communication through integrating written, oral (and aural), electronic, and visual modes and media. This new space will serve as the center for innovative community literacy initiatives. Russell received a Ph.D. in Texts & Technology at the University of Central Florida where he also earned B.A. and M.A. degrees in English. While at UCF, Carpenter contributed to Writers on the Move, a community literacy project that established pilot writing centers at area schools with Terry Thaxton. Russell received the 2010 Von Till award from the National Communication Association's Communication Center division for research, scholarship, and innovation in communication centers.

\* \* \*

**Patricia Aceves**, Ed.D, serves as director of the Faculty Center at Stony Brook University, in Stony Brook, NY. Previously, she was director of Distributed Learning at St. Cloud State University where she managed the Pathways Program for Incarcerated Students and served on the Partnership for Safer Communities, the higher education consortium for the Minnesota Department of Corrections.

**Robert Aceves**, Ed.D, is director of the City University of New York Aviation Institute at York College. While at St. Cloud State University, he taught the Introduction to Air Transportation course at the St. Cloud Correctional Facility and taught self-paced correspondence courses in the Pathways Program for Incarcerated Students.

**Marco Adria**, Ph.D., is professor of communications and director of the Graduate Program in Communications and Technology, University of Alberta. Adria teaches communications theory and the management of communications technologies. He is the author or co-author of many publications in the areas of organizational communication, popular culture, and nationalism, including most recently *Technology and Nationalism* (McGill-Queen's University Press). He has served as president of the Canadian Association of Library Trustees and as chair of the Edmonton Public Library Board. He received his Ph.D. from the Aston University Business School in Birmingham, U.K.

**Cora M. Allard** is a lecturer in Biological Sciences at Clemson University and works for the SC Life project (funded by the Howard Hughes Medical Institute). She completed an undergraduate degree in biology at Millikin University, a M.S. in entomology at the University of Kentucky, and is currently a Ph.D. candidate in wildlife biology at Clemson University. She has 15 years of experience in biological research, education, and outreach and five years of experience working with K-12 science educators and curriculum coordinators.

**Aria Altuna** is a lifelong resident of Tucson, Arizona. She is a student at Desert View High School and will graduate in 2012. She is currently a member of the Pride of the Jaguars Marching Band. She doesn't have any specific plan about how she will succeed in life, but plans to try her best at whatever makes her happy. She hopes to get into a good college and study something she will greatly enjoy (which could include chemistry, writing, dance, art, music, and/or biology). She became involved with the Wildcat Writers Student Research Team because she wanted an opportunity to experience new things.

**William P. Banks** is interim director of the University Writing Program and associate professor of rhetoric and composition at East Carolina University, where he teaches graduate and undergraduate courses in writing, research, and pedagogy. He has published articles on history, rhetoric, pedagogy, writing program administration, and sexuality in several recent books, as well as in *English Journal*, *College English*, *Computers & Composition*, *Dialogue*, and *Teaching English in the Two-Year College*, and he has guest edited the journals *Computers & Composition* and *Kairos*. He is currently working on two book projects: a single-authored book (*Queer Literacies*), which looks at the ways in which gay men and lesbians articulate literacies of queer(ed) identities and an edited collection on teachers-as-learners in online environments.

**Michael P.J. Benfield** is the Integrated Product Team (IPT) deputy program manager at the University of Alabama in Huntsville. Benfield has been project manager of one of the IPT Senior Design Experience projects for the past seven years and is the project manager of the Innovative Student Project for the Increased Recruitment of Engineering and Science Students (InSPIRESS) Level I project with the IPT program. Benfield holds a Ph.D. in industrial and systems engineering and engineering management from the University of Alabama in Huntsville and has worked in the Huntsville aerospace industry for the past twelve years supporting both NASA and the U.S. Army Aviation and Missile Command on Redstone Arsenal.

**Kristine Blair** is professor and chair of the English department at Bowling Green State University and 2010-2011 chair of the BGSU Faculty Senate. The author of over fifty publications on gender and technology, online learning, electronic portfolios, and the politics of technological literacy acquisition, Blair has served as the editor of the journal *Computers and Composition Online* since 2003. In 2004 and 2009, she was named the Outstanding Contributor to Graduate Education by the BGSU Graduate Student Senate; in 2007, she received the national Technology Innovator Award from the Conference on College Composition and Communication's Committee on Computers and Composition; and in 2010, she received the national Charles Moran Award for Distinguished Contributions to the Field of Computers and Composition. Blair currently directs the Digital Mirror Computer Camp, an outreach initiative for girls in grades 6-8 funded by a national American Association of University Women Community Action Grant.

**James Bliesner** holds an MA in social ethics from Boston University and has a significant background in community collaboration. He served 24 years as director of the San Diego Reinvestment Task Force, an agency authorized by the City and County of San Diego to "monitor lending practices and develop strategies for reinvestment." There, he garnered national awards and governmental appointments, and served as a faculty member for San Diego State University. Mr. Bliesner is currently a Visiting Scholar at the UCSD Department of Communications and has co-taught courses in online learning environments.

**Jode Brexa** teaches English as a Second Language at Arapahoe Ridge High School in Boulder Valley School District. She has been part of the Newcomer Program for the last seven years, developing a nationally recognized curriculum model for beginning students. In May 2010, she completed the Administrative Leadership and Policy Studies Program at the School of Education at the University of Colorado, Denver. She received a Department of State Teaching Excellence and Achievement Award in spring 2010, which took her to Tajikistan. She is currently working with Tajik teachers to develop a digital storytelling project there.

**Pat Byrne** is a lecturer in Information Technology and director of the Master's of Information Technology programme in the National University of Ireland, Galway. She teaches technical modules in the MIT degree, and acts as coordinator for the IT Project module. Pat has practiced as an independent IT consultant and also as programmer and systems analyst in industry. She brings her familiarity with the workplace environment to her current work, instilling in the students a professional approach in their practice of IT. Pat has also worked as a volunteer in local community organisations, applying her computing background to a variety of projects.

**Cheryl Cates**, Ph.D., is director of the University of Cincinnati Center for Cooperative Education Research and Innovation (CERI). In addition to her Ph.D., she holds an M.B.A. and a B.A. She has co-authored *Learning Outcomes, the Educational Value of Cooperative Education*, as well as chapters for *The Handbook for Research in Cooperative Education and Internships*, and *The International Handbook for Cooperative Education*. Cates has worked with cooperative education for 20 years and has served as the director of CERI since 2007.

**Alfredo Careaga** has a history of more than 30 years in research, development, and practice in areas of technology, dissemination of science, and sustainable development. He has Bachelor's degrees in physics and electrical-mechanical engineering and Master's and Doctorate degrees in mathematics. In the area of sustainable development, he was the founder of the Centro de Investigaciones deQuintana Roo (CIQRO), a research center that in the late 70s and early 80s, coined a model now known as sustainable development, developed a series of models of eco-technologies for the welfare of communities in the Maya area, and secured the protection of Sian Ka'an (now a world heritage site) under the decree as a Biosphere Reserve. For his merits in preserving the environment, Dr. Careaga received the National Prize for Ecological Merit in 2004. In science and technology, Dr. Careaga has publications in the field of mathematics, has served as founder and director of technology companies, conducted research on computer use policies for the National System of Higher Education and participated in the Popularization of Science Division at the National University of Mexico. Today, Dr. Careaga is a researcher at the Centro de Investigaciones Tropicales (CITRO), the RTPD project director (a project of the Ministry of Education of Veracruz) and president of the nonprofit organization Ibero-American Network for Sustainable Development (REDDES) that focuses on research and promotion of appropriate technology models for sustainable development.

**Thomas B. Cavanagh**, Ph.D., is assistant vice president of Distributed Learning at the University of Central Florida. In this role, he oversees the university's distance learning strategy, policies, and practices, including program and course design, development, and assessment. In his career, he has administered e-learning development for both academic (public and private) and industrial (Fortune 500, government/military) audiences. A regular presenter at academic and industry conferences, he is an award-winning instructional designer, program manager, faculty member, and administrator. His research interests include e-learning, technical communication, and the societal influence of technology on education, training, culture, and commerce. He is also an award-winning author of several mystery novels.

**Kettil Cedercreutz**, Ph.D., is associate provost and director of the Division of Professional Practice at the University of Cincinnati (UC), where he oversees the integrity of the cooperative education program originally developed by Dean Herman Schneider. He is a professor in the UC College of Engineering and Applied Science, School of Dynamic Systems. Cedercreutz has served as a department head and senior lecturer at the Swedish Institute of Technology, Helsinki, now part of Arcada Polytechnic, Finland.

**Caroline I. Collins** will receive her MFA in Writing from the University of California, Riverside in May of 2011. Ms. Collins is a seasoned researcher, program administrator, and fiscal analyst, and brings experience in both the corporate and academic arenas. She is Executive Director of the Center for Academic and Social Advancement (CASA), a non-profit community-based organization that helps

436

under-served youth build their educational and social skills. Ms. Collins facilitates the community-university partnership known as the *La Clase Mágica* after-school program, and she is presently assisting a UCSD research team design of *La Clase Mágica's* newest 21st century adaptation-- the *Hubs of Innovation* initiative.

**Trey Conner** is an assistant professor at the University of South Florida, St. Petersburg. His research interests include community literacy, the rhetoric of music and sound, digital pedagogy, civic engagement, ecology, rhetorics of science and technology, and the history and theory of rhetoric. He is currently working on a project that forges connections among ancient Greek rhetorical and musical practices, the theory and performance of Tala in Hindustani and Karnatic music, and contemporary improvisatory musical practices in order to formulate a theory and pedagogy of rhythm for composing in new media.

**Pamela Connor** is a professor in the Department of Preventive Medicine at the University of Tennessee Health Science Center in Memphis. She is also head of the department's Community Translational Research section as well as director of the Master's of epidemiology program. She has acknowledged expertise in family violence, project planning, implementation and evaluation, and conducting translational research and data analysis, and has written or co-authored multiple articles in peer-reviewed professional journals focusing on psychosocial behaviors within the family. Dr. Connor instructs physicians and UTHSC students in all aspects of research and planning, and is currently the primary investigator of four grants including a K30 initiative to expand clinical investigator training within the epidemiology program, along with an Office of Violence Against Women Campus Grant Program that will implement policies, procedures, training, and educational programs designed to build a community-campus infrastructure for responding to and preventing intimate partner violence.

**Timothy Crain** has lived in Tucson all of his life and is a member of the Wildcat Writers Student Research Team and a student at Desert View High School. His interest in writing came about when he was a freshman at Desert View. Before the transition to high school, he only viewed writing as a boring class that he believed would never help him in his future. He has entered several pieces of writing in city and nationwide contests. During 9th grade, he participated in a corrido contest and also in several scholarship-based contests.

**Debra Flanders Cushing** is a Ph.D. candidate in the College of Architecture and Planning at Colorado University-Denver and the coordinator for *Growing Up Boulder*, a child- and youth-friendly city initiative in Boulder, CO. Debra has also taught several service-learning courses in the Environmental Design Program at CU-Boulder. Her current research areas include youth-created digital stories as pathways to community engagement, varied formats for youth governance to create child- and youth-friendly communities, and youth participation in community planning. Debra received her Bachelor's in landscape architecture from Penn State and her Master's of science in landscape architecture from the University of Wisconsin-Madison with a focus in restoration ecology. Prior to beginning her Ph.D., Debra was a design practitioner for several years in Colorado.

**Curtis L. DeBerg**, founder and chief executive officer of Students for the Advancement of Global Entrepreneurship (SAGE), earned his Ph.D. and M.S. at Oklahoma State University in accounting and economics, respectively. Before that, he was employed as a CPA for the national accounting firm of Ernst & Whinney in Des Moines, Iowa. From September 1993 to May 2005, he was the Sam M. Walton Free Enterprise Fellow at Chico State. In 1999, his team of university students from Chico State was named International Champion for Students in Free Enterprise (SIFE). DeBerg has published several articles in refereed academic journals, and served three years as associate editor of the *Journal of Accounting Education*. From 1995-1997, he served as project co-director of a U.S. Department of Education grant entitled "Reengineering Elementary Accounting." DeBerg was a leader in reengineering principles of accounting during this time period when CSU Chico made significant changes in both content and pedagogy in principles of accounting.

**Amy Garrett Dikkers**, Ph.D., is assistant professor of educational leadership at the University of North Carolina at Wilmington. She earned a Ph.D. in comparative and international development education at the University of Minnesota, an M.Ed. in secondary English education from Wake Forest University, and a B.A. in English from the University of North Carolina at Greensboro. Before her doctoral study, she taught secondary school English domestically and abroad. The focus of her doctoral study was international development education, specifically the education of children in difficult circumstances, such as street children, ethnic minority children, refugee and immigrant children, and other groups often not served effectively in formal school settings around the world. She has taught face-to-face, hybrid, and online courses at the undergraduate and graduate levels. Her professional interests include the preparation of educational leaders and the use of technology-enhanced and online learning in higher education.

**Theresa Dolson** earned a B.A. in English literature from the College of William and Mary and an M.A. in English literature from Virginia Commonwealth University. As a participant for two summers in the National Writing Project, Dolson worked in the areas of composition theory, writing across the curriculum, and faculty development. While teaching at the University of Richmond, she noticed that when students were asked to apply what they were learning in a "real world" setting in a way that contributed to the community, they didn't just learn-they were transformed. Now Dolson works as the manager of the community-based learning program in the UR Bonner Center for Civic Engagement where she encourages other faculty to consider ways they might incorporate community-based learning into their courses. She is also a creative writer, an active member of the Professional and Organizational Developers Network, and the mother of three sons.

**A. Michael Dougherty** (Ph.D., Indiana State University) is professor emeritus of counseling at Western Carolina University (WCU) in Cullowhee, North Carolina. Dougherty joined the WCU faculty in 1976. He served as dean of the College of Education and Allied Professions and professor of counseling at WCU from 1998 until his retirement in 2009. He is author of *Psychological Consultation and Collaboration in School and Community Settings* (5th ed., 2009) and *Casebook of Psychological Consultation and Collaboration in School and Community Settings* (5th ed., 2009), both published by Cengage–Brooks/Cole. He currently teaches graduate-level courses in consultation, theories of counseling, and counseling children. He has consulted, taught courses, and made presentations in a variety of international settings including Barbados, Colombia, Cypress, El Salvador, Germany, Great Britain, Guatemala, Honduras, Jamaica, and Jordan.

**Debbie Faires** is assistant director for distance learning and a lecturer at San Jose State University's School of Library and Information Science. She earned her MLIS at SJSU in 2001. She administers projects that support the school's online degree programs and teaches classes in Web technology.

**Katelyn Foley** graduated from Harvard College (magna cum laude) with a degree in molecular and cellular biology, a minor in visual and environmental studies, and a citation in Spanish in December 2009. Her background consists of experiences in both science and entertainment, including stem cell research at the National Institutes of Health and the Harvard Stem Cell Institute, film production at Spyglass Entertainment, and space tourism marketing at Space Adventures. As an undergraduate, she co-founded the Digital Literacy Project (DigiLit), a nonprofit organization that provides laptops and computer classes for schools around the world. She is currently an associate consultant at Bain & Company in Los Angeles and will attend Harvard Business School through the 2+2 Program in 2012.

**Louis Cyril Henry Fourie** is professor, chair, and department head in Information Systems at the University of the Western Cape. He has taught at various other universities, including Fort Hare, North West, Johannesburg, Tshwane, Bond (Australia), West Florida (USA), Ndejje (Uganda) and Stellenbosch. Fourie is involved in various research projects regarding knowledge management, e-government, e-business, e-learning, bridging the digital divide, and concept maps as a business tool. He regularly consults and presents workshops in Kenya, Tanzania, and Uganda on knowledge management, e-commerce, and e-marketing. Fourie is also a qualified leadership consultant and regularly facilitates leadership development programmes. He frequently presents papers at national and international conferences, is featured weekly on national radio regarding the Internet, contributes regularly to several magazines, has published numerous papers in academic journals and contributed chapters to academic books, and has made many videos on business informatics and the influence of Information Technology on business.

**Lois Gander**, Q.C., B.A., LL.B., LL.M., is associate dean of academic planning and strategic development for the University of Alberta's Faculty of Extension. With almost 35 years of experience in providing university-based continuing education, Gander has worked in a variety of contexts, engaging with both mainstream and marginalized communities, and with governmental and non-governmental agencies that address contemporary social issues. Her particular area of expertise is public legal education. She is both an advocate and critic of community-university engagement.

**Karen Glum** spent summer afternoons chasing birds with a salt shaker, having been told she could catch one when it stopped to lick salt from its tail. A lack of success did not dampen her love for animals. Her favorite place in her hometown of Cincinnati is still the zoo, where she became an Elephant House and Education Department intern, and zoo camp leader. A love for science as well as nature led to a degree in biology. Today, she shares her passion with children and adults as a middle school science teacher and Science Department Chair at The Seven Hills School, and with her husband and sons.

**Morgan Gresham** is an associate professor at the University of South Florida St. Petersburg, where she serves as the writing programs coordinator. Her works span feminism, computers and composition, writing program administration, and civic engagement through writing.

**Meghan Griffin** is a doctoral student in the Texts and Technology program at the University of Central Florida and holds an M.B.A. from Palm Beach Atlantic University. She serves as assistant director and writing instructor at Palm Beach Atlantic University's Orlando Campus where she integrates service-learning practices with andragogy in order to meet the needs of working adult and non-traditional learners. Her professional writing courses incorporate digital composing tools, service-learning projects, and the use of emerging technologies for workplace writing. Meghan's dissertation research centers on food journaling technologies and embodiment theory within medical discourse related to body size modification.

**Aleshia Hall-Campbell** is associate director of cooperative agreements with the National Food Service Management Institute. Her prior experience includes serving as a program evaluator with the University of Tennessee Health Science Center Department of Preventive Medicine, where she was responsible for collaborating with community agencies in developing and conducting program evaluation activities. Additionally, she served as the program coordinator for the Tennessee Public Health Workforce Development Consortium, where she was responsible for coordinating all administrative functions of the statewide public health workforce program. She has significant experience in public health program planning and implementation and workforce development. Hall-Campbell has an M.P.H. in health administration from the University of North Texas Health Science Center and a Ph.D. in higher educational leadership from the University of Mississippi.

**Anton C. Harfmann**, M.Arch., is a registered architect and an associate professor in the School of Architecture and Interior Design at the University of Cincinnati College of Design, Architecture, Art, and Planning. He also serves as the associate dean for academic technology and facilities for the college. Professor Harfmann has produced "Voices of Practice," a documentary film capturing the life histories of practicing architects, and "Imagine Building," a documentary on the design and construction of the Lois and Richard Rosenthal Contemporary Arts Center.

**Amy C. Kimme Hea** is an associate professor in the Rhetoric, Composition, and Teaching of English Program and associate director of the Writing Program at the University of Arizona. Her research interests include Web-based teaching and learning, wireless technologies, new media, and professional writing theory and practice. She edited *Going Wireless: A Critical Exploration of Wireless and Mobile Technologies for Composition Teachers and Scholars* (2009) in Hampton's New Directions in Computers and Composition series, and has published print and hypertext essays in other peer-reviewed collections and journals.

**Jim Henry** is director of the Mānoa Writing Program at the University of Hawai'i at Mānoa. His book *Writing Workplace Cultures: An Archaeology of Professional Writing* (SIUP), a seven-year collaborative effort with 80-plus graduate students conducting autoethnographies of workplace cultures, received the Distinguished Publication award for 2001 from the Association for Business Communication. His article for the 2010 special issue of *Technical Communication Quarterly* on posthumanism, "(Re)Appraising the Performance of Technical Communicators from a Posthumanist Perspective," initiated the use of performance theory in technical communication studies. In addition to his research on community partnerships and technical communication (he always affiliates his undergraduate technical writing courses

440

with service-learning), he is researching intersections between cultural performance and organizational performance, as well as graduate student mentoring in first-year composition. In 2009, he received the University of Hawaii's Board of Regents Medal for Excellence in Teaching.

**Rebecca Hines,** Ph.D., is an associate professor in special education at the University of Central Florida. Her research interests include working with students with emotional/behavioral disorders and applications of instructional technology. Hines is co-principal investigator of the federal grant entitled "Teachers in Action with Persons with Disabilities through High-Tech High-Touch Service-Learning." Her most recent projects include a book on instructional strategies for inclusive secondary classrooms with colleague Lisa Dieker. She also has produced a DVD entitled *IMPROV for Educators: Simple Tips for Effective Collaboration*, featuring actress Cheryl Hines.

**Janice Holt** is director of Western Carolina University's School University Teacher Education Partnership (SUTEP) and Center for the Support of Beginning Teachers. Holt joined WCU in 2000. She served as a public school teacher from 1976–2000 and remains a National Board Certified Teacher. Holt also teaches methods courses for the Department of Elementary Education and Middle Grades and supervises teacher education interns. She has received grants totaling over $1.5 million dollars that focus on the support of beginning teachers. She has made numerous presentations at the national, regional, and state levels. She is currently in the process of completing her Ph.D. at Western Carolina University.

**Marcey Kinney** is an assistant professor at Bethune-Cookman University. She earned a Ph.D. in exceptional student education from the University of Central Florida. Dr. Kinney's research interests include technology as a tool for students with learning disabilities, service-learning, teacher education, and technology to enhance social communication skills for children and adults with autism. Kinney is an experienced teacher at the elementary and high school levels, having worked with students with a multitude of disabilities. She also has synchronous and asynchronous teaching experience at both the undergraduate and graduate levels.

**Karla Saari Kitalong** is associate professor of humanities at Michigan Technological University. Her research integrates visual communication, usability, and the design of interactive media. Her recent work has been supported by both the National Science Foundation and the National Endowment for the Humanities.

**James P. Lawler** is professor of Information Technology and service-learning at the Seidenberg School of Computer Science and Information Systems of Pace University in New York City. He is the originator of courses such as community empowerment through Information Systems and assistive device technologies, social networking systems on the Web, and Web design for nonprofit organizations that have been customized to connect hundreds of undergraduate students at the university with New York nonprofit organizations since 2003. Dr. Lawler is a recipient of the national Jefferson Award for Community Service, the Faculty Leadership Award for Service from Pace University, and Thinkfinity Awards for Service from the Verizon Foundation.

**Marianne W. Lewis**, Ph.D., is professor of management at the University of Cincinnati and the director of Kolodzik Business Scholars. Her research explores tensions, conflicts, and paradoxes that both impede and enable innovation. In particular, her work addresses the challenges of developing new products, implementing technological and organizational change, and building organization theory. She has published in such venues as *Academy of Management Review*, *Academy of Management Journal*, *Organization Science*, *Journal of Operations Management*, *Human Relations,* and *Journal of Management Education.*

**Jennifer Licata** received her B. S. in biology and M.Ed. in school counseling from Xavier University. She has enjoyed teaching sixth grade science at The Seven Hills Middle School for thirteen years. Jennifer has found teaching to be extremely rewarding and enjoys collaborating with colleagues and professional scientists. Outside of teaching, Jennifer enjoys spending time outdoors with her husband and two young children. As a family, they have begun to identify birds and her five-year old son is especially excited when he can identify a bird without any help from mom! Jennifer also enjoys cooking and gardening.

**Bernadette Longo** is an associate professor in the Department of Writing Studies at the University of Minnesota. Her research uses a cultural studies approach to understand technical communication practices situated within particular cultural contexts, mediated by technological devices. Dr. Longo's book *Spurious Coin: A History of Science, Management, and Technical Writing* was published by SUNY Press in 2000. Her co-edited collection *Critical Power Tools: Technical Communication and Cultural Studies* was published by SUNY Press in 2006 and in 2007 won the Best Edited Collection Award from the National Council of Teachers of English Committee on Scientific and Technical Communication. Before earning her Ph.D. at Rensselaer Polytechnic Institute in 1996, Longo worked for over 15 years as a contract writer and project manager with large clients in the medical and poultry processing industries. She has published numerous articles and has made many national and international conference presentations.

**Emily Wexler Love** completed her doctorate in educational foundations, policy, and practice at the University of Colorado at Boulder. Her research and teaching interests focus on immigrant education and education policy, specifically related to undocumented Latino youth. Using digital storytelling, her research considered young peoples' stories to understand how undocumented and documented youth are navigating school and community contexts. Her writing has examined youth engagement in protest related to immigrant issues, service-learning partnerships, and digital storytelling. She authored a chapter about the DREAM Act in *Current Issues in Educational Policy and the Law* (2008). She works closely with two youth-led organizations in Boulder County that are doing significant work to educate their community about the experiences of young people and how educators and community members can better support Latino youth. After studying in Chile and Mexico, Emily completed her undergraduate work in Spanish and English at Tulane University in New Orleans.

**Katherine Loving** has been the civic engagement coordinator at the University of Wisconsin-Madison's University Health Services since 1999. Her work focuses on building the capacity of the institution to engage in democratic community-university partnerships and creating opportunities for students to learn and apply the attitudes and aptitudes of engaged citizenship. Loving served as one of the founding team members of TechShop Madison and participated in the design, implementation, and ongoing

442

management of the community-based research project and subsequent service-learning program. She received her Master's of science in social work from UW-Madison and her Bachelor of arts in history and international studies from Washington University.

**Yuping Mao** is the academic developer of the Master of Arts in Communications and Technology program at University of Alberta in Canada. She teaches graduate courses on both qualitative and quantitative research methodologies and health communication. She has a Ph.D. in organizing and relating from Ohio University. Mao's research focuses on organizational communication and health communication with an emphasis on intercultural communication. Mao has presented her research in national and international conferences in both Canada and the U.S., and has published her work in *Review of Communication, Teaching Ideas for the Basic Communication Course, Howard Journal of Communications, Feminist Media Studies, China Media Research*, and *Italian Journal of Pediatrics*. She has also co-authored book chapters in communication. In 2008-2009, Mao worked with the City of Edmonton on the development of the Citizen Panel.

**Jill McCracken** is an educator, activist, and researcher. She is an assistant professor at the University of South Florida St. Petersburg, and her research interests include the rhetoric of marginalized communities, in particular that of sex work/trafficking, public policy, gender studies, reproductive technologies, civic engagement, and communication across the curriculum. She is currently working on an analysis of street sex worker representations and their effects on sex workers and society, which reveals the power of everyday language and its influence on the material conditions of street sex workers' lives.

**Lorraine McIlrath** has coordinated the Community Knowledge Initiative at the National University of Ireland Galway since 2004. There, she is responsible for developing and supporting civic engagement activities across the university including service learning and student volunteering. She is principal investigator of Campus Engage, a national Irish network to support civic engagement within higher education in Ireland (http://www.campusengage.ie). Since 2010, she has been a member partner in a nine university EU Tempus Funded Project to support the introduction of service learning to five universities in Jordan and Lebanon, entitled the Tawasol Project (http://www.tawasol.org). She spent the previous 10 years in Northern Ireland where she pursued postgraduate studies exploring the role of the media in contested societies and then became a lecturer at the University of Ulster's UNESCO Centre. In addition, she was worked on the development of the Northern Ireland curricula framework for "Local and Global Citizenship" in partnership with the Citizenship Foundation, UNESCO Centre and CCEA, and has published a 'Resource Directory' (2002) for all schools in Northern Ireland. Lorraine is co-editor of the recently published *Higher Education and Civic Engagement: International Perspectives* (2007) and *Mapping Civic Engagement within Higher Education in Ireland* (2009).

**Anne McKinney** began working with the WISE Consortium in March 2007 and taught Introduction to Online Pedagogy from July 2007 to August 2010. As the Visiting Coordinator of Instructional Design for WISE Pedagogy, McKinney's goal has been to help instructors learn effective practices for teaching online. McKinney created Introduction to Online Pedagogy, a free, wiki-based workshop. She has also taught professional and technical writing courses for the University of Illinois at Springfield.

**Cynthia McPherson** holds a Ph.D. in technical communication and rhetoric from Texas Tech University. Currently, she is director of business and technical writing in the English department at The University of Alabama in Huntsville. As a consultant and editor, McPherson has worked with scientists, engineers, and program managers from government and commercial sectors. Her research interests include technical communication pedagogy, principles and practices in editing workplace documents, and writing in the Department of Defense.

**Richard Miller**, Ph.D., P.E., FPCI, is a professor of civil and environmental engineering at the University of Cincinnati. His areas of expertise are pre-stressed concrete design, concrete bridges, and concrete materials. Dr. Miller is one of the initiators of the PCI Big Beam Contest for engineering students, and he serves as head of the rules and judging committee. He is chair of the Civil and Environmental Engineering Curriculum Committee and a member of the College of Engineering and Applied Science Curriculum Committee.

**David M. Mirvis** is a professor in the departments of Preventive Medicine and Internal Medicine at the University of Tennessee Health Science Center. He also serves on the graduate faculty of the program in health sciences administration and epidemiology. He received his M.D. from the Albert Einstein College of Medicine of Yeshiva University in 1970, and subsequently trained in internal medicine and cardiology at the National Institutes of Health and at the University of Tennessee. From 1987 through 1997, Mirvis served as chief of staff of the Memphis VA Medical Center and as an associate dean of the University of Tennessee College of Medicine. He was the founder and director of the University's Center for Health Services Research. Mirvis's research interests include health care delivery processes and health policy as well as theoretical and applied electrocardiology.

**James Kariuki Njenga** is a lecturer in the department of Information Systems, University of the Western Cape, and an e-learning consultant under the name eLearning Fundi. James's research interests include the use of information and communications technologies in education (eLearning), especially their use in higher education in Africa. He has previously worked as an instructional designer and a learning support technologist. Other research interests are in free and open source software, open access and open educational resources, as well as the use of Web 2.0 technologies in mentoring young people.

**Jody Oomen-Early** is a professor and Director of Undergraduate Programs in the School of Health Sciences at Walden University. She has worked in education for over 19 years and has served "on the front lines of health education" in a variety of community and non-profit settings. Dr. Early has a passion for exploring health and technology and for developing e-learning programs in the health sciences. Most recently, she was awarded the 2010 HEDIR Technology Award from the American Association of Health Education (AAHE) for pioneering one of the first fully online undergraduate health education programs in the U.S. Jody is currently involved with a number of research projects in and outside of the U.S. exploring the use of Photovoice as a community-based participatory tool for action research and social justice. She has presented her work at national and international conferences, and has published her research in journals such as the *International Electronic Journal of Health Education*, the *American Journal of Health Education,* and the *Journal of Online Teaching and Learning*. She is also a co-author of the 2ⁿᵈ edition of *The Process of Community Health Education and Promotion* (2010).

**Leann Parker** serves as associate director and director of research for University-Community Links (UC Links), a University of California initiative that promotes faculty and student engagement in a network of after-school programs for K-12 youth in California. Her areas of specialization center on learning environments and technologies that promote second language and literacy development for K-12 English language learners in and out of school. Among her other interests are issues in university-community collaborations, program sustainability, and evaluation. Previously, she directed several efforts for the University of California that focused on academic preparation of K-12 students, faculty research on new technologies for teaching and learning, high bandwidth Internet and university-developed digital resources for K-12, and technology in support of young English learners. She has also taught courses on second language acquisition and assessment at California State University-East Bay and worked with kindergarten, elementary school, and adult English learners. She holds a Ph.D. in education from University of California, Berkeley.

**John Patterson** spent time as a mechanical and production engineer upon leaving school and then retrained as a primary school teacher. Spending most of his time in challenging inner city schools and becoming a deputy head teacher, he recruited for a government office initiative to "raise educational standards through the innovative use of Information and Communication Technology." As an education and community consultant, this provided him with the opportunity to pilot community engagement initiatives across Merseyside in primary and secondary schools. Leaving this post after two years, John perfected the Schools Intergenerational Nurturing and Learning project (www.schoolsinteractive.co.uk) as a service-learning model working with the Dark Horse Venture Charity. In 2002, John was appointed as a Senior Lecturer in the Faculty of Education at Liverpool Hope University. To date, John has secured an M.Sc. researching the SIGNAL process alongside student teachers and is due to complete his Ph.D. focussing on volunteerism in 2011.

**Oksana Perez** is a student at Desert View High School in Tucson, Arizona, where she has lived all her life. She is a proud member of Desert View Drama and The Write Place Writing Center. After graduating in 2012, Oksana plans to attend the University of Arizona and become either a forensic psychologist or a music journalist for *Alternative Press* magazine. She became a part of this writing project because she and the other Wildcat Writers student research team members were interested in sharing the knowledge they accumulated through their work. Her inspiration to stay engaged in the project was the enthusiasm and friendliness she felt among the group.

**Alberto Ramírez Martinell** is an educator and researcher in the fields of multimedia production, multimedia learning, educational and student television production, digital literacy, technology enhanced learning, and information and communication technologies for development. He has a BSc in computer engineering from the Universidad Nacional Autónoma de México, a BA in humanities from the Universidad del Claustro de Sor Juana, Mexico, an MSc in computer science and media from the Hochshchule Furtwangen, Germany, and a Ph.D. in educational technology from Lancaster University, United Kingdom. He is currently the head of learning technology at REDDES, an NGO that concentrates on capacity-building for other NGOs who work on environmental, educational, and community development in Mexico and Latin America.

**Molly Reddy** graduated from the University of Wisconsin Madison in 2010 with Bachelor's of science in nonprofit & community leadership and Latin American, Caribbean, and Iberian studies. As a student at UW, she worked on the TechShop Madison project from its inception, as a service-learning student and researcher, and later as a student trainer and program manager. Reddy also worked as an organizer and trainer with nonprofits in Madison and university programs such as AIESEC International and Undergraduate Research Scholars. Her interest in Latin America has led her to work and study community and economic development in Colombia, Chile, and most recently Brazil, where she is currently located.

**Diane Rhyason**, B.Ed., MLIS, Ph.D., is executive director of the Legal Resource Centre of Alberta Ltd. Rhyason's involvement with public legal education extends back to 1975, when she was a founding member of the Legal Resource Centre. She served on its board until 2007 when she became its executive director. She has extensive experience in managing both large and small education, research, and development projects in conjunction with other community partners and with the University. Rhyason is also the publisher of *LawNow* magazine. Prior to coming to the centre, she was the vice president of administration at Lakeland College in Alberta. Her research interests are in the area of collaborative practices.

**David Russell** received his B.S. in entomology from University of California/Davis and his Master's and Doctorate degrees in zoology and molecular systematics from Miami University in Oxford, Ohio. A lecturer of zoology at Miami University, he teaches biology, environmental science, and advanced courses in field entomology and ornithology. One of only a handful of North American Banding Council (NABC) certified trainers in the U.S., Russell is also a master bird bander. He is the research/education director of the Avian Research and Education Institute (AREI), a nonprofit bird conservation, education, and advocacy organization and is the primary bander at the Hueston Woods Biological Station in Hueston Woods State Park, north of Cincinnati, OH. AREI has bird banding stations in Ohio's Miami Valley that serve as both research facilities and outdoor classrooms providing community members and students firsthand experience in environmental science.

**Jill Russell** received her B.S. in biology from the College of Mount St. Joseph in Cincinnati, OH. She received both her Master's in cardiac physiology and her Doctorate in neuroendocrinology degrees from Miami University in Oxford, Ohio. An assistant professor of biology at the College of Mount St. Joseph and an adjunct professor of zoology at Miami University, she teaches a variety of physiology courses as well as ornithology and various workshops on environmental science. Her work runs the gamut of expeditions to the arctic as part of a team building worldwide educational collaborative, to researching toxic compounds in arctic fungi, to being an invited ornithologist on a search for the Ivory-billed Woodpecker. She is the primary bird bander at the Clifford Bird Observatory in Cincinnati and is an invited lecturer/speaker at numerous colleges and universities as well as community groups nationwide.

**Erin Saitta** holds a Doctorate degree in materials chemistry and a Bachelor's degree in chemistry education from the University of Central Florida. Erin works as science education coordinator and postdoctoral research associate at the UCF Faculty Center for Teaching and Learning. She is currently leading a revision of the undergraduate chemistry II laboratory course to incorporate a guided inquiry methodology. In 2009, she led the first service-learning project to be included in a UCF chemistry course.

Erin is now working on the sustainability of service-learning in the STEM disciplines and is teaching faculty and graduate students how to implement this pedagogy in their courses. Her dissertation research was in environmental and industrial chemistry focusing on the removal of polychlorinated biphenyls from painted surfaces and their degradation through activated metal treatment systems.

**Savannah Sanchez** is a student at Desert View High School in Tucson, Arizona, where she has lived all her life. She is the drum major for Pride of the Jaguars Marching Band. She balances this fulltime job with Advanced Placement and other accelerated courses. Her interests range from yoga to sports to exploring nature. In 2007, she published a children's book entitled *Snow Day*. In 2009, she appeared in *Express Yourself! A Journal of Creative Expression*. That same year, her corrido "The Street Cleaner," placed in the top ten in the Bilingual Corrido Contest sponsored by the University of Arizona Poetry Center. She plans to pursue a degree in psychoanalytic anthropology and travel the world learning new cultures and new languages. She became involved in the Wildcat Writers Student Research Team because she knew it was a great opportunity to learn new things and expand her horizons and her network.

**Kathleen Schisa** is director of the Web-based Information Science Education Consortium (WISE) and associate director of Online Program Development at the Syracuse University School of Information Studies in Syracuse, New York. Schisa is a 2009 graduate of the school's M.S. in Library and Information Science Program and holds a B.S. in brain and cognitive science with a minor in social psychology from the University of Rochester.

**William Shewbridge** has over 25 years of experience in educational media. He is director of the University of Maryland, Baltimore County's New Media Studio where he focuses on advancing media literacy and exploring new technologies for learning. He is an affiliate assistant professor of modern languages and linguistics, teaching courses in intercultural media, television production, and digital storytelling. In 2008, the New Media Studio received the New Media Consortium's Center of Excellence Award in recognition of UMBC's digital story work. Shewbridge serves on the NMC's "Horizon Report" advisory board. Shewbridge holds a B.A. in history from UMBC, an M.S. in instructional design from Towson University, and a doctoral degree of communication design (D.C.D.) from the University of Baltimore.

**Linda C. Smith** is professor and associate dean for academic programs in the Graduate School of Library and Information Science at the University of Illinois at Urbana-Champaign, where she has been a member of the faculty since 1977 and teaching online since 1997. Smith is co-founder of Web-based Information Science Education Consortium (WISE).

**Barbara Speziale** is an associate dean and professor of biological sciences at Clemson University. She completed undergraduate majors in biology and English literature at the State University of New York at Binghamton, an M.S. in botany at the University of Minnesota and a Ph.D. in zoology at Clemson University. She has more than 20 years of experience in biology research, science education, and outreach, with support from more than $12 million in external grants. She currently directs a National Science Foundation project to recruit first-generation college students to science careers and an Undergraduate Science Education grant from the Howard Hughes Medical Institute. She directs Clemson University's Creative Inquiry program, supporting team-based research for undergraduate students. Her awards include the South Carolina Governor's Award for Scientific Awareness, Clemson's Martin Luther King Jr. Award for Excellence in Service, and the Menzie-Cura Environmental Education Award from the Society for Environmental Toxicology.

**Trae Stewart** is associate professor in the School of Teaching, Learning & Leadership in the College of Education at the University of Central Florida. He is co-principal investigator of "Teachers in Action, a service-learning program that engages pre-service teachers with persons with disabilities through high-tech, high-touch service-learning. He is also chair of the Board of the International Association of Research on Service-Learning and Community Engagement (IARSLCE). Dr. Stewart holds a Ph.D. in international and intercultural education (educational policy, planning, and administration) from the University of Southern California.

**Randy Stoecker** is a professor in the Department of Community and Environmental Sociology at the University of Wisconsin, with a joint appointment in the University of Wisconsin-Extension Center for Community and Economic Development. He moderates and edits COMM-ORG: The On-Line Conference on Community Organizing and speaks frequently on community organizing and development, community-based participatory research/evaluation, and community Information Technology. He has led numerous participatory action research projects, community technology projects, and empowerment evaluation processes with community development corporations, community-based leadership education programs, community organizing groups, and other nonprofits in North America and Australia. Randy has written extensively on community organizing and development and higher education engagement with community, including the books *Defending Community* (Temple University Press, 1994), *Research Methods for Community Change* (Sage Publications, 2005), and the co-authored books *Community-Based Research in Higher Education* (Jossey-Bass, 2003) and *The Unheard Voices: Community Organizations and Service Learning* (Temple University Press, 2009).

**Margaret Sullivan** earned her B.A. from The George Washington University and her M.A. from University of Colorado at Denver. She has worked in both the elementary school and high school during her 13 years of ESL instruction. During the last six years, she has also taught Advancement Via Individual Determination (AVID). Currently, she is a high school ESL teacher in Colorado.

**Nathan Tipton** is coordinator for the Academic Consortium for Applied Research (ACAR) unit in the Department of Preventive Medicine at The University of Tennessee Health Science Center in Memphis. He is responsible for writing, editing, and guiding departmental manuscripts to publication. He also assists in the researching, writing, and editing of departmental grants. Mr. Tipton received his Master's in textual studies from the University of Memphis in 1999 and is presently a doctoral candidate specializing in southern literature. He has published articles and reviews in *The Southern Literary Journal, Mississippi Quarterly, South Central Review, The Journal of Popular Culture,* and *Lambda Literary Review*. He was previously employed as editor in the Institute for Substance Abuse Research and Evaluation (I-SARE) at the University of Memphis and, prior to that, served as librarian/literature specialist at Memphis Public Library and Information Center.

**Matthew W. Turner** is the Integrated Product Team (IPT) deputy program manager at the University of Alabama in Huntsville. Turner has been project manager of the one of the IPT Senior Design Experience projects for four years and is the project manager of the Innovative Student Project for the Increased Recruitment of Engineering and Science Students (InSPIRESS) Level II project with the IPT program. Turner holds a Ph.D. in mechanical engineering from the University of Alabama in Huntsville and has worked in the Huntsville aerospace industry for ten years supporting NASA.

**Charles Underwood** is an anthropologist (Ph.D., University of California-Berkeley, 1986) who has worked internationally in a variety of educational and occupational settings in Scotland, India, Brazil, and the United States. He has directed several statewide University of California initiatives to promote innovative uses of digital resources for K-16 teaching and learning. Since 1996, he has directed University-Community Links (UC Links), a UC initiative that engages university faculty and students with K-12 youth in a network of after-school programs throughout California. From 2005 to 2008, Underwood was active in collaborative relief efforts providing educational resources for youth displaced by Hurricane Katrina. He has taught anthropology at Golden Gate University, the University of Sao Paulo, and UC Berkeley. His work continues to focus on the socio-cultural context of learning and the socio-cultural process of collaboration, working with university and community colleagues to pursue common goals across linguistic, cultural, institutional, and geographical boundaries.

**Lori E. Unruh** (Ph.D., University of Kansas) is an assistant professor at Western Carolina University (WCU) in Cullowhee, North Carolina. Unruh joined the WCU faculty in 2005 after working for over 15 years as a school psychologist. She is director of the school psychology graduate program at WCU, teaches graduate-level courses for that program, and supervises all school and clinic practicum students. She has provided research assistance to the WCU Center for the support of beginning teachers for the past four years.

**Dawn R. Utley**, P.E., received her Ph.D. from the University of Alabama in Huntsville, an M.S. in industrial engineering from the University of Tennessee and a B.S. in civil engineering from Tennessee Technological University. She is an associate professor and interim director of distance learning at UAH. She worked for the Tennessee Valley Authority as a structural civil engineer prior to her academic career. Her research interests include teaming processes in collaborative engineering efforts, motivation of knowledge workers, and quality systems implementation. Utley is an active member in ASEM and IIE, and has just completed her term as national president of ASEM.

**Terri Van Sickle** is a teacher consultant for the Tar River Writing Project at East Carolina University, a certified teacher in the field of English grades 6-12, and a contributing writer for parenting magazines in eastern North Carolina and the Crystal Coast. She earned a B.A. in English from East Carolina University and an M.Ed. in English education from the University of Georgia. Van Sickle taught for eleven years in public schools in Georgia and North Carolina. She served on the Red Clay Writing Project steering committee at the University of Georgia, and she currently serves as a member of ECU's Tar River Writing Project Leadership Team.

**Olga A. Vásquez** holds a Ph.D. from Stanford University and is an associate professor in the Department of Communication at the University of California San Diego. For over two decades, Vásquez has experimented with optimal learning environments at a research-based afterschool laboratory called *La Clase Mágica* situated in community institutions. These research-based after school laboratories represent a partnership between the local community and higher education to address the K-12 under-achievement of minority youth and their under-representation in higher education. Originally designed to serve Spanish-English bilingual learners from Mexican immigrant homes, *La Clase Mágica* also serves American Indian learners. Vásquez has written widely on bilingualism, literacy, and educational technology. Her recent work focuses on the need for educational change to meet the challenges of the 21$^{st}$ century.

**Jalina Vidotto** is a high school student in Tucson, Arizona, and a member of the Wildcat Writers Student Research Team. She volunteers in her school's mentoring program as well as its National Honor Society while taking rigorous Advanced Placement classes. Although her career choice is undecided, she plans to attend the University of Arizona in the fall of 2012. Jalina enjoys traveling and photography and hopes to own her own business one day.

**Ashley Walker** is an assistant professor of health education and promotion at Georgia Southern University in Statesboro, Georgia. She received her doctorate in health studies from Texas Woman's University in Denton, Texas. Dr. Walker is a Certified Health Education Specialist (CHES) and has seven years of experience working as a health educator in a variety of settings. She has worked in higher education for five years. In addition, Dr. Walker has experience in developing and sustaining campus-community partnerships and has completed both local and international community-based research projects. She has presented at both regional and national conferences regarding her work using community-based participatory research.

**Linda Walters** is a Professor in the Department of Biology at the University of Central Florida. She received her Ph.D. from the University of South Carolina followed by postdoctoral fellowships in Hawaii, India and Quebec. Dr. Walters has been at the University of Central Florida for 14 years and teaches a wide range of classes – from 1400-person lecture sections for Introductory Biology to small, graduate level seminars. Her research area is Marine Conservation Biology and all of her marine-oriented courses include research and service-learning components, the latter to improve the science communication skills of her students.

**Shannon Watson** is the advisor/activity coordinator at Anoka Ramsey Community College in Coon Rapids, MN, for federally funded TRIO student support programs. She served as the first graduate assistant assigned to coordinate the day-to-day operations of the Pathways Program for Incarcerated Students and provided advising and support to incarcerated students and their families.

**Rachael Wendler** is the coordinator of Wildcat Writers, an online service-learning program linking high school and college writing classes in Tucson, Arizona. She is a Ph.D. student and instructor at the University of Arizona, where she researches service-learning pedagogy in composition, the rhetoric of service, and the application of decolonial theory to university-community partnerships. Rachael also works for the Tucson Gear Up Project, a federally funded program that promotes college-readiness in area high schools, and she is a teacher consultant with the National Writing Project. In addition to college courses, Rachael has taught service-learning classes to high school students through Northwestern University's Center for Talent Development and to elementary students through AmeriCorps. Prior to entering academia, Rachael coordinated a literacy tutoring program at an urban elementary school in Chicago.

**Aimee L. Whiteside** teaches courses in technical communication, information design, learning technologies, and first-year writing. Aimee earned a Ph.D. in rhetoric and scientific and technical communication and a graduate-level certificate in adult learning technology integration at the University of Minnesota in August 2007. Her professional interests include the socio-cultural aspects of learning, blended and online learning, technology-enhanced learning, formal and informal learning environments, community partnerships in education, technical communication, and first-year writing. She has taught face-to-face, online, and blended courses at the undergraduate and graduate levels.

**Debbie G. Whittington** holds a B.S. in biology from the University of South Carolina and is employed by Florence School District Number Three in Lake City, SC. She has ten years of experience as a high school science teacher, teaching biology, environmental science, marine science, and anatomy and physiology to students from the technology preparatory to the advanced placement program level. For the last five years, she has served as a science master teacher with the district's middle schools, working with teachers and students to implement strategies that have successfully improved student achievement in science. She is working on her Master's in biological sciences at Clemson University and assists with graduate courses for in-service teachers offered by the SC Life project at Clemson. She also serves as secretary of the South Carolinians for Science Education, an organization that seeks to protect the integrity of science education.

**Jenny Wohlfarth** is an associate professor of journalism at the University of Cincinnati, where she is also coordinator of the journalism program's magazine/narrative nonfiction curriculum track, adviser of the student magazine, and adviser of the student chapter of the Society of Professional Journalists. Her articles have appeared in numerous national magazines for the past 20 years, spanning a wide range of subject areas, from art/architecture/design, to business and creativity, to nature/environment, and travel. Before joining the faculty at UC, she was executive editor of I.D. (International Design) Magazine and managing editor of HOW Magazine, both award-winning national magazines covering the world of design. Her academic research focuses on the scholarship of teaching and learning, and she has presented several papers at the Lilly Conference on College Teaching and the International Society for the Scholarship of Teaching and Learning Annual Conference. When she's not working with students in the classroom, she continues to write and publish magazine articles, primarily focusing on nature/environment and travel.

452

# Index

CPSIA information can be obtained at www.ICGtesting.com
Printed in the USA
267698BV00007BC/11/P

9 781609 606237